NAZI WIVES

NAZI
THE WOMEN AT THE TOP OF HITLER'S GERMANY
WIVES

JAMES WYLLIE

The
History
Press

I would like to thank my agent Sonia Land at Sheil Land Associates Ltd for her unswerving commitment and support, and Gaia Banks and the foreign rights team for getting this book out into the world. Thanks are also due to Laura Perehinec at The History Press for her enthusiasm and dedication, to Alex Waite for helping turn my manuscript into a book, and to the whole The History Press team for their excellent work. Finally, I'd like to thank my friends and family; without their loyalty and generosity this book would not have been possible.

First published 2019

The History Press
97 St George's Place, Cheltenham,
Gloucestershire, GL50 3QB
www.thehistorypress.co.uk

© James Wyllie, 2019

The right of James Wyllie to be identified as the Author
of this work has been asserted in accordance with the
Copyright, Designs and Patents Act 1988.

British Library Cataloguing in Publication Data.
A catalogue record for this book is available from the British Library.

ISBN 978 0 7509 9122 3

Typesetting and origination by The History Press
Printed and bound in Great Britain by TJ International Ltd.

MIX
Paper from
responsible sources
FSC® C013056

CONTENTS

INTRODUCTION

On the evening of 10 July 1937 the German-Jewish journal-ist Bella Fromm, who wrote the society column in a Berlin newspaper, went to the cinema to see the romantic comedy *Broadway Melody*. Loosely based on the 1929 original, it included the hit song 'You Are My Lucky Star', a bunch of characters trying to launch a Broadway show, farcical backstage intrigues and glamorous locations – penthouse apartments and rooftop pavilions – and a finale featuring two grand pianos gliding across the dancefloor next to a tap-dancing chorus line dressed in top hats and tails.

Arriving at the cinema, Bella parked her car and then suddenly noticed that she'd aroused the interest of two SS men. One of them noted down her licence plate while the other pointed his camera at her and 'took a quick snap-shot'. The reason for this level of surveillance became clear when several large automobiles with swastika pendants pulled up. Heinrich Himmler and his wife Margaret got out and entered the cinema, accompanied by their 'grim bodyguard'.[1] Once inside, Himmler and Margaret took their seats – flanked by his angels of death – and settled in for 101 minutes of fun and frolics. This surreal, almost comic scene is also rather unsettling given how Himmler is generally perceived: a humourless pedant and ruthless zealot obsessed by crackpot fantasies about a Germanic master race.

So why did he take Margaret to see a light-hearted MGM musical? Unlike others in the Nazi elite – including Hitler – Himmler wasn't a film buff eager to consume the latest Hollywood releases. Perhaps he fancied some carefree escapism to take his mind off the daily grind. Or did he view the film with a critical eye, regarding it as an example of the degenerate decadence of American society? Or maybe he was simply trying to please his wife. From the start, his long working hours and almost constant travelling had taken a heavy toll on their marriage. This was a rare opportunity to have a night out together. Dress up. Summon a fleet of cars and a uniformed escort. Treat her to a feel-good movie.

Sadly, we don't know if Margaret enjoyed *Broadway Melody*, or if she was pleased her husband had found time to indulge her; perhaps the most thrilling part of her evening was cruising the streets of the capital in an SS convoy, sending ripples of fear and awe through everyone who saw them speed past.

Among the thousands of books about Nazism barely a handful focus on the wives of the leading figures in Hitler's regime: Gerda Bormann, Magda Goebbels, Carin and Emmy Goering, Ilse Hess, Lina Heydrich and Margaret Himmler. While their men have left an indelible imprint on our collective memory the women who gave them vital support, encouragement and direction have largely remained relegated to the footnotes of history. While the overall experience of women in the Nazi period became a subject of serious study during the 1980s, opening up a whole field of enquiry and providing a complex and nuanced picture that challenged the stereotypes perpetuated by Nazi propaganda, the women at the very top of the system have been neglected.

Part of the reason for this is the nature of the source material, much of which has to be treated with caution. Although a lot more information has come to light in the last few decades, there are still considerable gaps and chunks of time missing from the diaries and letters that have survived, while the post-war autobiographies penned by several of the wives actively sought to portray their husbands as paragons of virtue and themselves as innocent bystanders; the memoirs and recollections of fellow travellers – each with their own agenda – have created an echo chamber of anecdotes, hearsay and gossip that make it harder to distinguish fact from fiction.

However, these sorts of issues affect any investigation into the past and are not sufficient to explain why historians have failed to give these women the prominence they deserve, thereby giving credence to their own claims that there was a clear distinction between their husbands' public and private lives. But this does not bear scrutiny. The Nazis set out to control every aspect of their citizens' existence – the food they ate, the clothes they wore, who they had sex with, what jokes they could tell, how they celebrated Christmas – making any separation between the public and the private meaningless. And despite their undoubted privilege, the wives were subjected to the same pressures as ordinary women. Their social lives were determined by political considerations. Friendships were jettisoned. Relationships – even with family members – abruptly terminated. Their behaviour was a factor in the struggles within the Nazi elite, particularly where Hitler was concerned; falling out of favour with the Führer could have serious implications for their husbands' careers.

Even though they might not have been privy to their husbands' daily decisions, the evidence of their murderous work was all around: the looted art on the walls; the furniture made from human skin and bones stashed in the attic; the fruit and vegetables taken from the local concentration camp gardens; the slave labour tilling their land. The rituals of family life – births, weddings, funerals – were inextricably linked to Nazi ideology. Perhaps this is why it has proved easier to take these women at face value and treat them as minor characters; treating them seriously means accepting that their husbands engaged in normal activities and experienced recognisably human emotions. Falling in and out of love. Worrying about the bills and their weight and where to send the kids to school. Planning dinner parties and picnics. Spending vacations sightseeing. Acknowledging that in many respects they were no different from the rest of us creates a form of cognitive dissonance: a deeply uneasy feeling.

Yet their story offers important insights into the nature of Nazi rule and the psychology of its leaders, providing a fresh perspective on the key events that shaped its rise and fall. The aim of this book is to chart their lives from the moment they became involved in the Nazi movement – in several cases before they even met their husbands – through the years of struggle, power, decline and destruction, and then into the post-war twilight of denial and delusion. While they enjoyed luxury lifestyles and VIP status, they also endured broken marriages, cheating husbands, suicide, assassination, desertion, impoverishment and incarceration. But despite all these trials and tribulations, their commitment to Hitler's cause never wavered.

Though they were each unique and fascinating individuals in their own right who coped differently with the demands placed on them, these women's backgrounds were strikingly similar. Well-educated, they all came from conservative middle-class families – representing the professions, business, the army and the lower gentry – where gender roles were rigidly defined; whatever her achievements, a woman's best hope was to find a good husband. Their parents, whether Protestant or Catholic, took religion seriously and their daughters were instilled with values that would shape their tastes, interests and political views: a belief in the supremacy of German culture, its music, art, literature and philosophy, the genius of its scientific achievements, its unbeatable army; devotion to the Kaiser and the state; a hatred of socialism and a fear that the unruly masses would devour them. As a result they had more in common with each other than they would ever have with a woman working in a factory.

They grew up in an era that saw the rapid transformation of Germany from a largely agricultural society to an industrial one, an uneasy trade-off between a democratic system and an imperial one, and a belligerent effort to establish Germany as a major global power with a large navy and a string of colonies. But despite the strident patriotism, there was also a pervasive feeling of crisis, of a country at war with itself, struggling to accommodate the pressures of modernity – not least the sharpening of class divisions – and surrounded by hostile neighbours.

The bourgeoisie were especially vulnerable to these stresses and strains, suffering from both an exaggerated sense of their own superiority and a nagging anxiety about the future.

The beginning of the First World War seemed to resolve these tensions, as the nation united in anticipation of glory. As the slaughter dragged on and on, the whole population was mobilised to support the war effort while blanket censorship and relentless propaganda made ultimate victory still appear inevitable, whatever the cost.

These women's young lives – at home and school – were monopolised by the conflict. Battlefield statistics and soldiers' stories entered the classroom. Priests prayed for success at the front. Everything from toys to playing cards were given a military theme. Mothers, particularly those from the middle classes, took part in a vast campaign of charity work, whether organising food drives or knitting socks and scarves for the men in the cold damp trenches.

The last year of the war delivered shock after shock to the already tottering system; the Bolshevik seizure of power in Russia threatened to spread revolution across its borders and inspire mutiny in the army; the failure of the massive do-or-die offensive on the Western Front that led to irreversible retreat; the collapse of Germany's main allies, Austro-Hungary and Turkey; the hunger, malnutrition and disease that wrecked civilian morale; the strikes and demonstrations; the calls for peace and the abdication of the Kaiser.

The chaos and violence that engulfed Germany in the wake of defeat and surrender continued into 1919, driving the country towards outright civil war. The radical left almost gained control before it was ruthlessly crushed by the *Freikorps* – right-wing paramilitary units made up of ex-soldiers and enthusiastic volunteers – who were given free rein by the embattled government of the new Weimar Republic, which was held responsible for the humiliating terms imposed by the Versailles Treaty.

As a result, these women became adults in profoundly insecure and volatile circumstances. Old certainties were gone. The civilised conventions of their parents' generation appeared increasingly irrelevant. Cut adrift, they each gravitated towards a self-styled saviour who promised them the world.

PART ONE

REACHING THE SUMMIT

1

EARLY RUNNERS

In the spring of 1920, Ilse Pröhl moved into a respectable student hostel on the outskirts of Munich, determined to benefit from the educational opportunities opening up for German women. In 1900, the year Ilse was born, women were admitted to university for the first time. Eight years later, the first female versions of the *Gymnasium* – exclusive fee-paying high schools that trained their pupils for the university entrance exam known as the *Abitur* – opened their doors.

These *Gymnasia* were restricted to daughters of wealthy families, but this wasn't a problem for Ilse: her father was a respected doctor who treated members of the Prussian court in Berlin and became a chief military surgeon at the elite Potsdam garrison. Aged 14, Ilse took up a place at one of these prestigious high schools. A bright, energetic and popular pupil, she was particularly keen on music and literature. She also enjoyed hiking and camping, outdoor pursuits that were extremely popular among middle-class adolescents seeking to escape the soullessness of urban life. This back-to-nature movement began as an all-male activity but by the time Ilse got involved it was thoroughly mixed.

Her carefree teenage years were overshadowed by the First World War. Though a firm supporter of the armed forces and a convinced patriot, the full reality of the catastrophe occurring in northern France was brought home to her when her father, who had been posted to a relatively quiet sector of the front, was killed in the spring of 1917.

This painful loss was compounded by the shock of defeat and the upheavals that threatened to break Germany apart. Then, during her last year at the *Gymnasium*, her mother remarried – to a museum director – and the family moved to Munich before Ilse could complete the *Abitur*. Rather than stay at her new home, Ilse signalled her desire for independence by taking a room at the hostel.

One evening, Ilse ran into a fellow lodger, a tall young man wearing a threadbare, tattered uniform, who gruffly introduced himself as Rudolf Hess. She was immediately struck by his gaunt appearance: the thick eyebrows that seemed destined to meet in the middle, the sunken eyes and haunted expression. Despite his curt manner, she was instantly attracted to him. Whether the 26-year-old Hess had a similar reaction is impossible to say. Of all the senior Nazis, Hess was the most enigmatic. Dozens of experts, from psychiatrists to historians, have struggled to make sense of him. Hess even puzzled himself. In a letter to a friend he confessed that he felt torn between two opposing sides of his personality: one craved an almost monk-like existence contemplating the mysteries of the universe, while the other was a bloodthirsty barbarian hungry for battle.

Yet it was precisely this combination of the thinker with the man of action that appealed to Ilse. The frayed uniform he was wearing that fateful evening – which Ilse instantly recognised – belonged to the notorious von Epp *Freikorps* regiment that he'd joined in 1919 during the violent overthrow of Munich's left-wing government.

Hess was also a decorated veteran – with an Iron Cross for valour – who'd been wounded twice. At the hellish Battle of Verdun, during which he witnessed 'every horror of death imaginable',[1] he was hit by shrapnel; while leading an infantry charge in Romania he was shot in the chest. His recovery complete, Hess trained as a pilot, satisfying a long-held urge to fly, but the war was over before he could test himself in combat.

When the conflict began, Hess had been at a critical juncture in his life. He wanted to go to university, but his father wanted him to enter the family business, an import-export firm based in the Egyptian port city of Alexandria where Hess grew up in a palatial villa on the edge of the desert, an environment that contributed to his sense of otherworldliness. His father was a strict disciplinarian who thought the most important day of the year was the Kaiser's birthday. Hess felt closer to his mother, a gentle, intelligent woman who encouraged his early interest in astrology.

In 1908, when Hess was 14, the family returned to Germany; having only spent summers there, Hess was thrilled by his first sight of snow. Packed off to boarding school, he remained an outsider. A hard-working pupil, he passed the *Abitur* and reluctantly enrolled on a business course; his poor performance provoked a clash with his father that was only resolved when Hess enlisted in the army.

With the war over – and his father's business requisitioned by the British – Hess was free to pursue a degree in history and economics. While he flirted with the *Thule Society* (a semi-secret group interested in Aryan mythology and prehistoric Nordic civilisations) Hess's main intellectual influence was the 50-year-old geo-politics professor Karl Haushofer, who had managed to combine a military career with academic study: Haushofer developed the concept of *Lebensraum* after visiting Japan and concluding that a nation's chances of success depended on the amount of *living space* available to it. Though Haushofer didn't think Hess was particularly intelligent, he admired his strength of character. The professor – and the rest of his family – treated Hess like an adopted son. This close friendship, which included Ilse, endured for decades, with mixed results for all concerned.

Despite Hess's aversion to fun, Ilse decided to pursue him and they began spending time together. It was a platonic affair. Still a virgin, Hess showed absolutely no interest in sex: for the next few years, their relationship lacked a physical dimension. Instead, they consciously cultivated a spiritual connection based on their shared love of German culture, especially the writers and composers of the late eighteenth and early nineteenth century. Their favourite was the poet and philosopher Friedrich Hölderlin: his early work worshipped nature, his later work worshipped God. Ilse gave Hess a copy of Hölderlin's metaphysical novel *Hyperion* and added a lyrical inscription; their love was 'full of power and yet tender as their spirit', while their 'hearts beat stronger waves even than the trident of the Sea God who is ruler of the waves'.[2]

However, it was their shared response to Hitler that forged an unbreakable bond between them, both convinced they'd stumbled on the man destined to drag Germany out of the abyss and set it on the road to glory. Soon after they first met, Hess heard Hitler speak at a tiny gathering. Unable to contain his excitement, Hess ran back to the hostel and burst into Ilse's room, raving about this amazing man and his electrifying message. A few weeks later, Ilse accompanied him to another Nazi gathering and was equally impressed. Her unquestioning enthusiasm for Hitler's poisonous ideology is evident in a letter she wrote to a schoolfriend, in which she made no attempt to soften her views; 'we are anti-Semites. Constantly, rigorously, without exception. The two basic pillars of our movement – national, and social – are anchored in the meaning of this anti-Semitism.'[3]

By the autumn of 1920, Ilse had completed her *Abitur*, begun a part-time university course in German and library science, and started work at an antiquarian bookshop. Asides from occasional trips outside Munich to ramble in the countryside, she spent the majority of her spare time working for the Nazi movement; delivering leaflets, putting up posters, helping out with the party newspaper and acting as Hess's secretary while he attached himself to Hitler and put his body on the line during the frequent brawls between Nazi supporters and their left-wing opponents.

In recognition of their efforts, Ilse and Hess were granted the privilege of being around Hitler during his downtime, unwinding with his most trusted companions. Ilse – and many others – described how much Hitler enjoyed a good laugh; not one for telling jokes, Hitler did impressions and liked nothing better than listening to a well-told funny story as long as it wasn't about him.

Shy and sensitive, Gerda Buch was a dreamy, artistic child on the verge of adolescence when she first met Hitler, who promptly took her under his wing. 'Uncle Adolf' had a special interest in young people – girls in particular – and was keen to adopt a quasi-guardian role, taking responsibility for their cultural, political and moral welfare. At the time, his main focus was Henriette Hoffmann, the 9-year-old daughter of Heinrich Hoffmann, one of Hitler's closest associates who would become his personal photographer. Every afternoon, while Henriette practised the piano, Hitler would test her knowledge of German myths and folklore. Though he spent less time with Gerda, Hitler lavished her with attention whenever he visited her home.

The reason Hitler was such a regular presence in Gerda's life was her father, Walter Buch, a career soldier. Buch was 19 years old when he joined the army in 1902. Gerda was born in 1909, a year after Buch married her mother. By 1914 he was a first lieutenant, one of the small number of officers who wasn't from an aristocratic background. Serving on the Western Front, Buch gained one promotion after another until he commanded a whole battalion. In 1918, he resigned his commission – disgusted by the Allied peace terms that reduced his beloved army to a meagre 100,000 men – and joined the other disgruntled ex-soldiers milling round Munich, licking their wounds after the disbandment of the *Freikorps* and the collapse of the Kapp Putsch, a military coup launched in spring 1920 and defeated by the largest general strike in German history. Pointed in the direction of Hitler, Buch quickly fell under his spell, declaring that Hitler 'had been sent to the German people by the grace of God'.[4]

Buch was exactly the kind of recruit Hitler was looking for; a representative of the officer class with an untarnished reputation. Buch's natural home in the movement was the Sturmabteilung (SA), better known as the Brownshirts. Hitler needed experienced men like Buch to transform this undisciplined mob of street fighters into an effective paramilitary force. During the summer of 1923, Buch took charge of the 275 SA men based in Nuremberg – some 100 miles from Munich – and began preparing them for action. Once again, Buch would be away from home. Reflecting on her childhood, Gerda complained that her father was 'merely a visitor. He never stayed with us for any length of time.'[5] Ultimately, Buch's most significant contribution to his daughter's young life was introducing her to Hitler.

Before Buch took over in Nuremberg, the Brownshirts acquired a new overall leader, the ex-flying ace and war hero Hermann Goering, whose aerial exploits – he was awarded the prestigious Blue Max for twenty confirmed kills and took over the elite Richthofen squadron after the Red Baron's death – had won him considerable fame. Fighter pilots were genuine celebrities; portrayed as knights of the air engaged in chivalric duels, they excited the public's imagination, offering relief from the grim unglamorous reality of trench warfare. Hermann was in the top rank, a household name. Even though he'd been in Stockholm for the past few years, his reputation still preceded him.

Hitler certainly understood what a potential asset he was. Goering could open doors to the military elite and aristocracy; local power brokers who could help Hitler realise his immediate ambition, to use Munich as the starting point of a national revolution. When they were introduced in late 1922 – shortly after Goering had arrived there and seen Hitler perform at a rally – Hitler invited him to join the movement.

Over the years, Goering made various statements about his decision to align with Hitler. Whether it was a deeply felt act of submission to the chosen one or a calculated gamble on Hitler's ability to mobilise the masses, there's no doubt the fledgling Nazi party offered Goering an opportunity to be a big fish in a small pond. But it was Goering's new Swedish wife Carin who sealed the deal. Already a confirmed anti-Semite, Carin worshipped the ground Hitler walked on. To her, Hitler was like a mythical superhero from a Norse legend: Carin did everything in her power to cement the relationship between the two men.

The first encounter between Carin and her future husband resembled something out of a romance novel. It was a wild stormy night. An icy blizzard was raging. Yet Count Eric von Rosen – a wealthy Swedish explorer – was intent on finding somebody to fly him from Stockholm to his medieval-style castle around 60 miles away where his wife and her sister, the 31-year-old Countess Carin von Foch, were waiting for him. The only pilot prepared to risk such a hazardous journey was Goering. The hair-raising flight tested his skill and nerve to the limit; with visibility almost zero, he managed to land the plane on the frozen lake that lay by the castle. Once Goering had entered its imposing interior – adorned with Aryan-themed tapestries, Nordic sculptures, antique weapons and two huge wrought iron swastikas – and settled by a roaring fire with a brandy, he felt completely at home.

Goering spent much of his childhood at two castles (one in Bavaria, the other in Austria) owned by his godfather and guardian angel Hermann Ritter von Eppenstein, a respected physician. In 1893, while on a trip to Africa, von Eppenstein met Goering's father, a colonial governor, whose young attractive and pregnant wife was suffering from a high fever. With Goering ready to drop, the situation was critical: von Eppenstein stepped in and saved the day. After Goering's father had retired on a barely adequate civil service pension, von Eppenstein offered to take the family in. His motives weren't entirely altruistic: he was having an affair with Goering's mother. Under his castle roofs, she split her time between her rapidly ageing husband and her benefactor.

Von Eppenstein was extremely proud of his noble status – born Jewish, he'd become a Christian to further his medical career, thereby gaining access to influential members of the Prussian elite – and flaunted it whenever possible; fond of pageantry and playing lord of the manor, he hosted baronial banquets accompanied by minstrels in medieval garb.

Carin grew up in similarly baroque surroundings. Her father was an aristocratic colonel, her Anglo-Irish mother came from a brewing dynasty. Carin had four sisters and with the other female members of the family they combined to form their own pantheistic Christian society, the Edelweiss Club – with the flower as their emblem – that boasted its very own chapel, a small but beautifully decorated stone building where they worshipped, sang folk songs and performed séances. Every day during the First World War they knelt and prayed for a German victory.

Carin and Goering's rarefied, fantastical upbringings gave them a grandiose sense of themselves; like lead actors in some great drama. But life had left them both deeply frustrated. At the end of the war, Germany's air force had been banned by the Versailles Treaty, leaving Goering angry and bitter. Addicted to action – from an early age he was obsessed with all things military, as well as hunting and mountain climbing – he became an overnight sensation in Sweden as the star of aerial shows, performing daredevil stunts in front of open-mouthed audiences. But the novelty wore off; he ceased to be the toast of the town. Depressed, he took the gig shuttling civilians back and forth. The fact Goering accepted von Rosen's request, despite the danger, indicates how desperate he was for adventure.

Carin was trapped in a loveless marriage to Nils von Kantzow, an army officer. Wed at 21, she fell pregnant three years later and endured a traumatic birth; though she loved her son Thomas she was ill equipped to be a mother and yearned to escape the suffocating atmosphere of polite society. Having left her 7-year-old son and husband in Stockholm, she'd taken refuge at the count's castle.

From the moment she joined Goering in the grand hall, the two of them were transfixed by each other. Drawn irresistibly together, they began a semi-clandestine affair that rapidly escalated. Carin told her sister that she and Goering were like Tristan and Isolde: 'We have swallowed the love potion and are helpless'; and her letters to him were full of melodramatic declarations such as 'you're everything to me. There is no other like you', and burning desire: 'I kiss everything that is near you.'[6] Inevitably, her husband found out. Divorce was the only option. Carin lost custody of her son in exchange for von Kantzow's financial support.

Once Goering was established in Munich, Carin joined him. After a businesslike civil ceremony in Sweden, they tied the knot again with family and friends present. They lived in a two-storey villa in the suburbs that quickly became a gathering place for Hitler and his cronies. Carin's sister Mary – who would become something of a fixture in their lives – fondly recalled that Hitler seemed totally at ease in Carin's company while she positively shone in his presence.

By late spring 1923, Goering had assumed authority over the Brownshirts and set about whipping them into shape with parade-ground drills and regimental exercises. Writing home, Carin boasted that Goering had transformed 'a rabble … into a veritable army of light': thanks to him, thousands of SA men were now 'a band of eager crusaders ready to march at the Führer's orders'.[7]

2

FUGITIVES AND PRISONERS

arly afternoon, 8 November 1923: Carin was stuck in bed wrestling with a serious case of pneumonia that had made her dangerously ill. Her intensely passionate spirit was contained in a physically frail body. Thin, slightly built, with a raft of health problems, she was especially vulnerable to chest infections. Then her husband appeared with some surprising news. The long-talked-about national revolution was going to begin that night at a beer hall where three of the most powerful men in Bavaria – the state governor, the chief of police and a senior army figure – were hosting a large political meeting. The plan was deceptively simple and wildly ambitious: hijack the event, persuade the triumvirate to hand over the keys to the city, and, with the masses rallying to their standard, march on Berlin.

Hyperinflation had unravelled the fabric of German society; the occupation of the Ruhr by French troops – prompted by disputes over the reparations demanded by the Versailles Treaty – had re-energised the foot soldiers of the nationalist right; there were serious left-wing revolts in Saxony and Thuringia. Conditions seemed ripe. Yet, there was also a growing sense that the worst had passed. Worried they may have missed their chance, Hitler and his cohorts decided to act.

At 8.30 p.m. Hitler, with Hess at his side, stormed into the beer hall, followed soon after by Goering and a squad of SA men. The dignitaries were hauled off stage and the crowd brought to heel. In an upstairs room, a deal was hammered out. The three leading officials promised to support the coup.

By around 11 p.m. a strange calm had descended. Hess, who'd acquired his own set of hostages – including a chief justice, a police president and a Bavarian government minister – was ordered to transport them to a pre-prepared, isolated house 30 miles from Munich and await further instructions. Goering, confident that events were going their way, asked somebody to inform Carin that everything was under control.

It wasn't. After Hitler left the beer hall to monitor events elsewhere, the triumvirate managed to slip away into the night. They immediately mobilised the army and the police, who moved to secure key locations. By morning, it was clear the Putsch had failed.

Determined to make a symbolic gesture of defiance, Hitler, Goering, and the other main players assembled their troops – around 2,000 men – and with banners aloft set off for the town hall, which was guarded by armed police. After a brief stand-off, shots were fired. Hitler dislocated his shoulder in the confusion, which left fourteen Nazis and four police officers dead, while a bullet struck Goering in the thigh, just below the groin. Bleeding profusely, he was whisked away from the chaotic scene and taken in by an elderly Jewish woman who lived nearby. From there, he was moved to a private clinic.

Carin – who had received Goering's upbeat late-night message – was now confronted by the truth. Dragging herself off her sickbed, she rushed to his side. Clearly, he needed proper treatment. Fast. Yet if he stayed in Munich, his arrest was inevitable. So, Carin got him into a car and drove to the villa of an acquaintance near the Austrian border. The following morning, the 10th, they tried to cross but the customs officials recognised the fugitive and dragged him off to the nearest police station. Presumably because of Goering's severe condition, the police were confident he wouldn't escape and left him unguarded, but he slipped out through a window and into a waiting car. At the frontier, the driver used a false passport and concealed Goering under blankets in the back seat. The ruse worked, and they made it across. For now, he was safe from justice.

In all the confusion, Ilse still had no idea what had happened to her boyfriend. Hess had dutifully remained at his post, holed up in the countryside villa with the captives he'd taken from the beer hall, tension mounting with each passing hour. Finally, around mid afternoon, Hess got word of his comrades' ignominious defeat. Afraid the police might arrive any minute, he bundled several petrified and confused hostages into a car and embarked on a bizarre round-around through the surrounding forests while he figured out what to do.

In the end, he abandoned them and disappeared on foot, hoping to find a phone and call Ilse. When Hess eventually did get through to her, Ilse grabbed her bicycle and pedalled off to meet him. Taking turns on her bike, swapping every few miles, they headed back to Munich and Professor Haushofer's house. After a brief discussion, Hess opted to flee. By the next day, he was in Austria.

Meanwhile, Gerda's father was in Nuremberg trying to decide how to respond to the rapidly unfolding events. Though rumours of the Putsch had reached Buch the previous evening, he'd elected to stay put. During the morning, news of the debacle filtered through. Incensed by reports that Hitler had been seriously injured, Buch told his SA men that 'the blood of Hitler would be avenged by the blood of the Jews',[1] but then thought better of it. Instead, Buch was faced with an ultimatum: the authorities had ordered all SA units to disband. Avoiding arrest, Buch refused to comply for another two days before falling into line. Yet he was determined to prevent the SA from disintegrating altogether and on 13 November he was in Munich trying to pick up the pieces.

By then the former head of the SA was in Innsbruck. After a couple of nights at the Hotel Tyrol, a delirious Goering was rushed to hospital. The doctors got to work; his bullet wound closed but re-opened again. He was in constant agony, as Carin explained to her mother in a letter dated 8 December 1923: 'It hurts so much that he bites the pillow, and all I can hear are inarticulate groans … they are giving him morphine every day now, it does nothing to diminish the pain.'[2]

While Goering suffered, Hess was hiding out with various contacts and moving back and forth to Munich to see Ilse – who had fallen ill – and discuss with Haushofer whether or not he should give himself up. As the trial of Hitler and his co-conspirators was going better than Hess could have expected (the judge was sympathetic towards Hitler and let him use the witness stand as a soap box, garnering him both national and international press coverage) he was increasingly tempted to hand himself in.

The verdicts on 1 April 1924 settled the issue. Though guilty of treason – a crime that carried a life sentence – Hitler was given only five years; various technicalities reduced it even further to around eighteen months, and he was eligible for parole after six. Encouraged by this show of leniency, Hess took the plunge, handed himself in on 12 May, received the same sentence as Hitler and joined him in Landsberg prison about 40 miles west of Munich.

Hitler and Hess were confined in a special wing – known as 'The Fortress' – reserved for political prisoners and convicted duellists. Conditions there were extremely relaxed: no prison uniform, no mandatory haircuts. They were allowed to decorate their light, airy cells with pictures and flowers. They could buy tobacco and alcohol and had a daily ration of a litre of beer. With no duties to perform, they lived a life of leisure. They had access to the prison garden. Lunch was at midday, tea and coffee at around 4.30 p.m., supper at 6 p.m. Hot drinks and pastries were served before lights out at 10 p.m. The whole wing resembled a Nazi holiday camp.

Hess, like the other inmates, was permitted six hours' visiting time a week, and Ilse showed up every Saturday. Greeted on the stairs by Hess and Hitler – who would always indulge her with a kiss on the hand – they would then sit down for lunch together. One weekend, Ilse took her previously 'totally un-political' mother to see Hitler; won over by his gracious manners, she joined the party 'as soon as she got back to Munich'.[3]

Given all the free time on their hands, Hitler decided to use it productively and embarked on writing a book. After trying various titles, he plumped for *Mein Kampf*. Furnished with a typewriter, Hitler would bang away with two fingers then go over the results with Hess, who acted as critic and sounding board.

Hess's constant stream of letters to Ilse enthusiastically detailed the development of his emotional bond with Hitler as they mulled over the progress of the manuscript. After reading Hess his First World War reminiscences, Hitler broke down in tears: 'Suddenly he dropped the page, buried his head in his hands, and sobbed.'[4] He also confided in Hess about his feelings regarding women and marriage; though he saw the attraction, Hitler stated that he would only be able to fulfil his destiny if he remained single, unencumbered by a wife and children.

All these revelations made Hess feel like he was being shown a rare glimpse of Hitler's soul, and he shared these intimate moments with Ilse. She responded by sending a collection of Hölderlin's poems to Hitler, hoping to further inspire him. Unfortunately for her, Hitler never read much poetry and he found Hölderlin's verse baffling. He was much more interested in what Hess's mentor, Professor Haushofer, had to say over the course of several visits he made to Landsberg, during which he outlined his philosophy of *Lebensraum*: given the size of its population, Germany could only survive and prosper if it grew beyond its current borders and expanded eastwards.

Professor Haushofer later claimed that Hitler was simply not educated enough to grasp the complexity of his theories – 'Hitler never understood these things and did not have the right outlook for understanding them'[5] – and wilfully misinterpreted their meaning. Haushofer preferred mass migration to conquest and never endorsed the genocidal violence that Hitler's racial imperialism demanded. But in Landsberg, Professor Haushofer may well have planted a seed in Hitler's oddly fertile brain. Over the coming years, his obsessive hatred of Jews and Bolsheviks found expression in a grotesque vision of a sprawling Eastern empire.

On 20 December 1924 – having spent eight and a half months in jail – Hitler walked out of prison to be greeted by a beaten-up rented car filled with well-wishers. Accounts vary as to whether Ilse was among them, but she was definitely there a week later when Hess was released. That evening, they met Hitler for dinner at his favourite restaurant and had ravioli, the house speciality. Reunited, they faced an uphill battle to get the movement back on its feet again.

Hitler was banned from any political activity and the party was outlawed. His first task was to raise the morale of his most dedicated followers. Almost immediately, Hitler reconnected with the Buch family. Gerda vividly remembered Hitler sitting by their 'tiled stove' as he reaffirmed his commitment to the struggle: 'If I saw the future as completely black, I wouldn't go on fighting.'[6]

In the meantime, Ilse and the music critic from the party newspaper were hard at work editing the very rough draft of *Mein Kampf* and turning it into a coherent text. On 18 July 1925, the first volume was finally ready for publication. By 1929, it had sold 23,000 copies; by 1932, nearly a quarter of a million; by 1945, 12 million.

One of the 350 people who visited Hitler in prison was Carin Goering. She turned up on 15 April 1924 with the intention of winning Hitler's support for her proposal; she and her husband would go to Italy and establish contact with Mussolini. Hitler was non-committal. Nevertheless, Carin left Landsberg re-inspired by her idol: 'He is a genius, full of love and truth and a burning faith.'[7]

It had been a tough winter. Though Goering had been released from hospital around Christmas, his condition continued to be serious and he was increasingly dependent on morphine. Money was tight, even though their hotel gave them a 30 per cent discount. The Austrian authorities were looking to expel their unwanted guest, and Italy appeared an attractive option. The couple landed in May 1924 and based themselves in Rome after brief stopovers in Venice and Florence.

At the time, Mussolini was busy consolidating his grip on the Italian state; Goering – and Hitler for that matter – were an irrelevance. Though Carin liked to pretend otherwise, Goering never got close to seeing *Il Duce*, his route blocked by a local fascist official who rebuffed his requests for an audience. Goering kept banging on his door, but to no avail.

Living hand-to-mouth in grotty lodgings, their situation became critical. Goering's weight ballooned. His morphine habit was now a full-blown addiction; he contemplated suicide. With her own health precarious, Carin knew they had to leave Italy before it was too late. Sweden was the obvious destination.

While nursing Goering was her main concern, Carin was worried that Hitler might forget about him. Before pitching up in Stockholm, Carin slipped across to Germany, saw Hitler and reassured him that a useful dialogue had been begun with Mussolini. She was careful not to reveal the full extent of Goering's spiral into drug-induced psychosis, his vicious mood swings, aggressive tantrums and erratic behaviour.

Back in Sweden, she contracted TB and was forced to pawn some of her possessions to feed his cravings. At her wits' end – and with her family's support – Carin had her husband admitted to a nursing home. Unable and unwilling to adjust to lower doses of painkillers, Goering ran amok, smashing medicine cabinets and assaulting staff. He was put in a straightjacket and carted off to the Långbro asylum. Locked in a cell and forced to go cold turkey, Goering's physical withdrawal was accompanied by nightmarish hallucinations and paranoid delusions. He ranted and raved about the Jews and their fiendish plots to kill him; according to his medical reports, he thought that a 'Jewish Doctor wanted to cut out his heart', and Abraham – from the Old Testament – was 'driving a red-hot nail into his back'.[8]

Yet Carin remained steadfast, convinced he'd recover. After ten weeks – and a brief relapse that led to another spell inside – he was fit enough to re-enter the world. Ashamed and reluctant to admit how far he'd fallen, Goering rarely spoke about this period in his life. Years later, he confessed to Carin's son that she saved him from oblivion.

3

MATCHMAKING

In the autumn of 1927, the government announced a general amnesty that meant Goering was able to return to Germany without fear of arrest: he found the party in the process of reconstruction and consolidation as it prepared itself to take a new route to power via the ballot box.

Hitler had spent much of his time since his release touring the country, uniting the fractured Nazi movement and reasserting his supreme leadership. Hess – who was now Hitler's personal secretary – stuck to him like glue wherever he went, leaving Ilse to her own devices. Though no less devoted to the Nazi cause, she was nevertheless losing patience with the snail-like progress of their relationship. After seven sexless years, Hess seemed no closer to popping the question. Despite shrugging off the delay – 'we were too busy to get married; he was away all the time and I was working'[1] – Ilse was contemplating moving abroad for a while. She'd completed her university course and her part-time job at the antiquarian bookshop was hardly enough to tie her to Munich. Which left Hess.

Ilse liked to claim that it was Hitler who settled the matter while the three of them were eating at the *Café Osteria*, one of his favourite hangouts. Ilse was debating her future when Hitler took her hand, placed it in Hess's and asked her if 'she'd ever thought about marrying this man?'[2] Her answer was obviously 'yes': unable to deny Hitler's wishes, Hess stopped procrastinating. After all – as he explained in a letter to his parents – Ilse was his 'good comrade' and 'loyal friend', they were 'fond of each other' and shared the same ideas about life. Compared to other women he'd encountered, she was 'an angel'.[3]

Having abandoned conventional religion, Ilse and Hess decided against a church wedding. On 20 December 1927, they got married at a small civil ceremony; Hitler and Professor Haushofer acted as witnesses. The newly-weds were very low on cash, but Ilse was able to obtain a loan through Winifred Wagner, mistress of the Bayreuth Festival that was held every year in the composer's honour. Winifred had briefly known Ilse before the war and they were re-introduced after Winifred befriended Hitler.

A huge Wagner fan, Hitler was delighted to make her acquaintance, while she regarded him with barely concealed awe. Her husband, Siegfried Wagner, was a bisexual bohemian twice her age who'd bowed to pressure from his mother —widow of Richard Wagner – to do the right thing and produce some heirs. Winifred had dutifully given birth to four children in rapid succession and together they provided Hitler with a kind of extended family. Her eldest daughter recalled how he would often drop by late at night and wake them in their nursery to tell them 'gruesome tales of his adventures'.[4]

Winifred was fond of Ilse and happy to help the young couple; in return, a grateful Hess kept her informed of Hitler's movements. With the money, Ilse and Hess got a small apartment in Munich. Not that co-habitation did anything to improve their sex life: Ilse complained to a friend that she 'felt like a convent girl'.[5]

Hess also insisted that she submit to the Nazis' new rules about female participation in the movement: she could retain her party membership – during this period around 8 per cent were women – but no more than that. Women were barred from taking on any official roles, while more mainstream conservative and right-wing parties had dedicated women's sections putting forward candidates for elections. Ilse could have joined one of the Nazi-orientated women's groups – like the German Women's Order (Deutscher Frauenorden, DFO) founded in 1923 – that were officially affiliated to the party in January 1928, but given her place in Hitler's hierarchy that option was closed to her.

However, this did not mean that Ilse was relegated to the sidelines. Her proximity to Hitler – who trusted her, respected her, and valued her loyalty – gave her a different but no less influential form of power. Her diplomatic skills and human touch were required when Hitler needed to find a solution to a tricky and sensitive personal matter; his relationship with his 19-year-old niece Geli Raubel.

Geli first caught Hitler's eye when she visited him in prison with her mother, who was Hitler's half-sister. Once she'd finished school, Geli was fully integrated into Hitler's inner circle after he invited her mother to become housekeeper at the modest cottage he was renting from Nazi sympathisers – who gave him a cut-price rate – near the small mountain town of Berchtesgaden; its spectacular location and tranquil atmosphere provided a perfect setting for long, lazy afternoons spent having picnics, swimming in lakes and strolling in forests. His entourage all embraced Geli; she was unpretentious, natural, light-hearted and full of fun. And she had a very positive effect on Hitler's moods. Ilse liked her. Hess thought she was sharp-witted. Heinrich Hoffmann called her 'an enchantress' who 'put everybody in the best of spirits';[6] even his daughter Henriette, who had every reason to resent Geli replacing her as Hitler's young protégée, found her 'incredibly charming'.[7]

In company, Hitler gave Geli the 'Uncle Adolf' treatment. Yet his feelings were far from pure; he'd become seriously besotted with her. The trouble was neither Geli nor Hitler's dashing chauffeur, Emil Maurice, realised this; they'd fallen for each other and were talking about marriage. Using her age as an excuse, a furious Hitler confronted Geli and demanded she drop Emil. Geli refused. Frightened of losing her, Hitler asked Ilse to broker a deal: the young lovers would have to wait two years to marry. In the meantime, they could only be together in Hitler's presence. Geli accepted these terms and on Christmas Eve 1937 she relayed them to Emil in a letter: 'Two whole years during which we may kiss each other only now and then and always under the watchful eye of Uncle Adolf.' Geli also acknowledged the key role Ilse played: 'She was so nice. She was the only person who believed that you really love me.'[8]

Hitler got what he wanted; within a few months Emil was gone and forgotten. In late 1929, Geli moved into a spare room in Hitler's new apartment. Ilse continued to take an interest in Geli's life, partly out of genuine concern, but mostly because Hitler needed a reliable source of information so he could keep track of Geli when he was away from Munich.

On 18 September 1927, Margaret Boden shared a three-hour train journey from Munich to Berlin with a bespectacled, unremarkable-looking young man called Heinrich Himmler. They struck up a conversation and by the end of the ride a connection had been made. Having gone their separate ways, they began exchanging letters, an almost daily habit that would continue throughout their relationship, largely because they were more often apart than together.

At 35, Margaret was eight years older than Himmler. From a comfortable land-owning family, she was just old enough to join the German Red Cross in 1914 and become a nurse. Established in the 1860s, it had 6,000 full-time angels of mercy available for duty when the First World War began. Nursing was considered a suitable vocation for women from upper- and middle-class backgrounds, like Margaret, and after completing her training she donned her uniform (which resembled a nun's habit) and was deployed to a field hospital. These were usually established in villages near the front, often in churches or schools, and furnished with 200 beds.

Vulnerable to shelling and air raids, the staff were rotated every six months. But no matter where Margaret went, she could not escape the cruel and heart-breaking parade of maimed, mutilated and traumatised casualties. The impact her experience of frontline nursing had on her is hard to quantify. How do you measure the loss of innocence? Of faith in the goodness of humanity? She was only 25 when the fighting stopped; from then on Margaret always seemed much older than her years.

Soon after the war, she got married. Very little is known about this union except that it was unsuccessful and the couple divorced after two years. In 1923, with financial help from her father, Margaret bought into a private clinic in Berlin run by a Jewish gynaecologist. As head nurse, her speciality was homeopathy – herbal cures and natural remedies.

Himmler was equally fascinated by alternative medicine. While he wasn't a technophobe, Himmler considered mass industrialisation to be an essentially alien force corrupting the essence of the German soul. He believed in revisiting peasant cultures and utilising the accumulated folk knowledge of earlier generations. More to the point, he had been afflicted by persistent and chronic stomach problems since childhood (during elementary school, he was off sick for 160 days) and the state of his guts was a recurring theme in their letters. Margaret put his condition down to stress and overwork – 'your stomach is just taking revenge for what you constantly put it through'[9] – and she recommended proper rest supplemented by doses of mustard, vinegar and onions.

Part of the attraction for Margaret could have been that Himmler reminded her of the young men she'd cared for during the war who often treated their nurses like surrogate mothers; in one letter she asked if Himmler had any pictures of himself as a little boy. Equally well, aside from finding her blonde hair and blue eyes very appealing, her sturdy frame and slightly severe manner gave her a matronly air that might have reminded Himmler of his doting mother. She'd always spoiled and indulged her sickly boy; she still sent him food parcels and did his washing.

Himmler's severe, stamp-collecting father was a head teacher at a well-respected *Gymnasium* – which Himmler attended – and he had tutored the son of Bavarian royalty, adding extra polish to the family name. Himmler grafted hard and did his best to live up to his father's high standards.

Aged 14 at the outbreak of the First World War, Himmler couldn't wait to be involved; yet in 1918, when he was finally old enough to begin basic training, he found it gruelling and was often homesick. The armistice came before he could be deployed at the front. Crestfallen, and reluctant to give up his uniform, he drifted in and out of various paramilitary groups, ending up in the SA in time to make a brief cameo appearance during the beer hall revolt.

By the mid 1920s he was working flat out for the party and had switched his allegiance from Gregor Strasser – who had emerged with a more left-wing orientated version of Nazism – to Hitler; Himmler's attachment to Hitler was total, a deep-seated emotional fixation that bordered on worship. Shortly before his train journey with Margaret, Himmler had been made deputy of the SS; formed to provide Hitler with an elite bodyguard, it was at that time a tiny fledgling outfit with no clear identity.

Though their early correspondence featured some tenderness and romantic word-play, it also revealed Margaret's essential pessimism – 'love without sorrow and worry is something I just cannot imagine' – and negative view of human nature. She was suspicious of new people and dreaded social interaction, yet at the same time felt a deep and crippling loneliness. Contemplating New Year's Eve, she bemoaned her fate: 'Tomorrow is a dreadful day when everyone is having a party and I must be alone. It really is awful.'[10]

During their second rendezvous at a hotel in a snow-bound Bavarian town, a three-day stay just before Christmas, they became physically intimate. Margaret was not a particularly sexual person and Himmler was a virgin. A few years earlier, he'd sworn off women altogether, having read a quasi-scientific tract that urged young men to remain chaste and channel their abundant and valuable sexual energy into more useful activities. Choosing celibacy was a convenient way for Himmler to make a virtue out of his abject failure with women; sex both scared and fascinated him.

In his student diaries, Himmler often wrote about how appalled he was by young women who were too free with their bodies, while fantasising about what it might be like to surrender himself to such wild, uninhibited creatures; at the same time, he managed to alienate his two closest male companions by falling for their girlfriends, whose rejection of him led Himmler to conclude that they were morally suspect as well. From his perspective, Margaret was an ideal mate; she had some experience but not enough to make him feel totally inadequate in the bedroom. Whether or not they had intercourse is unclear, but their letters after they parted again reflect this shift in their relationship. They started using nicknames and terms of endearment; Himmler even dared to make references to her 'beautiful dear body'.[11]

Having crossed this line together, they decided to get married as soon as possible. But there were several stumbling blocks: Himmler was intensely busy doing his bit to boost the Nazis' chances in the upcoming

Reichstag elections – scheduled for 20 May – and their wedding plans depended on Margaret selling her share of the Berlin clinic and using the money to purchase a plot of land; they were going to become farmers. This was a long-cherished ambition of Himmler's. In the autumn of 1919, he began studying agriculture in Munich, a course that combined book learning with work on a farm. After graduating in August 1922, he got job for a fertiliser company, which lasted a year before he quit to join the Nazi party. Margaret was raised on her father's large farm and was familiar with dealing with livestock and growing crops.

However, the process of disengaging herself from her Jewish business partner took longer than expected. In her letters, Margaret made snide remarks at his expense, calling him 'riff-raff' and 'Jewish rabble'; to her, he was living proof that all Jews were equally untrustworthy, noting that 'the others are no better'.[12]

Though there is little evidence to suggest Margaret held the same twisted and outlandish views as her fiancé, she shared the prejudices of the social milieu she was raised in, including its engrained racism and snobbery. Margaret's anti-Semitism was an instinctive reflex, as was her fear and mistrust of the lower classes, whether rural or urban. Keen to educate her politically, Himmler sent her copies of his speeches and pamphlets, and well-known racist tomes, which she dutifully read and tried to sound enthusiastic about. But she was not an extremist and often found Himmler's violent language troubling: 'Why do you reach for the dagger in such a bloodthirsty way? After all, being a conservative is a nice thing to be.'[13]

Ultimately, they spent more time completing the puzzle books they both enjoyed than discussing the philosophical and historical roots of Nazism. Reluctant even to attend a party rally, she was jealous of Hitler's hold over him and openly expressed her dissatisfaction: 'If only you didn't have to go around with the Boss anymore. He takes up so much time.' Himmler responded by reminding her that he was a revolutionary, not a 'spineless civil servant'.[14]

With the May election over, and the negotiations about her exit from the clinic almost complete, they wed in a Berlin registry office on 3 July 1928. Margaret's father and brother acted as witnesses. None of

Himmler's family were present; his parents were committed Catholics and struggled to accept his son's marriage to a Protestant woman. There was no honeymoon. Himmler was off attending both the annual party rally and the Bayreuth Festival during August. The newly-weds managed a three-day break away in early September before he disappeared again.

The Reichstag election results – the party got less than 3 per cent of the vote – were a sharp reminder of how far the Nazis were from achieving their aims. Their dismal showing was largely due to the phoenix-like recovery of the Weimar Republic from the low point of 1923, boosted by large loans from America, agreement over sustainable reparation payments, the thawing of diplomatic tensions with Germany's European neighbours, and the public's overwhelming desire for something resembling normal life.

One of the dozen Nazi delegates to enter the Reichstag was a rejuvenated Goering. With Carin back from Sweden, he quickly accepted a key role in the party's development, attracting the great and good and tapping them for much-needed funds. However, to raise money he needed money, or at least the appearance of it. Luckily for him, his wartime achievements still counted for something: Lufthansa – Germany's largest civil aviation company – was looking to boost its profile and picked Goering as its representative, bankrolling him to the tune of 1,000 RM (Reichsmark) a month.

He and Carin moved into an opulent apartment. The couple were soon hosting soirees for the cream of society; aristocratic and royal representatives of Germany's former imperial dynasties; captains of industry and influential bankers. To their guests, Carin and her husband presented a respectable, moderate front, allaying fears about Hitler's intentions. A decorative, charming hostess, Carin became a different animal when entertaining her fellow Nazis, diving head-first into their debates and arguments. Though Carin was a woman, her interventions were tolerated, even welcomed – apparently Goebbels particularly enjoyed these discussions – because of her undoubted radicalism and ideological fervour. In a letter she wrote to her mother around that time Carin spat venom at her enemies: 'Every-day the Communists parade with their crooked noses and red flags with the Star of David.'[15]

One of Goering's other colleagues who also managed to get elected that year was Gerda's father. Since the Munich Putsch, Walter Buch had toyed with various careers – lawyer, teacher, and wine and cigar salesman – but never abandoned hope that Hitler would rise from the ashes. His faith was rewarded in November 1927. Due to the fact that his father had been a high court judge, Buch was put in charge of the USCHLA, the Nazi Party Court, set up to deal with internal disputes and breaches of discipline.

By then, Gerda had finished high school, passed her *Abitur*, and was about to become a kindergarten teacher, a logical career for someone whose chief interests were arts and crafts, reading German children's stories and playing folk music on her guitar. Her younger brother recalled that 'she was never happier than when she was with children, drawing with them or making lino cuts'.[16] However, the fact she'd chosen to enter such a caring, nurturing profession did not mean she'd rejected her father's politics. Having grown up around Hitler and his ideas, Gerda failed to develop a mind of her own: her worldview was completely shaped by Nazism, her belief absolute.

If anything, Gerda was more fanatical than her father, something that would become clear after she became involved with a stocky, thick-necked, roguishly handsome macho man called Martin Bormann, who was a relative latecomer to the movement, joining the party in February 1927. He was briefly a press officer in his local area, then moved into the SA, which is how he first came into contact with Gerda's father. Though most of the Nazi elite regarded Bormann as their social inferior, a boorish yob lacking culture – one rival compared him to a pig – his background was solidly middle class. His father's family were from humble roots but he made a career as a trumpeter in a military band and after leaving his regiment he entered the postal service as a clerk and worked his way steadily up the ladder.

In later life, Bormann spoke proudly of his father's achievements, but the truth is he barely knew him; Bormann's father died when he was 3.

His mother, faced with the prospect of raising Bormann, his younger brother Albert, and two stepchildren from her dead husband's previous marriage, quickly got hitched to her widowed brother-in-law – the director of a local bank – who had five children of his own. As a result, Bormann grew up in a very large family, but he didn't like any of his siblings and felt neglected by his stepfather, who he came to despise.

Nevertheless, there was enough money around to send the young Bormann to a private prep school; other than displaying a talent for arithmetic, he struggled with most subjects. Not academic enough for a traditional *Gymnasium*, at 14 Bormann went to a technical high school – slightly less prestigious but no less exclusive – and was leaning towards agricultural studies when he was called up in June 1918, too late to see any fighting.

Demobbed, Bormann decided not to return home and got a job as the foreman on a large estate of 810 acres, where the owner recognised his head for figures and put him in charge of the accounts and the payroll. His boss was an arch-nationalist who mostly hired ex-*Freikorps* men to work his land. In this milieu, Bormann got involved in a variety of extreme right-wing anti-Semitic associations.

On the night of 31 May 1923 Bormann's life took a significant turn when he was involved in the sadistic murder of a former employee, Walter Kadow, who'd run up considerable debts and run off without paying them. For some inexplicable reason, Kadow made the fatal mistake of returning to the scene of the crime. Spurred on by rumours that Kadow was a communist agent, Bormann planned a nasty surprise for him; he convinced half a dozen estate workers to kidnap Kadow and give him a thorough beating. The assailants got Kadow stupidly drunk and then – using a horse and cart provided by Bormann – carried him to a nearby forest where they fractured his skull with a tree branch, cut his throat, shot him twice in the head, stripped him naked, burned his clothes and buried his broken body.

Bormann was arrested alongside the murderers – who included Rudolf Höss, the future commandant of Auschwitz – and spent over six months awaiting trial. On 12 March 1924, they had their day in court. The killers were sentenced to ten years; Bormann, one year. In prison, he knuckled down and adapted to the draconian rules and mind-numbing labour. Bormann remembered that he had to 'paste together all sorts of paper containers for cigarettes, drugs, candy, and gut strings for instruments' in order to fill his quota of 1,500 cartons a day. At the same time, he took advantage of the lack of distractions to contemplate his 'own ideas, especially political ones'.[17] He left prison even more convinced that the enemies of the German people needed to be punished.

Bormann returned to the estate to pick up where he left off, but on arrival discovered that he wasn't welcome there any longer; the owner had found out that Bormann had been having an affair with his wife, Ehrengard. Though Bormann never openly acknowledged their relationship, he maintained a correspondence with Ehrengard for the next twenty years and would occasionally pay her visits, usually late at night.

Bormann possessed a relentless and unrestrained libido that he made no effort to control, seeking to satisfy his sexual hunger whenever and wherever he could without any regard for social convention. It's not difficult to grasp why Bormann found Gerda so irresistible; slender and long-limbed, strikingly attractive, she emitted the radiance of youth. Equally, an association with the daughter of such a prominent Nazi could only smooth his passage through the ranks of the party.

His rugged masculinity appealed to the inexperienced Gerda. Dating him would also be an act of rebellion against her father; Buch thought Bormann was a worthless ruffian. However, he decided not to interfere on the basis that Gerda's schoolgirl crush would pass as soon as she realised how incompatible they were.

But events got the better of Buch. Every Sunday, Bormann would drive his Opel to the Buch home just outside Munich and spend the afternoon with Gerda under her mother's supervision. In April 1929, after returning from one of their long walks, Bormann formally asked for her hand in marriage. With the engagement official, the couple were allowed a little more freedom and at some point around the beginning of August, Bormann took Gerda's virginity. She immediately fell pregnant.

They were married on 2 September, with Hitler and Hess acting as witnesses. In the wedding photograph, there is a sharp contrast between Gerda – dressed in white and wearing a veil and a myrtle wreath – and her jack-booted husband and the other guests, all in full uniform: yet none of the men in the picture had any doubt that Gerda belonged with them.

Some miles outside Munich, Margaret Himmler was also expecting a child. But her husband had other priorities; since becoming head of the SS on 4 January 1929 – when he famously declared that he'd shoot his own mother if Hitler asked him to – he was totally absorbed by his mission to create an elite force of racially pure warriors.

Though Himmler had overseen renovations to their modest house and the construction of the chicken hutches, he was soon gone, leaving her to manage the farm. Her situation was not unusual. Much of the burden of running Germany's small farms was shouldered by the wives – nearly 80 per cent of those employed in this type of agriculture were female family members – while their husbands sought more lucrative work in the cities. Aside from the poultry, Margaret had to tend to geese, rabbits, turkeys and a pig, plus a variety of fruit and vegetables; as time went on, the couple also hoped to cultivate healing herbs.

The pregnancy only made her life more onerous and demanding. From the road, Himmler ordered her not to work too hard, but maintaining the farm was an all-consuming task, especially if it was ever going to break even. Her health suffered. Both Margaret and the baby were at risk. When Himmler returned home from the party rally on 7 August 1928, she was in agony. Himmler whisked her off to a clinic and the following day their daughter Gudrun was delivered by Caesarean section.

Margaret remained in hospital for the next three weeks. On her release, Himmler hired a nanny to help her when he was away. Unfortunately, Margaret couldn't stand her – she was 'disrespectful and lazy'[18] – and requested a replacement, the first of many domestic servants who failed to live up to her expectations.

By the New Year, Margaret was back to the daily grind. She dug potatoes, chopped wood, trimmed branches, carted manure, harvested elderberries and cranberries and tended to the mushrooms sprouting in the cellar. All this physical labour took its toll, and she stopped having periods. In a letter, Himmler advised her to take hot baths and drink mulled wine with cinnamon, and speculated that the problem stemmed from 'her inner anxiety';[19] he completely failed to recognise that his prolonged absences were the main reason Margaret was so stressed out.

Gerda suffered no ill effects from her pregnancy. On 14 April 1930 she gave birth to a son who was named Adolf, for obvious reasons. Since Hess had taken Bormann under his wing, he and Ilse became the god-parents. Eleven days later, Bormann was promoted and took control of the Party Aid Fund, which doled out insurance payments for the growing number of Nazis hurt or killed during violent confrontations with their opponents.

Aside from his official party duties, Bormann was successfully worming his way into Hitler's entourage and in 1930 Hitler gave him a task that required secrecy and discretion; checking out the ancestry of a 17-year-old girl whom Hitler had met at Heinrich Hoffmann's photographic studio, where she was working as an assistant. Hitler had taken a shine to her and wanted to know if she was from good Aryan stock. After completing a thorough investigation, Bormann was able to confirm that Eva Braun did not have a drop of Jewish blood.

4

ARRIVALS AND DEPARTURES

During the summer of 1930, the recently divorced Magda Quandt was looking for something to do. Her ex-husband had granted her a generous settlement: a spacious apartment in a fashionable part of Berlin, a healthy allowance and access to his country estate. Magda was sophisticated, multilingual, well-travelled, elegant, poised, at ease in elevated company and never short of male admirers; a life of gilded leisure beckoned.

She'd met her ex-husband, Gunther Quandt, in 1919 when he was 37 and she was 18. They spent a train journey together as she travelled from Berlin back to the elite finishing school she'd entered that year after passing her *Abitur*. Quandt was so overwhelmed by her that he kept showing up at Magda's college until they were granted sufficient time alone together for him to propose marriage. Flattered by the attention of such a successful man – Quandt had interests in textiles, chemicals and automobiles, including a controlling stake in BMW – Magda accepted. After a short grace period, they wed on 4 January 1921.

Magda's sudden plunge into married life suggested that she was seeking security after a disjointed childhood. Her mother divorced her father, an engineer, when Magda was 3, then remarried two years later. Magda's stepfather was a Jewish businessman whom she adored. The family moved to Brussels and Magda was sent to a strict Catholic convent school.

In 1914, Magda returned to Germany and was enrolled in a *Gymnasium*. During the war, her mother separated from Magda's stepfather. As a result, Magda was reunited with her biological father, who introduced her to Buddhism, while the older brother of a Jewish schoolfriend gave her a crash course in Zionism. Her genuine interest in both these wildly different philosophies withered when she became a housewife.

Magda inherited Quandt's two children from his first marriage. The couple then adopted three orphans, and in 1922 Magda gave birth to a son named Harald. Suddenly in charge of a large household and the servants that went with it, Magda did her best to cope while her husband focused on accumulating more and more wealth, locking himself in his study night after night, devising new ways to exploit Germany's see-sawing economy.

Quandt's idea of a good evening out was a formal dinner dance and home by ten; Magda was a stunning, lively young woman aching to sample what Berlin had to offer. The capital boasted the most spectacular and varied night-life in Europe, but Magda had to drag her heels at home. Perhaps sensing her restlessness, Quandt took her to London and Paris and together they made several transatlantic trips; a vacation to the USA and Mexico, and a longer visit to the east coast that combined business with pleasure; Magda was in her element, playing her part to perfection.

But opening Magda's eyes to the wider world only made the restricted nature of her Berlin existence more apparent. To make matters worse, her stepson – who was entering late adolescence – had developed a serious crush on her. Aware of the danger, Quandt and Magda decided to send him away to Paris to study. Shortly after his arrival there he was rushed into hospital suffering from acute appendicitis; sepsis set in following a botched operation, and within a few days he was dead.

The fraying connection holding the marriage together snapped. Soon after, Magda embarked on a torrid love affair with a young student. There are several competing theories about who he was, but no concrete evidence to support them. But those close to Magda agreed it was far more than a casual fling; she tried to break it off but couldn't, her feelings too strong to control. Quandt found out and divorce beckoned. Facing the prospect of losing everything – the divorce laws were heavily weighted towards the husband, especially if he was the injured party – Magda accidentally discovered some of Quandt's old love letters and used them to divert attention away from her and on to him. Fearing public embarrassment, Quandt gave her what she needed to continue living in style.

But Magda was dissatisfied and lacking purpose. Previously, she hadn't given much thought to politics, but in Berlin it was impossible to ignore the daily clashes between the Nazis and their opponents. Urged on by several friends, Magda attended a large Nazi rally where the main attraction was Joseph Goebbels.

Other than Hitler, Goebbels was the Nazis' most effective public speaker, peppering his invective with acerbic remarks and withering character assassinations, whipping up the audience as he went, bristling with aggression. He was extremely intelligent and highly educated, with a PhD in literature from Heidelberg University. Yet he was full of resentment and thwarted ambition; his attempts at being a writer – he produced several plays and a dire autobiographical novel – had proved fruitless, while his diminutive size, club foot and pronounced limp had marked him out for ridicule from a young age.

From a lower middle-class family where money was always tight (his father was a book-keeper in a factory) Goebbels was still able to attend a Christian-run *Gymnasium*; his parents were devout Catholics who hoped he'd enter the priesthood. Goebbels was a gifted student and his performance during his *Abitur* exams put him top of the class. Unfit for military service, he enrolled at the University of Bonn in April 1917, and studied there – and at several other institutions – before completing his doctorate in 1921. Three years later he joined the Nazi movement, attracted by its uncompromising attitude; Goebbels had nothing but contempt for the Weimar Republic, was thoroughly anti-Semitic and despised mainstream society.

Goebbels directed his anger at the upper class, the business elite and Jewish finance capital. Berlin based – where the movement adopted a more socialist stance, hoping to lure the city's working class away from the dreaded communists – he distinguished himself as an expert propagandist; his newspaper *Der Angriff* was a model of its kind. While initially uncertain about Hitler's credentials, by the late 1920s he was totally subservient to the Führer's genius: 'The born tribune of the people, the coming dictator.'[1]

Magda was inspired by the rally and Goebbels scorching rhetoric. She joined the party and dutifully read *Mein Kampf* and *The Myth of the 20th Century*, a rambling mishmash concocted by Alfred Rosenberg, the Nazi's self-appointed philosopher. Her early exposure to several all-embracing systems of thought – the Catholicism drilled into her by the Belgian nuns, her father's Buddhism, and her teenage friend's Zionism – had left her with a need to believe in something. She may not have fully realised it, but she'd always been searching for a cause to follow.

Magda quickly became leader of the local Nazi women's group, but her presence caused friction with the other members, who objected to taking orders from such an overprivileged lady. Frustrated, Magda set her sights higher and applied for work at Goebbels's propaganda department, where he couldn't fail to notice her. Struck by Magda's obvious class and beauty, Goebbels asked her to take responsibility for his private archive, hoping that working in such close proximity would make it easier for him to seduce her.

About six weeks before Magda entered Goebbels's life, the Nazis scored a spectacular breakthrough: on 14 September 1930 the party polled around 18 per cent of the vote in the Reichstag elections. The Wall Street Crash and the Depression that it unleashed ripped away the shaky foundations of the Weimar Republic, wiped out the centre ground of politics – pushing voters to the extremes – and concentrated power in the hands of a conservative clique around President Hindenburg, an ageing figurehead whose reputation rested on his exploits as one of Germany's most prominent military commanders during the First World War. Elected in 1925, he was meant to guarantee stability, but with the country plunged into deep despair, his influence proved largely malevolent.

In 1930, Hindenburg triggered Article 48 of the constitution, which gave him the authority to appoint the chancellor and govern without recourse to the Reichstag. Rather than deal with the economic emergency, the new cabinet simply poured oil on the flames by pursuing deflationary measures, sucking money out of the system;

banks folded, businesses went under and unemployment spiralled out of control. The immediate beneficiaries were the Nazis. For the first time they had the resources to mount a coordinated national campaign and their increased visibility, against a backdrop of mounting crisis, paid dividends.

Throughout the year, Goering had campaigned tirelessly. Despite persistent ill health, Carin gave her husband as much support as she could as he engaged in backstairs intrigues and addressed large crowds all across Germany. Her spirits lifted by the result, the couple staged a luxurious party on 13 October, attended by Hitler, Hess, Goebbels, and other prominent figures, to celebrate this transformation in their fortunes.

One of those flocking to Hitler's banner was the teenager Lina von Osten, whose older brother — already a confirmed Nazi supporter — persuaded her to accompany him to a party meeting and she left it a convert, energised by the dynamism of a movement geared towards the young; they would be the main beneficiaries of a bright new future. The party's anti-Semitism was also a factor. Lina loathed the Polish Jews who'd settled in her quiet corner of the world: to her, they were like an alien species.

Lina had seized the first opportunity she had to abandon her family home on the island of Fehmarn (on the north-eastern tip of Germany, facing the Baltic) and strike out on her own. Not that she disliked her parents, but her village was a parochial backwater, while her father's noble ancestry was a constant reminder of what was gone forever: descended from land-owning Danish aristocrats who had over time lost their extensive properties, her father was a humble teacher. During the hyperinflation of the early 1920s, Lina's family's assets dwindled even further and they had to move into the red-brick school building where her father worked.

Having decided to become a teacher herself — at the time, around a third of the teaching profession were women — Lina headed to the mainland port of Kiel to complete her training at a technical high school, staying at a boarding house for female students. As she neared the end of her course, Lina and a few friends attended a ball on 6 December 1930, and it was during what was otherwise a dull evening that Lina made the acquaintance of 27-year-old naval officer Reinhard Heydrich.

Much has been made of Heydrich's supposedly ideal Aryan physiognomy, at least in comparison to the other top Nazis. Tall, blond, with an athlete's build – a physically weak child, he'd taken up sports to get fitter and excelled at running, swimming and fencing – and no doubt impressive in a uniform, he also had an abnormally large head, narrow eyes, a slit for a mouth and jug ears. Lina found him intriguing – 'I felt sympathy for this purposeful yet reserved young man'[2] – and agreed to a rendezvous the next day. In her memoirs, she breathlessly described how Heydrich opened his heart to her over a series of long walks, a visit to the theatre and a meal in a restaurant, and then asked her to marry him during their third evening together.

Lina liked to suggest that their love was written in the stars and could not be denied; others have speculated that his sudden proposal was a necessary prelude to getting her into bed. But there is an alternative explanation. Heydrich was involved with another woman and though the evidence is somewhat confused it seems likely that she'd already had sex with him on the assumption that he'd do the decent thing. Was Heydrich in such a hurry to wed Lina because he was anxious to break free of this other entanglement? If so, his reprieve was only temporary: the jilted woman would come back to haunt him.

Beyond the powerful physical attraction between them, Lina and Heydrich shared some key characteristics. Both were fixed on escaping their backgrounds and forging a different destiny for themselves. They were stubborn and extremely ambitious. They each had a cold, calculating streak. Neither suffered fools gladly. Both had an inflated sense of their own worth and felt that the majority of people were inferior beings.

One of the things that set Heydrich apart was his musical talent. His father was a minor composer who ran a successful music school in their home town of Halle. Heydrich took up the violin at an early age and put in many hours of disciplined, dedicated and exacting practice. Not only did he develop a phenomenal technique – testimony to his work ethic and perfectionism – but his interpretations of classical pieces displayed a rare sensitivity and emotional range. Lina described him as an 'artist' who could 'translate feelings into sound'.[3]

Rather than follow in his father's footsteps, Heydrich chose the navy and joined up in 1922. Unpopular with his fellow cadets – who found him aloof and patronising – they considered his violin playing to be a sign of effeminate weakness, and constantly poked fun at him. But their insults bounced off Heydrich; he was used to being taunted. At school, his precociousness and persistent over-achievement made him a target from day one. All that mattered to him was whether his superiors thought he was officer material.

They did, and in 1926, after a six-month cruise, he was made a *Leutnant zur See* (ensign). In 1928, he became an *Oberleutnant zur See* (sub-lieutenant) and underwent special training as a wireless operator. Given further advancement was likely, Lina now saw no need to take up a teaching job; besides, nobody expected a professional woman to continue working after marriage. The couple visited both sets of parents and gained their approval. Then they hit the buffers: Heydrich's former girlfriend, distressed by the shabby way she'd been treated, was out for revenge.

The actual identity of this mystery woman is unknown; the general consensus is that her father was an important man with personal connections to the upper echelons of the navy. A complaint about ungentlemanly conduct – she accused Heydrich of trying to force himself on her – was made to the appropriate authorities and Heydrich had to appear before a naval court. All records of the proceedings were destroyed, though eye-witnesses contend that it was Heydrich's contemptuous and arrogant attitude that sealed his fate rather than the charges against him. On 30 April 1931 he was dismissed from the navy. Lina said that he was so shattered by the verdict that he had a total breakdown, locking himself in his room for days on end, smashing furniture and weeping uncontrollably, and she had to piece him back together again.

Whether true or not – and it's hard to imagine the man Hitler called 'Iron Heart' behaving like a hysterical child – the most startling thing about the whole incident is Lina's unswerving loyalty. Under the circumstances, nobody would have blamed her if she'd called off the engagement. She was only 19, so this was hardly her last chance of happiness. Clearly, Lina was convinced that with her guidance Heydrich could still rise to the top.

By late February 1931, Magda and Goebbels had begun sleeping together. From the start, the erotic charge between them was intense, a magnetic force that drew them together. Enraptured, Goebbels was walking on air: 'It's like I'm dreaming. So full of satisfied bliss.'[4] His sunny mood, however, did not last. The initial phase of the relationship was very volatile – if his diaries are anything to go by it was either agony or ecstasy without much in between – and they both had doubts about what they were doing. The trigger for screaming rows and agonised soul-searching was the re-emergence of Magda's younger lover.

One of the most corrosive aspects of Goebbels's character was his all-consuming jealousy. While it suited his gargantuan ego to be with a woman as desirable as Magda, he couldn't bear the thought of her with another man, despite the fact he rejected monogamy as an outdated bourgeois convention and made no secret of his own insatiable sexual appetite.

Magda was well aware of Goebbels's reputation as a shameless womaniser but he was also dynamic, motivated and obviously going places, while her young man had few tangible prospects. The lovesick student did himself no favours when he turned up at her apartment brandishing a gun and threatening to kill them both if Magda did not take him back. During a heated confrontation, he fired off one shot but the bullet whizzed past her and struck the doorframe instead. Magda called the police and had him carted away.

There were further complications when Magda was finally introduced to Hitler. However uncertain Magda was about Goebbels, there was no such ambiguity where Hitler was concerned. The feeling was mutual. In the spring of 1931, Magda and Goebbels spent some hours with Hitler and Otto Wagener, an ex-army *Freikorps* veteran and high-ranking SA man who for a while was a sort of special advisor to Hitler. Wagener observed 'the pleasure Hitler took in her innocent high spirits' and 'how her large eyes were hanging on Hitler's gaze'.

Afterwards, Hitler confessed to Wagener that Magda had made a big impression on him. Over the next few weeks, Hitler kept bringing her up in conversation. He told Wagener that Magda 'could play an important role in my life' and 'represent the feminine counterpart to my single-mindedly male instincts'. But what form could such a relationship take? Hitler believed that to perform his duties as the future leader of the Third Reich he had to appear single, dedicated solely to the welfare of his people, enduring self-enforced solitude for their benefit. Any contact with Magda would have to be as clandestine as possible; if she was with someone else it would be a lot easier to keep their liaison secret. Hitler remarked to Wagener that it was 'too bad she isn't married'.

Then, on a long walk alone together, Wagener relayed Hitler's thoughts to Magda and explained both Hitler's aversion to marriage and his desire to have a woman who could be like a wife to him; an intellectual, emotional and spiritual partner. Once Wagener was sure Magda understood what he meant – that if she wanted to form a special bond with Hitler she should consider marrying Goebbels – he asked Magda if she was prepared to accept the challenge. Magda didn't hesitate: 'For Adolf Hitler, I'd be prepared to take everything on myself.'[5]

Though Wagener's testimony lacks corroboration, there is no doubt that Magda was infatuated with Hitler. Perhaps with this bizarre *ménage à trois* in mind, she agreed to get engaged to Goebbels. They went public in July and marked the announcement with a small champagne-fuelled gathering alongside Hitler, Ilse and Hess, Wagener, and a few others. Yet Goebbels felt insecure about Magda's obvious feelings for Hitler, and he expressed his anxiety in an August diary entry: 'Magda loses herself a bit around the Boss … I am suffering greatly … I didn't sleep a wink.'[6] However, despite being tormented, Goebbels was too dependent on

Hitler's goodwill to confront him about it; ultimately, he was incapable of breaking up with his beloved leader.

Lina Heydrich liked to take the credit for pushing her husband into the Nazi fold; according to her, when they got together he had no political opinions of his own and considered most politicians to be incompetent, foolish civilians. Though it's true he'd not yet engaged with Nazism, all Heydrich's actions since late adolescence placed him firmly on the right of the ideological spectrum.

When his hometown was caught up in the post-war turmoil, Heydrich immediately signed up with the local *Freikorps* and acted as a messenger during clashes with the communists. The navy was virulently nationalistic and anti-Semitic, hostile to the Weimar Republic, bitterly opposed to the Treaty of Versailles and in favour of an authoritarian solution to Germany's problems. Heydrich didn't have far to travel to reach Nazism and Lina made sure he completed the journey.

In the spring of 1931 – while Heydrich was earning pocket money at a sailing club – his godmother spied an opening for him in the SS. Her son had joined Himmler's embryonic organisation and heard through the grapevine that he was looking for somebody to head up an intelligence-gathering section. Strings were pulled and Heydrich was granted an interview, much to Lina's delight.

However, at the last minute, Himmler cancelled due to illness. Heydrich decided to abandon his trip and reschedule but Lina, worried that he might not get another chance, telegrammed ahead to say he was still coming and then got him on the overnight train to Munich. Arriving the next morning, 14 June, Heydrich headed out to Himmler's home. Margaret opened the door, let Heydrich in and escorted him to her waiting husband.

Having Himmler at home was a rare treat for Margaret. Over the past year, she'd soldiered on with the farm, but the whole enterprise was close to collapse. The hens weren't laying well and she had to slaughter the geese because she couldn't afford to feed them any longer. The strain on her was palpable. But her husband was far too preoccupied to pay more than lip-service to her troubles. He had vastly increased SS membership and formalised its uniforms and rituals while carefully recruiting lawyers, academics, recent graduates and disaffected aristocrats for leadership positions. At the same time, he aspired to create a covert branch of the SS to monitor opponents.

The problem was that Himmler hadn't the faintest clue about intelligence work. As far as he knew, Heydrich had some experience in the field, based on his time in the navy, but he didn't realise that Heydrich had been engaged with purely technical stuff. So when Himmler asked him how he'd put together an intelligence unit, Heydrich fell back on his limited knowledge of espionage, based on the British spy novels he enjoyed reading. Himmler was impressed and offered him the job, beginning a partnership that would send millions to their deaths.

Since Geli Raubel had taken up residence in Hitler's Munich apartment – and his bed – she'd dabbled unsuccessfully in a number of things, including acting and singing, to fill her time while he was away. When Hitler was in town, she had no choice but to fall in with his routines and habits. Geli's social life revolved round his, whether it was a cosy lunch with Ilse and her husband, or paying Margaret Himmler a surprise visit. Margaret was shocked to find Hitler and Geli on her doorstep – 'I was speechless' – but enjoyed their stay: 'We had coffee together, which was very pleasant.'[7]

Often bored, Geli yearned to have a little fun. But that was easier said than done. Every year in the run-up to Lent, the Fausching Carnival was held in Munich and featured masquerades, dances, and street parades. Geli had persuaded Hitler to let her attend a fancy dress ball, on the condition that Heinrich Hoffmann and Hitler's publisher acted as chaperones. Despite this restriction, Geli was excited about going and had done a sketch of the type of dress she wanted to wear. While not overtly daring, it was relatively revealing. Hitler saw it and, according to Ilse, lost his temper; he yelled at Geli – 'you might as well go naked' – and started drawing an alternative design. Geli was so infuriated by his outburst that she grabbed the drawing 'and ran out the door, slamming it shut'.[8] Though Hitler apologised for his behaviour, she ended up going to the ball in a regulation white evening gown. With her two male escorts watching her every move, she was home by 11 p.m.

In the autumn of 1931, her frustration and unhappiness became too much to bear. Still only 23, she was a virtual prisoner who desperately wanted to escape. She begged Hitler to let her return to Vienna, where she'd grown up, and start afresh. Hitler wouldn't hear of it and bawled her out for even considering the idea; Geli knew then that he'd never let her break free.

On the evening of 18 September, while Hitler was in Nuremberg, Geli took the gun he'd given her for protection, placed the muzzle against her chest and fired. She fell to the floor. The bullet punctured her lung and lodged itself near the base of her spine. Lying face down, and in excruciating pain, Geli slowly bled to death.

The following morning, her body – which was already showing signs of rigor mortis – was most likely discovered by the housekeeper, though Ilse always insisted that her husband arrived there first, forcing the door to get in. Whether or not Hess found her, he was the one who had the thankless task of telling Hitler what had happened, managing to reach him on the phone as he was about to leave his hotel. Shocked and distressed, Hitler raced back to Munich – en route he got a ticket for driving at twice the speed limit – to face questions from the police, who had done a cursory search and spoken to witnesses, and the threat of scandal.

For forty-eight hours the rumours flew, left-wing newspapers cried murder, and it looked like Hitler's credibility was at stake. But then the fuss died down. The doctor who examined Geli was convinced she'd killed herself. The official investigation saw no reason to question his findings and the case was closed. Geli's corpse was transported to Austria and buried in Vienna. Hitler avoided the funeral, but made a solemn solo visit to her grave a week later. Geli's room in his apartment was left untouched.

Ilse was one of those who declared that Geli was Hitler's only true love and that after her death he was never the same again; he lost his capacity for joy and taking pleasure in simple things. However, this sentimental picture doesn't take into account the fact that Hitler had been seeing Eva Braun as well. He regularly dropped in on her at Hoffmann's studio, where she still worked, took her out to eat and occasionally to the cinema, and gave her presents. Geli was aware that Eva was on the scene; they accidentally bumped into each other during the 1930 Oktoberfest (sixteen days of funfairs and heavy drinking) and the two exchanged a few terse words and some spiteful glances. After Geli's suicide, Hitler and Eva's fairly innocent, mildly flirtatious relationship became a lot more serious; whether Eva realised it or not, she was about to step into Geli's shoes.

Though Goering wanted to be with Hitler in his hour of need, he was facing a crisis of his own. Since the beginning of the year, Carin's health had been in steep decline. By June 1931 she was in a sanatorium, her heartbeat weak, pulse faint, slipping in and out of consciousness, near death. Realising the end was near, she and Goering went on a last trip together in his new Mercedes, a present from Hitler. They travelled south to Bavaria and then into Austria, where Goering introduced her to his surrogate father, von Eppenstein, at his castle.

Then, on 25 September, Carin's mother died. She was determined to return to Stockholm for the funeral even though her doctors warned her it might kill her. Accompanied by her husband, they made the journey and were greeted at the station by her son Thomas – now in his late teens and fully reconciled with his mother – who remembered that 'she never looked lovelier'. It all proved too much, and Carin collapsed. Goering stayed at her bedside for days on end as she clung on; Thomas recalled how 'he would only steal away to shave or bathe or snatch a bite to eat … otherwise he spent all his time on his knees … holding her hand, stroking her hair, wiping the perspiration from her face and the moisture from her lips'.[9]

With Carin on the brink, Goering was suddenly required elsewhere; a meeting in Berlin with President Hindenburg, the man who ultimately held Germany's fate in his hands. Hindenburg was wary of Hitler but more sympathetic to Goering, the former war hero. Distraught, Goering didn't want to leave Carin, but she insisted he do his duty. Even then, her dedication to the cause outweighed all other considerations.

At 4 a.m. on 17 October, Carin passed away. Goering made it back for the funeral four days later, held at her family's private Edelweiss Chapel. Carin's death left a gaping hole in his heart that no amount of power or wealth could ever really fill.

The year ended with two weddings. The unresolved tensions between Magda and Goebbels over their relationship to Hitler had been laid to rest. Not long after Geli's death, there were a series of private meetings between Magda and Hitler, Goebbels and Hitler, and the three of them altogether, during which they reached an unspoken agreement. Magda and Goebbels would get married so they could stay close to Hitler and he could stay close to her. On 19 December 1931, Goebbels and Magda – who was probably already pregnant – tied the knot at a civil ceremony followed by a church service. Hitler was best man; when Magda thanked him with a kiss, his eyes were full of tears.

On 26 December Lina and Heydrich walked up the aisle; alongside family and friends were the local Nazi women's group – who'd provided a handmade swastika – and members of the SA and SS dressed in white shirts and black trousers (due to a temporary ban on both organisations they couldn't wear their full uniforms in public) who formed an honour guard outside the church, which was echoing to the strains of the 'Horst Wessel' song, the Nazis' favourite anthem.

Heydrich was now based in Munich, after a few months learning the ropes with the SS in Hamburg, renting a tiny flat from a sympathetic old lady and slowly constructing the framework for his intelligence unit, the Sicherheitsdienst des Reichsführers-SS (SD). His salary was poor – he earned less than a shop assistant – but just enough to enable Lina and him to begin their married life renting a small place in the suburbs of Munich.

Five days after their wedding, Himmler issued a set of guidelines to govern marriages within the SS. He wanted his SS clan to be descended from Nordic roots and free from racial impurities. All SS men would have to apply for a certificate that confirmed the biological suitability of their mates; anyone who married without it would be expelled. While Lina's Aryan heritage was flawless, Heydrich's own lineage would soon come under scrutiny.

5

BREAKTHROUGH

Despite the loss of their loved ones, both Goering and Hitler would find some consolation in the first few months of 1932. Though it's impossible to know for sure, most agree that Hitler began sleeping with Eva Braun early in the year.

Eva carried little of the traditional baggage with which an earlier generation of women had been burdened and in many respects she resembled the new breed of 'modern' women that shook up post-war German society: she smoked, followed the current dance crazes coming out of American jazz clubs, read fashion magazines and purchased the latest beauty products, idolised movie stars and celebrities, valued her independence – most young single women like Eva had jobs and usually worked in either retail, leisure or office administration – and had no intention of giving up her position at Hoffmann's, through which she'd acquired a serious interest in photography.

Yet in other ways, Eva embodied Hitler's ideal of natural womanhood. A true blonde, she was athletic and sporty – gymnastics and swimming – and kept herself in shape; she had almost no interest in politics or the state of the nation; she had few airs or graces and was refreshingly free-spirited; she was emotionally immature and easy for Hitler to manipulate. From her point of view, Hitler was courteous, often charming, indulgent and attentive, while his growing fame flattered and excited her. Eva hadn't yet grasped how cruel and indifferent Hitler could be towards those who dared get close to him.

That spring, a still heartbroken Goering renewed a brief acquaintance he'd made with a 38-year-old actress, Emmy Sonnemann, who was employed by the Weimar State Theatre. Goering was in town and after the show they ran into each other at the Kaiser Café; they went for a walk in a nearby park and Goering talked to Emmy at length about Carin and how her death had affected him: 'He spoke of his wife ... with so much love and genuine sadness that my esteem grew for him with every word.' Next time he was in Weimar they met for lunch and before long Emmy received an invitation to a reception in Berlin, where she spent 'a thrilling evening'.

Emmy liked to portray herself as an artist with no feeling for politics and claimed she did her best to avoid discussing Goering's work: 'I needed a great effort to interest myself in any political subject.' She was much happier talking to him about 'the theatre, books, paintings and human relationships'.[1] The most important thing for Emmy was that Goering respected her, both as a woman and as an actress. She had caught the acting bug aged 12 when she saw a production of *The Merchant of Venice*. Her father, an affluent entrepreneur who owned a chocolate factory, was dead set against her treading the boards, but her mother was more sympathetic. Emmy's chance came when a prominent director announced he was opening an acting school in Hamburg – where she grew up – and was offering two scholarships. Emmy's mother assured her that if she got one, her father would allow her to become an actress. Emmy duly did, and after completing her training she began her career working in small regional theatres.

In 1914, Emmy met a fellow actor, Karl Köstlin, while she was performing the role of Margareta in Goethe's *Faust*. They married a year later when they were both appearing in Vienna. For the rest of the war, they were often apart as he was required to serve in the Austrian army. Though Emmy found him 'intelligent, distinguished and extremely cultured', the relationship lacked passion – 'we were no more than good friends'[2] – and in 1920 they amicably divorced. Two years later, she was in Weimar, around 150 miles south of Berlin, which became her base for the next ten years. Emmy played a wide range of leading roles in both the classics and works by more modern playwrights, including Ibsen and Oscar Wilde.

These were happy years for her; she had a three-room apartment, loved her work, enjoyed the company of her fellow actors and spent her down-time in Weimar's bars and restaurants. Her first encounter with Goering occurred when her theatre group were giving an outdoor performance at a private party, performing a play written by their host. Goering was there with Carin, who Emmy found fascinating: 'She looked ill, but there emanated from her a charm which I could not resist.'

From the start of her relationship with Goering, Emmy showed great sensitivity and tact when it came to Carin's lingering hold over him. Not that she had a lot of choice: the first present Goering gave Emmy was a photograph of his dead wife. When she visited his apartment, Goering showed her the room he kept as a shrine in honour of Carin's memory: 'Her beautiful eyes looked down from innumerable frames on every wall.'[3] Nevertheless, Emmy had made up her mind: she would bide her time, convinced that Goering was the right man for her. But neither Goering nor Hitler would have much room for romance in 1932, the year of elections, which not only included two Reichstag elections but also a presidential one. Hitler decided to run against Hindenburg and though nobody really expected him to win, it seemed an ideal way to establish himself as a legitimate contender for high office.

In Munich, the party machine – with Hess at the controls – was working overtime. While not permitted to directly engage in the push for power, Ilse was able to take an informal role, maintaining lines of communication with allies, donors and potential supporters in and out-side her social circle, which took in representatives of the city's cultural scene – writers, painters, philosophers – many of whom she'd got to know through the world of antiquarian books.

The first round of the presidential election saw Hitler get 30 per cent of the vote; Hindenburg got over 49 per cent. In the next round, Hitler added 2 million votes but Hindenburg increased his share to 53 per cent. While there was some lingering disappointment, the contest had allowed Hitler to play the statesman on the national stage. The priority now was to convert this goodwill into votes in the upcoming Reichstag election.

When Hitler wasn't on the campaign trail, zigzagging the country by plane, he divided his time in Berlin between his suite at the grand

Kaiserhof Hotel and Magda and Goebbels's apartment, which had become his unofficial HQ. By now, Hitler had adopted a fairly strict vegetarian diet – he still ate eggs but no dairy products – so Magda made sure there was always suitable food available; because of Hitler's paranoia about being poisoned, she even delivered meals to him when he was at the hotel.

The whole campaign was disfigured by extreme violence. Political meetings frequently descended into anarchy; on one occasion, Goering plunged into a massive punch-up wielding a sword. The SA and its communist equivalent, the Red Front Fighters' League, brawled in the streets. There were targeted attacks and random assaults. In late May, Margaret and Gudrun had to stay with friends for a while after an unknown gunman shot at their house. Taking the hint, Heydrich dispatched Lina to the countryside for a couple of months.

Lina's safety wasn't the only thing troubling Heydrich. In June, an SS man from Heydrich's home town accused him of concealing the fact that he had Jewish ancestors. Alarmed, Himmler ordered a comprehensive investigation, which revealed the source of the problem: Heydrich's paternal grandmother. Her second husband had a surname that happened to sound Jewish. While this was embarrassing, it wasn't fatal. Heydrich's bloodline was not tainted. He was free to resume his SS career.

Tempting though it might be to suggest that Heydrich's systematic and ruthless persecution of the Jews stemmed from an insecurity about his roots – during Heydrich's childhood his father was targeted by local anti-Semites and jealous colleagues would continue to try and undermine Heydrich by dredging up this racial slur – there is virtually no evidence that Heydrich was driven by self-loathing. Certainly, Lina never gave any credence to the idea that he was motivated by the need to atone for his suspect past.

If anything, Heydrich suffered from overconfidence; rather than operating from a position of weakness, constantly looking over his shoulder, Heydrich never felt the least bit vulnerable; as far as he was considered, he was practically invincible.

With all the election turmoil, Bormann – as manager of the Nazis' insurance fund – was extremely busy. Dealing with the mounting toll of deaths and serious injuries and the claims of compensation arising from them, Bormann gained a reputation for scrupulous honesty; despite the considerable sums passing through his hands – there were 3 million RM at his disposal – Bormann never dipped his fingers in the till.

Gerda had her hands full too; a year earlier she'd given birth to twin girls, one named after Ilse, the other after Bormann's former lover, Ehrengard, but the child died a few months later. There is no record of how Gerda felt about this loss but by the autumn of 1932 she was pregnant again. With her husband working flat out, Gerda was left to cope with their rapidly expanding family on her own; she received no help from her parents due to a definitive falling-out the couple had with her father, Walter Buch.

Exactly what prompted the break is hard to establish. Buch was non-committal about the reasons for the split, simply citing the bad feeling that had always existed between him and Bormann. A letter from Gerda to her husband – written near the end of the war – refers to the termination of contact between them without being specific. Whatever the cause, Gerda never regretted losing the father she felt she never had.

As for Bormann, he was well aware of his father-in-law's low opinion of him; he had no qualms about driving a wedge between Gerda and Buch. Besides, Bormann had become indispensable: he no longer needed Buch's patronage to progress. Bormann also kept his own relatives at a considerable distance; as a result, Gerda's many children would grow up without grandparents. Instead, they found an alternative family among the Nazi elite.

On 31 July, Germany went to the polls: the Nazis scored a stunning success, gaining over 37 per cent of vote. The country's economic situation was catastrophic – over a third of the workforce was out of a job – yet the government seemed incapable of doing anything about it. In these dire circumstances, Hitler's undoubted charisma and well-crafted image, combined with the simple, clear message that he alone was capable of uniting a shattered nation and restoring Germany's pride and power, attracted a wide range of people.

They were now the largest party in the Reichstag. With the exception of the urban working class – which on the whole remained committed to the left – the Nazis gathered votes from across the socio-economic spectrum; impoverished rural labourers and struggling farmers; shop-keepers and artisans; civil servants and professionals; financial wizards and the beneficiaries of inherited wealth.

Many women who had previously voted for middle-of-the-road conservative parties switched their allegiance to Hitler. Six months earlier the Nazis had merged all their existing women's associations into a single entity, the National Socialist Women's Organisation (NFS). Reflecting the party's increased share of the female vote, the NFS grew rapidly in size over the course of 1932, rising from just under 20,000 members to just over 100,000.

Given Hindenburg's aversion to the main socialist party, which had come in second, his options were narrowing; granting the Nazis a role in government seemed increasingly unavoidable, but Hitler wanted to be chancellor, and despite intense discussions in late July and early August, nobody was prepared to offer him the job. During the summer and autumn there was a growing sense that the Nazis had missed their chance.

With the Reichstag in a state of paralysis, new elections were held in November that only confirmed this disturbing feeling; the Nazi share of the vote was down by 4 per cent, an ominous sign that the party had reached the limits of its popular appeal. Hitler faced a dilemma; con-tinue to wait to be invited to rule and risk seeing his support slip away, or attempt a violent seizure of power and risk a civil war the Nazis had little hope of winning.

Back in Munich, Heydrich was also wrestling with a serious problem. The SD was chronically short of money; its very existence was at stake. In September, he and Lina moved out of their tiny apartment and into a two-storey villa. They took the first floor while the ground floor was occupied by Heydrich's seven-man SD team and all their paperwork. Lina described herself as 'look-out, cook and housewife'. As a security precaution, Lina acquired two dogs to raise the alarm, while the villa's position, set back from a large garden some distance from the main gate, meant she'd have time 'to hide anything incriminating'.[4] Lina did her best to manage the household on a meagre budget. Meat and fish were too expensive so she cooked cheap vegetable soups instead; the highlight of the week was a traditional Bavarian potato salad washed down with beer.

Heydrich reached out to Ernst Röhm, leader of the Brownshirts; since its inception, the SS, though notionally independent, was technically part of this sprawling organisation that under Röhm's direction had swollen in size and influence. Röhm was an ex-frontline soldier with little time for civilians; to him, the parliamentary path to power was a sideshow, merely the prelude to a blood-soaked revolution that would wipe the slate clean and turn Germany into a vast military camp.

Lina claimed that she was instrumental in getting Röhm's backing. Needing to watch every pfennig, Lina kept careful count of the number of matches available for lighting the basement boiler. When she noticed they kept disappearing, she figured somebody was pilfering them. So Lina decided to expose the thief. She bought some novelty exploding matches from a joke shop and mixed them in with the regular ones – but she hadn't considered the fact that Röhm and Himmler were about to arrive for a crucial tour of inspection.

Before she could intercede, Röhm reached for his cigars and lit one. There was a loud bang; Lina recalled that Röhm 'went as white as a sheet'[5] and Himmler dived for cover. Allegedly, Röhm was so amused by her audacity and ingenuity that he was glad to authorise some extra funding. This piece of welcome news coincided with the revelation that Lina was pregnant. Nine months later, Röhm would become the child's godfather.

On 1 January 1933, llse and her husband were among a select few who attended a performance of Wagner's *The Master Singer* at the Munich State Theatre with Hitler and his special guest, Eva Braun. It was the most public acknowledgement yet that she was Hitler's girlfriend. His decision to bring Eva out into the open was prompted by her attempted suicide a few months earlier.

Having given herself to Hitler, Eva endlessly waited for him to pay her some attention but Hitler was barely in Munich during 1932; even when he was, he had precious little time for her. Eva took his absences and silences personally, as a sign of rejection. Anxiety turned to despair. Like Geli before her, she had her own pistol. Leaving a scribbled farewell note, she pulled the trigger. The bullet lodged in her neck, just missing the artery. Bleeding profusely, Eva managed to call a doctor – Heinrich Hoffmann's brother-in-law – who came immediately and got her to hospital, where the bullet was successfully removed.

Whether, deep down, Eva actually intended to kill herself is open to question; was it a cry for help? Did she think that this was the only way to get Hitler to take notice of her? Whatever her motives, Hitler was shocked into action. He vowed that he'd take better care of her. The outing to the theatre – with intimate associates like Ilse – was his way of showing Eva that she mattered to him.

Goebbels was meant to be at the opera with them, until an emergency sent him hurrying back to Berlin. Though Magda had successfully delivered their first child – a daughter named Helga, born on 1 September – it had aggravated a pre-existing heart condition. Not yet fully recovered, Magda became pregnant again. On 23 December she had a miscarriage and went into hospital. With her condition stable, Goebbels thought it was safe to head down to Bavaria to spend Christmas and New Year with Hitler.

It wasn't. Hitler's cottage at Obersalzburg – a mountainous area of forests and farms – didn't have a phone, so on New Year's Day Goebbels went to the nearby town of Berchtesgaden and called the hospital in Berlin. Magda had got an infection and was running a terribly high fever; she was perilously close to death. Beside himself with worry, Goebbels caught the first available train and travelled overnight to the capital to be at her bedside. On arrival, he was relieved to discover that she was out of danger. Over the next few hectic weeks, Goebbels visited her as often as possible while she slowly regained her strength.

Goering spent Christmas with Emmy Sonnemann. Since its tentative beginnings, Emmy and Goering's relationship had made discreet but steady progress. She was regularly staying overnight at his apartment.

Yet Carin was never far from his mind; once Christmas was over, he left Emmy to spend New Year with Carin's family in Sweden. On his return, Goering played a critical part in the unfolding drama that would decide the Nazis' future, smoothing out wrinkles during tense negotiations with Hindenburg and his fellow conspirators, who were caught between the need to obtain popular consent for their administration and the urge to impose some form of dictatorship.

As the month wore on, the old general and his allies were increasingly inclined to disregard their reservations about Hitler. If they gave Hitler what he demanded, the mass support he commanded would shore up their crumbling position and help defeat the communist menace, which they genuinely feared. If they didn't, they risked an armed revolt; the SA were now over a million strong. They agreed it was better to have Hitler on the inside – where they might be able to control him – than standing outside hammering on their door.

On 30 January, Hitler was named chancellor. The plotters who believed they could neuter the Nazis by bringing Hitler into office seriously miscalculated when they also made Goering Minister of Prussia, the largest state in Germany and home to its capital. With the title came control over all its police forces; Goering would use them to devastating effect. That evening Nazi supporters joined the SA and the SS for a massed torchlit victory parade; Hitler, Goering, Goebbels, Hess and Himmler – who were both in town for the big day – stood on a balcony at the Kaiserhof Hotel and revelled in their triumph. Aside from Emmy – for whom Goering had reserved a room so she could watch the march – none of their women were there to see it. The next morning, Hess bought himself a new watch, and in a daze wrote to Ilse: 'Did I dream all this or am I awake?'[6]

On 2 February, Magda was discharged from hospital and returned home to find Hitler waiting to greet her. A few weeks later, on the evening of 27 February, Hitler was dining with her and Goebbels. Magda made the mistake of serving Hitler some carp. Irritated, he was telling her off – didn't she realise he couldn't eat fish – when the phone rang. Somebody was calling to tell them the Reichstag was on fire.

Goering was first on the scene; he had lushly decorated quarters – containing valuable and very flammable tapestries – right next to where the fire was raging. Panicked, he called Emmy, who'd returned to Weimar to resume her role in Goethe's *Faust*, before going in search of help. Speculation that the Nazis actually started the blaze persisted for decades afterwards but no definitive link was ever established. The Dutch arsonist charged with the crime, who had vague links with the left, remains the most likely culprit; he'd already tried to set light to several public buildings.

Moving fast, the Nazis insisted that the attack heralded the beginning of a full-blown communist revolt. The next day, Hindenburg signed an emergency decree that effectively suspended the rule of law and a massive crackdown – already under way in Prussia – was set in motion; thousands were detained and tortured. Goering was at the forefront, granting SA squads police powers and forming the Gestapo. Within weeks, the prisons were bursting at the seams and improvised camps sprung up to accommodate the overflow, a measure Goering was unashamedly proud of; in his political tract *Germany Reborn*, he casually remarked that 'it was only natural that in the beginning excesses were committed. It was natural that here and there beatings took place.'[7]

Meanwhile, elections were called for 5 March: Hitler wanted to win a majority so he could dismantle the Reichstag altogether. Hitler spent the evening with Magda and Goebbels; they went to see Wagner's *The Valkyrie* and then headed to the Reich Chancellery to listen to the results on the radio. Despite the pervasive threat of violence and intimidation the Nazis only won 44 per cent of the vote. However, by bullying a small nationalist party to join forces with them and persuading the Catholic Centre Party to cooperate, the Nazis were able to push through the Enabling Act, which gave Hitler the freedom to suspend the Reichstag and do as he pleased.

Ironically – given its status as the cradle of the movement – the one province resisting Nazi domination was Bavaria; its conservative nationalist leadership were refusing to budge. This was a source of intense frustration for Lina; it was tortuous watching her enemies being crushed everywhere except in her own backyard while her husband festered on the sidelines.

However, the Enabling Act had given Hitler the authority to steamroller provincial politicians. On 9 March, Ritter von Epp – whose

Freikorps unit Hess had joined all those years ago – was made Bavarian State Commissioner and Himmler was put in charge of the police. The gloves were off; over a few days, hundreds of socialists, communists and obstructive officials were beaten, humiliated and arrested.

In a letter to her parents, Lina could hardly conceal her glee, giving a detailed account of what happened when the 'SA and SS enjoyed themselves'. Among their victims was a prominent Jewish citizen: 'They beat him with dog whips, pulled off his shoes and socks, and then made him walk home barefoot.'[8]

Lina's sense of triumph was not yet shared by Magda and her husband; they were both anxious about his place in the new regime. While Goering ran rampant in Prussia, Goebbels had nothing tangible to show for his endeavours. He craved control over all Germany's media and cultural activity. Finally, Hitler granted his wish – with the exception of the press – and made him head of the Ministry of Propaganda and Popular Enlightenment on 14 March; under its authority, Goebbels went on to establish sub-sections to govern each area of cultural production – music, theatre, art, literature and film.

Basking in the glow of his new status, Goebbels took Magda to the Berlin State Opera on 16 May to see a performance of *Madame Butterfly*, accompanied by the film director Leni Riefenstahl and her date. Leni was a former dancer whose career had been curtailed by injury, and who had appeared in a number of movies before stepping behind the camera. She'd come to the attention of both Goebbels and Hitler after the premiere of her first feature, *The Blue Light*. Hitler requested a private audience and at the 1932 party rally Leni received an invitation to one of Magda's exclusive parties. Leni was impressed by Magda – 'a perfect hostess whom I instantly liked' – but found Goebbels repellent.

Having negotiated the paparazzi gathered outside and settled in their box, Leni ended up next to Goebbels, who proceeded to shove 'his hand under my gown; it touched my knee and was about to move up my thigh'.[9] Leni snapped her legs shut, squeezing his hand until he was forced to wriggle it free. According to her autobiography, this was not Goebbels's first attempt to breach her defences. While Leni is not the most reliable source, her description of Goebbels's behaviour matches the type of sexual harassment he inflicted on numerous actresses and starlets.

Though she is vague about dates, it's possible that Goebbels began pursuing Leni while Magda was in hospital fighting for her life. Much to Leni's annoyance, Goebbels began calling her on a daily basis. After she asked him to stop, he showed up at her apartment on two separate occasions; he begged, he grovelled, he bullied and threatened, but she managed to resist.

The night at the opera was not the final insult; that summer, Goebbels lunged at her while they were driving together and nearly sent the car off the road. From then on Goebbels kept his hands off her, realising that he was on a hiding to nothing. Had he been able to destroy her career, he would have. But Leni had Hitler's stamp of approval, and she was far too talented to be easily dismissed.

Whether Magda suspected anything is impossible to say; the fact that she remained friendly with Leni suggests she didn't. For the time being, Magda operated on the principle that what she didn't know couldn't hurt her: besides, there was no shortage of men who'd be more than willing to take Goebbels's place.

During all this turmoil and excitement, Margaret Himmler was focused on domestic matters. In February, she and her husband sold the farm and moved into an opulent Munich apartment located on the same street as Hitler's. She'd begun keeping a 'childhood journal', a daily record of Gudrun's development in which she both fretted over minor instances of ill-discipline and celebrated her daughter's mischievous antics. At the same time, Margaret used the journal to monitor and assess her own parenting skills.

Then, in March, they adopted a 5-year-old boy, Gerhard; his father was an SS man who'd been killed in a Berlin street fight a month earlier.

Aside from being a gesture that reflected well on Himmler, it provided him with a male child, something he knew Margaret could no longer give him: after the severe difficulties she experienced giving birth to Gudrun, the doctors advised her not to try again. Margaret was initially pleased by the new addition. He seemed 'bright' and 'very obedient'[10] and she hoped he'd be a good influence on Gudrun. Margaret's positive attitude didn't last. Soon, Gerhard was simply something else for her to worry about. Having satisfied his yearning for a son and saddled Margaret with further responsibilities, Himmler began planning the next phase of SS expansion. Not only did he want the SS to monopolise the machinery of terror and surveillance, he wanted absolute power over its victims too.

By the middle of March, there were over 10,000 prisoners crammed into the local jails. To release the pressure, an abandoned munitions factory on the outskirts of the town of Dachau, 16 miles north-west of Munich, became an improvised concentration camp. Within a matter of weeks, Himmler had placed it under SS jurisdiction.

By taking control of Dachau, Himmler was making a statement of intent; all of the Nazis' concentration camps should belong to him. Yet even in his wildest dreams, Himmler could not have imagined that his ambition to purge Germany of its ideological enemies would lead him to the gates of Auschwitz.

PART TWO

HIGH SOCIETY

6

FIRST LADY OF THE REICH

On 20 April 1933, Hitler spent the evening of his forty-fourth birthday at the Prussian State Theatre watching the premiere of a stirring piece of propaganda dedicated to him and first performed on the radio in the run-up to the March elections. The gala night went well and included Emmy's debut on the Berlin stage.

Emmy's promising start in this new era in German theatre was given added impetus by her friendship and professional alliance with the celebrated actor and director Gustav Gründgens, whose fame was based on his interpretation of Mephisto in Goethe's *Faust*. But after the Nazis' assumption of power, there was a real danger that everything he'd achieved would be taken away from him.

Gründgens was a bisexual who'd supported the communists and worked in left-wing theatre during the 1920s. But he was spared the same fate that many like him suffered because of his connection to Emmy, who felt 'tied' to him 'both artistically and personally'. Leaning on Goering, who as Prussian minister had inherited control of its theatres, concert halls and orchestras, Emmy persuaded him to take affirmative action on Gründgens's behalf. After renewing Gründgens's contract at the Prussian State Theatre, Goering elevated him to the position of overall director in 1934.

These arrangements provided a huge boost to Emmy's career. Up to that point – despite her successes – she'd been a provincial performer, but now she was propelled onto the national stage; as she later remarked, 'I had reached the summit of ambition for any actress in Germany.' With Gründgens at the helm, she formed a mutually beneficial creative partnership: 'He helped me develop whatever talent I had.'[1]

After briefly reprising her well-worn role in *Faust*, she and Gründgens opened the autumn season with the comedy *The Concert*, a farce about an old pianist intent on seducing his young female pupils while his long-suffering wife tries to get him to mend his ways. The production received good reviews and went on tour in the summer of 1934, first to Munich and then on to Hamburg. The Munich leg almost proved fatal: en route to Obersalzburg, Goering and Emmy's car collided with another vehicle. On impact, the steering wheel rammed into Goering's chest, breaking two ribs, and Emmy gashed her scalp when her head smashed into the windscreen. Though their injuries were nasty, they knew they'd had a lucky escape.

Returning to Berlin, Emmy and Gründgens chose another comedy, *Minna von Barnhelm*, with Emmy in the lead. A perennial classic, there were over 200 productions of it during the Third Reich. Emmy and Gründgens's version ran for nearly a year. In the Nazi period, comedy was by far the most popular genre in German theatres. Though the regime's efforts to draw audiences to its self-produced political satire were a dismal failure, the Nazis appreciated the value of comedy as a safety valve, a form of release and escape from the demands they placed on their citizens. There was no shortage of uncontroversial material to draw on, whether the work of contemporary playwrights with titles like *Honeymoon Without a Husband* and *Uproar in the Courtyard*, or old favourites by both German and foreign writers; *Twelfth Night* and *The Taming of the Shrew* were Shakespeare's most performed works, while Oscar Wilde's witty comedies of manners were in great demand, as was Bernard Shaw, whose *Pygmalion* was filmed in 1935 with Gründgens as Professor Higgins.

Emmy did not simply use her fame and recently won influence to her own advantage. Throughout the theatre world, Jewish artists were running scared – deprived of employment or forced into retirement – and Emmy, with Goering's assistance, stepped in whenever and wherever she could to help her fellow artists. Bella Fromm, the society columnist, wrote in her diary that 'Emmy has been wonderful in her loyalty to her non-Aryan friends'.[2]

However, there were limits to what she could achieve – and what Goering was capable of doing for her. Henny Porten had been a major star since before 1914; with a string of hits under her belt, she'd spent time in Hollywood and successfully made the transition from silent pictures to talkies. But her husband was Jewish and Porten refused to divorce him. As a result, nobody would hire her. Emmy reached out to Goering, who said he could do nothing. Emmy refused to accept 'no' for an answer and kept pestering him. Eventually, at his wits' end, Goering turned to his younger brother Albert – a fervent anti-Nazi – who worked in the Austrian film industry and managed to find her some gigs in Vienna.

Emmy's increasingly high profile was a direct challenge to Magda's status as the First Lady of the Reich. Once the Nazis had seized power, Magda was the obvious candidate to assume this role. On Sunday, 14 May 1933, she gave the first Mother's Day radio address. After a grassroots campaign to establish Mother's Day as a national holiday had gained momentum during the 1920s – with enthusiastic support from the Association of German Florists – the Nazis made it official.

In her speech, Magda proudly declared that the German mother 'instinctively' understood Hitler's 'noble spiritual and moral goals' and was prepared to be 'his enthusiastic supporter and fanatical warrior'.[3] The response to her broadcast was overwhelmingly positive and she received hundreds of letters from across the Reich. Her mailbag – which contained, among other things, requests for money and advice on relationships – swelled to such an extent that she hired two secretaries to deal with it all.

Magda and her children were constantly being photographed for magazines and periodicals as an example of the perfect Nazi family. Though she certainly performed the essential function required of

German women and continued to produce children – between 1934 and 1937, she had two more daughters and a son – motherhood didn't come naturally to her. In the dozens of images featuring Magda and her children, she always appeared slightly removed, distant even, impeccably groomed in her designer outfits.

In the late spring of 1933, reflecting her interest in fashion, Magda was made honorary president of the newly created German Fashion Institute, set up to encourage a unique national style, put an end to decadent foreign influences and drive Jews out of the business: this last ambition was especially problematic given that much of the industry was Jewish owned (70 per cent of Berlin's off-the-rack clothes were produced by Jewish firms) and many of the top design-ers favoured by both Magda and Emmy were also Jewish. Though the elite designers were protected because of their prominent customers, by the late 1930s the fashion business had been thor-oughly Aryanised.

The other main aim of the Institute – to get German women to abandon the 'modern' look promoted by French fashion houses and Hollywood movies – was also fraught with problems. While splenetic criticism of foreign styles was widespread (as one Nazi commentator put it, 'the Parisian whores set the tone for the fashions offered to German women'[4]) efforts to convince them to adopt traditional folksy outfits like the dirndl, a Bavarian peasant costume, were not very successful. To further confuse matters, a Goebbels-sponsored journal featured regular photo-shoots with models in glamorous evening wear and swimsuits, plus a women's problem page; in an April 1934 edition it tackled the vexed question, short hair or long hair?

Magda embodied these mixed messages. Though the regime railed against cosmetics – everything from lipstick to false eyelashes – and favoured a 'natural' look (the SS periodical *The Black Corps* was fond of pictures of near-naked women in athletic poses) Magda used luxury brands like Elisabeth Arden toiletries, wore full make-up, and brushed her hair forty-two times before going out; in a public statement on the subject she said that 'the German woman of the future should be stylish, beautiful, and intelligent'.[5]

Magda also regularly made the front cover of *The Lady*, a high-end fashion magazine that held the German rights to *Vogue* and advertised clothes by Parisian designers like Chanel. On assuming her position at the Fashion Institute, Magda reaffirmed her commitment to making German women as 'feminine as possible'.[6]

Her husband was alarmed and swiftly moved to shut her down, instructing journalists that 'there is to be no mention made of Frau Goebbels in relation to the Fashion Institute'.[7] When the organisation held its first exhibition in mid August 1933, Magda was no longer involved. Goebbels may well have sacked her to prevent the ideological controversy her stance might have caused or because of the general hostility towards the wives of the top Nazis holding any public offices, but it is also possible that he was jealous and didn't want her stealing the spotlight.

Yet Goebbels continued to portray Magda as some kind of domestic goddess, a fairly futile exercise; after all, who could imagine her doing the washing up or scrubbing the floors? That's what the servants were for. Nevertheless, the Nazis went to great lengths to turn German women into super-efficient housewives, especially as their relentless drive to prepare the nation for war drained resources and materials out of the civilian economy and placed increasingly stringent limits on household goods. Butter, milk, eggs, sugar and coffee were all scarce, and there were shortages of textiles and furniture. Thousands of women attended courses lasting from a few days to a few weeks, covering such diverse topics as how to cook fish, provide a more sustainable alternative to the Sunday roast, turn old bed sheets into dresses, can and preserve food, and recycle their husband's suits as skirts or vests.

Deprived of a platform for her own ideas and uneasy about presenting herself as the housewife's choice, Magda did manage to find a domestic outlet for her frustrated creativity. She had a talent for interior design and decoration, and thanks to the number of residences the couple acquired, she had plenty to keep her busy. Even then, there was no escaping the demands of Nazi ideology, and in Magda's case, Hitler's views on art. Hitler loathed what he called 'degenerate art' – which essentially meant anything that was the slightest bit abstract or experimental – and was enraged when he saw that Magda had chosen a work by Emil Nolde, one of Germany's most prominent modernists, and hung it on the wall of Goebbels's official residence at the Propaganda Ministry. After Hitler threw a fit, the painting was quickly removed and stored discreetly away at the couple's lakeside property.

Despite being a contender for Magda's crown, Emmy still had to compete with Carin's legacy. In June 1934, Goering had Carin's remains transported from Sweden to Germany for reburial, prompted by the fact that her gravestone in Stockholm had been vandalised. Her zinc-lined coffin travelled by train under armed guard.* In every town it passed through, the church bells rang and the stations were draped in black. Arriving at Goering's new estate north of Berlin, the coffin was solemnly placed in an underground mausoleum, accompanied by the strains of Wagner's 'Twilight of the Gods'. Hitler laid a wreath and spoke a few words, paying tribute to the sacrifices Carin made for the movement.

Commentating on the ceremony, that month's edition of the Nazi's main newspaper for women extolled Carin's virtues: 'Let the life of this Nordic woman serve as a role model. We grow awe-struck, silent before so much self-evident loyalty and the inner greatness of a true woman.'[8] Her dutiful sister went on to write a glowing biography of Carin that became a bestseller; by 1943 it had sold 900,000 copies.

The site for her new resting place was in the grounds of Goering's country mansion, Carinhall, though the word 'mansion' hardly does it justice. Built to resemble a hunting lodge, it had a 150ft swimming pool, a movie theatre and a gymnasium in the basement, a map room, an office with a granite fireplace, a huge library, a vast banqueting hall serviced by uniformed footmen and surrounded by columns of red Veronese marble, state-of-the-art electronically controlled windows behind

---

* In 1991 a casket was discovered on the grounds of Carinhall, holding skeletal remains that were believed to belong to Carin Goering. In 2013 DNA evidence proved this theory to be correct and Carin was reburied in Sweden.

curtains that bore the letter *H* stitched in gold, a model railway with 60ft of track in the attic, and an imposing entrance hall lined with statues and paintings. Any awkwardness Emmy may have felt about occupying a home named after her lover's dead wife was trivial compared to the thrill of being the lady of the manor and living in the kind of splendour that was beyond the reach of even the top Hollywood actresses.

Then, in 1935 – perhaps following a nudge from Hitler – Emmy and Goering announced their engagement. Though the party staged at Carinhall to celebrate the announcement was hardly modest, it paled in comparison to the actual wedding. On 10 April, Berlin came to a standstill. In his dispatch to London, Eric Phipps, the British ambassador, described the scene: 'A visitor … might well have thought that the monarchy had been restored … the streets were decorated; all traffic was suspended … whilst two hundred military aircraft circled in the sky.'[9]

After a ceremony at the town hall, the 320 guests – who included Hitler and all the senior Nazi figures – moved to the cathedral and then on to a sumptuous feast. Emmy received a host of presents: the King of Bulgaria awarded her the country's highest honour along with a bracelet laced with sapphires, her hometown of Hamburg gifted her a solid silver ship, while the boffins at IG Farben – Germany's leading petro-chemical firm – gave her two synthetically produced gemstones.

The night before the nuptials, Emmy made her last stage appearance; whatever regrets she might have had, she recognised that it would be inappropriate for her to 'continue to act'.[10] In doing so, she was not only falling into line with the general prohibition against the top wives holding down jobs, but also the more general thrust of Nazi policy; a woman's place was at home, not at work.

However, like many of the regime's efforts to fit German women into the mould it had created for them, it was compromised by the overriding necessity of readying the country for war. With slight variations, the proportion of women in the workforce remained the same as in the Weimar period, at roughly a third. Reflecting the Nazis' priorities, there was a sharp decline in the level of female employment in the professions, including 15 per cent fewer high school teachers, but increases in agriculture, industry and office work. The majority of these working women were single; only about 35 per cent were married.

Emmy's retirement did not mean that she ceased to take an interest in the theatre world – she also became involved in defending and promoting her favourite classical musicians and conductors – or to exert her influence, especially when it came to Gründgens. In 1936, some critics expressed the opinion that Gründgens's production of *Hamlet* was ideologically suspect. Knowing that a bad review could land him in a concentration camp, Gründgens lost his nerve and fled to Switzerland. Alarmed by his sudden disappearance, Emmy sent her husband after him, and Goering was able to convince Gründgens to return; Goering even had the journalists involved arrested by the Gestapo and forced one of them to apologise to Gründgens in person. Nevertheless, Gründgens still felt vulnerable and decided to cultivate Goebbels as well. That same year, he married the screen star Marianne Hoppe. The relationship served a dual purpose; wedlock would help silence the rumours about his sexuality, while being with a movie actress brought him into Goebbels's orbit. Gründgens skilfully worked both sides of the fence and survived the Nazi era unmolested.

Firmly established as the Nazis' first couple, Emmy and Goering bestrode Berlin's social scene with considerable swagger, exhibiting their shared love of theatrical display; Goering was no less a performer than Emmy, and was well-known for his outlandish dress sense – he'd often greet visitors sporting a toga and Turkish slippers – and his habit of wearing a dizzying array of colourful and elaborate uniforms bestrewn with the medals he kept awarding himself as head of Germany's air force, the Luftwaffe.

His ever-changing wardrobe was a constant source of amusement for the general public, who never tired of inventing jokes about his fanciful attire; gags that were more affectionate than mean-spirited as his preposterous vanity made him appear more human and more relatable than the other Nazi leaders: 'Your Excellency,' reports Goering's adjutant, 'a pipe has burst in the Air Ministry!' Goering turns to his wife and cries out, 'Emmy, quick! Get me my Admiral's uniform!'[11]

A typical example of their ostentatious behaviour was the party they held to celebrate Goering's forty-third birthday on 12 January 1936. Over 2,000 guests paid 50 marks – the money went to charity – to attend the bash at the Berlin State Opera; there was a full orchestra playing waltzes and sanitised jazz tunes, an endless stream of champagne and a tombola – prizes included miniature tanks and machine guns made of marzipan, and a diamond-encrusted brooch in the shape of a swastika. Tellingly, Magda cried off sick, while Hitler, who had no wish to be upstaged, stayed at home.

The Goerings' reputation for behaving like an emperor and empress from ancient times was further enhanced by their decision to raise lions at home. Borrowing them from the Berlin Zoo, and returning them when fully grown, Emmy treated her lions as if they were harmless pets or very small children: 'Whenever a new lion cub came to us he was always greatly alarmed when we first put him in the bath-tub. But they soon got to know that they were washed once a week and let themselves be soaped all over.'[12]

For Emmy, all the roleplaying in which she indulged served to conceal the ugly truth of what Goering actually did for a living: his turbocharged Luftwaffe saw its first action in the Spanish Civil War fighting alongside Franco's right-wing armies and was responsible for the flattening of the small town of Guernica. Henriette Hoffmann – who married Baldur von Schirach, the Hitler Youth leader, in 1932 – made a psychologically acute observation about Emmy's flight into a fantasy world: 'She would have been content if … the uniforms had been stage costumes, her palace the scenery, the noise of war the sound effects behind the scenes and her magnificent presents only props. She never wanted reality.'[13]

Attempting to keep up with them were Magda and Goebbels. Certainly, most of those who encountered Magda on the endless round of receptions, diplomatic soirees and formal occasions found her enchanting – with the notable exception of Bella Fromm, who claimed she'd never seen 'such ice-cold eyes in a woman', full of 'determination and inordinate ambition'.[14]

But everywhere Magda turned, Emmy and her husband were there or thereabouts, putting their imprint on events and outdoing the competition. One of the highlights of the social calendar was a day out at the races. The Berlin Racecourse was run by the elite Union Club – founded in 1867 – and had 500 fee-paying members. The club expanded rapidly under the Nazis with bigger stands, more horses, off-track facilities that included a salon and a clinic for the animals, and a special enclosure reserved for high-ranking female punters like Magda and Emmy, where the ladies could eat, drink and gamble without being interfered with.

Goebbels attempted to put his stamp on the club by arranging an annual fashion show there – with help from Bella Fromm, of all people – but Goering easily trumped him by offering the largest cash prize ever awarded to the winner of the Berlin Grand Prix – renamed the Grand Prix of the Capital of the Third Reich – which was the premier race of the year.

The fact was that no matter how hard Goebbels and Magda tried to shine, they could never match Goering's vast income; behind Hitler, he was the second-richest Nazi. Most military experts believed that air power would prove decisive in the next major war and Goering's air force was a major beneficiary of Hitler's rearmament programme. Goering had the ultimate say over aircraft design and production; he awarded contracts and allocated the vast resources coming in from state and private investment. This enabled him to shamelessly siphon off a fortune from the Luftwaffe budget and illicit bribes from firms in exchange for contracts.

In 1936, his empire grew dramatically when Hitler made him the head of the Four-Year Plan, which was meant to gear the whole economy towards total war and encourage self-sufficiency in several key commodities: iron, steel, petrol and rubber. Hitler had lost patience with his economics minister, who was dragging his feet over the pace of rearmament. By creating the Four-Year Plan office and giving it to Goering – despite his complete lack of qualifications and relevant experience – Hitler was undermining the influence of the minister and promoting a man as hell-bent on war as he was. Once in charge of this sprawling conglomerate, Goering was able to commit larceny on a massive scale;

among the contributors to Goering Inc. were German companies like BMW and Bosch, the Swedish firms Electrolux and Ericsson, and the American corporations Standard Oil and General Motors.

Though Goebbels was no less corrupt than Goering, his sources of revenue were nowhere near as substantial. He and Magda had an official residence at the Propaganda Ministry and a house in Berlin, plus two lakeside properties not far from the city; the largest was at Schwanenwerder, an English-style country house with stables for the ponies and a four-bedroom guest annexe; the second, bankrolled by the state, was at Lanke, a slightly smaller manor house, but no less grand.

But Goering and Emmy had three Berlin addresses: the ever-expanding Carinhall, a large cottage at Obersalzburg, and Goering had inherited both his godfather's castles. Goebbels may have bought a sailing boat – which he was extremely proud of – but Goering had two massive yachts, *Carin I* and *Carin II*, while the chunk of forest Goebbels purchased could hardly compare with the 100,000 acres surrounding Carinhall, which Goering used as his private hunting ground. Guests to their respective homes would also be treated to better food – both in terms of quality and quantity – at Emmy and Goering's table: the meals served at the Goebbels residences were notoriously stingy and guests would often fill up beforehand.

Emmy and her husband even had better vacations. Both couples made frequent trips abroad, combining business with pleasure, some for only a couple of days, others more extended visits. Yet Goebbels mostly travelled alone as Magda was often either pregnant or recovering from giving birth. She saw Rome and northern Italy a few times, and joined her husband – and several other couples – on a ten-day jaunt to Greece in September 1936. After brief stopovers in Budapest and Belgrade, the group flew to Athens, where they were greeted by cheering crowds and a buffet lunch. Next up was a meeting with the king and a sit-down with the prime minister, followed by some free time to go sightseeing. Goebbels marvelled at the glories of antiquity – the Acropolis, the Parthenon, the amphitheatre at Delphi – but Magda felt under the weather, defeated by the heat. Then, on a four-day boat trip to various islands and their ancient sites, she came down with a severe case of seasickness.

Emmy, on the other hand, enjoyed numerous excursions on her yachts, whether gliding down the Rhine or sailing in the Adriatic. There were also state visits to potential allies. In the spring of 1939, she and Goering went to Libya and stayed at the summer house of the fascist governor Marshall Balbo, who'd waged a brutal war against indigenous rebels to secure Italian domination.

The day after their arrival, there was a huge welcoming party with 'big flood-lit fountains and Moorish guards' that reminded Emmy of 'a story from the Arabian Nights'. Other highlights of the trip were a military parade and camel riding in the desert, which Emmy compared to being 'in a ship on a rough sea'. The following year, they were in the Balkans as guests of both the Bulgarian and Serbian royal families, spending time at 'a real fairy tale castle by the sea-side'.[15]

The one tangible advantage Magda and Goebbels had over their rivals was their unique relationship with Hitler. This triangular arrangement continued to function uninterrupted after the seizure of power: Hitler frequently dropped in on Magda and the children, they celebrated their birthdays together, shared trips to the coast and had long discussions late into the night. On Magda and Goebbels's fifth wedding anniversary, as a token of his affection, Hitler gave them a mid-nineteenth-century oil painting by Carl Spitzweg that alluded to his own marital status; entitled *The Eternal Bridegroom*, it depicted a middle-aged gentleman offering flowers to a young maiden.

Goebbels was also a regular fixture at the lunches Hitler held at the Reich Chancellery, where he was expected to assume the role of court jester. Goebbels's talent for sarcasm was legendary and Hitler relished the way he would select a victim then mercilessly shred them with his razor-sharp tongue. At the same time, Hitler 'often asked Frau Goebbels to invite a few young actresses to tea, and he took a delight in attending these tea-parties'.[16]

Hitler had a guarded attitude towards Emmy; he didn't disparage or criticise her, but he was never relaxed around her either – maybe he sensed her lack of ideological commitment or was unsettled by the fact that she didn't treat him like some kind of demi-god. There was none of the intimacy or the meeting of minds that he experienced with Magda.

However, this special connection was nearly permanently broken during the 1935 party rally in Nuremberg. The cause of this falling out was the appearance of Eva Braun at the event, the first time she'd been introduced to Magda and many other of the leading Nazi personalities. This very public airing of Hitler's secret relationship occurred in similar circumstances to the trip to the theatre at the beginning of 1933; Eva had once again tried to kill herself.

Eva had seen a fair bit of Hitler during 1934, which lulled her into a false sense of security and made his neglect of her in the early part of 1935 much harder to bear. On 6 February, he forgot her birthday. For weeks on end, he didn't even call. She finally got to see him for two hours on 2 March. The next day he returned to Berlin without saying goodbye. Through the rest of March and all of April, she was left to her own devices. It was becoming unbearable.

A record of Eva's suffering is provided by the twenty-two pages of her diary – the only portion of it to survive – which cover this period. On 4 March she was 'on tenterhooks' as she clung to the forlorn hope that he might appear at her door. A week later, she bitterly complained that 'he only needs me for certain purposes'. On 29 April, she mournfully acknowledged that 'love seems not to be on his agenda at the moment'.[17]

Eva didn't know that Hitler was resting up after a minor surgery to remove a cyst from his throat. Towards the end of May, and still in the dark about his condition, Eva's moods fluctuated wildly and reached a near-hysterical peak on the 28th; that evening she took an overdose of sleeping pills. Her younger sister found her in time and a sympathetic doctor came to Eva's rescue.

Hitler realised he had to make amends and let Eva take her place among the other leading wives at the party rally that September. Perhaps not realising Eva's actual significance to Hitler – it wasn't unusual for him to have a young woman in tow – Magda made some negative remarks about her. One of Hitler's bodyguards recalled that Magda was 'completely shocked' by 'this capricious and dissatisfied looking girl sitting on the VIP rostrum'.[18] Word got back to Hitler. Furious, he refused to see Magda socially for over six months. Given the strength of her feelings for Hitler – his chauffeur rather caustically remarked that when Magda was with Hitler you could 'hear her ovaries rattle'[19] – it was torture for her to be denied contact with him and no doubt contributed to her growing dissatisfaction with her marriage. Without the regular visits from Hitler, the issues she had with Goebbels were harder to shrug off.

Goebbels suffered too, paranoid about losing favour with the man who meant everything to him; together, he and Magda tried to woo him back. They reserved a small cottage in the grounds of their Schwanenwerder property for Hitler's exclusive use. Finally, on 19 April 1936, Hitler came to see it for himself, and he and Magda were reconciled. Even so, this welcome development was not enough to lift her spirits. Only a few weeks after the reunion with Hitler, Goebbels made a note in his diary about her miserable state of mind: 'she weeps and is terribly sad' and 'sometimes has her moods: like all women'.[20]

Also causing a stir at the 1935 party rally – and friction with Eva – were two aristocratic English sisters, Unity and Diana Mitford, from the sort of vaguely artistic, eccentric and unconventional upper-class family that the writer Evelyn Waugh captured so well. Diana was the mistress of Oswald Mosley, an ex-Labour politician who founded the British Union of Fascists in 1932. However, it was Unity, the younger of the two, who fell hardest for Nazism, and particularly for Hitler.

Speculation raged at the time about whether Unity was romantically involved with Hitler. Diana didn't think so, saying that 'her admiration and even affection for him was boundless, but she was not in love', and she believed that Hitler simply appreciated Unity's fun-loving personality; Heinrich Hoffmann said Unity was both an example of Hitler's ideal woman, and potentially useful 'for propaganda purposes'. Hitler hoped to exploit Unity's 'blind devotion to him'[21] as part of the ongoing campaign to ensure British neutrality in the war he was determined to fight. But for that purpose, Hitler seemed to prefer Diana – whom he treated to a number of one-to-one meetings – not fully realising that her relationship with Mosley compromised her credibility back in the UK.

Once Unity had arrived in Munich in 1934 – and she and Diana had lurked in the wings of the party rally – she behaved like a deranged fan. She stalked Hitler, following his daily movements, learning his habits and patterns, waiting for the moment when he would acknowledge her presence, which he finally did at the Café Osteria on 9 February 1935. Now Unity had finally established contact, she convinced Diana to join her in Munich. The two of them received mixed reactions from the Nazi faithful; there was much grumbling about their low-cut dresses and liberal use of lipstick. Friedelind Wagner, Winifred's oldest daughter, was slightly more charitable; she said Diana was 'truly beautiful in a cool blue-eyed English way' and noted that Unity was 'an attractive girl' except when she smiled and 'revealed the ugliest set of teeth I have ever seen'.[22]

Magda was the only one who really warmed to Unity and appreciated her lively sense of humour. Whenever Unity was in Berlin they hung out together; they went shopping, watched movies and attended the opera. Magda also liked Diana, and she returned the compliment; as she put it in her autobiography, 'I became very fond of Magda Goebbels and her children'.

Magda went out of her way to help Diana and Oswald Mosley get married in Germany. Diana was a divorcee – her ex-husband was a member of the hugely wealthy Guinness family – and Mosley was recently widowed; they were both keen to avoid the negative publicity they'd receive if they got hitched at home. Diana asked Magda for help 'with all the form-filling'[23] and on 6 October 1936 the wedding went ahead. The ceremony was held in Goebbels's private rooms at the Propaganda Ministry. Diana was dressed in a pale gold tunic, and Hitler gave the newlyweds his blessing and a signed photograph in a silver frame; afterwards, Magda treated them to a wedding feast and presented Diana with leatherbound editions of Goethe's collected works.

A couple of months earlier, Hitler had personally invited the sisters to the 1936 Olympic Games – he provided them with a chauffeur-driven limo to ferry them back and forth to the stadium – and they stayed with Magda and Goebbels. For their amusement, Diana and Unity taught the couple the English parlour game 'Analogies'. Players had to guess the identity of a person by using an analogy; for example, what colour best represents them? In the case of Hitler, Goebbels's answer was 'fiery red'.[24]

During the Olympic Games, the Nazis engaged in a massive charm offensive; the streets of Berlin were cleared of anything that might spoil a visitor's day. Anti-Semitic propaganda was taken down, vagrants and petty thieves were systematically removed. For two weeks, with representatives of most of the participating nations descending on the capital, the main competitors for the title of First Lady of the Reich had a perfect opportunity to enhance their international prestige.

Setting the tone for the forthcoming events, Hitler presided over a banquet on the opening day of the Games. Goering picked up the baton and hosted an exclusive private lunch the following day – which featured kangaroo-tail soup on the menu – followed by a large and lavish official dinner on 6 August. Meanwhile, Goebbels and Magda were saving their energy for their big party, set for the 15th.

By then, Goering and Emmy had staged their final event in the grounds of the Air Ministry. After a splendid meal and a moonlit ballet, the arena was suddenly transformed into a fairground with roundabouts, a café and beer tents, while a procession of white horses, donkeys and actors dressed as peasants moved through the awe-struck crowd.

Two days later, Magda and Goebbels welcomed nearly 3,000 guests to Peacock Island, a magical wooded nature reserve connected to the mainland by pontoons. At first, it looked like the Goebbels' party might equal or even surpass their rivals' effort: the tree-lined pathways were illuminated by lamps, there were three orchestras providing dance music, an open barbecue and a spectacular fireworks display. However, as the night wore on – and young couples began disappearing into the bushes – things got increasingly out of control. The SS and SA men drafted in as security had been knocking back copious amounts of free alcohol and a minor disagreement turned into a riot; bottles and chairs were thrown and horrified guests scurried for cover. Ashamed, embarrassed and exhausted, Magda watched the dawn rise over the wreckage of broken glass, toppled tables and dishevelled survivors, and sobbed her heart out.

One fine morning in May 1937, Emmy claimed that she 'reached the peak of human happiness' when she and her husband opened a rest home for retired actors. Emmy had joined the board of governors of the Maria Seabach Foundation – established in the 1920s to provide accommodation for cash-strapped thespians – and convinced Goering to pump funds into the struggling organisation. Thanks to his generous donations, it was able to buy some land and build a new facility, situated in a picturesque forest location, which boasted thirty-five rooms, a large dining area and a library. Grateful for her contribution, the foundation took Emmy's name and under her direction it continued to thrive; the home was still taking in residents when Soviet troops arrived there in 1945.

Then, against all the odds, Emmy discovered that she was pregnant. Her joy was unconfined. Finally, she would join the other mothers of the Reich. Word of her condition spread fast and soon tongues were wagging all over Germany. Given that Emmy was 42 and Goering was 44 – and his marriage to Carin had been childless, even though the cause was her delicate constitution, not his alleged impotence – there was considerable doubt over the paternity. Emmy and Goering's sex life had already given rise to a number of wedding night jokes that focused on his performance in the bedroom (for example, that Emmy had stopped going to church after their honeymoon because she'd lost faith in the resurrection of the flesh), and now the gags flew thick and fast. Some were based on the wild rumour that Mussolini was the father – the Italian dictator spent time with the couple earlier that year – and some even accused his highly sexed son-in-law, Count Ciano, who was also said to have had a fling with Magda Goebbels, of doing the deed. More plausible were ones aimed at either the chauffeur or Goering's personal Luftwaffe adjutant: a senior air-force official asks Goering what they should do to celebrate if the baby is a girl. Goering replies 'A 100-plane fly-past'. And if it's a boy? 'A 1,000-plane fly-past'. And if there's no child? 'Court-martial my adjutant.'[25]

Goering liked to pride himself on his sense of humour and kept a notebook where he jotted down his favourite jokes, but with his manhood and Emmy's dignity at stake, he wasn't laughing any more. When a well-known Berlin night-club comic cut too close to the bone, Goering allegedly sent him for a short stay in a concentration camp. The accuracy of this oft-repeated story is hard to establish, and it is equally possible that it was Goebbels who cracked down on the hapless comic in 1936, dispatching him to Dachau before Goering got him released.

However, Goering was definitely very sensitive about the subject, and took exception to any suggestion he wasn't the father. When the founder and long-term editor of a rabidly anti-Semitic and shockingly crude Nazi tabloid made an indecent remark about Emmy in his paper, Goering tore him to pieces: the editor was dragged through the Party Court, barely escaped total excommunication and lost his place in the Nazi elite.

In the end, nothing could take away from Emmy and her husband's delight at the prospect of becoming parents. The only clouds on their horizon were health-related. There was concern that the pregnancy might aggravate Emmy's long-standing problems with sciatica, while Goering was having terrible trouble with his teeth and endured a series of dental procedures. To numb the pain, he was proscribed painkillers that contained a small amount of codeine. Though far less addictive than morphine, Goering carried on taking them once the course of treatment was complete, popping around five a day; not long after, he was up to ten a day.

On 29 October 1937, Magda and her husband held a glitzy reception at the Propaganda Ministry for the great and good of Germany's cultural scene. Guests included Hitler – who sat opposite Magda at dinner – the ubiquitous Heinrich Hoffmann, plus a bevy of famous film directors and well-known actors and actresses.

The whole evening was run with the precision of a military operation. Kicking off at 8.20 p.m., the various courses (a crab salad with asparagus, a clear soup, a main of goose with browned potatoes, dessert, a cheese platter with radishes on the side, and some fruit) were served at roughly ten-minute intervals. By 9.25 p.m. the guests had retired for coffee, pastries and cigars, before the VIPs were joined by less significant invitees for an hour-long concert featuring works by Schubert, Richard Strauss and Schumann.

Sitting at a top table was the 22-year-old Czech actress Lida Baarova, with whom Goebbels was having a passionate sexual relationship. As head of the movie industry, Goebbels was at the pinnacle of a booming business: during 1933–34, nearly 250 million cinema tickets were sold, and this had risen to 360 million in 1936–37. Fans queued up to enjoy the steady diet of comedies that accounted for over 50 per cent of all films produced; the biggest female star, Zarah Leander, specialised in rom-coms, playing women who had to choose between their jobs and finding a suitable husband.

With all that power came temptation, and Goebbels made vigorous use of the casting couch. While the more successful actresses were often able to fend him off without damaging their careers, the young hopefuls who rejected him suffered the consequences; Anneliese Uhlig was an up-and-coming star whose new film was pulled from the screens after she fought off his advances.

Goebbels's serial adulteries were common knowledge. Yet Magda continued to tolerate his excesses and turn a blind eye. In their Berlin home, Magda and Goebbels had separate bedrooms. One stormy night, Magda woke to discover the door connecting her room to his was locked, and in the morning she was confronted by the female guest who had shared her husband's bed. Magda let the incident pass without comment. In the end, she was convinced his one-night stands posed no threat to their marriage.

Equally, Magda was not above the odd dalliance herself; when provoked, she would taunt Goebbels with revelations about her own indiscretions. One such affair involved Kurt Ludecke, who had joined up with the Nazis in Munich in the early 1920s and then gone to the USA to build connections there. According to him, he first met Magda when she was in New York with her then husband Gunther Quandt and Ludecke renewed the acquaintance after his return to Germany in 1930.

Every so often, the two of them spent time alone together. Their last meeting was in 1936. Shortly after he was expelled from the movement for scandalous behaviour during his spell in America; Ludecke's powerful enemies included Gerda's father Walter Buch, who continued to be in charge of the Party Court. Ludecke made no direct reference to his liaison with Magda in his book *I Knew Hitler* (1937), but made no secret of his attraction to her, remarking on the 'warmth and charm with which nature had endowed her' and describing her as 'beautiful, cultured and intelligent'.[26]

Though Magda gained a measure of satisfaction from rubbing her husband's nose in it, his prolific infidelity was wearing her down, and things went from bad to worse after Goebbels encountered Lida Baarova. Born in Prague, Baarova had trained in the theatre and already had a number of screen credits before moving to Germany in 1934. With her dark hair, sultry look and seductive foreign accent she quickly became typecast as a sexy siren luring men to their doom; in her first German picture, released in 1935, she provokes a duel; in her second, a death at sea. Though these overblown melodramas were mediocre films she received positive reviews, and with a movie star boyfriend in tow, her career looked set to take off.

By 1936, Baarova was living with her celebrity partner in his villa close to Goebbels's home at Schwanenwerder, and she ran into him during a walk in the forest. From the start, Goebbels was extremely attracted to her – almost spellbound – and wasted no time letting her know how he felt. Baarova kept him at bay; she was involved with someone else and was well aware of Goebbels's reputation, but his persistence and the fact that his declarations of love seemed genuine – which they were – persuaded her to lower her defences.

Having consummated the relationship, Goebbels began energetically promoting Baarova's films. In 1937, she scored a big hit with *Patriots*. Set during the First World War, it followed the story of a German fighter pilot shot down in French territory. Taken in by a local theatre group, he has an affair with a French woman, played by Baarova, who must decide whether to hand him in or not. She does. Her lover is accused of spying; if convicted he faces the firing squad. Baarova's character makes an impassioned intervention and his life is spared. The critics ate it up, one reviewer gushing that Baarova was 'better than we have ever seen her'.[27]

Goebbels was in ecstasy and became more and more open about the relationship. Though he was playing with fire – and not just with Magda; according to the gossip hounds Baarova's partner, a hulk of a man, physically assaulted him – the propaganda maestro could not control himself. If Magda didn't want to attend a star-studded premiere, her husband would simply show up with Baarova on his arm.

Waking up to the danger, Magda confronted Goebbels and there were heated altercations. However, she was unable to summon enough energy to sustain her fightback. Earlier that year, she'd given birth to another girl – with the usual negative effects on her health – and friends noted that she seemed depressed. She was drinking and smoking more heavily. Then, in late autumn, she got pregnant again and lost the will to force the issue.

However, Goebbels didn't realise that his personal assistant had fallen hopelessly in love with Magda, couldn't bear to see his boss treating her so badly and was preparing to stab him in the back.

7

DOWN SOUTH

Gerda Bormann was in many ways the ideal Nazi wife. She didn't use cosmetics, had her blonde hair in a plait and wore traditional Bavarian dress, as did her children; in the few images of them that survived they look like they've just stepped off the set of *The Sound of Music*. At home, Gerda submitted without question to her husband's demands. She had no public profile and no place in the regime's publicity campaigns; at the party events she was obliged to attend, she remained hidden in the background. Most of all, she was a prodigious mother, producing children at a heroic rate: between 1933 and 1940, Gerda added five more to the two she already had.

As far as the Nazis were concerned, this was a woman's essential function: to drive population growth. Increasing the birth rate was an overriding goal and the regime mobilised its forces to achieve this aim: there were economic incentives and cash handouts for large families; the propaganda machine made films, broadcast radio shows and staged exhibitions that glorified motherhood; the medical profession and the scientific community – especially nutritionists and fertility experts – got in on the act; and the Gestapo policed those considered unfit to be mothers.

The regime also cracked down on abortion. During the Weimar period, it was reduced from a crime to a misdemeanour, but the Nazis introduced very harsh sentences and the number of convictions increased by 65 per cent. The policy towards contraception was more lenient, largely because the Nazis were worried about the spread of sexually transmitted diseases. Though frowned upon, condoms were available from vending machines at railway stations and in public toilets. A concerned Nazi doctor calculated that around 70 million condoms were sold every year.

Overall, Gerda was the exception rather than the rule. Though the birth rate increased – in 1933 there were just under fifteen live births per 1,000 people, which had risen to twenty by 1939 – it was still slightly less than it was in 1925, while the number of families with more than four children had dropped from a quarter in 1933 to a fifth in 1939. Lower-class women managing on tight budgets couldn't afford too many kids, and those women solvent enough not to work weren't prepared to give up the freedoms a smaller family gave them.

The Nazis knew they weren't meeting targets and launched a new initiative, the Honour Cross of the German Mother, a medal for the Reich's most productive women. Four offspring was enough to qualify for bronze, six or seven got you silver, while eight or over won a gold medal. Applicants were thoroughly vetted and their suitability assessed. Nevertheless, 3 million mothers were awarded the Honour Cross. Though Gerda's efforts were worthy of the top prize, she was not part of the grand inaugural ceremony held on the same day as Hitler's mother's birthday. Instead, Magda – who received a silver medal – was chosen to represent the leading wives.

Like Magda, Gerda didn't have to deal with her brood alone. There were nannies, cooks and cleaners. In the first few years after the Nazi takeover, the Bormanns' lifestyle was still relatively restrained. Because of his inexorable rise, by the mid 1930s they'd begun to enjoy the same privileged existence as other leading Nazis.

Bormann's career took a major leap forward thanks to Hess. On 21 April 1933, Hess was made Deputy Führer, and that year's Nazi party handbook outlined his duties: 'all matters of party leadership' and 'all the different aspects of the work performed inside the party' were 'under his supervision', as were 'all laws and decrees'.[1] Though this was a significant promotion for Hess, it didn't suit him. Hess was not a bureaucrat; he loathed paperwork and handed the vast bulk of the day-to-day business over to Bormann, who'd demonstrated his capabilities while managing the Nazis' insurance fund. In July of that year, Hess made Bormann his chief of staff. Bormann's power was unseen by the majority of Germans but no less real. The levers of the party were under his control; he delegated tasks, circulated directives to regional party bosses and dished out appointments. Before long, the whole structure was reliant on him. It helped that he had a brain like a filing cabinet where he stored a mine of information; Hitler knew he could depend on Bormann's memory – 'he never forgets anything' – and relentless efficiency, 'where others need all day, Bormann does it for me in two hours'.[2]

Bormann worked tremendously hard, existed on only a few hours of sleep a night, and pushed his subordinates to the limit. Christa Schroeder, Hitler's longest-serving secretary, wrote that Bormann 'expected from his staff the same enormous industriousness which distinguished himself'.[3] Demanding, impatient and unforgiving, Bormann was not a popular boss. His employees lived in fear of his quick-fire temper. According to Hitler's chauffeur, one minute Bormann could be charm personified, the next 'a sadist – belittling, offensive and wounding'.[4] Hitler knew Bormann was a terrible bully, but he got things done: 'I can rely on him absolutely and unconditionally to carry out my orders immediately and irrespective of whatever obstructions may be in his way.'[5]

By all accounts, Bormann behaved the same way at home, which gave rise to the widely held view that Gerda was an oppressed, brow-beaten housewife. A prominent Nazi characterised Bormann as 'the kind of man who takes delight in humiliating his wife in front of friends as if she was some lower form of being'.[6] If domestic standards slipped a fraction, or something was done incorrectly or landed in the wrong place, Bormann would lash out at Gerda. Hitler's valet said that everybody knew that Bormann terrorised his family: 'In moments of uncontrolled rage he would resort to physical violence against his wife and children.'[7] Bormann allegedly beat two of his children with a whip because they were frightened by a large dog, and kicked one for falling in a puddle.

It's hard to assess how Gerda felt about such degrading treatment. She'd didn't fight back. She didn't seek help. She didn't confide in anybody. Based on her Nazi ideology, Gerda believed it was her duty to obey her husband, and there's every indication that she was truly devoted to

Bormann. As far as her children were concerned, Gerda happily played with them, sang songs, drew pictures and read stories: it was their father's job to discipline and punish them. In a letter to him, in which Gerda contemplated the split with her own parents, she discussed her kids in a hard-headed and completely unsentimental way: 'Children are always selfish. They have their own interests and circles, and have no consideration for their parents.'[8]

In the early months of his rule, Hitler experimented with Reich Chancellery protocol by having one of the top Nazi wives on hand to welcome important guests and dignitaries. This system was dispensed with fairly quickly, but not before Ilse had demonstrated that she was totally unsuited to that sort of decorative role, especially when confronted by an awkward situation. Winifred Wagner's eldest daughter, Friedelind, was present for one such incident. A teenager at the time and something of a rebel, Friedelind left Germany for good in 1940, reached the USA a year later and penned a scathing critique of her mother and her Nazi associates.

Having portrayed Ilse as a 'plump, inelegant blonde with a deep voice' who scorned 'powder and make-up', Friedelind recalled how Ilse offered the guests some of 'Hitler's favourite candies' to keep them occupied while waiting for him to appear. Unfortunately, Hitler was in a foul mood; sitting next to Ilse at lunch, he fumed silently as Friedelind, her mother and the rest of the ensemble endured an unappetising bowl of noodle soup before retiring for coffee. No longer able to contain himself, Hitler flew into the next room and subjected one of his underlings to a ten-minute ear-bashing, screaming at full volume; Ilse and company heard every word of his blistering tirade. Mortified and paralysed by embarrassment, Ilse finally 'found the courage to tell him that his guests were leaving'.[9]

Ilse never felt at home in the perpetual whirl of the Berlin social scene; Bella Fromm noted that she rarely made an appearance. Despite the fact her husband's responsibilities obliged him to be in the capital more often, she visited as little as possible; Ilse's reluctance to embrace life in Berlin stemmed from its reputation as a citadel of sin, a toxic environment that sapped the moral fibre of anybody who stayed there too long. In Munich, she could remain true to the values that had animated her since her student days and uphold her and her husband's self-appointed mission; they would be the keepers of the Nazi flame. Years later, Ilse reminded Hess of their vow to 'never sell our birthright as idealists for the sake of external things'.[10]

While others enriched themselves at the party's expense, she and Hess led a frugal, typically bourgeois lifestyle. Their villa in a wealthy Munich suburb – with a large garden and several annexes – was a relatively modest abode compared to other prominent Nazi homes; the nearest they got to a country estate was a small lodge in the mountains that they used as a base for their hiking and camping holidays in the summer and skiing in the winter, cross-country rather than downhill. Hess's one indulgence was expensive motor cars; Mercedes was his brand of choice, and he liked nothing better than letting rip on the open road. Nevertheless, once he'd used up his monthly allowance of subsidised petrol, Hess paid for every extra drop of fuel out of his own pocket.

Because of Hess's honesty and disinterest in accumulating material wealth, he was dubbed 'the conscience of the party'; which was quite a label to live up to given the open criminality of the regime. After the Night of the Long Knives, in June 1934, when Hitler decapitated the leadership of the SA and settled a number of old scores – and the body count mounted in an orgy of violence – Hess had to clean up the mess caused when an innocent civilian was killed by mistake.

The intended target was a certain Dr Will Schmitt; instead the perpetrators butchered a respected music critic, Dr Wilhelm Schmidt. His widow described how four SS men came and took her husband away while he was practising the cello and she was preparing dinner. She heard nothing of his fate until his corpse appeared in a sealed coffin and the SS offered her financial compensation, which she angrily refused. Fed up with the SS men's repeated attempts to get her to accept the money, she marched over to the Brownhouse – the party's huge headquarters in Munich – and made a complaint.

The response was swift. On 31 July, Hess appeared at her door. This unfortunate sequence of events had come to his attention and he was there to make amends. Hess assured her that those responsible would be punished; as she recalled it, Hess then advised her to 'think of my husband's death as the death of a martyr for the great cause'.[11] Convinced that Hess's apology was sincere, she agreed to his offer of a monthly pension equivalent to her murdered husband's salary.

On a more personal level, Hess intervened on behalf of his and Ilse's close friend Professor Haushofer. The professor's wife was half-Jewish and he feared for her safety, his reputation and his son Albrecht's career prospects. Hess made Professor Haushofer head of two organisations designed to cater for the needs of the 20 million Germans living abroad. Hess also secured a post for Albrecht, a talented academic working in his father's field, at the Berlin High School for Politics. As Professor Haushofer remarked years later, Hess 'protected me and my family from bad experiences with the party'.[12]

Ilse also got in on the act; in late 1933, she wrote to Himmler complaining about the Gestapo's heavy-handed tactics and intrusive surveillance; her specific bugbear was its tendency to tap everybody's phones, no matter who they were, and she demanded to know why Himmler's agents kept tabs on loyal members of the regime. Unfazed, Himmler let Hess know about Ilse's letter. Hess blew his top at Ilse and ordered her not to raise her voice in protest again.

However, it's important not to read too much into Ilse's gesture of defiance; she was objecting to the Gestapo's methods, not the motives behind them. Neither she nor her husband made a fuss about the concentration camps and the torture chambers. Hess never questioned the raft of prohibitive measures that required his signature. He may have helped Professor Haushofer but he had no qualms about the Nuremberg Laws. Passed in 1935, the legislation formally separated Jews from the rest of the population; they effectively ceased to be German citizens. With a few minor exceptions, Jews were prohibited from entering into marriages or sexual relationships with non-Jews.

As it was, Hess and Ilse's fanaticism was undiminished, and she never failed to take her place in the front few rows on the podium during the

Nuremberg party rally every September, a week-long homage to Hitler that grew more elaborate and extravagant with every passing year. A more cultural, if no less mandatory event was the Bayreuth Festival; Ilse had remained friends with Bayreuth's curator and patron Winifred Wagner and enjoyed any chance to catch up with her, while carefully avoiding getting dragged into the controversies and running battles about which of the maestro's operas should be performed and who should conduct them.

Other members of the elite were not as keen to attend the Wagner jamboree and were only there reluctantly. The general public was even less interested and tickets proved difficult to shift. As Bayreuth's finances were in a poor state, these shortfalls were potentially ruinous. However, Hitler would always bail out Winifred and made sure the auditoriums were full and the seats filled. Bulk bookings were made by the SA, the National Socialist Teacher's Association, and the Nazis' women's organisations; from 1934, Goebbels's Propaganda Ministry covered a third of the festival's budget.

From her home base, Ilse diligently maintained a wide-ranging correspondence with the Nazi faithful, dispensing advice and dealing with a multitude of requests and queries. Though she liked to think of herself as a kind of honest broker, Ilse managed to rub people up the wrong way. Responding to a family member's request for a spare ticket to the 1935 Nuremberg rally, Ilse adopted a self-righteous tone, reminding her relative that they were 'not among the long-standing party faithful' so could hardly expect special treatment when tickets were in 'such short supply that even old comrades-in-arms in the movement are having to stay away'.[13]

Ilse's tendency to meddle in other people's private lives got her in hot water with Bormann when she involved herself in his younger brother Albert's marriage plans. Albert was the polar opposite to his brother; well-mannered, sophisticated and naturally conservative, he was a university graduate with a background in banking. Bormann plugged Albert into the party in 1931, landing him a job in Hitler's Private Chancellery, a purely administrative office that mostly dealt with Hitler's huge mailbag. The two men maintained a civil working relationship until Albert decided to marry a woman Bormann disapproved of because she wasn't Nordic enough.

But Ilse, who liked both Albert and his bride-to-be, encouraged them to take the plunge, which they did in 1933. Bormann was outraged and never spoke to his brother again; Christa Schroeder remembered how the two of them went to inordinate lengths to ignore each other; if either Bormann or his brother 'told a funny story', the other one would 'keep a straight face',[14] even if everyone else was laughing. As for Ilse, though Bormann was cordial in public, he bore a grudge against her from that moment on.

Ilse's behaviour also grated with Hitler, and by the mid 1930s he'd lost patience with her. Dr Karl Brandt – who was Hitler's personal physician for many years and a member of his inner circle – said that Hitler would frequently criticise Ilse because of 'her ambition', and complain about the way she would try 'to dominate men and therefore almost lose her own femininity'.[15] Ilse's unapologetic intellectualism clashed with Hitler's archaic view that women should not hold political opinions, and even if they did, they should keep their mouths shut.

On 13 June 1936, Gerda had her fifth child, a son named Heinrich after his godfather Himmler – Bormann had forged an uneasy alliance with the SS supremo – who gave the boy a teddy bear on his first birthday. That year, the family acquired two new properties, a larger house in the same exclusive Munich suburb as the Hesses, which was ready by mid September, though extensive renovations and refurbishments continued for another year, and a three-storey cottage in Obersalzburg.

Bormann purchased their place in the Bavarian Alps, sitting on a plateau that sloped away to trees below and was surrounded by towering mountain peaks, and began converting it; while he opted to retain some of the exterior features and outer walls, the interior was thoroughly remodelled and significantly enlarged. In autumn 1937, Gerda and her clan moved into what would be their almost permanent residence. A visiting journalist was bowled over by what he saw: 'From the cellar to the attic there was nothing but luxury and the best of everything.'[16]

Gerda's nearest neighbour in Obersalzburg was Hitler; he'd taken possession of a castle in the sky, the Berghof, which became an alternative command centre during his stays there. The Berghof emerged out of the cottage that Hitler had been renting since 1927 and subsequently bought in June 1933. Rather than raze it to the ground, a new structure grew upwards and outwards from its central core. Construction began in March 1936 and proceeded at lightning speed; by 8 July it was ready for occupation.

Money for both the Bormanns' and Hitler's new dwellings came from the Adolf Hitler Industrial Fund. The fund was the brainchild of a steel baron who convinced his fellow captains of industry to take a portion of their employees' wages and donate it to Hitler. From its inception, Bormann was in control of the treasure chest, making him Hitler's personal accountant and paymaster. Between 1933 and 1945, 350 million RM passed across his desk.

Though deliberately isolated, the Berghof complex was well connected to the outside world – it had a wireless station, three telephone exchanges and a post office – while the nearby market town of Berchtesgaden had a railway station and an airstrip for Hitler's personal use. Bormann arranged tight security. A 6ft-high electrified fence ran round the area, every one of the residents and staff carried ID and there was a barracks for a company of elite SS men.

At the Berghof, Hitler held court, relaxed, and pondered crucial decisions and questions of strategy. It was also where Bormann consolidated his place at Hitler's right hand, the executor of his every whim and idle request, and ultimately the gatekeeper of Hitler's domain. Over the years, under Bormann's management, it grew into a vast private estate for the Nazi elite with its own school and functioning farm: to give the many labourers who were employed on all the building work something to do other than drink and fight, there was a theatre and a brothel – with around twenty French and Italian prostitutes – in a barracks about 4 miles from Obersalzburg.

Initially, Bormann concentrated on removing more than 400 locals from their homes. Paying considerably more than the going rate, Bormann acquired their chalets and farms for modification or demolition.

On one occasion, Hitler pointed out a particular building that bothered him because it didn't blend in with the surroundings. Bormann promptly bought it, kicked out the inhabitants, had it torn down, and re-turfed the land on which it stood. The next time Hitler looked in that direction, he saw cows grazing in a field.

Hitler also had issues with the mobs of tourists who gathered outside the Berghof every day hoping to catch a glimpse of him; he would wander out and let them see their glorious leader as they paraded by. The process often took over an hour and in summer Hitler was forced to stand there in the blazing sun, which made him feel ill. In July 1937, Hitler casually mentioned this to Bormann. Immediately, his faithful servant got busy. Within twenty-four hours, Bormann had the head gardener and his team uproot a large lime tree and replant it in a spot where it could provide Hitler with the shade he needed.

Bormann also modified his personal habits to fall in line with Hitler's; a chain-smoker, Bormann refrained from lighting up in his master's presence – Hitler despised smoking – and complied with his vegetarian diet, though Heinrich Hoffmann observed that Bormann, having 'consumed raw carrots and leaves', would 'retire to the privacy of his room' and help himself to pork chops.[17]

In this new setting, Gerda slowly and tentatively began to emerge from her shell and gain a degree of independence, primarily because of her good relationship with Eva Braun. After Eva's 1935 suicide attempt, Hitler went out of his way to accommodate her; in August of that year, he rented a three-bedroom apartment for Eva and her sister; the following March, Hitler bought her a two-storey villa and a new car. More importantly for Eva, she was given the room adjoining Hitler's at the Berghof. It took her a while, and there were continued restrictions on her freedom of movement, but at the Berghof she came into her own.

Eva and Gerda were only three years apart in age, and Gerda's unthreatening demeanour went down well with Eva, whose main regret was that Gerda had so little free time because of her regular pregnancies and responsibilities as a housewife. Eva certainly knew that she had no reason to be jealous of Gerda. Hitler's abiding affection for her stayed within the bounds of his 'Uncle Adolf' persona; every year, he gave

Gerda a bouquet of red roses on her birthday. But Hitler also appreciated that Gerda was a model of German motherhood; according to a Berghof regular, he 'treated her with special respect'.[18]

Eva was less keen on Gerda's husband, and Bormann didn't care for her either. Yet they both recognised their mutual dependence on Hitler and the significance they both held for him and developed a marriage of convenience, presenting a united front where he was concerned, confining their rivalry to the minutiae of daily life; as time went on and Hitler was there less often, the power struggle between them for mastery of the Berghof bubbled up to the surface.

As Hitler made Bayreuth the home of opera, he wanted Munich to be the beating heart of German art. On 15 October 1933, at a ceremony broadcast on the radio and filmed by newsreel camera crews, Hitler laid the foundation stone for a new museum, the House of German Art. Three years later, the neo-classical building was complete. On 18 July 1937, Hitler opened its galleries with a speech that compared the new spirit in German art, which expressed 'the joy of life', with the 'deformed cripples and cretins' who practised modernism.[19] To commemorate this auspicious moment, the Nazis staged a massive parade in honour of 2,000 years of German culture and history. The chronologically themed procession was 6 miles long, took three hours and featured a Saxon warship, floats bearing medieval knights, mythological scenes, tributes to famous kings and military leaders, and tributes to cultural heavyweights like Wagner.

At the same time, in a hastily converted warehouse, the Degenerate Art Exhibition, which featured the work of prohibited artists, opened its doors and proved far more popular with the public than the House of German Art. Its collection of paintings of peasants, nude sculptures and heroic depictions of combat was no match for the degenerate alternative that included 730 artworks by German and foreign artists like Picasso, Matisse and van Gogh. Over 2 million people visited it at an average of 20,000 a day: the House of German Art only attracted around 3,000 a day.

Ilse and her husband liked to think of themselves as patrons of the art scene and aspired to turn their home into a sort of salon; one of their chosen artists was the modernist Georg Schrimpf. Munich based, Schrimpf's early Expressionist paintings reflected his left-wing attitudes, but by the late 1920s he'd moved to the right both stylistically and politically. This switch in style and viewpoint meant that Schrimpf escaped censure and in 1933 he became professor of the Royal School of Art in Berlin. Then, in 1937, the wind changed; Schrimpf was sacked and banned from showing his art, which was then removed from galleries and museums to join the others on display at the Degenerate Art Exhibition.

But the Hesses had his paintings hanging on their walls, and Hitler – who'd always hated Schrimpf's work – was disturbed to see these abominations when he visited Ilse and her husband in 1934. Up to that point, Hess seemed the logical choice to succeed Hitler; he was head of the party and had been at Hitler's side for over a decade. But after that evening, Hitler changed his mind. He told his press secretary that he couldn't possibly allow somebody with 'such a lack of feeling for art and culture' to be his second-in-command.[20] Shortly after this conversation, Hitler made Goering heir to the throne.

Hitler wasn't the only prominent Nazi who objected to an evening with the Hesses; Magda claimed that 'parties at the Hess home' were 'so boring that most people refused invitations'. Nobody was allowed to smoke. Instead of alcohol, Ilse served 'fruit juice and peppermint tea', and 'the conversation was as thin and dull as the drinks'; the guests were just thankful that Hess 'regularly broke up the party at midnight' so they could make an early getaway.[21]

Ilse did her best to compensate for her husband's reluctance to have fun, but it was an uphill struggle; when the director Leni Riefensthal dropped by for tea she remembered that Ilse 'chatted ... vivaciously' while 'her husband stayed silent'.[22] However, Hess did occasionally enjoy himself. In late October 1937, he and Ilse entertained the Duke and Duchess of Windsor. They were on a short trip to Germany and had spent the afternoon at the Berghof – where Magda played hostess – before dropping in on the Hesses.

The duke had briefly been King Edward VIII. He had acceded to the throne in January 1936 after the death of George V, but his love affair with the American socialite Wallis Simpson – who was on her third marriage at the time – led to his abdication eleven months later. With Simpson's divorce finalised, the couple got married in June 1937.

Ilse thought that the duke would have made an 'exceptionally clever king' and the duchess 'a fine' queen. During the course of a pleasant evening, Hess and the duke disappeared upstairs. After they had been gone an hour, Ilse went looking and 'found them in one of the attic rooms, where my husband had a large table with a collection of model ships from the German and English fleets of World War One'; the duke and Hess had arranged the models in formation and were 'excitedly' recreating one of its most dramatic sea battles.[23]

As for Munich's night-life, Ilse and her husband rarely ventured out except to go to classical concerts to hear music by their favourite composers, Mozart, Bach and Brahms. They studiously avoided the wild party crowd that inhabited Munich's sleazy underbelly and revelled in hedonistic excess.

Unity Mitford was part of this group; with Hitler rarely available to see her and her sister Diana mostly absent after her marriage to Mosley, she fell in with this fast-living Nazi clique as it ran around town, her energy and zeal never flagging. In fact, Unity was showing signs of becoming increasingly mentally unstable; she took poor care of herself, barely ate anything substantial and almost never slept. A string of unsuitable lovers and failed relationships didn't help matters. If anything, Unity would have benefited from Ilse's steadying hand on her shoulder, providing reassurance and guidance. It's not as if Ilse didn't have a reputation for looking out for the welfare of troubled young women, but Ilse and her husband viewed Unity as an interloper with no sense of decorum and no moral compass.

In the end, Ilse and Hess's quiet lifestyle suited them, with one notable exception. Hess had not completely lost his thirst for adventure and physical danger; drawing on his First World War training, he took up flying again, competing in an annual race to reach the peak of the Zugspitze, Germany's highest mountain. In 1932, he came in second. Two years later, he won the challenge cup and received a telegram of congratulations from the famous American aviator – and Nazi supporter – Charles Lindbergh.

No doubt Ilse was proud of her husband's achievement; if she'd known where his airborne antics would eventually take him, she might not have been so supportive. Hitler, on the other hand, was alarmed at the risks involved and promptly grounded Hess. For the time being, Hess only performed feats of death-defying speed when he was behind the wheel of his car; his adjutant remembered how Hess drove the Mercedes 'as if he were flying an aeroplane. At any moment one had the feeling that he was about to take off.'[24]

For all the apparent respect and hard-won status that Eva had gained at the Berghof, she was still operating within strict limits. On a regular basis, she was banished to her room, or back to her Munich villa, or told to disappear off-site for a few hours, often staying the night with Gerda. Her forced departures coincided with the arrivals of VIP guests and foreign statesmen at the Berghof. The same rules applied when Hitler was engaged in high-level political meetings with the senior Nazi leaders and officials such as Goering and Goebbels.

Eva usually took part in the social rituals of birthdays and seasonal holidays where the wives and children of the leading personalities joined their husbands at Hitler's table, but she kept a low profile when Magda stayed at the Berghof without her family in tow. These solo visits only occurred a handful of times and never for very long; when they did, Magda was seeking escape from her rocky marriage and a morale boost from her beloved Hitler.

Yet Magda never became part of the Berghof community; she and Goebbels didn't even have a property in the area. This was partly due to Eva; though Magda tried to assert her authority, Eva now felt secure enough to hold her ground. One story about them illustrates this shift in power; while having a chat, a heavily pregnant Magda asked Eva if she wouldn't mind tying her shoelace as she found it difficult to bend over; unfazed by this request to kneel before her superior, Eva calmly rang a bell and got her maid to do it.

Emmy and her husband did have a substantial home in the complex but were not Berghof insiders. Given that they had Carinhall, they weren't down south very often. However, there was also the Eva factor. For some reason – which is hard to pin down since Emmy was clearly not a competitor for Hitler's attention like Unity and Magda – Eva deliberately avoided her: perhaps she sensed Hitler's discomfort around Emmy; perhaps she objected to Emmy's pompous, regal manner; maybe she felt intimidated by her; maybe it was a generational conflict; or maybe she simply didn't like her.

Whatever the cause, Eva turned her back on Emmy. Evidence for this comes from a number of the Berghof staff who were privy to an incident that occurred while both Hitler and Goering were elsewhere. What seems to have happened is that Emmy, in an effort to break the ice, invited Eva – and her ladies-in-waiting – to tea one afternoon. But Eva and her little gang didn't turn up, and Emmy never received an apology or an explanation. Having been so rudely snubbed, Emmy didn't bother to extend the hand of friendship again.

Ilse, on the other hand, was always welcome; Eva regarded her as a long–term friend and potential confidante. However, Ilse – perhaps sensing that Hitler no longer appreciated her company – only visited the Berghof when she was obliged to. Instead, she often looked after Eva when she was exiled from the Berghof; Ilse recalled that the two of them 'would go on a walking tour in the mountains or something'.[25]

Eva valued Ilse's companionship; Ilse understood the difficulty of Eva's situation and treated her with kindness and sympathy. Yet no matter how complimentary Ilse was about Eva – praising her looks and sweet nature – she couldn't help comparing her to Geli, Hitler's one true love: Ilse thought Eva was a perfectly acceptable replacement, just not as good as the original.

When Hess stayed overnight at the Berghof – which he did every now and then – he occupied the Untersberg Room, which was rarely used except by him. On the top floor, the suite had a large wood-panelled living area with a desk, a bathroom and bedroom, and a balcony that offered stunning views across the mountains that stretched as far as

Salzburg. While this sleeping arrangement appeared to flatter Hess and confirm his elevated position in the movement, it also reflected his growing estrangement and detachment from the Nazi elite, including Hitler: to many, he was the eccentric weirdo in the attic, lost in his own world.

With Bormann dealing with the vast bulk of the administrative workload, Hess had more free time to indulge his esoteric interests. As an awkward adolescent, Hess was enthralled by astrology and in 1907 he was inspired by Daniel's Comet, the most brilliant to appear in the northern hemisphere for twenty-five years, which was visible at dawn from mid July until the end of August. Hess later recalled his first sighting of the comet: 'The tail shimmered swiftly across what was about a third of the sky. Every night I got up to observe its rapid flight and changing form. From that moment I never lost interest in the stars.'[26]

In 1933, Ilse introduced Hess to Ernst Schultz-Strathaus, whom she had first met in the early 1920s when she was working in the antiquarian bookshop. Strathaus was a literary scholar who had run several journals for bibliophiles; he was also an expert on the occult. Knowing Hess's fascination with the stars of the zodiac, Ilse brought the two of them together. In 1934, Hess secured Strathaus a position on his staff as an advisor on cultural affairs. At the same time, Strathaus acted as Hess's personal astrologer, providing him with a daily horoscope. Though Ilse was not quite as immersed in the occult as her husband, she endorsed his mystical outlook and believed, like him, that supernatural forces shaped human destiny. She once observed that 'in moments of extreme spiritual tension there comes to us, from regions lying outside the field of reason, knowledge that will not let us be deceived'.[27]

The regime's attitude to astrology was ambiguous. Officially, it was considered to be an alternative belief system and therefore a threat, not least because it was hugely popular with the general public. As a result, soothsayers suffered sudden waves of persecution. In 1937, the German Astrological Society was abolished and its periodicals banned.

Yet Hess – who was often singled out for his reliance on Strathaus's charts – was not alone. At various points, Himmler consulted astrologers, and there was speculation that Hitler saw a clairvoyant, a wizened old gypsy who was said to have the magic touch. But Hess was considered the main offender and there were rumours he dabbled in mesmerism and employed psychics to manipulate solid objects like metal.

Another of Hess's pet subjects was alternative medicine, which sprung from his own persistent health problems; the first sign of stress-related illness was a severe outbreak of boils during the tense autumn of 1932 that put him in hospital. From then on, he was afflicted by a range of problems: bloating, kidney pain, heart palpitations, rotten guts and insomnia. To combat these complaints, Hess adopted a macrobiotic diet. Both he and Ilse turned vegetarian when Hitler did – so even their digestive tracts could be in synch with his – but Hess was even more fastidious than Hitler when it came to his meals. At first, Ilse went to great lengths to prepare appropriate food for her husband, but eventually Hess hired a special cook who accompanied him everywhere. On a trip to Vienna, Henriette Hoffmann – who was living in the Austrian capital with her husband Baldur von Schirach – remembered that Hess 'carried with him a little pot of spinach with mysterious ingredients'.[28]

His stubborn refusal to ingest any other food – no matter what – was a bone of contention with Hitler: when Hess ate at the Reich Chancellery, he would spurn the vegetarian option chosen by Hitler in favour of the nourishment he'd brought with him; a lunch guest remembered how an annoyed Hitler offered to have his 'first-class cook' prepare whatever Hess liked. Hess declined, explaining that 'the components of his meals had to be of a special bio-dynamic origin'.[29] Hitler took Hess's refusal personally, suggested that he eat at home in future and rarely invited him again.

Hess's rigid regime was not just a personal quirk. With Ilse's backing, he devoted considerable time and energy to the promotion, study and development of alternative therapies and treatments. In 1934, Hess lobbied successfully for the incorporation of a wide range of associations – such as the German Natural Healer's Association, the Society for Spas and Climatic Science, and the League of Hydro-therapists – into the Nazis' official organisation for health professionals. Next, he set up the Rudolf Hess Hospital in Dresden as a centre for naturopathic medicine; run by a cancer specialist who admired the theories of the renowned psychotherapist Carl Jung – as did other senior staff members – its patients were treated to water cures, a variety of diets and periods of fasting.

In 1937, Hess hosted the World Conference of Homeopathy in Berlin; he began his opening speech with a plea to the medical profession to 'consider even previously excluded therapies with an open mind', then declared that homeopathy was the most appropriate 'form of science' for treating 'living creatures', confidently stated that the 'demand for holism' was getting 'stronger and stronger',[30] and assured his audience that political conditions in Nazi Germany provided an opportunity to make great strides forward.

As with astrology, Hess was unfairly victimised for being a sucker, duped by cranks and their irrational mumbo-jumbo. Asides from Himmler, whose interest in herbal medicine was hardly a secret, the regime sought to harness the power of natural healing. Its war on cancer was an overriding priority: it involved research into whether a plant-based diet could ward off the disease, and identified the use of chemicals in food and everyday household products as a potential cause.

At the root of Hess's experiments in organic medicines – and his reliance on mystical prophecies – was his and Ilse's failure to conceive a child. Given their self-image as the torch-bearers of the movement, it felt shameful not to have added one of their own to the Nazis' ranks. Together, they went to extreme lengths to make amends; Hess worked hard to overcome his aversion to sex. Though their efforts were fruitless, Ilse refused to give up hope; Magda told one of Goebbels's staff that Ilse 'assured her five or six times over a number of years that she was at last going to have a child – generally because some fortune-teller had said she would'.[31]

Desperate, Hess abandoned his principles and went in search of a pharmaceutical pick-me-up. In Munich, there was a chemist directly opposite Heinrich Hoffmann's studio. Every day, witnesses observed Hess enter the pharmacy and come out with a life-enhancing potion designed to boost his virility.

This wonder cure was probably one of the wide range of hormone-based anti-impotence pills available without a prescription. The biggest seller was Titus Pearls, created by Magnus Hirschfeld, the noted sexologist whose Institute for Sexual Science was shut down by the Nazis. However, the product containing his formula stayed on the shelves. The firm that manufactured it also made a breast enlargement drug for women; the sales pitch boasted that it would transform their figures 'from the inside out'.[32]

Around the same time Hess was taking his supplement, the advertisements for Titus Pearls were targeted specifically at men like him; jaded middle-aged executives looking to spice up their love lives. The marketing campaign's underlying message – which implied that a sexually inactive man was not a useful member of the community because of his failure to reproduce – applied directly to Hess; the general assumption was that Hess was the one with the problem, not Ilse, and the pressure was on him to rectify matters.

Whether it was the drugs, or the alignment of the stars, or the miraculous properties of his diet, Ilse finally became pregnant in early 1937. The couple were thrilled; now all Ilse had to do was deliver an all-important boy and their work would be done. Hess searched for favourable omens. According to folklore, if a larger than average number of wasps appeared during the summer, you could expect a higher percentage of male births; Hess kept careful count of the wasps buzzing round his and Ilse's garden by trapping them in honey jars.

The signs were good, and on 18 November, Ilse had a son – their only child – named Wolf Rüdiger Hess. Hitler was the godfather, and 'Wolf' was a nickname he'd used back in the early days. Ilse and her husband had become proud parents; but in doing so, Hess lost what was left of his credibility.

According to Magda and her husband, when Wolf was born, Hess 'danced with joy' in a manner that resembled 'South American Indians'. Hess then issued an order to all the regional party bosses asking them to send 'bags of German soil' to 'spread under a specially built cradle' so that his son could begin life 'symbolically on German soil'. Goebbels found the request highly amusing, considered sending a 'Berlin pavement stone'[33] to reflect his urban constituency, but in the end opted for a sealed package of manure taken from his garden.

8

SS WIVES' CLUB

Margaret Himmler and Lina Heydrich were not part of the Berghof clique. Margaret made no more than a couple of appearances at formal events; Lina never got past the front door. Despite their husbands' expanding empire they were not in the same league as Magda and Emmy – neither Lina nor Margaret had a public profile to speak of – or as established in Hitler's entourage as Gerda and Ilse.

Their secondary status annoyed them both. They expected to be treated with greater respect given their husbands' achievements, and granted the seniority due to them. Both complained incessantly that Himmler and Heydrich were not appreciated enough by Hitler or rewarded with the same generosity as other senior figures; the fact that her husband 'did not get enough recognition'[1] was a constant refrain in Margaret's diary.

However, rather than join forces and work together – as their husbands so successfully did – they were constantly at loggerheads. Margaret resented Lina's obvious ambition to be the most influential SS wife; Lina couldn't bear playing second fiddle to a woman for whom she had nothing but contempt. Lina thought Margaret was inferior to her in every way and never missed an opportunity to ruthlessly put her down. She mocked Margaret's more than full figure – '50 size knickers, that's all there was to her' – and called her a 'narrow minded, humourless blonde female', who was 'always worrying about protocol'.[2]

Lina wasn't alone in having such a negative view of Margaret; Heinriette Hoffmann thought she was 'a small bad-tempered woman who seemed born to be unhappy'. Many agreed with Lina that Margaret 'ruled her husband and twisted him round her little finger'.[3] The Nazi in-crowd refused to take her seriously, even Unity Mitford would 'laugh openly about Frau Himmler'.

Word of Unity's insults got back to Margaret and she complained to a mutual friend about that 'good-for-nothing Unity'; the acquaintance apologised on her behalf, then warned Unity to watch her mouth. This kindly woman – who'd been round the movement for years – expressed sympathy towards Margaret, 'a poor wretch who'd been through the First World War as a nurse', and had given her all; as a result, 'nothing was left of her'.[4] Others echoed this assessment, arguing that Margaret was the way she was because she'd suffered shell-shock, a piece of idle speculation that could be cruel or kind depending on the context.

Margaret was well aware of Lina's open hostility and raised the matter with her husband. Himmler already disapproved of Lina's tendency to speak her mind and interfere in SS business, which also got on Heydrich's nerves. Himmler asked another SS wife, Frieda Wolff – she knew both Margaret and Lina well and her husband was Himmler's personal adjutant – to have a quiet word with Lina, which Frieda did at a naval regatta. Lina didn't take kindly to being told she was out of order – 'I was accused of the most impossible things, my husband was accused of not being able to keep me within my limits' – and angrily rebuffed Frieda.

Having failed with this indirect approach Margaret allegedly persuaded Himmler to order Heydrich to either divorce Lina or quit the SS. Heydrich must have told Lina because she claimed she had a showdown with Himmler at one of Goering's garden parties when they were seated at the same table. Rather than being her usual voluble and assertive self, Lina kept quiet throughout; 'I put on my most mournful expression and sat stock still'. This unnerved Himmler, and he asked Lina if she was all right. She shrugged off his question and then they danced, which Himmler did 'badly'. And that apparently was that. Himmler told her everything was fine and never mentioned it again. Lina concluded that the whole incident was 'typical Himmler, on paper he ordered us to divorce, but when face to face with me, his courage left him'.[5]

In the end, regardless of what Margaret wanted, Himmler had no desire to jeopardise the excellent working relationship he had with Heydrich. The two made a formidable team. Heydrich never challenged the authority of his superior and did everything he could to fulfil his wishes; he might argue a point or grumble behind Himmler's back, but Heydrich's loyalty never wavered. Himmler was in awe of his subordinate's organisational capabilities and his 'absolutely amazing' ability to tell if someone was lying and judge whether somebody was a 'friend or foe'.[6] Their strengths and weaknesses complemented each other. Himmler was better in social situations; when Heydrich walked into a room the temperature dropped. Heydrich's thought processes were logical and linear; Himmler's were more abstract and convoluted.

For all the energy Margaret and Lina expended on doing each other down, they suffered from almost exactly the same problems in their marriages; a feeling of neglect and abandonment. Their husbands had no time for them or their children, only for their work.

On 23 December 1934 Lina gave birth to her second child, a son named Heider. Now she had two boys, and although there were servants to lighten her load, there was a lack of family support; her parents were a long way off on the Baltic island of Fehmarn, while Heydrich had virtually cut all ties with his parents and siblings.

Margaret, meanwhile, was having serious trouble with her adopted son Gerhard; he stole, he lied, he played truant. Punishing the boy made no difference, even though Himmler beat him with a riding crop. As far as Margaret was concerned, Gerhard was 'criminal by nature'. At her wits' end, Margaret tried to return Gerhard to his real mother but she wanted a big pay-off, so he was sent away to boarding school where he was ruthlessly bullied by the other pupils. Their daughter, Gudrun, on the other hand, was 'sweet and nice', yet she was still subjected to the same severe discipline and expected to meet Margaret's high standards.

Himmler's family were around to give her support but Margaret never got on with them. Her own parents had never approved of the marriage and stayed away, though from 1934 her younger sister, a trained seamstress, was a permanent resident and available to lend a hand, along with the servants, the cook and the gardener. However, Margaret was always clashing with her domestic staff. After firing one impertinent and 'lazy' couple, she remarked that 'people like that should be locked away and forced to work until they die'.[7]

Over Christmas and New Year 1934–35, Margaret and her husband had house guests: Walther Darré – head of the SS's Race and Settlement Office and Reich Minister for Food and Agriculture – and his wife Charlotte, the elegant well-educated daughter of an aristocratic landowner with right-wing anti-Semitic views. Having joined the SS in 1930, Darré, who'd served in the artillery during the First World War, worked as a farm manager and written extensively about animal breeding, quickly became friends with Himmler; Darré shared Himmler's vision of a racially pure peasant utopia and had coined the phrase 'blood and soil'.

Darré had hired Charlotte as his secretary in 1929 and they were married three years later. Charlotte and Margaret had a fair amount in common; they were roughly the same age and had both grown up on large farms. As a wedding present, Margaret and Himmler gave Darré and Charlotte two silver pots and a massive biography of Genghis Khan.

The families were enjoying the Himmler family's first Christmas at their new lakeside property in Tegernsee, which was not far from Munich. Bought from a singer, the substantial chalet-style house had a separate command post manned by four SS men, a private dock, land for livestock – sheep, ponies, pigs and deer – a fishpond, a greenhouse and a meadow used for croquet in summer and ice skating in winter.

That holiday season there was much for Himmler and Darré to celebrate; 1934 was a critically important year for their organisation as it expanded its power at the expense of Röhm's SA, which had become an obstacle to Hitler's plans to prepare Germany for war; he needed stability at home and abroad, and the full cooperation of the army. The SA, however, wanted to supplant the armed forces as the main source of military power and clean out the surviving remnants of the old order. In the meantime, Röhm refused to curb the street violence, vandalism and intimidation for which his men were infamous.

By spring 1934, the tension had built to a point where some kind of reckoning seemed inevitable. The question was who would strike first. This was Himmler's moment. In exchange for using the SS to suppress the SA, Goering agreed to give his police powers in Prussia to Himmler – who'd already assumed them in all the other regions – and control over the Gestapo.

During the night of 30 June–1 July, Himmler's hit squads struck. Anywhere between 83 and 200 people – including the unfortunate Dr Schmidt – were assassinated on the Night of the Long Knives. Röhm survived a few hours longer as Hitler and his cronies debated his fate; in the end he was gunned down in his cell. The fact that Röhm had befriended Lina and her husband, and was godfather to their first child, made no difference in the cutthroat world of Nazi politics; neither she nor Heydrich expressed any remorse. Hitler, meanwhile, was delighted: 'In view of the great services rendered by the SS … I hereby promote the SS to the status of independent organisation.'[8]

For all the goodwill flowing that yuletide, Christmas was a not a straightforward matter for the Nazi elite. The holiday was a muted affair at the Berghof due to the depression that always dogged Hitler at that time of year, brought on by the memory of his mother's death, which occurred on 21 December 1907 and still haunted him. Usually Hitler would spend Christmas Day alone in Munich; one Christmas Eve, he hired a taxi to drive him aimlessly round the city, killing time.

On a less personal level, Christmas was a key battleground in the Nazis' struggle to detach the German people from Christianity. Hitler considered it to be a religion that worshipped weakness and blunted the nation's fighting spirit. Though Hitler remained agnostic, most of his cohorts abandoned the faith of their childhoods and adopted paganism, reconnecting with the symbols and rituals of the old gods.

Himmler and Darré were practising pagans. So were the Hesses. Both Lina and Gerda's husbands despised Christians and did everything in their power to make life uncomfortable for them. Magda and Goebbels endorsed the anti-Church campaign; only Emmy and Goering maintained a notional commitment to its traditions.

Given Christmas's significance for Christians, the Nazis did their best to appropriate the holiday. There were Nazi-themed carols, Christmas cards emblazoned with swastikas, tree decorations bearing Nazi party insignia, and chocolate SA men. Mothers were encouraged to bake biscuits in the shape of runic symbols. Though Himmler tried to reintroduce a pagan holiday called the Feast of Midsummer, which he hoped would eventually be more popular than Christmas, he also pushed the SS brand every December – you could buy advent calendars with pictures of SS personnel and special yule candlesticks with the SS logo on them – and promoted the idea that Santa Claus was based on the Norse god Odin.

Himmler left no stone unturned in his efforts to discredit the Church. He commissioned a detailed investigation into the witch-hunts of the sixteenth and seventeenth centuries. Researchers collected a vast archive of material – amounting to nearly 34,000 pages – to prove that the so-called 'witches' were in fact good pagans who provided a hugely beneficial service to their communities because they knew how to exploit the magical properties of herbs and plants; by demonising and burning these wise and spiritually gifted women, the Christian authorities had committed an awful crime.

Himmler's 'Special Witch Project' was only one of a bewildering range of pseudo-academic initiatives that he launched, the majority of which were undertaken by his unique creation, the *Ahnenerbe*. This sprawling organisation employed ideologically sympathetic archaeologists, anthropologists and scientists who operated on the margins of their disciplines and were charged with uncovering the ancient and prehistoric lineage of the Aryan race and its crucial role in the development of the human species; there was even an attempt to prove that the very first *Homo sapiens* were of Aryan origin. Teams of experts visited potential sites of interest in North Africa, the Middle East and as far away as Tibet.

Quite what Margaret made of her husband's ideological obsessions is hard to gauge. She did continue to absorb the reading material that Himmler regularly gave her – from history books recounting the exploits of tribal chieftains who took on the mighty Roman Empire to archaeological papers analysing skulls. She would dutifully plough through these texts and referred to them in her diary and in her letters to Himmler. She usually expressed an interest without offering much in the way of comment or feedback. Clearly Himmler wanted Margaret to share his passions, or at the very least approve of them. On 25 May 1935 he took her to Wewelsburg to see the castle he was going to renovate and restore to its former medieval glory and use as a gathering place for his elite SS knights, like King Arthur's Camelot. When Margaret visited, it was still a ruin.

Perhaps Margaret tolerated Himmler's bizarre enthusiasms in the same way that countless wives put up with their partner's pet projects, encouraging them while keeping their real feelings to themselves. In the end, the time Himmler spent on his castle and myriad other schemes was time he wasn't spending with her and Gudrun. Throughout the whole of 1935, Himmler only managed to fit in six weeks at their Tegernsee home.

Lina said that she and Heydrich found Himmler's eccentricities amusing – 'we laughed about his hobbies' – but essentially harmless; 'my husband and I just had a well-meaning smile for them', she remembered, and they listened 'without emotion to his theories about pagan stones'.

Even so, Heydrich was not totally disinterested in Himmler's 'mysticism'.[9] On the summer solstice 1935, he was being shown round Fehmarn – the island where Lina grew up – by a local historian who led him to a well-known eighteenth-century farmhouse that stood on the site of a much older building that had ancient stone graves beside it. Given Himmler's interest in early Scandinavian cultures – the *Ahnenerbe* explored Denmark, Sweden, Norway, Iceland and Finland – Heydrich proposed establishing a big museum there and a foundation to pay for it. Fehmarn was also where Lina and her husband had their holiday home; work on it was finished the day Heydrich made his archaeological discovery. With money borrowed from the son of a rich industrialist who'd inherited his father's fortune, they bought a good-sized plot of land by a beach overlooking the Baltic and erected a traditional timber-framed house with a thatched roof. Lina loved it and the family spent most of their summers there.

One of the results of the SS's elevation after the Night of the Long Knives was that Lina and Margaret acquired apartments in Berlin. A new world of possibilities was opening up for them. In Munich, Lina always felt out on a limb, excluded from the upper echelons of Nazi society; now, in Berlin, she was determined to mix with suitably distinguished and influential people.

Coming to her aid was the 25-year-old Walter Schellenberg. Handsome and intelligent, Schellenberg was a student at Bonn University who'd done two years of medicine before switching to law; he enrolled in the SS in 1933 and entered the SD after being recruited by two of his professors. Soon he was socialising with Heydrich and Lina. According to Schellenberg, Lina 'was glad to find … someone who could satisfy her hunger for the better things in life, her longing for more intelligent and cultivated society in the world of literature and art.' He took the couple 'to concerts and the theatre' and they 'began to frequent the best circles in Berlin society'.[10]

Entertaining was made easier for Lina in February 1937 when the family moved to a new nine-room house – each one with its own alarm – spread over three floors with two extra rooms for the servants, SS guards at the front gate, and a large garden where Lina installed a playground and a hen-house.

Lina was hampered in her endeavours by her husband; not only was Heydrich thoroughly bored by polite society – he preferred trawling the bars and nightclubs accompanied by his SS comrades – he also had little interest in making friends. Lina observed that he never had 'any personal friends' and 'tried to avoid any social contact between neighbours and fellow workers'.[11]

Nevertheless, there were exceptions. Herbert Backe and his wife Ursula, together with their children – who were roughly the same age as Lina's boys – were regular guests in the Heydrich home, spending weekends and evenings with them. Backe, who'd joined the SS in 1933, was an agricultural expert and protégé of Darré. Backe then got Darré's job after Himmler ditched him and ended their friendship. Like Lina, Ursula was a wholehearted Nazi and acted as her husband's unofficial secretary, PA and archivist combined; her diary was essentially a forensic record of Backe's activities.

Yet the relationships Lina did manage to foster were fragile, subject to the machinations of Nazi politics and the rivalries in which her husband was constantly engaged. A case in point is the Heydrichs' relationship with Wilhelm Canaris and his wife Erika. Canaris was a war hero who'd joined the navy in 1905 aged 18, commanded a brutal *Freikorps* regiment, and by 1923 was an officer aboard the same ship as the young trainee Heydrich. Erika was a cerebral, cultured woman with a passion for music. A capable violinist, she held tea parties where she'd perform with a string quartet. When one of them dropped out, Canaris suggested Heydrich as a replacement; Erika was delighted by his sublime violin playing and Heydrich became a permanent member.

The friendship was short-lived and Canaris and Heydrich went in separate directions. By 1933, Canaris's career was stalled, but with the ascension of the Nazis his fortunes changed and on 1 January 1935 he became head of the *Abwehr*, the army's espionage section. Not long after, Lina and Heydrich ran into Canaris and Erika as they were out walking with their children and discovered they were neighbours.

Lina appreciated Erika's refined character while Heydrich and Canaris seemed pleased to renew their acquaintance. They went riding in the nearby Grunewald forest, played croquet in the afternoon, and held a weekly music evening with Heydrich on first violin, Erika second, his younger brother on cello and a friend on viola. Canaris, who was a keen cook, provided fine food; his specialities were wild boar in a red wine sauce and herring salad served with brandy and caviar.

However, despite Lina's claims that the professional rivalry between Canaris and her husband 'did not touch our private and social life',[12] tension between them was never far from the surface. The *Abwehr* and the SD were natural opponents, especially as Heydrich wanted to control every aspect of intelligence work both at home and abroad. Though the two of them hammered out a deal – known as the Ten Commandments – that defined and clarified their areas of responsibility, they never trusted each other. When Heydrich noticed one of Erika's daughters taking an interest in the desk in his study, he accused her of spying, while in his diary Canaris referred to Heydrich as a 'brutal fanatic with whom it will be difficult to have open and friendly cooperation'.[13] They may have maintained a civilised exterior, but the two men were locked in a deadly struggle for dominance.

Once settled in Berlin, Margaret became immersed in the world of a First Lady of the Reich. She was now part of the diplomatic party circuit and faithfully recorded her reactions to each event in her diary: she thought the French Ambassador was 'the funniest, most amusing person I have ever met'; at the Argentinian embassy she saw 'many people I know'; the Egyptian embassy was 'very nice'; a soiree hosted by Hitler at the Reich Chancellery for 200 people featured 'gorgeous flowers everywhere, just marvellous'; and five days later, she was at the Ministry of Propaganda, which was 'very boring, we left early'.[14]

Aside from getting on well with the odd countess and being intrigued by the Japanese ambassador's German wife – who told her 'many intimate and interesting things' – Margaret struggled to fit in with the crowd and was clearly out of her comfort zone in high society: 'New invitations are starting again. If only I didn't need so much sleep.' A good night out for Margaret was a trip to the theatre – she preferred comedies like the farce *All Lies*, which she found 'very funny'[15] – and sometimes the cinema. Otherwise, she was perfectly happy having a quiet evening in, playing bridge and retiring early with a good book.

Despite her social awkwardness, Margaret wanted to be seen as an important figure, worthy of respect. Every Wednesday, she hosted a tea party in her new fourteen-room villa for the leading SS wives. Normally anywhere between six and ten women showed up. Margaret's guests were all from middle- and upper-class families, like Frieda Wolff, whose aristocratic father had worked for the Grand Duke of Hesse, run a district court and owned shares in a paper company. Frieda's husband, and the spouses of the other wives in the club, had similar professional backgrounds – lawyers, economists, political scientists and businessmen – that reflected Himmler and Heydrich's recruitment strategy.

Lina was dead against Margaret's initiative and set about sabotaging it. Her first move was to bring the wives into her orbit. With the help of one of them, an ex-dancer, Lina staged a one-off musical performance that began with the SS ladies singing folk songs and ended with them doing the cancan. Next, Lina organised a fitness class; scheduled to clash with Margaret's tea parties, it combined gymnastics and calisthenics, and was run by an instructor provided by Heydrich.

After their first gruelling session, Lina's exercise group were all hot and sweaty, but they were embarrassed about using the gym's communal showers. To encourage them to overcome their shyness, Lina stripped off and stood naked in full view of them, which was enough to get her fellow SS wives to shed their inhibitions and their clothes. Overall, the class was a success; at the end, eight of the ladies won a gold sports badge, while another twenty got silver.

In 1936, sport offered Lina another chance to get one up on Margaret. Her husband was on the German Olympic Committee and during the games Lina and Heydrich were given much better seats than Margaret and Himmler – an arrangement that delighted Lina because it 'did not suit Himmler. He was used to my husband being second to him'[16] – and they were invited to all the gala events. They even sat at a top table during the International Olympic Committee ball, a six-course feast of the finest food at the magnificent White Hall in Berlin Castle held the night before the opening ceremony. Lina and Heydrich were also awarded VIP status at the Winter Olympics earlier that year and had their own fleets of cars and a private plane at their disposal.

Of all the sports Heydrich excelled at, fencing was the most important to him. He practised with the best and competed at a high level; at the SS Fencing Master's tournament in November 1936, Heydrich was fifth in the rapier class and third in the sabre class. This was a more than creditable performance, but Heydrich hated losing, often ignored fencing etiquette, and challenged the referee's decisions.

Himmler's sport was tennis, and he was a keen player. For a time, Margaret took up the game; aside from needing the exercise – she was in her forties and had problems with her weight – it was one activity she could share with her husband. The effort obviously proved too much for her and she soon stopped taking to the court with racquet in hand. Himmler, however, kept up his tennis on a regular basis.

Himmler's genuine interest in the sport did not mean he was prepared to compromise his principles. The aristocratic Gottfried von Cramm – twice winner of the French Open and twice runner-up at Wimbledon – was the undisputed no. 1 German tennis player. Though von Cramm had gone through the necessary motions and married in 1930, his preference was for men, and before the Nazi era he was relatively open about his sexuality, taking advantage of the liberated atmosphere of Weimar Berlin. Himmler deeply feared and hated homosexuality; in a 1937 speech, he declared that it was the reason why 'the male state is in the process of destroying itself'.[17] Initially, the Nazis continued using the Weimar law on homosexuality that made it illegal for two men over the age of 21 to have penetrative sex. Under its provisions, 4,000 men were convicted between 1933 and 1935. Then the scope of the law was widened to include any 'indecent activity between men'.[18] This change produced a dramatic escalation in convictions; from 1935 to 1939, 30,000 men were sent to prison or concentration camps.

After being denounced by a hustler, von Cramm was picked up in April 1937 by two Gestapo agents, grilled for several hours and released. He was spared jail because he was about to contend the inter-zonal final of the Davis Cup, a competition Germany had never won despite getting close in recent years.

The decisive match, played on the Centre Court at Wimbledon, against Don Budge from the US team, has gone down in tennis history as a classic; millions in Germany, including Hitler – who'd called von Cramm just before the match to wish him luck – tuned in to hear ball-by-ball radio commentary, willing von Cramm on to victory. With the stakes incredibly high, he came close but was beaten in five nail-biting sets.

Had von Cramm won, his fate might have been different. But defeat left him totally exposed and, worse still, his wife divorced him. Himmler seized the chance to put him behind bars; in May 1938 he was sentenced to a year's imprisonment for a relationship with a young Jewish actor, but was paroled after six months. In 1939, von Cramm tried to make a comeback but was stopped in his tracks when the All England Club – using his criminal record as an excuse – prevented him from playing at Wimbledon.

By 1936, Lina was convinced that Heydrich was cheating on her; in a brutally honest statement about her husband, she said that 'he was keen on anything in a skirt'.[19] Lina didn't have any clear idea about who the women concerned might be, but she was sure she wasn't imagining things; why else would her husband stay out all night – which he frequently did – returning at dawn reeking of booze and perfume? Lina repeatedly confronted Heydrich about it and hurled accusations at him, but he denied everything.

Her fears on that front were unfounded; Heydrich was not having affairs or keeping any mistresses hidden away. Several of his SS colleagues, however, testified that he regularly visited prostitutes and gained a reputation for treating them badly. One SS officer claimed that after being with Heydrich 'even the most pitiful whore would not want him a second time'.[20] The same man recounted a visit to a brothel in Naples where Heydrich emptied a purse of gold coins on the floor and watched the prostitutes and the madam fight over them.

Taking into account the questionable reliability of the witnesses who had every reason to make their boss appear as twisted and depraved as possible – thereby making themselves appear less appalling – there is definite pattern to Heydrich's sexual behaviour. In May 1926, he was on a naval exercise that included a spell in Barcelona. One of his fellow officer cadets remembered that Heydrich went in search of a brothel the second he disembarked. The former cadet also recalled an unsavoury incident during a function at the German Club; Heydrich took 'a young lady of impeccable social background' for a stroll in the garden and 'behaved in such a manner that the girl slapped him in the face'.[21] Soon after, Heydrich caused a scene at a dinner dance when he repeatedly asked the wives of some English officers to dance. Then there are the circumstances surrounding his dismissal from the navy and the distressed girlfriend he dumped for Lina.

These actions – added to the revelations of his fellow SS men – are strong indications that Heydrich's treatment of prostitutes wasn't merely malicious gossip; they offer further confirmation of his sociopathic tendencies. Emotionally stunted and lacking empathy, Heydrich viewed other people as objects, things that could be manipulated to serve his own needs. He also loved the thrill of pushing boundaries and proving to himself that he was untouchable; if his nocturnal habits had become public knowledge, Heydrich would have been ruined.

Fearing the spread of sexually transmitted diseases, the Nazi regime was extremely tough on street-walkers – during 1933 thousands were arrested – but it was more flexible when it came to brothels. Having been closed down in the Weimar era, brothels began to open for business again, especially in the big cities. In 1937, it became legal for a prostitute to rent a room in a building as long as there were no children under 18 living there. However, that same year, prostitutes were caught up in mass arrests of 'anti-social' elements. They were also subject to regular health tests; if a prostitute showed any signs of VD, she was sterilised.

Regardless of the severe punishments inflicted on those in the sex trade, Heydrich decided to become a brothel owner. According to Schellenberg, Heydrich wanted an 'establishment where important visitors from other countries could be "entertained" in a discreet atmosphere where they would be offered seductive feminine company' and hopefully 'reveal some useful information'.

For this purpose, an elegant house in a fashionable quarter of the capital was requisitioned, a leading architect chose the furnishings and decor, and there were double walls with microphones in them, connected by 'automatic transmission to tape recorders which would record every word spoken throughout the house'. Three technical experts – 'bound by an oath' – ran the apparatus. An experienced madam, known as 'Kitty', was put in charge of sixteen carefully selected high-class prostitutes, who all spoke a number of foreign languages.

Salon Kitty did a roaring trade; everybody from foreign dignitaries to high-ranking Nazis and government ministers, military men and figures from showbusiness, uttered the password – 'Rothenburg' – and went through its doors. Schellenberg said the collected pillow talk yielded a plentiful haul of 'diplomatic secrets'.[22]

Though Lina remained ignorant of her husband's night-time pursuits, she was nevertheless convinced that Heydrich was playing around. However, Lina was not the type of woman to let anybody take advantage of her. She was attractive, still only in her twenties, and had needs and desires that were not being satisfied by her workaholic husband; the evidence is circumstantial, but it does appear that Lina sought out the company of other men.

One of Lina's alleged trysts was with Walter Schellenberg. In Schellenberg's version of events, he deflects any suggestion that he was actually engaged in a relationship with Lina by focusing on Heydrich's paranoia. Suspicions alerted by what was probably no more than a harmless flirtation, Heydrich tried to catch Schellenberg and Lina in the act. Schellenberg had been at the Heydrichs' island retreat attending an SS conference with other senior personnel and stayed on an extra day after his boss flew back to Berlin, during which he and Lina visited a lake, had coffee together, and according to Schellenberg 'talked about art, literature and concerts'.

Four days later, and back in the capital, Heydrich asked Schellenberg to join him and the head of the Gestapo, Heinrich Mueller, for a night on the town. Following their meal, they went to an obscure bar and ordered drinks. Once Schellenberg had taken a few swigs, Mueller – a veteran policeman – switched into interrogation mode. Had Schellenberg enjoyed his little outing with Lina? Didn't he realise he was being watched all the time? Rattled, Schellenberg insisted nothing untoward was going on. Then Heydrich coolly informed Schellenberg that his drink was poisoned; if he swore on his honour that he was telling the truth, Heydrich would give him the antidote. Having insisted that he was, Schellenberg was immediately handed a dry Martini, which he thought tasted a bit odd; it 'certainly seemed to have an added dash of bitters'.[23] After that, nothing more was said and the three of them caroused the night away.

It's possible that Schellenberg's story was exactly that; he was not above spinning an elaborate yarn to conceal the truth and preserve his reputation. But whether or not Heydrich set the honey trap, it seems unlikely that Schellenberg, who was fixated on advancing his own career, would have risked incurring Heydrich's wrath in order to sleep with Lina.

The other potential contender was Wolfgang Willrich, painter, poet, art critic and polemicist whose views were extreme even by the standards of the SS. His paintings were pure propaganda, all rosy cheeked farm girls and young SS recruits, with titles like *Guardians of the Race*. Willrich's articles and essays divided opinion and he was a controversial choice as one of the six-man panel responsible for selecting the artists for the Degenerate Art Exhibition, an appointment that inspired Willrich to write a book, *The Cleansing of the Temple of Art* (1937).

Heydrich made the mistake of asking Willrich to paint Lina's portrait. It's not hard to imagine Lina being drawn to Willrich's dynamic character during the long hours she spent posing for him, aroused by the strange intimacy that develops between an artist and their subject. Heydrich was obviously worried, and seized on an opportunity to intimidate Willrich.

In March 1937, a magazine called *People and Race* put the finished portrait of Lina on its front cover. Rather than confront Willrich directly, Heydrich had Frieda Wolff's husband write a stiff letter to the editors demanding that they cease publishing Willrich's work. Though Willrich was barely affected by this ban, it was warning enough, and if there was an affair between him and Lina it ended around this time.

Shortly after, in an effort to save their marriage, Lina and her husband decided to go on holiday together, just the two of them, hoping that a few weeks away from everything would revitalise their relationship. They went on a Mediterranean cruise – as regular tourists – and stopped off in Italy, Greece, Tripoli, Tunisia and Carthage. After this welcome break, their marriage seemed to stabilise, for a while at least, and the following summer Lina became pregnant for the third time. But the underlying factors that fuelled her discontent were not so easily resolved. Lina continued to play a secondary role in her husband's life, which was about to get even busier. Heydrich and his partner in crime were planning to conquer new territory.

On 12 March 1938, within a few hours of German troops marching unopposed into Austria, Margaret and Lina's husbands arrived in Vienna. They'd been preparing for months. At their disposal was the data they'd been accumulating about potential Nazi opponents; the remnants of the left; prominent Austrians who might dare to resist; intellectuals, writers and artists with suspect CVs; and the large Jewish community – concentrated in Vienna – and especially its richest members and their businesses.

From the moment Heydrich formed his intelligence service, he recognised the value of information. Almost immediately, he began compiling a library of colour-coded index cards containing precise details about individuals of interest. This filing system that Heydrich had once stored in boxes in his and Lina's apartment in Munich had swollen in size and now included thousands of people. By the time Heydrich and Himmler landed in the Austrian capital all the relevant cards had been sorted and they were ready to put all their knowledge to work.

In the first few days after their arrival, between 20,000 and 70,000 people were seized and given a taste of Nazi justice. On his way home, Himmler stopped off at Mauthausen near the Danube and decided it was the perfect location for a new concentration camp. In her diary entry for 27 March , Margaret wrote that her husband 'returned from his performance in Austria with great satisfaction, almost jubilant'.[24]

The unification of Germany and Austria – the *Anschluss* – had always been a high priority for Hitler, and he was committed to bringing his homeland and the Reich together. The Nazis had been chipping away at Austrian independence for years. A failed coup attempt in 1934, launched by the Austrian Nazi party and approved by Hitler, resulted in a more cautious approach, but by 1938 he was intent on overthrowing the Austrian government, whose chancellor made himself a hostage to fortune when he announced a plebiscite to decide whether his people wanted to be part of Germany or not. Fearing a 'no' vote would derail his plans, Hitler went on the offensive. He issued an ultimatum backed up by Goering's threat to unleash the Luftwaffe, and the Austrian chancellor caved in to Hitler's demands.

Six weeks later, on 2 May, Hitler and a large retinue set off on a state visit to Italy. His alliance with Mussolini had been further strengthened by *Il Duce*'s last-minute decision to grant Hitler a free hand in Austria – whose territorial integrity he'd previously guaranteed – and the five-day tour was meant to demonstrate the harmony between them. For Margaret, this was the one and only occasion when she truly experienced First Lady of the Reich treatment.

Margaret had been on a semi-official whirlwind tour of Italy six months earlier. In Rome, she loved the food, went to the hairdressers, visited the Colosseum and the Forum, and had a drive round the Vatican garden thanks to 'the accommodating policies of the police, and the SS flag on our car'. Next up was Naples, then Pompeii and Herculaneum, where she was affected by the sight of 'people surprised by sudden death'. While viewing the ancient Roman ruins at Catania, Margaret came to the conclusion that 'countries are so poor nowadays' because 'there are no slaves any more'.[25]

The state visit to Italy, however, was on a different order of magnitude, especially since both Emmy and Magda were about to give birth and stayed at home, and although Eva was allowed to tag along, she was not permitted to join the main party. Once in Rome, Eva did some sightseeing, filmed the big public events with her new camera and went shopping; she visited the premises of her favourite shoemaker, who thought she was an actress and remembered that Eva 'had good, normal feet and anything would fit her'.[26]

In the absence of Emmy and Magda, Margaret, Ilse and Anneliese von Ribbentrop got top billing: Anneliese was the wife of the Nazis' foreign minister and a good friend of Margaret's. Together, the wives did not exactly impress their hosts, whose fears were realised when Ilse and Margaret went against protocol and refused to curtsey before Queen Elena, the wife of King Victor Emmanuel who technically remained head of state. Their actions affronted the Italian dignitaries but gained approval from their own side. Hitler was ill at ease with all the bowing and scraping and resented the king's attempt to overshadow Mussolini.

Despite this shaky start, the trip passed off without further difficulties. Though Ilse tried to boss the wives around – Margaret noted that 'Mrs Hess wanted to lecture Mrs Ribbentrop' – the women got on reasonably well. Margaret was in fine spirits. She enjoyed the huge naval display in Naples and thought a sports demonstration given by fascist youth groups at the Mussolini Stadium was 'fantastic'.[27]

After all the years of sacrifice, of feeling alone and undervalued, Margaret finally had something to show for it. But her good mood didn't last: from then on, life was only going to get more difficult.

9

A LEAP IN THE DARK

On the evening of 20 April 1938 – Hitler's forty-ninth birthday – the Nazi elite joined him and the cream of the movie business for the premiere of the director Leni Riefensthal's *Olympia*, her film about the 1936 games. Leni's propaganda masterpiece of the previous year, *Triumph of the Will*, had gone down very well with Hitler, and even Goebbels, who still resented Leni for rejecting his amorous advances, had to admit that her work was touched by genius. With her star in the ascendant, Leni was commissioned to produce a film about the Olympics.

During the two weeks of competition, Leni's massive camera crew were everywhere, using innovative techniques to shoot trackside and capture the action close up. At the end, she had miles of footage and would spend the next year or so locked in an editing room trying to make sense of it all. By the time Leni's movie was ready to screen, *Olympia* had gone hugely over budget and schedule, much to Goebbels's annoyance. However, the film was ecstatically received and gained widespread critical acclaim, including first prize at the Venice International Film Festival.

In the audience for opening night was the Czech actress Lida Baarova, whose affair with Goebbels had become progressively more serious. While Goebbels had quickly tired of other actresses and tossed them to one side, he couldn't get enough of Baarova, and she was beginning to believe that she might soon to be more than just his mistress. Perpetually worried that Magda would grasp the true extent of his feelings for Baarova, and concerned that his own phone was not secure enough, Goebbels went out on limb and asked for Emmy's help; could he use her phone to make a few calls? Emmy agreed, but when she realised Goebbels 'had begun to use our private telephone to maintain contact with Frau Baarova'[1] she had to remind Goebbels that the Gestapo tapped everybody's lines, including hers.

Pregnant again, Magda had been weighed down by health issues – like her long-standing heart problem – that always afflicted her when she was expecting a child and continued to bother her after she gave birth to another daughter, Hedda, on 5 May. Once this hurdle was negotiated, the seriousness of her husband's infatuation with Baarova was brought home to her by Goebbels's private assistant, Karl Hanke.

A diligent man, with a fondness for all things military, Hanke was nevertheless something of a nonentity, and was working as an instructor at a technical high school when he entered the Nazi party in 1928 as part of the SA. After Hanke lost his job in 1931 due to his Nazi affiliations, he worked full time as a secretary in Goebbels's office, and within a year was permanently at the propaganda minister's side. Hanke had been nursing a crush on Magda for some time and had compiled a scrupulously precise dossier detailing Goebbels's infidelities and his relationship with Baarova, which he showed to Magda. Shocked, Magda could no longer deny what was right before her eyes.

These revelations coincided with a period of doubt and disillusionment for Magda. In conversations with her only confidante, Ello Quandt, her ex-husband's younger sister, Magda expressed her doubts about the direction Nazism was taking – she objected to the militarisation of German society, which was robbing it of its 'culture', its 'mirth' and its 'joy' and replacing them with 'blind obedience, regulations' and 'commands' – and she questioned Hitler's judgement, especially the way he let the regime treat women as second-class citizens when they deserved 'to receive more consideration'.[2]

Matters came to a head at the beginning of August when Goebbels – who could no longer cope with his double life – confessed all to Magda and begged her to consider the possibility that the three of them could find a way to co-exist. Confused and disorientated by this sudden and unexpected suggestion, Magda agreed and grimly sat through tea with Baarova and Goebbels. He took Magda's stoic silence as a positive sign and arranged a weekend on his yacht. The sight of Baarova sunning herself on the deck and acting as if she'd already won the battle was too much for Magda to bear and she abandoned ship. Soon after, in an unusually intimate conversation with Emmy, Magda called her husband a 'devil in human form'.[3]

Magda had survived one divorce and was prepared to go through another. As it happened, recent changes in the marriage laws had made it easier for couples to separate. Though the Nazis vigorously promoted marriage, the divorce rate steadily increased from 1933 onwards, and the regime did little to reverse this trend; ultimately, it wanted productive unions not failed ones. Alongside the other grounds for divorce – like adultery or biological or racial unsuitability – the new law, introduced on 6 July, added 'irretrievable breakdown' to the list. This meant that Magda would not have to prove in court that her husband was unfaithful.

But before Magda could take such a serious step, she had to consult Hitler. Divorce would break the unique bond between them. It was weaker than it had been, but was still strong, and Hitler did not hesitate to answer her distress call. At first, Hitler didn't want to believe Magda, but when Hanke verified her account Hitler turned his anger on Goebbels, mad at him for betraying Magda. Then he brought them together and laid down the law. Divorce was out of the question. They would have to try and mend their marriage and Goebbels would have to dump Baarova. But this was easier said than done, and neither Magda nor her husband left the Berghof with much hope that their relationship would survive the test.

That summer, Hitler had every right to rest on his laurels and relax at the Berghof. He'd restored Germany's status as a major European power and gone a long way to delivering on his promise to dismantle the hated

Treaty of Versailles. At home, though some of the early gloss had worn off his regime and the return of economic hardship and uncertainty was beginning to erode support, his personal popularity was unaffected and the *Anschluss* had given it a huge boost. But he was restless and in a hurry to achieve his vision of empire and a brave new world. Hitler's greatest fear was dying before he'd completed his historic mission and fulfilled his destiny, and he was increasingly preoccupied with his own mortality. Earlier that year, on 2 May, he'd drawn up a will: Eva was the first beneficiary named and would receive a decent monthly income for the rest of her life. With his affairs in order, Hitler was contemplating how to subdue his next victim. The amalgamation of Czechoslovakia with the Reich appealed to Hitler; he was keen to get his hands on its raw materials, including coal, and one of Europe's largest armaments manufacturers – Skoda.

Also within the Czech borders was the Sudeten region, which had been carved out of Germany under the Treaty of Versailles and contained a substantial German population. Detaching the Sudetenland, as a prelude to the full absorption of the rest of the country, was Hitler's immediate focus as nervous European leaders scrambled to prevent him from moving forward, but Hitler would not yield an inch and began mobilising his army.

The possibility that Britain might feel obliged to use force to resist Hitler's plans was weighing heavily on Unity Mitford. With her hair bleached to 'a more Nordic gold', Unity had followed Hitler's triumphal trip to Austria after the *Anschluss* and toured the Czech-German border in May; she continued to fully support everything Hitler did. Yet, Britain was still Unity's homeland and as the stakes got higher she seemed determined to destroy herself. When she contracted bronchitis she refused to take it seriously. According to Friedelind Wagner, Unity defied her doctor by 'pouring her medicine out of the window, standing there in a thin night-gown' and 'courting pneumonia'.[4] Inevitably, Unity deteriorated and had to be transferred to a clinic, where all the bills were covered by Hitler.

The escalating threat of outright war over Czechoslovakia wasn't just affecting Unity; there was a fraught and strained atmosphere backstage at the party rally in Nuremberg, which spilled over into a head-to-head confrontation between Margaret and Lina. Since her grand state visit to Italy, Margaret had been dealing with the same old domestic problems, Himmler's absences – 'he is never here any more' – and clashes with the domestic staff; she had to fire yet another 'shameless maid'.[5]

However, Margaret was looking forward to the rally and she'd drawn up a timetable of events and meetings for the other SS wives to follow. Lina balked at the idea of being micro-managed by Margaret and convinced Frieda Wolff that Margaret was deliberately preventing them from having a good time. Together, they ignored Margaret's schedule, did their own thing, and revelled in the late-night party scene that existed on the fringes of the rally.

Incensed at their blatant disregard for her authority, Margaret confronted Lina and Frieda and gave them a good telling off. They promptly went straight to their husbands to complain about Margaret's overbearing behaviour and Heydrich and Wolff felt obliged to report what had happened to Himmler, who neither defended nor condemned Margaret for losing her cool. Instead, he merely shrugged helplessly and suggested they forget the whole thing.

The tension that had pervaded the rally evaporated at the end of September because of the Munich conference, during which Hitler, Mussolini, Neville Chamberlain and Léon Blum haggled over the future of Czechoslovakia. In exchange for promises of peace and an end to further territorial expansion, Hitler was granted control of the Sudetenland. The Czech government was not invited to the talks and had little choice but to accept the deal, and on 3 October the Nazis claimed their prize.

Mission accomplished, Hitler had time to show off his latest toy, the Eagle's Nest, a guesthouse perched on top of a mountain, the Kehlstein, which was visible from the Berghof. For months, the silence that normally reigned over the peaks at Obersalzburg had been shattered by an almighty din; Hitler's press secretary observed that the local oxen had been usurped by 'gigantic trucks and diggers' and 'the rumble of dynamite detonations'.[6] A small army of construction workers was labouring round the clock to complete the building, which Bormann hoped to able to present to Hitler on his fiftieth birthday the following April.

As it was, Bormann pushed his workers so hard – several died during avalanches and torrential rains – that the construction was complete seven months early. Hitler's housekeeper called the finished structure 'a true masterpiece of architecture, engineering and workmanship'.[7]

Throughout October, Hitler took a steady stream of foreign dignitaries up the Kehlstein: the first phase of the journey was by car along a 4-mile road that had been carved out of the rockface and led to a car park over a mile above sea level, next to a tunnel whose entrance was guarded by a massive brass gate; the tunnel ran deep into the mountain itself and ended at a copper hall with a lift big enough to hold forty people, which took guests another 400ft upwards in less than a minute and deposited them directly into the Eagle's Nest, with its bedrooms, reception room, dining room, conference room, kitchen, basement, guardroom, balcony and panoramic circular picture window.

Among the early visitors to the Eagle's Nest were Magda and Unity, who were treated to a tour of Hitler's penthouse in the sky on 21 October. Spirits lifted by the Munich Agreement, Unity had recovered her strength and irrepressible exuberance, while Magda was in Obersalzburg to resume her discussions with Hitler about the crisis in her marriage. Magda was still bent on a divorce but Hitler remained dead against the idea. Two days later, they were joined by Goebbels – who had failed to shake off Baarova – and he and Magda agreed to a three-month trial separation during which Goebbels would have to behave himself or risk losing everything: if he failed to keep his end of the bargain, Hitler would accept that a divorce was unavoidable and Goebbels would have to resign.

With a measure of calm restored, Emmy and her husband felt free to go ahead with the christening of their daughter Edda, who'd been born on 2 June. The delighted parents – Emmy recalled that her husband 'claimed with absolute conviction that it was the most beautiful child he had ever seen'[8] – received 628,000 telegrams of congratulations, while their baby daughter was given two paintings by the German Renaissance painter

Lucas Cranach the Elder, one of which, *Madonna and Child*, was a gift from the city of Cologne.

Edda's christening took place at Carinhall on 4 November, and the ceremony was performed by Reich Bishop Mueller, the most senior figure in the German Protestant Church and a convinced Nazi and anti-Semite. Despite Hitler's aversion to Christianity, he showed up to give the baby his blessing. Also present were photographers from *Life* magazine, who captured an image of Hitler cradling the baby in his arms.

Five days later, as an affirmation of their pagan beliefs and rejection of Christianity, Ilse and her husband held a ceremony to mark their son Wolf's entry into the world. The rites performed involved the soil that Hess had ordered delivered from all over the Reich a year earlier, which was arranged in piles round Wolf as he lay in his crib. The ritual coincided with a deeply significant day in the Nazi calendar; 9 November was the anniversary of the 1923 Beer Hall Putsch and every year the survivors of that botched coup gathered for a series of ceremonies that commemorated the fourteen Nazis who'd died during it. Each year, the celebrations grew more elaborate and pompous as Hitler – and Goering, who'd taken a bullet that day – consecrated the memory of the fallen heroes, laying a wreath in a temple surrounded by flaming torches.

That November, the atmosphere in the city was even more charged than usual, seething with violent undercurrents. Two days earlier, a German diplomat in Paris had been shot by a young currently stateless Polish Jew. Since then, as the official fought for his life in hospital, Goebbels had been ramping up the anti-Semitic rhetoric and promising bloody revenge if he failed to recover from his wounds.

Wolf's pagan baptism went ahead anyway on the early afternoon of 9 November. Hitler was in attendance along with a few close friends including Professor Haushofer. Once the ritual was over, Haushofer and Hitler disappeared into a side room and the professor proceeded to give Hitler a lecture on the current European situation and the importance of maintaining good relations with the British, which only served to put Hitler in a bad mood: he never sought Professor Haushofer's advice again.

By the time Hitler had left Ilse and her husband, and was on his way to give a speech to the old fighters at the infamous beer hall, the diplomat had passed away. News of his death reached Hitler at around 9 p.m. when he was having dinner with his comrades. After a brief meeting with Goebbels, Hitler authorised a pogrom that was carried out by his SA thugs and quickly became known as *Kristallnacht*, the Night of Broken Glass.

According to Lina, the action took her husband by surprise; apparently Heydrich only realised what was going on when he looked out of his hotel window and saw a synagogue in flames. Both Heydrich and Himmler were alarmed by the wanton violence and unsupervised mayhem; it went against the methodical persecution they favoured, what they liked to think of as a 'scientific' approach. Lina said her husband thought the Jewish question was a 'medical problem' not a 'political' one, and compared the Jewish community to a parasite that 'clung like leeches to the body of another nation'. Yet Heydrich's view of himself as a surgeon clinically removing a poisonous growth was underpinned by an almost existential revulsion, which Lina shared; the Jews were 'unbearable to him and to me in the soul and in the psyche'. The only solution as far as they were concerned was 'that the Jews should be forced to emigrate from Germany'.[9]

At 1.20 a.m. on 10 November, as the pogrom raged and SA men ran riot, Heydrich attempted to impose some order on proceedings and issued instructions to all Gestapo and SS units: no attacks on foreigners; no looting of wrecked Jewish homes; and with the overall total of 20,000 'healthy men' in mind, the arrest of 'as many Jews, especially rich ones' that could be 'accommodated in the existing jails'.[10] The following morning, Heydrich sat down and calculated the overall loss of property and life, but his figures fell well short of the real number. In the end, 267 synagogues were destroyed, 7,500 businesses vandalised and 91 Jews killed, while hundreds more committed suicide or died in detention.

On 12 November, Heydrich was present at a major conference with a host of ministers, plus Goering – who was fretting about the potential blow to the economy from all the *Kristallnacht* destruction – and Goebbels, who was supremely satisfied by his handiwork. Together they proceeded to draft a series of decrees that accelerated the absolute segregation of Germany's Jews and their exclusion from society, forced them to pay for the damage done during the pogrom and stripped them of their remaining assets.

With everything that had been going on, the Christmas break offered a momentary respite for the Nazi elite. At the Berghof, the New Year's Eve party – attended by Gerda, her husband, Eva and the rest of the Berghof in-crowd – was a livelier gathering than usual and there was a buzz about the place as the guests prepared for the evening's entertainment. Eva's sister, Gretl – who was slowly edging her way into the Berghof world – noted that 'the hairdressers are under siege by the women, and the gentleman are fondly looking forward to their tuxedos'.[11] After dinner, there was a firework display, then everybody moved into the great hall for traditional toasts and the countdown to 1939. Normally teetotal, Hitler forced himself to have a drink of champagne before retiring just after midnight, signalling that it was time to start winding things down.

The kind of parties with drinking and dancing until dawn were never a feature of life at the Berghof, at least when Hitler was there. Most evenings culminated in either a screening of a movie, or one of Hitler's endless fireside chats where he spun out his thoughts into the early hours while his audience struggled to stay awake. Gerda was usually there – a Berghof regular observed that she would sit 'by the fireplace among the wives of Hitler's closest staff, not saying a word all evening'[12] – but she was spared the late nights. Bormann had imposed a 10 p.m. curfew on her, because it was inappropriate for a mother like her (she had another new infant to contend with, a five-month year old girl she'd named Eva) to be out too late; Gerda needed her rest if she was going to keep their household in order.

So once the evening movie had finished or the clock struck the appointed hour in the room where Hitler held court, Gerda was sent home. Hitler's valet remembered that even when Bormann 'threw his own seasonal parties', where the guests were 'principally film actresses who interested him personally', Gerda was 'not permitted to circulate' despite the fact she had to 'do all the arranging and the chores'.[13]

Five days after the New Year's Eve bash, Goebbels arrived in Obersalzburg. He'd had a miserable couple of months, contracted an ulcer and was taking heavy-duty sleeping pills to fend off bouts of insomnia. But after twelve days rest and less fraught discussions with Hitler, his batteries were recharged and he was ready to face Magda in Berlin. Her health had also been poor and though she was not yet pre-pared to forgive her husband, she consented to an official statement of intent regarding their marriage.

A lawyer was brought in to draw up a contract – which the couple signed on 22 January 1939 – that postponed a final decision for a year, enough time for Goebbels to demonstrate that he was truly a reformed character. In the wake of this, Baarova – who'd been waiting patiently in the wings – was exiled back to Czechoslovakia, and not allowed to return, while all her films were removed from circulation; as far as the viewing public were concerned, she had ceased to exist.

Margaret spent her New Year's Eve in bed suffering with a stomach ailment that had blighted her Christmas and exacerbated her usual wor-ries: 'The maid situation is catastrophic. What I have to put up with is unbearable. I don't feel well.' Yet only a few weeks earlier Margaret had been enjoying a vacation in Salzburg with her husband that was almost perfect – 'we spent beautiful days together and talked a lot' – and left her feeling contented and fulfilled: 'Today I am firmly convinced that I have earned my place in the sun, and love and happiness.'[14]

Little did she know that Himmler had fallen in love with his 26-year-old secretary, Hedwig Potthast. Born on 6 February 1912 to middle-class parents who put her through a *Gymnasium* and finishing school, where she picked up a smattering of English, Hedwig sub-sequently got her degree at the Economics Institute for Interpreters in Mannheim. Graduating in 1932, at the height of the Depression, she ended up getting a job as a clerk in a post office. Bored and seek-ing a challenge, Hedwig applied for a position with the Gestapo's press department in autumn 1935; this was still not enough to satisfy her ambitions and in January 1936 she became Himmler's personal secretary.

Hedwig was friendly and upbeat – her friends nicknamed her 'Bunny' – and she enjoyed gymnastics and rowing. She was popular with her colleagues; in October 1937, she joined other members of staff for Himmler's birthday at Lake Tegernsee and was welcomed into the SS family. As they worked in close proximity, Hedwig and Himmler's relationship snowballed and sometime over Christmas 1938 – perhaps at the equivalent of the SS office party – they admitted their feelings for each other, as Hedwig explained to her sister: 'We had a frank conversation during which we confessed that we were hopelessly in love.'[15]

Though the couple kept their affair under the radar as much as possible – according to Hedwig they were trying to find an 'honourable way … to be together'[16] – those in the know included Lina, who liked and respected Hedwig, whom she considered 'an intelligent woman characterised by warm-heartedness'. Unlike Margaret, Hedwig wasn't 'a narrow minded petit-bourgeois', nor was she 'an eccentric', or 'one of the SS sophisticates'. As far as Lina was concerned, Hedwig was a genuine, well-meaning person who helped Himmler 'achieve true stature'.[17]

Margaret apparently had no idea what was going on. As it was, her poor health continued into January, and she went into the Hohenlychen clinic, a former sanatorium for tuberculosis just north of Berlin. Himmler had converted this turn-of-the-century building with Gothic spires into a centre for orthopaedic care and a health spa for the SS elite; it had a large swimming pool with a retractable roof, a state-of-the-art operating theatre, and rooms fitted out with all kinds of exercise equipment. The facility was run by Professor Karl Gebhardt, an old schoolfriend of Himmler's who'd qualified as a surgeon in 1932. An expert in sports medicine, Gebhardt did pioneering work with disabled patients improving their strength and coordination. Having joined the SS in 1935, Gebhardt gained considerable recognition after successfully treating a number of athletes during the 1936 Olympics.

Margaret stayed at Hohenlychen for a couple of weeks and apart from the fact that her only visitor was Himmler and the only person who bothered to call her was Anneliese von Ribbentrop, she enjoyed the peace and quiet and the chance to catch up on some reading. But back in Berlin, Margaret struggled with the demands of the hectic diplomatic social scene, her energy flagging: 'Many invitations. I am terribly tired again.' Even Margaret's regular trips to see stage plays – which included the classic comedy *The Concert* that Emmy had previously starred in, and a production of *Hamlet* – were not giving her the same pleasure as before; in her opinion, the theatre was 'getting worse and worse'.[18]

Margaret could at least feel pleased by her husband's contribution to the next phase of Hitler's plan to reshape the map of Europe. In early March, he increased the pressure on the Czech president and hurled a barrage of threats at him as German troops massed on the border and Goering pledged to obliterate Prague if the Czechs refused to go quietly. With no sign of either Britain or France coming to the rescue, the Czech president gave way. On 15 March, Margaret's husband was in Prague with Hitler. As with the *Anschluss*, Himmler and Heydrich had accumulated a database of people to be arrested and quickly put in place what was needed to execute the round-ups and crush any dissent.

A few weeks later, on 9 April, Lina gave birth to a little girl called Silke, her first daughter. Though pleased about the new addition to his family, Heydrich was barely at home to see her grow. He was engaged in a major reorganisation of the SS and the Gestapo, consolidating all their various functions into one agency – the RHSA – divided into six departments. Aside from this, Heydrich had also been ordered by Goering to assume responsibility for the 'emigration and evacuation'[19] of all the Jews in the Reich. Nevertheless, despite his bulging in-tray, Heydrich did manage to squeeze in some holiday time with Lina and his children at their beach house in Fehmarn.

By the time Magda arrived at the Bayreuth Festival on 25 July 1939, she was on the verge of a breakdown. Even though she'd signed the contract with Goebbels, Magda had not made up her mind about whether or not to take him back and was torn between his pleading and bullying and her ardent admirer Hanke; having driven the wedge between

Magda and her husband – and convinced her to sleep with him – Hanke believed that she would eventually be his. The strain affected her health and in the spring she retired to her preferred clinic in Dresden, which was becoming like a second home to her. To add to her agony, Hitler was keeping his distance; perhaps he didn't want to be seen playing favourites, or perhaps he'd been disappointed by her conduct.

At the same time, Hitler was also giving Goebbels the cold shoulder. Goebbels knew full well that his only hope of restoring Hitler's confidence in him was to save his marriage, and he went all out to persuade Magda to forgive and forget, except she was blowing hot and cold; on 17 March, Goebbels noted in his diary that Magda had been 'so sweet', but on 30 May, she was seeing everything 'in a false, distorted light'.[20]

Crushed by pressure from all sides, Magda escaped for a few weeks' holiday in Sicily and southern Italy with Dr Karl Brandt, Hitler's chief physician; Albert Speer, Hitler's pet architect; Arno Breker, Hitler's favourite sculptor, and their wives. Away from the madness, Magda was more like her usual self, comfortable in her own skin. The return to Berlin shattered any equilibrium she'd regained; Hanke, who had nothing to lose since he'd quit working for Goebbels and joined the army, was pushing her to make a commitment to him and Goebbels was threatening to take the children away from her if she did.

At Bayreuth, it all caught up with her during a production of the tragic love story *Tristan and Isolde*. Sharing a box with her husband, Hitler, Winifred Wagner and Speer, Magda 'cried silently throughout the whole performance' and spent the interval 'racked with incessant sobs in the corner of one of the drawing rooms'. According to Speer, Hitler was appalled by such a publicly embarrassing scene, and after the opera finished he told Goebbels that 'it would be better if he left Bayreuth immediately with his wife' and 'dismissed' him without shaking hands or waiting for a reply.[21]

By the end of July, Margaret was back at Lake Tegernsee after a holiday at a Baltic resort with her daughter, but not with her husband, who was otherwise engaged. Margaret had a reasonable time without Himmler – 'peaceful days and the weather quite good' – but expressed concern about Gudrun; she was doing poorly at school and her reading was 'really quite bad'.[22] On 14 August, Margaret noted in her diary that Himmler was with Hitler at the Berghof awaiting news of von Ribbentrop's trip to Moscow. Hitler was seeking an alliance with Stalin that would keep them from each others' throats for the time being and ensured they both got a piece of Poland, and had dispatched his foreign minister to thrash out a deal.

In between consultations with Hitler, Himmler was packing in lots of games of tennis – between mid July and mid August he played thirteen times – a trend that continued when he returned to Berlin at the end of the summer. No doubt Himmler was trying to burn off the anxiety and stress that was accumulating inside him and caused his chronic stomach problems; that year, his condition got so bad that he hired a Swedish healer to give him massages on an almost daily basis.

His apprehension was mixed with excitement; Himmler had Poland in his sights. It promised to be a land of opportunity for the SS. Not only were he and Heydrich expected to decapitate the Polish intelligentsia, the aristocracy, political and Church leaders and any representative of Polish nationalism, there was its huge Jewish population to deal with and the prospect of launching the great *Lebensraum* experiment of colonisation in the East.

To accomplish the SS's primary task of murderous suppression, Heydrich established eight special task forces – the Einsatzgruppen – which would accompany the German army once the invasion began. Heydrich himself planned to be there in the thick of things and hoped to see some action one way or another.

Before the campaign began, Heydrich wrote to Lina a letter to be opened in the event of his death. In it he adopted a formal, almost bureaucratic tone as he instructed Lina to educate their children to be 'true to the ideas of the Nazi movement', asked her to 'remember our life together with respect and fondness', and gave her permission, 'once time has healed the wounds', to find a new father for their children, as long as he was like 'the kind of man I aspired to be'.[23]

Margaret was also preparing to serve her country by putting her First World War nursing experience to good use: 'If there is a war I have to work with the Red Cross.' After the Nazi-Soviet pact was signed on 23 August, and the way was clear for the invasion of Poland, Margaret told Gudrun about her decision, which would mean them being apart for long periods; 'she, of course, cried a lot and cannot calm down'.

When it came to the moment when Margaret had to leave Lake Tegernsee for Berlin and her new duties, Gudrun saw that her mother was weeping and tried to put on a brave face; Gudrun 'heroically laughed' even though 'tears kept streaming down her face'. Yet despite this traumatic parting, Margaret was 'glad' she could 'participate' and believed that 'the war will be over soon'.[24]

The day before Hitler's armies steamrollered into Poland, Emmy and her husband went for a walk after breakfast at Carinhall. Goering's mood was sober and he confessed to Emmy that the war was 'going to be appalling, more terrible than we can yet imagine'. The only hope of avoiding a protracted bloodbath was to keep Britain out of it and Goering asked Emmy to 'pray that I can bring peace'. That night, as Hitler's tanks rolled into action and Goering's planes took off from their airstrips to pummel the enemy, Emmy was consumed by premonitions of doom: 'The future rose up … like a high wall, sinister and threatening.'[25]

For all his boasting about the devastating strength of the Luftwaffe, Goering knew that it wasn't as powerful as he pretended, and he was well aware of the difficulties the economy would face if it needed to sustain a long war, particularly one fought on two fronts. The memory of defeat in the First World War loomed large; during that conflict Britain's navy was able to blockade Germany's coastlines – which contributed massively to the slow starvation of the civilian population – and maintain a steady flow of men and material from its empire.

Goering feared a repeat performance. And he wasn't the only one. Hess, another First World War veteran, was equally wary of taking on the British and getting mired in a two-front conflict, especially as Hess understood better than most that Hitler would never abandon his cherished dream of laying waste to the Soviet Union; the truce with Stalin was only temporary. Ilse remembered that her husband thought 'a new war would be a disaster for Europe and the whole world'.[26]

However, Hess was no longer able to influence Hitler's decisions. He was still an important figure in the public eye, performing his many duties and speaking engagements, but behind the scenes Hess was yesterday's man, isolated from power. Ilse was also out of the loop for much of 1939 and focused on domestic life. She was devoted to their son Wolf and engaged in supervising major extensions to their Munich home. Ilse wanted a telephone exchange installed, extra accommodation for more staff and enough garage space for up to ten cars. When Ilse's mother heard about these expensive additions, she wrote her daughter a stern letter condemning her extravagance. Sensitive to any suggestion that she was letting herself be corrupted, Ilse rejected the accusation that she and her husband were over-indulging themselves: 'We're not suffering from megalomania Mama: we haven't got any more cars ... we haven't even got a new one.'[27]

In the midst of all this, and the worsening international situation, Ilse and Hess managed to have their annual hiking holiday in the mountains, which he recalled with great fondness. On their return, Hess set about trying to forge a clandestine link to members of the British government through Professor Haushofer's son Albrecht, who was a firm opponent of the Nazi regime. Albrecht Haushofer's academic position as a foreign policy expert – which had been secured by Hess – allowed him to travel and in the autumn Albrecht began seeking out potential contacts in Switzerland and Spain. But beyond a tentative and cautious exchange of communications nothing much was achieved.

Goering's peace efforts also came to nothing. Several of his Swedish business associates agreed to help and managed to set up a meeting at a remote farmhouse with Goering and half a dozen British industrialists but the discussions went nowhere, which was a disappointment to the British ambassador in Berlin; having visited Carinhall numerous times and gone hunting with Goering, the ambassador thought he was a thoroughly decent chap and Emmy a fine woman. On their last night together, Goering and the ambassador contemplated the coming war and Goering promised that if one of his Luftwaffe bombers happened to kill the ambassador during a raid, he would personally fly over to London and drop a wreath on his grave.

The first casualty of this failure to find an agreement was Unity Mitford. When Britain and France reacted to Hitler's annexation of Czechoslovakia by announcing their readiness to defend Poland if necessary, Unity found herself looking into the abyss; all her efforts to exploit her celebrity to convince her countrymen that Britain and Hitler's Germany were natural allies had come to nothing, and she started telling people she'd kill herself if they came to blows. Her sister was with her during the Bayreuth Festival, and after a meal with Hitler, Diana remembered that Unity 'said once again that she would not live to see the impending tragedy'. For Diana, her sister's sombre words made that evening's performance of *Twilight of the Gods* even more poignant: 'Never had the glorious music seemed so doom laden.'[28]

On Sunday, 3 September, after Britain declared war, Unity wrote a series of farewell letters and headed over to the HQ of the regional party leader, left an envelope containing her prized signed portrait of Hitler and gold Nazi party badge with instructions to have them buried with her in Munich if anything happened to her, then drove to a park, sat on a bench, took a pistol from her handbag, fired one round into the ground to make sure it was working and shot herself in the right temple.

Unity was found slumped unconscious by the police a few hours later and whisked straight to a top private clinic; a doctor who examined her said she looked 'very white and corpse like'.[29] The bullet was jammed into the left side of her brain and could not be removed. It had caused severe and irreparable neurological damage; Unity could barely speak or move. Hitler was shocked when he heard the news: Heinrich Hoffmann said that 'Unity's attempted suicide made a profound impression' on him[30]; Hitler paid for her treatment, sent her flowers every day and made one brief visit, during which Unity simply stared into space.

Hitler knew that with the war now in progress, Unity couldn't stay in Germany, so he had her possessions put in storage and arranged for her to be taken in a reserved train carriage – accompanied by a doctor, a nurse and a nun – to a Swiss clinic, and from there back to Britain. An invalid, Unity died in 1948, at the age of 33. Reflecting on Unity's involvement with Nazism, Diana wrote that her sister had 'adopted' their 'creed … including their anti-Semitism, with uncritical enthusiasm'.[31] Unity had sacrificed everything on the altar of Hitler's obsessions; she'd wasted her young life on a toxic fantasy that was about to send millions more to their deaths.

Carin Goering stares thoughtfully into the distance. (AKG)

Hermann Goering in the courtyard of Carinhall – his country estate – inspecting a parade of Japanese recruits. (Wikimedia Commons)

Emmy Goering and her husband on their wedding day standing on the steps of Berlin Cathedral saluting the crowds of well-wishers. (Bundesarchiv)

Emmy Goering modelling one of her many fur coats. (Wikimedia Commons)

Emmy Goering and her husband attend a concert in Berlin. (Bundesarchiv)

Emmy Goering cuddles her pet lion cub while her husband and Mussolini look on. (AKG)

New Year's Eve at the Berghof 1939: Eva Braun by Hitler in the front row, Gerda Bormann two rows back. (AKG)

Gerda Bormann on her wedding day sitting between her husband and father – Walter Buch – with Hitler in the front passenger seat. (AKG)

Ilse Hess looks relieved that her husband has survived the Zugspitze Mountain Flying Race, coming in first place. (AKG)

Ilse Hess and her husband follow the action at the Olympic Games 1936. (AKG)

Magda Goebbels, the 'First Lady of the Reich'. (Bundesarchiv)

A family portrait – staged for propaganda purposes – featuring Magda Goebbels, her husband, their six children, and Magda's son from her first marriage, Harald, – wearing his uniform. (AKG)

Magda Goebbels and her husband are greeted by the faithful at Berchtesgaden railway station. (USHMM)

The triumvirate; Hitler next to Magda Goebbels, her husband and three of their children. (AKG)

Lina Heydrich, her husband and their young son Klaus enjoying some fresh air. (Bundesarchiv)

Lina Heydrich accompanies her husband through the corridors of the Wallenstein Palace in Prague on their way to watch a classical music concert. (Bundesarchiv)

The young Margaret Boden
a decade before she met
Himmler. (Bundesarchiv)

The newly wed Margaret Himmler and her husband outside their
farm near Munich. (USHMM)

Margaret Himmler does her best to enjoy the great outdoors. (USHMM)

Eva Braun and Hitler pose with their beloved dogs on the Berghof terrace. (Bundesarchiv)

Geli Raubel and Hitler relaxing on a summer's day. (AKG)

The main entrance to the Oberzalzburg complex. (Bundesarchiv)

One of the many vast drawing rooms at the Berghof. (Bundesarchiv)

PART THREE

A LONG WAY DOWN

10

WAR AND PEACE

By the end of 1939, Magda and her husband were at peace. Despite all the quarrelling and emotional turmoil, the terms of the marriage contract they'd signed at the beginning of the year had been fulfilled and the couple reconciled. Their reunion met with Hitler's approval and on 30 October he invited them for tea at the Reich Chancellery, then on 15 January 1940 he paid them a visit at their country house – bringing a puppet theatre for the children – and was back again on 1 February. Hitler and Magda and her husband reminisced about the time when the three of them were inseparable; according to Goebbels, they 'revived old memories'.[1] Soon after, Magda discovered she was pregnant again; the First Family of the Reich were back in business.

On 29 December, Goebbels had attended the premiere of the film *Mother Love*, which traced the different stages of a widow's life, from youth to old age, as she raises her four children while running a laundry business to keep food on the table, sacrificing her own happiness as she battles against the odds to turn her troubled children – one son gets involved with a married woman, another impregnates one of her employees, another loses his eyesight, while her daughter becomes a dancer – into useful members of the community. Publicity for the film claimed that it aimed 'to represent the image of the mother, to reveal her unending love and kindness, and by doing so erect a monument of fidelity and thanks to all mothers'.[2] Goebbels sobbed during the screening and in his diary wrote that it was 'a victory for German cinema'.[3]

Margaret Himmler was equally moved when she saw *Mother Love* shortly after it came out. She thought it was 'a beautiful movie',[4] which was high praise from her; she rarely expressed such strong feelings about a film, except when she didn't like it. Perhaps Margaret identified with its message and themes, the lone protagonist giving her all and receiving very little in return, ground down by the burdens of motherhood, yet always doing her best.

Margaret's worries about her own family were more acute now she was doing her bit for the war effort. In the first few months of the conflict, she'd been based at a Berlin hospital and was 'looking forward to surgical work',[5] but she kept clashing with the senior doctors and staff, who weren't keen on having Himmler's bossy wife breathing down their necks. Frustrated, she quit and on 3 December 1939 she took up a supervisory position for the German Red Cross, monitoring its field hospitals and the treatment facilities near the main railway hubs that cared for injured and wounded soldiers in transit.

By the mid 1930s, the German Red Cross had fallen into the hands of the SS. Its titular head was Charles Edward von Saxe-Coburg-Gotha – who went from the *Freikorps* to the SA and then onto the SS – but real authority was wielded by the SS physician Ernst-Robert Grawitz, a favourite of Margaret's husband and her overall boss.

From the end of 1937, all 9,000 German Red Cross units were merged into one organisation under the control of the Ministry of the Interior. Once nurses had been vetted for their political and racial fitness, they had to join the party and swear an oath of allegiance to Hitler. As war approached, the German Red Cross stopped treating civilians and began preparing for military casualties; the number of emergency staff swelled from 13,500 in 1933 to 142,000 in 1938, ready to be deployed in reserve hospitals on the home front, or field hospitals in the war zone, situated 15 miles behind the frontline with 200–1,000 beds. A network of soldiers' homes were established for those who required long-term rehabilitation or were permanently disabled.

Margaret's separation from 10-year-old Gudrun hit her daughter hard – she was having trouble sleeping and wept down the phone – and her distress was compounded by the fact that she hardly ever saw her father. Not that Margaret fared any better; as she glumly noted in her dairy. Himmler was 'almost never home evenings although he is in Berlin'.[6] That year, Margaret would face a reckoning in her marriage. Himmler and his mistress Hedwig had decided that they wanted to have children, and as a result felt they had to tell Margaret the truth about their affair.

On 12 September 1939, fifteen days before Poland capitulated, Heydrich took to the skies in a Heinkel plane as a turret gunner, risking death to fire on retreating Polish soldiers. Lina's husband had begun his quest to see action in 1935 when he trained as a sports pilot, becoming skilful enough to participate in aerobatics shows. During the summer of 1939, he completed a course that qualified him to fly a fighter plane and had an airstrip marked out in a field near the family's Fehmarn villa so he could fly from Berlin to the house at the weekends; Heydrich would gun his engine to announce his imminent arrival and Lina would get the dinner on. Lina, who viewed his new hobby with some alarm, went up with him once and they flew round the island; Lina loathed it and never got in his plane again.

Once Poland was occupied, Heydrich made a number of trips there to check on the brutal progress of his Einsatzgruppen death squads and begin herding the local Jewish population into ghettos. To make his absences more bearable, Lina had acquired some new editions to her small Berlin social circle, including Walter Schellenberg's new wife, Irene. Her mother was Polish, which would cause problems getting an SS marriage certificate, but Heydrich helped Schellenberg out and persuaded Himmler to allow the couple to wed. Lina and Irene got on exceptionally well; they hung out, shopped, had lunch and dinner, and went to the movies.

The other couple brightening her days were Max de Crinis and his wife Lilli, a former actress. Lina met de Crinis and Lilli in 1939 when he was made professor of psychiatry at the world-renowned Berlin University teaching hospital, Le Charité. De Crinis was about to become a key figure in the regime's euthanasia programme – known as T4 – and on 10 August he attended a meeting with around a dozen other psychiatrists to select technical staff capable of implementing its mandate, which was endorsed by Hitler, and stated that 'patients who … are considered incurable can be granted mercy death after a critical evaluation of their health'.[7]

De Crinis's involvement with T4 was based on both his professional and ideological credentials. The son of a doctor, de Crinis was born in Austria in 1889. By 1924, he'd become an associate professor of neurology and from then until 1934 he was very active in the Austrian Nazi party. That year, he took up a chair at Cologne University. In 1936, he joined the SS and the SD. His personnel file described him as 'a well-known pioneer in the anti-Semitic realm'.[8]

De Crinis was an enthusiastic advocate of the sterilisation programme that had paved the way for the regime's adoption of euthanasia. The 'Law for the Prevention of Hereditarily Diseased Offspring' was drafted on 14 July 1933, and supplemented by the 'Law Against Habitual Criminals', which enforced the castration of anyone over 21 who had done more than six months in jail for a second offence. Four of the nine conditions named in the legislation covered mental health: manic depression, schizophrenia, 'congenital feeblemindedness' – which included those with criminal records, prostitutes, the unemployed and the homeless – and 'anyone suffering from chronic alcoholism'.[9]

Potential victims were selected by psychiatrists like de Crinis – who had done studies on both epilepsy and alcoholism – and appeared before one of the 220 local health courts, where their fate was decided. By 1939, 345,000 people had been sterilised: 200,000 'feeble-minded', 73,000 schizophrenics, 37,000 epileptics and 30,000 alcoholics.

Though the first to die were children, the T4 programme focused on adults. In mid January 1940, the decision was made to use carbon monoxide gas; at the beginning of February, de Crinis was on a panel recruiting suitable doctors and forms went out to health officials at asylums and sanatoriums for registering potential 'patients'. During a conference in March, de Crinis discussed T4 with psychiatrists from state mental hospitals. Killings were initially carried out at four different locations; around twenty 'patients' were gassed at a time in a room designed to look like a communal shower. All the deceased had their gold teeth removed.

In August 1941, T4 was halted after protests from the Catholic Church; by then 70,000 had been murdered. De Crinis was one of prime movers behind the reintroduction of the programme in the autumn of 1943, and it continued until the end of the war. In 1939, there were between 300,000 and 320,000 people in German mental health institutions; by 1946, there were only 40,000.

Schellenberg regarded de Crinis as his best friend, a fine man with a 'most pleasant and cultivated household'.[10] Heydrich thought he was 'a very nice fellow'.[11] Lina and her husband would often go riding with de Crinis and his wife in the early morning, galloping round the Grunewald forest on horses from a Berlin stables. Afterwards, they would go back to de Crinis's villa on Lake Wansee for a champagne breakfast.

During April 1940, Heydrich spent four weeks in Norway with a fighter squadron, strafing the enemy, drinking in the officers' mess and playing cards. His participation in this short campaign ended on 13 April when his Messerschmitt 109 overshot the runway on take-off and crashed; the plane was wrecked and Heydrich broke his arm. The next day he was back behind his desk in Berlin with an Iron Cross Second Class.

After the rapid conquest of Poland, there followed several months of stasis as Hitler waited to see if Britain or France – particularly Britain – were prepared to rethink their decision to go to war. With no clear sign that either of them were going to back off, Hitler resumed hostilities and attacked Norway in order to secure vital sea routes.

Job done, Hitler turned his attention westwards towards the old enemy France; he craved revenge and redemption for the defeat of 1918, a chance to erase that shame and humiliation from the pages of history. What he didn't have was the means to wage a long campaign. Out of this necessity arose the infamous Blitzkrieg strategy: the concentration of force to achieve a rapid breakthrough, punching a hole through the enemy's defences with a combination of tanks and aircraft, racing through the gap and deep into its territory, leaving those left behind vulnerable to encirclement. The results were nothing short of spectacular. On 10 May, the attack was launched; on 17 June, six weeks later, the French surrendered.

Soon after, Emmy – who was wearing the latest Parisian fashions – and her husband had a special dinner to celebrate this stunning victory and the Luftwaffe's role in it. Goering had brought some pâté de foie gras from Paris to accompany different coloured vodkas from Poland, and they also consumed 'roast salmon done in the Danzig style with Moselle … and then a tiny very light Viennese torte'[12] with white wine. The meal was provided by Otto Horcher, Emmy and her husband's personal chef and caterer, who ran Horcher's restaurant in Berlin. Opened in 1904 by his father Gustav, it served solid German fare, dishes such as smoked eel with horseradish sauce, lentil soup with frankfurter, and potato salad with Pommery mustard and poached egg. Goering had started going there in the late 1920s to wine and dine aristocrats and industrialists. Otto catered all the Goerings' big parties, including the Olympics banquets, as well as receptions and private dinners at Carinhall.

The Horcher brand benefited from Nazi expansion. After the *Anschluss*, Otto took over the top restaurant in Vienna. When the war began, Goering made sure all of Otto's waiters and cooks were exempt from military service. In Norway, Otto set up exclusive Luftwaffe Clubs serving food and drink to officers and opened two for the public in Oslo. After the fall of France, Otto acquired the legendary Maxim's in Paris so his patron would have somewhere to eat on his frequent trips to the city, as he orchestrated one of the greatest art thefts in history.

In early March 1940, Margaret arrived in Poland for an inspection tour of German Red Cross sites. She visited Posen – which had a school and boarding house for nurses – Lodz, which was the centre of German Red Cross activity in Poland, and finally Warsaw. Like many of her colleagues, Margaret complained about the primitive living conditions and poor hygiene in the hospitals and transport trains, what she called 'indescribable filth'. She was also offended by the appearance of the local inhabitants:'This Jew trash, these Pollacks, most of them don't even look like human beings.'[13]

Prejudices confirmed, Margaret returned to Berlin, where, at some point, Himmler told her about Hedwig. However much this must have hurt her, Margaret never contemplated divorce. For her, it would have amounted to a shameful humiliation. Then there was Gudrun to think of; Himmler was devoted to her and she idolised him. Given she was already struggling to cope with both her parents away most of the time – according to her mother, she was 'very nervous and doing poorly at school'[14] – neither of them wanted to disrupt Gudrun's life any further. Himmler continued to put in appearances at Lake Tegernsee, tried to call every day and wrote regular letters. Himmler's willingness to maintain appearances was not simply because he wanted to spare Margaret and Gudrun unnecessary pain. He was dead set against divorce; 77 per cent of the SS leadership cadre were married, as opposed to around 44 per cent of the general population, and any SS man who wanted to leave his wife had to get Himmler's permission; if they defied him, they were expelled from the SS.

An example of Himmler's uncompromising attitude was the way he treated his old comrade, Karl Wolff, who wanted to split from Frieda and marry his long-term mistress, a widowed countess with whom he'd been conducting an affair since 1934; she had borne his child in 1937 and was housed in a love nest in Budapest with ten rooms and a bath house. But Himmler refused to let Wolff dump Frieda. In the end, Wolff appealed over Himmler's head to Hitler, who gave him the go-ahead to divorce.

Throughout this drawn out process, Frieda – who had written to Himmler to say that she did not want to stand in the way of Karl's happiness – stayed at their Lake Tegernsee home with her children. Though she and Margaret were neighbours who'd known each other for nearly a decade and their daughters were good friends, the bitter quarrel between their husbands impacted on their relationship. Once it became clear that Karl was defying Himmler's orders, Margaret distanced herself from Frieda, abandoning her in her hour of need.

Perhaps Frieda's experience was too close for comfort; Margaret's unhappiness, her sense of loss and abandonment, began appearing in her diary. On 9 June 1940, she wrote that 'so much sadness makes it hard to be alone … so in the evenings I mostly play Solitaire and read a little'. On 4 January 1941, she reflected that 'the old year has gone by. It took a lot of courage to go through it.' A month later, she bemoaned the fact that 'every young girl craves a man' without realising 'how bitter life is' and hoped that she would be able to 'protect my daughter from the worst'.[15]

One of the pieces of art proudly displayed in the Bormanns' Munich household was a bronze bust of Gerda done by the regime's most visible and lauded sculptor, Arno Breker. Breker was known for his monumental, classically themed works – with names like *Prometheus*, *Torchbearer* and *Sacrifice* – featuring naked men in dynamic and heroic poses. Breker's portraits in bronze were mostly private commissions; he did busts of Hitler, Goebbels, Magda's son Harald Quandt, and Edda Goering.

Born in 1900, the son of a stonemason, Breker spent time in Paris in the 1920s after qualifying from the Dusseldorf School of Arts. He was in Rome in 1932 when Goebbels tracked him down and tried to persuade him to return to Germany, which he did in 1934. Two years later he entered two sculptures into the Olympic arts competition, won silver, met Hitler at the reception and was very impressed. The feeling was mutual; in 1940 Hitler awarded Breker the golden badge of the Nazi party.

Breker was also the richest Nazi artist, earning a fortune from state commissions, prizes and his own factory, which used slave labour to mass-produce versions of popular works like his portrait of Hitler. Gerda sat for Breker in 1940 and after the bronze of her was complete, she befriended Breker and his wife, the glamorous Demetra Messala, an ex-model who'd sat for Picasso in Paris; by the time she joined Breker in Germany, she was a successful art dealer. They married in 1937 and had five children.

That Gerda felt comfortable in such sophisticated company is indicative of her rising status as a Nazi wife. Gerda was an integral part of life at the Berghof, which had settled into a fixed daily routine revolving round Hitler's habits. He slept late, appearing around noon; lunch was taken a few hours later and then most days at around 4 p.m. Hitler, Eva and their guests would take a twenty-minute stroll downhill to the Little Tea House instead of scaling the heights to reach the Eagle's Nest: aside from the fact it was often very cold up there, the thin air at that altitude made Hitler queasy.

The Little Tea House was much cosier. According to Hitler's faithful secretary Christa Schroeder, Hitler and Eva always had cocoa rather than tea or coffee, and though the 'selection of cakes and pastries was very tempting', Hitler 'always had apple pie, its pastry breath thin, low in calories, with slices of baked apple'. In this relaxed atmosphere, 'Hitler would love to hear amusing stories, and people who could tell them were very welcome.'[16] Sometimes, if the company was not stimulating enough, Hitler would fall asleep in his chair.

The evenings were monopolised by Hitler's monologues, whether delivered over dinner or at the fireside. On 5 July 1941, a member of Bormann's staff began work on an ambitious project to record all of Hitler's pearls of wisdom. The end result – known as *Hitler's Table Talk* – covered every meal at the Berghof up to mid March 1942; after that, the entries were intermittent, with large gaps between sessions.

Until recently, historians believed that the final text, which ran for hundreds of pages, was a verbatim reproduction of Hitler's speeches, but recent research suggests that Bormann's assistants transcribed the material from memory each morning and then handed their notes over to Bormann for shaping and editing. Bormann took the whole process of capturing his master's voice very seriously, performing the role of a faithful disciple and curator of Hitler's thoughts, preserving them for future generations.

That summer at the Berghof, Hitler was pondering a dilemma. Despite the subjugation of France in record time, Britain refused to fold. Invasion was an option and plans were assembled, but it was a risky prospect. Then Goering stepped forward and offered to resolve the problem by using the Luftwaffe to bring Britain to its knees. Goering's solution appealed to Hitler and for six months, beginning in August, his air force tried to do just that, initially attacking the RAF and its infrastructure and then switching to bombing London and other economically significant cities.

However, for all the destruction and mayhem caused, it was clear by the end of February 1941 that Goering was not going to keep his promise to Hitler: the Luftwaffe was losing planes and experienced pilots at a fearsome rate, while Goering's poorly managed, institutionally corrupt, wasteful and inefficient Four-Year Plan office had become a sprawling behemoth incapable of producing enough aircraft to subdue a whole nation, especially one fighting so tenaciously while manufacturing its own planes at a faster rate and in greater numbers.

Throughout this critical period, the most challenging of his Nazi career, Goering dedicated a lot of time and energy to his art collection, which he'd begun building seriously in 1936 after setting up a private fund for purchasing art. The main contributor was the cigarette manufacturer, Philip Reemstama, who accounted for 75 per cent of the market. Goering did him a number of favours, fending off the competition, getting him out of legal scrapes and winning him army contracts that amounted to billions of cigarettes. The tobacco king was understandably grateful and every three months he donated 250,000 RM to Goering's fund.

Goering bought through a number of dealers and sought out work by sixteenth- and seventeenth-century German artists, the Dutch masters, and Italian Renaissance painters, sometimes paying above the odds, sometimes below. Otherwise, he shamelessly stole from Jewish owners and galleries, and by 1940 he had acquired 200 pieces.

After the war started, his agents scoured Poland, coming back with thirty-one drawings by Albrecht Durer, which Goering gave to Hitler, and ransacked the art market in Amsterdam, buying whole collections of paintings from big private owners, including a fake Vermeer. At the same time, Goering used degenerate art as collateral. He exchanged paintings by Cezanne, Van Gogh and Munch for hard cash, and on 3 March 1941, he swapped eleven works – including one by Degas, two by Matisse, two by Picasso, a Braque and a Renoir – for a Titian. A month later, in a similar deal, he got a Rembrandt and two tapestries for twenty-five degenerate paintings. Once France fell, however, the real bonanza began. In Paris, a massive warehouse was filled to the brim with art confiscated from the city's Jewish community. Between 3 November 1940 and 27 November 1942, Goering made twenty-five visits to the warehouse and removed 700 items, mostly paintings but also tapestries and sculptures.

All these treasures were transported by rail to Carinhall, where Emmy could enjoy them. Like her husband, she claimed they had no intention of keeping the art for themselves; they were its custodians, keeping it safe and secure. Once the war was over, Emmy said her husband would open the Hermann Goering Museum and put it all on public display.

Magda spent much of 1940 in and out of hospital, her heart condition aggravated, as always, by her pregnancy. In August, she was fit enough to return home, but by early October she was – according to her husband – 'suffering badly with her heart'. On the 10th, she was 'nervous and irritable' and towards the end of the month, as delivery day beckoned, Magda faced 'her critical time' with 'great courage'. On the 29th, her ordeal was over and she gave birth to their sixth child, another daughter.

The following day there was a party for her husband's forty-third birthday. Magda and her children – with some professional assistance – had put together a special present for Goebbels, a short home movie featuring them walking in a forest, playing with a toy castle and hunting rabbits. Once Goebbels had been treated to a private screening, the film appeared in the cinemas as a piece of morale-boosting propaganda. Goebbels was delighted by this celluloid gift, inspiring 'laughter and tears' because it was 'so beautiful'.[17] In return, he laid on 'a small party for Magda's birthday' on 12 November. Pleased that she was 'dazzlingly beautiful again', Goebbels was also thrilled that Hitler decided to drop by: 'The Führer arrives towards ten in the evening, and stays until four in the morning. He is absolutely confident and relaxed, just as in pre-war times.' The trio discussed 'vegetarianism', the 'coming religion', and Goebbels proudly noted that with them Hitler could be 'a proper human being again'.[18]

But such scenes of domestic tranquillity were repeated less and less during 1941. That year, Magda and Goebbels were increasingly apart and leading separate lives. This was due to Magda's persistent health issues – a minor heart attack in February, bronchitis in March – Goebbels's packed schedule, which included a fair amount of foreign travel, and the potential threat of British bombers over Berlin, which encouraged them to send their children down south; for a time they stayed at Obersalzburg and other locations in Bavaria. Later, they were shipped off to the Upper Danube region.

During all this, relations between Magda and her husband remained cordial, with plenty of goodwill on either side. Yet they were drifting away from each other, the gulf between them steadily growing. Soon, the familiar problems that had dogged their marriage from the outset would make a mockery of the contract they signed.

During late October 1940, Margaret was in the Balkans for a couple of weeks on German Red Cross business, accompanied by Professor Gebhardt, who ran her favourite health spa, the Hohenlychen clinic. They travelled to Romania via Budapest – where they were entertained by 'gypsy music' in their hotel – had a quick stopover in Belgrade and went to see a 'German resettlement' in the Bessarabia region of northern Romania. This area had been ceded to the Soviets as part of the 1939 Hitler–Stalin pact; it was subsequently reclaimed by the Romanian army, who descended like locusts on its Jewish population, killing around 8,000, and dumping 250,000 in concentration camps.

As a result, whole villages and towns were emptied and a large amount of land was made available, which prompted Margaret's husband to include the region in his plans to resettle ethnic Germans in places where they could establish model farming communities. Margaret and Professor Gebhardt were given a tour of one of these so-called *Volksdeutsches* villages, and she was impressed by how 'clean' it was.[19]

Back in Berlin, Margaret's social life had dwindled to almost nothing; the diplomatic soirees were over for her and she saw very few people.

One of them was Anneliese von Ribbentrop. Out of all the leading Nazi wives, Anneliese was Margaret's closest friend. Strong-willed, ambitious, intelligent and stylish, Anneliese was roughly the same age as Margaret and came from the Henkel family, who had grown wealthy selling their unique brand of sparkling wine. She married Ribbentrop in 1920 after meeting him at a tennis tournament, and together they had an enviable lifestyle. Their elegant Berlin villa had its own tennis court while their country estate boasted a nine-hole golf course. After inviting Hitler to dinner in 1932, Anneliese converted to Nazism and pushed her husband into his inner circle.

Unfortunately for Margaret, their friendship was abruptly terminated because their husbands fell out with each other. The two men had become close after Ribbentrop joined the SS in 1934, bonding over their shared love of tennis. However, once Ribbentrop had been made foreign minister, they squabbled over their respective spheres of influence in Allied and neutral countries. Matters came to a head in 1941. Angered by the SD's support for a failed coup against the Nazi-friendly government in Romania, Ribbentrop forced Himmler to sign an agreement that underlined his authority over foreign affairs.

On 8 May 1941, Margaret noted in her diary that 'the relationship' between her husband 'and Herr von Ribbentrop has ended' because 'Ribbentrop had too many pretensions'.[20] At the same time, Margaret ended her association with Anneliese; without her for company, Margaret's isolation in Berlin was complete.

During the winter of 1940–41, Ilse Hess suspected that her husband was planning something out of the ordinary, as 'he was extremely busy with all sorts of activities and his state of tension was visible'. Hess was flying again, using the airfield at Augsburg so often that Ilse found it hard to believe he was simply seeking some 'distraction from the cares of office'.

The mystery deepened when 'a large brand new radio apparatus appeared in the work room of our home … and was used behind closed double doors'. She investigated it and discovered that it was tuned to receive reports from a weather signals station. Most curious of all was 'the astonishing amount of time – and in the middle of a war – that my husband spent with our son'.

On Saturday, 10 May 1941, Hess had scheduled an early lunch with an old comrade, Alfred Rosenberg, but Ilse was feeling unwell and didn't join them. After Rosenberg left, Hess popped upstairs to see Ilse and asked her to take tea with him at the 'usual hour'. When he appeared at 2.30 p.m., Ilse was surprised that he was 'wearing bluish-grey breeches and high airman's boots' and 'even more astonished to see he had on a light blue shirt with a dark blue tie, a colour combination I had so often advocated without the slightest effect'. When Ilse questioned him about his attire, Hess replied that he was trying to please her. Ilse was not convinced. Later she realised that her husband had been sporting a Luftwaffe officer's uniform.

After tea, Ilse remembered that 'he kissed my hand and stood at the door of the nursery, grown suddenly very grave, with the air of one in deep thought'. Hess bade his sleeping son farewell and left for the airfield at Augsburg, where he took off in his Messerschmitt plane, embarking on a mission to bring about peace between Britain and Germany.

Ilse started to worry when he didn't return home that night: 'The next two days, Sunday and Monday … we knew absolutely nothing of what had happened.' On Monday evening, the 12th, Ilse had 'arranged for a show in our little cinema at home' for Hess's staff, the chauffeur and the servants. During the film, Hess's youngest adjutant appeared in a terrible state; he'd just heard on the radio that Hess had crashed in the North Sea, having suffered a 'mental aberration'.

Ilse immediately rang the Berghof, fully intending 'to speak to the Führer and give him a piece of my mind', but she was connected to Bormann instead, who said he knew nothing, which at that moment was true. Ilse did not believe him and 'expressed' her 'indignation with an emphasis and rhetoric I had never employed before or since'. Bormann – who had everything to gain from Hess's disappearance – promised her that a ministry official would bring her more news as soon as possible, but when the official arrived long after midnight he had nothing meaningful to say.

The next morning, the 13th, Hess's old friend and mentor, Professor Haushofer, dropped by; he was 'deeply shaken and filled with despair' because he thought Hess was dead. Once Haushofer had limped off, Ilse, who was overcome with exhaustion, took her son and went to bed, falling instantly 'into a deep sleep'. When she awoke, her prayers were answered; her husband had landed safely in Scotland.[21]

Before she had time to digest the news, Ilse was summoned to her husband's Berlin apartment to find Bormann waiting for her. After giving her a thorough grilling, Bormann asked to her to list what items in the flat belonged to the state – which would be seized – and what belonged to Hess, which she could keep. As it turned out, only the carpets were hers, while the rest of the fixtures and fittings were government property. Having set her this deliberately degrading task, Bormann added insult to injury; if Ilse wanted to buy the bedroom furniture, he'd give her a 50 per cent discount.

Ultimately, Ilse's fate depended on Hitler. He was at the Berghof the morning after the flight when Hess's adjutant arrived with a letter from his boss. Having read it, Hitler reacted with a mixture of rage and incomprehension that only increased as more details emerged. Some close to Hitler – including his valet – thought he knew what Hess was going to do and had given his approval; his enraged response was nothing more than a performance from a gifted actor. But Ilse categorically denied this: 'I have certain knowledge that my husband desired to make a personal sacrifice without being ordered to do so, without any knowledge of this act as far as Hitler was concerned.'[22]

Hitler immediately had all of Hess's private staff arrested; some of them languished in camps until 1944. Hess's brothers were also picked up then released after being given the fright of their lives. Professor Haushofer was already a marked man – Hitler referred to him as 'the Jewish tainted professor'[23] – and he was held in custody by the Gestapo for four months. His son Albrecht was dragged before Hitler and asked to account for himself.

Albrecht wrote a report about his contacts with the Duke of Hamilton – whom Hess had briefly met at the Olympics – and the letter he wrote to the British peer on Hess's behalf that outlined proposals for peace between the two countries. As a result of this confession, Albrecht was imprisoned for two months at Gestapo HQ in Berlin and fired from his job. Fearing further harassment, Albrecht took refuge in the Bavarian mountains.

Hess's own version of events did not mention Albrecht Haushofer or his father. In an official statement Hess made to his British captors, he explained his reasons for taking such precipitous action: 'After the end of the war in France, Hitler made an offer to reach an understanding with England; but this was turned down. This served to make me more sure than ever that my plan must be put into practice' to prevent 'an endless line of children's coffins with weeping mothers behind them, both English and German; and another line of coffins of mothers with mourning children.'[24]

Hess's concern for the lives of the innocent did not extend to Soviet civilians; he was fully aware that Hitler was about to launch the long-awaited invasion of the Soviet Union – scheduled for that summer – and realised that the campaign would be waged with unprecedented savagery. By attempting to convince the British to lay down their weapons, thereby removing the threat of a two-front war, Hess was doing what he could to help Hitler annihilate his Bolshevik enemies. In his letter to Hitler, Hess acknowledged that his 'project' had only 'a very small chance of success' and was likely to end 'in failure'. If so, Hess thought the best way for Hitler to avoid any 'detrimental results' and 'deny all responsibility' was to heap the blame on him and tell the world that he 'was *crazy*'.[25]

Whether it was down to Hess's suggestion or not, this was the explanation given by the regime as it attempted to neutralise speculation about what had happened, downplay its significance and minimise the effect of the propaganda being produced by the British media. Goebbels was in charge of getting the message out there, and he had no doubts about who was responsible for the fiasco: 'Professor Haushofer and Hess's wife were the evil geniuses in this affair … the whole thing can be traced back to his mystic obsession with healthy living and all that nonsense about eating grass … I'd like to give a good thrashing to that wife of his!'

On 14 May, the main Nazi newspaper – under Goebbels's direction – referred to Hess's 'delusions' and criticised his reliance on 'magnetic healers' and 'astrologists'. This was bad news for Hess's personal astrologer Ernst Schulte-Strathaus, who was arrested that afternoon. Allegedly, Strathaus had made a series of positive predictions about Hess's mission, one in January, one in March, and one the day before Hess flew off. Strathaus was interrogated for two weeks, then moved to Gestapo HQ in Berlin where he was placed in solitary confinement for eleven months before being transferred to Sachsenhausen concentration camp; he was released after two miserable years there.

On 16 May, Goebbels observed that 'the Hess affair is still a big talking point' but 'the rumours are cancelling themselves out'. The following day, he was pleased to note that 'the public is slowly calming down and already jokes about it are doing the rounds'.[26] But the jokes showed how confused and bewildered the German people were; Hess had always been the reliable stalwart, the dependable man at Hitler's side. After all, he gave the Christmas radio address every year and now they were meant to believe he'd gone mad. One joke ran: Two friends meet in a concentration camp, and one asks the other 'Why are you here'? Answer: 'Because on May 5th I said to someone that Hess was crazy. And why are you here?' Answer: 'Because on the 15th I said he wasn't crazy.'[27]

Hess was definitely not a well man. He was suffering from severe hypochondria. After he landed in Scotland, the British Medical Research Council analysed the twenty-eight different sorts of medicine Hess had brought with him. There was an elixir for his gall bladder, opium derivatives for pain, aspirin for headaches, atropine for colic, barbiturates to stay awake, amphetamines for fatigue and a saline mixture for constipation. In addition, there were 'mixtures of unknown products made up along homeopathic lines' that were 'so diluted it's impossible to say what they are'.[28]

11

CASUALTIES

At around 4 p.m. on 10 June 1941, twelve days before the largest invasion force ever assembled – 3 million German soldiers plus another half a million foreign troops – rolled like a tidal wave into the Soviet Union, a terrifying storm hit the Berghof. According to the housekeeper, it had been 'an unbelievably hot day' with 'a heavy storm brewing in the north' when 'all of a sudden it started getting dark everywhere, as if it were a real solar eclipse' and there was 'an incredible crack' accompanied by 'a deafening explosion'. A bolt of lightning had obliterated the 33ft-long pole – adorned with a huge swastika flag – which jutted proudly out of the Berghof, leaving 'thousands of wood splinters' the size of 'match-sticks' scattered everywhere.[1]

Stunned, the housekeeper was frantically trying to figure out what to do when a call came in from Bormann; he'd seen the lightning strike from his house down the hill. Bormann instructed the housekeeper to remove the identical flagpole that stood in the car park and use it as a replacement and warned him not to breathe a word to anybody in case this freakish accident was interpreted as a bad omen, a warning of imminent disaster.

Dealing with this minor emergency was but one of the many tasks Bormann performed in his role as the Obersalzburg estate manager. His pride and joy was the 200-acre Manor Farm. Though the poor quality of soil on the lower slopes made it difficult to grow crops, the farm's cattle and pigs provided the Obersalzburg residents with meat and dairy products, the chickens laid eggs, and an apple orchard produced cider. There was also a greenhouse for fruit and vegetables and mushrooms sprouting in the Berghof cellars.

Yet both Bormann and his master were increasingly absent. After the invasion of the Soviet Union, Hitler moved to a series of Führer HQs; first, he based himself at the Wolf's Lair, then the following year he moved to Werewolf; both were massive concrete bunkers buried deep in thick forests populated by swarms of mosquitoes. According to Christa Schroeder, Hitler's long-term secretary, those at the Wolf's Lair were at their worst in July, while Werewolf was blighted by 'the dangerous Anopheles strain whose bites can give you malaria'.[2] Bormann spent a lot of his time at both complexes, shuffling back and forth from Berlin.

With the two dominant males away from Obersalzburg, the Berghof increasingly became Eva's domain. With a select group of women to keep her company, Eva indulged her love of photography and shot hours of footage with her film camera, sunbathed on the terrace, and frequently went swimming in Lake Königsee, which was only 5 miles away. Aside from her own friends with whom she would run around Munich and invite to tea at the Berghof, two women who were part of the Nazi elite – Anna Brandt and Margarete Speer – were the most constant members of her little gang.

Anna Brandt caught the dictator's attention in the 1920s when she was a champion swimmer. Her speciality was backstroke; between 1924 and 1928 she won five national titles, broke seven German records and took part in the Amsterdam Olympics. Her achievements made her a celebrity and she graced the covers of newspapers and magazines. Anna was introduced to Hitler at his cottage in Obersalzburg and she joined the Nazi party before her husband did. Karl Brandt was made one of Hitler's personal doctors in the mid 1930s, had considerable influence over the regime's health policies and was overall head of the T4 euthanasia programme.

Margarete Speer was not a world–class athlete but she and her husband Albert enjoyed outdoor activities like hiking and camping; on their honeymoon they went canoeing. At the same time, they were fans of the theatre, literature and classical music. Speer's father was a successful architect while Margarete's was a master joiner with his own small firm, and the young couple had to overcome his parents' misgivings about their son marrying beneath him. Speer, who'd taken up his father's profession, first heard Hitler speak at his university. Intrigued, he joined the party. Initially, Goebbels was his patron, but then Hitler adopted him and came to treat Speer like a long-lost son.

With much of her time occupied by her offspring, Gerda was on the fringes of Eva's group. Though her eldest son was now at an exclusive and extremely strict boarding school – the National Socialist Education Institution – her most recent child had been born in October 1940 and she had another son in March 1942, followed by one more in September 1943. As her other six kids got older, Gerda, the qualified kindergarten teacher, took a serious interest in their education, recording their progress in letters to her husband as if she was completing an end of term report.

A sign of Eva's growing assertiveness was the offer of help she extended to Ilse not long after Hess's flight; 'I like you and your husband best of all. Please tell me if things become unbearable, because I can speak to the Führer without Bormann knowing anything about it.'[3]

Allegedly, Eva intervened with Hitler to stop Bormann from having Ilse arrested, ended his surveillance of her and demanded she receive a monthly pension. Though Eva insisted Ilse was treated with dignity and respect, Bormann did everything he could to make Ilse's life difficult. He blocked and delayed the payments due to her, tried unsuccessfully to have her Munich home confiscated and haggled with her over the furniture in the Berlin residence, charging her twice what it was worth. Ilse may have been shielded from worse treatment than this, but she was still an internal exile, a pariah with an uncertain future, her destiny out of her hands.

Her husband was also at the mercy of forces beyond his control. He'd put his case to a number of dignitaries, including the Duke of Hamilton, but his pleas fell on stony ground. The British government had no intention of coming to terms with Hitler. Hess had made a fundamental error of judgement. Like others in the Nazi elite, he believed that Britain was ruled by its aristocracy; as long as you secured the backing of a few important lords, you were bound to get what you asked for.

Demoralised and dejected, Hess attempted suicide. At around midnight on 15 June 1941, Hess distracted his guard by asking for a whisky to help him sleep. Dressed in his Luftwaffe uniform and polished leather boots, he slipped out of his room, crept onto the landing, and threw himself over the bannister. He dropped 25ft and broke his leg on impact. In July, after observing Hess for eighteen days, one of his psychiatrists wrote that Hess believed 'poison of a subtle kind' was being added to 'his food and medicine' that affected 'his brains and nerves' with the 'intention of driving him insane'. On the basis of his 'bizarre ideas of persecution and torture', the psychiatrist concluded that Hess was paranoid.[4]

Ilse had no idea about what her husband was going through. A glimmer of hope appeared on the horizon that summer when Hitler agreed to let her write to Hess, although this gesture was not entirely benevolent. The Nazi leadership were anxious to have some way of monitoring Hess's situation and Schellenberg was put in charge of handling the correspondence: 'I had to organise measures for him and his wife to write to each other. After a time, the British allowed him to correspond, within limits, by the way of the International Red Cross in Switzerland, and it fell to me to supervise the arrangement.'[5] But as it took up to eight months for Ilse's letters to reach her husband, it would be some time before she got a reply.

The final phase of retribution for Hess's actions was set in motion by Heydrich in early June 1941 and targeted the purveyors of 'occult doctrines and so-called occult science'. Lina's husband relished this particularly assignment. Himmler's affection for mystics and prophets irritated him; Heydrich thought they were misguided fools who exerted a malign influence on society. On his hit list were 'astrologers, occultists, spiritualists, supporters of occult radiation theories, sooth-sayers' and 'faith healers'.[6] Hundreds were arrested by the Gestapo. Thousands of books, magazines and pamphlets were seized. Goebbels, who supported the clampdown, couldn't resist making a joke at their expense; in his diary he noted that 'not a single clairvoyant predicted that he would be arrested. A poor advertisement for their profession!'[7] However, most of those detained were released after a short stay in a camp, having been beaten and humiliated, while *Aktion Hess*, as it was known, failed to undermine their popularity: in 1943 there were an esti-mated 3,000 tarot card readers in Berlin.

Much as Heydrich enjoyed locking up astrologists, his main con-cern at the time was preparing for the invasion of the Soviet Union. On 17 June, he assembled the leaders of four Einsatzgruppen task forces and gave them unambiguous instructions for the coming campaign: they were to act with 'unprecedented severity'; all Jews in the service of the Communist Party were to be 'eliminated', plus all other Soviet officials and 'radical elements'.[8]

Heydrich's orders dovetailed neatly with the responsibility he was given by Goering on the 31st to find 'a total solution of the Jewish question in the German sphere of influence in Europe'. By the end of 1941, Heydrich's Einsatzgruppen had butchered 500,000–800,000 people, most of whom were Jewish. Dispatching their victims with bullets and blunt objects, the killings took a heavy toll on the perpe-trators, quite a number of whom went insane or committed suicide. As a result, Heydrich and his boss began considering a less hands-on approach to mass murder and looked to the euthanasia programme for inspiration.

On 20 July, Heydrich re-joined his fighter squadron – without Himmler's authorisation – which was operating over the Soviet Union. Two days later, just after 2 p.m., his plane was hit by flak, his engine malfunctioned and he was forced to make an emergency landing behind enemy lines. Forty-eight hours passed before he was found by mem-bers of an Einsatzgruppen death squad who'd killed forty-five Jews and thirty other hostages on the day they found him. Lina remembered that her husband arrived home 'dirty, unshaven and very upset'.[9]

After this adventure, Heydrich was grounded and took no further part in the campaign, which was making giant inroads into Soviet territory, seizing the Baltic states, Belorussia, and driving deep into Ukraine. By the autumn, the Germans had captured over 3 million Soviet soldiers and had reached the outskirts of Moscow before grinding to a halt.

In the midst of all this, Heydrich managed to find time for fencing, an hour every morning and more at weekends. Earlier that year he'd become president of the International Fencing Federation after out-manoeuvring his rivals. In June and July, while he was in the Soviet Union with Himmler, he was training for the German National Championship; he came fifth. During September, he was preparing for a sabre-fencing match with Hungary, the reigning champions, and won his three bouts. This packed agenda was guaranteed to make Lina miserable: 'It was terrible for me. He was never, never at home.'[10] Even when her husband was in Berlin, he continued to go out on the town at night, trawling the bars and clubs. On one occasion, Heydrich kept the happily married Schellenberg up until 5 a.m., hopping from one venue to another, engaging 'in stupid conversations' with the bar staff, who all 'knew him and feared him, while pretending devotion'.[11]

During March 1941, Margaret went on a two-week tour of German Red Cross facilities in France and Belgium. Travelling alongside Emmy's sister-in-law, Margaret covered a lot of ground and visited various soldiers' homes – the largest of which was at Amiens – a number of field hospitals and several railway stations that handled incoming wounded. Along the way, Margaret was also able to take in regular tourist attractions; chateaus in the Loire, the cathedral at Chartres, the palace at Versailles, and a day of shopping and sightseeing in Paris, where she stayed at the Hotel Ritz and was wined and dined by the local SS chieftains. Overall, Margaret was 'very pleased', and thought 'the trip was very harmonious'.[12]

Not long after, on 22 July 1941, Himmler treated her and Gudrun to a tour of the vast herb and spice garden for homeopathic medicines he'd established at Dachau. Work had begun in 1938 to drain 200 acres of marshy land near the camp. Some 1,000 prisoners toiled and sweated to lay garden soil, mixed soil and sand. Using only natural manure and compost – fertilisers and pesticides were forbidden by Himmler – the garden, which the camp inmates called the 'plantation', produced thyme, basil, estragon, rosemary, peppermint, caraway, marjoram, sage, and gladioli for its vitamin C.

On 23 January 1939, the plantation came under the management of the German Research Institute for Nutrition and Food Provision (one of the many SS businesses) with the aim of supplying herbal medicines to domestic and foreign markets, carrying out experimental research and maintaining laboratories, and selling livestock, honey from its bee colony and fruit and vegetables – potatoes, leeks, tomatoes, cucumbers, swedes, and onions – from its greenhouses.

Gudrun wrote to her father after their visit and told him she'd seen 'the large nursery, the mill, the bees' and 'how all the herbs were processed', gushing about how 'magnificent' and 'lovely' it all was.[13] For Margaret, the plantation was the end result of the plans she and her husband had nurtured in the early days of their relationship, the homeopathic nurse and the agriculture student who wanted their own small herb garden. To see their dream realised on such a grand scale must have been deeply gratifying. Not once did she stop to consider what it cost in human suffering: the back-breaking work, long hours, poor food rations, severe cold and outbreaks of deadly diseases.

Margaret's enjoyment of the day was probably undermined by the fact she was still suffering the after-effects of a domestic accident a month earlier:

The water heater exploded while I sat in the bath tub and the porcelain shattered all over me. Had to get stitches that night at the hospital in Tegernsee. I bled like a pig and had to be bandaged in six places; they spent two hours on my right arm and on the left side of my abdomen there is a big wound, which got infected and often hurt terribly.

On 19 July, Professor Gebhardt made a house call to see how she was doing and was satisfied with her condition; a few weeks later he wrote her a 'very calming letter'. By then, she was 'doing much better', and thought things were 'gradually getting back to normal'.[14]

However, this meant dealing with her errant stepson – 'terrible things are happening continuously' – and with her worries about Gudrun, who'd had her appendix out in March, who was 'doing very poorly at school',[15] and who was missing her father terribly; though she had a party for her birthday with nine guests and loads of presents, Himmler couldn't make it. Instead, he sent her photos of him playing tennis in Berlin.

Reading the correspondence he exchanged with Margaret that autumn, it's hard to find any sign that their marriage was irretrievably broken. In one letter, Margaret told 'her good husband' that she and Gudrun were waiting for him 'with so much longing';[16] for Margaret's birthday, he sent her coffee and roses. But at the same time, Himmler's mistress, Hedwig, was expecting their first child and he was busy plotting their future together.

Hedwig described these plans in a letter to her sister: 'As soon as the war is over he wants to buy us a house in the country on a piece of land', that could be made 'profitable' by planting 'a small tree nursery' or 'breeding small animals' or 'cultivating berries'. Enchanting as this was, Hedwig was an urban creature and had her doubts: 'The idea is not bad. I have not quite decided about it yet. It would certainly be a huge adjustment, and I would have to learn so much.'[17]

On 13 February 1942, Hedwig gave birth to a son named Helge at the Hohenlychen clinic. Professor Gebhardt was present at the birth and became the child's godfather. It was now a matter of some urgency to find Hedwig a secure and appropriate home in which to raise her child, especially as her parents had disowned her. Himmler found her a cosy woodman's lodge in the Mecklenburg forest, about 50 miles north of Berlin, with lakes dotted around it and a tiny village nearby.

Hedwig's new residence was 5 miles away from Ravensbrück concentration camp, the first SS facility solely for women prisoners. Opened in May 1939, by August 1940 there were 3,200 inmates lodged in crowded barracks with around fifty female guards watching over them and high-voltage electric fences to deter any thoughts of escape.

Also 5 miles away, but in the opposite direction, was the Hohenlychen clinic. That Christmas, Professor Gebhardt wrote Hedwig a fawning letter:

> When I think back to the hour of the birth of your little son, my god-child, and on all the responsibility and joy that we felt at the time, then I am at a loss for words to express myself … I can only give you the assurance that I will endeavour to be an absolutely faithful follower of Himmler.[18]

Did Margaret know about her husband's love child? A few weeks after the birth, Himmler spent three days at Lake Tegernsee. Whether he told her then or not, Margaret did eventually become aware of what had transpired: 'Sometimes I cannot believe what I live through each day. We poor women.' A later diary entry was even more explicit: 'Surrounded by lies and betrayal. I can't bear it any more … I am always alone.'[19]

One evening in mid September, Lina went to the cinema with Schellenberg's wife Irene and returned home to find him and her husband breaking open the champagne to toast Heydrich's new appointment as the 'Protector of Bohemia and Moravia', the Nazi-run chunk of the former Czechoslovakia. The Protectorate's armaments industry was crucial for the war effort but production was down due to sabotage. Heydrich's mission was to get the assembly lines back on track, something he achieved with a mixture of the carrot and the stick; he arrested and executed hundreds of subversives, real and imagined, while increasing food and beer rations for key workers.

Though this was a significant career move for her husband, Lina was less than happy when he departed on 27 September 1941, particularly when she realised she was pregnant again. Her mood improved, however, after it was decided that she and the children could join him in Prague. Three months later, Lina arrived at her new home, the imposing Prague Castle, and felt overwhelmed by the majesty of it all: 'I am standing at a window in the castle and looking down over the gleaming, golden city. I am seized by sublime feelings. I feel that I am no longer an ordinary human being. I am a princess in a fairy tale land.'[20]

Her initial euphoria wore off. The castle was too much like a museum for her tastes and she found the weight of its accumulated history oppressive. She longed for a space she could make her own for her family and husband to enjoy. Meanwhile, Heydrich was commuting back to Berlin two or three times a week. On one of these visits, he chaired the notorious Wansee Conference, during which representatives of various government and state departments were informed about the Final Solution and discussed the logistics and timetable for the eradication of all Europe's Jews.

Lina's desire for a more suitable domestic arrangement was finally answered and the family moved to a neo-classical manor house that had been seized from its Jewish owner by Heydrich's predecessor. Situated 12 miles north of Prague, a mere half an hour's drive away, the house had thirty refurbished and redecorated rooms with central heating, a 7-hectare garden and 125 hectares of forests. Concentration camp labour was drafted in to build a swimming pool.

As the family settled in, Lina was the happiest she'd been since the early days of her marriage. When he wasn't in Berlin, Heydrich was home every evening at a decent hour to be with her and play with the children. At weekends, Lina and her husband went riding; the kids had a pony; the boys got fencing lessons. Lina started collecting antique German porcelain. Some evenings, she helped Heydrich prepare his speeches, giving him advice and stern criticism. There were music evenings. The couple often had guests, including Heydrich's old friend Canaris and his wife Erika; Lina remembered their stay with some affection; 'they were happy days'. Otherwise, Heydrich 'liked being able to be less formal ... he stretched out on the sofa and read, often into the small hours'.[21]

There were also public events to attend. On 15 May 1942, Heydrich opened the city's first 'cultural festival' with works by Bruckner, Mozart and Dvorak, performed by the German Philharmonic Orchestra of Prague. In his programme notes, Heydrich stated that 'music' was 'the everlasting manifestation of the cultural workings of the German race'.[22]

On 21 February 1942, a British psychiatrist noted that Hess was displaying 'a distinct loss of memory'.[23] On the 27th, Major Foley – an officer from military intelligence who was familiar with Hess – observed similar symptoms and wondered if they were 'genuine or simulated'. Neither Major Foley nor the nurses believed that Hess was 'such a consummate actor that he is able to consistently pretend he has forgotten things which should have impressed themselves strongly on his memory'.[24] Hess's amnesia was a transitory phenomenon; his memory would slip in and out of place, his ability to recall events came and went from one day to the next. In his first letter to Ilse, dated 20 May 1942, he discussed the Nazis' war on cancer, reflected on the fact that his son Wolf was about to start school – 'it is almost impossible to think of him as a schoolboy, confronted for the first time with the serious side of life' – and made an unambiguous reference to the period before his flight, remembering Wolf as 'the tiny wide-eyed child who was sitting' in his nursery 'when I last saw him'.[25]

By then, Hess had been moved to a former mental hospital near Abergavenny in Wales that was being used to accommodate wounded soldiers. Hess had a whole wing to himself and was guarded by thirty men. He read a lot of Goethe, jotted down notes for an autobiography, and was sometimes allowed to take a walk after lunch. Hess found the 'colours of the landscape ... unusual and attractive' and relished witnessing the change of seasons as 'the red earth, lying between meadows and fields of green' turned 'yellowish ... when ripe'.[26]

Despite this apparently relaxed routine, Hess remained convinced the British were trying to poison him. He kept a secret record of what he believed was a systematic attempt by his captors to ruin his digestion and prevent his bowels from functioning properly with the overall aim of 'destroying his memory';[27] according to Hess there was caustic acid mixed in with his food, which was so salty that he got kidney infections, and poisons in his water that affected his ability to urinate. He was plagued by insomnia and had become hypersensitive to noise. Yet in his letters to Ilse, Hess never ranted or raved about his situation. His tone was always measured and thoughtful, even philosophical: 'The world is out of joint in every respect. But one day the joints will be fitted together again – and we too shall be reunited.'[28]

During 1942, Magda did her best to live up to her image as the First Lady of the Reich and performed a number of public duties. She visited a military hospital where 'the head physician was not able to handle the wounded right, and their morale is pretty low', and delivered a speech to 'a thousand Berlin women on Mother's Day'.[29] There was also a sequel to the home movie made for Goebbels's birthday two years earlier. The 1942 version was a much more professional effort and had been carefully planned; there was a classroom scene, humorous antics, the kids playing games and wearing Mickey Mouse masks, and a sequence showing the war hero Rommel – who was giving the British a pounding in North Africa – visiting the family at home. Unlike its predecessor, the film was pure propaganda.

Perhaps it was inevitable, but the truce between Magda and her husband did not last; slowly but surely the cracks reappeared. Magda was in her forties and all the years of sickness and ill health had taken their toll on her looks; Goebbels no longer desired her like he used to. He regarded her with affection, respected her intelligence and strength of character and probably loved her in his own utterly selfish and possessive way, but the erotic spark was gone, so he started cheating again. As Magda wearily conceded to her confidante Ello Quandt, 'I'm getting old. I often feel exhausted and I can't change matters. Those girls are twenty years younger than me and have not brought seven children into the world.'[30]

Goebbels began seeing his secretary. One night in February, Magda spotted her climbing from the garden into his study. Enraged, she threatened him with divorce and went to see her lawyer. However, Goebbels was able to talk her down. There was no repeat of the intense battle of wills that occurred over Lida Baarova; neither of them had the energy for that again, and Hitler had made it brutally clear what the consequences would be if they divorced. So Magda withdrew her challenge and didn't protest when the secretary came to their home for meals and private parties. In the end, the secretary dumped Goebbels because she was worried her fiancé would find out about the affair.

Unable to prevent her husband from sleeping around, Magda amused herself by playing tricks on his girlfriends. One of them used a special key to enter a passageway where the door was usually closed, so Magda had the locks changed. She prank-called another, informing her that Goebbels would send a car to meet her at a crossroads in the Grunewald forest at 11 p.m. Magda let her wait there for an hour before telling Goebbels what she'd done.

On 27 May 1942, the Heydrich household was moving at a more leisurely pace than usual; the previous night Lina and her husband had been the guests of honour at a special event held at the Wallenstein Palace as part of the Prague cultural festival. That evening, alongside an opera, the programme featured a violin concerto written by Heydrich's late father and played by a quartet of his ex-students from Halle. Afterwards, a reception was held for guests and performers at the swish Hotel Avalon. Lina remembered that Heydrich was in his element, 'a master of etiquette, entertaining, interested in everyone, a charming conversationalist'.[31]

After a late breakfast, Heydrich strolled the grounds with Lina and played with his kids. At 10 a.m. he climbed into his dark green Mercedes and his SS chauffeur set off for the capital. At a crossroads on the outskirts of Prague, Heydrich's car was ambushed by two members of the Czech resistance, who'd been parachuted in from Britain some months earlier. One had a gun, but it jammed; the other threw a bomb that landed on the back seat and exploded, tearing holes in Heydrich's midriff. Bleeding heavily, Heydrich fired a couple of shots at the fleeing assassins, collapsed, and was rushed to hospital in a baker's van.

Two Czech doctors immediately extracted a small piece of metal from the wound in his back and sent him for an X-ray, which revealed puncture wounds, damage to the pancreas, and signs of a foreign body – possibly a bomb splinter or a piece of the car's upholstery – in the spleen area, which would require another operation. Heydrich wanted it performed by a German surgeon, so his Czech carers tracked down a suitable candidate and he got to work at around midday. A steel fragment, 8cm x 8cm, was removed from his spleen, but bits of leather and horse-hair were still embedded in Heydrich's guts. Nevertheless, he seemed fit enough and they stitched him up and put him to bed. Lina arrived soon after. Hitler phoned the hospital at 12.30 p.m. Professor Gebhardt flew in that night. On the morning of 31 May, Himmler showed up. Lina brought her husband home-cooked meals. Heydrich seemed to be on the mend.

But on 2 June his temperature soared to 102°F (39°C). At this point, one of Hitler's personal doctors – who'd arrived on the scene to give his verdict on Heydrich's recovery – suggested they use the drug sulphona-mide to fight the infection. Professor Gebhardt rejected this suggestion and on the 3rd he phoned Himmler to tell him the fever was receding and the wound was draining freely. After lunch, however, Heydrich lost consciousness. Lina rushed to his bedside. In the early hours of the 4th, he came round and deliriously uttered his last words to Lina: 'Go back to Fehmarn.'[32] Distraught and overwhelmed, Lina took a sedative. By the time she awoke, he was dead. Heydrich passed away at 4.30 a.m., killed by septicaemia.

When Hitler heard the news he couldn't contain his anger. Why had Heydrich ignored protocol? Driving about with his car roof down with no bodyguards or SS escorts? All the top Nazis had bulletproof vehicles and their own protection squads. How could he have been so irrespon-sible? Reflecting on her husband's casual attitude to his own safety, Lina was convinced he'd harboured a death wish: 'It seemed to me he had long embraced the idea of dying soon … I know it sounds trite, but I believe he wanted to sacrifice himself.'[33]

For two days, his coffin sat in the courtyard at Prague Castle. Tens of thousands of ethnic Germans and Czechs filed past to take a final peek at their 'Protector'; no doubt some of them were just making sure that he was dead. On 9 June, the coffin went by train to Berlin for a ceremony that began in the Mosaic Room at the Reich Chancellery with Wagner's 'Twilight of the Gods' playing in the background.

Himmler spoke first and praised his colleague's steely determination and unflinching dedication to his work: 'I know what it cost this man to be so hard and severe despite the softness of his heart: to make tough decisions in order to act in accordance with the law of the SS.'[34] Hitler went next. Visibly moved, he kept it brief; Heydrich was 'one of the best National Socialists' and 'one of the greatest opponents of all the enemies of the Empire' who'd 'died a martyr for the preservation and protection of the Reich'.[35]

His oration finished, Hitler passed by Heydrich's two sons – who were in the front row next to Professor Gebhardt – and patted them on the cheek. The coffin was then taken away to the strains of Beethoven's *Eroica*, and a carriage drawn by six black horses ferried Heydrich's corpse to the Invalides cemetery where a swastika was draped over the coffin, there was a three-gun salute, and all the senior SS officers and police leaders solemnly gathered at the graveside for a final tribute.

Lina was not in any condition to attend the funeral. Her nerves were shattered and she had the health of her unborn child to consider; on 23 July, she gave birth to her second daughter, Marte. In Heydrich's old stomping ground, eighteen Czech towns were renamed in his honour, along with dozens of streets in the capital. A year later, a bronze bust of him was erected at the spot where the attack took place.

The retribution dished out by Heydrich's successor, Kurt Daluege – a hard-headed, crude and violent SS man – was comprehensive. The assassins and their team were cornered and eventually killed in a church crypt in the city centre; 3,188 Czech civilians were arrested and 1,327 of them sentenced to death; 4,000 others were deposited in camps. The most shocking atrocity occurred at the village of Lidice: all the adult male inhabitants were executed, the children were farmed out to SS orphanages and the women were transported to Ravensbrück.

At the Hohenlychen clinic, not far from the Lidice women's final destination, Professor Gebhardt was also facing the consequences of

Heydrich's death; Gebhardt had refused to use the drug sulphonamide to combat the infection that killed him and now he feared that he might get the blame.

In order to demonstrate that his judgement had been correct, Gebhardt organised a series of experiments at Ravensbrück. Trials began at the end of July. The first victims were male prisoners from Sachsenhausen concentration camp. Their legs were fractured and infected with virulent bacteria; half of them were given sulphonamide, the other half nothing at all. The results were mixed, so Gebhardt selected around seventy Polish women from Ravensbrück – known as 'the rabbits' – and subjected them to horrific treatment: large incisions were made in their legs, and dirt, small pieces of wood, fragments of glass and, in one case, a curved surgical needle, were inserted in the gaping wounds.

Margaret's boss at the German Red Cross, Ernst-Robert Grawitz, even suggested shooting the women with bullets in order to reproduce battlefield injuries, but Gebhardt decided to stick with severe tissue damage. In the end, Gebhardt got what he wanted; five of the women who'd taken the sulphonamide died, confirming his claim that the drug was ineffective. Gebhardt presented his findings to over 200 army doctors at the Third Working Conference of Advisory Physicians, 24–26 May 1943, and his assistant gave a lecture on 'Special Experiments with Sulphonamides'.

During July and August 1942, Margaret spent four weeks in Latvia at the town of Mitau, 20 miles from Riga, for the anniversary of its liberation from the Soviets. Though she found the trip 'interesting and instructive'[36] and she visited a SS-run field hospital, she came down with smallpox and was in bed most of the time.

Back at Lake Tegernsee, and recovering from her illness, Margaret was on the receiving end of care packages sent by Himmler that were stuffed with basic household goods and domestic products that were in extremely short supply and beyond the reach of the majority of the population: tissues, wax paper, toilet paper, two little lamps, two wash cloths, a wooden tray and a wooden bowl, a laundry bag for travelling, scouring powder and an old toothbrush for polishing shoes. He also sent her so much caviar that she didn't know what to do with it; should she give it away?

In September, Margaret returned to Berlin to resume her German Red Cross duties, which was good for her morale: 'Without any work outside the house, I could not live through the war.'[37] That month, she wrote to her husband about Gudrun and the difficulties she was having finding anybody at school who was prepared to be her friend. In the evenings, Margaret filled the lonely empty hours sewing, reading and making preserves.

Every Christmas, Emmy hosted two parties. One was at the Goering's official residence in Berlin, where 300–400 guests mingled beneath coloured decorations hanging from chandeliers, stood next to walls covered with the branches of pine trees and listened to Emmy's friends from the Berlin Opera singing carols. The other was at Carinhall, a more intimate affair for family – which included Carin's son Thomas and her sister – and the staff. A well-known actor from the State Opera dressed up as Santa Claus, there was a ballet performance, and on Christmas Eve a professional organist played 'Silent Night' before everyone opened their presents.

That year, the festivities were overshadowed by the unfolding disaster at Stalingrad. The German spring and summer offensives had pushed its armies even further into the Soviet Union and a thrust to take this industrial city on the Volga began in the autumn; the whole Sixth Army was sucked into an urban quagmire, bitterly contesting every inch of the ruined city, reduced to rubble by Goering's Luftwaffe. As the Germans battled away, the Soviets counterattacked, rolling back their lightly defended flanks and trapping them in Stalingrad.

All the while, Goering had assured Hitler that his planes could continue to supply the beleaguered troops with what they needed to survive and fight on as winter asserted its fearsome grip. However, Goering's mission of mercy was doomed from the start. It would take 300 flights a day to fulfil the soldiers' needs, but the weather made that impossible; in freezing temperatures aircraft couldn't start their engines, there was ice on the wings, zero visibility and heavy snow meant planes had to be dug out before take-off. To make matters worse, the airfields were in range of Soviet guns and planes. In the effort to feed the troops, 488 transport planes were lost and 1,000 aircrew killed.

As a consequence, the surrounded army starved and eventually its commander defied Hitler's no surrender order and capitulated on 31 January 1943. This was Hitler's first major defeat of the war, one from which he would never recover; the momentum that had taken him so far had gone.

12

UNDER PRESSURE

On 18 February 1943, Magda was in the huge Berlin crowd gathered to witness her husband give a speech – also broadcast on the radio – in which he called for total war; the absolute mobilisation of every facet of German society for the titanic struggle ahead. Anything that wasn't useful, any economic or social activity that didn't contribute directly to the war effort, or diverted resources away from it, was to be terminated.

Goebbels directed some of his invective at women and urged them to 'devote all their energy to waging war, by filling jobs wherever possible to free men for action!'[1] By that point, over 50 per cent of the workforce was female but Goebbels and other leading figures were keen to maximise any untapped potential. Compulsory labour conscription was introduced for women aged 17–45, although the recruitment drive was hampered by the exceptions available for those with poor health or difficult domestic situations. By the end of June, 3.1 million women had registered at employment offices but only 1,235,000 were suitable for work, and half of those only part-time. The shortfall was filled by hundreds of thousands of labourers imported from across Europe, many of them women, who endured unspeakable living conditions and inhumanly long hours.

Inspired by her husband's words, Magda was determined to make a contribution: Goebbels noted that she was 'absolutely uncompromising and radical on the question of total war'.[2] Magda found herself a position at a local factory – owned by Telefunken, a major communications company –

and commuted there by tram. The demands of the job were immediately too much for her, and by 1 March she was back in the Dresden clinic again.

On 18 March Goebbels noted that Magda was 'having a hard time recovering from her illness … the war depresses her not only physically but psychologically'.[3] Her heavy mood was not improved by the fact that her husband had told her about what was going on in the East. A year earlier, Goebbels had met with Hitler and got a clear indication of what the answer to the Jewish question would be: 'The Führer was as uncompromising as ever. The Jews must be got out of Europe, if necessary by applying the most brutal methods.'[4]

Himmler had assumed full control of the Final Solution after Heydrich's assassination; on 19 July 1942, Himmler launched *Aktion Reinhard* – named in honour of his fallen comrade – to exterminate Poland's Jews. The first transports to Treblinka death camp, which was equipped with gas chambers and crematoriums, began three days later. Two other killing sites, Belzec and Sobibor, were soon up and running. By the summer of 1943, when *Aktion Reinhard* was wound down, around 2 million people had been murdered.

Though Hitler had instructed the senior figures who knew about the camps not to discuss them with their wives, Goebbels shared the burden with Magda and she spoke to Ello Quandt about his revelations: 'It's terrible all the things he's telling me now. I simply can't bear it any more. You can't imagine the awful things he's tormenting me with.' But she was sworn to secrecy – 'I have no-one to pour my heart out to. I'm not supposed to talk to anyone' – and stopped herself from giving Ello the whole terrible truth.

Bewildered by what she'd learned, Magda was having doubts about Hitler: 'He no longer listens to reason … And all one can do is stand by and watch what is happening. It's all going to end badly – it can't possibly end otherwise.'[5]

Ilse was at home in Munich when the city experienced its first significant bombing raid; on the night of 20 September 1942, sixty-eight bombers dropped their deadly cargo, killing 140 civilians and injuring over 400. Ilse had no intention of abandoning the city at the first sign of danger. However, by early 1943, she'd had enough of her Munich home; it was too expensive to manage and too big for just her and her son Wolf. Instead, she wanted to convert it into a convalescent home for wounded soldiers. In March, she asked if she could proceed with her plan. The answer was no; Himmler wrote to her and explained that 'the Führer's decision concerning your house is very clear. You should keep the house … and not sell it. You may ask for all the expenses necessary to keep up the house so that you are not burdened in maintaining the valuable piece of property.'[6]

But Ilse knew this was a false promise; any money for the house would have to come through Bormann, and she was well aware of how tricky that would be. So she boxed up her possessions, boarded up the main house and moved into the vacant chauffeur's apartment; her husband's extensive library was stored at their small chalet about 100 miles from Munich.

The city was rocked by another raid in March 1943, much bigger than the previous one; nearly twice as many of its citizens were killed or wounded, while 9,000 were left homeless. Over in Wales, Hess was apparently oblivious to the threat his wife and son were facing. In his letters to Ilse, he focused on Wolf's development, regretting the fact that his talents lay 'in the direction of technical science', when he and Ilse had always hoped that their child would become 'a great poet or musician who would bring happiness to mankind'.[7]

Only once did Hess describe how he felt about what happened to his personal staff, his friends and his family after his departure. Though their persecution angered him, Hess appreciated that Hitler was 'under a nervous strain hard to imagine – a strain responsible for states of excitement, in which decisions have been made which would not have been made in normal times'.[8] He was also 'happy to see' from her letters that Ilse remained loyal to Hitler and that nothing had changed in her '*inward relationship* to the man with whose destiny we have been so closely linked in joy and suffering, for more than twenty years'.[9]

One of the many restrictions imposed on civilian life by the pursuit of total war was the ban on the manufacture and sale of cosmetics. As a woman who was fond of her make-up, Eva was less than pleased by this measure, and having made her feelings known, she made sure her supply was not interrupted. Equally, Eva was not affected when the same thing happened with sanitary towels; by the end of the year, there were none available and ordinary women had to come up with home-made alternatives.

The rationing of clothing made no impact on her either. Eva continued to wear three new dresses a day – one for lunch, one for tea, and one for dinner. Like Emmy and Magda, she was able to source her outfits from a handful of German designers and French and Italian fashion houses. The clothing ration that applied to the rest of the population came into effect in 1939. Every individual was given vouchers worth 150 points to last them a year, reduced in 1942 to 120 every sixteen months. Under this system, a winter coat was 100 points, a woman's skirt 20, a blouse another 20, and it cost 40 for a dress or a new pair of stockings.

Despite all her privileges, Eva suffered from Hitler's prolonged absences. On Christmas Day that year, while Gerda spent the after-noon with her kids having 'a birthday party for all the new dolls and for the old rejuvenated ones, complete with cocoa and cake', Eva was all alone at the Berghof. Gerda felt sorry for Eva, but also for Hitler, who had to put up with 'telephone conversations and letters impreg-nated with this mood of hers instead of something positive that would make him feel happy'.[10]

While Bormann was away almost as much as his boss, Gerda and her husband constantly wrote to each other and their letters demonstrate the intense bond between them. Bormann called her 'the superlative of all the women I know or ever knew'.[11] Contemplating an upcoming visit from him, Gerda was 'overjoyed at the thought of having you here again. So full of longing to have you in my arms and not let you go.'[12] Yet for all the sweet nothings, Bormann could still treat Gerda like she was his servant. During a big reception at their Obersalzburg home, Hitler's chauffeur remembered that at 'about two in the morning Bormann suddenly decided he should wear a smoking jacket' and 'asked for a particular shirt to go with it that he had worn a few days ago'. When Gerda informed him that his shirt was in the wash, her husband 'erupted into a screaming fit'[13] and ordered her to go straight to their Munich residence and bring him back the type of shirt he wanted.

Nevertheless, Gerda increasingly saw herself as a senior figure in the Nazi elite. Her husband had been made secretary to the Führer on 12 April 1943; to get to Hitler you had to go through Bormann first, and he now felt strong enough to move against Gerda's estranged father Walter Buch, who was still head of the Nazi Party Court. In autumn 1943, Hitler put Bormann in charge of party jurisprudence and the court lost its independence. According to Buch, Bormann had the 'power to decide the court's judgements' beforehand. Though Buch 'opposed the change', his protests fell on deaf ears; Hitler had 'stopped listening to him years ago'.[14]

Gerda demonstrated her growing sense of self-importance by befriending Himmler's mistress Hedwig, beginning a correspondence after meeting her. In one letter, she commented on the photographs of Himmler that Hedwig had sent her: 'I have never seen such a relaxed picture of him as these together with his son.'[15] The fact that Himmler was married did not bother Gerda. For her it was the natural order of things: Himmler's behaviour was merely the healthy expression of a man's biological need to reproduce. Her open-minded attitude applied to her own marriage. Bormann never made any secret of the fact that he chased any stray female who happened to wander across his path. During an excursion on a steamer boat, one of Hitler's valets saw Bormann through a half-open cabin door with his trousers round his ankles and his boots still on, having sex with a 'prominent lady'.[16]

Up until 1943, Bormann's infidelities were largely one-night stands or short-term liaisons; once he'd satisfied himself, Bormann lost interest. However, the actress Manja Behrens got under his skin. Born 1914 in Dresden, Manja was the daughter of a lawyer and an actress, and briefly studied English in Prague. Until 1935, she worked as a dental assistant while taking private acting lessons before making her stage debut. Soon after, she appeared in two films: *Stronger than Paragraphs*, where she played a woman in love with the man who murdered her uncle and is faced with a dilemma when the wrong person is arrested and sentenced to ten years; and *Susanna in the Bath*, a sexed up melodrama where an art teacher imagines her nude, paints the results, exhibits the picture and causes a scandal.

Before she could make another movie, Manja's screen career abruptly ended when she rejected Goebbels's attempt to seduce her, telling him she'd rather clean stages than go to bed with him. Without any more film work, she went back to the theatre, did a couple more plays and was introduced to Bormann at a ball in 1940. He found her attractive but nothing happened. They met again in similar circumstances in October 1943; he was overwhelmed by desire, and confessed to Gerda a few months later that he 'fell madly in love with her'.[17] With his usual bull-headed determination, he kept pestering Manja until she gave in.

But Manja was concerned about Gerda's feelings. She needn't have worried. Gerda was glad to welcome Manja into the family – 'I am so fond of M ... and the children too love her very much, all of them' – and was excited at the prospect of establishing a polygamous house-hold together:

> One year M has a child, and the next year I do, so that you will always have a wife that is mobile. Then we'll put all the children together in a house on a lake, and live together, and the wife who is not having a child will always be able to come and stay with you in Obersalzburg or Berlin.

To put this arrangement on a proper legal footing, Gerda suggested they draw up a new marriage contract that would give Manja the same rights as Gerda, something she believed could be repeated on a national scale as part of regime policy to boost the birth rate: 'It would be a good thing if a law were to be made at the end of this war ... which would entitle healthy, valuable men to have two wives.'[18] Keen to put her ideas into practice, Gerda invited Manja to stay with them in Obersalzburg, but the threesome proved unsustainable, Manja struggled to adjust and fled the love nest. By 1944, she was working in an armaments factory doing fifteen-hour shifts.

After her husband's assassination, Lina spent the summer recovering at Fehmarn. Having decided to make her future in the Protectorate, she put her Berlin house on the market and returned to Prague on 7 December 1942. Technically, her Czech manor house belonged to the Reich, but when Hitler gave her permission to stay there indefinitely, she declined his offer; Lina didn't want to own it herself, fearing it would cost too much for to manage on her widow's pension and any income she might earn, so instead she rented the estate.

Rather than dwell on Heydrich's death or wallow in self-pity, Lina showed her resilience and determination to keep fighting. In a letter to her parents, she said her decision to return to the scene of the crime was 'a political commitment' and she was proud of the fact she was 'perhaps the only woman in public life who has not disappeared into anonymity through the death of her husband'.[19] On a trip to Denmark, she argued with the SS chief there about his policies, and was planning similar interventions in Norway and France. Alarmed, Himmler put the brakes on; it was simply too dangerous for Lina to go wandering around Europe. Confined to her estate, Lina concentrated on developing the grounds. She added an orchard, a vegetable patch, and kept rabbits and poultry. Jewish labourers from the Theresienstadt camp were shipped in to landscape the gardens and turn them into an English-style park with a stream.

Life without her husband was made more palatable by his SS chauffeur, who was particularly good with her two sons, and a riding companion of Heydrich's – an SS officer and ex-policeman – who acted as her financial and legal advisor, regularly joined the family for dinner and taught the kids to swim and ride horses. At weekends, he and Lina would hunt hare and pheasants in the forest. To help look after the children, Lina employed a full-time live-in governess, while the house was kept ship-shape by the domestic staff, who did their best not to incur her wrath. One of them remembered that Lina 'liked ordering people around … if she hadn't slept well, she would go about shouting at everybody, telling them they were lazy and so on, even the SS guards. When she was in a good mood she ignored us all.'[20]

On 24 October 1943, Lina experienced another sudden and violent death. Her two boys – Klaus was 9 and Heider was 8 – were riding their bikes round the gardens in the late afternoon. The main gates were open as a visitor was expected and Klaus and Heider zipped in and out of them. After a bit, Heider went back to house, but Klaus stayed out on his bike. At 4.45 p.m., Klaus whizzed past the SS guard, who tried to stop him, and sped into the road, where a truck suddenly appeared out of nowhere and drove straight into him. Lina and the SS guard carried her unconscious son into the house; he was covered in blood and had serious injuries to his neck and chest. One of Lina's Jewish workers was a doctor and he examined Klaus before her personal physician arrived. It was too late; Klaus died within thirty minutes of the collision. He was buried on the estate in a metal casket, dressed in his Hitler Youth uniform.

The long delays that affected the correspondence between Ilse and her husband made life difficult for both of them. On 15 January 1944, Hess complained that it was over four months since he'd received a letter from her, and asked her to send him some more books because they were 'of the greatest value' and helped relieve the monotony of his 'solitary confinement'.

The real reason why Hess was so keen to exercise his mind was that his amnesia had returned: 'I may as well tell you: I have completely lost my memory. The whole of the past swims in front of my mind in a grey mist. I cannot recollect even the most ordinary things.'[21] Though his confession disturbed her, Ilse refused to admit defeat. Having consulted a number of doctors, she reassured her husband that his memory would return after the war was over.

Meanwhile, during June and July, Munich was subjected to a series of massive raids that left thousands dead and hundreds of thousands homeless. Reflecting on the 'destruction of our beautiful, beloved Munich', Ilse was struck by the fact that Hitler had inspected the devastation and 'stood before the rubble deeply shaken'. She wondered how he could bear to stand by as 'one after another of the things closest to his heart is annihilated' while waiting for the right moment to strike back and snatch the victory that Ilse still believed was within his grasp: 'It is 1944 and we will never give up hope.'[22]

That same July, Hamburg was razed to the ground; on the 24th, 1,500 residents were killed along with 140 animals in Hamburg zoo. Three nights later, 787 aircraft dropped loads of incendiaries, creating a terrifying firestorm that accounted for an estimated 40,000 victims. Emmy had grown up in Hamburg and she lost family members and friends, while three of her husband's nieces died in the conflagration.

The capital was also under fire. From March until the end of the year, there were sixteen major raids. It was all too much for Emmy. She was 'unhappy and desperate' and 'crushed by the stupidity of this war'. Rather than let these feelings of hopelessness paralyse her, she did what she could to alleviate the suffering. Each time Emmy was in Berlin, she visited 'the wounded in hospitals to bring them cigarettes, books and other little comforts'.[23] For the bombed out homeless, she donated linen, clothing and furniture from the guest lodge at Carinhall.

On 24 November, during yet another attack, a bomb struck Magda and Goebbels's Berlin residence: 'The top floor is burned out completely. The house is full of water ... and all the rooms are filled with pungent smoke.' When Magda drove in from their country house to inspect the damage she passed through some of the city's poorest districts, which had borne the brunt of the assault with 'terrible' results.[24] Having assessed the smouldering remains, Magda and her husband spent the night in the bunker beneath the wrecked building.

To combat the stress and tension of being constantly under threat, tackle her depression and blot out her sense of foreboding, Magda re-engaged with Buddhism, which had intrigued her for a while when she was young. Whether it helped her cope is hard to say; certainly she needed all the Zen-like calm she could muster when Goebbels threw a tantrum that Christmas. According to Rudolf Semmler, Goebbels's PA, 'the traditional movie session' featuring 'an American film' was compromised because the 'big decorated Christmas tree' had been placed in front of the screen. On seeing this, Goebbels lost 'all self-control. Then Frau Goebbels arrived ... we could hear the row going on behind closed doors.'[25] Magda was unable to stifle his rage and Goebbels stormed out of the house to spend Christmas Day on his own.

While Magda and her husband were fighting, Emmy was busy with charitable activities, sending 'clothes and toys to thousands of children of numerous families whose fathers had been killed in action during the war'[26] and enclosing a card signed by both her and Goering. This was not simply a wartime measure. The leading Nazi wives had been giving generously to the needy at Christmas time since 1933 when Hitler opened the Winter Relief Agency to fight 'hunger and cold'. Its network of nationwide district branches and staff of over a million volunteers accepted cash donations as well as food, clothing and heating supplies.

Christmas was the focal point of the campaign: SS and SA men dressed up as Santa Claus and dished out presents to street urchins; members of every Nazi organisation – especially the youth and women's groups – stood on busy intersections with their collecting tins, went door to door selling badges in the shape of Christmas decorations, as well as handcrafted gifts at markets and seasonal festivals, and went carol singing. In addition, the agency provided hundreds and thousands of free Christmas trees. Emmy, Magda, and the other wives made their gestures of goodwill on the Day of National Solidarity, which was held on the first Sunday in December, setting up stall in a prominent public place and distributing presents from the piles of goodies heaped up next to them.

By 1939, the agency was harvesting nearly twice as money as it had in 1933, but much of it came from a compulsory 10 per cent tax on workers' incomes that was increasingly resented as people struggled to make ends meet. By the winter of 1943, there was little enthusiasm left for the charity drive; the Allied bombing campaign had sucked the joy out of Christmas and there was a joke going round that offered advice to shoppers looking for the ideal gift: 'Think practically, give coffins.'[27]

Goering had promised the German people that they'd never be bombed so he was held responsible for their flattened cities. At the same time, his and Emmy's luxury lifestyle had lost its popularity. It had ceased to be endearing; it was just insulting. Goering's excessive weight and expanding waistline were no longer sources of mirth but evidence of his greed, and people strongly disapproved of Emmy's conspicuous consumption. In April, an SS man criticised her for inviting the wives of eighty generals for coffee and laying on an obscene amount of food: 'The table fairly groaned under the weight of delicacies.'[28]

At the beginning of 1943, food rations had been reduced by roughly a third from the levels set in 1939, which were 2,570 calories a day for regular civilians, 3,600 for members of the armed forces and 4,652 for those engaged in heavy labour. Ration cards for different items were issued on a monthly basis and amounted to 10kg of bread a month, 2.4kg of meat, 1.4kg of fats, including butter, and 320g of cheese. On paper these quantities were sufficient, but the problem was supply; there were severe shortages of meat, fresh fruit and vegetables, sugar was scarce and people's diets relied more and more on bread – the quality of which deteriorated all the time – and potatoes.

As part of his total war initiative to stamp out wasteful indulgence, Goebbels closed down the half a dozen high-end restaurants in Berlin, including Horcher's, Emmy and Goering's favourite eatery. Goering was furious and fought to keep it open for another six months but in November 1943 Otto and his staff decamped to Madrid and opened a restaurant there. Before the war, Goering would have won this tussle with Goebbels; not any more. Goering had become damaged goods.

Goering's steady loss of power and influence – during 1943 he'd ceded control of the war economy to Albert Speer – had a dire effect on Emmy's efforts to help her Jewish friends. Rose Korwan was an actress who'd met Emmy in the early 1920s and worked with her in Weimar and in Berlin. As the persecution of Germany's Jews worsened, Emmy claimed that she 'tried not to lose sight of her and stay close to her just precisely because she was a Jewess'. When Rose was no longer permitted to perform, Emmy gave her a weekly allowance and encouraged her to flee the country, but Rose had fallen in love with a local Jewish man and refused to budge.

In March 1943, when transports to the East were leaving Berlin, Rose married her boyfriend and asked for Emmy's protection after he was arrested for arguing with an SS man and not wearing his yellow star. Emmy called Himmler, who was reluctant to help: 'You must realise Frau Goering … that millions of German women have their husbands at the front and do not know what has happened to them. How can you expect that I can concern myself with the fate of one particular Jewess?'

Emmy implored him to do her a 'personal favour', and Himmler agreed to look into it. An hour later, he rang Emmy back and told her that Rose's husband would be dispatched to Theresienstadt, 'one of our very best camps', and assured her that he would 'be very well there'. When Rose heard the news, she asked Emmy if she could accompany him. Not wanting to push her luck, Emmy told Goering to ring Himmler about it, and:

> After some equivocations, Himmler agreed to send the woman to the camp. Everything would be all right, he assured us. He would personally see to it that the couple got a room, and even someone to clean it for them. The promise set both our minds at rest.[29]

But Himmler was lying through his teeth. A mutual friend of Emmy and Rose went to the station to see the couple off, but the train they were put on steamed off in the opposite direction. On hearing this troubling news, Emmy asked her husband to intervene again but Himmler would not take his call. Instead, a note was delivered confirming that Rose and her husband had arrived safely at Theresienstadt. Unable and unwilling to challenge Himmler further, Goering left the matter there; meanwhile, Rose and her husband were on their way to the gas chambers.

According to one of the Jewish prisoners working on Lina's estate outside Prague, she 'strode about like an Amazon, whip in hand' and 'loved the crack of it against her riding boots. The impression was she was cruel and arrogant'. Lina spat at her workers, called them 'Jewish pig' and though she never assaulted anyone herself, she would get her SS guards to do it for her if she spotted anybody slacking off: 'She had the

SS man … beat our comrade … until his back drew blood' because he was 'unable to run with his fully laden trolley'.

Lina housed the prisoners in the stables, where they were 'all crammed together in the smallest possible space', while 'the bugs ensured that we got no rest after each day's 14–18 hours toil. The food was deficient in all respects.' None of them had any doubts about who was responsible for their miserable existence; the 'inhuman treatment' and 'the constant threat of deportation to Auschwitz if the job was not carried out satisfactorily' was the 'exclusive handiwork of Lina Heydrich'.[30]

In January 1944, Lina's Jewish labourers were sent East to the camps and were replaced by fifteen female Jehovah's Witnesses from Ravensbrück. In 1933, Lina's husband had announced that any Jehovah's Witness – there were 25,000 of them in Germany – could be taken into custody by the Gestapo. In 1935, it was the first religious organisation banned by the Nazis. Over the years, 10,000 were imprisoned and over 1,000 killed; in the camps they wore a purple triangle and were especially harshly treated because of their stubborn adherence to their faith.

During July 1943, Margaret was in Berlin with the German Red Cross supervising the opening of an SS-run hospital for those 'hurt by the bombings in the West'. In mid August, she inspected her railway transit facilities and declared that they were in 'perfect condition'. On 3 September, four days before her fiftieth birthday, Margaret expressed her conviction that Germany would prevail: 'Our country is neither destined to, nor can, go under.' She was more concerned about her domestic situation, wondering 'about all the things that are going to happen to me in the next year of my life. And I don't mean in this war.'[31] Himmler's adulterous relationship was a never-ending source of grief and Margaret fretted about the corrupting influence it was having on Gudrun: 'She is only 14 and should not know more about life's difficulties. She already hears so many things she should not know about.'[32]

Though Himmler's visits to Lake Tegernsee were never longer than a three-day stopover, he compensated by increasing the volume and frequency of the packages he sent to his wife and daughter. On Mother's Day, there were flowers for Margaret. Sweets, candied fruits, brandy-filled chocolate beans, cans of condensed milk, and packets of glucose and marzipan arrived with the mail. Alongside these treats, Himmler sought to reinvigorate the intellectual exchange that had been a feature of his correspondence with Margaret until he got involved with Hedwig. As before, history books were at a premium. One parcel that Margaret received from him contained biographies of Empress Constance, who was Queen of Sicily during the Middle Ages; the King of the Vandals, who conquered Carthage; and Bismarck. Another included a glossy SS annual that had photographs of soldiers, workers and farmers engaging in sport and folk-dancing, plus several books on Japan.

On 6 August, Gudrun's birthday, Himmler wrote a wistful letter to Margaret that revisited the day 'fourteen years ago' when she gave him 'our sweet little daughter, with so much pain and in danger of your life'. The memory prompted him to sign off with 'special affection and … many kisses'.[33] This uncharacteristic outpouring, combined with his diligent present giving, suggests he might have been having regrets about Hedwig, perhaps realising that he had more in common with Margaret than with his younger lover. Or was he just guilty now that Hedwig was expecting their second child?

Himmler was certainly worried about how isolated Hedwig was in her forest home and he wanted to find her somewhere to live close to Obersalzburg; however, he had a cashflow problem. While the SS's wealth grew and grew, his private income remained relatively static, so he turned to Bormann – the party's paymaster – for a loan. Bormann was happy to have one of his rivals in his debt and came up with the money. Himmler bought Hedwig a modest cottage near Berchtesgaden, not far from the Nazi reservation.

On 3 July 1944, at the Hohenlychen clinic, Hedwig gave birth to a daughter under the watchful eye of Professor Gebhardt. Sadly for her, Himmler could not be there, as he was a guest of honour at an extravagant wedding – the party went on for three days – that was being held at the Berghof. One of Himmler's protégés, Hermann Fegelein, a dashing but sadistic SS cavalry officer, was getting married to Eva's younger sister

Gretl. Six months later, as the Soviet army massed on the borders of the Reich, Fegelein deserted Gretl and was preparing to flee Berlin with another woman and some stolen gold bars when he was apprehended by the SS and executed.

At around 12.45 p.m. on 20 July, a bomb hidden in a suitcase and planted under a table exploded during a conference at Hitler's HQ. It blew out the windows, sending glass flying through the air and shattered the table, scattering sharp splinters everywhere. In all the smoke and confusion, Hitler was momentarily trapped under fallen beams. According to an account he gave afterwards, 'I was able to get up and go on my own. I was just a little dizzy and slightly dazed.'[34] However, his forehead was bloody from a cut, the hair was burned off the back of his scalp, there was a saucer-sized burn on his calf, his right arm was so swollen he could hardly lift it and there were burns and blisters on his hands and legs; more seriously, both his ear drums had burst, which temporarily deafened him and took some time to heal. The attempted coup by a conspiracy of army officers, intelligence operatives and concerned civilians was fatally compromised by Hitler's miraculous survival, and within twenty-four hours its leaders were either dead or under arrest. Nevertheless, it sent shockwaves through the Nazi elite.

Eva was on a swimming excursion at Lake Königsee when the bomb went off; the second she knew what had happened, she wrote him a letter: 'Darling, I am beside myself. I am dying of fear. I feel close to losing my mind … I have always told you that I will die if anything happens to you.'[35] Not far away at Obersalzburg, Gerda was deeply shocked: 'How could that fellow put his briefcase with the bomb down there, how did he get it into HQ at all? I've been racking my brains about it a lot.'[36] On her estate outside Prague, Lina wasn't surprised by the attack, given her husband's belief that the officer corps was a nest of traitors capable of anything. At Lake Tegernsee, Margaret was appalled: 'What a disgrace. German officers wanted to bump off the Führer … nothing like this ever happened in the history of Germany.'[37]

Emmy – who'd last seen Hitler on Edda's sixth birthday in early June – was more cautious in her appraisal: 'I cannot pass judgement on these men or congratulate their actions,' while her demoralised, lethargic and fatalistic husband did 'not disapprove of the bomb attempt itself as much as the manner in which it had been carried out',[38] implying that the oath of loyalty the army plotters had made to Hitler was too sacred to break whatever the circumstances.

In Wales, Hess heard the news on the radio. According to his orderly, Hess became 'extremely talkative with much gesticulating in a very exhilarated manner. He appeared very pleased that the Führer had escaped assassination.'[39] Earlier in the year, Hess had abandoned all hope and on 4 February he made a feeble attempt to commit suicide by stabbing himself in the chest with a bread knife, a flesh wound that required two stitches and left a tiny scar. Having refused food for the next eight days, he suddenly announced that his amnesia had lifted again. Now Hitler had escaped death, Hess felt more like his old self, for the time being at least.

Hess's long-suffering friend, Professor Haushofer, was caught up in the retribution that followed the assassination attempt, like hundreds of others who were arrested because they had offended Hitler at one time or another. Professor Haushofer spent a gruelling month in Dachau before being released. On 25 July, his son Albrecht managed to evade the Gestapo when they came knocking on his door and hid out for nearly six months until they caught up with him on 7 December. Two days later, Albrecht was driven straight from Munich to Berlin and slung in the dreaded Moabit prison.

Magda was in the Dresden clinic during the attempt on Hitler's life, recovering from the surgery she'd had to treat a problem with her trigeminal nerve, which had paralysed the right side of her face and caused her awful agony. The condition had bothered her for months and the therapy she was getting failed to improve it. After delays and complications – including Hitler's concern that facial surgery might ruin her looks – Magda had the operation that spring. As predicted, it was only partially successful. Her features were still twisted and she was in serious pain; a prolonged period of convalescence beckoned.

But suddenly Magda was galvanised by Hitler's brush with death. Clearly, Fate had spared him for a reason and she began to believe that victory, or at the very least an honourable outcome, was possible. Magda bought into all the talk of the wonder weapons that were going to reverse the course of the war. While the regime did manage to unleash its V1 and V2 rockets over the south-east of England – spreading fear, panic and carnage – it was too little, too late, and the promise that even more decisive weapons were on the way sounded increasingly hollow.

Another false assumption that Magda clung to was the conviction that the Allied coalition would collapse the closer it got to German territory; after all, how could the world's foremost capitalist state – America – and the previous holder of that accolade – the UK – stay on friendly terms with Stalin's Soviet Union?

These ideas sustained Magda for a while, but for a woman as intelligent as she was, the dire reality of the military situation was impossible to ignore. However blinded she may have been by her faith in Hitler, Magda was no fool. The Soviets were pushing relentlessly forward, closing in on Warsaw and penetrating the Balkans. Mussolini had fallen and much of Italy was in Allied hands. After the D-Day landings, the Allies had finally broken out of the coastal regions and with the German army in headlong retreat the way to Paris was open.

The weight of events once again undermined her physical, emotional and psychological health; Magda booked herself back into the clinic, as if she was already preparing for the end.

13

DEAD END

In the summer of 1944, Gerda and her children made the short journey to Berchtesgaden to visit Hedwig's new cottage. Pretty much alone with her two small infants, Hedwig appreciated the company. Gerda thought Hedwig seemed pleased with the house and its location, and was struck by how 'ridiculously like her father'[1] Hedwig's daughter was, just like the pictures Hedwig had showed her of Himmler as a child.

After tea, Hedwig invited them all to the attic to see something special: furniture made from human body parts. Gerda's eldest son, Martin Adolf Bormann – who was home from school for the holidays – remembered how Hedwig 'clinically and medically' explained the process behind the construction of a chair 'whose seat was a human pelvis and the legs were human legs – on human feet'.[2] Hedwig also had copies of *Mein Kampf* bound with human skin that had been peeled off the backs of Dachau inmates. 'Shocked and petrified', Martin Adolf and his siblings went outside with their mother, who was 'equally stricken'. Gerda told them that when Himmler tried to give Bormann a similarly unique edition of *Mein Kampf* he refused to take it; Gerda said it was 'too much for him'.[3]

Gerda had been living in a Nazi bubble since she was a teenager, and in the otherworldly seclusion of Obersalzburg for nearly a decade. Until recently, the war had seemed a faraway thing. Though she was still 'utterly convinced of our victory', Gerda was now having to confront the prospect of defeat. She viewed the war as a 'struggle between

Light and Darkness', and 'a fight of Good against Evil' that resembled the myths and fairy tales that had always fascinated her. Bormann shared her apocalyptic vision; defeat would mean the 'extermination of our race' and 'the destruction of its culture and civilisation'. Faced with such horrors, Gerda refused to accept this outcome – 'it cannot possibly be the meaning of history that Jewry should make itself the master of the world' – and urged her husband to ensure that every German child realised 'that the Jew is the Absolute Evil in this world'.[4]

Margaret was in Berlin during August. There was less for her to do at the German Red Cross, so she 'spread a lot of happiness' distributing clothing to bombed out citizens, even though 'standing in cellars on flagstones for four hours every day is none too easy for me'.[5] At Lake Tegernsee, she supervised construction of an air-raid shelter; the workers came from Dachau and Margaret complained to camp officials about their poor quality.

The letters between her and her husband kept going back and forth, and the packages for her and Gudrun kept coming with rare luxuries like soap and chocolate. In mid November, Himmler was at Lake Tegernsee, and he and Margaret discussed the difficulties Germany faced; both agreed that they would be overcome and 'the war would end favourably'.[6] Himmler departed after three uneventful and unexceptional days, promising that he'd try to make it back for Christmas.

On 3 December, Magda and her husband were honoured by a visit from Hitler. It had been over four years since he'd come to their home. At that moment, with the Allies inexorably pushing forward, it was a deeply symbolic gesture that ensured that they would remain with him no matter what. Hitler arrived at tea-time. Rudolf Semmler, Goebbels's PA, recalled how 'the children received him in the hall with bunches of flowers in their hand' and 'Goebbels stood to

attention with his arm stretched out as far as it would go. The children made their little curtsies and Hitler said how surprised he was at the way they had grown.'

Hitler gave Magda some flowers – a 'modest bunch of lily-of-the valley' – and 'explained that it was the best that could be found', as Goebbels 'had closed all the flower shops in Berlin'. Hitler was accompanied by a servant, an adjutant, six SS officers and a bodyguard. He brought his own tea in a thermos flask and his own cakes. He only stayed half an hour, but having 'enjoyed the family atmosphere', and the chance to escape his 'monastic life for half an afternoon', Hitler 'promised to come again soon'. Delighted and bursting with pride, Magda remarked that Hitler 'wouldn't have gone to the Goerings'.[7]

While Germany starved, Emmy and her family had one final feast at Carinhall to celebrate Goering's birthday on 12 January 1945. They polished off the caviar from Russia, duck and venison from his forests, Danzig salmon, the last of the pâté de foie gras, and washed it all down with vodka, claret, burgundy, champagne and brandy.

At the end of the month, a Soviet tank entered the forests round Carinhall. Emmy, Edda and the other women left the next afternoon and headed for the relative safety of Obersalzburg, where the house had an underground shelter with twelve rooms. Following close behind was Goering's art collection. Over the next two and a half months, two special trains, eight freight cars and over a dozen box cars shunted hundreds of valuable works between various locations in Bavaria and Austria, where they were unloaded and hidden away. Nine freight cars ended up parked on the tracks at Berchtesgaden station, close to Obersalzburg. From their cargo, Goering removed two paintings of the Madonna and four miniature angels by Hans Memling, a fifteenth-century German artist, and gave them to Emmy as a nest egg, something to sell if she fell on hard times.

As the Allies drew closer and nobody appeared to be in charge any more, the locals thoroughly ransacked Goering's train, taking carpets, rugs, tapestries and paintings, and carting off gold coins, sugar, coffee, cigarettes and expensive liquors.

By early January 1945, Himmler had made Hohenlychen his almost permanent base. The roof of the clinic had a Red Cross symbol on it so it wouldn't be bombed, and the ever-loyal Professor Gebhardt was on hand, as was Himmler's Swedish masseur; his persistent stomach ailments were causing him serious grief and he needed to rest. As a result, Himmler did not make it to Lake Tegernsee for Christmas. Instead, he phoned and talked to Margaret. She remembered that 'he had a cold again … he was sick' and 'in very delicate health'.[8]

Himmler also wrote her a sentimental letter: 'This is the first time we have not celebrated Christmas together; but just yesterday I was thinking so much of you.'[9] He also sent her a silver tray, different coloured silks – blue, black and white – a handbag, some underwear and some stockings: on 9 January he mailed her coffee, gingerbread cookies, liver pâté and a book on the Prussian army.

In her diary, Margaret tried to maintain a positive outlook; she noted that her husband was 'happy and in good form' when they spoke on the phone and she was proud that 'all of Germany looks up to him'. Margaret was also relieved that her difficult stepson Gerhard had finally found his calling – 'he is very courageous and loves it with the SS' – having joined the organisation's military wing. Nevertheless, she was not taken in by false hope: 'The war situation is unchanged and very grave.'[10]

On 6 January, Lina had a private meeting with Himmler in Berlin that lasted an hour and forty-five minutes. They discussed the security situation in the Protectorate and the risks she faced staying there; Lina had received a threatening letter earlier that month and communist partisans were causing more and more disruption.

But Lina returned to her estate, and a few weeks later she wrote to her parents about her plans. For the moment, she was staying put: 'I wouldn't know where we could be safer than here, to flee, as other women do, is out of the question for me.' Ultimately, it didn't matter where she was. Whether in the Protectorate or in Germany, defeat would mean the end for her, as 'the Russians will know where to find us to liquidate us' or the 'British and Americans will come. And with them the Jews. With our Jewish laws we burned our bridges. The Jews will be able to get at us. There is no point in deluding ourselves.'[11]

Eva was in Berlin until 9 February, then returned again for good on 7 March. She explained her decision to stay with Hitler to his faithful secretary Christa Schroeder: 'I have come because I owe the Boss for everything wonderful in my life.'[12]

Bormann also remained in Berlin. Aside from there being no question of him leaving his master's side, he was still running the party machine with his usual hyper-efficiency and productivity, refusing to accept the inevitable. Gerda saw him in February then returned to Obersalzburg. Despite everything, she continued to believe that 'one day the Reich of our dreams will emerge … even if we no longer survive'.[13]

On 25 February Magda asked one of Hitler's physicians for enough poison 'for herself and her six children'. It was not an easy request for her to make. According to Semmler, she 'could not bear the thought of ending the lives of her children'; the very idea of it drove her 'crazy with grief and pain'.[14] Yet Magda saw no future. She knew that what had been done in Hitler's name would never be forgiven or forgotten, and the Soviets were unlikely to show her family any mercy. On 4 March, her husband informed Hitler that they intended to stay put 'even if Berlin is attacked and surrounded'.[15] Understanding what that meant, Hitler hesitated before giving his approval.

Goebbels's diary entries for that month had a routine, businesslike quality about them. He was still running his Propaganda Ministry, and on the 16th he hosted a reception for all his staff. On the 21st, he was studying 'the latest film statistics', which were 'very good despite all the difficulties. It is surprising that the German people still wants to go to the cinema at all.'

Magda barely featured in Goebbels's notes. He was irritated when she 'got one of her headaches' on the 8th, and annoyed when she retired to bed feeling unwell on the 27th because she'd 'over-done it' organising the move from their country estate to Berlin. By 4 April they were settled in the capital and spent 'a somewhat melancholy evening during which one piece of bad news after another descends on our house. One sometimes wonders desperately where it will all lead.'[16]

Over the night of 7–8 January 1945, 645 Lancaster bombers attacked Munich and Ilse's house received a direct hit. Salvaging what she could, Ilse took her son Wolf and headed for the Bavarian Alps, where they found shelter in a small village. There, Ilse would patiently see out the rest of the war, waiting for the moment danger passed and she could turn her attention back to her husband and their future together.

In Wales, Hess was lost in his own world, passing the time reading novels by obscure eighteenth-century German novelists and marvelling at the 'infinite breadth of form and style in character and presentation'.[17] Knowing he was currently beyond harm, Ilse could imagine a life ahead of her, even if the regime collapsed and Hitler was no more.

For Albrecht Haushofer there would be no future. In the early hours of 23 April, Albrecht – who'd been languishing in jail since the previous December – and fifteen other prisoners were assembled in the yard, given back their personal effects and asked to sign release forms. Any hopes that this meant freedom were quickly dashed when they saw thirty-five SS men armed with machine guns standing outside the gate.

An SS officer informed them that they were being transferred to another facility and his men would escort them to the station. When they got close, Albrecht and fellow inmates were directed towards a stretch of bombed out wasteland. They were put up against a wall and executed. According to his father, Professor Haushofer, Albrecht was shot in the back of the neck.

In March, Lina had an unexpected visitor: Himmler turned up at the house looking tired and dishevelled, and asked her for a hot bath and breakfast. Refreshed, he chatted with her and played with her children. When Lina tried to pin him down on the state of the war and the prospects of reversing the Allied advance, he was evasive, which led her to assume the worst. But Lina was not yet ready to abandon the estate she'd worked so hard to maintain and in which she'd invested so much of herself.

Himmler skulked back to Hohenlychen. All his grand aspirations, his dreams of fostering a rebirth of the German spirit and forming a new aristocracy to govern a racial paradise, were in tatters. By the end of March, American troops were closing in on his fantasy SS castle at Wewelsburg. Himmler evacuated his staff and on the 31st demolition teams arrived, dynamited the castle's west and south towers and set the interior on fire by lighting curtains and anything else that was flammable.

When they left, the locals spent two days looting the smouldering remains, emptying the wine cellar and clearing out the on-site museum, which contained skulls, coins, knives, ancient pottery, Viking swords, Bronze Age helmets, Scythian bronze arrowheads and the fossil of an ancient marine reptile, a 9ft-long ichthyosaur.

After visiting Himmler at Hohenlychen on 22 March, Hedwig made her way back to Berchtesgaden. Her last call from him was on 19 April. They discussed 'personal matters' and the fact that the situation was 'more difficult every day'. Himmler said he'd call her again but never did. He ended the conversation with the 'hope that God would protect her, the children, and Germany'.[18]

At Lake Tegernsee, Margaret received a final phone call from her husband around Easter time. Once again, the main topic was his guts: 'He is very ill again, and had trouble with his stomach.'[19] On 20 April Margaret, her daughter, her sister Lydia, an aunt and several other female relatives crammed themselves into their car and left their home behind. Margaret's driver was heading for the South Tyrol, a region of Austria on the border with Italy that had already been identified as a safe haven with its mountains and secluded valleys. As the Allies neared Berchtesgaden, Hedwig followed in the same direction, taking her children with her.

In early April, Karl Wolff – Frieda's ex-husband – dropped in on Lina to warn her that Soviet forces were not far off and local resistance was mounting. It was time to leave. By the middle of the month, Lina had packed up the house, slaughtered all her livestock, and bought a circus caravan to transport her family's belongings and her dead son's casket. Also in her luggage was the bloodstained uniform her husband had been wearing when he was assassinated.

On the day of departure, the lady of the manor gathered her staff together, thanked them and promised them a small gratuity after the war. Lina, her three children and their governess, plus a certain amount of baggage, squeezed into two cars. With the caravan behind them, they set off for Germany. However, within a few miles, the convoy was attacked by Soviet aircraft. The caravan was blasted off the road. Lina rescued her dead son's damaged casket and what was left of his remains was hastily reburied in the woods.

En route, Lina left her other son and eldest daughter in the care of some friends who promised to get them to Fehmarn when the time was right. Then Lina, with her 3-year-old daughter, carried on through Bavaria to Lake Tegernsee, where they took refuge at Frieda Wolff's house – the two SS wives together again – until US troops turfed them out at the beginning of May.

The atmosphere at Hitler's birthday party on 20 April was more down-beat than usual. A month earlier, the Soviet army had reached the outskirts of Berlin. Their assault began four days before Hitler's clos-est followers gathered to wish him many happy returns of the day. That morning, Soviet artillery started shelling the city centre, within range of the bunker.

A sombre mood descended on proceedings and most of his guests – including Goering and Himmler – made a hasty exit. Hitler retired early to bed. Eva, however, was determined to have some fun. According to one of Hitler's young secretaries, 'a restless fire burned in her eyes'; Eva wanted 'to dance, to drink, to forget'. Wearing a new dress – 'made of a silvery blue brocade' – she swept towards her apartment in the Reich Chancellery, gathering up Bormann and anybody else she came across. In her living room, Eva cracked open the champagne and dug out her gramophone; she found a record – the popular wartime hit 'Blood in Red Roses Speaks of Happiness to You' – and played it over and over again as 'she whisked everyone into a desperate frenzy'.[20]

While terrified residents tried to flee the city, one woman was desperately trying to get in. Hanna Reitsch was Germany's most famous female pilot and a committed Nazi; she somehow found somewhere to land in the devastated capital and make it to the bunker unscathed on the 26th. She was offering to airlift people out of Berlin. Hitler refused, as did Eva, who handed Reitsch a letter for her sister Gretl in which she asked her to destroy all her private papers and correspondence with Hitler, and said that she was 'glad to die at the side of the Führer; but most of all glad that the horror now to come is spared me. What could life still give me? It has already been perfect.'[21]

Magda also gave Hanna Reitsch a letter, addressed to Harald Quandt – her son from her first marriage – who had served in the infantry throughout the war and was currently a British POW. Written with an eye to posterity, it reads like a last piece of propaganda, courtesy of the First Lady of the Reich. In the letter, Magda laid out her reasons for the course she had chosen:

> For me there is no alternative. Our beautiful idea is being destroyed, and with it goes everything in life I knew to be fine, worthy of admiration, noble and good. Life will not be worth living in the world that will come after Hitler and National Socialism. Therefore, I have brought the children with me. They are too precious for the life that will come after us.

Having extolled their virtues, she asked God to 'grant' her 'the strength to accomplish the last and most difficult task of all … to be true unto death to the Führer'.[22]

Magda's words reflected her unique position in Hitler's entourage, her personal connection to him and her proximity to power. But her motivation was not that different from the scores of other women who chose suicide during the last days of his rule. Over the course of 1945, 7,000 people killed themselves, of whom 3,996 were women. Many justifiably feared they would be raped by Soviet soldiers. At least 100,000 were sexually assaulted, and some small towns and villages in the path of the advancing Soviet army committed mass suicide rather than face its wrath.

In Berlin, women carried cyanide and razor blades in their handbags or on their person. During April and May, the city witnessed 5,881 suicides. In an upmarket Berlin suburb, the wife of an army captain killed herself and her 8-year-old daughter. She'd made the decision to use poison that February and told her husband that 'she feared that she and her child would fall into Russian hands' and 'would end her life before that happened'.[23]

At Obersalzburg, Gerda received her last letters from her husband and some of Hitler's early watercolours. When Bormann managed to reach her on the phone, he told her not to worry as he had a car ready to whisk him out of Berlin at a moment's notice, and assured her that they'd see each other again.

Though Bormann had overseen the construction of a network of underground shelters at Obersalzburg – work began in August 1943 and 3,000 labourers, mostly Italian, built 4 miles of tunnels and bunkers with walls 5ft thick – and the one beneath his house was large enough for his whole family and their staff, he wasn't leaving anything to chance. Gerda's escape plan had been worked out in advance, her destination the South Tyrol. She acquired a school bus and painted a Red Cross on the roof. Aside from eight of her own nine children – her eldest son was making his own way home from his elite Nazi boarding school and would end up missing the bus – Gerda had collected seven other stray infants. Along with her sister-in-law, Gerda and the equivalent of a kindergarten class set off on their trip. She was carrying with her Bormann's precious typewritten copy of *Hitler's Table Talk*, the manuscript he had so diligently compiled from the countless hours he'd spent hanging on Hitler's every word.

Goering went straight to Obersalzburg after Hitler's birthday on 20 April. The day before he'd said goodbye to Carinhall: any art too big to carry was buried in the grounds, demolition teams mined the building and blew it to pieces. The following morning, he was reunited with Emmy and Edda at their mountain retreat.

Unaware of what was happening in Berlin, Goering's egomania prompted him to interpret the silence and lack of news from the bunker as proof that Hitler was dead, making him the new Führer. On the 23rd, he sent Hitler a telegram; as his anointed successor, should he now assume control? If the Führer was alive, however, Goering hoped he would 'decide to leave Berlin and come here'.

Emmy never commented on her husband's last-ditch grab for supreme power, as futile as it was ludicrous. Having heard nothing by 6 p.m. that evening, Goering got back on the line: 'In view of your decision to remain at your post in fortress Berlin, do you agree that I take over, at once, the total leadership of the Reich; with full freedom of action at home and abroad.'[24]

Hitler had shrugged off Goering's first telegram; given the confusion, it was an understandable error of judgement. The second message pushed him over the edge. Feeling hurt and wounded, Hitler ordered Goering's arrest and Bormann was able to activate the SS unit stationed at Obersalzburg. They immediately surrounded Goering's house. Emmy and Edda were separated from him, with a guard stationed outside their room. Before they were parted, Goering told Emmy it was a mistake that would be resolved the next day.

But the following morning, Wednesday, 25 April, at around 9.30 a.m., 359 Lancaster bombers and sixteen Mosquitos pulverised Obersalzburg. Emmy, her husband, Edda, Emmy's sister, and their staff – a maid, a nurse, a governess and an adjutant – were allowed to go into the shelter beneath the house while their SS captors watched over them. During a lull in the bombing, they all transferred to the main Obersalzburg bunker where the Berghof residents were gathered.

Then the second wave hit half an hour later. When Christa Schroeder emerged from hiding, she saw that the Eagle's Nest had been destroyed and the Berghof had been 'badly damaged'. The walls still stood but the roof 'hung in ribbons' and 'doors and windows had disappeared. Inside the house the floor was thickly covered with debris and much of the furniture had been demolished. All the ancillary buildings had been destroyed, the paths scrambled to rubble, trees felled at the root. Nothing green remained, the scene was a crater landscape.'[25]

Scared as she was, Emmy realised this was a crucial moment; with their lives hanging in the balance, she turned to the SS officer in charge of them and gave a virtuoso performance, evoking a pact she'd made with Hitler on her 'wedding day' when he 'promised to grant me a wish'. If for any reason, Hitler considered it necessary to execute her husband, he'd agreed to have Emmy and Edda 'shot at the same time'.[26] This gave the SS man pause for thought. Though he'd received a communiqué from Bormann ordering him to kill the traitors, he was getting cold feet. A compromise was reached. His SS unit would accompany Goering and family to his Austrian castle 150 miles away; it took their convoy of vehicles thirty-six hours crawling along jam-packed roads to get there.

The Goerings' Obersalzburg house had been wrecked by the bombing. A US soldier noticed part of the roof in the swimming pool and two dead bodies floating on the surface. On the bottom of the pool, he saw something glistening in the sun. He dived in and recovered a Roman-style gladiator's sword that had been crafted by Napoleon's personal armourer; the soldier sold it in 1978 to a private collector for an undisclosed sum.

Bormann's house had been hit as well; 1,000 watercolours by Rudolf von Alt – the prolific landscape painter who had inspired Hitler to become an artist – were found unscathed in the underground shelter. After the war, von Alt's paintings were supposed to hang in the galleries of the grandiose museum Hitler was planning to build in Linz. Over 350 of these salvaged works disappeared without a trace.

At the Berghof, French and American troops helped themselves to the copious supplies of alcohol, the artwork and anything that had Hitler's initials on it; his stationery, silverware, porcelain, crystal glasses and goblets. Several days later, a US colonel inspected the site: all that remained standing was the fireplace and the toilet.

Nearby Berchtesgaden was also targeted by the raid and Hedwig's cottage was badly damaged. Scavengers removed the entire bedroom suite, a chandelier, a desk and a small tapestry, but they left Himmler's library untouched.

After Hitler's birthday on 20 April, Himmler headed straight back to Hohenlychen to resume the peace initiatives in which he had been engaged since the beginning of the year. Himmler had approached the International Red Cross through Swedish intermediaries in the vain belief that the Western Allies and the Nazis would join together to fight the Bolsheviks. To demonstrate his good intentions, Himmler authorised the release of some camp survivors, the dwindling number of whom were being driven from place to place on pitiless forced marches in which hundreds perished.

On the 28th, Reuter's news agency exposed Himmler's treachery. While Goering's betrayal had disappointed Hitler, it wasn't a complete surprise; the man he'd admired, trusted and valued had ceased to exist some time ago and it was only his lingering affection for his old comrade that prevented him from jettisoning Goering sooner. But Himmler was a real shock, a body blow that sent Hitler into an apocalyptic fury, and he condemned Himmler to the gallows. However, at this late point, the chances of the order reaching anybody capable of carrying out the death sentence was almost zero. For the time being, Himmler was safe at Hohenlychen, waiting for the Allies to offer him a role in their imminent struggle with Stalin.

On 29 April, Eva and Hitler became husband and wife; with a stroke of a pen his secret mistress – who was a mystery to the majority of Germans

– sealed her place in history and gained a form of immortality. In the hours before the wedding, Hitler had written his last will and testament: 'I have now, before ending this earthly existence, decided to take as my wife the girl who, after years of loyal friendship, has voluntarily returned to the almost besieged city to share her fate with mine. It is her wish to join me in death as my wife.'[27] At the ceremony, attended by Magda, Goebbels, Bormann and a selection of the staff, Eva wore a silk taffeta dress and her finest jewellery. Though the bunker was being rocked by shellfire that made the walls shake, Hitler's chauffeur remembered that the mood was 'festive'. There was champagne and sandwiches, and the 'conversation turned to earlier experiences' as they 'reflected with nostalgia on the past'.[28]

On the 30th, Hitler spoke about the future over lunch. Eva said goodbye to Magda, the two rivals united by their decision to die with their beloved Hitler. Then Magda had a private talk with him. Afterwards, she told his valet about her last moments with Hitler: 'I fell to my knees and begged him not to take his own life. He lifted me up benevolently and explained to me quietly that he had no choice.'[29]

At 3.15 p.m., Hitler and Eva retreated into their shared quarters. His valet and Bormann waited outside for a suitable time before entering. On seeing Hitler and Eva dead on the sofa, Bormann 'turned white as chalk'. Hitler had taken poison – hydrocyanic acid, a clear liquid with the scent of bitter almonds – then shot himself in the temple with his 7.65mm pistol, which lay on the floor near his feet. Eva was slumped next to him, her legs tucked under her. She was wearing 'a black dress of light material'. According to the valet, the poison had left its mark on her; Eva's 'contorted face betrayed how she had died'.[30] She was 34 years old.

Having wrapped the corpses in carpet, Bormann, the valet, the chauffeur and two SS bodyguards carried them outside and into the Reich Chancellery garden. Petrol siphoned from the tanks of the cars in the bunker garage was poured over Hitler and Eva as Soviet artillery shells pounded into the earth nearby and strong winds whistled around them. After repeated attempts to ignite a match failed, Bormann set fire to some papers and tossed them into the pit. The mourners gave a final salute and hurried inside. Five and a half hours later, Hitler and Eva's blackened bones were buried in a shell crater.

For the next twenty-four hours, the survivors existed on autopilot, wandering around in a daze. Magda sunk into a deep gloom. Her husband, Bormann, and what remained of the leadership cadre went through the motions. A request to negotiate peace with the Soviets was rebuffed. They named Hitler's successor – Admiral Donitz, head of the navy – and formed an emergency cabinet. When the play-acting was done and Goebbels had made a few last jottings in his diary, Magda readied herself for the final act. Her children were given cocoa laced with a powerful sedative and fell almost instantly asleep.

Nobody knows for sure what happened next. Nobody who might have been in the children's room when they died lived to tell the tale. From the reminiscences of those close to the scene, several versions of the truth emerged. There is general agreement that the SS physician Dr Stumpfegger was involved in the murder of Magda's children, but there are differences of opinion over her exact role. Several accounts claim that she was in the room at the time and may even have administered the poison herself. But this seems unlikely. Would Magda really have crushed cyanide into her children's mouths? Since moving into the bunker, she was almost incapable of being near them. One of Hitler's young secretaries remembered that Magda 'hardly had the strength to face her children with composure now. Every meeting with them made her feel so terrible that she burst into tears.'[31]

However strong-willed she was, by then Magda was a shadow of her former self. She simply could not cope with the horrific reality of the choice she'd made. And why should she when there was an experienced professional ready and willing to do it for her? Hitler's valet recalled seeing her waiting 'nervously' outside the room 'until the door opened and the Doctor came out. Their eyes met, Magda Goebbels stood up, silent and trembling. When the SS Doctor nodded emotionally without speaking, she collapsed.'[32]

Afterwards, Magda allegedly sat in her room, ashen-faced, playing solitaire and chain smoking. At 8.40 p.m., her and Goebbels's funeral pyre was ready. Wearing their golden Nazi party badges, they walked arm in arm to the bunker exit and took a step into the garden. Magda bit on her capsule. Her husband shot her in the head to make sure, swallowed his poison and turned the gun on himself. Their bodies were shifted into a shallow grave and doused in petrol. The air was calm enough to light a match. Magda and Goebbels went up in flames: the fire burned all night.

Bormann was in one of two groups that decided to make a break for it. They left the battered bunker and disappeared into the ravaged city where death waited on every street corner. But Bormann had only one thought in his mind: survival.

PART FOUR

HOLDING ON

14

CAPTIVES

ontemplating the fall of Nazism a few weeks after the war ended,
Hess struck an optimistic note in a letter to Ilse. The ideals they'd
followed for the last twenty-five years would have their day again:
'History has not ended. It will sooner or later take up the threads apparently broken off for ever, and knit them together in a new pattern.' As for
Hitler, the time they'd shared with him had been 'full of the most wonderful human experiences' and it was a privilege to have participated 'from
the very beginning in the growth of a unique personality'.[1]

Hess was on his way to the International War Crimes Tribunal in
Nuremberg, where he would appear alongside Goering and a handful
of other senior figures. The ghost at the proceedings was Bormann, who
was tried in absentia. Despite the fact several witnesses testified that he
died in Berlin, the Allied authorities were not convinced. After leaving Hitler's bunker, Bormann had tried to negotiate his way through
the battle-scarred city – where fighting still raged – in the company
of the SS doctor who'd poisoned Magda's children. As they made their
way, they met up with three Panzer tanks and fell in with them. They
were joined by Hitler's valet and his chauffeur and were making slow
but dogged progress when they ran into a Soviet anti-tank barrier and
came under heavy attack. According to Hitler's chauffeur, 'the Russians
opened up with everything they had. A second later, a hellish tongue of
fire bust out'[2] and Hitler's valet saw Bormann and the doctor 'tossed in

the air like dolls by the explosion'.[3] Fleeing the scene, neither of Hitler's subordinates stopped to check if Bormann was alive or not.

Shortly after, Arthur Axmann, a Nazi Youth leader, 'came across the bodies of Martin Bormann and his companion'. Axmann told the Americans that 'they lay close together without movement'. Initially, he thought 'they were unconscious or sleeping' but when he bent to examine them he noticed 'they were not breathing'. Seeing no visible wounds, Axmann assumed Bormann 'had taken poison'.[4] But the lack of a corpse led to speculation, which fuelled doubts, and a consensus quickly emerged that Bormann had somehow survived and was on the run. Investigators were especially keen to speak to Gerda about his possible whereabouts.

But Gerda had no idea where her husband might be or whether he was dead or not. Gerda's school bus party had made it over the Alps and reached the South Tyrol, where they were met by the Nazis' regional boss, who had secured a place to stash all Gerda's sensitive material and found them a home in a small village in a valley 30 miles from Bolzano.

Though safe for the time being, Gerda was in dreadful agony. Her sister-in-law, who had made the journey with her, observed that 'Gerda was getting worse. She was normally a very quiet person … now she couldn't hide her pain.'[5] Together, they found a local Italian doctor who immediately recognised the seriousness of her condition; Gerda was suffering from the advanced stages of ovarian cancer and needed an operation as soon as possible. By then, the Allies were on her trail. A distraught parent in Munich had approached the authorities and told them that Gerda had kidnapped his child and taken it to the Tyrol. Two intelligence agents tracked her down and informed the British unit stationed in the area. Having consulted the doctor who diagnosed Gerda, a British army major – who thought Gerda was 'a very nice woman'[6] – turned up on her doorstep.

Gerda panicked, thinking he was going to take her to a concentration camp, but the major assured her that she was in no danger. Instead, she went straight to a hospital for POWs in Merano. Surgery took place but without effect. Facing her imminent demise, Gerda sought solace in religion and converted to Catholicism. She died on 23 March 1946, a few months shy of her thirty-seventh birthday. Aside from the correspondence between her and her husband covering the years 1943–45 (which was found in Berlin and offered a striking contrast to the general view of her as a gentle, introverted soul) Gerda left no trace of herself behind.

The one item of real value stored among her possessions was Bormann's copy of *Hitler's Table Talk*, which Gerda had brought with her from Obersalzburg. The Italian official in charge of her property sold the manuscript to Françoise Genoud, a Swiss-French banker and Nazi spy who laundered money for them during the war. Genoud translated the document into French – and probably made minor adjustments to the text along the way – then his version was acquired by a British publisher, who brought out the English language edition in 1953.

Though its accuracy and authenticity as an exact record of Hitler's monologues is questionable, Bormann had succeeded in capturing his master's voice, fulfilling his mission to present future generations with the opportunity to experience what it was like to be at the Berghof listening to Hitler deliver tedious and long-winded lectures on his favourite topics.

Following Gerda's instructions, her many children were placed in the care of Rev. Theodor Schmitz, a German army Catholic chaplain. Though several of them died young, the rest were fostered by ordinary Italian families. Gerda's eldest, Martin Adolf – who was eventually reunited with his siblings after staying incognito with a farmer and his wife – became a Jesuit priest.

Gerda's father Walter Buch, who had set his daughter on the Nazi path, was picked up by the Allies at the end of April 1945. Due to Buch's long association with Hitler, they treated him as a major player. But Buch denied that he had much influence, deprived of power because his son-in-law loathed him and undermined any authority he might have had. Buch was also tight-lipped about his own devotion to Hitler, avoiding making any personal statement about his allegiance; according to Buch, Hitler had succeeded because of his 'persuasive power and his love for the German people' and their 'need for a leader'. During several interrogations, Buch insisted that he was 'a man who for seventeen years was forced to do against his will a job which he didn't like. I kept asking to be relieved of my functions, and to be permitted to return to my original position as a regular army officer.'[7]

Yet the Allies were not buying his excuses and they kept Buch locked up until November 1949. Only 67, but with nothing left to live for, the old soldier took what he considered to be the honourable way out: shortly after his release, Gerda's father slit his wrists and threw himself in a river.

Gerda's husband, however, continued to live on, if only in the imaginations of those trying to track him down. After Nuremberg, there were alleged sightings of Bormann in northern Germany, Denmark, Italy and Spain. Then from around 1952, attention shifted to South America and there were claims that he was at various times in Argentina, Chile and Peru. The CIA had an open file on him, wrote regular reports, followed leads, kept tabs on obscure informers and tracked anybody who may or may not have come into contact with Bormann since the war. The discovery of Adolf Eichmann – who masterminded the logistics of the Final Solution – in Argentina, his kidnap by the Israeli secret service and subsequent trial in Jerusalem, focused minds on the Nazi diaspora in South America, which included the Auschwitz camp doctor Joseph Mengele, and added to the rumours about Gerda's husband.

In the late 1960s, a number of writers and investigative journalists went in search of Bormann, piecing together any clues that might point them in the direction of his lair; several of them claimed they found incontrovertible proof of his existence, while one actually said he'd been face to face with Bormann. Together, these writers helped promote the idea that Bormann was at the head of a powerful secret organisation – a global network of Nazis – plotting to bring about the Fourth Reich, a notion that inspired a number of best-selling novels at the time.

In December 1972, construction workers on a building site in Berlin found two skeletons with their skulls intact, near to where Bormann was last seen; dental records and facial reconstruction confirmed that the bones belonged to him. Further examinations revealed the cause of death. It seems that the Soviet barrage had incapacitated Bormann – perhaps burying him under rubble – and, unable to move, he took cyanide rather than be captured by Soviet soldiers. The mystery surrounding Bormann's fate was solved and the spectre of Gerda's husband was finally laid to rest.

In the early summer of 1945, Ilse was taken into custody by French troops and spent fourteen days as their guest, during which she was well treated, before being moved to a location close to Nuremberg. The Allied authorities were hoping she might be able to help them break through the wall surrounding her husband, whose amnesia was back with a vengeance. Hess's short-term and long-term memory were shot, or at least they appeared to be. In the dock, he cut a bizarre figure, reading novels, muttering to himself and sleeping, while in his cell he refused food and threw violent tantrums.

The team of psychiatrists working on Hess were inclined to believe him – one of them described Hess's condition as 'hysterical amnesia' – but were still not 100 per cent sure. One person who had their doubts was the American in charge of the prisoners, Colonel Burton Andrus: 'From the moment the man in the old coat and the flying boots began talking about chocolate,' which Hess thought had been poisoned, 'I made up my mind that his madness was a sham.'[8]

Real or not, the Allies had no option but to take Hess's amnesia seriously. Ilse advised an American officer that the best way to draw him out was to concentrate on his personal life rather than his political activities. She provided the officer with eighty family photos, including recent ones of their son Wolf, and suggested 'as possible therapy for her husband the use of classical music',[9] preferably Mozart's *The Magic Flute* or Rossini's *Barber of Seville*.

Although they didn't try this, the Allies were running out of time and ideas. A plan to have Ilse and Wolf visit him was frustrated by Hess's refusal to see them under any circumstances. Desperate, the Allies resorted to a form of shock therapy, putting Hess in a room with a succession of people who ought to have been very familiar to him. Goering went first. On seeing his old comrade, Hess's bemused reaction was 'Who are you?' Goering took this response as an insult, replying 'You ought to know me. We have been together for years.' Hess conceded that Goering's name was familiar but that was all. Exasperated, Goering pressed on: 'Don't you remember that I visited your family and your wife? I saw you and your wife together repeatedly. You also visited my family with your wife.' Hess shook his head helplessly and blamed his amnesia, which was like 'a fog, behind which everything has disappeared'.[10]

Two of Hess's secretaries failed to register. Even Professor Haushofer drew a blank. Haushofer was no stranger to the Allies and was picked up at his farmhouse and taken to Nuremberg. He swore to do everything in his power to break through to his old friend: 'I am prepared to see him even in the critical state of mind he is in now ... I am prepared ... to go in front of the Devil's eye and talk to him.'[11]

Rather than confront Hess directly, as Goering had done, Professor Haushofer tried to coax him out of his shell. He showed Hess a picture of Ilse – whom Hess recognised – told him that Ilse had shown him all their letters, which meant he'd 'remained in contact' with Hess's 'spiritual life and ... feelings',[12] and talked to Hess about his mother. Yet when the professor brought up the subject of Ilse and Hess's home in Munich, Hess denied ever living there. The shutters had come down again.

The encounter deeply disturbed Professor Haushofer, who was already at a very low ebb. A few days before his meeting with Hess, he'd had a minor heart attack, and his interrogators had been extremely hard on him. They wanted Haushofer to admit that his theories had underpinned Hitler's genocidal imperialism. He thought this accusation was absurd given that Hitler 'and his disciples' had 'little knowledge of world events'. At the same time, Professor Haushofer had 'been happily married to a non-Aryan for the last fifty years'; once Hess's protection was gone, he was under constant threat. His inquisitors weren't persuaded and implied guilt by association, showing the professor one of his journals that had articles about the USA being the home of 'Jewish plutocrats'. The effect was instant; his interrogator reported that 'on reading it, Haushofer breaks down emotionally, tears came into his eyes and he could barely speak'.[13]

Eventually Professor Haushofer was released, but he faced the prospect of being re-arrested at any moment. He was 76. His son Albrecht had been brutally murdered, and now his surrogate son – who had both shielded him from and exposed him to great danger – appeared to be a lost soul wandering through perpetual darkness. In March 1946, Professor Haushofer and his wife Martha took a walk in the woods. About a half a mile away from their house, they stopped under a willow tree. They both took poison, then Haushofer hanged Martha from a branch and died at her feet. Their lifeless bodies were found the next day.

On 30 November 1945, Hess suddenly rose out of his slumber and announced to a stunned courtroom that his amnesia was fake – 'simulated' for 'tactical' reasons – and now his 'memory' was 'again at the disposal of the world'. If this wasn't startling enough, he proceeded to 'assume full responsibility for everything that I have done, everything that I have signed, and everything that I have co-signed'.[14]

It seemed that Hess had fooled everybody, including Ilse. However, the effort required to sustain the charade for such long periods over many years and convince the phalanx of experts who poked and prodded him that his amnesia was genuine, was not without consequences for Hess's mental health. To trick his captors he had to trick himself as well, which was a dangerous game, as he acknowledged in a letter to Ilse: 'When I was in England, playing the part of a man who had lost his memory, I learned many things by heart as a means of saving myself from the fate which I was carefully pretending to have suffered.'[15] His behaviour in captivity suggests, however, that the role absorbed him to such an extent that he became a victim of the condition he was trying to simulate. Within weeks of his dramatic statement in court, Hess was stumbling about in the shadows again.

On 1 October 1946, Hess was given life in prison. The fact that he flew to the UK when he did, before the mass murder of the Jews had begun in earnest, saved his neck. Goering and eleven others were sentenced to death by hanging.

Once Emmy and her husband had reached their castle in Austria in the dying days of the war, and their SS escort vanished into thin air,

Goering was removed by the Americans. As Emmy watched him depart her sciatica flared up: 'As I began to brush my hair, my right arm suddenly dropped inertly and I felt a violent pain. It was the beginning of a paralysis. Two years went by before I was able to use my arm properly.' Not long after, Emmy and her 7-year-old daughter Edda were dispatched to Goering's Bavarian castle, only to find it had been stripped bare by US troops: 'What a state the house was in! It was absolutely empty! Not even an electric bulb had been left in it. I later learned that the Americans had taken away twelve lorry loads of furniture.'[16] To add insult to injury, a GI conned her out of some emeralds by telling her that her husband was going to be set free.

On 19 November 1945, one of the Nuremberg psychiatrists brought her a letter from Goering, the first she'd received since they'd been parted. In it, Goering was unconcerned by his own situation. Instead, his worries were focused on Emmy; 'I am desperate when I think of what you have to suffer on my account, only because you are my wife. The only thing that worries me and weighs me down, is the thought of you.'[17]

Five days later, Emmy, her sister and her niece were dumped in Straubing prison in a cell with a straw mattress and a commode. Edda arrived after three days with her teddy bear and running a high temperature. It took a couple of weeks before she was on her feet again. Over the New Year, they were lodged with some Catholic nuns, then moved to a chalet in a forest with a chambermaid, though the building was no more than a hut with no electricity or running water. These basic living conditions were an inconvenience, but what troubled Emmy most was the lack of contact with her husband. At her wits' end, she wrote a passionate letter to Colonel Andrus, begging him to let her visit Goering: 'I haven't seen my husband for nearly a year and a quarter and I am longing so terribly for him that I don't see any way out; I need strength to carry on without my husband. A few minutes when I see him and could hold his hand would help me no end.'[18]

Her request was refused. The Nuremberg officials did not want to give a further boost to Goering's morale. In captivity, Goering had been forced to go cold turkey and quit his addiction to painkillers. As a result, he'd lost weight and regained his fighting spirit. Rather than wilt under cross-examination in court or during lengthy interrogations, Goering came out all guns blazing, questioning the legitimacy of the tribunal and arguing that the war crimes charges were bogus because waging war was inevitably criminal.

He'd also become the ring leader of the other high-profile prisoners – with the exception of Albert Speer, who chose to denounce Hitler and everything he stood for – and tried to coordinate a united front. Emmy was proud of her husband's defiance and told yet another of the Nuremberg psychiatrists that Goering wanted to show the world that he had nothing to be ashamed of and wasn't 'backtracking like a coward'. When her visitor asked her about the Final Solution, Emmy simply stated that 'Hitler must have been insane.'[19]

For all his bluster, the evidence against Goering was overwhelming and clearly demonstrated his involvement in the extermination of the Jews. He was made particularly uncomfortable by revelations about gruesome experiments that were performed on camp inmates for the benefit of the Luftwaffe.

Emmy and Edda were finally permitted to visit Goering on 12 September 1946. They were allowed half an hour with the prisoner, who was chained to a guard. The three of them were divided by a glass wall; Emmy and her husband engaged in trivial chit-chat. Edda read him poems she'd written.

Over the next couple of weeks, they returned to see him eight times. Their final meeting was on 7 October. Emmy put on a brave face and told Goering that he could 'face death with a clear conscience now' having done all he could 'at Nuremberg' for his comrades and 'for Germany'.[20] But outside the prison, Emmy let her guard down; the thought of her beloved being strung up like a piece of meat was tearing her apart. Another visiting wife recalled that 'there were tears in her grey-green eyes. They rolled down her cheeks. She looked utterly desolate and helpless.'[21]

Yet Goering's last words to her were 'They will not hang me.' The idea of dying that way offended him. He'd asked to be executed by firing squad but his request was denied. So on the evening before he was due to climb the scaffold, at around 10 p.m. on 15 October, Goering took cyanide. It will never be known for sure how Goering got hold of the poison; in his suicide note, he claimed he'd had it with him since he was arrested, secreted on his person. This is unlikely given the number of searches Goering was subjected to before entering his Nuremberg cell. Probably one of the American guards he'd befriended smuggled it in for him. When Emmy told Edda what had happened she had her own theory: 'An angel came from the ceiling of his cell to give him the poison.'[22]

Goering's ashes were dumped in an unknown spot somewhere outside Nuremberg. Reflecting on the manner of his death, Emmy could not comprehend how 'such a man' – who had 'always given so much to others, who had radiated understanding' and was 'devotion and goodness incarnate' and a 'model of compassion and fidelity' – could have been treated so harshly.[23]

Emotionally crushed and physically compromised, Emmy received medical care during the months immediately following Nuremberg. On 29 March 1947, she was considered well enough to join around 1,000 other women – including concentration camp staff, prostitutes and wives of SS men – at Göttingen, a former labour camp for Soviet women, which was separated by a barbed wire fence from thousands of male prisoners. The facility had five low barracks, floodlights, sirens and roll-call in the middle of the night.

At first, Emmy was in kept in the clinic, but then moved to a hut that had 'two enormous rats'. One of her fellow inmates was Henriette Hoffmann, whose husband Baldur von Schirach had avoided the death penalty at Nuremberg. During the war, Henriette had fallen from grace after she challenged Hitler about the mistreatment of Jews she'd witnessed while on a trip to Holland. Hitler took her complaints badly and Henriette was no longer welcome; the child prodigy had disappointed 'Uncle Adolf'.

Henriette remembered that Emmy was one of the few women who took her appearance seriously and was the only inmate who 'looked splendid, like a famous actress playing Faust's Gretchen in prison'. Emmy had one nightdress with her – which resembled 'an evening gown' – and as she was 'a glutton for cleanliness' she 'washed it at least three times a week, although it was a complicated job. She would not entrust it to anybody in the wash house and washed it herself, in a charming little wash bowl as smooth as silver.'[24]

A few weeks after Emmy was installed at Göttingen, Ilse arrived; Henriette recalled that she 'wore her hair long and looked like an itinerant preacher'.[25] Ilse shared a hut with sixteen other prisoners – according to her they were all 'wonderful'[26] – and she was especially fond of an old woman who'd worked as a cleaner at Hess's party HQ in Munich. Her mood was lifted further when her request to have her son Wolf with her was granted, and Emmy was reunited with Edda soon after.

Meanwhile, Hess had been transferred to Spandau prison in Berlin with six others on 18 July 1947, at 4 a.m. The jail covered 8 acres, had two outer rings of electric fences, nine concrete watchtowers and an inner wall that was over 26ft high. Hess occupied a cell that was 8ft long and 5ft wide, freshly painted with a metal bed, a mattress, a chair and a table, a commode, a bar of soap and a towel on a shelf, and a barred window.

Hess and Ilse continued to correspond, both keeping the tone light; Ilse told him that she'd retained her 'sense of humour' and formed 'a splendid literary study circle' with some other women, and they were tackling the work of the poet Rilke. Yet time moved slowly. By Christmas 1947, there was still no sign of an end to her confinement. But Ilse was more worried about Emmy's well-being than her own; not only was Emmy 'ill', she had also 'been through more than I have in the last two years'.[27]

Ilse was right; Emmy was struggling to deal with her protracted incarceration and that October she wrote an indignant letter to a government minister about the injustice of her situation: 'I am completely un-political … my only fault is that I am Hermann Goering's wife. You cannot possibly punish a woman for loving her husband and being happily married to him.'[28]

Both Emmy and Ilse were waiting to appear before denazification courts. While the Allies concentrated on prosecuting major figures and those closely associated with the Final Solution, the West German judiciary assumed responsibility for the hundreds of thousands who'd worked with the regime. Every suspect was ranked according to five categories of guilt, of which Category (I) – Major Offender – was the most serious.

The courts were generally quite lenient. Given that it was impossible to recruit totally new legal personnel, many of the judges involved had Nazi sympathies – by September 1950, when the process was being wound down, over 950,000 people had been tried, of whom 270,000 were pardoned.

In March 1948, Ilse finally appeared before a denazification tribunal and was completely exonerated. Hess's flight and its consequences had saved his life; now it spared Ilse any further retribution for her years of unwavering dedication to Hitler.

Emmy went to trial two months after Ilse. The proceedings lasted two days. Sixteen witnesses testified on her behalf; Jewish friends she'd helped, residents from the retirement home for actors that Emmy had founded, famous female movie stars, and even her old sparring partner Gustav Gründgens. But Emmy was too high-profile a figure to be discharged with just a slap on the wrist. As the judge observed, Emmy had 'not only shared in a large number of personal honours, but also the exceedingly luxurious lifestyle of her husband'.[29] She was placed in Category (II) – Offender – and sentenced to one year behind bars, which she'd already served. Thirty per cent of her assets and property were seized, and she was banned from acting for five years.

When news of the verdict got out, there was shock and dismay. How could Emmy Goering, who'd flaunted her power so blatantly for so many years, have got off so lightly? In Stuttgart, 300 women gathered to express their anger and disgust.

15

REMEMBERING AND FORGETTING

On 13 May 1945 Margaret and her daughter Gudrun were discovered in the Tyrol and taken into custody by the Allies. They spent two nights at an American-run hotel near Bolzano, one night in Verona, flew to Florence, and ended their journey in a British-run camp and interrogation centre near Rome, where they were the only female prisoners.

Margaret remained ignorant about her husband's fate until 20 August when she was interviewed by Ann Stringer, an American reporter with the United Press. Once it was obvious that the Allies were not going to do business with him, Himmler tried to lose himself among the thousands heading west. However, he was arrested by British soldiers and on 23 May, just as his captors realised who they were dealing with, he took cyanide.

On hearing this news, Margaret barely reacted. Stringer remembered that when she informed Margaret 'that Himmler was buried in an unmarked grave' she 'showed no surprise, no interest. It was the coldest exhibition of complete control of human feeling that I have ever witnessed.' What Stringer didn't realise was that Margaret would have considered it beneath her dignity to display emotion in front of an American journalist.

Margaret had seen press coverage about the death camps and knew her husband would be blamed; facing the prospect of having to account for his actions, she chose to plead ignorance, and told Stringer that she was 'just a woman' who 'did not understand politics'.[1]

From Rome, she and Gudrun were transported to Nuremberg. On arrival, Margaret was strip-searched and 'a vial of potassium cyanide was found stitched into the shoulder padding of her coat'. Margaret and Gudrun were placed in a bare cell with two planks for beds. Recognising that Nuremberg jail wasn't exactly an ideal environment for a teenage girl, Colonel Andrus attempted to make Gudrun's time there as normal as possible: 'I was determined that the girl's education should go on. We shopped around Nuremberg city ... to find school-books and water-colours for the child. She showed her appreciation by shyly sending me a painting she'd done surrounded by yellow and blue flowers.'[2]

Nevertheless, Gudrun was interrogated on 22 September 1945; she was asked about her final meeting with her father and whether she travelled round a lot in the war. Gudrun replied that she'd spent 'the last five years' either 'at home' or at 'school'. She talked briefly about her tour of the Dachau herb plantation, and when she was questioned about whether her parents had ever discussed their post-war plans, or anything else of significance, Gudrun's response was unequivocal: 'My mother never told me anything.'[3]

Four days later, it was Margaret's turn in the hot seat. Unsurprisingly, her interrogator was primarily interested in her husband's organisation of the Final Solution and how much Margaret knew about what was going on. At first, she claimed that Himmler never discussed the extermination camps with her, but after persistent probing she confessed that she knew some 'existed' but couldn't remember who told her about them – 'maybe' Himmler – she wasn't certain. Pushed further, Margaret admitted that she'd visited Ravensbrück – 'I have seen the concentration camp for women myself' – but didn't say when or why she went; Ravensbrück's grounds included a herb garden, though not as big as the one at Dachau, and German Red Cross nurses were employed there. Margaret didn't mention Ravensbrück in her diary, but she probably inspected the camp when she was on one of her official trips, either on her way to Poland in 1940 or to Latvia in 1942.

As to whether her husband was the driving force behind the annihilation of the Jews, Margaret shifted the blame on to Hitler: 'I think that these matters were determined by the Führer.' Otherwise, Margaret was keen to stress that her separation from Himmler meant she only saw him '15 or 20 times' during the entire war and for merely three days at a time. When it came to Hedwig, however, she was reluctant to go into detail. She pretended not to recall her first name or how many children she had, though Margaret did concede that Himmler was not a 'faithful' husband.[4]

Hedwig had made it to Austria at the end of the war but was easy to find. She was interrogated on 22 May 1945, during which she described Himmler as 'an idealist with tremendous faith in Germany and in the Führer'. Her interrogator observed that Hedwig was 'an attractive woman in her early thirties' and concluded that she was an 'unassuming woman rather than a forceful or calculating one'.[5]

Considered of no importance, Hedwig was released. She did not face a denazification hearing and settled down in Bavaria, where she kept in touch with some of Himmler's old colleagues and members of his family. In 1953, Hedwig decided to cut all connections to her past, moved to Baden-Baden, married and worked as a secretary, glad to be forgotten. Hedwig gave one interview before she died in 1994 and insisted that she knew nothing about what Himmler did during the war; there was no mention of the human furniture she'd stored in the attic of her Berchtesgaden home.

Lina and her youngest daughter were staying with Frieda Wolff at Lake Tegernsee when the war finished and were promptly ejected by US troops who wanted to commandeer Frieda's house. For a short while Lina and her daughter slept in their car before finding beds in a local hospital. Having given her child to friends for safe-keeping, Lina embarked on the long haul back to Fehmarn; she went by train from Tegernsee to Munich, by bicycle to Augsburg, hitched to Stuttgart, then took a train via Hanover to the Baltic coast. She arrived at her parents' house on 7 September 1945 and registered with the British authorities administering the region.

About a year later, Lina heard some unsettling news. She was wanted by the authorities in Prague for crimes against humanity. Scared that the British might hand her over, Lina procured false papers and went south, landing first in Munich before crossing the border into Austria where she worked as a milkmaid on a farm. Lina hated every minute, gave up, and returned to Fehmarn.

On 19 October 1947, the People's Special Court in Prague – which had heard testimony from workers on Lina's Czech estate – sentenced her to life in prison with twenty years' hard labour for starving prisoners and letting her SS guards beat them. The Czech authorities applied to have Lina extradited but the British declined to cooperate. Instead, they picked her up themselves.

Lina's denazification trial took place on 29 June 1949; she was designated as a Category (IV) – Follower – and let off without a custodial sentence. Perhaps her husband's assassination was considered punishment enough. Even by the standards of the denazification tribunals it was a strangely generous judgement given the indictment against her in Prague and Heydrich's instrumental role in shaping and directing the Final Solution, which had been systematically exposed during the 1947–48 trials of the surviving Einsatzgruppen leaders. Lina was surprised by the court's clemency: 'I became one of the few Nazi women who never got locked up, and I was a bit sorry not to have had to do some time.'[6]

Nevertheless, Lina appealed, and in January 1951 she was downgraded to Category (V) – Exonerated – and permitted to keep her assets, including her and Heydrich's Fehmarn villa. Lina converted it into a guesthouse and restaurant. Many of her visiting trade were SS veterans and through them she was introduced to a charitable organisation called Silent Help that had been formed by a core of twenty or thirty members in November 1951 to 'help all those who, as a consequence of wartime and post-war conditions, have forfeited their liberty through imprisonment, internment or similar circumstances'.[7]

Founded by Helene Elisabeth von Isenburg, a staunch Catholic and neuropath whose late husband had been a fervent Nazi and professor of family and family research in Munich, Silent Help raised money for former SS men – whether concentration camp staff or high-ranking officials – who were rotting in jail, secured them representation and paid their legal fees, pestered the authorities about their treatment and helped them adjust to civilian life after release.

Though Lina would have recognised the faces and names of the SS stalwarts who stayed at her guesthouse, her friends from her Berlin days were not among them. Schellenberg had re-invented himself as an international man of mystery and assisted US agents in their efforts to catch Nazis on the run. Max de Crinis, the euthanasia expert, and his wife Lilli poisoned themselves on 2 May 1945. Herbert Backe – who was in charge of the production and distribution of food during the war and was responsible for starving millions to death – hanged himself in his cell at Nuremberg on 6 April 1947; his wife Ursula was the only one of Lina's close-knit group who stayed in touch and helped out Lina's son Heider; he lodged with Ursula while studying engineering at Hanover University in the early 1950s.

Heider graduated and went on to work for the Dornier aircraft company. Lina's youngest daughter Marte married a local farmer and opened a small fashion shop in Fehmarn. Her other daughter Silke became a model, lived for a while in Mexico, but later returned to Fehmarn and settled down. Ever concerned about her finances, Lina launched a series of legal challenges over her right to receive the full pension owed to a widow of a German general killed in action – which was equivalent to that paid to the wife of a government minister. Despite the detailed evidence presented in court about Heydrich and the Holocaust, Lina won her case.

From as early as 1949, when Lina gave an interview to a journalist from *Der Spiegel*, she rarely missed an opportunity to talk about her husband. In 1951, she was contacted by Jean Vaughan, a writer and Nazi sympathiser, who wanted to collaborate with her on a book about Heydrich. They wrote to each other for several months. In some of their exchanges, Lina answered his specific questions, and in others she presented fragments of detail alongside more lengthy reflections.

Lina's recollections were hesitant at times, her thoughts muddled, especially when it came to the Final Solution. Her starting position was denial. Her husband was innocent of that particular crime, based on the fact that the extermination programme began after his assassination: 'As to the orders concerning the Jews in Russia, they were issued from the highest places, as far as I know, and I don't know whether they were already issued in the lifetime of my husband. But the more I think about it, the more I doubt it.' In that sense, Lina was glad Heydrich 'died in 1942' and was able to keep 'his faith and his ideal'.

Lina also pointed out that Heydrich had no authority over the camp system, which was overseen by Himmler and run by a specific branch of the SS. Heydrich might have been responsible for putting people in cages but once they walked through the camp gates his power over them ended; as Lina put it, 'never is a judge held responsible for the condition of the prison'. Yet she couldn't shake the disquieting feeling that her husband must have been aware of Himmler's mission and may well have been involved in the planning stages. But even if Heydrich was aware of the horrors to come, he didn't share any of it with her: 'He kept an absolute silence, and if he knew of what was to happen, he certainly succeeded in keeping it from us.'[8]

The process of raking over the recent past unsettled Lina and she broke off her correspondence with Vaughan. The events were still too fresh, the emotions too raw to process, Lina needed more time and distance before she could erect a monument to her husband.

After Nuremberg, Margaret and her daughter Gudrun were detained in a women's camp until November 1946; sick, depressed and dysfunctional, they were both admitted to a Church-administered mental hospital, alongside 2,500 epileptics and 800 other patients, while Margaret awaited denazification.

Between 1948 and early 1953, Margaret was involved in three different trials with three different outcomes. In 1948, she was placed in Category (III) – Lesser Offender. In 1952, following an appeal, this verdict was reduced to Category (IV) – Follower. Her reclassification was met with howls of protest – after all, she was Himmler's wife – and

Margaret was bumped up to Category (II) – Offender – which meant forfeiting any property or money linked to her husband and losing the right to vote. Margaret was not happy with this decision and for several years she battled to get the various widow and state pensions she thought were owed to her.

By then, Margaret had moved to a small apartment in Munich; she wanted a quiet life and was content to disappear into obscurity. Her old friends and colleagues were dead. Ernst-Robert Grawitz, her boss at the German Red Cross, used a grenade to obliterate himself and his family. Professor Gebhardt of the Hohenlychen clinic was arrested for his gruesome experiments on camp inmates and in the autumn of 1946 he joined other members of his profession – including Karl Brandt, whose wife had been such a close companion of Eva's – at Nuremberg for what was known as the Doctors' Trial. Professor Gebhardt was sentenced to death and executed on 2 June 1948.

More heartening for Margaret was the return of her stepson Gerhard from nearly a decade in the Soviet Union. Gerhard – who'd joined the military wing of the SS in the last months of the war – was captured by Soviet troops and deposited in a labour camp. The Soviet authorities knew about his connection to Himmler and gave him a twenty-five-year sentence. After Stalin's death, the authorities began slowly emptying their sprawling network of camps and Gerhard was freed in 1955. He headed for Munich and stayed with Margaret for a year before striking out on his own. He married, worked as a truck driver, and kept in touch with both his stepmother and stepsister.

Gudrun's relationship with Margaret had become strained; unlike her mother, she was not ready to bury the past. Having graduated high school, Gudrun left Margaret and trained to be a dressmaker. But building an independent life for herself was not easy. When her employers or co-workers discovered who she was, Gudrun was out of a job. Struggling to make ends meet, she moved back in with Margaret when her health went into steady decline.

Gudrun did find some validation, however, among the ranks of Silent Help, and worked tirelessly on its behalf for over forty years. Gudrun entered the SS self-help association when it was established and its members treated her with a degree of respect and admiration that bordered on reverence.

At the same time, Gudrun helped to set up a barely legal neo-Nazi group for her own generation called the Viking Youth. In 1958, Gudrun attended a gathering of SS veterans and fellow travellers held in Austria near an ancient Celtic site deep in the Bohemian forests. Gudrun was the guest of honour at what would become an annual celebration of her father's achievements; she considered it her 'life's work to show' Himmler 'in a different light'. Though he was 'branded as the greatest mass murderer of all time', she wanted 'to try and revise this image' and 'get the facts straight about what he thought and what he did'.[9]

Her mother died on 25 August 1967; she was 74. Margaret's silence about her husband and their lives together meant she was largely ignored by historians, who concluded that their marriage was effectively over by 1935. Only recently, after her correspondence with Himmler and portions of her diary entered the public domain, has it been possible to gain some insight into this strange sphinx-like woman, who was determined to take her secrets with her.

Other than a brief three-year marriage of convenience to a Finnish theatre director, Heydrich was the only man in Lina's life; she confessed to a women's magazine in 1967 that 'even today I still dream about my husband nearly every night. He wants to separate himself from me. He wants to leave me. I reproach him that he has deserted me. Almost every night it is the same.'[10] In 1969, Lina's Fehmarn guesthouse burned down when the thatched roof caught fire, but thanks to the insurance payment she was able to purchase a new, smaller property and resume her business. Her main concern, however, was safeguarding Heydrich's legacy. Lina was obsessed by the idea that he was being treated unfairly by posterity. In a letter to a Dutch historian, she bemoaned the fact that her husband was being judged so harshly for committing acts that he thought were 'an unavoidable political necessity', and pointed out that it was easy to condemn 'the decisions of those times from today's warm bed'.[11]

To help create a more balanced assessment, Lina spoke at great length to a number of historians. Given that she wanted to be taken seriously, Lina only agreed to work with candidates she approved of on the basis that they were going to be thorough, objective and interested in the real truth about her husband. Her most unusual encounter was with Shlomo Aronson, an Israeli academic from Tel Aviv. After covering the trial of Adolf Eichmann, Aronson decided to study Nazism in greater depth and went to Germany, where he enrolled at the Free University in Berlin and completed a thesis about the early days of the SD and the Gestapo in Munich. Aronson put to one side any hostile feelings he may have had towards Heydrich's widow and sought Lina out. Despite her anti-Semitism, Lina was prepared to indulge Aronson and gave him many hours of her time.

Lina also talked to Heinz Höhne, who became interested in the SS when he wrote a series of articles for *Der Spiegel* about former SS men who'd avoided denazification and held prominent positions in West German society. This investigation inspired Höhne to embark on his monumental, ground-breaking and definitive study of the SS; Lina was a willing interviewee and provided him with brutally frank anecdotes about Margaret and her husband. In the early 1970s, Lina gave another grandstanding performance to the American author John Toland, who was writing a biography of Hitler.

Nevertheless, Lina was still not satisfied with how Heydrich was being represented. Alongside these scholarly tomes, there were a raft of other books about Heydrich that portrayed him as Hitler's executioner and the most evil man in the Third Reich, an ice-cold sadist and butcher; the uber-Nazi. It was all too much for Lina to tolerate without fighting back, so she wrote her own book. Candid and disarmingly honest – as if she was presenting the unvarnished truth – Lina's account of her life with Heydrich featured no guilt or doubt or regret about what she was recounting. She was unapologetic about their ideological convictions and shameless about their racism and anti-Semitism, while at the same time downplaying Heydrich's direct involvement in the Final Solution.

Ultimately, she wanted the reader to appreciate that Heydrich was a supremely gifted individual. There was his talent as a musician – 'if things had not gone so horribly wrong, I would not be the widow of a war-criminal but without doubt the wife of a brilliant violinist'[12] – his athletic prowess, his courage, his diligence and work ethic, his intellect and powers of reason, and his patriotism; in the end serving Germany was the most important thing for him. He was in short, a great man. Lina's appeals fell on deaf ears. Her book – *My Life with a War Criminal* – which was published by a small German imprint in 1976, made little impact and has never been translated into English. Undeterred, she kept talking to whoever wanted to listen.

Lina died on 14 August 1985; she was 74. Not long before she passed away, Lina gave a brief TV interview. Sitting straight-backed and motionless in a book-lined study, poised and polished, her clothes conservative but smart, staring straight ahead with an unblinking stare and delivering her answers in a dry emotionless tone, she let the world know that she was proud to be Lina Heydrich.

16

THE FINAL YARDS

After her spell at Göttingen prison camp, Ilse settled in Munich and reconnected with former friends and acquaintances like Winifred Wagner. Though the Queen of Bayreuth was not taken into custody, she went through two denazification hearings. At the first, in 1947, Winifred was placed in Category (II) – Offender; at her re-trial in 1948, she was rewarded with a lower ranking, Category (III) – Lesser Offender. Nevertheless, her reputation was tainted and she gave up running the festival.

Winifred's social circle included Emmy and Edda – Emmy was full of admiration for Winifred and wrote that 'my child and I love and respect this wonderful woman with all our hearts'[1] – but ultimately, Winifred was closer to Ilse; unlike Emmy, they'd experienced the Nazi movement's early years together, and to them the 1920s seemed like an innocent and carefree time when Hitler was more easy-going and approachable, before his dreams became an appalling reality.

Though over the years Ilse and Winifred saw less of each other, they kept in touch by letter, exchanging gossip about surviving members of Hitler's clique and criticising their memoirs, and debating the merits of each year's festival programme. In 1975, five years before her death, Winifred gave an ill-judged interview during which she extolled Hitler's virtues and practically declared her love for him.

On 14 December 1955, *Der Spiegel* printed a short announcement: Ilse had opened a guesthouse and rooms were available at reasonable nightly rates. She had converted an old farmhouse high in the Bavarian Alps; it had stunning views and a room set aside for her husband that contained his books, his manuscripts and papers, a radio, and some of the toys he and Wolf used to play with together. Ilse had reserved this private space for Hess because she was convinced that one day he'd walk out of Spandau. However, she didn't expect the Allies to reconsider his life sentence unless they were forced to.

To help gain publicity for her cause, Ilse produced *Rudolf Hess: Prisoner of Peace* in 1954, the first of a series of collections of her correspondence with her husband. According to one of his fellow inmates, when Hess learned about the book he 'became feverishly excited', delighted that he had gone into print before any other of the Spandau prisoners.

On the basis of Hess's letters to her – in *Prisoner of Peace* and later editions – a casual reader might think that Ilse's husband enjoyed his incarceration; his monastic life seemed to suit him as he worked on his patch of the Spandau garden, revelled in the odd classical recital played on the chapel organ by another one of the prisoners, and read voraciously, consuming the stacks of books Ilse kept sending him – on one occasion he ordered as many as sixty. Hess delved into history, musical biography, architecture, astronomy and nuclear physics, while keeping a close eye on current events. But this was only half the story. From 1950 onwards, Hess was as difficult and disruptive as he had been in the UK and at Nuremberg. He refused to sleep. He wouldn't work. He wouldn't eat. He kept everyone awake at night with his moaning and groaning. His amnesia made regular appearances, like an annoying neighbour you can't quite get rid of.

Once again, his jailers had to decide whether it was all an act or not. Albert Speer – who was serving a twenty-year sentence – thought it was; on 1 July 1956, Speer noted in his diary that he saw Hess emerge from his cell looking 'relaxed and cheerful' but as soon as he realised Speer was watching him, Hess's 'expression changed in a fraction of a second. Suddenly a tormented, suffering man confronted me. Even his gait changed abruptly. His springy step became stiff and faltering.'[2]

Matters came to a head after one of his fellow inmates was released early due to ill health. During November 1957, there were rumours that Hess was eating small amounts of laundry detergent to give himself stomach cramps. Towards the end of the month, while he was performing his gardening duties, Hess tried to commit suicide and was found in his cell lying under his bed-sheets covered in blood.

The medical staff patched him up and the next day Hess told Speer what had happened:

> There was no guard in the vicinity, I quickly smashed my glasses and used a piece of glass to open the veins of my wrist. For three hours nobody noticed anything. I lay in the cell and had plenty of time to bleed to death. Then I would have been freed of my pain forever.[3]

On the outside, Ilse was striving to get him released. In 1956, she appealed to the UN, then in 1957 to the European Commission for Human Rights. Her argument was simple: Hess had risked everything to be an ambassador for peace and the sixteen years he'd already spent in captivity was surely sufficient punishment for his Nazi activities, not to mention the effect it had on his well-being.

On 1 October 1966 Hess became the sole prisoner at Spandau when Speer and Baldur von Schirach left the jail. Both had done their allotted time. Speer would return to his wife Margarete and become a best-selling author. Von Schirach was not so blessed. Henriette had divorced him in 1950; she remarried and spent the rest of her colourful life offending people with her provocative opinions.

Ilse and her son Wolf – who had qualified as an engineer and was married with children – realised that this was a crucial moment in their quest to liberate Hess. Not only did Hess's solitary confinement highlight his predicament, the eyes of the media were on him. On the 10th, Ilse and Wolf issued a 'Declaration to all Thinking People in the World' that condemned Hess's 'cruel' imprisonment for being 'hitherto unknown in the annals of modern law',[4] and sent it to the pope, the UN Human Rights Commission and the World Council of Churches.

At the beginning of 1967, Ilse formed the Freedom for Rudolf Hess Support Association and issued a petition for her husband's release that gained over 40,000 signatures from people in forty different countries, while the association's rallies drew an average crowd of around 500. At the same time Ilse fired off letters to politicians, intellectuals, bishops, journalists and historians asking for their backing. Many of them went on record to say they agreed with her.

During November 1969, Hess was incapacitated by a perforated ulcer and was transferred to the British Military Hospital in Berlin on 8 December. His condition was critical. Now it looked like he might actually die, Hess wrote to the Spandau director and asked if Ilse and Wolf could visit him; after twenty-eight years, Hess wanted to see his wife and child again.

On 24 December 1969 Ilse and Wolf arrived at the hospital. Forty reporters and photographers were waiting for them. Ilse was wearing a fawn, camel-hair coat and a scarf round her head. Once inside, she removed her outer garments to reveal a two-piece suit and a blouse with a white collar. She and Wolf took the lift to the third floor. Ilse had brought her husband a large bunch of winter flowers but was not permitted to give them to him. During the half-hour meeting that followed, Ilse, Wolf and Hess were flanked by four prison directors and a warden.

As Ilse and her son entered the room, Hess spontaneously leapt up to greet them, remembered that they weren't allowed to touch and made a hand-kissing gesture instead. For a moment, the atmosphere was charged with emotion, and Wolf could tell his mother was 'on the edge of tears',[5] but Ilse held her feelings in check and they began chatting about Hess's health, Wolf's engineering career, and other family members. It all went by in a flash; Ilse recalled that 'time passed very quickly, and before the conversation really got into its stride visiting time was over'. As they left, Ilse gave the Spandau director her husband's Christmas presents; a sandalwood box of Mousson lavender soap, pale blue cotton pyjamas and a recording of Schubert.

Hess recovered and returned to Spandau, against the wishes of the Western powers – Britain, America and France – who shared jurisdiction over Hess with the Soviets. They'd decided that it was no longer necessary to keep him locked up. But the Soviets felt differently. They thought Hess was just as culpable as the other defendants at Nuremberg, considering the longevity of his service to Hitler and his influence on the movement and its ideology, and were angry he'd been spared death. As for his so-called peace mission, it was only undertaken to make it easier for Hitler to crush the Soviet Union.

The Soviets also pointed out – quite correctly – that Hess remained an unreconstructed Nazi. Hess's extensive prison writings are full of contempt for liberal democracy, which he thought was feeble and corrupt, US-style capitalism, which was soulless and culturally barren, while communism was just as awful as always. His anti-Semitism was alive and well, and in the future, Hess firmly believed that Nazism would again capture hearts and minds; commenting on the prospects of converting young people to the cause, Hess was confident that when 'they become more detached from the past events, and when normal times return, they will again resume an attitude that will correspond to *ours*'.[6]

On this basis, the Soviets rejected any suggestion that Hess should be released. As a minor concession, they agreed he could receive one visitor a month for an hour at a time. Undaunted, Ilse kept up the pressure. In 1973, she delivered a complaint to the European Commission for Human Rights at Strasbourg which claimed the British government had contravened Article Three of its Human Rights charter. Her appeal was rejected in May 1975.

On 2 February 1977, Hess tried to sever an artery with a knife. On 28 December 1978, he suffered a stroke that left him almost blind. At the end of his tether and 'convinced that I have only a short time to live', Hess wrote to the Spandau directors on 4 January 1979 and asked to be released 'because of my poor state of health, and because I would like to see my grandchildren'.[7] His request was denied.

In the early 1950s Emmy got a modest apartment, which she shared with her daughter Edda, and enjoyed a pleasant existence, sustained by her memories: 'The years have gone by. Edda and I like Munich very much. Fate has brought me many sorrows but also incomparable happiness. My marriage was a gift from God and my daughter is my whole life.'[8]

Yet Emmy was not entirely satisfied. Ever since US personnel had emptied her husband's various castles and storage facilities, Emmy had resented the appropriation of Goering's immense collection of art; the Allies found a total of 1,375 paintings, 250 sculptures, 108 tapestries, 75 stained-glass windows and 175 other objets d'art. But that wasn't all of it. Numerous valuable pieces were stolen; Goering's silver-topped baton; a gold-handled sword awarded to Emmy on her wedding day; several priceless diamond-encrusted daggers; and the paintings by Memling that Goering had removed from his art train and given to Emmy.

What hurt most was the loss of the *Madonna and Child* by Cranach the Elder, which the city of Cologne presented to Edda on the day of her birth and took back after the war. Emmy agitated unsuccessfully for its return until Edda stepped into the fray. Edda had passed her *Abitur* and studied law at Munich University. In 1964, she put her newly won knowledge to use and persuaded the courts to give her back the painting, beginning a four-year wrangle with the Cologne authorities that eventually ended in victory for them; Edda's most prized possession was gone for good.

Emmy died on 8 June 1973, aged 80, and was buried at the Waldfriedhof cemetery in Munich. It was a relatively low-key, quiet affair, in keeping with the life she'd led since moving back to the city after her denazification tribunal.

After Emmy's death, Edda inhabited a neo-Nazi milieu. Her only relationship of any significance was with a wealthy journalist and Nazi follower who'd bought Goering's yacht *Carin II*. During frequent media appearances – she did a three-hour interview for Swedish TV – Edda stubbornly defended her father, and continued to cherish him until her death in 2018: 'I loved him very much, and it was obvious how much he loved me. My only memories of him are such loving ones. I cannot see him any other way.'[9]

Like her daughter, Emmy never denied her love for Goering and was distressed that so many people thought he was a monster; as far as she was concerned, he wasn't guilty of many of things of which he'd been accused. To set the record straight, in 1967 she wrote a book – *My Life with Goering* – that attempted to paint a more flattering picture of the man she adored, and give her perspective on his actions. Nowhere in the book did Emmy address her husband's decisive role in Hitler's rise to power, his development of the Luftwaffe as an instrument of terror aimed at civilians, or his management of the war economy; 'a woman in love thinks only of her partner's success, and it is of little importance to her how he obtains it'. Nor did Emmy dwell on his addictions or his insatiable appetite for material wealth. Instead, she described him as a perfect husband and father whose only crime was his loyalty to Hitler, which itself was a product of Goering's noble character, duty-bound to follow the Führer's orders however wrong-headed they might be; besides, trying to get Hitler to change his mind was like 'baying at the moon'.

Nevertheless, there is an uneasiness in her text, a sense of uncertainty and incomprehension about what the Nazis did and to what extent she and her husband were responsible. Emmy admitted that 'one never knows whether one has acted rightly or wrongly', and she was haunted by the disturbing thought that she was partly to blame: 'I often wonder now if we should not … have been a little more vigilant, and when we saw injustices being done if we should not have put up stronger resistance, especially to Adolf Hitler over the Jewish question.'[10]

On 24 February 1981, a federal court quashed a civil action brought against the West German government by Ilse's lawyer in 1977 on the basis that Hess's detention was unconstitutional. Another door had slammed in Ilse's face. That October, she saw her husband for the last time and it must have been heart-breaking for her to see him in such terrible shape, affected by pleurisy, a dodgy heart, skin rashes and knotted intestines.

In 1984, Ilse wrote the introduction to a book by her son about Hess's predicament. Ilse described how she and her husband always had a sympathetic attitude towards the British that encouraged Hess to believe he would receive a fair hearing rather than the 'inhuman treatment'[11] the British subjected him to: Ilse sincerely hoped they would finally see the error of their ways. The British authorities were already on her side, and together with their French and American partners made another approach to the Soviets about granting Hess his freedom, citing his advanced age and deteriorating health. The Soviets were unmoved and blocked their proposal.

Ilse was in her 80s by now and the accumulated stress of running the campaign and banging her head against a brick wall was weighing her down. As she took a back seat, Wolf maintained the momentum, staging candlelit vigils and protests outside Spandau, while one particularly aggrieved neo-Nazi hurled a petrol bomb into the prison. There was renewed hope that the Soviets might reconsider their inflexible position when their new premier, Mikhail Gorbachev, signalled his desire to reform the communist regime. But in the end, Hess took matters into his own hands.

On 17 August 1987, Hess was tending to the Spandau garden and asked the guard if he could retrieve something from the tool shed. The guard agreed and left Hess to his own devices. Seven minutes later, the guard went to check on his prisoner and found him sprawled awkwardly across the tool-shed floor. He was stone dead.

Apparently, Hess had stood with his back against the wall, taken hold of an extension cable, tied it to the window handle, wound the loose end round his neck and slid slowly downwards, legs stretched out, the noose tightening all the time until it strangled him to death.

Ilse and Wolf immediately cried foul. How could a frail, weak 93-year-old man have managed to kill himself like that? Ilse demanded a second autopsy and accused the British of murdering her husband. But Hess had tried to commit suicide on four previous occasions, and there is no hard evidence to suggest that this wasn't his fifth attempt. The official autopsy was carried out on the 19th and confirmed that Hess had died by his own hand. The case was closed and Spandau demolished.

Hess's body was flown to an airstrip north of Nuremberg and handed over to Wolf. He took it straight to Munich for a second autopsy, performed on 21 August, which failed to find an alternative cause of death. On the 22nd, Wolf met Ilse to discuss plans for a secret burial; the local authorities in Wunsiedel, where the Hess family had a plot, refused to accommodate Hess's coffin. The following day, Wolf had a heart attack.

Eventually, the police performed the burial over the course of three nights, depositing Hess's corpse in an undisclosed location. In March 1988, the authorities caved in to Ilse's demands and his body was dug up and interred in the Hess communal grave at Wunsiedel.

The ugly nature of her husband's death and the trauma surrounding it left Ilse exhausted, and in the early 1990s she went into a nursing home. Her son Wolf recovered from his heart failure but was never quite the same again; he died in 2001. He was only 63 years old.

On 7 September 1995, Ilse passed away. She was 96. The ceremony at her funeral was performed by Gerda's eldest son, Martin Adolf Bormann, the trained Jesuit priest who'd spent his adult life trying to make sense of the misery his father had helped cause, arranging encounter groups for the victims and perpetrators of Nazi persecution. The mourners included Gudrun Himmler, ever faithful to her father and still heavily involved with neo-Nazi organisations; Gudrun died in 2018, clinging to the belief that Himmler had done no wrong.

Ilse's funeral was held at the Wunsiedel cemetery and she was buried next to her husband in the Hess family plot. On 21 July 2011, they were separated again. Ilse and Hess's grave had become a neo-Nazi shrine that attracted a steady stream of pilgrims. The local mayor was tired of them turning up in his town to pay homage to their fallen heroes and decided to act. Ilse and her husband's gravestone was removed; Hess's remains were exhumed and cremated, and his ashes were scattered in the sea.

CONCLUSION

On paper, Gertrud Scholtz-Klink was the most powerful woman in Hitler's Germany. Born in 1902, Scholtz-Klink qualified as a nurse, joined the Nazi party in 1930 and fully supported its plans for women. In 1934, she was made Reich Women's Leader and put in charge of the Nazi Women's League; over the next few years, she became head of the Women's Bureau – set up to get women into work – and established the Nazi Mothers' Service, which taught women about their duties and responsibilities as mothers.

These organisations intruded on the lives of millions of women, and Scholtz-Klink tackled her many tasks with tremendous zeal. She designed posters and invented slogans, wrote dozens of books and pamphlets, gave hundreds of speeches at meetings and rallies, went on lecture tours, broadcast on the radio, and talked to foreign journalists.

Yet Scholtz-Klink was never in the running to be First Lady of the Reich. She was never on display at receptions or high-profile public events. She never obtained the same exalted status as the other leading women. The wives of the Nazi elite ignored her; there is no record of Scholtz-Klink ever receiving an invitation from any of them. Crucially, Hitler couldn't stand her.

The top Nazi wives were able to enjoy their many privileges and their gilded lifestyles because Hitler allowed them to. His interest in them was bound up with his need for an extended family – he took great care choosing Christmas and birthday presents for the wives and their children – and the fact that he was more relaxed and comfortable in the company of women, as long as they openly and unconditionally adored him, didn't discuss politics and conformed to the stereotypes he found attractive.

Any power the top Nazi wives had was entirely dependent on his goodwill. One false move was enough to ruin them; Hitler could reduce them to nothing with a wave of his hand. Ilse understood what it meant to incur his displeasure, as did Emmy in the final weeks of the war, while Magda felt the consequences of his anger during her separation from Goebbels.

Each of the women in this book had a different relationship to Hitler, his ideology and the Nazi regime. During the twelve years of his rule, Magda was consistently portrayed as the Reich's leading lady. The grotesque final hours of her life, full of nightmarish images and bloody tragedy, cemented her reputation as the archetypical Nazi wife. But Magda's actions were not determined by her devotion to Hitler's philosophy – she subscribed to his main ideas but began questioning them as early as 1936 – and once the war started, aside from the odd moments of euphoria when she glimpsed victory, her attitude was largely negative. Obeying her husband's wishes was also of secondary importance; pleasing Goebbels was never Magda's sole motivation, and under different circumstances she would have divorced him.

In the end, it was Magda's emotional and psychological attachment to Hitler that governed her behaviour. What made Magda different from the other women was the nature of this relationship. From the beginning, Hitler appeared to feel as strongly about her as she did about him. It seemed they were a perfect match, an idea that was given greater allure by the fact that they could never be together, creating a seductive fantasy that trapped her in Hitler's deadly embrace.

Next to Magda stands Carin Goering, whose connection to Hitler was both personal and political. Though she did not commit suicide, she seemed to consciously choose martyrdom. Given her awful health problems, an early end was always possible. If she'd wanted to live to a ripe old age, Carin could have pursued a life of leisure, a sedate existence taking long vacations in warm climates and seeking out clean mountain air. But she took a different path and threw herself into the Nazi movement, expending every ounce of energy on the struggle, dragging her husband through hell and back, all to help bring about Hitler's revolution. The effort was too much for her. But Carin's sacrifice was not forgotten; she was sanctified by the Nazi regime and held up as a shining beacon for German women to follow.

Though Carin and Magda became icons, Gerda was the closest of all the wives to the Nazi ideal of womanhood; she fitted the image created by the propaganda machine. Her husband once reminded her that 'as a Nazi child' she was 'dyed in the wool'.[1] And he was right; Gerda was exposed to Hitler before she was even a teenager, brought up by a rabidly Nazi father, married off to a Nazi hard man, and sealed away from the outside world. She lived and breathed Hitler's ideology. It was second nature to her, and Gerda's early death ensured that her beliefs were never compromised.

Lina only met Hitler once at a reception in the early 1940s and exchanged a few words with him. Nevertheless, her dedication to his mission was total and unwavering. Any doubts Lina had were related to the state of her often tense marriage, while her criticisms were directed at those she thought were failing to do their duty properly. There's no doubt that if Lina had been given real power she would have used it ruthlessly, without hesitation or remorse; a merciless warrior ready to wipe her foes off the face of the earth.

For all their differences, Lina and Margaret had one thing in common; they were both snobs who looked down their noses at most of humanity. But Margaret was from another generation to Lina, her character had been shaped by the end of the imperial era and her experiences in the First World War. Though she appeared to endorse her husband's ideas, she rarely expressed an opinion of her own. When she did, it was usually a petty complaint about a particular individual. Margaret's ingrained pessimism meant she was never able to share Himmler's utopian visions. In her own mind, she always tried to do the decent thing, conduct herself properly and act in a morally correct manner. However, she was fundamentally incapable of appreciating the suffering of others and lacked the imagination to truly comprehend the horrors that her husband inflicted on millions of people.

Emmy was the least interested in Nazism and would have played out her days on the stage if she hadn't met and fallen in love with Goering. Her wilful blindness about what that meant was not accidental and was typical of many Germans who benefited from the regime and preferred to ignore its brutal excesses and look the other way, rationalising their lack of resistance and passive complicity. Though Emmy firmly disapproved of the Nazis' radical anti-Semitism, she shrugged helplessly as the persecution intensified, deceiving herself about what was happening in the East. Emmy's excuse was that she was theatre folk, part of a select and distinctive breed that existed apart from everybody else, for whom the concerns of the 'real world' were an irrelevance.

Ilse also saw herself as part of a unique tribe; she was an idealist. Her whole identity was wrapped up in her beliefs; she was the movement's patron saint, who'd held on to her warped principles throughout all her trials and tribulations. It never occurred to Ilse that she might be wrong.

A few years before her death, a German film crew got into Ilse's nursing home hoping to interview the Grand Old Lady of Nazism. They found Ilse sitting in a crowded room and managed to come away with a few minutes of footage. Watching her skilfully fend off their questions with monosyllabic, non-committal answers, a twinkle in her eye and a smile on her lips, it's hard to shake the feeling that despite everything that had happened, Ilse still believed it had all been worthwhile.

NOTES

INTRODUCTION

1. Fromm, *Blood and Banquets*, p. 248.

PART ONE

Chapter 1
1. W. Hess, *My Father Rudolf Hess*, p. 30.
2. I. Hess, *Prisoner of Peace*, p. 81.
3. Görtemaker, *Eva Braun*, p. 74.
4. Reiche, *Development of the SA in Nürnberg*, p. 26.
5. Bormann, *The Bormann Letters*, p. 34.
6. Irving, *Goering*, p. 47.
7. Ibid., p. 55.

Chapter 2
1. Reiche, *Development of the SA in Nürnberg*, p. 48.
2. L. Mosley, *The Reich Marshal*, p. 118.
3. Toland, *Hitler*, p. 199.
4. Knopp, *Hitler's Henchmen*, p. 184.
5. NA: IMT − RG 59:73088690.
6. Bormann, *The Bormann Letters*, p. 93.
7. Irving, *Goering*, p. 70.
8. Ibid., p. 88.

Chapter 3

1. Toland, *Hitler*, p. 950.
2. Schwärzwaller, *Rudolf Hess*, p. 78.
3. Manvell and Fraenkl, *Hess*, p. 38.
4. Wagner, *Heritage of Fire*, p. 31.
5. Schwärzwaller, *Rudolf Hess*, p. 78.
6. Hoffmann, *Hitler Was My Friend*, p. 148.
7. Von Schirach, *The Price of Glory*, pp. 178–9.
8. Sigmund, *Women of the Third Reich*, p. 132.
9. Himmler and Wildt (eds), *The Private Heinrich Himmler*, p. 30.
10. Ibid., p. 49; Longerich, *Heinrich Himmler*, p. 106.
11. Himmler, *The Himmler Brothers*, p. 79.
12. Ibid., pp. 66 and 83.
13. Longerich, *Heinrich Himmler*, p. 107.
14. Himmler, *The Himmler Brothers*, pp. 69 and 71.
15. Irving, *Goering*, p. 93.
16. Whiting, *The Hunt for Martin Bormann*, p. 50.
17. Von Lang, *Bormann*, p. 36; Whiting, *The Hunt for Martin Bormann*, p. 45.
18. Himmler, *The Himmler Brothers*, p. 112.
19. Ibid., p. 118.

Chapter 4

1. Wyllie, *Goering and Goering*, p. 37.
2. Heydrich, *Mein Leben mit Reinhard*, p. 23.
3. Knopp, *The SS*, p. 120.
4. Read, *The Devil's Disciples*, p. 216.
5. Wagener, *Hitler*, pp. 241, 255 and 258.
6. Ullrich, *Hitler: A Biography*, p. 284.
7. Himmler, *The Himmler Brothers*, p. 132.
8. Toland, *Hitler*, pp. 229–30.
9. L. Mosley, *The Reich Marshal*, p. 164.

Chapter 5

1. E. Goering, *My Life with Goering*, pp. 11–12 and 14.
2. Ibid., pp. 52 and 54.
3. Ibid., pp. 8 and 12.
4. Dederichs, *Heydrich*, p. 52.
5. Deschner, *Heydrich*, p. 57.
6. D'Almeida, *High Society in the Third Reich*, p. 37.
7. H. Goering, *Germany Reborn*, p. 129.
8. Gerwath, *Hitler's Hangman*, p. 68.
9. Riefenstahl, *A Memoir*, pp. 124 and 168.
10. Himmler, *The Himmler Brothers*, p. 58.

PART TWO

Chapter 6
1. E. Goering, *My Life with Goering*, pp. 28 and 46.
2. Fromm, *Blood and Banquets*, p. 197.
3. Reuth, *Goebbels*, p. 183.
4. Guenther, *Nazi Chic?*, p. 151.
5. Ibid., p. 132.
6. Ibid., p. 172.
7. Ibid.
8. Sigmund, *Women of the Third Reich*, p. 23.
9. Wyllie, *Goering and Goering*, p. 101.
10. E. Goering, *My Life with Goering*, p. 56.
11. Hillenbrand, *Underground Humour in Nazi Germany*, p. 25.
12. E. Goering, *My Life with Goering*, p. 78.
13. Von Schirach, *The Price of Glory*, p. 87.
14. Fromm, *Blood and Banquets*, p. 66.
15. E. Goering, *My Life with Goering*, p. 83.
16. Hoffmann, *Hitler Was My Friend*, p. 141.
17. Sigmund, *Women of the Third Reich*, pp. 158–9; Knopp, *Hitler's Women* p. 19; Görtemaker, *Eva Braun*, p. 92.
18. Görtemaker, *Eva Braun*, p. 98.
19. Kempka, *I was Hitler's Chauffeur*, p. 13.
20. Klabunde, *Magda Goebbels*, p. 233.
21. Hoffmann, *Hitler Was My Friend*, p. 165.
22. Wagner, *Heritage of Fire*, p. 141.
23. D. Mosley, *A Life of Contrasts*, p. 130.
24. Ibid.
25. Hillenbrand, *Underground Humour in Nazi Germany*, p. 28.
26. Ludecke, *I Knew Hitler*, p. 378.
27. Romani, *Tainted Goddesses*, p. 159.

Chapter 7
1. Schwärzwaller, *Rudolf Hess*, p. 90.
2. Schroeder, *He Was My Chief*, p. 8.
3. Ibid.
4. Kempka, *I was Hitler's Chauffeur*, p. 39.
5. Schroeder, *He Was My Chief*, pp. 9–10.
6. Von Lang, *Bormann*, p. 52.
7. Linge, *With Hitler to the End*, p. 93.
8. Bormann, *The Bormann Letters*, p. 35.
9. Wagner, *Heritage of Fire*, pp. 85–87.
10. I. Hess, *Prisoner of Peace*, p. 129.
11. Manvell and Fraenkl, *Doctor Goebbels*, p. 59.

12. NA: IMT – RG 238: 57322925.
13. Görtemaker, *Eva Braun*, p. 100.
14. Schroeder, *He Was My Chief*, p. 19.
15. MC: US/MISC/14; Brandt, 'The Brandt Interview', p. 22.
16. Von Lang, *Bormann*, p. 96.
17. Hoffmann, *Hitler Was My Friend*, p. 202.
18. Von Lang, *Bormann*, p. 116.
19. Toland, *Hitler*, p. 415.
20. Manvell and Fraenkl, *Doctor Goebbels*, p. 47.
21. Semmler, *Goebbels*, p. 36.
22. Riefenstahl, *A Memoir*, p. 163.
23. Irving, *Hess*, p. 57; Schwärzwaller, *Rudolf Hess*, pp. 143–4.
24. Ibid., p. 108.
25. Pryce-Jones, *Unity Mitford*, pp. 138–9.
26. I. Hess, *Prisoner of Peace*, p. 144.
27. Ibid. p. 22.
28. Von Schirach, *The Price of Glory*, p. 155.
29. Speer, *Inside the Third Reich*, p. 179.
30. Ernst, 'Rudolf Hess (Hitler's Deputy) on Alternative Medicine'.
31. Semmler, *Goebbels*, p. 35.
32. Taylor, Timm and Hern (eds), *Not Straight from Germany*, p. 319.
33. Semmler, *Goebbels*, p. 35.

Chapter 8

1. USHMM: Doc: 1999. A.0092; *Frau Marga Himmler Diaries 1937–1945* (trans), p. 10.
2. Höhne, *The Order of the Death's Head*, p. 164.
3. Von Schirach, *The Price of Glory*, p. 61.
4. Pryce-Jones, *Unity Mitford*, p. 157.
5. L. Heydrich and J. Vaughan *Correspondence*, 7 March 1951 from Real History www.fp.co.uk and Höhne, *The Order of the Death's Head*, p. 165.
6. Ibid., p. 166.
7. USHMM: M. Himmler, pp. 11–12.
8. Höhne pp. 128–9.
9. L. Heydrich and J. Vaughan, *Correspondence*, 12 December 1951; Williams, *Heydrich*, p. 69.
10. Schellenberg, *The Schellenberg Memoirs*, p. 34.
11. L. Heydrich and J. Vaughan, *Correspondence*, 12 December 1951.
12. Ibid.
13. Bassett, *Hitler's Spy Chief*, p. 99.
14. USHMM: M. Himmler, p. 9.
15. Ibid.
16. L. Heydrich and Jean Vaughan, *Correspondence*, 7 March 1951.
17. Longerich, *Himmler*, p. 233.
18. McDonough, *The Gestapo*, p. 180.

19. Gerwath, *Hitler's Hangman*, p. 112.
20. MacDonald, *The Killing of SS Obergruppenfuhrer Reinhard Heydrich*, p. 14.
21. Ibid.
22. Schellenberg, *The Schellenberg Memoirs*, pp. 35–6.
23. Ibid.
24. USHMM: M. Himmler, p. 11.
25. Ibid., pp. 2 and 5.
26. Lambert, *The Lost Life of Eva Braun*, p. 346.
27. USHMM: M. Himmler, p. 14.

Chapter 9

1. E. Goering, *My Life with Goering*, p. 92.
2. Meissner, *Magda Goebbels*, p. 140.
3. Read, *The Devil's Disciples*, p. 491.
4. Wagner, *Heritage of Fire*, p. 203.
5. USHMM: M. Himmler, pp. 15–16.
6. Ullrich, *Hitler: A Biography*, p. 609.
7. Döhring, Krause and Plaim, *Living with Hitler*, p. 126.
8. E. Goering, *My Life with Goering*, p. 81.
9. Heydrich, *Mein Leben mit Reynard*, p. 71; Knopp, *The SS*, p. 131; Heydrich, *Mein Leben mit Reynard*, p. 81.
10. Friedländer, *Nazi Germany and the Jews*, p. 115.
11. Ullrich, *Hitler: A Biography*, p. 632.
12. Von Lang, *Bormann*, p. 116.
13. Linge, *With Hitler to the End*, p. 94.
14. USHMM: M. Himmler, pp. 17–18.
15. K. Himmler p. 189.
16. Ibid..
17. Himmler, *The Himmler Brothers*, p. 244.
18. USHMM: M. Himmler, p. 19.
19. www.history.com/this-day-in-history
20. Goebbels, *Diaries 1939–1941*, pp. 4 and 14.
21. Speer, *Inside the Third Reich*, p. 220.
22. USHMM: M. Himmler, p. 21.
23. Gerwath, *Hitler's Hangman*, p. 139.
24. USHMM: M. Himmler, p. 23.
25. E. Goering, *My Life with Goering*, pp. 2–3.
26. I. Hess, *Prisoner of Peace*, p. 15.
27. Irving, *Hess*, p. 57.
28. D. Mosley, *A Life of Contrasts*, p. 145.
29. Pryce-Jones, *Unity Mitford*, p. 235.
30. D. Mosley, *A Life of Contrasts*, p. 142.

PART THREE

Chapter 10

1. Goebbels, *Diaries 1939–1941*, p. 109.
2. Fox, 'Everyday Heroines', p. 28.
3. Goebbels, *Diaries 1939–1941*, p. 79.
4. USHMM: M. Himmler, p. 24.
5. Ibid., p. 23.
6. Ibid., p. 24.
7. Bryant, *Confronting the 'Good Death'*, p. 38.
8. Kater, *Doctors Under Hitler*, p. 129.
9. Stephenson, *Women in Nazi Germany*, p. 34.
10. Schellenberg, *The Schellenberg Memoirs*, p. 86.
11. Ibid., p. 265.
12. L. Mosley, *The Reich Marshal*, p. 312.
13. USHMM: M. Himmler, p. 24.
14. Ibid., p. 25.
15. Ibid., pp. 25 and 27.
16. Schroeder, *He Was My Chief*, pp. 160–1.
17. Goebbels, *Diaries 1939–1941*, p. 157.
18. Ibid., p. 171.
19. USHMM: M. Himmler, p. 26.
20. Ibid., p. 30.
21. I. Hess, *Prisoner of Peace*, pp. 12 and 19–24.
22. Ibid., p. 25.
23. Toland, *Hitler*, p. 665.
24. I. Hess, *Prisoner of Peace*, p. 14.
25. Ibid. p. 27.
26. Goebbels, *Diaries 1939–1941*, pp. 364 and 367.
27. Hillenbrand, *Underground Humour in Nazi Germany*, p. 39.
28. Hutton, *Hess*, p. 110.

Chapter 11

1. Döhring, Krause and Plaim, *Living with Hitler*, pp. 140–1.
2. Schroeder, *He Was My Chief*, p. 112.
3. Hutton, *Hess*, p. 100.
4. McGinty, *Camp Z*, p. 181.
5. Schellenberg, *The Schellenberg Memoirs*, p. 203.
6. Kurlander, *Hitler's Monsters*, p. 120.
7. Goebbels, *Diaries 1939–1941*, p. 408.
8. Gerwath, *Hitler's Hangman*, pp. 189–90.
9. Williams, *Heydrich*, p. 101.
10. Deschner, *Heydrich*, p. 191.
11. Schellenberg, *The Schellenberg Memoirs*, p. 239.

12. USHMM: M. Himmler, p. 29.
13. Himmler, *The Himmler Brothers*, p. 199.
14. USHMM: M. Himmler, p. 30; K. Himmler, p. 211.
15. USHMM: M. Himmler, p. 30.
16. Himmler, *The Himmler Brothers*, p. 218.
17. Himmler, *The Himmler Brothers*, pp. 233–4.
18. Ibid., p. 232.
19. USHMM: M. Himmler, pp. 30 and 32.
20. Knopp, *The SS*, p. 160.
21. Williams, *Heydrich*, p. 160.
22. Ibid., p. 176.
23. McGinty, *Camp Z*, p. 299.
24. Ibid., p. 300.
25. I. Hess, *Prisoner of Peace*, p. 43.
26. Ibid., p. 46.
27. Schwärzwaller, *Rudolf Hess*, p. 190.
28. I. Hess, *Prisoner of Peace*, p. 43.
29. Goebbels, *Diaries 1942–1943*, pp. 175 and 218.
30. Meissner, *Magda Goebbels*, p. 213.
31. Gerwath, *Hitler's Hangman*, p. 270.
32. Williams, *Heydrich*, p. 189.
33. Dederichs, *Heydrich*, p. 145.
34. Gerwath, *Hitler's Hangman*, p. 199.
35. Ibid., p. 279.
36. USHMM: M. Himmler, p. 32.
37. Ibid., p. 33.

Chapter 12

1. Stephenson, *Women in Nazi Germany*, pp. 56–7.
2. Goebbels, *Diaries 1942–1943*, p. 260.
3. Ibid., p. 309.
4. Ibid., p. 138.
5. Klabunde, *Magda Goebbels*, p. 301; Meissner, *Magda Goebbels*, pp. 224–5.
6. Schwärzwaller, *Rudolf Hess*, p. 179.
7. I. Hess, *Prisoner of Peace*, pp. 44-45.
8. Ibid., p. 46.
9. Ibid.
10. Bormann, *The Bormann Letters*, pp. 37–8.
11. Ibid., p. 6.
12. Ibid., pp. 8–9.
13. Kempka, *I was Hitler's Chauffeur*, p. 43.
14. NA: IMT – RG 238:57318818.
15. Himmler, *The Himmler Brothers*, p. 249.
16. Knopp, *Hitler's Hitmen*, p. 158.
17. Bormann, *The Bormann Letters*, p. 39.

18. Ibid., pp. 42 and 45.
19. Dederichs, *Heydrich*, p. 167.
20. Ibid., p. 163.
21. I. Hess, *Prisoner of Peace*, p. 47.
22. Görtemaker, *Eva Braun*, p. 219.
23. E. Goering, *My Life with Goering*, p. 106.
24. Goebbels, *Diaries 1942–1943*, p. 524.
25. Semmler, *Goebbels*, p. 115.
26. E. Goering, *My Life with Goering*, p. 146.
27. Perry, 'Nazifying Christmas', p. 604.
28. Irving, *Goering*, p. 518.
29. L. Mosley, *The Reich Marshal*, p. 365.
30. Dederichs, *Heydrich*, p. 164.
31. USHMM: M. Himmler, p. 34.
32. Ibid., p. 35.
33. Himmler, *The Himmler Brothers*, p. 259.
34. Ohler, *Blitzed*, p. 192.
35. Sigmund, *Women of the Third Reich*, pp. 174–5.
36. Bormann, *The Bormann Letters*, p. 66.
37. USHMM: M. Himmler, pp. 35–6.
38. E. Goering, *My Life with Goering*, p. 112.
39. Irving, *Hess*, p. 395.

Chapter 13

1. Bormann, *The Bormann Letters*, pp. 119–20.
2. Knopp, *Hitler's Hitmen*, p. 146.
3. Lebert and Lebert, *My Father's Keeper*, p. 113.
4. Bormann, *The Bormann Letters*, pp. 67, 37, 173 and 104–6.
5. USHMM: M. Himmler, p. 36.
6. NA: IMT – RG 238: 57323277.
7. Semmler, *Goebbels*, pp. 174–5.
8. NA: IMT – RG 238: 57323277.
9. Himmler, *The Himmler Brothers*, p. 277.
10. USHMM: M. Himmler, p. 36.
11. Dederichs, *Heydrich*, p. 167.
12. Schroeder, *He Was My Chief*, p. 146.
13. Bormann, *The Bormann Letters*, p. 177.
14. Semmler, *Goebbels*, pp. 185–6.
15. Goebbels, *Diaries: Final Entries 1945*, p. 45.
16. Ibid., pp. 192, 83, 254 and 317–18.
17. I. Hess, *Prisoner of Peace*, p. 48.
18. NA: IMT – RG 238: 6242149.
19. NA: IMT – RG 238: 57323277.
20. Junge, *Until the Final Hour*, pp. 159–60.

21. DNTC: IMT – Vol. 004 – Subdivison 8/Hitler Section 8.15.
22. Ibid.
23. Goeschel, 'Suicide at the End of the Third Reich', p. 164.
24. L. Mosley, *The Reich Marshal*, p. 378.
25. Schroeder, *He Was My Chief*, p. 188.
26. L. Mosley, *The Reich Marshal*, p. 382.
27. NA: RG 242: 6883511.
28. Kempka, *I was Hitler's Chauffeur*, p. 70.
29. Ibid., pp. 89–90.
30. Linge, *With Hitler to the End*, p. 199; Kempka, *I was Hitler's Chauffeur*, p. 78.
31. Junge, *Until the Final Hour*, p. 174.
32. Linge, *With Hitler to the End*, p. 207.

PART FOUR

Chapter 14

1. I. Hess, *Prisoner of Peace*, p. 49.
2. Kempka, *I was Hitler's Chauffeur*, p. 95.
3. Linge, *With Hitler to the End*, p. 210.
4. Kempka, *I was Hitler's Chauffeur*, p. 152.
5. Whiting, *The Hunt for Martin Bormann*, p. 35.
6. Farago, *Aftermath*, p. 163.
7. NA: IMT – *RG 238: 573188178.*
8. Andrus, *The Infamous at Nuremberg*, p. 73.
9. NA: IMT – RG 238: 57323137.
10. Ibid.
11. NA: IMT – RG 238: 57322925.
12. NA: IMT – RG *238: 57323137.*
13. NA: IMT – RG 59: 73088690; RG 238: 57322925.
14. Irving, *Hess*, pp. 496–7.
15. I. Hess, *Prisoner of Peace*, p. 38.
16. Goering, *My Life with Goering*, p. 135.
17. DNTC: IMT – Vol. 014 Subdivision 35/Goering Section 35.03.
18. Andrus, *The Infamous at Nuremberg*, p. 161.
19. Persico, *Nuremberg*, p. 297.
20. Sigmund, *Women of the Third Reich*, p. 63.
21. Von Schirach, *The Price of Glory*, p. 87.
22. E. Goering, *My Life with Goering*, p. 159.
23. Ibid.
24. Von Schirach, *The Price of Glory*, pp. 134 and 137.
25. Ibid., p. 138.
26. I. Hess, *Prisoner of Peace*, p. 89.
27. Ibid., p. 96.

28. Sigmund, *Women of the Third Reich*, p. 64.
29. Ibid.

Chapter 15
1. Crasnianski, *Children of the Nazis*, p. 16; Himmler, the Himmler Brothers, p. 287.
2. Andrus, *The Infamous at Nuremberg*, pp. 69 and 139.
3. NA: IMT – RG 238: 57323267.
4. NA: IMT – RG 238: 57323277.
5. NA: IMT – RG 238: 6242149.
6. Dederichs, *Heydrich*, p. 171.
7. Knopp, *The SS*, p. 336.
8. L. Heydrich and J. Vaughan, *Correspondence*, 7 March 1951.
9. Lebert and Lebert, p. 106.
10. Dederichs, *Heydrich*, p. 175.
11. Ibid., p. 174.
12. Knopp, *The SS*, p. 120.

Chapter 16
1. E. Goering, *My Life with Goering*, p. 87.
2. Speer, *Spandau*, pp. 216 and 291.
3. Ibid., p. 343.
4. Posner, *Hitler's Children*, p. 62.
5. Ibid., p. 65; W. Hess, *My Father Rudolf Hess*, p. 288.
6. Schwärzwaller, *Rudolf Hess*, p. 16.
7. Posner, *Hitler's Children*, p. 69.
8. E. Goering, *My Life with Goering*, p. 168.
9. Posner, *Hitler's Children*, pp. 212–13.
10. E. Goering, *My Life with Goering*, pp. 15 and 95.

CONCLUSION
1. Bormann, *The Bormann Letters*, p. 49.

BIBLIOGRAPHY

ARCHIVE SOURCES

Donovan Nuremberg Trials Collection, Cornell University Library (DNTC).
Institute for Contemporary History, Munich (ICH).
Musmanno Collection, Gumberg Library, DuQuesne University (MC).
National Archives, Washington DC (NA).
Swiss Federal Archives, Bern (SFA).
United States Holocaust Memorial Museum (USHMM).

Books
Alford K.D., *Nazi Plunder: Great Treasure Stories of World War II* (De Capo Press, 2000).
Andrus, B., *The Infamous at Nuremberg* (Leslie & Frewin, 1969).
Ascheid, A., *Hitler's Heroines: Stardom and Womanhood in Nazi Cinema* (Temple University Press, 2003).
Bach, S., *Leni: The Life and Work of Leni Riefenstahl* (Knopf/Doubleday, 2007).
Bassett, R., *Hitler's Spy Chief: The Wilhelm Canaris Story* (Cassell, 2005).
Bird, E., *The Loneliest Man in the World: The Inside Story of the 30-year Imprisonment of Rudolf Hess* (Sphere, 1974).
Black, M. and Kurlander, E. (eds), *Revisiting the 'Nazi Occult': Histories, Realities, Legacies* (Camden House, 2015).
Bloch, M., *Ribbentrop* (Abacus, 2003).
Boak, H., *Women in the Weimar Republic* (Manchester University Press, 2013).
Bormann, M., *The Bormann Letters: The Private Correspondence between Martin Bormann and his Wife from January 1943–April 1945* (Weidenfeld and Nicolson, 1954).
Bramwell, A., *Blood and Soil: Walther Darré and Hitler's Green Party* (Kensal Press, 1985).
Bridenthal, R., Grossmann, A. and Kaplan, M. (eds), *When Biology Became Destiny: Women in Weimar and Nazi Germany* (Monthly Review Press, 1984).

Browning, C. and Matthias, J., *The Origins of the Final Solution: The Evolution of Nazi Jewish Policy 1939–1942* (William Heinemann, 2004).

Bryant, M., *Confronting the 'Good Death': Nazi Euthanasia on Trial 1945–1953* (University of Colorado Press, 2005).

Calic, E., *Reinhard Heydrich: The Chilling Story of the Man who Masterminded the Nazi Death Camps* (William Morrow Company Inc., 1985).

Cocks, G., *Psychotherapy in the Third Reich: The Göring Institute* (Oxford University Press, 1985).

Crasnianski, T., *The Children of the Nazis: The Sons and Daughters of Himmler, Göring, Höss, Mengele and others – Living with a Father's Monstrous Legacy* (Arcade Publishing, 2018).

D'Almeida, F., *High Society in the Third Reich* (Polity, 2008).

De Courcy, A., *Diana Mosley* (Vintage, 2004).

Dederichs, M., *Heydrich: The Face of Evil* (Greenhill, 2009).

Deschner, G., *Heydrich: The Pursuit of Total Power* (Orbis, 1981).

Dietrich, O., *The Hitler I Knew: Memoirs of the Third Reich's Press Officer* (Skyhorse Publishing, 2010).

Döhring, H., Krause, W.H. and Plaim, A., *Living with Hitler: Accounts of Hitler's Household Staff* (Greenhill, 2018).

Dornberg, J., *Munich 1923: The Story of Hitler's First Grab for Power* (Harper & Row, 1982).

Douglas-Hamilton, J., *Motive for a Mission: The Story Behind Hess's Flight to Britain* (Macmillan, 1971).

Evans, R., *The Coming of the Third Reich* (Penguin, 2004).

——*The Third Reich at War: How the Nazis led Germany from Conquest to Disaster* (Penguin, 2009).

——*The Third Reich in Power: 1933–1939* (Penguin, 2006).

Farago, L., *Aftermath: Bormann and the Fourth Reich* (Hodder and Stoughton, 1975).

Fest, J., *Inside Hitler's Bunker: The Last days of the Third Reich* (Pan, 2004).

——*Speer: The Final Verdict* (Weidenfeld & Nicolson, 2001).

——*The Face of the Third Reich* (Penguin, 1979).

Fisher, M.J., *A Terrible Splendor: Three Extraordinary Men, A World Poised for War, and the Greatest Tennis Match Ever Played* (Crown Publishers, 2009).

Friedländer, S., *Nazi Germany and the Jews 1933–1945* (Phoenix, 2009).

Fromm, B., *Blood and Banquets: A Berlin Social Diary* (Carol Publishing Group, 1990).

Gadberry, G., *Theatre in the Third Reich, the Pre-war Years: Essays on Theatre in Nazi Germany* (Greenwood, 1995).

Gerwath, R., *Hitler's Hangman: The Life of Heydrich* (Yale University Press, 2011).

Gilbert, G., *Nuremberg Diary* (Da Capo Press, 1947).

Goebbels, J., *The Diaries of Joseph Goebbels: Final Entries 1945* (ed. H. Trevor-Roper) (GP Putnam's Sons, 1978).

——*The Goebbels Diaries 1939–1941* (ed. and trans. F. Taylor) (Sphere, 1982).

——*The Goebbels Diaries 1942–1943* (ed. and trans. L. Lochner) (Doubleday, 1948).

Goering, E., *My Life with Goering* (David Bruce & Watson, 1972).

Goering, H., *Germany Reborn* (Elkin Mathews and Marrot, 1934).

Goeschel, C., *Mussolini and Hitler: The Forging of the Fascist Alliance* (Yale University Press, 2018).

Görtemaker, H.B., *Eva Braun: Life with Hitler* (Penguin, 2011).

Graber, G., *The Life and Times of Reinhard Heydrich* (McKay, 1980).

Grange, W., *Hitler Laughing: Comedy in the Third Reich* (University Press of America, 2006).

Grunberger, R., *A Social History of the Third Reich* (Penguin, 1974).

Guenther, I., *Nazi Chic? Fashioning Women in the Third Reich* (Bloomsbury, 2004).

Gun, N., *Eva Braun: Hitler's Mistress* (Meredith Press, 1968).

Hake, S., *Popular Cinema In the Third Reich* (University of Texas Press, 2001).

Hamann, B., *Winifred Wagner: A Life at the Heart of Hitler's Bayreuth* (Granta, 2005).

Haste, C., *Nazi Women* (Channel 4 Books, 2001).

Hayman, R., *Hitler and Geli* (Bloomsbury, 1997).

Heins, L., *Nazi Film Melodrama* (University of Illinois Press, 2013).

Helm, S., *If This is a Woman: Inside Ravensbrück, Hitler's Concentration Camp for Women* (Abacus, 2015).

Henderson, N., *Failure of a Mission 1937–1939* (GP Putnam's Sons, 1940).

Herzog, D., *Sex after Fascism: Memory and Morality in Twentieth-Century Germany* (Princeton University Press, 2005).

Hess, I., *Prisoner of Peace* (Institute for Historical Review, 1954).

Hess, W., *My Father Rudolf Hess* (WH Allen, 1984).

Heydrich, L., *Mein Leben mit Reinhard: Die Persönliche Biographie* (Druffel & Vowinckel, 2012).

Hillenbrand, F., *Underground Humour in Nazi Germany 1933–1945* (Routledge, 1995).

Himmler, K., *The Himmler Brothers: A German Story* (Macmillan, 2007).

Himmler, K. and Wildt, M. (eds), *The Private Heinrich Himmler: Letters of a Mass Murderer* (St Martin's Press, 2014).

Hoffmann, H., *Hitler Was My Friend* (Burke Publishing, 1955).

Höhne, H., *Canaris: Hitler's Master Spy* (Doubleday, 1976).

——*The Order of the Death's Head: The Story of Hitler's SS* (Penguin, 1969).

Hutton, J.B., *Hess: The Man and his Mission* (David Bruce & Watson, 1970).

Irving, D., *Goebbels: Mastermind of the Third Reich* (St Martin's Press, 1994).

——*Goering: A Biography* (Focal Point, 1989).

——*Hess: The Missing Years 1941–1945* (Macmillan, 1987).

Junge, T., *Until the Final Hour: Hitler's Last Secretary* (Phoenix, 2005).

Kater, M., *Doctors Under Hitler* (Chapel Hill, 1989).

Kelley, D., *22 Cells in Nuremberg* (WH Allen, 1947).

Kempka, E., *I was Hitler's Chauffeur: The Memoirs of Erich Kempka* (Frontline, 2012).

Kershaw, I., *Hitler: 1889–1936 Hubris* (Penguin, 1999).

——*Hitler: 1936–1945 Nemesis* (Penguin, 2000).

——*The End: Nazi Germany 1944–45* (Penguin, 2012).

King, D., *The Trial of Adolf Hitler: The Beer Hall Putsch and the Rise of Nazi Germany* (Pan, 2017).

Kirkpatrick, C., *Women in Nazi Germany* (Jarrolds, 1939).

Klabunde, A., *Magda Goebbels* (Little Brown, 2001).

Knopp, G., *Hitler's Henchmen* (Sutton, 2000).
——*Hitler's Hitmen* (Sutton, 2002).
——*Hitler's Women* (Sutton, 2003).
——*The SS: A Warning from History* (The History Press, 2008).
Kurlander, E., *Hitler's Monsters: A Supernatural History of the Third Reich* (Yale University Press, 2017).
Lambert, A., *The Lost Life of Eva Braun* (Arrow, 2007).
Leasor, J., *The Uninvited Envoy* (McGraw-Hill, 1962).
Lebert, S. and Lebert, N., *My Father's Keeper: The Children of the Nazi Leaders – An Intimate History of Damage and Denial* (Little Brown, 2001).
Le Tissier, T., *Farewell to Spandau* (The History Press, 2008).
Lifton, R., *The Nazi Doctors: Medical Killing and the Psychology of Genocide* (Basic Books, 1988).
Linge, H., *With Hitler to the End: The Memoirs of Adolf Hitler's Valet* (Frontline, 2013).
London, J., *Theatre Under the Nazis* (Manchester University Press, 2000).
Longerich, P., *Goebbels: A Biography* (Vintage, 2015).
——*Heinrich Himmler* (Oxford University Press, 2012).
Lower, W., *Hitler's Furies: German Women in the Nazi Killing Fields* (Vintage, 2014).
Ludecke, K., *I Knew Hitler* (Jarrolds, 1938).
MacDonald, C., *The Killing of SS Obergruppenführer Reinhard Heydrich* (Papermac, 1989)
Manvell, R. and Fraenkl, H., *Doctor Goebbels: His Life and Death* (Frontline, 1960)
——*Goering* (Greenhill, 1962).
——*Hess* (MacGibbon & Kee, 1971).
Meissner, H., *Magda Goebbels: First Lady of the Third Reich* (Nelson Canada Ltd, 1980).
McDill, J., *Lessons from the Enemy: How Germany Cares for her War Disabled* (Lea & Febiger, 1918).
McDonough, F., *The Gestapo: The Myth and Reality of Hitler's Secret Police* (Coronet, 2016).
McGinty, S., *Camp Z: How British Intelligence Broke Hitler's Deputy* (Quercus, 2011)
McGovern, J., *Martin Bormann* (Arthur Barker Ltd, 1968).
Middlebrook, M. and Everitt, C., *The Bomber Command War Diaries: An Operational Reference Book 1939–1945* (Penguin, 1990).
Mosley, D., *A Life of Contrasts: The Autobiography* (Gibson Square Books, 2009).
Mosley, L., *The Reich Marshal: A Biography of Hermann Goering* (Pan, 1977).
Nicholas, L, *The Rape of Europa: The Fate of Europe's Treasures in the Third Reich and the Second World War* (Vintage, 1995).
Ohler, N., *Blitzed: Drugs in Nazi Germany* (Penguin, 2017).
Overy, R., *Goering: The Iron Man* (Routledge, 1984).
Padfield, P., *Himmler: Reichsführer SS* (Papermac, 1990).
Persico, J., *Nuremberg: Infamy on Trial* (Penguin, 1994).
Petropoulos, J., *Art as Politics in the Third Reich* (The University of North Carolina Press, 1996).
——*Artists under Hitler: Collaboration and Survival in Nazi Germany* (Yale University Press, 2014).

——*The Faustian Bargain: The Art World in Nazi Germany* (Penguin, 2001).

Phipps, E., *Our Man in Berlin: The Diary of Sir Eric Phipps 1933–1937* (Palgrave, 2008).

Picknett, L., Prince, C. and Prior, S., *Double Standards: The Rudolf Hess Cover-Up* (Time Warner, 2001).

Pine, L., *Nazi Family Policy 1933–1945* (Bloomsbury, 1997).

Pope, E., *Munich Playground* (GP Putnam's Sons, 1941).

Posner, G., *Hitler's Children: Inside the Families of the Third Reich* (Heinemann, 1991).

Pringle, H., *The Master Plan: Himmler's Scholars and the Holocaust* (Harper Perennial, 2006).

Proctor, R., *The Nazi War on Cancer* (Princeton University Press, 1999).

Pryce-Jones, D., *Unity Mitford: A Quest* (Weidenfeld & Nicolson, 1976).

Read, A., *The Devil's Disciples: The Lives and Times of Hitler's Inner Circle* (Pimlico, 2003).

Regin, N., *Sweeping the Nation: Domesticity and National Identity in Germany 1870–1945* (Cambridge University Press, 2007).

Reiche, E., *The Development of the SA in Nürnberg 1922–1934* (Cambridge University Press, 1986).

Reiss, C., *Joseph Goebbels: A Biography* (Hollis & Carter, 1949).

Reitsch, H., *The Sky My Kingdom* (Bodley Head, 1955).

Reuth, R.G., *Goebbels* (Constable, 1993).

Rhodes, R., *Masters of Death: The SS-Einsatzgruppen and the Invention of the Holocaust* (Alfred Knopf, 2002).

Riefenstahl, L., *A Memoir* (St Martin's Press, 1967).

Romani, C., *Tainted Goddesses: Female Film Stars of the Third Reich* (Sarpedon Publishers, 1992).

Roseman, M., *The Villa: The Lake, The Meeting: Wansee and the Final Solution* (Penguin, 2003).

Scheck, R., *Mothers of the Nation: Right Wing Women in Weimar Germany* (Berg, 2004).

Schellenberg, W., *The Schellenberg Memoirs: A Record of the Nazi Secret Service* (Andre Deutsch, 1956).

Schmidt, U., *Karl Brandt: The Nazi Doctor – Medicine and Power in the Third Reich* (Bloomsbury, 2007).

Schroeder, C., *He was My Chief: The Memoirs of Adolf Hitler's Secretary* (Frontline, 2012).

Schwärzwaller, W., *Rudolf Hess: The Deputy* (Quartet, 1988).

Semmler, R., *Goebbels: The Man Next to Hitler* (Westhouse, 1947).

Sigmund, A.M., *Women of the Third Reich* (NDE Publishing, 2000).

Speer, A., *Inside the Third Reich* (Phoenix, 1995).

——*Spandau: The Secret Diaries* (Macmillan, 1976).

Steinacher, G., *Nazis on the Run: How Hitler's Henchmen fled Justice* (Oxford University Press, 2011).

Stephenson, J., *Women in Nazi Germany* (Longman/Pearson Education Ltd, 2001).

Strobl, G., *The Swastika and the Stage: German Theatre and Society 1933–1945* (Cambridge University Press, 2007).

Taylor, M., Timm, A. and Herrn, R. (eds), *Not Straight from Germany: Sexual Politics and Sexual Citizenship Since Magnus Hirschfeld* (University of Michigan Press, 2017).

Toland, J., *Hitler* (Wordsworth Editions, 1976/1997).

Tooze, A., *The Wages of Destruction: The Making and Breaking of the Nazi Economy* (Penguin, 2007).

Trevor-Roper, H., *The Last days of Hitler* (Macmillan, 1947).

——(ed.) *Hitler's Table Talk: His Private Conversations* (Enigma Books, 1953/2000).

Ullrich, V., *Hitler: A Biography – Volume 1: Ascent 1889–1939* (Vintage, 2016).

Von Lang, J., *Bormann: The Man Who Manipulated Hitler* (Book Club Associates, 1979).

——*SS General Karl Wolff: The Man between Himmler and Hitler* (Enigma, 2005).

Von Schirach, H., *The Price of Glory: The Memoirs of Henriette von Schirach* (Muller, 1960).

Wachsman, N., *KL: A History of the Nazi Concentration Camps* (Abacus, 2015).

Wagener, O., *Hitler: Memoirs of a Confidant* (Yale University Press, 1985).

Wagner, F., *Heritage of Fire* (Harper & Brothers, 1945).

Walters, G., *Berlin Games: How Hitler Stole the Olympic Dream* (John Murray, 2006).

Weale, A., *The SS: A New History* (Abacus, 2010).

Wehler, H.U., *The German Empire 1871–1918* (Berg Publishers, 1985).

Welch, D., *Propaganda and the German Cinema 1933–1945* (IB Tauris, 2001).

Wertham, F., *A Sign for Cain: An Exploration of Human Violence* (Macmillan, 1966).

Whiting, C., *The Hunt for Martin Bormann: The Truth* (Pen & Sword, 1973).

Williams, M., *Heydrich: The Dark Shadow of the SS* (Fonthill, 2018).

Wilson, J., *Hitler's Alpine Headquarters* (Pen & Sword, 2013).

——*Hitler's Alpine Retreat* (Pen & Sword, 2005).

Wyllie, J., *Goering and Goering: Hitler's Henchman and his Anti-Nazi Brother* (The History Press, 2010).

Zwar, D., *Talking to Rudolf Hess* (The History Press, 2010).

JOURNAL ARTICLES AND THESES

Badger, W. and Purkiss, D., 'English Witches and SS Academics', *Prenature: Critical and Historical Studies on the Preternatural*, 6.1 (2017).

Carrier, R., '"Hitler's Table Talk": Troubling Finds', *German Studies Review*, 26.3 (2003).

Fox, J., '"Everyday Heroines": Nazi Visions of Motherhood in Mutterliebe (1939) and Annelie (1943)', *Historical Reflections*, 35.2 (2009).

Goeschel, C., 'Suicide at the End of the Third Reich', *Journal of Contemporary History*, 41.1 (2006).

Harris, V., 'The Role of the Concentration Camps in the Nazi Repression of Prostitutes 1933–1939', *Journal of Contemporary History*, 45.3 (2010).

McDonogh, G., 'Otto Horcher: Caterer to the Third Reich', *Gastronomica*, 7.1 (2007).

Montgomery, J., 'Sisters, Objects of Desire or Barbarians: German Nurses in the First World War', thesis, University of Tennessee, 2013.

Nilsson, M., 'Hugh Trevor-Roper and the English Editions of Hitler's Table Talk and Testament', *Journal of Contemporary History*, 5.1 (2016).

Palumbo, M., 'Goering's Italian Exile 1924–1925', *Journal of Modern History*, 50.1 (1978).

Perry, J., 'Nazifying Christmas: Political Culture and Popular Celebration in the Third Reich', *Central European History*, 38.4 (2005).

Quirin, K., 'Working Women and Motherhood: Failures of the Weimar Republic's Family Policies', *The Gettysburg Historical Journal*, 13.8 (2014).

Roos, J., 'Backlash against Prostitutes' Rights: Origins and Dynamics of Nazi Prostitution Policies', *Journal of the History of Sexuality*, 11.1/2 (2002).

Sigel, R., 'The Cultivation of Medicinal Herbs in the Concentration Camp', Studies, Reports, Documents, vol. 2, *Dachau Review History of Nazi Concentration Camps* (1990).

Silver, J., 'Karl Gebhardt (1897–1948): A Lost Man', *Journal of the Royal College of Physicians at Edinburgh*, 41, (2011).

Timm, A., 'Sex with a Purpose: Prostitution, Venereal Disease and Militarised Masculinity in the Third Reich', *Journal of the History of Sexuality*, 11.1/2 (2002).

Zroka, A.L., 'Serving the Volksgemeinschaft, German Red Cross Nurses in the Second World War', thesis, University of California, 2015.

WEBSITES

Carrier, R., 'Hitler's Table Talk; An Update', www.richardcarrier.info/archives/10978.

Ernst, E., 'Rudolf Hess (Hitler's Deputy) on Alternative Medicine', edzardernst.com?2015?01?rudolf-hess-hitlers-deputy-on-alternative-medicine

Irving, D., 'Frau Marga Himmler Diaries 1937-1945: Himmler's Diary Jan 1934-Dec 1935.

1939: The Vaughan Papers', Real History, www.fp.co.uk.

INDEX

March 1918, after an intensive artillery bombardment, one million German soldiers attacked British lines on a 50-mile front at 09.35 hours.

The British Fifth Army, commanded by General Hubert Gough, holding the line between St Quentin and Amiens, were unprepared for this assault as German stormtroopers swiftly advanced through the mist and penetrated the British lines. Gough's line collapsed and his soldiers were forced to withdraw. On the first day of the offensive, the British sustained 38,000 casualties, while the Germans lost 78,000. The Allies were close to defeat and a new strategy was needed to prevent a German victory. At the Doullens Conference held on 26 March 1918, Allied leaders agreed to unify British and French forces by appointing Field Marshal Ferdinand Foch as commander of the Allied Forces. The agreement signed by French Prime Minister Georges Clemenceau and Lord Alfred Milner, on behalf of the British War Cabinet, decreed that:

> General Foch is charged by the British and French governments with co-ordinating the action of Allied Armies on the Western Front. To this end he will come to an understanding with the Commander-in-Chief, who are requested to furnish him with all necessary information.[2]

This decision was a turning point in the war, because Foch's new strategy would prevent an Allied defeat. Foch recalled:

> Instead of a British battle to cover the Channel ports and a French battle to cover Paris, we would fight an Anglo-French battle to cover Amiens, the connecting link between the two armies.[3]

Haig supported the decision to appoint Foch as overall commander and made some changes within the British command structure by replacing Gough with General Sir Henry Rawlinson as commander of the remnants of British Fifth Army on 28 March. These exhausted units would eventually be used to re-form the Fourth Army. French troops were sent into the British lines to bolster their depleted strength, which would prevent German forces from advancing. On 4 April, Haig sent three Australian brigades to stem the German tide at Villers Bretonneux. Haig released his 'backs to the wall' order on 11 April, in which he wrote:

> Three weeks ago to-day the enemy began his terrific attacks against us on a fifty-mile front. His objects are to separate us from the French, to take the Channel Ports and destroy the British Army.

In spite of throwing already 106 Divisions into the battle and enduring the most reckless sacrifice of human life, he has as yet made little progress towards his goals.

We owe this to the determined fighting and self-sacrifice of our troops. Words fail me to express the admiration which I feel for the splendid resistance offered by all ranks of our Army under the most trying circumstances.

Many amongst us now are tired. To those I would say that Victory will belong to the side which holds out the longest. The French Army is moving rapidly and in great force to our support.

There is no other course open to us but to fight it out. Every position must be held to the last man: there must be no retirement. With our backs to the wall and believing in the justice of our cause each one of us must fight on to the end. The safety of our homes and the Freedom of mankind alike depend upon the conduct of each one of us at this critical moment.[4]

The Germans continued to push forward their attack, but they became the victims of their own success for their advances were so rapid, they had overstretched their lines of supply to the extent that it was difficult to replenish their advancing waves with fresh troops, arms, munitions and equipment. By the time Haig issued his desperate order to fight to the last man, German forces had lost 239,000 soldiers and commanders had abandoned Operation Michael. The Allies, who were close to defeat, sustained 255,000 casualties. Successive German offensives took place during the spring of 1918. Ludendorff launched Operation Georgette on 7 April in an effort to capture Ypres; on 27 May Operation Blücher-Yorck was launched to establish a bridgehead across the River Aisne. In June, the aim of Operation Gneisenau was to capitalise on ground captured on the Aisne sector westwards. Ludendorff ordered a final offensive to expand eastwards from the Aisne salient in July in an operation named Friedensturm, but the initiative failed and Germany's last-ditch attempts to defeat the Allies had faltered.

The German penetration into Allied lines had put enormous pressure upon the Allied armies. With great reluctance, General Pershing dispatched temporarily some American divisions that were trained and available to support the Allied armies.

Three weeks after its stint on the Ansauville sector, the American 1st Division was assigned to the First French Army, which was holding the Montdidier sector. It entered the line opposite Cantigny during the evening on 24th/25th April in between the French 45th and 162nd Divisions. German forces became aware that American forces were present and ordered artillery and gas attacks upon their positions in a desperate effort to intimidate and undermine their confidence before they launched an offensive.

At the beginning of May 1918, the German Army still held superior numbers against the Allied divisions on the Western Front, but General Erich Ludendorff was under great pressure to accomplish his prime objective of defeating the BEF in Flanders and winning the war. His armies were suffering from exhaustion and during the Lys Offensive in April 1918 discipline started to deteriorate when some soldiers refused to fight. His main concern was that his numerical advantage had been reducing quite considerably since the intervention of the Americans into the war. Time was on the side of the Allies, and with American support they could potentially deny Germany a victory. By the end of May 1918, the size of the AEF in France had increased to 650,000, but only the American 1st Division was in the line, because General Pershing continued to insist that his force would only carry out offensive operations once fully trained and as a distinct composite force, commanded only by American officers.

The AEF launched its first large-scale attack upon Germany forces when 1st Division captured Cantigny on 28 May 1918 at the cost of approximately 100 casualties. Its success at Cantigny demonstrated to its French and British allies that the AEF was able to conduct operations and to capture ground. It also demonstrated that it could be relied upon to play its role in the war and gave the Allies hope that the strength of the AEF, with its vast numbers, would help to shift the balance of power in the war and would help them to achieve ultimate victory over Germany.

The battle also raised the morale of the American soldiers and gave them experience and confidence. Cantigny was an ominous warning to the Germans, who realised that once the might of the AEF entered the battlefield, the Allies would hold the advantage of having more troops and resources, which would ultimately severely diminish their chance of victory.

Despite his reservations, Pershing had to release further divisions into the frontline to bolster the Allied lines. The American 2nd and 3rd Divisions were given responsibility to defend the line at Belleau Wood and Chateau Thierry a week after the Cantigny operation, and they successfully stopped the German advance upon Paris. On 6 June, 2nd Division, including US Marines, began a month-long battle for Belleau Wood. Their lack of experience was buoyed by their determination and their large numbers augmented the depleted ranks of the French, British and Dominion forces.

The Allies were able to turn the tide of war to their favour during July 1918. General Sir Henry Rawlinson, commanding the British Fourth Army, ordered Australian Corps commander General John Monash to launch a small-scale operation at Le Hamel to capture the village and ridge that overlooked their lines east of Villers Bretonneux. They were supported by the US 33rd Division, and this was the first time that American soldiers fought alongside British and Australian troops in a combined operation. During the assault upon Le Hamel on 4 July 1918, General Monash had devised a strategy that enabled Australian and American troops supported by British tanks and aeroplanes to capture this village within ninety-three minutes. Monash had provided Rawlinson with a template for victory that would be deployed on a larger scale at Amiens on 8 August 1918, where the Allies overran the German lines. Ludendorff would declare this to be 'the black day of the German Army in the history of this war'.[5] After that day German forces were in retreat, their morale was low, and their ranks comprised inexperienced soldiers, since many of their seasoned troops had already been consumed during the past four years of war.

The BEF had also lost many experienced soldiers during those years. In 1914, the average strength of a division was 13,000 infantry, but by 1918 that figure had been reduced to 8,000. During an Allied War Conference held at Villa Romaine, Versailles, on 7 October 1918, British Prime Minister David Lloyd George explained to Marshal Ferdinand Foch the problem of maintaining British forces with manpower conflicted with the challenge of ensuring that there were sufficient resources at home working in industry to support the war effort during 1918. The minutes recorded:

> We had made a very special effort in 1918 to meet the desires of the Marshal, and had scraped up every man we could. We had denuded home defence with the result that General Robertson, the Commander-in-Chief, had sent a written protest, pointing out the risk. The Government had decided to take the risk. We had pulled out men from many essential industries, including the munitions industry. One result was the present coal crisis, and we were not able to furnish our Allies, particularly France, with her full demands. At the present time very strong pressure was being put on the Government to take 50,000 men back from the army for the coal mines. We were short of 20,000,000 tons of coal for munitions and ship building industries. The difficulty was that the miners were about the best soldiers we had, so the army was very reluctant to spare them. This year our casualties would amount to 800,000, and

we could only find a total 700,000 drafts. Consequently, by the end of the year the army would be down by 100,000 men. He had reminded Marshal Foch, that we had put boys of 18 into the line and were the only nation who had done this. One result was to reduce the numbers available next year when they normally would have come into the army. Excluding returned wounded men, who might amount to 190,000 men for the whole year, the total number of drafts we had for the navy, army and air service was 300,000 men. Of these, the navy had asked for 50,000. The exigencies of anti-submarine warfare necessitated a great increase in small craft. Most of the patrolling, even to cover the American troops, was done by the British Navy. The Government were pressing the Admiralty to comb out men so that all the 300,000 who were to be called up should be available for the army. Some 50,000 men were required for tanks, and approximately the same number for aeroplanes. If these numbers were met, only 200,000 would be left as drafts for the army. Canada had conscription and could maintain her forces, but this was not the case with Australia, and the Australian divisions would gradually wither away. The only other source of supply for British troops were Ireland. Irish recruits, however, could only be obtained by facing something not far short of civil war. Marshal Foch himself could estimate the value of this source of recruiting, which at the best must be precarious. On these figures it was impossible to maintain the British divisions, and certainly not enough at their present strength.[6]

The French Army was also challenged with replenishing their ranks with fresh troops. French Prime Minister Georges Clemenceau wrote to Marshal Foch on 21 October 1918:

> The French and the British Army, without a moment's respite, have been daily fighting, for the last three months, battles which are using them up at a time when it is impossible for us to reinforce them immediately with fresh effectives. These two Armies are pressing back the enemy with an ardour that excites world-wide admiration.[7]

French–American forces were driving their advance along the Meuse–Argonne sector while British and French forces were pursuing the Germans to the German border. Once the Hindenburg Line had been breached towards the end of September, General Erich Ludendorf realised that they had lost the war and recommended that German politicians seek an Armistice. Once German leaders had declared their serious desire for peace, German soldiers with low morale would soon lose the motivation to continue fighting and there existed growing public support at home for peace. A short space of time elapsed between Germany requesting peace terms based on President Wilson's fourteen-point plan in early October and 11 November 1918, during which time the German Army collapsed on the Western Front, while the flames of revolution were sweeping across the German nation. The Allies were caught off guard by the rapidity of events. They had engaged in limited discussions on their expectations for peace, but no draft of Armistice terms existed for they did not expect Germany to request an armistice before peace terms could be negotiated. This provided an opportunity to include their prime war objectives within the terms of the Armistice.

Some people were unaware of what an armistice meant and its implications. As the Allies waited for the German response to their terms, a journalist from the *Birmingham Gazette* pondered upon the meaning of the word 'armistice':

> One journalist filled up the anxious hours of waiting for news during the weekend by hunting up the correct meaning of 'armistice'. His investigation showed that the word so spelt comes immediately from the French, and indirectly from Spanish and Italian, and finally of course from Latin. Literally it could be said to mean that 'arms stand,' or more intelligibly 'arms stand still.' An armistice, according to one authority, leaves the question of war unsettled – 'it is an interval in war, and supposes a return to it.'[8]

As negotiations continued through October 1918, the Allies continued offensive operations and by the end of the month the German Army was on the brink of capitulation and close to defeat. Haig recognised the importance of maintaining the momentum of the Allied advance and to continue to exert pressure upon the German soldiers that they were pursuing. Haig wrote to Winston Churchill on 3 October:

> It is of the highest importance to keep on pressing the enemy at every possible point, because if we allow him any breathing time at all, he will be able to reorganise his forces, to construct new defences, and make new plans, and much of the work of 'wearing him out' will have to be started afresh.[9]

By the first week of November 1918, Germany had been broken and with revolution erupting at home, it was ready to agree and sign an armistice.

The aim of this book is to provide an account of events that took place during the final days of the First World War through using personal accounts, letters, official reports and minutes from cabinet meetings and Allied war conferences. The 1914–18 conflict was a world war and the conditions agreed during the Armistice signed on 11 November 1918 had far-reaching consequences across the globe. However, this volume will focus upon the events concerning north-western Europe. The book details the political events that led to the signing of the Armistice, beginning with the German peace initiatives in 1916 and 1917, before chronicling the period during autumn 1918 when the German Government sent serious overtures to the Allies requesting peace. Allied leaders were left with a dilemma for they wanted to end the war, but they wanted peace on their terms. They wanted to impose harsh conditions, but they ran the risk of Germany not agreeing to those terms and continuing the bloodshed of the war, and this book shows the quandary that Allied politicians faced.

As Allied and German leaders discussed peace, the fighting continued unabated during the days before the signing of the Armistice. British, French, Canadian, American, Australian and New Zealand soldiers fought the German Army as they pursued them to the German frontier. The soldiers on the frontline on all sides were aware that the war was drawing to a conclusion and this news would have a drastic effect upon their morale and motivation to continue the fight. This book describes some of the bitter battles fought during the last days of the war and explores the emotions of both Allied and German soldiers as the conflict came to an end. Some soldiers would die knowing that within days the war would be over. Men were thrown into needless battles during the final hours, and many were slaughtered unnecessarily because some units did not get notification of the Armistice and continued fighting after 11.00 hours on 11 November 1918. This book uses sources from Britain, France, America, Canada, New Zealand, Australia and Germany to detail those violent last days of the First World War and to show how news of the Armistice was received by soldiers and civilians. Here are their voices.

Part I

THE PATH TO PEACE

Chapter 1

German Approaches to Peace 1916–17

The Verdun and Somme campaigns fought during 1916 had a drastic impact upon German forces on the Western Front. The official French war history published in 1916 estimated French losses at Verdun to be 377,231, including 162,308 killed. German losses were estimated at 337,000, including 100,000 killed.

German forces unleashed their Verdun offensive on 21 February and although they captured ground, they became worn down by France's determination to defend this fortified town, which held significant symbolic national importance to the people of France. General Eric Ludendorff wrote:

> Verdun had exacted a very great price in blood. The position of our attacking troops grew more unfavourable. The more ground they gained the deeper they plunged into the wilderness of shell-holes, and apart from actual losses in action, they suffered heavy wastage merely through having to stay in such a spot, not to mention the difficulty of getting up supplies over a wide, desolate area. The French enjoyed a great advantage here, as the proximity of the fortress gave them a certain amount of support. Our attacks dragged on, sapping our strength. The very men who had fought so heroically at Verdun were terrified of this shell-ravaged region. The command had very early declared himself in favour of breaking off the attack.[1]

The Somme campaign fought with attrition brought approximately 400,000 British losses, 200,000 French losses and 680,000 German casualties from 1 July to 13 November 1916. The campaign succeeded in wearing down German resolve and they were fearful that if the Allies

1

continued to press forward their advances, they would eventually be fighting on German soil. General Eric Ludendorff realised that the Allies held the advantage over Germany on the Western Front, when he was appointed First Quartermaster-General on 29 August 1916. He recalled:

> The longer the war lasted, the more acutely we felt the overwhelming superiority of the enemy in numbers and war material ... The equipment of the Entente armies [The allied nations of Britain, France, Russia, and Italy were known as the entente during the First World War] with war material had been carried out on a scale hitherto unknown. The Battle of the Somme showed us every day how great was the advantage of the enemy in this respect.[2]

Field Marshal Paul von Hindenburg concurred with Ludendorff's pessimistic view regarding Allied numerical superiority and agreed that the toll of two campaigns severely impacted upon German forces:

> There was no doubt that, at the end of 1916, the position as regards relative numbers between us and our enemies had developed even more to our disadvantage than had been the case at the beginning of the year.[3]

Hindenburg doubted that German forces on the Western Front would be strong enough to resist Allied offensives in 1917:

> On our Western Front we had to expect that in the coming spring our enemies would reappear in the arena in full strength, in spite of the heavy losses they undoubtedly had suffered in the past year.[4]

With the likelihood of further Allied offensives being launched upon German lines and the inability to launch their own offensives in 1917, Ludendorff convinced the German High Command that a defensive strategy should be adopted. To this end, he conceived a plan where he would order the withdrawal of German forces 25 miles across the Somme to newly established defensive positions. Since he admired the works of Richard Wagner, he named the defensive system the Siegfried Stellung, after the principal protagonist from Wagner's opera *The Ring*. This line of fortified trenches, deeply excavated concrete dugouts and gun emplacements protected by acres of high density barbed wire entanglements would be known to the British as the Hindenburg Line. Measuring 85 miles, it was built east of Arras and stretched through the village of Bullecourt to positions in the Champagne region near

Soissons. By initiating a tactical withdrawal, Ludendorff would shorten the front by 27 miles and free ten infantry divisions to be deployed in reserve to bolster sectors where the enemy was making breakthroughs. Work commenced on building the new defensive line during September 1916 as the Somme campaign was being fought, unbeknown to the Allies. Ludendorff wrote:

> These strategic positions had the advantage of shortening the front and economizing men, and their occupation according to plan was prepared. Whatever we should retire on them, and how the positions would be used, was not of course decided in September 1916.[5]

Hindenburg commented:

> So it was a case of retreat on the Western Front instead of attack![6]

As the German Army was preparing to continue the fight on a shorter frontline with the construction of the Hindenburg Line, it became apparent to the German Government in Berlin that it could not win the war it had begun and it was considering negotiating a peace settlement with the Allies with the purpose of ending the fighting in 1916. Prince Maximilian of Baden served on the Headquarters Staff of Fourteenth Army Corps, but during the autumn of 1914 his health deteriorated. After recovery he was involved with the Red Cross, where he focused upon the welfare of prisoners of war. Prince Max wrote:

> The campaign of 1916 ended in bitter disillusionment all round. We and our enemies had shed our best blood in streams and neither we nor they had come one step nearer to victory. The word 'deadlock' was on every lip. In Germany, too, the impossibility of purely military decision was realised by many in whose presence the words 'peace of understanding' could not hitherto have been uttered. People looked to the leading statesmen with a certain insistent expectancy: 'The forces on either side have obviously reached a condition of rigid equilibrium: the war must become senseless; what are you going to do to end it?'
>
> People – and they were not isolated individuals – came to me in the autumn of 1916 full of a vague anxiety: 'Things are not going well with the war.' At the same time I became acquainted with a well-informed and reasoned line of criticism which attacked the essence of our war policy and claimed to prove with weighty arguments that we should lose the war if it went on in this fashion.[7]

3

The German Government set about drafting a peace note to be sent to the Allies during December 1916. Hindenburg, who was consulted over the wording, recalled:

> I considered it my duty in this matter to strive for such a solution that neither the Army nor the Homeland should suffer any injury. Main Headquarters had to co-operate in settling the wording of our peace offer. It was a difficult and thankless task to avoid creating an impression of weakness at home and abroad while giving all provocative expressions a wide berth. I was able to see with what a devout sense of duty to god and man my All-Highest War Lord devoted himself to the solution of the peace problem, and I do not think that he regarded a complete failure of this step as probable. On the other hand, my own confidence in its success was quite small from the outset. Our adversaries had vied with one another in putting forward excessive claims, and it appeared to me out of the question that any of the enemy Governments could and would voluntarily go back on promises which they had made to each other and their peoples. However, this view did not in any way affect my honest intention to co-operate in this work for the good of humanity.[8]

On 12 December 1916, Chancellor Theobald von Bethmann-Hollweg delivered a speech at the Reichstag in Berlin, declaring Germany's desire to open peace negotiations. During the address he read the following peace proposal requesting American diplomats to communicate it to the Allies on its behalf. Chancellor Bethmann-Hollweg wrote:

> Mr Chargé d'Affaires,
>
> The most formidable war known to history has been ravaging for two and a half years in a great part of the world. The catastrophe that the bonds of a common civilisation more than a thousand years old could not stop, strikes mankind in its most precious patrimony; it threatens to bury under its ruin the moral and physical progress on which Europe prided itself at the dawn of the twentieth century. In that strife Germany and her Allies, Austria–Hungary and Turkey, have given proof of their indestructible strength in winning considerable successes at war. Their unshakeable lines resist ceaseless attacks of their enemies' arms. The recent diversion in the Balkans was speedily and victoriously thwarted. The latest events

4

have demonstrated that a continuation of the War cannot break their resisting power. The general situation much rather justified their hope of fresh successes. It is for the defence of their existence and freedom of their national development that the four Allied Powers were constrained to take up arms. The exploits of their armies have brought no change therein. Not for an instant have they swerved from the conviction that the respect of the rights of other nations is not in any degree incompatible with their own rights and legitimate interests. They do not seek to crush or annihilate their adversaries. Conscious of their military and economic strength and ready to carry on to the end if they must the struggle that is forced upon them, but animated at the same time by the desire to stem the flood of blood and to bring the horrors of war to an end, the four Allied Powers propose to enter even now into peace negotiations. They feel sure that the propositions which they would bring forward and which would aim to assure the existence, honour, and free development of their peoples would be such as to serve as a basis for the restoration of lasting peace.

If, notwithstanding this offer of peace and conciliation the struggle should continue, the four Allied Powers are resolved to carry on to an end, while solemnly disclaiming any responsibility before mankind and history.

The Imperial Government has the honour to ask through your obliging medium, the Government of the United States, to be pleased to transmit the present communication to the Government of the French republic, to the Royal Government of Great Britain, to the Imperial Government of Japan, to the Royal Government of Roumania [sic Romania], to the Imperial Government of Russia, and to the Royal Government of Serbia.

I take this opportunity to renew to you, Mr Chargé d'Affaires, the assurance of my high consideration.[9]

There were no terms or conditions that would form a basis for peace and the Allies were not convinced that this was a sincere desire to end the war. The French felt acrimony towards Germany for it had invaded part of its country, many of its towns and villages had been destroyed; and it had lost hundreds of thousands of its men during the fighting. There was remote prospect of the French engaging in peace talks unless Germany surrendered. French Prime Minister Aristide Briand was suspicious of the German peace initiative. In a speech to the French Chamber of Deputies, the legislative assembly of the French Parliament, on 13 December he expressed his reluctance to accept this German peace proposition and feared that it was an attempt to split the Allied coalition. Briand declared:

> There is one cry constantly on German lips: 'We were attacked; we are defending ourselves; we are the victims!' To this cry I make answer for the hundredth time: 'No, you are the aggressors; no matter what you might say, the facts are there to prove it. The blood is on your heads. Not on ours.'[10]

Prime Minister Georges Clemenceau wrote:

> The Boches are in a merry mood. They are speaking of peace. Why did they not have this idea when they entered on the campaign, for it is they who declared war?[11]

The Russian Duma was only interested in talking peace after Germany was defeated. Neutral countries, such as America, encouraged the Allied nations not to reject the peace offer and to engage in negotiations with Germany. The Vatican also advised the Allies to request peace terms from Germany.

David Lloyd George, who had become Prime Minister after Herbert Asquith's resignation on 6 December 1918, was not convinced that this was a genuine peace proposal. He regarded the German peace note as a contrived manoeuvre to raise morale and maintain support for continuing the war among the German population, who had seen reports of heavy losses on the battlefields and were feeling the effects of deprivation, including food shortages. He also felt that Germany was making an artificial attempt to talk peace to regain some moral ground amongst neutral countries and the civilian population of the nations that opposed it, demonstrating that Germany had offered a chance of peace, but the Allies were prolonging the war by continuing the conflict. Germany still occupied much of Belgium and France, which put it in a strong negotiating position if the Allies accepted its peace offer. Lloyd George wrote:

> This was not the language of an enemy suing for peace after a crushing defeat in the field, or of a foe conscious that on the whole the tide was beginning to turn against him, or even an adversary who realised that although he had no fear of being beaten, nevertheless, if the war continued both parties in the end would be ruined. It was rather in the nature of an overture from a Power of unbreakable strength of its armies, boasting of a succession of

resounding triumphs against its enemies and of its abilities to hold its own in future against every effort to dislodge its grip on the vast territories it had conquered, but anxious to cast upon its enemies the responsibility for prolonging the War. German statesmanship, which was entirely under military control and direction, had three objects in view when it launched this peace offensive. The first was to reconcile that part of the German population who were beginning to feel that brilliant victories without number brought nothing but heavier burdens, more and more privations, and mounting casualties to the triumphant Fatherland. It was necessary to convince these that ultimate victory was the only alternative to an unsatisfying peace. The second was to persuade neutral countries which were becoming increasingly hostile to Germany and also the people behind the Governments of belligerent countries, that the prolongation of the War was due entirely to the bloodthirsty stubbornness and insatiable ambition of the Allied Governments. The third was to enter into peace negotiations whilst military conditions were more favourable to Germany than to the Allies, the German Armies being quartered in Allied territory and on the whole having beaten off the assaults made on their positions there on every front.[12]

The German press assisted its government to propagate the propaganda by apportioning responsibility for continuing the war upon the Allies if they refused the offer of peace. The *Vossische Zeitung* proclaimed:

> The German proposals rest on the basis of strength and sharpness of our arms. If peace, which we freely offer, is not accepted, we will force peace with the sword and with all the means of land, sea and aerial warfare.[13]

As the Allied governments deliberated how they were to respond, the British press regarded the German initiative with disdain. British newspapers were sceptical about the peace proposal and thought that Germany was opportunistic in taking advantage in the downfall of the Asquith Government and that it was looking for an armistice with the intention of rebuilding its forces strength in preparation for further campaigns. Germany and her allies occupied parts of France, Belgium, Serbia, Montenegro, Russia and Rumania. Britain and her allies were not prepared to concede this ground to Germany as part of a peace settlement and treated the German proposal with contempt. Hindenburg recalled:

> On December 12 our readiness to conclude peace was announced to our enemies. Our answer from enemy propaganda, as well as the hostile camps, was only scorn and a rebuff.[14]

In Britain, Lord George Curzon, Leader of the House of Lords, encouraged the nation to continue the fight until the end to ensure that future generations would not need to experience such a conflict:

> We are not fighting to destroy Germany. Such an idea has never entered into the mind of any thinking human being in this country. But we are fighting to secure that the German spirit shall not crush the free progress of nations and that the armed strength of Germany, augmented and fortified, shall not dominate the future. We are fighting that our grandchildren and our great grandchildren shall not have, in days when we have passed away, to go again through the experience of the years 1914–17. This generation has suffered in order that the next may live. We are ready enough for peace when these guarantees have been secured and these objects attained. Till then we owe to the hundreds of thousands of our fellow countrymen and our Allies, who have shed their blood for us, to be true to the trust of their splendid and uncomplaining sacrifice and to endure to the end.[15]

Prince Max recalled:

> On 21st December, 1916, President Wilson dispatched his first peace note, in which he called on the belligerent countries to state precise war aims, so that the war might no longer be fought in the dark. On 26 December the German Government courteously declined to state its aims. A direct exchange of ideas between the belligerents, it said, seemed to be the most appropriate method.[16]

After consultation among the Allied governments, it was agreed to reject the German offer and on 30 December 1916 the French Government handed to the United States Ambassador in Paris their written response, which was to be conveyed to the German Government. The reply began by rebuking the assertion in the German note that the Allies were responsible for the war and that Germany and her allies were victorious:

> The Allied Governments of Russia, France, Great Britain, Japan, Italy, Serbia, Belgium, Montenegro, Portugal and Rumania, united for the defence of the freedom of nations and faithful to their

undertakings not to lay down their arms except in common accord, have decided to return a joint offer to the illusory peace proposals which have been addressed to them by the Governments of the enemy Powers through the intermediary the United States, Spain, Switzerland and the Netherlands.

As a prelude to any reply, the Allied Powers feel bound to protest strongly against the two material assertions made in the Note from the enemy powers, the one professing to throw upon the Allies the responsibility of the war, and the other proclaiming the victory of the Central Powers.

The Allies cannot admit a claim which is thus untrue in each particular, and is sufficient alone to render sterile all attempt at negotiations.

The Allied nations have for thirty months been engaged in a war which they have done everything to avoid. They have shown by their actions their devotion to peace. This devotion is as strong today as it was in 1914; and after the violation by Germany of her solemn engagements, Germany's promise is no sufficient foundation on which to re-establish the peace she broke.

A mere suggestion, without statement of terms, that negotiations should be opened, is not an offer of peace. The putting forward by the Imperial German Government of a sham proposal, lacking all substance and precision, would appear to be less an offer of peace than a war manoeuvre ... In reality these overtures made by the Central Powers are nothing more than a calculated attempt to influence the future course of the war and to end it by imposing a German peace.

The object of these overtures is to create dissension in public opinion in Allied countries. But that public opinion has, in spite of all the sacrifices endured by the Allies, already given its answer with admirable firmness, and has denounced the empty pretence of the declaration of the enemy Powers.

They have the further object of stiffening public opinion in Germany and in the countries allied to her; one and all, already severely tried by their losses, worn out by economic pressure and crushed by the supreme effort which has been imposed upon their inhabitants.

The endeavour to deceive and intimidate public opinion in neutral countries whose inhabitants have long since made up their minds where the initial responsibility rests, have recognised existing responsibilities, and are far too enlightened to favour the designs of Germany by abandoning the defence of human freedom.

Finally these overtures attempt to justify in advance in the eyes of the world a new series of crimes – submarine warfare, deportations, forced labour and forced enlistment of inhabitants against their own countries and violations of neutrality.

Fully conscious of the gravity of this moment, but equally conscious of its requirements, the Allied Governments closely united to one another and in perfect sympathy with their peoples, refuse to consider a proposal which is empty and insincere.[17]

The Allied reply concluded by reiterating Belgium's plight and the conditions for a peace settlement to be agreed:

Belgium before the war asked for nothing but to live in harmony with all her neighbours. Her King and her Government have but one aim – the re-establishment of peace and justice. But they only desire a peace which would assure to their country legitimate reparation, guarantees and safeguards for the future.[18]

The Germans took offence at the Allied response. Prince Max wrote:

On 30th December the note containing the reply of the Entente to our peace offer was handed over. It was full of insults designed to stamp us afresh as bearing the sole blame for the outbreak of the war as well as for its lawless conduct.[19]

Further initiatives to end the war were continued during 1917. Pope Benedict XV presented his own peace proposal on 1 August 1917, where he condemned the conflict as a futile slaughter and recommended that Germany should produce a paper that would guarantee Belgium's political and economic independence.

During September 1917, as Allied and German forces were fighting the Third Ypres campaign, a message was sent by the German Government via a neutral diplomatic channel to the British Government indicating its willingness to engage in peace talks. Arthur Balfour, Foreign Secretary of State, notified Allied governments of Germany's proposal and replied to it positively that the British Cabinet would be willing to receive any proposals submitted and discuss with their allies. However, no proposal was submitted by Germany.

Chapter 2

Proposals for Peace – 1918

As the world entered its fifth year of war, some Allied leaders considered their own expectations for peace in 1918. David Lloyd George announced the following conditions for a ceasefire at an address to trade unionists on 5 January 1918, which included:

1. Independence for Belgium, Montenegro and Serbia;
2. Return of Alsace and Lorraine to France;
3. Creation of Poland as an independent state;
4. Restoration of territory to Italy and Rumania;
5. Home Rule for the Slavs in Austria–Hungary;
6. Turkish control of Constantinople and the internalisation of the Dardanelle Straits;
7. Recognition of nationalities of Arabia, Armenia, Mesopotamia, Syria and Palestine;
8. Independence for countries colonised by Germany;
9. German reparations paid to countries for violations of international law;
10. Creation of a League of Nations.

President Woodrow Wilson, twenty-eighth President of the United States, announced his own fourteen-point proposal for world peace to Congress on 8 January 1918. These proposals would form the basis of Wilson's vision of a new international order, which called for open, transparent diplomacy. This would aim to address the problems that caused the outbreak of war in 1914, when secret agreements and alliances between countries resulted in a global conflict. The proposals were as follows:

1. Open covenants of peace, openly arrived at, after which there shall be no private international understandings of any kind, but diplomacy shall proceed always frankly and in the public view.

2. Absolute freedom of navigation upon the seas outside territorial waters, alike in peace and in war, except as the seas may be closed in whole or in part by international action for the enforcement of international covenants.

3. The removal so far as possible of all economic barriers, and the establishment of an equality of trade conditions among all the nations.

4. Adequate guarantees given and taken that national armaments will be reduced to the lowest point consistent with domestic safety.

5. A free open-minded, and absolutely impartial adjustment of all colonial claims based upon a strict observance of the principle that in determining all such questions of sovereignty the interests of the populations concerned must have equal weight with the equitable claims of the Government whose title is to be determined.

6. The evacuation of all Russian territory and such a settlement of all questions affecting Russia as will secure the best and freest co-operation of the other nations of the world in obtaining for her an unhampered and unembarrassed opportunity for the independent determination of her own political development and national policy, and assure her of a sincere welcome into the society of the free nations under institutions of her own choosing: and more than a welcome, assistance also of every kind that she may need and may herself desire. The treatment accorded Russia by her sister nations in the months to come will be the acid test of their goodwill, of their comprehension of her needs, as distinguished from her own interests, and of their intelligent and unselfish sympathy.

7. Belgium, the whole world will agree, must be evacuated and restored without any attempt to limit the sovereignty which she enjoys in common with all other free nations. No other single act will serve as to restore confidence among the nations in the laws which they have themselves set and determined for the government of their relations with one another. Without this healing act the whole structure and validity of international law is forever impaired.

8. All French territory should be freed and the invaded portions restored, and the wrong done to France by Prussia in 1871, in the matter of Alsace–Lorraine, which has unsettled the peace of the world for nearly fifty years, should be righted, in order that peace may once more be made secure in the interest of all.

9. A readjustment of the frontiers of Italy should be effected along clearly recognised lines of nationality.

10. The peoples of Austria–Hungary, whose place among the nations we wish to see safeguarded and assured, should be accorded the first opportunity of autonomous development.
11. Roumania, Serbia and Montenegro should be evacuated; occupied territories restored, Serbia accorded free and secure access to the sea, and the relations of the several Balkan States to one another determined by friendly counsel and historically established lines of allegiance and nationality, and international guarantees of the political and economic independence and territorial integrity of the several Balkan States should be entered into.
12. The Turkish portions of the present Ottoman Empire should be assured a secure sovereignty, but the other nationalities which are now under Turkish rule should be assured an undoubted security of life and absolutely unmolested opportunity of autonomous development, and the Dardanelles should be permanently opened as a free passage to the ships and commerce of all nations under international guarantees.
13. An independent Polish State should be erected which should include the territories inhabited and indisputably Polish populations, which should be assured a free and secure access to the sea, and whose political and economic independence and territorial integrity should be guaranteed by international covenant.
14. A general association of nations must be formed under specific covenants for the purpose of affording mutual guarantees of political and territorial independence for great and small states alike.[1]

In the Points 1 to 5, President Wilson focused upon ending clandestine diplomacy, preserving freedom of movement on the seas, stopping trade wars, promoting disarmament and bringing an end to the arms races between nations and to settle colonial conflicts. Wilson addressed the issues of frontiers in the remaining points. Germany did not accept the plan and its response was defiant. Prince Max wrote:

> On 12 January the Entente replied to President Wilson. War aims were proclaimed such as the Central Powers could only accept after a crushing defeat.[2]

Germany was granted an opportunity to turn the balance of power on the Western Front in its favour when Russia signed the Treaty of Brest-Litovsk on 3 March 1918, ending its war with Russia and allowing it to transfer its divisions on the Eastern Front to the West. However, despite several campaigns launched during the spring of 1918, the

Germans were unable to deliver a decisive victory over the Allies before the Americans were trained and able to bolster their depleted ranks.

General Erich Ludendorff had led successful campaigns on the Eastern Front during 1915 and 1916 and succeeded in deploying a defensive strategy on the Western Front during 1917. However, his attempts to capture Paris during the spring 1918 offensive and end the war before American troops could be deployed on the Western Front had failed. After successive offensives which led to advances deep into Allied lines to the extent that the Germans could see the Eiffel Tower through field glasses, the tide of fortune turned against them. The Allies rallied and defended their lines. German commanders became complacent by not constructing strong defences because they expected to continue their advance. When the Allies opened offensive operations during the summer 1918, German forces were defending shallow trenches and weak positions. The success at Le Hamel on 4 July 1918, when Australian and American troops, supported by aeroplanes and British tanks, captured Le Hamel and the German defences of the Wolfsberg within ninety-three minutes, bolstered their confidence. General Monash, commander of the Australian Corps, had devised a successful approach to break through the German lines and provided the Allies with an effective strategy that would lead them to victory. At that time, the German Army was in no position to launch large-scale offensives, as Ludendorff confirmed:

> By the beginning of August we had suspended our attack and reverted to the defensive on the whole front ... I considered that the enemy might continue his attacks ... but I further assumed that these operations would only take the form of isolated local attacks for the enemy was also tired, on the whole not less than ourselves.[3]

The success at Le Hamel was emulated on a larger scale at the Battle of Amiens on 8 August 1918, when eleven divisions comprising of British, Canadian and Australian infantry belonging to General Sir Henry Rawlinson's Fourth Army and troops from General Marie-Eugene Debeney's First French Army created a massive breach within the German lines on a 12-mile front, penetrating 7 miles deep.[4] Within three days, the Allies had captured approximately 22,000 German prisoners and 400 guns. Field Marshal Sir Douglas Haig was confident that Germany would be defeated by the autumn providing that the Allies maintained momentum and continued to place pressure upon

Germany. Haig told Field Marshal Sir Henry Wilson: 'We ought now to hit as hard as we could, and try to get peace this autumn.'[5] General Erich Ludendorff, feeling dejected, wrote:

> August 8th was the black day of the German Army in the history of this war.[6]

Lacking men, munitions and resources, the Germany Army was unable to launch offensive counter-attacks, as Hindenburg wrote:

> On this August 8 our orders to counter-attack could no longer be carried out. We had not the men, and more particularly the guns, to prepare such an attack, for most of the batteries had been lost on the part of the front which was broken through.[7]

The defeat at Amiens undermined Ludendorff's confidence in Germany's ability to win the war and in his own abilities as quartermaster general, to the extent that he offered his resignation to Hindenburg and Kaiser Wilhelm on 9 August. Ludendorff recalled:

> The 8th of August put the decline of that fighting power beyond all doubt and in such a situation as regards reserves. I had no hope of finding a strategic expedient whereby to turn the situation to our advantage. On the contrary, I became convinced that we were now without that safe foundation for the plans of G.H.Q., on which I had hitherto been able to build, at least so far as this is possible in war. Leadership now assumed, as I then stated, the character of an irresponsible game of chance, a thing I have always considered fatal. The fate of the German people was for me too high a stake. The war must be ended.
>
> The 8th of August opened the eyes of the staff on both sides; mine were certainly opened, and so, according to his statement in the Daily Mail, were those of General Foch. The Entente began the great offensive, the final battle of the world war, and carried it through with increasing vigour, as our decline became more apparent.[8]

Ludendorff's resignation offer was declined by Hindenburg and Kaiser Wilhelm, however it became apparent to the latter that Germany was heading for certain defeat and was considering ending the war. The Kaiser commented:

15

I see that it is necessary to review conditions. We have come to the limit. The war must be brought to an end. Accordingly, I shall expect the Commanders-in-Chief at Spa in the course of the next few days.[9]

As Allied forces continued to liberate German-occupied France, Germany's Allies were seeking peace on other fronts. Austria sent a Peace Note on 15 September 1918. Turkey was losing the war in the Middle East; Damascus fell on 20 September 1918 and it was close to defeat.

Meanwhile, on the Western Front soldiers of the German Army were exhausted as they fought relentless defensive and rear-guard actions during the summer and autumn of 1918. There was no opportunities for respite and reorganisation. After sustaining casualties and lacking reserves, they were becoming outnumbered by the Allies, who had a continuous supply of fresh American troops. An anonymous German soldier wrote:

> Now we have begun to retreat at the whole front, not because we were forced to do so, since the German is too good a soldier to be forced to do that … but because our fighting troops do not want to hold out any longer. Why should one sacrifice oneself, for what? Perhaps for the sake of the Fatherland and its most holy goods? No, they have all buried their patriotism a long time ago. They do not want to fight in a war of conquest any longer. This is the view shared by 95 per cent of all branches of the service in the field.[10]

As their numbers swiftly dwindled the situation became so desperate that German staff officers fought alongside the ranks. Hindenburg reported:

> With regard to the last fearful struggle it is written with the blood of our sons in letters that can never fade. What terrible demands were made in these weeks on the physical strength and moral resolution of the officers and men of all Staffs and formations! The troops had now to be thrown from one battle into another. It was seldom that the so-called days in rest billets were enough to allow us to reorganise the decimated or scattered units and supply them with drafts, or distribute the remains of divisions we had broken up among other formations. Both officers and men were certainly beginning to tire, but they always managed to find a new impulse whenever it was a question of holding up some fresh enemy attack.

Officers of all ranks, even up to the higher Staffs, fought in the front lines, sometimes rifle in hand. The only order issued in many cases was simply 'Hold out to the last.'

...We had not the men to form a continuous line. We could only offer resistance in groups, large and small. It was only successful because the enemy, too, was visibly tiring. He seldom attempted a large operation unless his tanks had opened a way or his artillery had extinguished every sign of German life. He did not storm our lines directly, but gradually slipped through their many gaps. It was on this fact that I based my hope of being able to hold out until the efforts of our enemies were paralysed.

Unlike the enemy, we had no fresh reserves to throw in. Instead of an inexhaustible America, we had weary Allies who were themselves on the point of collapse.[11]

Although the Allies could rely on the inexhaustible supply of American reserves, albeit many were untrained, the British and French armies were losing considerable casualties and were experiencing their own serious resource problems. Marshal Foch recalled:

The British Army had lost, from July 1st to September 15th, 7,700 officers and 166,000 men; and, as with the French army it was unable to fill the gaps in ranks.[12]

Germany suffered further setbacks on 29 September 1918 because Bulgaria surrendered on that day and British, Australian and American troops had breached the Hindenburg Line, along the St Quentin Canal section. This line of defence, as previously mentioned, stretched from Arras to St Quentin, was heavily fortified and considered impregnable. Holding this line was the Germans' last hope of preventing the Allies from marching into Germany and it gave them a bargaining position to discuss peace. Thirty British divisions, including the Australian Corps and two American divisions, overwhelmed thirty-nine German divisions. Some 35,500 German prisoners and 380 guns were captured.[13] When the Allies had broken through this line it became apparent that German forces on the Western Front were about to collapse. The breakthrough of the Hindenburg defences and the capture of the St Quentin Canal on 29 September 1918 was a psychological blow to the Germans from which they would not recover. Germany had lost the war. Field Marshal Haig wrote the following letter to Winston Churchill on 3 October 1918:

17

In my opinion, it is of the highest importance to keep on pressing the enemy at every possible point, because if we allow him any breathing time at all, he will be able to reorganise his forces, to construct new defences, and make new plans, and much of the work of 'wearing him out' will have to be started afresh.[14]

General Ludendorff wanted to use an armistice as a mechanism for Germany to avoid defeat and to prevent the Allies from entering Germany. Ludendorff met Hindenburg and the Kaiser at Spa during the morning of 29 September and immediately recommended that an armistice be sought in order to save Germany. Kaiser Wilhelm wrote:

After our failure of August 8th, General Ludendorff had declared that he could no longer guarantee a military victory. Therefore, the preparation of peace negotiations was necessary. Since diplomacy had not succeeded in initiating any promising negotiations and the military situation had become even worse in the meantime, on account of revolutionary agitation, Ludendorff, on the 29 of September, demanded that preparations be made for an armistice instead of for peace negotiations.[15]

Colonel Hans von Haeften, as representative of the German Supreme Command of the Foreign Ministry, reported to Prince Max of Baden:

Our military situation had become decidedly worse. On 29 September Headquarters had decided to appeal to President Wilson, accept his Fourteen Points, and request him to mediate an armistice.[16]

Prince Max was conscious that another German peace offer would highlight German weakness and raise Allied morale. He wrote:

The peace offer of December 1916, the July resolution, Kuehlmann's speech – every official peace feeler up to now had horrified the Supreme Command, because peace feelers 'strengthened the enemy morale and weakened ours'.[17]

By October 1918 the German Army was exhausted and demoralised. Lacking food, equipment and since General Ludendorff had expended his last reserves, it were not in a position to continue the fight for much longer. The arrival of American troops on the Western Front, despite being inexperienced, had given the Allies an overwhelming advantage over German forces. Meanwhile, in Germany there was a shortage of food and an outbreak of civil disturbances. Kaiser Wilhelm's position as Head of State was rapidly becoming untenable. In order to prevent revolution in Germany, the Kaiser was advised to install a democratic government. Chancellor von Hertling refused to serve with a democratic government and tendered his resignation. Germany could continue to fight until the end, but Ludendorff favoured instigating peace talks to bring the war to a conclusion. The German Government concurred with Ludendorff's view.

Prince Max of Baden was appointed Chancellor on 1 October. Prince Max had supported peace moves and opposed the policy of unrestricted submarine warfare. Germany now had a leader, heading a government that included social democrats, and Prince Max was regarded as a person with whom the Allies could negotiate peace. He was the Kaiser's cousin and regarded as a liberal who had strongly advocated peace, but was reluctant to sign a peace note to President Wilson until the new government had been formed. Requesting an armistice was also a strong signal to the Allied nations and the German population that Germany was defeated. Prince Max would have preferred to continue the fight while negotiating for peace. It was not until the following day, when Ludendorff revealed that the German Army on the Western Front was on the verge of collapsing and that an armistice was required urgently to salvage the situation, that the Chancellor, Prince Max succumbed to pressure from Ludendorff to initiate peace and began drafting a peace proposal to President Woodrow Wilson on 3 October 1918:

> The German Government requests the President of the United States of America to take in hand the restoration of peace, to bring this request to the notice of all belligerent states and to invite them to send plenipotentiaries for the initiation of negotiations. They accept as a basis for the peace negotiations the programme laid down by the President of the United States of America, in his message to Congress of 8 January, 1918 and in the subsequent announcements, particularly in his speech of 27 September, 1918.
>
> To avoid future bloodshed, the German Government requests the President to arrange the immediate conclusion of an armistice on land, by sea and in the air.[18]

By addressing the proposal directly to President Wilson, Prince Max was aligning the German desire for peace with the US President's fourteen-point plan. American troops were bolstering the Allies and

19

America's peace proposal was considered less harsh than what France and Britain would propose. By using President Wilson's plan as a basis for peace, the war would be brought to an end and all Germany had to do was to vacate the French and Belgian territory that it occupied and return its soldiers to its own frontier. Hindenburg wrote:

> I hoped I could fight down pessimism and revive confidence. Unfortunately, the State had already been shaken too greatly for me to achieve my purpose as yet. I myself was still firmly convinced that, in spite of the diminution of our forces, we could prevent our enemy from treading the soil of the Fatherland for many months. If we succeeded in doing so the political situation was not hopeless. Of course it was a tacit condition for this success that our land frontier should not be threatened from the east or south and that the public at home stood firm.
>
> Our peace offer to the President of the United Sates went forth in the night of October 4–5. We accepted the principles he had lain down in January of this year for a just peace.[19]

On 4 October 1918, Prince Max sent the peace note via the Swiss Government in Berne to President Woodrow Wilson requesting the opportunity to negotiate peace terms to end the war, using Wilson's original fourteen points as a basis for negotiation. Hindenburg recalled:

> We accepted the principles he had laid down in January of this year for a 'just peace'.[20]

Crown Prince Wilhelm, commander of Army Group Crown Prince, failed to initiate peace in 1917 to end what he viewed as a senseless war. During October 1918 he was responsible for operations in the Verdun sector, where he became distracted by the events at home: He recalled:

> And while my thoughts were concentrated upon the battle and upon the German soldiers entrusted to me, there reached me from home news that sounded distant and strange: the wording of our Peace Note to President Wilson; the brusque refusal voiced by the Paris press: the reply that evaded replying and demanded our consent to evacuate all occupied territory as a condition of an armistice …
>
> We fought. The battle began to die down slowly at the end of the second week during which it had raged. Both sides were completely exhausted. We had yielded ground under the enormous pressure, but we were still standing; and nowhere had the enemy broken

through. On the 10, the Third Army stood in the new Brunhilde position from St. Germainmont on the north bank of the Aisne, passing through Bethel to the east of Vouziers and west of Grandpré. Gallwitz was fighting the Americans in the area between Sivry and the Forest of Haumont. By the 12, the First Army had occupied, according to plan, the Gudrun–Brunhilde position, and the Seventh Army had retired to the Hunding position behind the Oise–Serre sector. A review of the military situation showed that the threatened collapse of the west front had been prevented by the transfer of the lines of resistance to stronger and narrower sectors. Despite the seriousness of the situation, we stood for the moment fairly secure; and, while the enemy was preparing for the fresh concentration and new offensives, we could ourselves be recuperating and getting ready for defence – and such a breathing-space was more than necessary to the over fatigued and over-taxed troops. There remained, therefore in my opinion, the faint hope that the peace efforts now being undertaken might lead, before the winter began, to a conclusion of the war that would be honourable for Germany by reason of its being a righteous peace of reconciliation. Failing this, we could – again, according to my personal views – reckon with a possibility of holding out till the spring of 1919 at the furthest.[21]

On receiving the German peace note, President Wilson was sceptical and questioned whether this was a serious peace initiative or was it just a manoeuvre to avoid the consequences of defeat? Without consulting directly with fellow Allied leaders, Wilson replied to Prince Max's proposal for peace on 8 October in a message signed by Robert Lansing, US Secretary of State, through the Swiss Chargé d'Affaires. Wilson challenged the sincerity of the offer and whether the Germans would accept his fourteen-point proposal. If they were serious President Wilson added the stipulation that Germany should evacuate all occupied territory, before the talks could begin. Wilson was offering Germany a peace that would be achieved by the Germans withdrawing to their own frontier. Wilson's response is detailed:

> Before making a reply to the request of the Imperial German Government, and in order that the reply shall be as candid and straightforward as the momentous interests involved require, the President of the United States deems it necessary to assure himself of the exact meaning of the Note of the Imperial Chancellor.
>
> Does the Imperial Chancellor mean that the Imperial German Government accepts the terms laid down by the President in his

address to the Congress of the United States on January 8th last, and in subsequent addresses, and that its object in entering into discussions would be only to agree upon the practical details of their application?

The President feels bound to say, with regard to the suggestion of an armistice, that he would not feel at liberty to propose a cessation of arms to the Governments with which the Government of the United States is associated against the Central Powers so long as the armies of those Powers are upon their soil.

The good faith of any discussion would manifestly depend upon the consent of the Central Powers immediately to withdraw their forces everywhere from invaded territory.

The President also feels that he is justified in asking whether the Imperial Chancellor is speaking merely for the constituted authorities of the Empire who have so far conducted the war?

He deems the answer to these questions vital from every point of view.[22]

At Versailles, European Allied leaders were discussing the current situation now that Bulgaria had pulled out of the war on 6 October. They were infuriated to learn that the US President was talking peace with the Germans, via an article written in *The Times*. They were seeking harsher peace terms than the terms proposed by President Wilson and once they became aware of the new German peace note they set about considering their own conditions. On 7 October, Prime Minister Georges Clemenceau instructed Marshal Foch to begin preparing a draft of terms that would be imposed upon Germany. Clemenceau wanted reasonable conditions that Germany would accept; he was anxious that the war be brought to an end in order to prevent further loss of life. At an Allied Conference held on that same day at the Quai d'Orsay, Paris, in the presence of Lloyd George, Clemenceau stressed that 'the principle which the Allies should adopt should be to ask all that is necessary from Germany, but not more. The Allies must not open themselves to the reproach of exposing thousands of men to be killed simply because they would not accede to reasonable conditions.'[23]

Foch proposed that war would only come to an end if Germany evacuated from Belgium and France, including Alsace and Lorraine. This would allow the Allied Armies to occupy Germany up to the western bank of the River Rhine, and enable Germany to pay reparations and surrender military assets and trains.

The Allied leaders met again on 9 October. There were no changes to Foch's proposed conditions, but the minutes of the meeting expressed the concerns of Lloyd George, who felt grieved that President Wilson had not consulted them. At the same time, he did not want anything to damage relations between the American President and the European Allies:

> Mr. Lloyd George said that he was as anxious as anyone else to avoid offending President Wilson, but he was even more anxious not to fall into a German trap. He considered that President Wilson's action was a very grave matter. It was all very well to say that we had not been consulted, but it would be very difficult to avoid being compromised by the action that President Wilson was now taking. The difficulty was to prevent the Germans from converting a negative into an affirmative, President Wilson practically says: 'I consider that, as a guarantee of good faith, you must evacuate the occupied territories before we have an armistice.' But it would be difficult to prevent the enemy putting the matter the other way and saying 'If we evacuate the occupied territory we are entitled to an armistice,' and yet evacuation, was, according to our military advisers, totally inefficient. If Prince Max of Baden should accept the fourteen points – which, by the way, were capable of any number of interpretations – we should be in an awkward position. In three months we might have reached the situation which Marshal Foch had warned us, namely, that the enemy had retired into a position where he could reconstitute his forces. Unquestionably the enemy was now very much frightened. The Peace party had come to the top. He reminded the Conference, however, that we had seen that before in 1917. In three months' time the military party, by working steadily and quietly, might get on top again. Then they might be in a position to reconstitute their army under much better conditions. Another point which he wished to impress on the Conference was that once an armistice was declared, we should never be able to start the war again. If the enemy was made to evacuate Alsace–Lorraine, the Trentino and Trieste, as well as the conquered positions, we should never want to begin again, because we should be in possession of what we aimed at, since the German colonies were already in possession of the Allies. On the other hand, if the evacuation of the occupied territories only took place, and the negotiations broke down, we should be in a position of not possessing what we were fighting for, since the enemy would remain in possession.[24]

Marshal Foch was of the view that President Wilson's fourteen-point plan would only form the basis of an armistice, but advised caution, as the minutes verified:

Marshal Foch said that he understood that President Wilson's conditions were a minimum, but did not profess to give all the conditions of an armistice. They merely laid down a preliminary condition of which must be fulfilled before the terms of an armistice could be discussed. The actual conditions of an armistice must be based on the facts existing on the day when the armistice was agreed to. If we tried to lay down these conditions finally now, the conditions might change and they might become altogether unacceptable to us.[25]

The conference on 9 October of Allied leaders at Versailles was adjourned without firmly agreeing to Armistice terms. They doubted that they could impose these conditions upon Germany at that moment, but at the same time they wanted nothing less than Foch's terms. Haig, who discussed the situation with Foch at Mouchy-le-Châtel on 10 October, wrote:

I remarked that the only difference between his [Foch's] conditions and a 'general unconditional surrender' is that the German Army is allowed to march back with its rifles, and officers with their swords. He is evidently of the opinion that the enemy is so desirous of peace that he will agree to any terms of this nature which we impose.[26]

Despite the reservations held by the European leaders, Prince Max of Baden, through German Secretary of State Wilhelm Solf, replied to President Wilson's response on 12 October as follows:

In answer to the questions of the President of the United States of America, the German Government declares:

The German Government has accepted the principles of which President Wilson laid down in his speech of January 8th and in his later speeches as the basis of enduring the just peace (Reichsfrieden). Its object in entering upon a discussion would, therefore, be solely that of reaching an agreement regarding the practical details of their application.

The German Government assumes that the Governments of the Powers associated with the United States also place themselves upon the ground of the proclamations of President Wilson.

The German Government, in accord with the Austro–Hungarian Government, declares itself willing, in order to bring about a truce, to fulfil the President's proposals for evacuation. It suggests to the President that he shall bring about the appointment of a mixed commission the duty of which shall be to make the necessary agreements for evacuation.

The present German Government, which bears the responsibility for this peace step, has been constituted as the result of negotiations with and in agreement with, the great majority of the Reichstag. Supported by the will of this majority in his every action, the Imperial Chancellor speaks in the name of the German Government and of the German people.[27]

Crown Prince Wilhelm recalled:

On October 12, in reply to the inquiry of President Wilson, Berlin gave a binding acceptance of the conditions drawn up by him and also signified that we were prepared to evacuate the occupied areas on certain conditions.

In all the news from the other side I seemed dimly to discover, as through a veil, two minds struggling for mastery. There was Wilson, who wanted to establish his Fourteen Points; there was Foch, who knew only one aim – our annihilation. Which would win? The pair were equally matched – sprinter Wilson and Foch the stayer. If things were quickly settled, Wilson's chances were good; if the negotiations were protracted, time was in Foch's favour. Every day's delay in arriving at an understanding was a gain to him; it allowed the dry-rot in the homeland to spread: it enfeebled and wasted the front, which was mainly buttressed upon auxiliary and defensive positions.[28]

The news of the acceptance of President Wilson's conditions for peace did destabilise the confidence of German soldiers fighting on the Western Front. After fighting hard for four years, and losing heavy casualties in the process, it was hard for them to accept Armistice terms and walk away from the ground that they had bitterly captured, contested and held. Captain Herbert Sulzbach had enlisted in August 1914 and was a recipient of the Iron Cross serving with the 63rd Field Artillery, 9th Division. Salzbach wrote in his diary on 12 October:

Our reply to Wilson states that we will comply with his request and evacuate the whole of the occupied territory. For us soldiers, who have fought victoriously for four years, this step is a hard and saddening one, but nevertheless – and perhaps it has to be like this – it is no use now racking our brains and considering all the possibilities, we have to look the bare facts in the face. Outnumbered

25

in the West, Bulgaria's defection, the defeat of Turkey, internal chaos in Austria, shortage of food and clothing at home – all these factors oblige us to engage in the soberest reflection. But it is quite incredible that we might have been able to make peace on better terms in 1916. Rumours of an armistice are already going the rounds.[29]

The prospects for peace were nearly jeopardised when the German submarine *UB-123*, commanded by Oberleutnant Robert Ramm, sank the passenger ship *Leinster* on 10 October 1918 in the Irish Sea. She was sailing from Kingstown (now named Dun Laoghaire) to Holyhead when she was hit by two torpedoes. A total of 771 passengers were aboard, mainly military personnel but also 180 civilians, and approximately 600 lives were lost. Mr Dane received the following letter from his son, who was serving with the West Kent Yeomanry and was aboard *Leinster*, returning to his home in Dover on leave:

Just a few lines to let you know that I am still alive and quite well, with the exception of a few bruises and I think I am very lucky to get off so lightly after the terrible time I went through. I suppose you have heard by now that I was on-board the ill-fated '*Leinster*' coming home for fourteen days' leave. Well, we left, Kingstown at 8.55. All went well for about forty minutes, when all of a sudden I saw a very small torpedo coming towards the bow. At first I thought it would miss us, but we were unlucky, and the explosion was enough to stop us. The ship now started to go down by the head, but not far, and I think that she would have kept up all right until help arrived. Anyway, I was not leaving anything to chance, so I got ready for a swim. I first took off my overcoat, by the way, these drowned a good many men, and then put my lifebelt on. Then I started to take my puttees and boots off, and had one boot undone when the next explosion came, and I can tell you it was a terrible one. It seemed to lift the whole ship out of the water, and when she dropped back again she simply went to pieces. I might mention people were blown sky high by this second explosion. No sooner had this occurred than she began to sink at once. I was, at this time, in the stern of the ship. The stern came clean out of the water, and I should imagine from the top of the deck where I stood to the water was quite sixty feet. There was nothing else to do but go down with the ship or slide down the side into the water, and I can tell you it was a slide that I shall never forget. When I reached the water I swam for all I was worth, as I did not want to get caught in the suction and dragged down. I made straight for a lot of wreckage that

26

was floating, and I succeeded in getting hold of a couple of planks which kept me up quite well for a time, but the sea was so rough at the time it was very hard work to hang on to them. Then a boat got mixed up with this lot of wreckage, and I thought to myself I'm making for that to see if I can manage to get into it. I found she was overloaded, so I had to hang on to the life lines that run round the sides. This I succeeded in doing, but every now and again the sea would almost knock you off, but I hung on. There were quite twenty hanging on to her, besides being over loaded, and I thought every sea that came would sink her. Some of the men who were hanging on became exhausted and dropped off (poor devils). I then having more room to move, I managed to get my left leg over the top of the rope which runs round the sides of the boat. That got me out of the water a bit, but I was getting very weak when one of the chaps in the bow of the boat put a bit of rope round my shoulders, and hung on to me for a time. Then after about an hour and a half in this awful position, there came four destroyers to our assistance. I remember seeing one of them come up, but I don't remember our boat getting alongside. The next I remember was getting down in the bottom of the boat, which was by this time swamped. When I fell down I came to my senses, and all there was in the boat was myself and a sailor. He came and got hold of me and put a rope round my shoulders, and I was dragged on board the destroyer. I believe I was more dead than alive, as I could not walk. I was taken down below, and they stripped me and knocked a bit of life in me. We were then taken back to Kingstown, and I was sent straight into hospital, where I have been in bed ever since, but I am feeling all right in myself, only for my legs, which are terribly bruised by my hanging on to the planks, and then the boat, but never mind, I am alive, and that's worth something. I cannot describe to you the awful scenes that I saw and the screams of people who were drowning, so I will say no more about it, as it does not bear thinking about.[30]

American citizens were among the passengers who drowned, which infuriated President Woodrow Wilson, as he commented:

At the very time that the German government approaches the government of the United States with proposals of peace its submarines are engaged in sinking passenger ships at sea and not the boats alone, but the very boats in which their passengers and crews seek to make their way to safety.[31]

Wilson sent a stern letter on 16 October requesting that Germany provide evidence that it was a democratic state and dictated that any peace discussions would be negotiated with Allied military commanders. Wilson also stipulated that Germany must immediately stop submarine warfare. *UB-123*, the submarine that sunk the *Leinster*, struck a mine in the North Sea on 19 October. Oberleutnant Robert Ramm and the entire crew perished and were probably unaware that the war was coming to an end.

Meanwhile, on the Western Front German forces were unable to resist the onslaught of co-ordinated Allied attacks on various fronts. Rumours of Armistice had a demotivating effect upon the German soldier, who found it difficult to find the strength and determination to continue the war and hold his ground. Crown Prince Wilhelm recalled that these attacks and the talk of Armistice had a significant negative impact upon his soldiers:

> On the 15th, formidable attacks were launched afresh against the Army group of Crown Prince Rupprecht, against me and against Gallwitz. The terrific onslaught. Loss of ground here and there. The troops were nearly played out. Next day, Lille fell. Things were worst with the Crown Prince of Bavaria. Losses were sustained wherever the enemy attacked. Now that they had heard something of a possible armistice and approaching negotiations, it was as though our people could no longer find their full inner strength to fight. Also as though, here and there, they no longer wanted to. But where was the dividing line between could and would with these men, who had a thousand times bravely risked their lives for their country, and whose heads were befogged by hunger, pain and privation? Does that one last failure make a coward of the man who has a hundred times shown himself a hero? No! Only it deprives him of one thing – the prize for which he has risked his life a hundred times.[32]

On 17 October the German Government, together with military commanders led by Ludendorff, discussed Wilson's note of 16 October. Ludendorff had rallied from his period of ill health and changing his perspective, becoming confident that if the German Army could continue a defensive war and hold out until 1919, the situation might change with divisions between the Allies, or their armies might collapse due to exhaustion or for lack of resources. Prince Max overruled his military commanders' intentions to continue the war and ordered the continuation of peace talks and the cessation of unrestricted submarine warfare.

While German politicians spoke of peace, the flames of revolution were spreading across their cities. The morale of the German soldier on the Western Front was severely affected; losing their motivation, they became reluctant to continue the fight. Why would they continue to risk their lives in battle when it was certain that the war was likely to end within days? One soldier recorded the following in his diary on 18 October:

> The discipline is relaxing. You can see signs of it everywhere. Nothing to be said of these continual retreats.
>
> Is it true that our troops flee every time the enemy attacks? Is our morale shaken to that degree? It's certainly not so in my battalion. We have always withdrawn in perfect order. But haven't we the strength to counter attack? The discontent from the rear is beginning to pervade the army. The word armistice flies from mouth to mouth, and no one wants to sacrifice his life three minutes before peace. Max, Max, you have played your country a dirty trick! How can we still have courage and confidence when our government sacrifices everything behind our backs? It's hard these days to fight with a firm heart.[33]

The talk of Armistice became a catalyst for German officers and soldiers to desert their posts. One captured German regimental order stated:

> The morale in the front line leaves a good deal to be desired. Phrases such as 'If we're not relieved tonight, we'll go to the rear ourselves,' become more and more frequent. I must express my utter dissatisfaction with this attitude. Men and officers apparently don't realise that it is now a question of life and death for our country. We are struggling against a whole world of adversaries. Every day of resistance brings us nearer peace. The enemy must realise that the German Army always had been and always will be invincible. We are still deep in the enemy's country. The more we defend these positions tenaciously, the more the enemy will realise that our army has not faltered. Men who are unfortunately taken prisoners must continue to serve their country by showing an unshaken confidence and by declaring that, far from capitulating, we are ready to fight for our country to the last man. If everyone does his duty, the enemy won't break through us. I know how tired and exhausted we are. The High Command knows it too. But on other fronts the fighting is even worse. And all we need to do is hold, hold even though at first sight that seems beyond our force. Men under no pretext must leave front lines at night except by special permission. Officers and under-

29

officers must thwart by every means in their power, even by the use
of fire-arms, this cowardly conduct. The troops must keep the good
reputation they have won so far in the field.[34]

While German soldiers were losing the will to fight, Allied soldiers were
opposed to the prospect of an Armistice for different reasons because
they were keen to finish the job by continuing the fight until the German
Army had been totally destroyed or surrendered unconditionally.
Captain Oliver Sichel, 2/6th Royal Warwickshire's, wrote on 16
October:

The peace terms are all rot and we are all against it out here. Why
should not Foch finish it?[35]

Sichel would not live to see the end of the war because he was killed on
25 October, being buried in Awoingt British Cemetery.

Chapter 3

Allied Response to the German Peace Initiative

Although Germany was now keen to accept President Wilson's proposals as an initial basis for peace, the Allied politicians and military leaders in Europe had not been consulted. General Sir Henry Wilson, Chief of the Imperial General Staff, sent the following telegram to Field Marshal Sir Douglas Haig:

> President Wilson's 14 points are in no sense the definition of an armistice, and the Prime Ministers in Paris last week made this quite clear to him, and he agreed that when it comes to discussing a question of armistice, the terms must be laid down by the Allied Naval and Military Representatives. This point has not yet been reached, and until it has and until the terms of an armistice have been laid down by the Allies and agreed to by the enemy, the operation now going on should be continued with all vigour you consider safe and possible.[1]

There was a feeling that further conditions needed to be explored before approving the final draft. British admirals had not been consulted and they had their own thoughts regarding an armistice. They were concerned that there were no terms to inflict damage upon Germany's Navy, hindering their ability to go to war again. Admiral Sir David Beatty, Commander-in-Chief of the Grand Fleet, wanted to maintain Britain's supremacy on the seas as a superior naval power and was making demands for sanctions to be imposed upon the German Navy to diminish its strength. Beatty wanted to enforce such terms that would reduce Germany's naval strength as if it had been defeated in a large-scale naval battle. Beatty and Admiral Sir Rosslyn Wemyss, First Sea Lord and Chief of the Naval Staff, considered naval terms for the

31

Armistice with the Board of Admiralty on 16 October. Beatty's suggestions for naval Armistice terms were reported:

> Admiral Beatty had replied that we ought to demand the surrender of two out of three squadrons of the German battleships, which, in his view, should be brought to our ports. These squadrons contained the newest of the German battleships. In addition he demanded the surrender of all the battle cruisers, a certain number of light cruisers, and 50 destroyers, in addition to all the German submarines.[2]

The Admiralty Board also agreed that the blockade of German ports, which was having a devastating impact upon German civilians and food supplies, should continue throughout an Armistice until peace had been finalised.

The War Cabinet convened a meeting on 19 October 1918 in Whitehall, where Admiral Wemyss was given the opportunity to present the proposed naval terms for an Armistice. The War Cabinet also considered the contentious issue relating to the extent the Armistice terms should be imposed upon the German Navy, and there was a strong consensus to reduce its effectiveness and strength. Andrew Bonar Law, Chancellor of the Exchequer, commented:

> We must completely reverse the naval situation, and in view of the difficulty of starting the war after an armistice, we should secure this as part of the terms.[3]

No decision about the naval terms was reached during this particular meeting, however Lloyd George, chairing the War Cabinet, advised 'that the Navy must keep these considerations in view'.[4]

During the same meeting, Lloyd George asked Field Marshal Sir Douglas Haig to provide an outline of terms for an Armistice from the British Army's perspective.

Haig replied:

> In the event of the enemy asking for an armistice the nature of the reply should depend greatly on the answers which we can make to the following two questions:-
>
> 1.) Is Germany so beaten that she will accept any terms dictated by the Allies?
> 2.) Can the Allies continue to press the enemy sufficiently vigorously during the coming winter months to cause him to

> withdraw so quickly that he cannot destroy the railways, roads, etc., up to the German frontier?[5]

Haig then continued to present a detailed, comprehensive memorandum to the War Cabinet, containing his appraisal of the state of German, British, French and American forces in order to answer these two fundamental questions:

> A very large part of the German Army has been badly beaten, but the whole Field Army has not yet been broken up. Owing to the large number of Divisions of which it consists general disorganisation (which follows a decisive defeat) is not yet apparent.
>
> In my opinion the Germany Army is capable of retiring to its own frontiers and holding that line against equal or even superior forces.
>
> The length of that line is about 245 miles as against the front of 400 miles which he was holding only a week ago. The situation of the Allied Armies is as follows:-

> The French Army seems greatly worn out. Many of the rank and file seem to feel that the war has been won. Lille, Roubaix, Tourcoing and other big centres of industry have been taken. Reports say that many of their men are disinclined to risk their lives. Certainly neither on the right, nor on the left of the British have the French attacked vigorously during the past six weeks. Even in July it was the British and American Divisions which carried the French forward on the Marne. Next year a large proportion of the French Armies will probably be Black!
>
> American Army is disorganised, ill-equipped and ill-trained, with very few N.C.O.s and officers of experience. It has suffered severely through ignorance of modern war and it must take at least a year before it becomes a serious fighting force.
>
> The British Army has fought hard. It is a veteran force, very confident in itself, but its infantry is already 50,000 under strength. If infantry effectives could be maintained and rest given during winter it would remain what it is now, the most formidable fighting force in the world. On the other hand with diminishing effectives we must expect morale to decline.
>
> If the French and American Armies were capable of a serious offensive now, the Allies could completely overthrow the remaining efficient enemy divisions before they could reach the line of the Meuse.
>
> They are not. We must reckon with that fact as well as with the

fact that the British Army alone is not sufficiently fresh, or strong to force a decision by itself.

This means that the Allies are not in a position to prevent the enemy from doing an immense amount of material damage to railways, roads, etc., during the winter months and <u>during his retirement</u>.

The advance of the Allies, when active operations again begin, will, therefore, be greatly hampered and progress must be slow.

In the coming winter, too, the enemy will have several months for recuperation, and absorption of the 1920 class, untouched as yet.

So we must conclude that the enemy will be able to hold the line which he selects for defence for some time after the campaign of 1919 commences.

To sum up then:-

A careful consideration of the military situation on the Western Front, and keeping British interests in view, forces me to the conclusion that an armistice with Germany should be concluded on the following basis:-

1.)   Complete and immediate evacuation of Belgium and occupied French territories.
2.)   Alsace and Lorraine must also be evacuated and Metz and Strasburg handed forthwith to the Allies.
3.)   Rolling stock of French and Belgian railways or equivalent to be returned, inhabitants repatriated, etc.

The effect of this would be that the Allied Armies would be established on the enemy's frontier with their communications intact and adequate rolling-stock.

From such a position a resumption of hostilities would enable the war to be prosecuted under favourable conditions on the enemy's soil. Moreover, with Metz, Strasburg and Alsace-Lorraine in a position to invade South Germany. The military and political advantages of an advance in this direction would be very considerable.[6]

Based on Haig's report, the War Cabinet considered that given the current conditions, Germany would not agree to such severe Armistice conditions. Lloyd George 'did not think … that they were sufficiently defeated to concede such terms'.[7]

Andrew Bonar-Law was not convinced that Germany would accept such drastic conditions for peace. The minutes of the meeting reported his comments:

> MR. BONAR LAW observed that this amounted to a complete defeat to the enemy. No nation would ever accept such terms unless they were in desperate straits. So far as he could see there was nothing in the military situation to compel him to accept such terms.[8]

Haig was confident that German commanders had overestimated the strength and morale of the Allied forces, highlighting that 'the enemy might think that the Allies were stronger than they were in reality'.[9]

Bonar Law reaffirmed that the question during the winter months would be which armies would become the stronger. However, Lloyd George ascertained that:

> The real point was whether the German morale would be strong enough to enable them to resume the offensive, in the event of a breakdown of Peace negotiations, to recover the territories they had evacuated under the terms of the Armistice.[10]

Lloyd George was also concerned that if the Allies asked for too much in terms of conditions for an Armistice that would be unacceptable to the Germans, then the opportunity of ending the war would be lost.

The Prime Minister pointed out the danger of losing a good bargain through asking too much. 'We knew exactly what we required, and if we obtained that we should be safe.'[11]

On 20 October, Prince Max agreed to President Wilson's terms for a military armistice to happen. Germany would evacuate occupied lands and that any conditions for an Armistice would be decided by Allied military leaders. The fact that he had rejected Ludendorff's strategy to continue the war was evidence that Germany was ruled by a democratic government. Wilson was satisfied with Prince Max's answers and assurances, and he was confident that he could approach the Allies with Germany's proposal for an Armistice. Crown Prince Wilhelm recalled:

> On the 21, we learn the terms of the Government's reply to Wilson. Everything has been done to meet his wishes. Surely, on this basis, he can find ways and means to conclude an armistice and to set peace negotiations on foot. Will he indeed do so? Will he still do so? More days pass during which thousands of Germans and men of all nations are mown down, during which the gentlemen at the green-

baize table take their time, during which our position at the front does not improve. The voice of Wilson's note of the 24th, and the arrogant and haughty voice, was the voice of Marshal Foch – or the voice of a Wilson who had sunk to be the puppet of the French wirepuller and now equalled his master in hawking and spitting.[12]

In London, a further meeting of the War Cabinet took place on 21 October, where members reflected upon the memorandum that Haig presented at the previous meeting on 19 October:

> Mr. Balfour [Secretary of State for Foreign Affairs] pointed out an apparent inconsistency in the Field Marshal's terms. He stated that the Allies had not the strength to finish the war this year. Hence, the object of an armistice would be to enable them to finish it on better terms next year. It had generally been assumed, however, that an armistice would mean the end of the war. He did not see how these conflicting hypotheses could be reconciled. He further pointed out that the Field Marshal's plan gave no security for any terms of peace beyond ensuring the territory that was occupied by the Allies. It provided no gauge for obtaining the reparation to Belgium or North France.[13]

Lloyd George was confident that the blockade of Germany would ensure that Germany paid reparations to France and Belgium. However, Austen Chamberlain, member of the War Cabinet, posed the question what would happen if the Armistice broke down?

> Mr Chamberlain asked the Field Marshal whether, supposing an armistice were granted on the terms suggested by him, namely the occupation of all territory up to the German frontier of 1870, and supposing the negotiations for peace break down, say, in January or February, and he was told that he must begin fighting again; in these conditions, could he smash the enemy?[14]

Haig was prepared to resume the war if the peace negotiations collapsed and if they were in possession of Germany's industrial heartlands west of the Rhine, it would make the prospect of Germany putting up a fight more remote. Haig's response to Chamberlain was recorded in the minutes:

> Field Marshal Haig said that he would be in a better position than he was now, since the Allies would have possession of a large part of the coal and other sources of munitions supplies of the enemy.[15]

Also at the War Cabinet meeting on 21 October, Admiral Wemyss enforced the view that it was important to align the Naval conditions at sea for Armistice alongside the military terms on land. It was recorded:

> He [Wemyss] felt that both the naval and military situations ought to be considered together. He admitted that the terms suggested by the Board of Admiralty were so stiff that they were not likely to be accepted, but he pointed out the great difficulty in reducing them. If the principle was accepted that hostilities were not likely to recommence after an armistice had once been declared, it was necessary that the terms of the armistice should approximate to what it was desired to obtain in the peace. This was why it was so difficult to cut the naval conditions down. To do so might mean that while we had been victorious on shore, we should not reap the fruits of our victory at sea. This naval victory was no less real because it was not spectacular, for the Admiralty claimed by their strategy to have imposed their will upon the enemy.[16]

Admiral Sir David Beatty was given another opportunity to present his case for naval terms to be considered alongside the military conditions to the War Cabinet on 21 October. It was reported:

> ADMIRAL BEATTY said that, in preparing his list of the ships which the enemy should surrender as the naval conditions of an armistice, he had based himself on the assumption that our object in the war now, as ever before, was to destroy German militarism, that is to say, both the military and naval power of Germany. If this was not accomplished, the war might break out again, as soon as the enemy recovered sufficiently. Like the First Sea Lord, he also based his views on the assumption that hostilities were not likely to recommence after an armistice, and consequently that the terms of an armistice must be as near as possible to the terms of peace. From a naval point of view it was necessary by these terms to reduce the forces of the enemy to such an extent as to prevent him from reducing our strength, as he had done in the past, by the attacks of his submarines. He must not again be allowed to approach to such a position. If the enemy was left with the power of building submarines, and with sufficient surface craft to enable those submarines to put to sea – and submarines could be only really effectively dealt with close to their point of departure – that is to say, if the enemy was left with sufficient naval power to protect the nests of his submarines, then he would be powerful at sea as before. Sir

David Beatty associated himself with what Admiral Wemyss had said in regard to the success of our sea power. It was true that we had obtained no decisive active victory, but we had obtained a passive victory. Because it was passive there was no reason why the nation should give up the object with which it had entered the war, namely, the destruction of German militarism. Admiral Beatty said that the terms he would impose would include the surrender of 2 out of 3 squadrons of Dreadnaughts; all the German battle cruisers; a number of light cruisers; fifty of the most modern destroyers; as well as all the submarines. The basis on which he calculated the number of dreadnaughts to be handed over as follows: – If the Grand Fleet should encounter the High Sea Fleet, he hoped and expected to accomplish the entire destruction of the latter, but in achieving this he expected to have heavy losses which he estimated at 8 or 9 capital ships. His proposal was to leave the enemy the equivalent of what he should lose, and to take the remainder. Sir David Beatty said it might be contended that if we contented ourselves with taking the enemy's submarines, his High Sea Fleet would soon become obsolete.[17]

The meeting was interrupted by the news that Turkey was seeking an Armistice and the talk about naval conditions was halted. Lloyd George did say that it would be wise to consider both naval and military terms together when the moment came and advised Wemyss and Beatty to consider what would be the minimum terms that the Royal Navy would accept.

In Germany there was concern that the army was so dejected that it would be unable to defend its own frontier if required. Field Marshal Paul von Hindenburg was disappointed in the German Government's position in seeking reconciliation, believing it was having a serious impact upon the fighting ability of his soldiers. He wrote of his concerns for the morale of the German soldier and loss of impetus to fight in a letter to Prince Max on 24 October:

> I cannot conceal from your Grand-Ducal Highness that in the recent speeches in the Reichstag I missed a warm appeal of goodwill to the Army, and it caused me much pain. I had hoped that the new Government would gather together all the resources of the whole nation for the defence of our Fatherland. That hope has not been realised. On the contrary, with few exceptions they talk only of reconciliation and not of fighting the enemies which threaten the very existence of our country. This has had first a depressing and

then a devastating effect on the Army. It is proved by serious symptoms.

If the Army is to defend the nation, it needs not only men, but the conviction that it is necessary to go on fighting, as well as the moral impetus this great task demands.

Your Grand-Ducal Highness will share my conviction that realising the outstanding importance to be attached to the morale of the nation in arms, the Government and the representatives of the nation must inspire and maintain that spirit in both the army and the public at home.[18]

On 25 October, Marshal Foch convened a meeting with Allied commander-in-chiefs at Senlis to assess the military situation and discuss the proposed terms of an Armistice that was based upon German withdrawal from occupied territories and the surrender of war material.

There were major differences between the Allied leaders in their expectations for an Armistice. President Wilson did not want Germany to be destroyed as a nation, he did not want to place responsibility for the outbreak of the war upon Germany and he wanted to establish a League of Nations. The French Premier Clemenceau was not interested in the creation of a League of Nations. He sought vengeance and wanted to punish Germany by imposing strict Armistice terms that would make it pay reparations as compensation. These should consequently cripple the country economically, include the return of Alsace and Lorraine, lead to the creation of the Rhineland as a nation and ensure the disarmament of the German Army, meaning that Germany could never attack France again. Lloyd George was not seeking vengeance, but wanted justice resulting in Germany paying reparations and maintaining its ability to trade. He also wanted to sustain Britain's naval supremacy.

The different expectations of the Allied leaders in their conditions for an Armistice were apparent to their German adversaries. Crown Prince Wilhelm wrote in his diary:

There is at the moment a marked contrast between Wilson and Foch. Wilson desires a peace by justice, reconciliation and understanding. Foch wants the complete humiliation of Germany and the gratification of French vanity.

Every manifestation of firmness on the German front and the German diplomatic attitude strengthens Wilson's position: every sign of military or political weakness strengthens Foch.

Wilson demands surrender on two points only:

1. Submarine warfare: no more passenger ships to be sunk.
2. The democratization of Germany. (No deposition of the Kaiser: only constitutional monarchy: position of the Crown as in England).

A military humiliation of Germany is not aimed at by Wilson. Foch, on the other hand wants, with every means in his power, to bring about a complete military capitulation and humiliation (gratification of French revenge). Which of the two will get the upper hand depends solely and simply upon Germany. If the front holds out and we preserve a dignified diplomatic attitude, Wilson will win. Yielding to Foch means the destruction of Germany and the miscarriage of every prospect of an endurable peace.

England's position is an intermediate one. The main difficulty in the peace movement is France.[19]

In Whitehall, the British Admiralty continued to discuss proposed terms with the British War Cabinet on 26 October. If the Allies expected Germany to surrender its military assets on land, then the Admiralty expected Germany to surrender its modern surface ships and all its submarines. Arthur Balfour wanted to challenge President Wilson's 'Freedom of the Seas' clause:

> That we might state that we could not agree to the doctrine of Freedom of the Seas until the League of Nations had proved itself to be an effective instrument.[20]

Lloyd George 'pointed out that if the League of Nations was effective there would be no wars, and the question would not arise'.[21]

The War Cabinet was in a dilemma because it could not agree to President Wilson's 'Freedom of the Seas' condition, but it did not want to jeopardise the attempts to initiate peace and wanted to maintain good diplomatic relations with the US Allies without offending President Wilson.

Admiral Wemyss pointed out that the British Government had always contended that the manner in which submarines were used was illegal. 'If we were to treat it as a legal method of war we might get ourselves into great difficulties. That was why the Admiralty insisted on the surrender of all submarines.'[22]

Lloyd George was concerned that the inclusion of the surrender of the surface and submarine fleet would possibly threaten the peace initiative. The British War Cabinet remained concerned that Germany would not agree to such terms and they would threaten its objective of ending the war. General C.H. Harington, Deputy Chief of the Imperial Staff, provided further detail about the condition of the opposing armies on the Western Front:

> General Harington, at the request of the Prime Minister, gave his views as to the present military situation of the German Army. He admitted that our own Army was extended to the full and was the only Army fighting properly. The French Army was extremely tired, and was, so to speak, leaning against the enemy, only advancing when the enemy gave way. The American Army was not in a much better situation. On the other hand, from all the information we had, it was clear that some portions of the German Army were in such a bad state that anything might happen. It was true the weather might give the enemy some respite. Nevertheless, the German High Command must be seriously anxious about the state of their troops, and must be willing to accept very stiff terms of an armistice.[23]

Major General C.H. Harington reassured Lloyd George that an Armistice would still be achievable if the naval conditions were included:

> In his view, the German Army was in such a state that they might accept harsh terms for an armistice.[24]

If Germany was allowed to retain its surface ships and submarines Austen Chamberlain 'looked with horror to the day when, after the armistice had been declared, a huge Vote of Credit was asked for in Parliament in order to build up the fleet against Germany'.[25]

General Jan Smuts, member of the War Cabinet, regarded the issue 'not a legitimate one for an armistice, but was part of the terms for peace'.[26]

Lord Rufus Reading, Lord Chief Justice, affirmed that 'we should make it clear that the question of the reduction of German naval power was one that we should be bound to bring up as part of the terms for peace'.[27]

Bonar Law supported the Admiralty, asserting that: 'President Wilson had said that the terms of an armistice must be such as to prevent the enemy from fighting again. Therefore, from this point of view, it was desirable to include the surrender of the battleships and cruisers.'[28]

Lloyd George proposed a way of emphasising their reservations and reluctance to agree to the 'Freedom of the Seas', but prevent embarrassment to President Wilson:

> To say that the doctrine of the Freedom of the Seas was not acceptable to us, but that we would be willing to debate it at the Peace Conference.[29]

The War Cabinet therefore agreed to include this meagre and vague insertion into the conditions:

> The naval conditions of the armistice should represent the admission of German defeat by sea in the same degree as the military conditions recognise the corresponding German defeat by land.[30]

This conclusion kept the Navy's issue with President Wilson's 'Freedom of the Seas' condition in his fourteen points, and gave it more time to enforce the issue to a result that was suitable at a later date.

On 29 October Allied leaders gathered in Paris, where a meeting was convened at the office of M. Pichon (French Minister for Foreign Affairs) at Quai d'Orsay. Among the attendees were Prime Ministers Georges Clemenceau and David Lloyd George and Edward House, President Woodrow's representative, who although having no prior military experience was referred to as Colonel House. They agreed:

> That the Associated Governments should consider the terms of an armistice with Germany, and the terms of an armistice with Austria. They should then forward these to President Wilson. If President Wilson agreed in the terms, he should not notify them to the German or Austrian Governments, but should advise these Governments that their next step was to send preliminaries to Marshal Foch and General Diaz [Italian Chief of Staff] respectively.[31]

As Germany still continued with hostilities, its Allies were considering their own positions regarding the war. On 27 October 1918, Austria began initiatives for making peace and on 30 October 1918 Turkey signed an Armistice. Germany now stood alone and it was now under pressure to agree to an Armistice. This encouraged the Allies that they could now impose stringent and excessive terms upon Germany. On 1

November the first session of the Supreme Council of War took place at Versailles. Haig wrote:

> I was present at the Supreme War Council at Versailles. The paper embodying the proposed peace terms for an armistice which had been approved in general by the Prime Minister was read. The terms are very stiff, and include retirement beyond the Rhine with a strip of 40 kilos, on the eastern bank. The surrender of 5,000 guns (heavy and field) railway waggons, locomotives, etc. The fact that Turkey and now Austria have abandoned Germany seems most important and means that they at any rate expect the early downfall of Germany. So probably the Allied Governments are justified in demanding stiff terms. On the other hand, the determined fight put up by the enemy today shows that all the Divisions in the German Army are not yet demoralised![32]

Although talks of Armistice were being conducted, Haig's diary entry shows that the German Army was still determined to continue the war. Despite the prospects of peace and the end of war in sight, the conflict would still be fought with vigour during the final days of the First World War.

Chapter 4

German Situation at Home and at the Front

Gerrman soldiers fighting on the Western Front were often oblivious to the dire situation back home. Throughout the autumn of 1918 the German Army was withdrawing eastwards. Hans Spieß served with the 5th Reserve Cavalry Rifles Regiment and wrote to his family on 10 October:

> The war can't last much longer, we are always moving backwards. We are busy holding up the enemy troops, they are attacking us every day. You can imagine how many of our men that does cost.[1]

The situation continued to deteriorate because on 21 October Spieß wrote what could possibly have been his last letter home, as he was killed by a gunshot wound to the chest the following day:

> My dears ... I am presently still alive. I can't tell you what is happening on the German side. There is no quiet moment any more. We had to move back more than 100 km within a few days. Whoever can't run, is taken prisoner. Please don't be upset. There is nothing we can do. There are no men left. It won't be long this way. All my love, your Hans.[2]

While Prince Max was discussing peace Hindenburg and Ludendorff wanted to continue the fight. The Chancellor felt undermined by his generals, especially when on 25 October he ordered them to remain in Spa, but instead they defied his order and were heading for Berlin. Ludendorff also circulated the following Army order with the purpose of generating a fighting spirit among his deflated troops, at the same time, attempting to destabilise the efforts to reach a peaceful conclusion to the war:

Wilson says in his answer that he is ready to propose to his allies the opening of armistice negotiations, but that any such armistice must render Germany powerless to take up arms again. He will only negotiate peace with Germany, if she is ready to comply entirely with the Allies' demands for her internal re-organisation; otherwise he will only consider unconditional surrender.

Wilson's answer is to demand for the army to capitulate, and is therefore inacceptable for us soldiers. It is the proof that the will for our annihilation which in 1914 let loose the war upon us is today as strong as ever. It is further a proof that the phrase 'Peace of Justice' is in the mouth of our enemies merely a trick to undermine our resistance. Thus, for us, soldiers, Wilson's answer can only be an inducement to prolong our resistance to the utmost of our power. When once the enemy recognises that no sacrifice will avail to break through the German front, they will be ready for a peace which secures Germany her future – in particular a future for the great mass of her people.[3]

Although this communiqué did not act in accordance with the German Government's aim to reach a peaceful agreement, Prince Max did recognise that Ludendorff did sincerely believe that 'he was acting in full accord with the Government; he was led to do so as a result of telephone messages in which Haeften had presumably not always distinguished very accurately between his own personal opinion and that of the Government'.[4] This message undermined the efforts of the Chancellor to prove to President Wilson that the German Government was acting independently and not influenced by the Army.

The effects of the war were also taking its toll upon the health of General Erich Ludendorff. While he was leading the German Army to defeat, he was simultaneously grieving for the loss of his stepsons. His stepson, Franz Pernet, was killed in aerial combat on 5 September 1917. His youngest stepson, named Erich Pernet, had also been killed in action in air combat on 22 March 1918.[5] Ludendorff had by chance come across the graves of two unidentified German flying officers and he identified one of them as Erich. 'The war has spared me nothing,' he lamented.[6]

Towards the end of October 1918 there existed widespread concern from various quarters about Ludendorff's welfare. Rumours were circulating that he had suffered a nervous breakdown. Prince Max wrote:

My wish to tap new sources of military advice at once provided indignant protest from the Supreme Command. General Ludendorff declared himself ready to come to Berlin within the next few days and to supply me with every kind of military information.

I was naturally willing to await the personal conversation with Ludendorff, but I did not feel reassured any more than did my Cabinet.

Our anxiety was increased by rumours with regard to General Ludendorff's health. Colonel Bauer was in Berlin on official business and had expressed himself very pessimistically to several heads of departments with regard to the General's condition.

Then in a moment the cry of alarm: 'Ludendorff must go; he has lost his nerve,' got through to the public in spite of all the habits of discipline in which the Press had so patiently submitted for four whole years.[7]

On their arrival at Schloss Bellevue, Berlin on 25 October, Ludendorff and Hindenburg went before Kaiser Wilhelm to demand the break off of negotiations and for Germany to continue the fight. Ludendorff recalled:

On the 25th October the Field Marshal and I place our views before His Majesty in Berlin, wither we had again travelled. We expressed the view that we must fight on. The new Chief of the Civil Cabinet, His Excellency von Delbrück, was present. While keeping his own opinion in the background, he adopted the same standpoint as Prince Max. We were surprised to learn that he was ignorant of the fact that we had discussed the question of peace with the Chancellor as early as the middle of August. His Majesty came to no decision, but he showed full confidence in me. He referred us to the Chancellor. The latter was ill and von Payer received us and Admiral Scheer at nine o'clock in the evening. He seemed personally ill-deposed towards us, in contrast to his previous attitude. He knew well that the Cabinet wanted me to go, as I was for fighting on.[8]

Ludendorff had suffered a nervous breakdown due to the family bereavements that he had recently suffered and Germany's failure to hold back the Allied advance. During the following day, 26 October, the pressure was too much to bear and Ludendorff offered his resignation to Kaiser Wilhelm. Ludendorff recalled:

At 8 o'clock on the morning of the 26th, still in the mood of the previous evening, I wrote tendering my resignation. In this I adopted the point of view that, in the discussion of the previous day with Vice-chancellor von Payer, I had gained the impression that the Government would not act in the crisis, that His Majesty, the country and the army were thus placed in an untenable position, that I was considered anxious to prolong the war, and that, in view of the attitude taken by the Government to Wilson, my departure might ease their position. I therefore begged His Majesty to graciously accept my resignation.

In accordance with his usual practice, the Field Marshal came to see me at 9 o'clock on the morning of the 26th. I had placed my letter on one side, as I had made up my mind not to speak to him of it until the letter was before His Majesty. The Field Marshal was master of his own destiny, and I did not want to influence him. He saw the writing, however. The form of the letter attracted his attention, and he begged me to dispatch it, but to retain office. I ought not to desert the Emperor and the army at this time. After an inward struggle I consented. I became convinced that I ought to retain my post, and proposed to the Field Marshal that we should make another effort to see Prince Max. He did not receive us, he being still ill. While I was waiting for the news on this point, Colonel von Haeften reported to me that the Government had succeeded in persuading His Majesty to dismiss me … His Majesty would shortly send for me at Bellevue Castle.

On the way from the General Staff Office to the Bellevue Castle I told the Field Marshal what I had just heard. Later I heard it stated that Prince Max had put the question of my dismissal forward to His Majesty as a cabinet question.

The Emperor seemed wholly changed in comparison with the previous day… I said respectfully to His Majesty that I had gained the painful impression that I no longer enjoyed his confidence, and that I accordingly begged most humbly to be relieved at my office. His Majesty accepted my resignation.[9]

Ludendorff had offered his resignation in the past, but it was always declined. Field Marshal Hindenburg also offered his own resignation on that day. He wrote:

His Majesty had granted General Ludendorff's request to be allowed to resign and refused my own.[10]

General Wilhelm Groener was appointed Chief of Staff as Ludendorff's successor.

Meanwhile, there were acts of dissension within the German Imperial Navy when false reports circulated German ports that an American–

British fleet was heading for the German coast and that the Admiralty was preparing to send the High Seas Fleet to confront it. Crown Prince Wilhelm recalled:

> On October 28, my adjutant, Müller, returned from an official journey to the homeland. He brought the first evil news of mutiny in the navy. From his report, it appeared evident that the revolution was already menacingly at hand in Germany; but that apparently nothing was being done at the moment to suppress the rising movement.[11]

On 29 October orders were issued at Kiel for the High Seas Fleet to set sail and engage the Royal Navy in one last battle. The sailors from this fleet had languished in this German port for most of the war. With the end of the war in sight, the sailors were not prepared to be sacrificed in a futile battle. They were also suffering from food shortages while their officers consumed whatever rations were available. They shared the deprivations of German civilians and were keen for the war to end. Reluctant to participate in a desperate battle days before the war was likely to end, the crews of several warships refused to obey the order to put to sea. The order to leave port was issued five times for the next two days until 31 October, and each order was repeatedly ignored.

Seaman Richard Stumpf, aboard SMS *Wittelsbach*, witnessed the revolution that was beginning to take place in the German port at Wilhelmshaven:

> On Sunday the *Strasburg* was put out to sea. Some of her stokers deserted and went on shore. Those who remained put out the fires (in the boilers) and tried to sink the ship by opening the flood gates. On a ship of the Posen class, a lieutenant was beaten to death.
>
> ... It became evident last Monday afternoon that the fleet was about to sail out. Apparently an Anglo–American fleet of a hundred and fifty ships was sighted off Heligoland. We all knew within our hearts today is the last time we shall ever see many of our ships. My mind contemplated what would happen if we were engaged and destroyed the enemy fleet. I toyed with the utmost grotesque possibilities. In the final analysis this might still result in our victory. Soon, however, an impregnable veil of fog descended upon the sea. The weather made any thought of sailing out impossible. In the sea of fog and fine rain one could no longer make out the stern of the vessel from amidship.
>
> Soon thereafter we heard that the stokers of three battlecruisers had deliberately allowed the fire to die down and had even extinguished them. At this time about a hundred men from *Von der*

Tann were running loose about town; *Seylitz* and *Derffinger* were missing men. Thus the fleet could not have sailed even if there had been no fog … What has happened to the almighty power of the proud captains and staff engineers? Now at last, after many years, the suppressed stokers and sailors realise that nothing, no, nothing can be accomplished without them …

On the *Thüringen*, the former model ship of the fleet, the mutiny was at its worst. The crew simply locked up the petty officers and refused to weigh anchor. The men told the captain that they would only fight against the English if their fleet appeared in German waters. They no longer wanted to risk their lives uselessly. Six destroyers and a submarine were summoned, and aimed their guns at the ship. A company of naval infantry then occupied all the compartments and arrested three hundred men.[12]

Thüringen and *Helgoland* were the first German ships to hoist the Red Flag in Wilhelmshaven, however this revolt was suppressed when a submarine, *U-135*, with a torpedo boat came alongside these vessels and other mutinous ships and threatened them into surrendering. Prince Max was concerned by events occurring in German ports:

Alarming news from the navy had reached the Chancellery; on several ships in the port of Wilhelmshaven there had been cases of refusal to obey orders. The reports were still vague. Had discipline been restored? Was Bolshevist agitation at the bottom of it or merely local discontent? Ritter von Mann [Minister of Marine], Simons told me, had appeared with a very grave face at the Cabinet meeting and had reported as follows:

The crews of several big ships had refused to obey the order to put to sea (29th and 30th October). They had quite openly mutinied and barricaded themselves in, so that Admiral von Hipper had had to have them surrounded by torpedo-boats and even to have the torpedoes trained on them. Then the men who had refused duty were arrested. The mutineers had stated in explanation of their conduct that the officers and commanders of the fleet did not want peace and had intended to sacrifice the fleet in a great battle.[13]

Approximately 1,000 sailors were arrested and the mutiny was temporarily supressed at Wilhelmshaven. However, at Kiel on 3 November a demonstration conducted by 3,000 sailors, soldiers and civilian dockyard workers took place sympathising with those forty-seven sailors from SMS *Markgraf* who were incarcerated in a Kiel prison, demanding their release. As they marched towards the centre of Kiel a patrol of German soldiers blocked their path and when their orders for the demonstrators to stop were ignored their officer ordered them to open fire, which resulted in eight demonstrators killed and twenty-nine wounded. This incident would transform this local demonstration to release the prisoners into a national revolutionary movement.

Sailors aboard ships and ashore in barracks formed councils on 4 November and took control of Kiel with little opposition. Raising the Red Flag above their vessels and barracks, they demanded the release of all political prisoners. Approximately 20,000 soldiers who were based at Kiel, which was 50 per cent of the garrison, joined them in their protest.

German troops belonging to IX Corps District were mobilised and sent to Kiel to suppress the mutiny. Instead, they fraternised with the mutineers and joined their cause. Prince Max recalled:

> On the night of 4th–5th November fresh news reached us from Kiel ... Kiel was in the hands of the mutineers. On the morning of the 4th the insurrectionary movement had leaped from barracks to barracks, the workers making cause with the sailors.
>
> At the first moment a counter action on the part of the Governor of Kiel, Admiral Souchon, seemed as if it would be successful; he had succeeded, according to his own report, in partially disarming a band of mutineers on the march, whereupon the rest threw their arms away. But a few hours later the revolt had broken out on all sides, and made an impression of having been deliberately prepared over a long time. The sailors got possession of the arms including four machine-guns, and attacked the Detention Barracks guard, reinforced though it had been. The great majority of the guard refused to shoot. Souchon estimated the advancing mob at 2,000 well-armed men, so that the movement could only have been put down at the cost of considerable bloodshed.[14]

The leadership of the Social Democratic Party and USPD (Unabhängige Sozialdemokratische Partei Deutschlands, translated as the Independent Social Democratic Party of Germany) were taken by surprise by the scale of this uprising. Wilhelm Dittmann, a member of the Council of the People's Delegates, later wrote that 'no one among the Social Democrats thought it possible that the military could break down as suddenly and catastrophically as in fact happened, step by step, in October and November 1918'.[15]

By 5 November approximately 40,000 sailors had complete control of Kiel with red flags flying around the port. Revolution and dissent was rapidly spreading across to other German ports at Rostock, Hamburg, Bremen and Wilhelmshaven. Supported by the German workforce and socialist political parties, the revolution gathered momentum within the German cities Cologne, Stuttgart, Frankfurt and Leipzig,

A peaceful coup that usurped the rule of the monarchy took place on 8 November in Munich, where the pacifist Kurt Eisner from the Independent Social Democratic Party proclaimed Munich and Bavaria a republic with himself as head of the socialist government in the region. Eisner's declaration was reported in newspapers as follows:

> The peasants will supply towns with food-stuffs. The old antagonism between town and country will disappear. Distribution of food-stuffs will be rationally organised. Workers and citizens of Munich, trust in the great and tremendous change which is being prepared in these difficult times. Let all assist, so that unavoidable revolution may take place quite peaceably. At this time of insane fratricide we loathe all bloodshed. Every human life must be saved. Keep calm and co-operate in building up a new world. The fratricidal struggle of Socialists is, so far as Bavaria is concerned, at an end.
>
> Long live the Bavarian Republic! Long live peace! Long live the creative labour of all workers!
>
> Munich Lanchtag Building, midnight of November 7–8. In the name of the Council of Workers, Soldiers and Peasants.
>
> President Kurt Eisner.[16]

Gefreiter Adolf Hitler had been gassed during a British attack on the night of 13/14 October 1918 on a hill south of Werwick, south of Ypres. Incapacitated and suffering from temporary blindness, he was sent to hospital at Pasewalk in Pomerania and it was there, while recovering, that he heard news of the revolution that was spreading across Germany. Hitler wrote:

> I was sent into hospital at Pasewalk in Pomerania, and there it was that I had to hear of the Revolution. For a long time there had been something in the air which was indefinable and repulsive. People were saying that something was bound to happen within the next few weeks, although I could not imagine what this meant. In the first

instance I thought of a strike similar to the one which had taken place in spring. Unfavourable rumours were constantly coming from the Navy, which was said to be in a state of ferment. But this seemed to be a fanciful creation of a few isolated young people. It is true that at the hospital they were all talking about the end of the war and hoping that this was not far off, but nobody thought that the decision would come immediately. I was not able to read the newspapers. In November the general tension increased. Then one day disaster broke in upon us suddenly and without warning. Sailors came in motor-lorries and called on us to rise in revolt. A few Jew-boys were the leaders in that combat for the 'Liberty, Beauty, and Dignity' of our National Being. Not one of them had seen active service at the front. Through the medium of a hospital for venereal diseases these three Orientals had been sent back home. Now their red rags were being hoisted here. During the last few days I had begun to feel somewhat better. The burning pain in the eye-sockets had become less severe. Gradually I was able to distinguish the general outlines of my immediate surroundings. And it was permissible to hope that at least I would recover my sight sufficiently to be able to take up some profession later on. That I would ever be able to draw or design once again was naturally out of the question. Thus I was on the way to recovery when the frightful hour came. My first thought was that this outbreak of high treason was only a local affair. I tried to enforce this belief among my comrades. My Bavarian hospital mates, in particular, were readily responsive. Their inclinations were anything but revolutionary. I could not imagine this madness breaking out in Munich; for it seemed to me that loyalty to the House of Wittelsbach was, after all, stronger than the will of a few Jews. And so I could not help believing that this was merely a revolt in the Navy and that it would be suppressed within the next few days. With the next few days came the most astounding information of my life. The rumours grew more and more persistent. I was told that what I had considered to be a local affair was in reality a general revolution. In addition to this, from the front came the shameful news that they wished to capitulate! What! Was such a thing possible?[17]

The Berlin correspondent for the *Nieuwe Rotterdamache Courant* reported the sombre and despondent mood in the German capital on 8 November:

Complete calm so far prevails in Berlin. One sees hardly anybody whose face does not wear a depressed expression. People in the streets are oppressively quiet. Everywhere reigns a fatalistic and yet tense feeling in connection with the armistice and peace conditions. One gets an impression that the development of the domestic and political situation in Berlin itself is closely connected with the solution of the Kaiser question.

I was in the town last night and tonight. At critical points military posts were standing one or two men strong, but there was nothing for them to do. Moreover, extensive measures have been taken to suppress all disturbances.[18]

The nation was on the precipice of a civil war as the revolution had spread across Germany. Workers and German soldiers were collectively in revolt. The Swedish newspaper *Social Democraten* reported:

A general railway strike has broken out in Germany. In Berlin there are at present 200,000 deserters.[19]

Kaiser Wilhelm's position as head of state was in jeopardy. Prince Max of Baden received the following report from a close confidant:

The spread of the revolt through the length and breadth of the country is no longer to be avoided … it is owing to the success of the revolutionary movements at Hamburg and Kiel that the danger of infection is so overwhelming as it is. We must be prepared for civil war. The question of today is: Who is going to win it?

There can be no doubt that Bolshevism will for the moment get the upper hand all over the country, unless indeed the popular Government is able to dispose of the necessary loyal troops. And that is unthinkable until the question of the Kaiser has been dealt with. The mass suggestion: 'The Kaiser is to blame!' provides a point of contact between the insurgents and the troops who are expected to put them down. We shall see wholesale desertions, even on the part of troops who have proved their loyalty at the front.

The Majority Socialists have acted rashly in issuing their ultimatum; but they really are not in a position to remain any longer in the Government unless the question of the Kaiser is settled. Should the Kaiser remain, the Majority Socialists are today bound to join the revolutionary movement, if they are not to let the Independents and the Spartacus Group have it all their own way with the masses. On the other hand, when the question of the Kaiser is once solved we can be quite sure that the Majority Socialists will put their whole organisation and propaganda resources at our service for the fight against Bolshevism.[20]

Friedrich Ebert, leader of the Social Democratic Party, declared its aim 'to seize the Government resolutely and energetically, as in Munich, but without bloodshed, if possible'.[21]

Social unrest and revolution prevailed in Berlin, together with the flu epidemic that was spreading, it was not safe for Kaiser Wilhelm to remain in the capital; therefore on 30 October he went to the German Army Headquarters at Spa, Belgium, where he could be protected by his troops if there was an assassination attempt upon his life. Kaiser Wilhelm wrote:

> I now resolved to go to the front, acquiescing in the desire expressed to me by the army that I might be with my hard-fighting troops and convince myself personally of their spirit and condition.
>
> I could carry out this resolve all the sooner in view of the fact, ever since the new Government had been set up, no further claims were made upon my time either by it or by the Imperial Chancellor, which made my staying at home seem useless.
>
> The notes to Wilson were discussed and written by Solf [Wilhelm Solf, German Foreign Minister], the War Cabinet, and the Reichstag, after sessions lasting hours, without my being informed thereof; until, finally, on the occasion of the last note to Wilson, I caused Solf to be given to understand very plainly, through my chief of Cabinet, that I demanded to know about the note before it was sent.
>
> Solf appeared and showed the note; he was proud of his antithesis between *laying down of arms* ('Waffenstreckung'), which was demanded by Wilson, and *armistice* ('Waffenstillstand'), which was proposed. When I spoke about the rumours of abdication and demanded that the Foreign Office adopt an attitude, through the press against what was unworthy in the newspaper polemics, Solf replied that already everybody on every street corner was talking about abdication and that, even in the best circles, people were discussing it quite unreservedly.
>
> When I expressed my indignation at this, Solf sought to console me by observing that, should His Majesty go, he also would, since he could serve no longer under such conditions. I went, or – to put it much more correctly – I was overthrown by my own Government, and Herr Solf remained.[22]

While revolution spread across the German home front, the Allies on the Western Front were beginning to initiate their final offensives of the war.

Part II

FINAL BATTLES

Chapter 5

Battle of Valenciennes
1 November 1918

As Allied leaders contemplated the conditions of an imminent Armistice, their armies continued the war unabated and with a strong determination to drive German forces from occupied Belgium and France. The British First Army was advancing upon the French city of Valenciennes and it was necessary to capture it in order to secure jumping off positions that were in line with the Third and Fourth British Armies, which had advanced further south in preparation for a further operation. The First Army needed to reach the lines of these armies before the Sambre offensive, which was scheduled to commence on 4 November 1918, could take place. Canadian Corps, British XXII Corps, together with 61st Division, from the First Army were designated to carry out this preliminary operation. Valenciennes was protected by the Schelde Canal to the west. Also known as the Canal d'Escaut, its eastern bank was heavily defended by German machine-gun posts. Valenciennes was defended by six German divisions, with a further two in reserve. To complicate matters, the Germans had flooded the low land west and south-west of the city. This meant that the main thrust of the attack to secure Valenciennes was to attack it from the south.

During the early hours of 1 November, German artillery launched a barrage using HE Shells and gas before the Allied operation had begun. Later that morning at 05.15 hours, following a creeping barrage, British divisions and the Canadian Corps began their advance upon German lines south of Valenciennes.

Sergeant Major A.H. Cook was a recipient of the Distinguished Service Cross and the Military Medal while serving with the 1st Somerset Light Infantry, 4th Division. He had participated in the attack upon the Somme on 1 July 1916 and two years later he was taking part in the assault upon Valenciennes. Sergeant Major Cook recalled:

The attack commenced at 5.15 a.m. under the most terrific barrage I had seen or heard. They said there were some 2,000 cannon, and hundreds of machine guns, carrying out indirect fire. The din was indescribable, speech was impossible, no matter how much one shouted, whistles were hopeless, and signals were out of the question as it was still dark. We just blundered on blindly, close up to the line of blasting and bursting shells.

The flash of the bursting shells showed the blanched faces of the lads, and the barrage intended to terrify and break the morale of the enemy was scaring our young warriors stiff. They were half stunned by the unearthliness of our own barrage, but it was sweet music to us old campaigners.[1]

As they advanced towards Préseau, Sergeant Major Cook recalled:

I saw a section of my company, about twenty-five yards to my left, killed to a man by a short burst, a shrapnel shell had burst a few yards in rear and sprayed them with bullets; they all went down as one man and did not rise again. That is the danger of these creeping barrages.[2]

Second Lieutenant A.P. Bowers and eight men from the 1st Somerset Regiment were probably the section that was wiped out by advancing into the creeping barrage and they were all buried at Préseau Communal Cemetery Extension.

There was no time for the withdrawing German armies to establish defensive lines with deep trenches, which meant that the shallow trenches that they had hastily dug provided inadequate protection from the intensive Allied artillery barrages. Sergeant Major Cook recalled:

Dawn commenced to break as the attack progressed, and one was able to see what was going on. The earth was vomiting forth clods, bodies, trees, houses, and anything that came in the way of this blasted line. It was hell let loose; surely no human could survive such a hell. There was no deep dug-outs here, what trenches we passed were shallow and hurriedly dug by a retreating enemy.[3]

The Canadian 44th and 47th Battalions led the advance along the western bank of the Rhonelle. The 44th Battalion (Manitoba) was ordered to capture Mont Houy, but the battalion war diary reported that it encountered strong resistance after it had secured this objective:

The barrage opened promptly at 5.15 a.m. and was well defined over the whole front. Companies got well away, clearing enemy outpost line without trouble except beyond Mont Houy and on the extreme right flank where some fighting with enemy machine gunners took place.[4]

The 47th Battalion (British Columbia) war diary reported that German artillery was firing gas into its positions and when it encountered entrenched German infantry it became engaged in a bitter struggle:

> Barrage opened and the attack commenced. From the start enemy counter barrage was considerable and a large percentage of gas was used. A particular concentration was placed on B.H.Q. Serious resistance was not met with until POIROR STATION was passed then the enemy were met in great numbers well dug in and prepared to defend the position – Despite the fact that the artillery had accounted for a large number there was severe fighting and in most cases enemy posts did not surrender until many had been killed by the bayonet or shot down.[5]

By 07.10 hours, the 47th Battalion had secured its objective line, but it was coming under substantial fire from German personnel positioned within Valenciennes.

> The final objective was gained on time and consolidated in depth – M.G. [machine gin] and T.M. [trench mortar] fire was heavy from Valenciennes on the companies holding the line of the railway and the support companies from artillery fire N.N.E. direction. Touch could not be made with the 38th Battalion on the left, and many enemy were seen in the streets presenting some good L.G. [Lewis Gun] targets.[6]

Lieutenant T.G. Newitt MC, MM and eighteen men from the 47th Battalion were killed in this action. However, the Canadians secured the position and then moved northwards.

The 46th Battalion (Saskatchewan) was following behind the leading battalions and before it reached the line where it was meant to leapfrog those battalions it became embroiled in mopping up small pockets of German resistance. A desperate close quarter battle ensued. Lieutenant-Colonel H.J. Dawson DSO, commanding 46th Battalion, reported:

The fighting that took place along the Famars–Valenciennes and Aulnoy–Marly roads was deadly work. Many enemy were killed by the parties of 46th Btt'n and working with bayonet, bombs and Lewis guns. The area was packed full of Germans. Every cellar contained numbers. Those that offered any show of resistance were killed and the rest were sent back as prisoners … At points trenched resistance was encountered. At one point in the main road, a field gun was firing point blank at our men and also two trench mortars were in action with machine guns sweeping the streets. The Lewis guns got in their work on these parties and No. 292383, Pte. W. J. Wood, pushed up close with his Lewis Gun, disposed part of the crew and forced the remainder to surrender.[7]

Private Skeates from the 46th Battalion recalled:

Bob Irvin, Sergeant Irvin, he was a darn good fellow – came from Fort William. He had some rum there and we emptied that bottle and we told our fellows, 'Come on!' and we went over. Machine gun bullets were like hailstones, coming four or five feet right in front of us. You couldn't believe it unless you had experienced it. Just like hailstones! But we beckoned our fellows on and we got them machine-gunners.[8]

Lieutenant-Colonel Dawson reported that these machine-gun positions had escaped the attention of the preparatory barrage and how this German resistance was subdued:

The barrage had missed these and they were very strongly entrenched. Here followed a remarkable and most gallant attack by Major Gyles, C.S.M Gibbons, Sergeant Cairns, and eleven other men. Fire was opened from our Lewis guns and rifles in reply to the heavy Boche fire. Then C.S.M. Gibbons, Sergeant Cairns, and four other ranks with two Lewis guns moved down to the right to outflank the enemy. This party made its way under covering fire to within 75 yards of the enemy and opened fire, causing such casualties that the remainder surrendered. Here, three field guns, 1 T.M., 7 M. Guns and over 50 prisoners were captured and the ground was strewn with dead Germans.[9]

Sergeant Hugh Cairns was among those from the 46th Battalion killed during this battle. Cairns, who originated from Ashington, England, had received a Distinguished Conduct Medal for his actions at Vimy in

1917. He died from his wounds on 2 November and was buried at Auberchicourt British Cemetery. He was later awarded a posthumous Victoria Cross as a result of the action at Valenciennes. His citation reported:

> For most conspicuous bravery before Valenciennes on 1st November, 1918, when a machine gun opened on his platoon. Without a moment's hesitation Serjt. Cairns seized a Lewis gun and single-handed in the face of direct fire, rushed the post, killed the crew of five, and captured the gun. Later, when the line was held up by machine-gun fire, he again rushed forward, killing 12 enemy and capturing 18 and two guns. Subsequently when the advance was held up by machine-guns and field guns, although wounded, he led a small party to outflank them, killing many, forcing about 50 to surrender, and capturing all guns. After consolidation he went with a battle patrol to exploit Marly and forced 60 enemy to surrender. Whilst disarming this party he was severely wounded. Nevertheless he opened fire and inflicted heavy losses. Finally he was rushed by about 20 enemy and collapsed from weakness and loss of blood. Throughout the operation he showed the highest degree of valour, and his leadership greatly contributed to the success of the attack. He died on the 2nd November from wounds.[10]

The 12th Canadian Brigade simultaneously launched a direct attack upon Valenciennes from the western banks of the Scheldt Canal. Artillery bombarded the German-occupied houses and machine-gun positions that lined the eastern bank of the canal prior to the infantry assault. It was decided not to bombard Valenciennes because of the risk of killing French inhabitants and Belgian refugees who lived in the city. The 72nd Battalion (Seaforth Highlanders of Vancouver) attacked the north-western corner of Valenciennes and experienced great difficulty in crossing the canal under hostile fire. The war diary reported:

> At 11.30 hours 'A' Company proceeded to cross the CANAL DE L'ESCAUT, but owing to difficulty with the cork float bridge which broke in two or three places while being pushed across the canal, the whole company was ferried across in collapsible boats.
>
> The outstanding work of No. 2025243, Pte. D. Clawson, might here be given mention, he stripped, dived into the canal, and by swimming he managed to push the end of the bridge and get it fastened on the eastern side of the bank. This he did in the face of an enemy machine gun post which was within 75 yards of the crossing. Unfortunately

Pte. Clawson was killed later on in the day while clearing out an enemy post in the railway yards on the east bank of the canal.[11]

Private D. Clawson was an American citizen who originated from Johnsonburg, Pennsylvannia. He was buried at Valenciennes (St Roch) Communal Cemetery.

Other attempts were made to get across the canal. Some boats were sunk by German machine-gun and trench mortar fire. However, units from the 72nd Battalion succeeded on reaching the other bank, but were unable to consolidate their position, which meant that they were compelled to withdraw. At dusk they used the crossings established by 38th Battalion (Eastern Ontario) in order to enter Valenciennes.

The 38th Battalion had crossed the Canal d'Escaut at 12.40 hours, but had to search through the south-western sector of the city for snipers and machine-gun positions that were operating within this urban environment. One officer was killed together with three killed and seven wounded. The war diary recorded:

> Considerable resistance encountered from enemy machine guns and snipers and four posts were mopped up. Battalion established for the night along railway and touch was established with the battalion on our left and 10th Canadian Infantry Brigade on our right. Patrols were sent through the city at night and met with considerable resistance from machine gun and trench mortar fire.[12]

British troops further south kept pace adjacent to the Canadian advance. The 182nd Brigade, 61st Division had to cross the Rhonelle at Artes using seven footbridges that were constructed by 476th Field Company, Royal Engineers. Intelligence reported:

> River RHONELLE believed to be 15 feet broad, 2 ft. 6 inches deep with steep banks 6 to 10 feet high and to be fordable.[13]

By 04.30 hours the 2/8th Worcestershire and 2/7th Royal Warwickshire Regiment had secured the eastern bank. The 2/8th Worcestershire's war diary reported:

> At 01.30 hours the Bttn. marched out of VENDEGIES and moved via LA JUSTICE to the forming up positions north of the RHONELLE preparatory to the attack on MARESCHES. Heavy rain during afternoon which continued throughout the march to the line made cross-country tracks muddy and slippery.

In crossing the forward face of the slope leading down to the railway running between SEPMERIES and ARTES the Bttn. had to pass through a barrage of H.E. and gas shells and were again shelled while crossing the RHONELLE by footbridges place in position by RE's earlier in the night.[14]

Maresches was secured by 07.15 hours and 761 prisoners captured. Their left flank came under German machine-gun fire from St Hubert, but by 08.30 hours they had secured their objectives.

German forces were desperate to recapture lost ground, and the 28th German Reserve Division launched a counter-attack that pushed the British line back towards the Rhonelle. The 2/8th Worcestershire Regiment war diary reported:

> At 10.00 hours the German infantry supported by captured British tanks counter attacked. The 4th Division were driven out of PRESEAU. The 2/7th Bttn. Warwick's were forced back and the left flank of the Bttn. turned. 'C' and 'D' Companies occupying the open ground E and NE of MARESCHES had no means of fighting the tanks and were obliged to withdraw. The left half of 'A' Coy also came back, but the remainder of the Coy moving to the right crossed into the loop of the RHONELLE River s[outh] of the mill. In this position they could not be followed by the tanks, but were exposed to their fire.[15]

Sergeant Major A.H. Cook, 1st Somerset Light Infantry, 4th Division, observed the chaos and confusion:

> In the late afternoon the Germans launched another counter-attack, this time it was on the 49th Div. on our left. There was another retirement, which exposed the left flank of 'light' Coy. of the Somerset's, who also had to retire. We were able to watch three counter-attacks with comparative calm from our trenches, wondering when our turn was coming. We could not give effective covering fire, as we were not certain who was who. Tanks could be seen manoeuvring about, firing as they went. They started to head towards us, but fortunately changed their direction.[16]

Although some of the Worcestershires' line had been pushed back, they still occupied Maresches, where they dug outpost positions along the northern and eastern perimeters of the village. Meanwhile, on their right flank, the 146th Brigade, 47th Division reported:

At 05.15 the attack started. It was a little too dark at first and the leading companies found a little difficulty in keeping in touch. Bridges 20 feet long were carried down to the RHONELLE and at least three of these were placed in position. Some men waded across, the depth of water varying considerably. The attack went forward behind the creeping barrage with complete success.

There was a twenty minute pause in the barrage just east of the Rhonelle and this gave our troops plenty of time to get across the stream and get ready to go forward. The large mill by the stream on our immediate left did not give the trouble that had been expected. Prisoners began coming down very rapidly and a large number of the enemy troops put up an extremely poor fight. Two platoons were detailed to mop up that part of Aulnoy within the Brigade boundary and they captured about 70 prisoners in the village besides killing numbers of the enemy. There were a large number of civilians in the village, but they kept in their cellars and probably suffered very little as only a shrapnel barrage went over the buildings.[17]

On 2 November the attack upon Valenciennes and the villages south of the city was resumed. Food supplies were not brought up to the front line, which meant that some soldiers were continuing the battle without eating. Sergeant Major A.H. Cook had been on active service since 1914 without being wounded, but during the final days of the war he was hit for the first time. He recalled:

Owing to the confusion of reliefs, my company did not get orders till after zero hour, when our instructions were to mop up the village of Preseau. We hurried forward on our empty stomachs over the ground we had captured, and started mopping up the houses.

Now this is a dangerous and thankless task. You are an exposed target from all angles. Practically all houses in France have cellars, and these were the danger spots. When verbal persuasion failed, a smoke or Mills bomb soon vomited forth its contents, obstreperous ones were quickly disposed of, docile ones were disarmed and packed off back, no escorts were sent and none were necessary.

Snipers began to pick off the men and these are very difficult to locate and dislodge. Several shots were certainly meant for me, a sniper does not usually miss. One man came out of a house twenty yards away and fired point-blank at me, the bullet shrieked past – a miss, my turn – a bull. And as we worked our way around, death lurking at every corner.

Shells began to fall in the village, making our task still more unpleasant. The men began to group together, probably feeling there was safety in numbers. But I realised a shell amongst us would have a disastrous result for the relics of my poor old company, now about 30 strong. I warned them of the danger and ordered them to spread out more; but it was too late, death was on its way and burst right in the midst of us.

The result was ghastly, it burst on the hard cobbles and flew in all directions; even the broken cobblestones scattered, and did as much damage as the shell. Several were killed and the remainder of us shared the flying pieces – some more so than others. 2/Lt. Harrison got it in the foot, and I got it in the knee. It was as if a cart-horse had kicked me.

I could scarcely believe I was wounded; I thought I was immune, after dodging it for four and a quarter years. I had been with the 1/Somersets from the beginning of the war, and now had the misfortune to be hit on what proved to be the very last day they were in action. The whole of the 4th Division were relieved that night and did not go into action again.[18]

On 2 November, the 12th Canadian Brigade entered Valenciennes. German snipers and machine-gunners were still present within the city, concealed behind barricades and positioned within houses. By daybreak, German forces had withdrawn, and by 07.20 hours the town was cleared of resistance by the 12th Canadian Brigade and it had established contact with the 11th Brigade east of Valenciennes. Once German forces had vacated the city, its artillery bombarded it vehemently with gas, high explosive and incendiary shells.

The operation to capture Valenciennes was completed on 2 November at a cost of eighty killed and 300 wounded. The capture of the city allowed the First Army to align itself with British Armies further south in preparation for the Sambre offensive. Lieutenant R.J. Holmes, Canadian 46th Battalion, reflected:

> In that one morning our little brigade captured about 1,800 prisoners and there were between 800 and 900 dead Germans in our area. I never saw anything like it. We surely got ours back for almost a month of hard chasing and dirty fighting.[19]

News of the capture of Valenciennes was wired to British newspapers. Later that day the *Nottingham Evening Post* reported:

VALENCIENNES IN OUR HANDS, CANADIANS ENTER THE TOWN THIS MORNING. Fighting yesterday south of Valencienne was of a very severe nature and was continued until this morning. On the battlefront of six miles large numbers of the enemy were killed. Many hostile counter-attacks were repulsed and 4,000 prisoners were taken. The 17th Corps under General Ferguson and 22nd Corps under General Godfrey gained the high ground south of Valenciennes and have now passed their troops through the town, which is wholly in our possession.[20]

The strategy to capture Valenciennes was reported by a Press Association correspondent:

FLEE OR SURRENDER: GERMANS ONLY CHOICE AT VALENCIENNES. The fall of Valenciennes is the inevitable result of the patient and persevering tactics of the past fortnight. We might have made another Arras of the place and rendered it impossible for the Germans to live in it. Instead we carried out a series of progressive outflanking attacks. The enemy had to face the certainty of being cut off or get out, and skilled in the methods of retreat, he chose the latter alternative, and during Friday afternoon, Canadian troops entered the town, which is unscathed by our shells.

The numerous street barricades and wreckage, and barbed wire mingled with the scattered masonry, make Valenciennes more than it really is. There are still many civilians remaining, and stray Germans have continued to emerge from sundry hiding places and give themselves up ever since we entered the place. There was apparently slight resistance when the Canadian patrols cautiously advanced into the streets. Some fires were burning, and a good deal of smoke hung over the town. The troops pushed on through Valenciennes leaving only working parties of sappers to clear up and look out for traps.

The fighting had been particularly intense before the Germans suddenly fell back, and around the town itself the prisoners were taken from no less than 21 battalions, representing five divisions. The Canadians found the ground littered with dead.[21]

Chapter 6

American Sector

Meuse–Argonne Offensive

General Henri Gouraud's French Fourth Army and General John Pershing's American Expeditionary Force (AEF) were responsible for driving their lines of advance through the Meuse–Argonne sector during the autumn of 1918 until the signing of the Armistice. Approximately 50,000 French soldiers and 400,000 American Doughboys were supported by heavy artillery, aeroplanes and tanks.

Field Marshal Sir Douglas Haig valued the American soldier, but he was conscious that their staff officers had a lot to learn in regards to leading these men in a modern industrialised war. At a meeting of the British War Cabinet his views were recorded:

> Field Marshal Haig said that the American men individually were very good material. The staff, however, were very inexperienced and hardly knew how to feed their troops.[1]

Pershing remained insistent that the American Army should fight together as one unit, while Haig favoured assimilating this expansive resource within the Allied ranks in order to utilise them more effectively:

> There were two methods of working the American troops, either keep them together as an army, or to distribute them among the Allies. If they could be brought in with the Allies, it would be possible to achieve good results from them.[2]

On the Meuse–Argonne sector the AEF continued the line from La Harazee in the middle of the Argonne Forest to Clemery, advancing upon an 18-mile front. Their German adversaries expected an advance through the Meuse valley and were fearful that if the Allies penetrated

25 miles into their own lines on this sector, Sedan would be captured and the lines of railway communications that ran from Belgium to the Metz area would be severed. Anticipating an attack in this region, German forces had fortified the Meuse–Argonne sector during the past four years with three defensive lines comprising German machine-gun bunkers that could provide deadly enfilading fire upon an attacking force. They had utilised the terrain to incorporate these formidable defences within the entangled undergrowth and ravines of the Argonne Forest on the west flank, Montfaucon Ridge in the centre and the high ground on the eastern flank that skirted along the River Meuse. Lieutenant-Colonel George English, 89th Division, described the terrain of the sector:

> The terrain in which this great battle was fought was what is known as the Argonne region, from the Forest of Argonne which lies in it. It is a rough and hilly country lying between the marshy plains of the Woevre on the east and the level, chalky Champagne district on the west. The Meuse River flows through it in the general direction of southeast to northwest. There are many forests besides the Argonne, most of the woods and forests lying on high ground. The valleys are cultivated as far as possible, but there are many steep hills and deep ravines.
>
> Both sides of the Meuse valley are bordered with high, wooded hills. Protected by the range of hills beyond the Meuse ran the important railway from Metz, through Mézières and Sedan to the districts of Belgium and northern France. In the southern border of the Forest of Argonne and across the Meuse to the north of Verdun had run the enemy's lines for four years. Strongly organised for defence, both by the nature of the country and by every device of military art, this line had held, though strong attacks had been made upon it by the French earlier in the war.[3]

The Meuse–Argonne offensive began on 26 September 1918. Despite making steady progress in this sector, within three weeks, the First Army had suffered 100,000 casualties, half of which were soldiers incapacitated by influenza. Marshal Foch appreciated the problems faced by American forces in this sector:

> By the middle of October, after three weeks of bitter and costly fighting, the American First Army had reached the defile of Grandpré on its left, and, on its centre, the heights of Romagne-sous-Montfaucon.

The advance through the Argonne from south to north had presented undeniable difficulties to the American Staffs. Most of the roads in this region run from west to east, and the hilly nature of the country makes easy organization of the new lines of communication impossible. Hence the varied difficulties encountered in supplying the numerous American troops engaged in the battle; and yet their enthusiasm had to be kept up ... and their violent efforts sustained.[4]

Due to the extension of the American front, Pershing decided to create a Second US Army, commanded by General Robert Lee Bullard, which was tasked with the advance towards the heights overlooking the River Meuse. Hunter Liggett was appointed commander of the First Army, with the rank of brevetted lieutenant-general, on 12 October. Liggett devoted the following two weeks to allow the soldiers under his command to rest, reorganise and train for the final phase of the Meuse–Argonne offensive. He recalled:

> I took command of the First Army on the sixteenth [October]. It then consisted of seventeen American and four French divisions with the usual army and corps artillery, aviation and other troops – a total of more than 1,000,000 men.[5]

German commanders recognised the importance of defending their lines in the Verdun sector. General Von der Marwitz, commander of the German V Army, realised that if American and French forces broke though the German lines on this sector, then their nation's border would be threatened. He affirmed to his soldiers:

> The heaviest part of the task will fall on the V Army ... in the coming weeks, and the safety of the Fatherland will be in its hands. It is on the firm resistance of the Verdun front that depends the fate of a great part of the Western Front, perhaps even of our nation.[6]

Although the German soldiers from V Army were determined in their defence of the Verdun sector, Field Marshal Paul von Hindenburg acknowledged that the troops, despite their experience, were disadvantaged:

> It was plain that this situation could not last. Our armies were too weak and too tired. Moreover, the pressure which the American masses were putting upon our most sensitive points in the region of the Meuse was too strong.[7]

Lieutenant-General Liggett suggested that the US First Army should launch a simultaneous attack with General Gouraud's Fourth French Army, to press forward their advance 5 miles into the German lines and secure the Barricourt Heights that were positioned south of Sedan. Liggett recalled:

> We made plans for the proper liaison of the two armies, and I left convinced that we would work together nicely. As I went I reiterated that I would attack at 5.30 of the first [November 1918]. Morally certain that a simultaneous attack by Gouraud's army could be arranged. I drove direct to First Army headquarters, where General Pershing still was, and at a conference that evening I recited my talk with Gouraud and dwelt on the necessity of the two armies striking together. He readily assented and saw Marshal Foch the following day, as a result the battle orders were changed to November 1 and the Fourth Army was directed to attack simultaneously.[8]

The First Army was ordered to penetrate the last German defensive line, known as the Freya Stellung, in an effort to severe the railway lines that passed through Sedan. This would hinder German forces in their ability to bring forward reinforcements into the region or to evacuate from the sector.

The final phase of the American offensive on the Meuse–Argonne sector started at 03.30 hours on 1 November with a concentrated artillery barrage targeting German advanced positions, strongpoints, headquarters, reserve units and lines of communication. The firepower was awesome and devastated the German defences. D Battery, 129th Field Artillery, 35th Division was among the US batteries that shelled the German lines that morning. Captain Harry Truman was the battery commander and would later become the 33rd President of the United States of America. In a letter dated 1 November, to his fiancée, Bess Wallace, Truman wrote:

> I have just finished putting 1,800 shells over on the Germans in the last five hours. They don't seem to have had enough energy to come back yet. I don't think they will. One of their aviators fell right behind my Battery yesterday and sprained his ankle, busted up the machine, and got completely picked by the French and Americans in the neighbourhood. They even tried to take their (there were two in the machine) coats. One of our officers, I am ashamed to say, took the boots off of the one with the sprained ankle and kept them.

The French, and Americans too for that matter, are souvenir crazy. If a guard had not been placed over the machine, I don't doubt that it would have been carried away bit by bit. What I started to say was that the German lieutenant yelled 'La guerre fini' as soon as he stepped from the machine. He then remarked that the war would be over in ten days. I don't know what he knew about it or what anyone else knows, but I am sure that most Americans will be glad when it's over and they can get back to God's country again. It is a great thing to swell your chest out and fight for a principle, but it gets almighty tiresome sometimes. I heard a Frenchman remark that Germany was fighting for territory, England for the sea, France for patriotism, and Americans for souvenirs. Yesterday made me think he was about right.[9]

Two hours later, at 05.30 hours, American infantry advanced behind creeping barrages into the German lines. Captain R.C. Hilton, Machine Gun Company, 9th Infantry Regiment, 2nd Division recalled:

The attack started from a position about four hundred yards south of Landres-et-St. Georges at daybreak Nov. 1st. with the Marine Brigade attacking, the 3rd in support. The 9th Infantry went forward in a column of battalions, this company taking a position near the trenches with the mission of delivering a barrage on the enemy lines at and around Landres-et-St. Georges from 'H' hour minus two to 'H' plus one. After three hours of continuous firing this company joined the 3rd Battalion of the 9th for the attack. The company had to march through the other two battalions to join its own battalion near Landres-et-St. Georges. The enemy fired machine guns in our direction, wounding Sgt. Tom Polman, who had been wounded by just sixteen machine gun bullets before this engagement, forming a perfect cross on his body.[10]

Although this was the last week of the First World War, German forces were showing a strong defence of their positions in the Argonne Forest. Colonel Albertus Catlin, who commanded 6th Marine Regiment, 4th Marine Brigade, 2nd Division, during the battle for Belleau Wood during June 1918, wrote of the strong German defence they encountered during the final week of the war on the Meuse–Argonne sector:

Finally, on November 1, General Pershing started the drive that proved to be the last great struggle of the war. It was that mighty sweep towards Sedan, that reaching for the very heart of the Hun.

71

The Germans massed their best troops and a tremendous artillery and opposed every step of the advance with the utmost bitterness. It was a fight to the death. An interminable line of murderous German machine guns, for a few feet apart, was thrown across the American advance. The casualties were terrific.[11]

The 89th Division began its advance from a small salient at the Bois-de-Bantheville that protruded into the German lines. The 2nd Division advanced on its left, while 90th Division carried its right flank. During the previous four days, they had been subjected to intensive German artillery fire comprising of high explosive shells and gas. Their objective was to secure several ridges, culminating in the capture of Barricourt Ridge, which overlooked the River Meuse. Sergeant Rudolph Forderhase, 356th Infantry Regiment, 89th Division, recalled:

We were awakened by a messenger at 5 a.m. to the sound of artillery fire and bursting shells nearby. The acrid smell of exploded TNT assailed our nostrils when we stepped outdoors. The artillery preparation had begun at 3.30 a.m. We had slept soundly through all of it. We ate breakfast of sorts, and then watched the first of the prisoners our comrades of the 177th Brigade, had taken as they were being marched to the rear. After they had passed, we started up the road in the direction from which the prisoners had come. Our battalion was, at this time, a part of the Division reserve. Although possibly still within range of their rifle or machine gun fire. Their artillery was not active, at present, as they were very busy moving it back to avoid its capture by our troops. We hiked through open fields towards Ramonville, our first objective. As it got dark, we approached a road when we came near the village and we had instructions to remain there and wait for orders.

With the fresh American troops attacking all along the Argonne front, the war weary Germans were using every means to slow down the advancing Americans and get as much of their supplies and equipment out as possible. To slow down the advancing Americans they were making excellent use of their machine guns. They took advantage of the forest cover and favourable terrain and, after being driven out of the trench system, they were able to delay us by strategically placed machine guns and, occasionally, a single field gun.[12]

On the first day of the offensive on 1 November, the American 89th Division encountered strong resistance from the German 88th Division, which had just been deployed to this sector during the night of 29/30 October. The 88th, comprising fresh soldiers, were meant to have relieved the 13th Division, but this unit was retained in support. Buttressed by machine-gun and strong artillery support, they were able to offer a stout defence. The soldiers from these two German divisions were highly respected by their American adversaries. Lieutenant-Colonel George English wrote:

> While there is no question, but at the time of this drive the morale of the German troops as a whole had fallen, still these two divisions were rated highly in the German Army. There were among them replacements of older men who had been doing garrison and frontier guard duty and young men from the class of 1919. Yet the greater portion of the German troops opposite this division were young, vigorous, aggressive soldiers – the best that the German Army had to furnish to hold the most critical point of the entire line at the time.[13]

Numerous machine-gun positions proved particularly troublesome and were effective in slowing down and stopping the advance of the 354th Infantry Regiment, 89th Division. Sergeant Arthur Forrest charged ahead of his company to overwhelm a series of six well-positioned German machine-gun nests close to Remonville. Forrest, who prior to the war was a professional baseball player, was awarded the Congressional Medal of Honor for this valiant act. His citation stated:

> When the advance of his company was stopped by bursts of fire from a nest of 6 enemy machine guns, without being discovered, he worked his way single-handed to a point within 50 yards of the machine gun nest. Charging, single handed, he drove out the enemy in disorder, thereby protecting the advance platoon from annihilating fire, and permitting the resumption of the advance of his company.[14]

Another Congressional Medal of Honor was awarded on that same day for a similar act of bravery to First Lieutenant Harold Furlong, 353rd Infantry Regiment, 89th Division, at Bois-de-Bantheville. His citation recorded:

> Immediately after the opening of the attack in the Bois-de-Bantheville, when his company was held up by severe machine-gun fire from the front, which killed his company commander and

several soldiers, Lieutenant Furlong moved out in advance of the line with great courage and coolness, crossing an open space several hundred yards wide. Taking up a position behind the line of the machine guns, he closed in on them, one at a time, killing a number of the enemy with his rifle, putting four machine-gun nests out of action, and driving 20 German prisoners into our lines.[15]

Private John Childers took charge of his platoon when his commander and sergeant were wounded. After calling out and receiving no response for remaining corporals to lead the surviving members, he took control of the situation and led the platoon to secure their objectives, encountering strong German resistance. His Distinguished Service Cross citation confirmed:

> After all his superiors had become casualties, he assumed command of the platoon and, reorganising the scattered groups, he led them forward against great resistance and gained his objective.[16]

Proficient German soldiers took advantage of some of their inexperienced American counterparts, allowing them to enter exposed positions where they became isolated before firing upon them from their concealed nests. Private Malcolm Aitken, serving with 'D' Company, 5th Marine Regiment, 2nd Division, was an experienced soldier who fought at Belleau Wood and during the final days of the war he was involved in the final phase of the Meuse–Argonne Campaign. Aitken recalled the savage fighting in the Argonne Forest:

> From November 1st until 9th it was one continuous scrap. We would clean up one nest and then find another twice as bad. Woods and brush and individual spots hid these machine guns and they were very difficult to dislodge. You see there was so much cross-fire from the riflemen and other machine guns, that you didn't know which one to get first. This resulted in such affairs as the famous Lost Battalion. They found comparatively little resistance ahead of their logical position, resulting in loss of liaison on either side and finally in being practically surrounded by enemy emplacements. The Bosch were wise, all right, and played on our inexperienced men by waiting in cover until an organisation had passed and then opened on their rear. Our outfit cleaned up thoroughly as we went, having enuf [enough] of heads among us to guide the destinies of the rest, so, although we were late getting to the line of objectives, we could honestly report a clean country to the rear. We were flanked several

times for a little bit during the seven or eight day advance, but always managed to turn the tables. We were seasoned troops, so of course bore the brunt of the advance for the first few days, then advanced as moppers up.[17]

German lines began to crumble as they were unable to stem the tide of the overwhelming might of the AEF. The American 89th Division captured the entire German 2nd Battalion 88th Division on 1 November at Remonville.[18] Major-General William Wright reported:

The infantry succeeded in its attack by faithfully following the barrage without hesitation to its objectives. The German machine gunners in their fox holes cowered under the effects of the heavy barrage. Some were killed by this fire, but for the main part they were killed or captured by the infantry before they could get the machine guns out of the holes and into action. Chaplains throughout the Division who rapidly followed up the infantry and buried the dead, report that the majority of the German dead had rifle bullets in their heads or upper bodies. The enemy resistance with Artillery fire was strong at the start, but decreased later in the day as our infantry pressed steadily forward.[19]

The 89th Division continued to push forward on the second day of the final onslaught. Sergeant Rudolph Forderhase recalled:

Ahead of the supporting troops, on the morning of Nov. 2, was an area of high ground known as the Heights of Barricourt. The Germans were driven from this position early in the morning of November 2. It was said that when Marshal Foch was told 89th Division troops had occupied the Heights of Barricourt, he said 'good, the war is over'.[20]

However the German artillery continued to target the advancing 89th Division, as Forderhase recalled:

The planes were hardly out of sight when we got to our feet and we took few steps when the artillery began to cover the entire area with artillery fire. Our men, still in open order, again hit the ground. The shells that fell in the area I could see, appeared to be from heavy field guns. There may have been some from the 77mms, but anyway, the firing continued until the green meadow was dotted with many deep shell holes. Again it seemed incredible that I saw no casualties, and learned of none. One of the early projectiles struck the ground and some twenty paces from where I lay. A jagged fragment of the shell, buried itself within ten or twelve minutes. There were, probably, at least a thousand craters four or five feet deep for the poor French peasants to fill some time in the future. The events of that morning, made many of us wonder if we were leading a charmed life.[21]

The Meuse–Argonne battle was fought under challenging conditions. A combination of misty weather and rugged terrain made it difficult for advancing waves to maintain order and direction. General Hunter Liggett wrote:

The Meuse–Argonne was a battle fought under lowering, misty skies in a country so rough and tangled men without a natural instinct for direction were astray the moment they lost sight of their nearest neighbour. It was a battle pursued more by ear and senses of touch than with the eye. Troops moved by the dead reckoning of pocket compasses, as ships in fog.[22]

American soldiers were able to use the cover of fog for their own advantage to move through the Argonne Forest and some came into close contact with German soldiers, who were unaware of their presence. Captain R.C. Hilton, Machine Gun Company, 9th Infantry Regiment, 2nd Division, testified:

On the night of the 3rd, the famous night march through the German lines took place. The 9th was commanded by Colonel Van Horn and it took up advance guard formation and led the march in a column of two's at dusk. Machine gun resistance was met from the beginning, but these guns were soon put out of action. German soldiers were soon heard talking all through the woods, but our move was so quiet and orderly that the Germans evidently thought that we were their troops and they did not fire on us. At two points on the road German camps were located. Lt. Colonel Corey, in command of the column, ordered Major Janda, who commanded the 3rd Battalion, to attack as we came to these camps. The regiment was held up occasionally on this account while a lively fire fight took place. The Germans were so surprised and confused that they did not put up much of a fight. Our objective, about 8 kilometres through the woods, was reached with very few casualties and we took up a defensive position north of the woods facing Beaumont.

A farmhouse at La Tuilerie at the north edge of these woods was used as a signal post by the enemy and we found it lighted and full of Germans. The house was surrounded and fifty prisoners, several horses and pieces of artillery were taken. There was no occasion to fire machine guns during the march; however, they were used to good advantage to organise and strengthen the infantry position as soon as the halt was made.

At 9.00 a.m. on the 4th, the 2nd and 3rd Battalions attached to gain a ridge east of Beaumont, where we met strong machine gun resistance and suffered many casualties. Most of the hostile machine gunners were killed or captured. This was reduced to two skeleton platoons.[23]

On 3rd November, Major-General William Wright, at the 89th Division's Headquarters, received orders that they were to be relieved by the 1st Division, but Wright remarkably requested that his soldiers were not withdrawn. Lieutenant-Colonel George English confirmed:

> During the evening of this day, orders were received at Division Headquarters from 5th Corps that the 1st Division, would send a column through our lines and that we were to be assembled in the rear. General Wright immediately called the Corps by telephone and asked permission to remain in the line and to continue the advance. He stated that his troops were in fine condition, were in touch with the situation and could certainly make further progress the next day. He desired to gain possession of the Forest of Dieulet, which would afford artillery positions for long guns to break the German railroad beyond Stenay, and also to endeavour to get the bridgehead at Laneuville. The Corps Commander granted that request.[24]

After advancing through the Forest of Dieulet and reaching Laneuville on 4 November, General Wright declined a further offer to withdraw his men, who had been fighting continuously for four days.

By 4 November, the First Army had advanced 20 miles within four days and had broken the German defences. The German Army resolve had been shattered and its forces were compelled to withdraw to a new defensive position along the River Meuse. Captain R.C. Hilton, Machine Gun Company, 9th Infantry Regiment, 2nd Division, wrote:

> During the night of Nov. 4th, the 23rd Infantry marched through our lines and drove the enemy further back. The following night the 9th marched through the 23rd and continued the advance. This 'leap

frog' movement continued until we reached the Meuse River and the enemy was driven across the Meuse.[25]

The 5th Division had already reached the bank of the River Meuse by 3 November. At 01.00 hours the division began to cross the river at Brieulles and had established a bridgehead before dawn. There was a canal located east of Brieulles and attempts by engineers to construct a bridge across this waterway were thwarted by German fire, resulting in heavy casualties. Despite the German shellfire at Brieulles, Sergeant Eugene Walker, assisted by Corporal Robert Crawford and Privates Noah Gump, John Hoggle and Stanley Murnane, all belonging to 'D' Company, 7th Engineers, 5th Division, went into the river to secure one of those bridges. Submersed in cold water, under hostile fire, they physically held the deck of the pontoon bridge so that the infantry could get across the river. They all received the Distinguished Service Cross for their courage, physical endurance and determination. Their individual citations all reported:

> When 3 boats in a pontoon bridge across the Meuse River were destroyed by artillery fire, he volunteered and waded into the river under heavy shell fire and, by holding up the deck until new boats were launched and placed in position, although under great physical strain, permitted the uninterrupted crossing of the infantry.[26]

Two footbridges were constructed during the night 3/4 November, and infantry from 5th Division were able to charge across the canal and establish a bridgehead on the German side.

Further north at Clery-le-Petit, the 60th Infantry Regiment, 5th Division, tried to establish a bridgehead across the River Meuse using two pontoon bridges at around 16.00 hours on 4 November. When German artillery observers spotted these bridges they immediately notified their batteries, who destroyed them with barrages.

Later that night, another bridge was constructed across the Meuse at a different location close by. Also, a bridge had been built across the nearby canal. During the following morning, 5 November, these crossings were discovered by German batteries and they were soon destroyed by shellfire. This caused a major problem for the 60th Infantry Regiment, because part of the unit was pinned down in the swampy marshland between the River Meuse and the canal. Others were trapped on the eastern bank of the canal, which meant they were unable to withdraw. German fire was coming from the Côte de Jumont, which overlooked the Meuse, the canal and ground occupied by 5th Division.

Despite the awesome German machine-gun fire that focused upon the canal, Captain Edward Allworth, 60th Infantry Regiment, leapt into the cold water and swam across to the other bank, followed by his men. After reorganising their ranks, Allworth led an assault upon the German-occupied ridge, which was known as Hill 260. Many of Allworth's party were now wearing wet clothes after swimming across, but despite feeling cold they fought a strongly contested battle for the ridge that overwhelmed the German defenders. Captain Allworth was awarded the Congressional Medal of Honor for his courage. His citation recorded:

> While his company was crossing the Meuse River and canal at a bridgehead opposite Clery-le-Petit, the bridge over the canal was destroyed by shell fire and Captain Allworth's command became separated, part of it being on the east bank of the canal and the remainder on the west bank. Seeing his advance units making slow headway up the steep slope ahead, this officer mounted the canal bank and called for his men to follow. Plunging in he swam across the canal under fire from the enemy, followed by his men. Inspiring his men by his example of gallantry, he led them up the slope, joining his hard-pressed platoons in front. By his personal leadership he forced the enemy back for more than a kilometre, overcoming machine-gun nests and capturing 100 prisoners, whose number exceeded that of the men in his command. The exceptional courage and leadership displayed by Captain Allworth made possible the re-establishment of a bridgehead over the canal and the successful advance of other troops.[27]

On 6 November, Pershing ordered the First Army to capture Sedan, but the French also wanted to capture the town to settle old scores with the Germans. The 1st and 42nd Divisions from the US First Army reached the ridges that were positioned south of the town on 8 November. They had crossed into the French Fourth Army's sector and became entangled in their advance upon Sedan. The 42nd Division was known as the Rainbow Division and was able to isolate the town from these ridges with its artillery, which targeted the railway lines. The German occupants soon withdrew from the town. Since the town held sentimental importance to the French, the Americans held back to allow the French Fourth Army to capture it; though there was a misunderstanding when General Frank Parker commanding the 1st Division ordered his soldiers numbering 25,000 men to march through First Corps towards Sedan. It lead to an embarrassing moment resulting in the mistaken capture of General Douglas MacArthur, when the vanguard elements of 1st Division reached positions held by 42nd Division at Bulson, who paused their advance while the French entered the town. Major-General Hunter Liggett recalled:

> Douglas MacArthur, then commanding the Rainbow Division, affected a peculiar cap, not unlike that of a German officer. He and some of his staff were grouped about a map this night on the division front when some elements of the First Division burst through and captured him and his party under the impression that they had bagged a German division command … MacArthur had taken his 'capture' as something of a joke, but not First Corps headquarters.[28]

MacArthur had received complaints from some of his superior officers, as he recalled:

> Without my knowledge, criticism of the fact that I failed to follow certain regulations prescribed for our troops, that I wore no helmet, that I carried no gas mask, that I went unarmed, that I always had a riding crop in my hand, that I declined to command from the rear, were reported to G.H.Q. All of this was entirely specious, as senior officers were permitted to use their own judgement about such matters of personal detail. I wore no iron helmet because it hurt my head. I carried no gas mask because it hampered my movements. I went unarmed because it was not my purpose to engage in personal combat, but to direct others. I used a riding crop out of long habit on the plains. I fought from the front as I could not effectively manipulate my troops from the rear. But someone at headquarters foolishly sent an officer to conduct confidential interviews of my comrades, with reference to my actions.[29]

Some officers may have exaggerated the situation in order to embarrass MacArthur, because he did not mention in his report that he was mistaken for a German officer and captured by American troops, writing:

> Have decided to establish my headquarters in Bulson for the night. Awakened just before daybreak by an aide with the startling information that a brigade commander of the 1st Division had just entered Bulson, coming from the south, a direction practically perpendicular to that over which we advanced. The officer proved

to be Colonel Erickson, who showed me the orders issued by General Parker, commanding the 1st Division, indicating that the 16th Infantry of his brigade was advancing along the river road. This would bring that regiment under the fire of my brigade. Feeling that in the obscurity of early morning the 16th Infantry might be mistaken by my men for the enemy. I at once hastened to the right of my line to inform Colonel Tynley, commanding the 168th Infantry, of the circumstances and to caution him against any debacle. I had barely reached his position when in the distance I saw troops moving up the river road. Guessing it was the 16th Infantry, I pushed out in front of my line, accompanied by Major Wolfe, my executive and one of my aides. We suddenly stumbled on a patrol of American troops of the 1st Division, under the command of Lieutenant Black. He recognised me at once and told me that the troops I saw were the leading battalion of the 16th Infantry, under the command of Colonel Harrell. Harrell was a classmate of mine at West Point. Explained the situation to Lieutenant Black and directed him to return at once and contact Colonel Harrell and explain to him the position of my troops and the danger involved in the situation. As I finished talking to Lieutenant Black I noticed that one of the soldiers in the patrol was looking at me in a rather wishful way. I was smoking a Camel cigarette and presumed he was watching me enjoying what was then a rare possession at the front – American tobacco. So I offered him one from the rather dilapidated pack I was using. He thanked me and as he lit it said, 'I was thinking, if you had just a'bin a Boche general 'stead of an American one we would all of us got the DSC.' I laughed and gave him the pack saying, 'If you don't get a medal in any event you do get a packet of cigarettes.' He grinned and blurted out, 'To tell you the truth, sir, I would rather have the cigarettes than the medal.' As they disappeared down the hill he was the rear point of the patrol. He turned and waved his musket and I raised my cap to him as he disappeared in the morning mist. That afternoon the 16th Infantry and the troops of the 42nd were together engaged in bitter fighting at the gates of Sedan. I was told my patrol friend had been killed.[30]

Reconnaissance patrols from the 89th Division confirmed during the morning of 5 November that the majority of bridges crossing the Meuse on their sector had been destroyed, with the exception of the Pouilly Bridge which had been damaged, but could be crossed by soldiers on foot. Sergeant Rudolph Forderhase, 356th Infantry Regiment, recalled:

We found the rest of the Battalion near the summit of the hill. Division headquarters had been dissatisfied with the slow progress made after the Heights of Barricourt had been taken. They seemed unable to visualize the effectiveness of the enemy's rear guard tactics, and the handicap of not having assistance from our artillery until November 4. The enemy had been able to get almost all their weapons and supplies across the river. They had gathered up all the boats, and all materials, from which rafts could be constructed.[31]

Captain Arthur Wear sought volunteers from the 3rd Battalion, 356th Infantry Regiment, to swim across the cold waters of the Meuse to the other side at Pouilly and gather intelligence about the German strength and positions. Forderhase recalled:

> Captain Arthur Y. Wear was now in command of the Battalion. He had orders to get men across the river. He now called for men to volunteer to swim across the river and attempt to get information as to the strength, and disposition, of the German troops. The stream was near bankfull, due to the fact that the enemy had placed obstructions on the upstream side of the bridges, which hindered the normal flow of the stream. The water was cold and deep. Only about half of those who volunteered were selected. Of these, only a few succeeded in getting across. About half were killed by the enemy, or drowned in the cold water. Only about half of those who got back were able to give information of any value.[32]

Conscious that he had sent his men to their deaths on what he regarded as a futile operation, Captain Wear tragically committed suicide during the early morning on 6 November, as Sergeant Forderhase wrote:

> When the surviving swimmers returned and informed Captain Wear of what had been accomplished, he walked a short distance into the dark and sombre woods and shot himself in the head with his service pistol. The captain had been ill and had gotten out of the hospital only a few days earlier. One would be inclined to think that his judgement was not as good as it would normally have been. He was a very conscientious man and, doubtless felt guilty about sending these men on such an unpromising mission. His suicide demonstrated dramatically the very severe strain field officers come under when the higher command, a mile or more to the rear, and probably never having had actual combat experience, given orders

that are not reasonably possible of execution. I happened to be only about fifty yards away when I heard the shot. The Captain did not transmit his orders. The news of his suicide, and the fate of the swimmers, was promptly transmitted to Division Headquarters, and there were no more efforts to swim the river.[33]

Lieutenant-Colonel George English suggested that Captain Wear was probably suffering from shell shock, or what is now regarded as post-traumatic stress, and that he had returned to duty prematurely:

Captain Wear had recently been discharged from the hospital and was weak and nervous. His command had been through severe fighting and had an exhausting march beginning in the early morning. Evidently his mind gave way under the strain of the events and of his depleted physical condition. He ordered his battalion to withdraw from its position along the railroad tracks and bank of the canal to a position in the woods above the town; he sent word to Captain Puffer to take command of the battalion; but did not transmit to Captain Puffer the orders which he had received; then going a little aside from his headquarters in the dismal woods, at about 3 o'clock in the morning, he ended his life by shooting himself through the head. This was one of those tragedies of the war indicative of the frightful strain of the times. Captain Wear's abilities and courage had been tested in the previous fighting and had given promise of a glorious career as a soldier. As a result of his own over-zeal in coming back to hard field service before he was physically fit, the Division lost one of its promising officers.[34]

Captain Arthur Wear, who won the Bronze medal for tennis doubles at the St Louis Olympics in 1904, was buried at the Meuse–Argonne American Cemetery.

Major Mark Hanna, commanding 2nd Battalion, 356th Infantry Regiment, also made a dauntless reconnaissance patrol alone into the town of Pouilly on 6 November. He crossed the Meuse across the damaged bridge and got to within close proximity of German soldiers, who entered the town for meals. During the two hours he spent in Pouilly he gathered vital information about the locations of German machine-guns within the town. He returned to the American-occupied bank of the river in broad daylight and it was only after he crossed the damaged bridge that he was fired upon by German machine-gun fire. His citation for the Distinguished Service Cross recalled:

Major Hanna displayed extreme courage on Nov. 6 by making a daring reconnaissance of the town of Pouilly, near Stenay. This town was held in strength by the enemy, with evident indication of determination to prevent a crossing of the River Meuse at this point. He remained in the town over two hours, returning with information of great value.[35]

During the night of 8 November, further orders were received by 356th Infantry Regiment, 89th Division, to send reconnaissance patrols across the Meuse to identify suitable positions to land rafts, locate German positions and capture prisoners to identify units and gather intelligence. However, there were no rafts available and attempts to construct makeshift boats using logs bound together and bags of charcoal failed. Captain Schwinn, commanding 1st Battalion, sought volunteers to swim across the Meuse. Lieutenant-Colonel English recalled:

> So that ultimately to carry out the mission, many of the members of the patrols made the attempt to cross by swimming. All were volunteers who essayed this perilous feat. The river was 150 to 200 feet in width, with a swift current. The water was ice cold, the season being substantially that of winter. The men who so bravely dared this crossing had been ten days in active battle; they had only the clothes upon their backs, not even blankets to wrap in when they came out of the water. A determined enemy held the opposite shore and they knew that if they survived the perils of the crossing they would probably have to fight upon the further shore, wet and exhausted as they would be. The prospect might well have daunted the stoutest heart: but when volunteers were called for, more men responded than were needed.[36]

Schwinn's plan to reconnoitre the eastern bank of the Meuse involved sending three patrols, each comprising two men across at different sections of the river. They were covered by riflemen on the western bank as they swam across the cold tidal river. Two men succeeded in reaching the other bank while two drowned and another patrol had to abandon its attempt.

Sergeant Waldo Hatler and Corporal John McAfee were among the volunteers who went into the freezing waters, entering on 356th Infantry Regiment's left flank. McAfee suffered from exhaustion and exposure to the cold, and drowned before reaching the other bank. Hatler was able to swim to the eastern bank, located German positions and returned to the western bank to report the vital intelligence gathered. Awarded the Medal of Honor, Hatler's citation confirmed:

> When volunteers were called for to secure information as to the enemy's position on the opposite bank of the Meuse River, Sergeant Hatler was the first to offer his services for this dangerous mission. Swimming across the river, he succeeded in reaching the German lines, after another soldier, who had started with him, had been seized with cramps and drowned in midstream. Alone he carefully and courageously reconnoitred the enemy's positions, which were held in force, and again successfully swam the river, bringing back information of great value.[37]

Lieutenant Creaghe and Lieutenant Hayes made two attempts to carry out their reconnaissance of the eastern bank, but the first was thwarted by a German patrol boat and they had to abandon a second attempt further along the river bank when German patrols were seen on the other side.

The third patrol was conducted on the 356th Infantry Regiment's right flank at Pouilly and comprised of Sergeant Harold Johnston and Private David Barkeley. They entered a little creek called the Wame, which was a tributary of the Meuse, and were able to get across to the German-occupied side of the river and identified ideal banks on which to land rafts. Barkeley drowned as he swam back to the American side, but Johnston succeeded in returning to report to battalion headquarters. Barkeley was awarded posthumously the Congressional Medal of Honor, which confirmed:

> When information was desired as to the enemy's position on the opposite side of the River Meuse, Private Barkeley, with another soldier, volunteered without hesitation and swam the river to the exact location. He succeeded in reaching the opposite bank, despite the evident determination of the enemy to prevent a crossing. Having obtained his information, he again entered the water for his return, but before his goal was reached, he was seized with cramps and drowned.[38]

Sergeant Harold Johnston was awarded the Medal of Honor. His citation recorded:

> When information was desired as to the enemy's position on the opposite side of the River Meuse. Sergeant Johnston, with another

soldier, volunteered without hesitation and swam the river to the exact location of the enemy. He succeeded in reaching the opposite bank, despite the evident determination of the enemy to prevent a crossing. Having obtained his information, he again entered the water for his return. This was accomplished after a severe struggle which so exhausted him that he had to be assisted from the water, after which he rendered his report of the exploit.[39]

At Mouzon on 9 November, Sergeant Ludovicus Van Iersel, 9th Infantry Regiment, 2nd Division, conducted a reconnaissance patrol, under German fire, that resulted in him being awarded the Congressional Medal of Honor:

> While a member of the reconnaissance patrol, sent out at night to ascertain the condition of a damaged bridge, Sergeant Van Iersel volunteered to lead a party across the bridge in the face of heavy machine-gun and rifle fire from a range of only 75 yards. Crawling alone along the debris of the ruined bridge he came upon a trap, which gave away and precipitated him into the water. In spite of the swift current he succeeded in swimming across the stream and found a lodging place among the timbers on the opposite bank. Disregarding the enemy fire, he made a careful investigation of the hostile position by which the bridge was defended and then returned to the other bank of the river, reporting this valuable information to the battalion commander.[40]

The 365th Infantry Regiment was ordered to capture positions within the Bois Frehaut on the eastern bank of the Moselle River, north of Pont-à-Mousson, Marbache sector, as 92nd Division advanced upon the German stronghold at Metz. The African-American soldiers from this division had to assault the German line, which was well defended by uncut barbed wire defences that had remained untouched by the Allied bombardment. They would fight from 07.00 hours on 10 November until 11.00 hours on 11 November. The scene was more reminiscent of the experience of British and French soldiers during the early stages of the conflict instead of the penultimate day of the First World War. Major Warner Ross wrote:

> Promptly at seven as scheduled, our barrage jumped and in a few seconds practically all of our shells were falling beyond the wire. This was our time to get through and quickly, if ever. All along the front the boys went for those entanglements ... they had recently

been repaired and strengthened. Most of the wire was the heavy new German type, with barbs an inch and a half long and less than an inch apart. It required heavy two-handed cutters with handles two and a half feet long to cut. Small cutters were useless for cutting here. The wide belts were not only criss-crossed back and forth in all directions on stakes and chevaux-de-frise, but woven in every conceivable way as high as a man's head back among the trees.

There were pits and trenches with wire thrown in loose and in coils covered with light limbs and leaves for men to fall into. We had no tanks. They set off mines, many of which blew holes sixty to seventy feet in diameter. Grenades and bombs were suspended from limbs and in the brush such a way that stepping on or touching a certain stick or wire would explode them. Machine guns were placed at varying distances back in the wood, some on little camouflaged platforms in trees, some in trenches, some in cement 'pill-boxes' located so as to sweep and enfilade every section of the wire.

High ranking officers from the rear as well as low ranking ones who swarmed up to visit the place after the armistice were amazed at the strength of the position, and when they saw it at close range, the predominant question was, 'How did they ever get through?' And they only saw it from the outside edge, for no one was allowed in the wood. It was saturated with gas for days.

The entire Bois Frehaut … was wired every few hundred yards in front of trench systems and enfilading machine guns. There were deep rocky ravines, steep hills, large patches of undergrowth filled with wire, traps, mines and pitfalls of every description, also magnificent dugouts and a most complete system of phone and signal lines.[41]

Ralph W. Tyler, the African-American war correspondent, wrote of the 365th Infantry Regiment's exploits at the Bois Frehaut on 10–11 November:

And so the 2nd Battalion went into action with but one white officer, the Major. No unit in the advance had a more difficult position to take and hold than the position assigned to the 2nd Battalion, 365th. The Bois Frehaut was a network of barbed wire entanglements, and the big guns in Metz had nothing to do but sweep the woods with a murderous fire, which they did most effectively.

French and Senegalese in turn had failed to hold these woods, for it was worse than a hell – it had become the sepulchre of hundreds. I was over and through these woods; I saw the mass of barbed-wire entanglements; I saw the nests in the trees in which Germans had camouflaged machine guns that rained a fire upon the Allied troops.

It is impossible to describe the scene of carnage. The order to the colored men of the 365th was to 'take and hold' although it was believed, almost to a certainty, that they could not hold it, even if they could take it. But they did take and hold it, and these men of the 2nd Battalion, with Spartan-like courage; with an endurance unbelievable, would be holding the position at this writing had not the armistice been signed or had they not received the order to retire.[42]

The African-American soldiers of 365th Infantry Regiment defied German machine-gunners and snipers and breached the defences of the Bois Frehaut. However, once they had captured the wood on 10 November they had to hold their position until the Armistice and were the target of unrelenting heavy Germany artillery fire from batteries close to Metz.

Major Warner Ross recalled:

It seemed to me that almost all the big guns that side of Metz were firing on Bois Frehaut and the old no-man's land just behind it. And I learned afterward that they were, for we were the only ones that had taken and were holding any special territory. They had been expecting a drive on Metz for some time and their artillery especially was well prepared. Shrapnel and high explosive contact shells of all sizes fell on all parts of the area. They knew more about the armistice than we did and his artillery seemed to do all the damage it could while the war lasted. Just before dark on the tenth he began throwing over great quantities of gas and continued to mix it in all night long. They seemed determined to run us out or exterminate us.[43]

By 11.45 hours Bois Frehaut was captured. Major Warner Ross bore witness to gruesome sights during the battle for Bois Frehaut as his soldiers were slaughtered on the day before the war came to an end:

One little scene has bobbed up in my memory – the death of an E Company Runner. Late on the afternoon of the tenth I left my P.C. to get a view of a certain position. I had gone but a short distance when I stepped on something that attracted my attention. It was a human hand! Near it was a large spot of blood and a trail as though something had been dragged in the general direction of where our First Aid Station had been before it was blown up. My course lay a little to the right, but I followed the gruesome marks for about fifty yards and there huddled up in a gulley laid the 'E' Company Runner I had sent out with a message for Captain Sanders about two hours before.

Not only was his right arm off at the elbow, but his right side and leg were badly mangled. I thought he was dead, but bent over and put my hand on his forehead. His eyes opened. In them was a wistful, faraway look. I spoke, and with an apparent effort he got them focused, they brightened with recognition, and immediately almost to my undoing, his body straightened! His right shoulder and the stub of an arm jerked! Utterly helpless, trembling on the very brink of eternity, he had come to 'Attention' and had saluted his Major! Then I noticed he was making a pitiful effort to talk, and in some way, I can't explain just how, I got the impression that there was something in his pocket he wished me to see. I took out a wallet and found what I knew he wanted. It was a post-card photo of a pretty colored girl holding in her arms a dark, smiling baby. Shells were screeching over. Just then one tore the earth nearby and sprinkled us with dirt. I propped his head against my knee and held the picture close to his eyes. A proud satisfied look came into them, then a calm, tired smile. He seemed looking farther and farther away. Another terrific bouncing jar and the bloody, mud smeared form relaxed. Another brave comrade had 'gone west'.

A little farther on I saw a big private leaning against the splintered trunk of a tree, his bowels all hanging out. No one else was near. He seemed to be in delirium and was crying pitifully like a little child for 'Mamma'. When he saw he stared for an instant, then jumped up and yelled, 'Major Ross is with us! Go to it boys!' and fell over – dead. Then I thought about all I had heard to the effect that you have to treat soldiers like dogs – especially colored ones – to gain discipline and inspire respect. I thanked God I didn't have to.[44]

Private Levy Buchanan, 131st Infantry Regiment, 33rd Division, was another US soldier who was killed within hours of the war coming to an end. Private Theodore Thomas recalled:

In the attack on the Bois de Warville, Nov. 10, 1918, we had retired to our trenches, where we had started the attack, and about three hours later, around 9 o'clock in the evening, the Germans began shelling our position. Pvt. Buchanan was lying down about twenty-five feet from me. A high explosive shell hit him, mangling his body and killing him instantly, as well as a comrade, John Karel. Dazed myself, I went over to the boys, but nothing could be done for them.[45]

The final phase of the Meuse–Argonne offensive was a success as within a week First Army had penetrated 24 miles into German-occupied ground. The Second Army also performed well and drove its advance towards Metz. Colonel Albertus Catlin wrote:

> For two weeks the Germans succeeded in beating back the most determined American attacks in front of Landres and St Georges. Then the battling Second Division was hurled in. Operating at the centre, they started an irresistible push on the very afternoon that the Germans began to show signs of weakening and pressed forward until they controlled the heights below Beaumont. They broke through that livening fortress for five kilometres the first day, leading all other divisions, and for the first time since the beginning of the war the official German communiqué admitted that the line had been pierced.
>
> This advance made possible the shelling of the vital Mezieres–Metz railway. The advance became a pursuit, with the Germans on the run and the Second Division ever in the van. Forty kilometres were covered in seven days, German soldiers surrendered in companies, and the end of the war was in sight.[46]

General Hunter Liggett also confirmed that German soldiers were in a state of panic and hysteria. He wrote:

> The German was leaving on the run, throwing his packs away in his haste, and trying to hold us with rear-guard machine-gun detachments. Between the Meuse and the Bar rivers his army was particularly disorganised ... In this closing battle we had an American Army in the full sense of the word for the first time in the war. For the first time we were on our own.[47]

Field Marshal Paul von Hindenburg wrote of the failure of exhausted German forces to hold back the American advance towards the Meuse:

> It was plain that this situation could not last. Our Armies were too weak and too tired. Moreover, the pressure which the fresh American masses were putting upon our most sensitive point in the region of the Meuse was too strong. Yet the experiences of these masses will have taught the United States for the future that the business of war cannot be learnt in a few months, and that in a crisis lack of this experience costs streams of blood.[48]

Chapter 7

French Sector

Meuse–Argonne Offensive

General Henri Gouraud's French Fourth Army was responsible for the line from Rheims to La Harazee, in the middle of the Argonne Forest. The French 61st Division was advancing on the American First Army's left flank in pursuit of a German Army retreating towards the River Aisne. By 4 November, 219th Régiment d'Infanterie had reached this river and patrols were ordered to cross the Aisne to confirm if German forces remained in the vicinity. The battalion war diary reported:

> A raid made by Lieutenant Cornetau on the northern bank of the Aisne with the objective to ensure the enemy presence confirms the occupation of its positions with machine gun fire; however activity of the artillery is decreasing.[1]

On 5 November the 219th Régiment d'Infanterie continued to push forward its advance behind retreating German forces:

> The enemy retreats on our left between Condé sur l'Escaut and Crécy sur Serre. On our right also in the Argonne Forest, the march in advance is ordered.[2]

As the 219th Régiment d'Infanterie advanced into the Argonne and liberate French villages on 7 November, it came under German artillery fire:

> The regiment forms in column to march. The regiment gets the order to form the left flank guard with two battalions, an Engineer squad, a battery of the 251st Artillery Field Regiment. At 5 a.m. the advance march starts again. The 5th Battalion in front, Battalion Leussier in

91

support. The 6th Battalion detached forms the rear guard of the main part of the column. The villages of Chesnoy, Aubaucourt and Wignicourt are occupied. The enemy makes harassing artillery fire with 77mm and 105mm, the spearhead gets machine gun fire. At 2 pm the village of Hagnicourt is reached, 90 civilians are rescued. At the end of the day the Battalion Van Den Vaero holds the ridge of Brunet and the line of observation is established along the railway line on the South side of Montigny-sur-Vence.[3]

After the 219th Régiment d'Infanterie crossed the River Vence, further French civilians were liberated on 8 November:

At 6 a.m. the spearhead of the advanced party crosses the Vence on improvised footbridges and occupy Montigny-sur-Vence, where 205 civilians are liberated. At 10 a.m. Guignicourt is reached, occupied with still 200 civilians. Around noon the Battalion Van Den Vaero gets out of St. Pierre-sur-Vence. Two machine gun platoons open fire on an enemy group, which run away in disorder leaving two light machine guns.[4]

By 9 November the Battalion Leussier continued to pursue the retreating German Army, which was in a state of disarray, towards Mézières and the Meuse:

Battalion Leussier goes beyond Battalion Van Den Vaero. On the outskirts of Mathieu Farm the Commanding Officer Leussier is wounded by a machine gun bullet. The Adjutant Major takes command of the Battalion, which is the first to enter Mézières by Pierre suburb, in touch on the left with the 93rd Infantry Regiment and on the right with 264th Infantry Regiment. The Meuse is crossed. The Citadelle suburb is reached. At the end of the day the line of observation edges the canal, reserve of advanced post at the Citadelle, HQ of Commandant at the crossroad of Givet and Mohon roads – Battalion Van Den Vaero at Mathieu Farm, where the 6th Battalion commanded by Captain Courtois soon arrived.[5]

The 93rd Régiment d'Infanterie was also advancing towards Mézières on that same day:

9th November: The advanced company (Beucler) arrives at the edges of Mézières at 8.45 am. All the bridges of the Meuse have been blown up. A crossing sited at 200 metres from St Pierre Bridge has allowed the first party of Beucler's battalion to cross on to the other bank. Eight prisoners are captured, but the crossings on a small arm of the Meuse and the canal that connect the two branches of the Meuse bend are broken. We work all day to re-establish them under fire from enemy artillery and machine guns, which are on the other canal bank and in the quarries of Ridge 222.[6]

On 10 November, the 93rd Régiment d'Infanterie, together with the 219th Régiment d'Infanterie, encountered strong resistance as it reached Mezières and the banks of the Meuse:

The 93rd Régiment d'Infanterie and the 219th Régiment d'Infanterie, under command of the Lieutenant-Colonel of the 93rd Régiment d'Infanterie, get the order to force the crossing of the canal on the east of the Citadelle and to advance in order to establish a strong bridgehead, of which the centre would be Saint Laurent. The canal crossing is attempted by surprise at dawn. It does not succeed. The enemy was on its guard and gets our first party with hand grenades and machine gun fire. An assault with Stokes mortar preparation and 37 mm guns are prepared for 10 a.m. It succeeded in part. The canal is crossed first by the 2nd Coy of the 93rd Régiment d'Infanterie then by half a company of the 219th Régiment d'Infanterie. These elements reach the railway line at 300 m east of the canal. The 27th Coy of the 93rd Régiment d'Infanterie (Lieut. Fine) has reached the tunnel. In one day it has taken 32 prisoners, among them 1 officer. On our side we had some casualties. The enemy always resists strongly and the action keeps going till night. During the night the regiment gets the order to be relieved.[7]

For its part, the 219th Régiment d'Infanterie reported on 10 November:

At 5 a.m. the 5th and 6th Bns advance towards Mezières on the Meuse River left bank. Headquarters of the Colonel is situated 700 meters from the Citadelle. Parts of the 13th and 14th Companies cross the canal on a footbridge built during the night by the platoon of Lieutenant Pitois (11th Company, 13th Battalion Engineers) and take positions on the Western slope of the railway line in direction of Saint Laurent. The enemy violently shells Mézières and especially the suburb of the Citadelle and the hospital, which is fired upon.

During the night the regiment is relieved by the 8th Cuirassiers à Pieds and billeted at Guignicourt and Yvermont.

Casualties: 2 wounded.[8]

The 264th Régiment d'Infanterie also came under fire as it crossed the River Meuse on 10 November. The battalion war diary reported:

Operation of 5th Battalion (Brégeon)
With the help of Engineers and Sappers of the Regt, a raft is built to allow the crossing of the selected party on the Northern bank of the Meuse. The assault is scheduled at 10 a.m. At 9.40 a.m. the Stokes mortars begin their fire and oblige the enemy machine guns to disclose themselves. At 10 a.m., assisted by a strong fog, Sub-Lieutenant Alix and 4 men succeed in crossing the river and to take foot on the northern bank. The crossing can only be made by 3 or 4 men at once. No artillery reaction. More and more machine guns disclose themselves. At 11.35 a.m. 25 men have crossed with one machine gun. But the advance is impossible. The fog breaks out and the enemy machine guns oblige Sub-Lieutenant Alix and his party to hide themselves. However, at 12.10 a.m. he succeeds in establishing a liaison with the troops of the 219th Regiment assault from the Citadelle of Mézières.

At 1.35 p.m. the order is given to push on and to cross the rest of the 17th Coy on the North bank. After several different unfruitful tries due to artillery and enemy machine gun fire, the Captain of the Brégeon Company of the Battalion reports at 2.10 p.m. that it is impossible to cross the Meuse. The detachment on the north bank cannot move. By order all actions are suspended. 1 KIA 2 Wounded.

Operation 6th Battalion (Baumann)
After the crossing of the 1st party of the 93rd RI and 219th RI, the 23rd Coy of the 264th RI get across the canal east of the citadelle and advance to the railway line on the east of the canal followed by the rest of the Battalion. Sub-Lieutenant Thiedot is killed. 2 KIA, 12 WIA.

The shelled Hospital of Mézières is on fire and the Germans keep firing all night with shells and bullets to prevent us from extinguishing the fire, the 240 patients are evacuated with great difficulty.[9]

Sub-Lieutenant Marcel Thiedot, 264th Régiment d'Infanterie, who was born in Troyes, was aged twenty-five when he was killed in action on 10 November 1918, the day before the war ended.

Chapter 8

British Assault Upon the Sambre Canal

The Battle of the Sambre was the final offensive launched by British forces during the First World War and began on 4 November 1918 across a 30-mile front that stretched from Guise to Conde. It involved the British Third and Fourth Armies, together with the French First Army commanded by General Marie-Eugène Debeney carrying the right flank.

The major obstacles that faced the British Fourth Army on its sector between Oisy in the south and Hecq in the north was the Sambre Canal and the Forest of Mormal. Although under German occupation for four years, the battlefield conditions were different in comparison to the muddy, shell-cratered terrain of trench warfare in other sectors, for the battle of the Sambre would be fought among populated villages, hedges and land that had not been touched by war.

Many of the officers during the last months of the war were serving in acting ranks, replacing fallen or wounded officers, who were promoted in the field. Captain Dudley Johnson, who had been recently appointed Acting Lieutenant-Colonel and commanding officer of the 2nd Royal Sussex Regiment, reported:

> The country on both sides of the canal was very enclosed with hedges and orchards making it impossible to distinguish any marked tactical features or pick out any landmarks which would serve as distant direction guides during an advance.[1]

German forces had been routed from Valenciennes, but they were determined to stop the Allied advance along the banks of the Sambre–

Oise Canal. This canal took five years to construct from 1834, was 44 miles long (71km), consisted of thirty-eight canal locks and connected the Oise and Sambre rivers. Inaugurated in 1839, the economic purpose of this canal was to supply Belgian coal from the Charleroi coal mines to Paris, because French coal production from Valenciennes coal mines was not sufficient to meet demand.

The Sambre–Oise Canal was a difficult obstacle to overcome for some sections were seventy feet wide from bank to bank and forty feet wide at water level with the exception of the locks, which were seventeen feet wide. The Germans had either demolished existing bridges, or prepared them for demolition, so there was no expectancy that these bridges would be used during the operation and responsibility befell upon the Royal Engineers to establish bridgeheads across the canal.

This was a considerable challenge for the sappers, for bridging the canal was the first objective of the operation. The Germans complicated any attempt by the Allies to advance in this region by flooding the ground, creating swamps where troops would find themselves in water at ankle depth, hindering their movement. The streams that flowed adjacent to the Sambre–Oise Canal near Ors and Catillon were swollen and increased to a width of fifteen feet and three feet deep, causing a further obstruction for British troops to pass. German forces could foresee that the Sambre–Oise Canal would be attacked and this could possibly be the only place where they could offer a last stand defence before the German Army capitulated and the Allies reached the German frontier. Trees had been felled on the eastern banks of the canal south of Catillon and used as a defensive position that machine-gun crews and riflemen could use as firing positions. Barbed wire had been erected upon these felled trees and in front of them. 1st Division intelligence reports indicated that German engineers were strengthening defences along the banks of the canal. One patrol noted on 2nd November:

> Work on E. Bank of the Canal was frequently heard during the night. Hammering and digging were plainly heard and wiring is suspected.[2]

German engineers had destroyed the major road bridges crossing the Sambre Canal, leaving small footbridges for their personnel to use if they needed to swiftly withdraw from the west bank, but these bridges had been prepared for demolition. This meant that a rapid dash would be required in order to capture these vital crossings before engineers detonated these mines. Royal Engineers officer Lieutenant-Colonel C. Sankey DSO referred to IX Corps Intelligence Report, which stated:

Road bridges were in existence at Ors and Catillon and at Oisy. Prisoners state that those bridges have been blown and this has been confirmed by our cavalry patrols. Prisoners report that footbridges were recently constructed at 50 metres intervals. Prisoners state that all the bridges have been mined and connected by electric wires.[3]

The 105th Field Company, R.E., commanded by Major F.W. Richards, was responsible for the construction of rafts to get infantry across the canal at Landrecies, but influenza was spreading rapidly throughout the company. Lieutenant-Colonel R.J. Done, Commander Royal Engineers 25th Division, reported:

> Besides Major Richards and Captain Ridge, the 105th Field Coy., and now only two subalterns fit for duty, as there were going to be three distinct operations, I attached 2nd Lieut. Reeve from 130th Coy. R. E. to Major Richard's Company; but he was obliged to go sick the next day; and as a good many men in the 105th Field Coy. R.E. had now gone sick with influenza I attached a whole section of 130th Field Coy., under 2nd Lieutenant Wells to Major Richard's Company.[4]

Lieutenant-Colonel Done was also concerned that they were unable to fully practise the operation. Instead, the sappers gave the infantry a demonstration of the intended Sambre operation on the River Selle. 1/8th Worcestershire Regiment was allotted the objective of crossing the canal at Landrecies and was held in reserve at Pommereuil from 31 October to 3 November. Done recalled:

> Although we could not have a full rehearsal, on the afternoon of the 2nd November, we gave a demonstration using the Selle River and 6 rafts and 8 pieces of superstructure made in addition for this purpose. The Selle River was only some 32' wide, but served for our purpose. A platoon of infantry made a demonstration attack on it followed by Sappers carrying rafts and superstructure. On reaching the river, the Sappers, duly paddled across, the platoon of infantry was ferried across and the rafts were made into a bridge. The realistic nature of the operation was somewhat marred by the enormous crowd of spectators; who found amusement in the efforts of one or two of the infantry to balance themselves on the rafts. There was some general feeling of doubt I think, as to whether the operation would really be feasible under fire. One C.O. gave it as his opinion, that it would be a 'Sporting Event'. However as far as

the bridging equipment went the rafts seemed practical; and no one could offer a suggestion for anything better.

This demonstration undoubtedly did a great deal of good. It showed the infantry what was being projected to help them; and what they might look for on arrival at the canal; and gave them confidence that the rafts would carry them safely across; especially if they balanced themselves well in the centre of the raft; instead of the extreme edge; as with some men seems to be the natural instinct. All the infantry destined to cross on rafts were provided with life-belts in case they should become wounded while actually crossing.[5]

After midnight a thick mist prevailed over the region during the morning of 4 November 1918. This mist provided adequate cover for the British soldiers and sappers as they assembled before the attack near to the Sambre–Oise canal at 03.30 hours.

On the 1st Division's sector, 2nd Brigade comprising 2nd Royal Sussex Regiment, 2nd King's Royal Rifle Corps and 1st Northamptonshire Regiment, carried out the main assault across the Sambre–Oise Canal at Lock No.1, which was situated 1½ miles south of Catillon. Before they could cross the canal, 409th (Lowland) Field Company, Royal Engineers, commanded by Acting Major George de Cardonnel Emsall Findlay, MC and Bar, was responsible for constructing bridges to enable them to cross a stream and the canal so that they could establish a bridgehead. They had four days to conduct reconnaissance patrols to assess the dimensions of the stream and canal, assemble bridging equipment and to construct bridges that would be sufficiently long enough to reach the eastern bank of the canal. At Lock No.1 the width of the canal was confirmed to be seventeen feet. They gathered and prepared material for thirty footbridges, measuring twenty-three feet long, that would cross the canal and various streams in the vicinity.

No.4 Section, 1st Australian Tunnelling Company, led by Captain Oliver Woodward MC and Bar, was attached to Findlay's 409th Field Company Royal Engineers. Woodward was a mining engineer before the war. His men had much experience for they were involved with the mining at Hill 60 during 1915 and at Messines in 1917. During the last week of the First World War, 1st Australian Tunnelling Company was ordered to build a tank bridge as soon as the tactical situation permitted, which consisted of heavy steel beams that would be used by tanks and motor vehicles to cross the Sambre–Oise Canal. These were delivered to a position 300 yards from Lock One, where they were assembled during the night of 3/4 November. Lieutenant-Colonel Sankey stated that:

The tank bridge at the Lock was too heavy to be carried up complete, but it was designed in such a way that it consisted of only two types of members, steel joists and chassis, thus enabling a large party to be employed without fear of confusion.

The shore transoms were identical with the chassis, and the only constructional work required at the site was the prizing out of the coping stones of the Lock and the spiking down of the ribands.[6]

Captain Woodward had a difficult task ahead of him because this would be carried out under hostile fire. The west bank of the canal was subjected to sporadic German artillery fire and there were small pockets of German resistance located along the west bank of the canal.

The Battle of the Sambre began with a machine-gun barrage at 05.44 hours followed by the preparatory artillery bombardment a minute later. This barrage fell along the line of the canal and the eastern bank. As soon as the preparatory artillery barrage started, 2nd Royal Sussex Regiment supported by 409th Field Company, Royal Engineers, brought up bridges for it to cross the canal. Lieutenant-Colonel Dudley Johnson, commanding 2nd Royal Sussex Regiment, reported:

> At 05.45 hrs the artillery barrage opened on the line of the canal and on the lock. There had been no preliminary bombardment of the lock houses. As the barrage opened No.11 platoon 'C' coy and No. 5 platoon 'B' coy and 1 section M.G.C. advanced with the sappers carrying the bridges and all closed up to within 100 yards of the barrage and waited for the lift.[7]

Three minutes after Zero Hour the first waves with the bridge-carrying teams charged towards the canal bank and the lock. Their path was interrupted by German shellfire and the bridges were dropped upon the ground. Several casualties among the sappers were caused by this artillery fire before they started to construct a bridge. Unperturbed by the pandemonium that reigned, the bridges were picked up and they continued the advance. Planks that were intended to be used as a bridge to cross a small stream across swampy ground west of the canal lock were too short to fulfil the task. Lieutenant-Colonel Johnson recalled:

> The bridges turned out to be of insufficient length to span the stream. So some of the men of the leading platoons waded the stream and scrambled up the lock bank and one man actually scrambled across the remnants of the broken lock gate.[8]

In some places it was impossible to erect two of the footbridges because of the debris of fallen trees, hedges, roots and barbed wire that obstructed them and a more suitable place was sought. Soldiers belonging to the German 19th and 29th Divisions were defending the canal along this sector and much fire was coming from the direction of a derelict house near to the lock, which caused heavy casualties among the carrying parties and the infantry. This hindered the sappers' ability to get their bridges across the canal. Private Walter Grover, 2nd Royal Sussex Regiment, recalled:

> We had to go up to the Sambre Canal and our job, 2nd Brigade's job, was to capture the lock on the Sambre Canal ... it was all open fighting then, no trenches. The trees with autumn leaves and the hedges were like English countryside ... we had a cup of tea and a smoke. It was pouring with rain. We had a cigarette and had a chatter. We knew that the end was very near, just one week before the Armistice was signed. Austria had packed up and the Germans were on the run. We thought is this our exodus. The battle orders were that at Zero, at 5.15, dawn was just breaking. When dawn broke, we could see the canal and we could see the outline of the canal and we could see the trees. We knew what we were up against because we knew that the Germans had got a machine gun in the lock house. Before we got onto the canal itself we had to get across a dyke, and they got duckboard bridges for the dyke which we was supposed to cross on, but they were too short. They were supposed to be over the canal before we got there. We were the second line, the first platoon had to get across where the duckboards were too short. So they were waiting there for the next lot to come up with duckboards to come across; and they were all piled up along the bank. We overcame a salvo of shells amongst us; that is where we lost a lot of men. At last the engineers brought these longer boards, which we managed to get across, and then they threw the larger ones across the lock itself ... Once we got across, captured the strongpoint, the war was finished as far as we were concerned ... We had a bullet go right through our Lewis Gun I was carrying. As we were going across I heard a ping, during all the rattle of machine guns and shells, I remember I had heard a ping, in the evening we had gone about six miles, over the canal, we could not find any Germans, they had gone. When we stood down to clean the gun, we could not get the striking arm out, when we looked at it we found a bullet through it ... I always carried something in front of me, like a spade and I was carrying this gun with me, it would have gone

through me if it did not go through that. That was the end of the war for me.

We tried to get across this narrow path, but we were all bunched up, the duckboard bridges being too short we were all bunched up, we could not get across ... whether some of our shells were dropping short I don't know ... one or two may have been dropping short.[9]

The German barrage that fell upon the western bank of the stream caused chaos and mayhem, as casualties fell and supporting waves became intermingled with leading waves. Lieutenant-Colonel Johnson reported:

> At this time waves of infantry and sappers with the bridges for the bridging were approaching the stream when several shells landed amongst the sappers as well as the infantry, thus delaying the time table for getting the bridges in position. This caused the rear waves to close up on the leading waves and bridge crews, and there was now a considerable crowd of men held up owing to disorganisation of the bridge carriers. Officers then hurriedly got any men near to pick up the bridges and advance to the stream, but just as they arrived there, further salvos of shells landed right amongst them, literally blowing them back again on to the rear waves.[10]

Some of the bridges that were to be used to bridge the lock employed instead across the stream west of the canal. One of the bridges was laid across a stream and enabled forward parties from the 2nd Royal Sussex Regiment to cross to the other side, where they lined the canal bank. There they established a firing position to provide covering fire and suppress German fire from the eastern bank of the canal and from the four houses that stood adjacent to the lock. Lieutenant-Colonel Sankey wrote:

> The first subsidiary bridges of the southern group arrived at the stream immediately west of the Lock placed over the stream by men wading up to their waists; the remaining two subsidiary bridges of this group arriving shortly after, we used in conjunction with a V-form to make a single crossing. Infantry, of whom some scrambled over the stream and some crossed the bridges, advanced over the wire and up the bank, and silenced the enemy post in the ruined house west of the lock, which up to this time had caused much trouble and some casualties by bombs.

Great assistance was given at this time, and indeed throughout the whole bridging operation, by the infantry who helped to carry the bridges over the stream and up the bank; foremost in giving this assistance was Lt. Colonel Johnson DSO, MC, commanding the 2nd Royal Sussex Regiment.[11]

Lieutenant-Colonel Dudley Johnson, 2nd Royal Sussex Regiment, wrote:

Once more scratch parties were told to man-handle the bridges and the leading waves advanced to the stream and this time succeeded in getting one of the bridges (intended for the main crossing of the lock) laid across the stream. Men soon crossed this and lined the bank of the canal engaging the canal on the opposite bank with fire – some of the Lewis gunners standing on top of the bank firing their Lewis Gun from the hip, traversing as they did so. Under the cover of this fire a second bridge was pulled across the one already laid and hauled up the bank to the edge of the lock. The wheels and launching lever were then fixed and the bridge laid across the lock at 06.10 hours.[12]

This was the first bridge built by the sappers that reached the western bank of the lock and it was left to Major George Findlay and two NCOs to manoeuvre it into position to cross the lock. Since most of this bridging party had become casualties, they were assisted by infantry belonging to the 2nd Royal Sussex Regiment. These bridges were designed to be wheeled to the canal bank and lowered by a lever to the other side. Lieutenant-Colonel Sankey reported:

The first-wave infantry bridges at Crossing No.1 were designed as single-span bridges, as light as possible consistent with their being able to support 4 to 6 men on them at one time. They were fitted with a lever and a pair of wheels, so they could be launched from the near abutment without requiring anyone on the far side to receive them.[13]

According to Captain Oliver Woodward, he observed Major Findlay lead his sappers across the lock by jumping across the partially open lock gates at 06.00 hours and then they stormed a German machine-gun emplacement that was positioned in a boiler house. Woodward offered his assistance to Findlay, which he gladly accepted. They overwhelmed this position and the occupants within this garrison soon surrendered. Findlay, who had previously been awarded the Military Cross and Bar, was awarded the Victoria Cross for the role he played near Catillon. His citation recorded:

> For most conspicuous bravery and devotion to duty during the forcing of the Sambre–Oise Canal at the lock, two miles south of Catillon, on 4 Nov. 1918, when in charge of the bridging operations at this crossing. Major Findlay was with the leading bridging and assaulting parties which came under heavy fire while trying to cross the dyke between the forming-up line and the lock. The casualties were severe, and the advance was stopped. Nevertheless, under heavy and incessant fire he collected what men he could and repaired the bridges, in spite of heavy casualties in officers and other ranks. Although wounded, Major Findlay continued his task and after two unsuccessful efforts, owing to his men being swept down, he eventually placed the bridge in position across the lock, and was the first man across, subsequently remaining at this post of danger till further work was completed. His cool and gallant behaviour inspired volunteers from different units at a critical time when men became casualties almost as soon as they joined him in the fire swept zone, and it was due to Major Findlay's gallantry and devotion to duty that this most important crossing was effected.[14]

Once this bridge was secured across the lock, Lieutenant-Colonel Dudley Johnson came forward with the 2nd Royal Sussex Regiment, dashed across the bridge and attacked the German machine-gun position that was located within the ruins of the four lock houses. It was for this action that Johnson received the Victoria Cross. His citation stated:

> For most conspicuous bravery and leadership during the forcing of the Sambre Canal on the 4 November 1918. The 2nd Infantry Brigade, of which the 2nd Battn. Royal Sussex Regiment formed part, was ordered to cross the lock south of Catillon. The position was strong, and before the bridge could be thrown a steep bank leading up to the lock and a waterway about 100 yards short of the canal had to be crossed. The assaulting platoons and bridging parties, Royal Engineers, on their arrival at the waterway were thrown into confusion by the heavy barrage and machine-gun fire, and heavy casualties were caused. At this moment Lieut.-Colonel Johnson arrived, and, realising the situation, at once collected men to man the bridges and assist the Royal Engineers, and personally led the assault. In spite of his efforts heavy enemy fire again broke

up the assaulting and bridging parties. Without any hesitation, he again reorganised platoons and bridging parties, and led them at the lock, this time succeeding in effecting a crossing, after which all went well. During all this time Lieut.-Colonel Johnson was under a very heavy fire, which, though it nearly decimated the assaulting columns, left him untouched. His conduct was a fine example of great valour, coolness and intrepidity, which, added to his splendid leadership and the offensive spirit that he had inspired in his battalion, were entirely responsible for the successful crossing.[15]

Once the houses at the lock had been secured, the remainder of the 2nd Royal Sussex Regiment were able to cross to the eastern bank of the canal, followed by the 2nd King's Royal Rifle Corps, where a significant number of German prisoners were captured. Private Walter Grover, 2nd Royal Sussex Regiment, recalled the capture of German prisoners after overwhelming the machine-gun position in the lock house:

> They knocked it down at the finish, they shelled it. They found out where the strongpoint was and put two or three shells into it. That was when the Germans gave up. I never saw any more Germans after that, apart from a few we found in a little hole in the ground, we came across a party of them. They just threw their hands up when we got there. I could never stick a bayonet in any of them, they threw their hands up and that was that. I thought that the quickest way, if I was attacked, was to use the rifle. I could not see myself sticking a bayonet in them. I suppose if it came to the point I would have to. Funny part about it, when we got into Germany, our attitude towards them completely changed.[16]

As Lieutenant-Colonel Johnson was subduing the German machine-gun in one of the lock houses, a second footbridge was brought to the lock and successfully laid, followed by two subsidiary bridges that were meant to bridge the stream before the west bank. By 06.35 hours six infantry bridges had been established across the lock.

The bridge building work of the sappers from 409th Field Company R.E. was completed by 06.45 hours and they were assembled in the cellar of the lock building for a brief rest, before they started to search for mines and booby traps in the lock and neighbouring buildings. The 409th Royal Engineers sustained thirty-five casualties, including one officer killed and three wounded; eleven men killed and twenty wounded. Every officer was a casualty, along with 45 per cent of the ranks.

The 2nd Royal Sussex Regiment and 2nd King's Royal Rifle Corps were able to cross the canal and establish a bridgehead, successfully reaching their targeted objective line by 09.00 hours.

While a bridgehead was being extended on the eastern bank, at 07.30 hours Findlay considered it safe for Captain Woodward's No.4 Section, 1st Australian Tunnelling Company to commence constructing the tank bridge over the canal. The first joist arrived at 08.20 hours after being physically carried for 500 yards. Although the machine-gun positions along the canal bank had been neutralised, at 09.00 hours German artillery began targeting the canal and made the task of building this bridge hazardous. Once these Australian sappers got the first beam across the canal the task became easier and after three hours the work was completed by 10.30 hours, but at a cost of four killed and five wounded.[17]

As soon as the tank bridge was constructed, the 1st Australian Tunnelling Company was then ordered to search for German mines and booby traps along the banks of the canal. Woodward reported to Commander Royal Engineers, 1st Division:

> The tank bridge which was to be erected by this section was successfully erected by 10.30 4/11/18 ... I have to advise that 80 T.N.T. high explosive charges were removed by this Section from the foundations of the building on the West side of the bank.[18]

The last Australian soldiers killed during the First World War were from 1st Australian Tunnelling Company and died as they built this tank bridge over the Sambre Canal. Their names were Sapper C. Barratt 8271, 2nd Corporal A. Davy 5581 and Sapper Arthur Johnson 7680, and they were buried adjacent to each other in Le Rejet-de-Beaulieu Communal Cemetery.

Note that three Australian Flying Corps pilots were killed in action during the last days of the war. They included Captain Thomas Baker DFC, MM and Bar, killed on 4 November, who was buried at Escanaffles Communal Cemetery; Lieutenant Arthur Palliser, killed on 5 November, buried at Anvaing Churchyard; and Lieutenant Whitley Symons, also killed on 5 November and buried at Cement House Cemetery. These fatalities demonstrate that the airmen belonging to the Australian Flying Corps, German Imperial Air Force, French Air Force and Royal Air Force continued to fight during the last days of the war in order to contest control of the skies.

As the sappers laboured in bridging the canal, battalions from the 2nd Brigade pushed forward their advance eastwards from the canal.

The battalions became mixed and visibility, which had been obscured by the morning mist, was worsened by the smoke from the barrage. The infantry had been well briefed and were able to reorganise themselves. The 2nd Royal Sussex advanced on the left while the 2nd King's Royal Rifle Corps advanced on the right.

The 2nd Royal Sussex Regiment did not encounter much significant German resistance and many surrendered. Lieutenant-Colonel Johnson reported:

> Once the canal had been crossed the resistance put up by the enemy was small and beyond rounding up a few machine guns which gave battle here and there, there was no infantry fight worthy of mention as the enemy infantry seemed only too ready to 'Kamerad'.[19]

The 2nd Royal Sussex lost one officer killed, seven wounded and four missing; eight men killed, six wounded and eighty-four listed as missing. They had captured approximately 200 prisoners, two field guns and fifty machine-guns.

North of Catillon, the 96th Brigade was given the objective of crossing the Sambre canal at Ors and forming a bridgehead as far as the Landrecies to La Groise Road. Once the five-minute bombardment of German positions east of the canal was completed, the 2nd Manchester on the right, 16th Lancashire Fusiliers in the centre and the 15th Lancashire Fusiliers carrying the left flank, rushed to the western bank of the canal, 1,000 yards north-east of Ors, to provide covering fire in support of the 218th Field Company, Royal Engineers, in its attempt to build two cork float bridges to the eastern bank. German forces positioned along the eastern canal bank used machine-guns, trench mortars and gas to defend their position. Their attack was just south of where there was a bend in the canal.

The 218th Field Company, R.E. supported by 2nd Manchester's, was tasked with crossing the canal just north of Ors. Acting Major Arnold Waters, commanding the 218th Field Company, R.E., and Sapper Adam Archibald, from the same company, were awarded the Victoria Cross for their courageous attempt to construct a bridge in this sector across the Sambre–Oise Canal under heavy enemy fire. Major Waters had already been decorated with the DSO and MC earlier in the war. The bridging operation was carried out under close range enemy machine-gun and artillery fire, together with the German release of gas that hindered the construction. Heavy casualties were sustained and the bridge itself was being damaged as it was being built. These were difficult conditions that made the task almost impossible to achieve. The two bridges were destroyed as soon as they were completed and needed to be rebuilt. When Second Lieutenant Thomas Barker, aged twenty, was killed and two other officers were wounded Major Waters, with disregard for his own safety, personally went forward to supervise the completion of the bridge. He was in the canal supported by cork floats, wet and under close range fire as he oversaw the building of the bridge. His citation recorded:

> From the onset the task was under artillery and machine gun fire at close range, the bridge being damaged and the building party suffering severe casualties. Major Waters, hearing that all his officers had been killed or wounded, at once went forward and personally supervised the completion of the bridge, working on cork-floats while under fire at point blank range. So intense was the fire that it seemed impossible that he could escape being killed. The success of the operation was due entirely to his valour and example.[20]

It was miraculous that Major Waters escaped death – he survived the war to receive his VC from King George V. Waters died peacefully aged ninety-four on 22 January 1981.

Sapper Adam Archibald was part of the bridge building team that worked on the cork floats on the canal and he was exposed to heavy artillery and machine-gun fire, fired from within a few yards. This fire was annihilating the engineers and Sapper Archibald and Major Waters were the only sappers working on this bridge. Despite the danger of being wounded or killed, Archibald proceeded with the construction of the bridge until completion, when he collapsed from the effects of gas poisoning. Archibald's citation for the Victoria Cross stated:

> For most conspicuous bravery and self-sacrifice on 4 Nov 1918, near Ors, when with a party holding a floating bridge across the canal. He was foremost in the work under a very heavy artillery barrage and machine gun fire. The latter was directed at him from a few yards' distance while he was working on the cork floats; nevertheless, he persevered in his task, and his example and efforts were such that the bridge, which was essential to the success of the operations, was very quickly completed. The supreme devotion to duty of this gallant sapper, who collapsed from gas-poisoning on completion of his work, was beyond all praise.[21]

Sapper Archibald survived the war. He recovered from gas poisoning at a hospital at Le Havre and lived a peaceful life until he died aged seventy-eight at his home in Leith in 1957.

Determined German resistance and unrelenting fire frustrated the sappers from 218th Field Company, Royal Engineers, who were unable to build the bridge without support. It was necessary for 2nd Manchesters to maintain a sustained covering fire upon German forces on the eastern bank. The war diary of the 2nd Manchesters reported the pressure that the sappers encountered:

> The attempt to bridge the canal under most terrific machine-gun fire, heavy trench mortar fire, and spasmodic artillery fire. The R.E.'s in throwing over the bridge worked in a magnificently gallant manner, but were decimated with perishing fire.[22]

Second Lieutenant Wilfred Owen MC, the renowned war poet, led one company from the 2nd Manchesters to the canal and assisted in providing covering fire for the Royal Engineers while they bridged the canal. When this ineffectual attempt to build a bridge along this section of the canal was realised, men of the 2nd Manchesters resorted to rafts to paddle across the canal. The situation was chaotic amidst the dawn mist, shell and machine-gun fire and gas, and it was reported by those who survived the battle that Owen was shot and killed while paddling across the canal in a raft. His mother received notification that her son had been killed just as the church bells signalling the Armistice were being rung seven days later.

While the Sappers bravely constructed the bridge, Second Lieutenant James Kirk was another officer from the 2nd Manchesters who made an audacious and self-sacrificing attempt to protect them with machine gun cover. Kirk was twenty-one when he was killed on that day and was buried in Ors Communal Cemetery. His posthumous Victoria Cross citation is worth quoting in its entirety:

> For most conspicuous bravery and devotion to duty north of Ors on 4 November 1918, whilst attempting to bridge the Oise Canal. To cover the bridging of the canal he took a Lewis gun and under intense machine-gun fire paddled across the canal in a raft, and at a range of ten yards expended all his ammunition. Further ammunition was paddled across to him, and he continuously maintained covering fire for the bridging party from a most exposed position till killed at his gun. The supreme contempt of danger and magnificent self-sacrifice displayed by this gallant officer prevented many casualties and enabled two platoons to cross the bridge before it was destroyed.[23]

After two platoons from the 2nd Manchester Regiment got across to the eastern bank, German artillery fire soon destroyed the bridge. Despite repeated efforts to repair it, the operation had to be abandoned due to overwhelming German fire and the remnants of the 2nd Manchesters had to be withdrawn.

The 16th Lancashire Fusiliers attacked between Ors and where the canal bended eastwards. Sappers from 218th Field Company, R.E., supported by the 16th Highland Light Infantry (Pioneers), successfully lashed cork floats to the poles of the bridge and, despite heavy machine-gun fire, were able to complete construction of the bridge within thirty minutes. This bridge was positioned 1,500 yards north-east of Ors.

A platoon commanded by Second Lieutenant Stapley crossed the canal, but when Captain Pemberton followed them, the anchors that secured the bridge to the eastern bank became detached, creating a breach. The bridge could not be used and there was just one platoon on the eastern bank. Despite attracting considerable enemy machine-gun fire, Stapley and Pemberton secured the bridge to the bank, allowing Second Lieutenant G.H. Potts, the battalion adjutant, to cross with three other men. Then an enemy shell struck the structure of the bridge, rendering it unusable. Acting Lieutenant-Colonel James Neville Marshall, with a respected reputation for being a 'strict disciplinarian', was seconded from the Irish Guards to stiffen the effectiveness of the 16th Lancashire Fusiliers. As their commanding officer, he personally intervened in directing his men and the sappers to repair the bridge from the embankment while exposed to enemy fire. The first party of engineers and Lancashire Fusiliers were killed or wounded. Leading by example, his leadership and presence inspired further volunteers to come forward to attempt to repair the bridge. When the bridge was repaired, Marshall was killed as he led a charge towards the other bank. There are conflicting reports of Marshall's death, as his Victoria Cross citation recorded that:

> When a partly constructed bridge came under concentrated fire and was broken before the advanced troops of his battalion could cross, Lieut.-Colonel Marshall at once went forward and organised parties to repair the bridge. The first party were soon killed or wounded, but by personal example he inspired his command, and volunteers were instantly forthcoming. Under intense fire and with complete disregard of his own safety, he stood on the bank encouraging his men and assisting in the work, and when the bridge was repaired attempted to rush across at the head of his battalion, and was killed while doing so.[24]

The war diary of the 16th Lancashire Fusiliers reported:

> Lieutenant-Colonel Marshall M.C. and Bar came forward when his battalion was held up and fearlessly worked on the canal embankment encouraging the men in their efforts to repair the Bridge. Fully exposed to the enemy fire he was shot through the head.[25]

Second Lieutenant G.H. Potts confirmed that Marshall was 'killed trying to cross on one of the duck-boards floating on petrol tins. We had probably a hundred casualties without moving an inch.'[26] Private Frank Holding, 'B' Company, 16th Lancashire Fusiliers, recalled:

> We were on the Sambre, we were at a little place called Ors … it was at evening time, we had to go across this river, it wasn't a very wide river, the Royal Engineers had built some small bridges that could get across, they built about 5 or 6, and our CO, Colonel Marshall, he was always leading the troops wherever he went, you got a gold coloured wound strip, well he had nine of them like a cuff, previous wounds, he'd come from the Grenadier Guards to us as CO. He was only Acting Lieutenant in the Guards, and he finished up as Colonel in the Lancashire Fusiliers. Anyway, he was first across this river at Ors and he was shot clean through the head. He received a VC for that. He was a grand fellow in every way … We got across the Sambre Canal fairly easy after that, and we overrun a four gun battery, which would be of our equivalent of 6-pounders. They had been causing all the damage as we were crossing the canal.[27]

Nonetheless, Marshall's bravery in directing the operation motivated the men that he led. Leading by example and devoted to carrying out his duty, Marshall would sacrifice his life for this commitment. Captain Harold Pemberton witnessed Marshall's last moments during the battle:

> … the heroic nature of Colonel Marshall's death will live in the memory of all those who were with him on that day. We had to cross the Sambre Canal in the face of the most desperate resistance. Many attempts were made resulting fatally when Colonel Marshall hurried up from battalion Headquarters and took charge of operations. He immediately jumped up on to the Canal bank in spite of the heavy fire and encouraged the men to cross. It was then that he was hit – I saw him fall with a smile on his face and I know for he had often told us, that he had died in the manner after his own heart – the death of a soldier and a gentleman.[28]

Second Lieutenant Potts wrote a fitting tribute to Marshall:

> He was a character of guts and determination, he didn't fear anybody or anything, it was a complete tragedy that a man of this quality should have been lost at the end of the war.[29]

By 07.00 hours it was apparent that attempts to cross the canal north of Ors had failed. It was an impossible task for the 2nd Manchesters and the 16th Lancashire Fusiliers to cross along this stretch of the canal, as was evident by the two hundred casualties and the sacrifices made by Owen, Marshall and Kirk. The futility of an offensive on this sector of the canal was acknowledged by 32nd Divisional Staff, who realised that further attempts would only resort in further loss of life for no purpose and ordered these two battalions to withdraw and cross the canal over the kerosene tin bridge consolidated by the 1st Dorsetshire Regiment south of Ors. These orders reached 2nd Manchesters and 16th Lancashire Fusiliers at 08.30 hours, when remnants from both battalions entered Ors and crossed the canal. On crossing the canal, the 2nd Manchester Regiment moved northwards, working along the canal. By midday, two companies belonging to the 2nd Manchester Regiment were in line with the 14th Brigade, where they resumed their attempt to achieve their objective of securing the eastern bank and capturing La Motte Farm, which was strongly defended by German defenders.

The 16th Lancashire Fusiliers and the 2nd Manchesters, who suffered the most casualties in the 32nd Division, followed the advance. The 14th Brigade had captured 342 prisoners, twenty-eight guns, fifty-one machine-guns, one trench mortar and 1 anti-tank rifle.

During the day, the 32nd Division had sustained 700 casualties. It had played a significant part in the Battle of the Sambre–Oise Canal, for the Fourth Army had secured a bridgehead on a front of 15 miles that penetrated 2½ miles into enemy-occupied territory.

Further north, the infantry belonging to 18th and 50th Divisions had to capture several miles of German-occupied ground, including several villages and the Forest of Mormal, before they reached the Sambre Canal. Their tanks assisted in overwhelming the strong German machine-gun positions, however it was extremely difficult for tank drivers to navigate their vehicles through the Forest of Mormal in fog and under continuous German artillery fire and gas attacks. It made the task of locating the strategically well-placed German machine-guns within the forest very difficult and it was necessary for some of the drivers to drive their tanks with the forward port holes open to see where they were going and look for German targets. As a result, they were exposed to German machine-gun fire and shrapnel that was flying around. Private Arthur Hunter from 9th Battalion, Tank Corps, was overcome by gas as he drove his tank through the forest. His citation for the Military Medal confirmed:

> Although suffering from gas poisoning, Pte. Hunter continued to drive his tank continuously for nine hours, no one else being available. Driving in a gas mask, in a thick fog, although under very heavy machine-gun fire, he kept his front windows open and exposed himself all the time in order to pick up targets for his gunners, showing great devotion to duty.[30]

Private Alexander Hodge also drove his tank into the Forest of Mormal, with the front port holes open at great personal risk. This tank driver, also from the 9th Battalion, Tank Corps, was awarded the Military Medal. His citation stated:

> This driver, by his coolness and very skilful driving, took his tank through thick woods and destroyed several machine-gun posts that were holding up the infantry. For three hours in a thick mist and under heavy machine-gun and artillery fire, he drove with open front windows, displaying an absolute disregard of personal danger.[31]

When the crew of the tank commanded by Temporary Second Lieutenant Henry Gravelle was overcome by gas, Gavrelle had to replace most of his tank crew from the infantry ranks from the 2nd Royal Dublin Fusiliers. This meant that he had to swiftly train these men, who had no experience of driving a tank, under difficult circumstances during the battle. This act was rewarded with a Military Cross. His citation stated:

> During the action near Mormal Forest on 4 November 1918, although suffering from the effects of gas and only one of his crew left, he brought his tank into action. Under a very heavy barrage he taught a crew of infantrymen, whom he collected, to man the guns and went forward and caught up his infantry. He beat down all opposition, and by his determined courage and skill placed the infantry on their objective.[32]

The 54th Brigade had to capture Preux-aux-Bois, including the orchards north of this village before they could secure a line along the edge of the Forest de Mormal. They were supported by tanks belonging to 'B'

Company, 14th Battalion Tank Corps. Tank 9196 supported the 11th Royal Fusiliers, but when it malfunctioned the infantry found it difficult to penetrate through the thick hedges. The battalion war diary reported:

> At zero plus 113 our barrage opened, rather wide of the mark and we suffered a few casualties. Tank No. 9196, which was detailed to assist us in our attack, joined us by this time and moved forward at zero plus 118 minutes. It assisted us in breaking through two hedges, but after crossing the stream moved off to the left to engage a reported enemy post and broke down. Beyond engaging the enemy with the 6 pdr. gun it was of no further use to us. The company then experienced great difficulty in breaking through the hedges, but picked up a dozen prisoners from a post on the left flank.[33]

The tanks that supported the 2nd Bedfordshire Regiment also broke down during the attack upon Preux-aux-Bois, but the infantry were able to adapt tactics for the terrain in order to capture the village. Lieutenant-Colonel A. Percival hailed the successful capture of Preux-aux-Bois in his report:

> The success of the attack and the small number of casualties suffered appears to have been due firstly to the well-conceived plan of taking the village from the north. Most of the enemy machine gun positions were sited in hedges facing west and by attacking them in flank it was possible to work along the hedges and get close to them before being seen.
>
> Secondly I consider the success to have been due to the adoption of principles recently taught in training, namely the value of local flanking movements when dealing with enemy machine guns. The thick hedges and enclosed nature of the country was peculiarly adapted to these tactics. Thirdly to the dash and drive and quickness to take advantage of an opening shown by all ranks.
>
> The tanks were useful in breaking down hedges, but were not on this occasion of much assistance in helping the advance as one broke down and two others were put out of action before they had gone very far.
>
> Bill-hooks were carried and were exceedingly useful in getting through hedges.[34]

Some tanks were knocked out by German shells in the battle for the village of Hecq, but this did not stop their crews from leaving their vehicles and continuing the fight with the infantry. Temporary Second

Lieutenant Phillip Chittenden's tank was knocked out by a German shell before reaching the village. His citation for the Military Cross confirmed:

> His tank received a direct hit and became immobile. He went forward with all his guns and the remainder of his crew to fight with the infantry. He assisted 2nd Lieut. Atley (7th Royal West Kents) to capture a formidable machine-gun position which was still holding out. One of his guns having been disabled, he replaced it with one of the captured enemy machine-guns, and continued at the head of the infantry, later personally capturing eight prisoners in a house. Held up by several enemy strong points he got into touch with 2nd Lieutenant R.U. Robinson's tank, with the assistance of which these strong points and twenty-five prisoners were taken. Having left the Royal West Kents on their objective, he moved forward, with his crew now reduced to two; venturing into positions still held by the enemy, he continued fighting in the forefront of the advance entirely without support. He only withdrew when the last of his guns had been put out of action by enemy fire. His initiative, courage, fighting spirit, and cool grasp of situations reflect the utmost credit on this young officer.[35]

Private George Buckmaster was driving the tank commanded by Chittenden. When he abandoned the disabled vehicle he supported Chittenden with the infantry in the attack on Hecq, an action that would earn him the Military Medal:

> He accompanied his officer, who went on fighting with the infantry on foot with his Hotchkiss guns. Always in the forefront of the infantry, this man displayed exceptional coolness in every situation in which his party found themselves. Besides capturing several of the enemy on his own initiative, and using a captured enemy machine-gun with great effect, he immediately volunteered to go through very heavy machine-gun fire and take a message to a tank which was moving off in the distance. This he successfully accomplished, and personally led the tank back across the enemy's front to the village of Hecq, where the infantry were held up, with the result that this tank cleared the village and enabled the infantry to advance.[36]

Temporary Second Lieutenant Richard Robinson's tank was able to support the 7th Royal West Kents and also played a significant role in the capture of Hecq, as his citation stated:

114

Having knocked out several machine-guns in the orchards west of Hecq, which he systematically traversed, he completely mopped up the village of Hecq, causing by his fire the surrender of many prisoners and enabling the infantry to advance. He then very successfully complied with a request from the O.C. Royal Fusiliers to obliterate a machine-gun nest south of Englefontaine, mopping two more machine-guns en route. He found the infantry held up north of Hecq by strong points, consisting of two machine-guns and two trench mortars. One of these he knocked out and the others bolted into wooded country impassable for tanks. At this point the tank was under an intense fire from machine-guns and trench mortars and was rendered immobile by one shot entering the radiator. 2nd Lieutenant Robinson evacuated his crew and guns and continued to fight with the infantry, assisting in the capture, about 15.00 hours, of the machine-guns and trench mortars in this area.[37]

Corporal Alfred Glaysher and Lance Corporal Wilson Kinsbury belonged to Robinson's crew and when they abandoned their tank they carried on the fight. Their Military Medal citation reported:

When finally knocked out by a direct hit, the crew went on fighting with Hotchkiss guns on foot until it had assisted the infantry to clear the whole area of machine-guns and trench mortars.[38]

Infantry of the 38th Division were tasked with assaulting German lines east of Englefontaine, which were defended by the German 14th Division and 58th Saxon Division. 3rd Westfalian Regiment No.16 was determined to hold the line at Raucourt, close to the Forest of Mormal. The regimental history provided details of its primitive defences, which were a lot different in comparison to the trench systems established on the Western Front that caused the stalemate for four years:

The front near Raucourt was held by battalions of the 16th and 57th Regiments, interspersed with the heavy machine guns of the regiment behind the front line. The whole position consisted of rifle pits connected up irregularly. There were no dugouts. There was no field of view owing to hedges, houses, wall and gardens. The battle headquarters were in small cellars hardly splinter proof. In these inadequate positions the weakened and used up troops awaited the attack of an overwhelming enemy. The hostile artillery and air activity were so great that attacks were expected hourly and the division was in a constant state of readiness.[39]

The German Army was in retreat and there was only a short time to establish shallow trenches for firing positions and shelter. Although hedges and villages, with their houses and walls, posed a problem for the attacking British as they advanced, these obstructions denied German machine-gunners and snipers a clear field of fire. Despite poor defensive lines, the 3rd Westfalian Regiment No.16 offered a stubborn defence of its position at Englefontaine throughout the morning. The regimental history recorded:

On 4 November at 6.30 a.m., the enemy's great attack began with an enormous expenditure of ammunition and supported by numerous aeroplanes and tanks. It fell on opponents thoroughly exhausted by the hardships of the past few months. The regiment maintained itself with the courage of despair and only succumbed to superior force when both its flanks had been turned. No reserves were available to counter-attack. The portions of the regiment which had not already succumbed to the effects of the bombardment were over-run and killed. A few were taken prisoner and still fewer were able to escape to bring back news of the glorious end of the regiment. From 9 a.m., the regiment had no longer any communications to the rear. About 1 p.m., Capt. Peips reported from the artillery protective position that he had repulsed the enemy; but on his right flank long columns of artillery, infantry and tanks were on the march. Notwithstanding this, orders were issued by the regiment to offer further resistance. Five minutes later a despatch rider from the brigade reported that British cavalry and tanks had occupied Jolimetz. Col. von Abercron thereupon decided to give the order to retreat; but the battalion was not any longer in a position to do so … An hour later the regiment had the account of the last stand of the 1st Battalion from scouts who had fought their way back … the remnants of the 3rd Battalion succeeded in fighting their way out. About 2.30 p.m., it was reported from all sides that the enemy was advancing. As there were now only about 30 or 40 men left, Col. von Abercron retired with about 20 men. A few officers with two machine guns and about 20 men covered this retirement. This detachment was attacked about 3 p.m. in rear and flank and was forced to retire pell-mell. At the same moment the enemy emerged everywhere from the wood under the cover of his barrage. On the Herbignies–Grande Carrière road the remnants of the regiment fell in with fresh troops. The casualties sustained by it were 16 officers and over 500 men. The remnants of the regiment (57 men) were placed under Cavalry Captain von Hesse in readiness to protect the right flank of the 18th Reserve Division.[40]

However, it was difficult for 121st Brigade, Royal Field Artillery, to follow the retreating German soldiers with its guns once they were out of range after the initial advance, due to the poor conditions of roads. This meant that the leading British battalions were vulnerable because they did not have artillery support. Lieutenant-Colonel MacClennan testified:

> The infantry meanwhile had gone right on. It was absolutely impossible to get field guns along to support them, the only type of battery which could have competed with the situation being pack, or mounted, of which there were, of course, none. The enemy had blown huge craters on every road and track, most carefully sited where the ground on each side was a bog, and making passage by wheels impossible until they had been dealt with by the Pioneers, which was done during the night.[41]

Infantry belonging to 37th Division struggled in their advance as they were opposed by strong German resistance from the hedges and orchards close to Louvignies and from the railway east of Ghissignies. The 13th King's Royal Rifle Corps war diary reported:

> In many cases, as soon as our men were within hand-to-hand fighting distance, the enemy surrendered, but here and there more determined resistance was met with and considerable bayonet work took place. On the right front Coy about 70 dead Germans were counted. The Field Ambulance informed our M.O. that an unusually large number of enemy wounded passed through suffering from severe bayonet wounds.[42]

The 13th King's Royal Rifle Corps captured Louvignies with seven officers and 270 prisoners, and reached its first objective line to schedule at 08.15 hours. During the process of clearing the houses within the village, gruesome work was carried out. The battalion war diary reported:

> Several gory individual contests took place in cellars. One N.C.O. of 'B' Coy fought with 3 Huns in a cellar and killed the lot. His weapon was a small hand axe which he was carrying for cutting his way through hedges.[43]

The last offensive conducted by British forces on the Sambre was a success. The Fourth Army had crossed the Sambre and Oise Canal, establishing a bridgehead 2½ miles deep on a sector 15 miles long, while further north they had penetrated 3½ miles into German-occupied territory. The British breakthrough had contributed to forcing Germany into accepting an Armistice. Lieutenant-General Sir Henry Rawlinson wrote on 4 November:

> We attacked all along the front at 5.45 a.m. this morning, in conjunction with the armies on our right and left. A moving mist helped us very much in forcing the passages of the Sambre Canal, which the 1st Division did in grand style. The 32nd Division had some difficulty at and north of Ors, where German cyclists and Jaegers put up a strong resistance, and there was heavy fighting. But by grit and determination they too got across, and the IXth Corps were on, or beyond, all their objectives by dusk this evening. Braithwaite did a very difficult job very skilfully. The XIIIth Corps also got on well through the Mormal Forest, and they appear to have had no difficulty in capturing Landrecies. In fact, all divisions did splendidly, and I have sent them all congratulatory telegrams. The only thing that bothers me is the continual explosion of delay-action mines on the railway. Six or seven went up today, well behind our front, and this has caused a serious block in the traffic and supplies and ammunition are not coming forward as well as I could wish. However, the Fourth Army today had captured over 4,000 prisoners and 80 guns and the Third Army on my left has caused had an even better bag, and got 6,000 prisoners and 150 guns. This will be a heavy blow to Berlin, and may well decide them to accept our armistice terms, stiff as they are. The Americans are through the Argonne, and have taken Beaumont, some 15 miles south of Sedan. I don't think the Boche can last much longer.[44]

Chapter 9

The New Zealanders Capture
Le Quesnoy

The medieval town of Le Quesnoy was built on high ground and had been surrounded by ramparts since the middle of the twelfth century, but this formidable defence did not prevent its capture by Louis XI in 1447, Henry II of France in 1552 and Spanish forces during 1568. The strengthening of the ramparts at Le Quesnoy during 1678 by the engineer Vauban was not perfect as the Austrians were able to penetrate its defences in 1793.

The objective of capturing Le Quesnoy was given to the 3rd (Rifle Brigade), The New Zealand Division, as part of the Sambre offensive on the British Third Army sector on 4 November 1918. Enveloped by high ramparts, it could potentially cost high casualties in assaulting the town if its German occupants decided to hold their ground. Brigadier-General James Edmonds described the defences at Le Quesnoy in the official British history of the war:

> The town was enclosed by a seven-sided bastion enceinte, with a covered way tenaille (a continuous rampart of salient and re-entrants) outside it, the space between the two lines forming a dry ditch with mounds of earth, with trees growing on them, scattered over it.[1]

Colonel H. Stewart, the chronicler the New Zealand Division history, provided a more detailed description of the complex fortifications at Le Quesnoy:

> The moat, unlike that under the Ypres walls, is not a single broad ditch, but is divided into an inner and outer moat by a line of 'demilunes' or disconnected fortifications, which act as an outlying

rampart. The outer moat is about 50 feet wide and 36 feet deep. The "demilunes" are some 20-30 feet high. Their sides are faced with brick or sandstone supported by thick banks of earth. In some places there is a single, in others a double line of these outlying bastions. By some stretch of the imagination they maybe compared to bold islets, but the banks and transverse walls, which connect them, and the trees and the thick undergrowth which crown their summits and cover the earth banks make the whole of this outer rampart a bewildering labyrinth, in which, owing to circumscribed view and the different orientations of the various walls, it is extremely difficult to reserve an idea of direction. Picturesque in appearance, they form also admirable defensive positions. They were now held in some strength as outposts by German snipers and machine gunners. Beyond them the inner moat lies at the foot of the rampart proper. A small stream, a tributary of the Rhonelle, enters the fortress from the lakes south-east of the town by a sluice and flows along the inner moat, washing the foot of the final rampart. It leaves the fortress on the north by a second sluice. It was considered not unlikely that the enemy would utilise this stream for flooding the inner moat, and a supply of cork mats had been obtained for crossing it. He had, however, either neglected or been unable to strengthen the defence in this way, and the moat contained only the normal amount of water. From the inner rampart, a redoubt projected every 200 yards to give flanking fire. This final rampart was a solid continuous brick wall about 60 feet high. For crossing these defences the Rifle Brigade had provided themselves with half-a-dozen scaling ladders.[2]

The assault upon Le Quesnoy began at 05.30 hours on 4 November 1918 when Allied artillery commenced their bombardment of German positions. Q Special Company projected 300 cylinders of burning oil upon the town's ramparts for the purpose of clearing German snipers and machine-gunners.

Artillery could have destroyed the medieval town, but New Zealand commanders were reluctant to proceed with this strategy. There were an estimated 5,000 French civilians living in the town and the commanders preferred to isolate it with the hope that would encourage its German occupants to surrender and prevent civilian and New Zealand casualties so close to the end of the war. Under the cover of an artillery barrage and a smoke screen, the 1st, 2nd, 3rd and 4th Battalions, New Zealand Rifle Brigade, advanced north and south of Le Quesnoy. Captain Malcolm Ross, a war correspondent with New Zealand Expeditionary Force, reported:

The initial barrage was magnificent and even terrorising to our own men, who in some places thought twice before starting after it. The noise and concussion were so great that officers told me they suffered from headaches so severe that they could not sleep that night.[3]

The artillery searched the ramparts for targets, but stopped firing upon the western perimeter after fifteen minutes to allow patrols to reach the outer moat and to ascertain whether German forces still occupied the town.

At 07.29 hours, the 1st Battalion approached Le Quesnoy from the south-west to the first objective line, which it was scheduled to reach at 08.01 hours. The battalion war diary reported:

The attack on our front proceeded very fast and nothing deterred our boys even though they suffered a good many casualties, from right enfilade machine gun fire. An unexpected attempt at counter attack was made by the enemy on our right and rear between 7 and 7.30 a.m. After our forward companies had gone forward to their objectives a body of enemy troops numbering about 5 officers and 150 O/R [Other ranks] were seen coming from the right along the Railway Line and 'C' Coy, which was resting on Railway Line as Reserve Coy, immediately detached a Platoon to deal with them and within a few minutes the whole body threw up the sponge. Our casualties totalled O/R's 15 KIA, 53 wounded, 5 missing. Officers 9 wounded. Capt. Harding VC commanding 'B' Coy recalled to act as Battalion Commander.[4]

The projection of burning oil upon the fortifications had failed to clear German machine-gunners, because the 3rd Battalion encountered German machine-gun fire from the ramparts as it approached Le Quesnoy. The battalion war diary reported:

The town of LE QUESNOY was not attacked, but troops moved round the north and south to encircle it. The operation was entirely successful. LE QUESNOY was completely encircled during the morning. On attempts being made to mop up, the town was found to be strongly held and defended by machine guns firing from the ramparts.[5]

German sniper fire came from Le Quesnoy throughout the morning. There were snipers on the ramparts and perched in the trees within the moat. The 2nd Battalion, New Zealand Rifle Brigade, approached the moat from the north and a party of four men were able to reach the ramparts that protected Le Quesnoy. The battalion war diary reported:

> At 08.00 hours one NCO and three men managed to cross the moat and gain the inner ramparts of LE QUESNOY. They captured a machine gun, which they threw into the moat, but the enemy was too strong and the patrol had to re-cross the moat. A platoon of 'B' Coy' covered by a platoon of 'D' Coy next attempted to cross, but the enemy drove off the covering platoon and 'B' Coy's platoon had to remain in the moat under cover until the town was taken.[6]

In order to subdue the German snipers and machine-gunners positioned along the ramparts, it was necessary to provide some protective covering fire for the platoon that was unable to cross the moat and had to remain at the base of the ramparts. Other parties from the battalion continued to move towards positions north-east of Le Quesnoy in an effort to isolate the bastion, but for several hours were targeted by German fire from the ramparts. The 2nd Battalion war diary reported:

> At 09.00 approx. 3 inch Stokes were got into position just forward of the railway and opened fire on the enemy trench mortars and machine guns in the town and Lewis guns did good work in keeping down the enemy fire.[7]

Parties from the 4th Battalion, New Zealand Rifle Brigade, attacking from the south-west, also got close to the ramparts of Le Quesnoy, but they experienced the same problems as their sister battalions as they were pinned down in the moat that surrounded the town. Lieutenant-Colonel H.E. Barrowclough DSO, MC, commanding the battalion, together with Second Lieutenant L. Averill, MC, his intelligence officer, and a couple of personnel from his staff went forward in the fog to locate the positions of his companies that had advanced towards the moat. Barrowclough reported:

> On the left, 'C' Company, under Lieut. Rabone were successful in getting right up to the outer defences, and then came under very heavy machine gun fire, which held them up all day. 'B' and 'A' Coys were practically in the same predicament, but owing to the roughness of the ground they were able to find covered approaches etc., which enable them to manoeuvre freely.

The space between the outer and inner ramparts were pitted over by a series of lofty islets crowned with trees and thick undergrowth. The sides of these islands were steep, faced with brick or stone and all of them about 20 to 30 feet in height. Boche snipers and machine gunners were persistent in firing from these excellent defensive positions. Both 'A' and 'B' Coys however set to work to endeavour to perpetrate the defence. The town was surrounded and it was obvious the Boche must give in. It remained to be seen which battalion of the brigade would be the first to enter the town.[8]

Although German howitzers were targeting the moat, a small party led by Second Lieutenant Francis Evans got close to the ramparts. Evans immediately became trapped by the German sniper and machine-gun crews defending the ramparts. Lieutenant-Colonel Barrowclough wrote:

2nd Lieut. Evans with a platoon of 'B' Coy made a very daring advance and were cut off by the Boches. They were pinned down by enemy machine gun fire and were entirely cut off for about 5 hours. 2nd Lieut. Evans with his batman was killed in a gallant attempt to discover a way out.[9]

The divisional history provided more detail in regards to Evan's tragic demise in the moat at Le Quesnoy as he tried to climb the ramparts:

Snipers and machine gunners were still in some numbers on the bastions, but no enemy post appeared to linger now in the broken ground of the outer moat itself. The approaches towards the island ramparts afforded admirable cover and reasonable freedom of manoeuvre. Under Barrowclough's personal direction the centre company deluged one of the outer bastions with rifle grenades, the light trench mortars not being for the moment available, and Evans' platoon clambered up its wall by a scaling ladder and occupied it. From here Evans himself, with 4 men and a Lewis gun, went forward to reconnoitre further. They reached the obvious gap which Averill and Lummis had seen, climbed some 3 feet of broken steps on to the buttress of another outer bastion and then scrambled through the trees on its narrow top towards an inner bastion.

It was close on 9 a.m., and the fog and smoke were lifting. The explorers were discovered and fired on by a machine gun post on their right flank from the top of a projecting salient of the final rampart. They jumped into a shallow hole. After a moment, on the machine gun's ceasing fire, Evans tried to scale the steep side of the inner bastion. He was immediately shot through the brain and rolled back dead into the hole. One of his men in trying to get the Lewis gun into action against the machine gun was similarly shot through the head and killed instantly. The other 3 men were pinned to this very inadequate shelter in the heart of the fortifications for 6 hours with their dead companions. The latter were subsequently buried close to where they had fallen.[10]

Evans, who originated from Wellington, was aged twenty-four when he was killed at Le Quesnoy and he was buried at Romeries Communal Cemetery.

The 4th Battalion could do no more but to hold its positions around the moat. Barrowclough was reluctant to sacrifice further men while he knew that, once Le Quesnoy was encircled, the German occupants would realise they were isolated and it would result in their eventual surrender without further fighting.

The 3rd Battalion had reached Landrecies Gate, which led into the town from the south-east. Around 11.00 hours this battalion sent three German prisoners through this gate in order to explain to their comrades that they were surrounded and to encourage them to surrender. There was no response and the defenders continued to fire their machine-guns and rifles in defiance.

The 2nd Battalion also sent a prisoner into Le Quesnoy across the northern entrance into the town via the Valenciennes gate, warning that further attempts to defend the town were futile. The German occupants, however, remained disinclined to surrender.

According to Captain Malcolm Ross, a war correspondent with the New Zealand Expeditionary Force, a Maori belonging to a pioneer battalion was one of the first to enter Le Quesnoy, albeit only briefly, as he approached the Valenciennes Gate from the north.

The first man to enter was a Maori – one of our pioneer battalion. After stiff fighting and several casualties to officers and men, a battalion of the Rifle Brigade found themselves within three hundred yards of the Porte de Valenciennes. Already the Boche had laid a mine. Presently there was a loud explosion, and the bridge was hurled into the air … At 2.30 the battalion commander (who is one of our most determined fighters) decided to try a sortie. Two officers and ten others went forward. To this party they had attached themselves some Maoris of the pioneer battalion, who for the moment, having nothing else to do, joined the fighting troops. One of these, seizing a Boche rifle, led the way, and shot the first German he saw. There can be no better account of the incident than his own terse and humorous description: – 'When I see the Boche 1 shoot and kill one. Then I shoot again and miss. Then I fire the third time, but no plurry bullet.' (There had been only two bullets in the magazine of that Boche rifle). The Maori then realising that there was little more that he could do, returned to his unit and exchanged the rifle for a shovel, well content that he had killed at least one Boche. Like some demon in a pantomime, he faded out of the picture, and no one knows his name or number; but the battalion commander is still looking for him to recommend him for a well-earned decoration.[11]

With the German occupants of Le Quesnoy continuing to offer a strong and determined defence, the position seemed to be impregnable despite it being surrounded. Around 15.00 hours an Royal Air Force aeroplane dropped a message with a demand that they surrender, with a promise that they would be treated fairly. The message read:

> To the Commandant of the Garrison of Le Quesnoy:
> The position of Le Quesnoy is now completely surrounded. Our troops are far east of the town. You are therefore requested to surrender with your garrison. The garrison will be treated as honourable prisoners of war.
> The Commander of the British Troops.[12]

At the same time, the 3rd Battalion sent another two German prisoners into the town to make a further appeal for the German garrison to surrender and prevent further loss of life. Malcolm Ross, the war correspondent, reported:

> By 3.00 p.m. German soldiers from the ranks were persuaded to surrender and left the town, but the officers refused and continued their stubborn defence.
> Later on this battalion commander sent a German officer into Le Quesnoy with a message, asking the garrison to surrender. A platoon commander took him up to the inner gates, before which the German burst into tears, being afraid that his own men might shoot him for a deserter. The diggers however, insisted that he should go in. They saw no more of him. About three in the afternoon two more Germans were sent in with a message to say that if the garrison did not come out in batches of five at a time, the New Zealanders would

slaughter the whole lot. These two peace envoys returned, and stated that the German soldiers were willing to surrender, but the commandant would not agree. Apparently, however, this dire threat had some effect, for afterwards resistance gradually slackened, and the next thing this battalion commander heard was that the New Zealanders were over the top of the highest wall and into the citadel.[13]

Meanwhile, south of the Le Quesnoy, the 4th Battalion New Zealand Rifle Brigade was preparing to find a way to climb the ramparts and enter the town. Lieutenant-Colonel Barrowclough brought up all available Lewis Guns and Stokes mortars. Lewis guns were positioned so that they could target the top of the ramparts, while the Stokes mortars focused their fire upon the machine-gun positions defending islands in the inner moat. This fire succeeded in subduing German resistance from the inner moat and it cleared the upper ramparts of machine-gunners and snipers. Lieutenant-Colonel Barrowclough reported:

Meanwhile 'A' Coy under Lieut. Kenwick, systematically pushed patrols forward. Each lofty island was searched with rifle grenades and Stokes mortars. Then under cover of two or three Lewis Guns, a long scaling ladder was reared, and a patrol with a Lewis Gun established itself on the top. In this way the enemy were driven back to the inner wall. This was too high for our 30 foot ladder, and at first it looked as if it would be impossible for us to effect an entry. At last a place was discovered where a traverse wall gave us sufficient height to put up the scaling ladder. The first attempts to rear it were met with volleys of stick grenades from the defenders; but after a short bombardment with Stokes it was found possible to get the ladder into position.

2nd Lieut. Averill, M.C. of Battalion H.Qrs and 2nd Lieut. Kerr of 'D' Coy with No. ____ Platoon, then climbed up the ladder at 4 p.m. and gained the top of the ramparts. A few shots and the Boche rapidly surrendered. The whole Battalion then mopped up the town. All prisoners being collected into the Place D'Armes. The whole Battalion climbed up that single ladder.[14]

Second Lieutenant Averill, who was aged twenty-one and had spent seven months on active service, later recalled:

We knew that the enemy was on the run and that his morale had been seriously weakened by the outcome of recent battles. His fire had been mastered and it happened that I was to go up the ladder first. When halfway up I looked to the right and was ready to run down again. Earlier in the day 2nd Lieutenant Evans and one of his men had been killed by bullets from a machine-gun nest there and I knew that it would have been foolhardy to proceed if it was still working. I saw the gun. It was deserted. The ladder reached a foot below the rampart and I ran up. Once over the top, I was quickly followed by Lieutenant Kerr and a machine-gun section. Then the rest of the battalion followed. I heard a crackling in the undergrowth and fired a shot at two Germans who ran for cover. That's all there is to it. Later, I walked round the Valenciennes Gate and met Lieutenant-Colonel Jardine whose men had just gained the entrance.[15]

A memorial commemorating the capture of Le Quesnoy was built into the ramparts, close to where the 4th Battalion placed its ladder to enter the town. The moment when Second Lieutenant Averill led the battalion as it ascended the ladder on to the ramparts is depicted in stone on the memorial. There is also a road within the town walls that is called Rue D'Averill in honour of Second Lieutenant Averill, the first man to climb the ladder.

The 2nd New Zealand Rifle Battalion gained access into the town from the north by using the partially destroyed road bridge. Some New Zealand casualties were caused by friendly fire. The war diary reported:

At 16.00 the enemy fire practically ceased and a party moved forward and crossed the bridge into the town. Our barrage was reported by all Coys. to be very good. There were very few shorts until the objectives were taken. After that shells fells short in considerable numbers, particularly on the eastern end of the railway triangle. 2nd Lt. Bates, DCM, was killed at the assembly point by a short and several men were wounded.[16]

The German commandant in command of the garrison at Le Quesnoy at that point realised that it was futile to continue to resist and offered his revolver as a token of surrender. Le Quesnoy surrendered and 711 German prisoners were captured, with several offering to assist in the location and removal of mines and booby traps within the sector. German casualties amounted to forty-three killed and 251 wounded.[17]

The capture of Le Quesnoy was a joyous moment for its citizens, who had lived under German occupation for four years, as they realised that they were now liberated. Lieutenant-Colonel Barrowclough reported:

The civilian population gave the troops a wildly enthusiastic meeting, thrusting flowers, cakes, and flags upon the men. Old men and women, and a few of the 'Mademoiselles', pressed forward eager to shake hands or embrace the 'Diggers'. The town was well searched and yielded a goodly store of souvenirs, such as Boche revolvers and binoculars. By 6 p.m. the cookers were in the town and the men got a good meal; after which they were billeted in houses round the Place D'Armes.[18]

The war correspondent Malcolm Ross recalled:

People excitedly crowded about them, and they were hugged and kissed and presented with flags and flowers. The frenzied delight of these Frenchmen and French women was unbounded. Later, into one of the vaulted chambers lately occupied by the enemy, went the battalion commander and another officer. Thither the Boche had conveyed much French furniture – beds, mattresses, pillows, mirrors – and some of the poorer people now rushed in, anxious to get their own back. Near the door was a piano stolen by the Boche. In a moment of inspiration a Frenchman sat down at it and commenced to play the 'Marseillaise'. The effect was electrical. Men, women, children and soldiers joined in the stirring strains of the splendid hymn, the echoes of which resounded from the vaulted roof. The thin faces and poorly clad forms of the liberated civilians, in the light of two candles held by the battalion commander and one of his men, made an unforgettable scene that only a Rembrandt could do justice to. The place was strewn with Boche equipment; and one excited old Frenchman began hacking at it with a German bayonet that he had picked up. Then the battalion band marched in along the Rue Thiers, and so on to the Place D'Armes, followed by a wildly excited throng, waving the tricolour, singing and cheering. The band struck up the 'Marseillaise'. That put the townspeople on fire. One moment, you would see women shouting and singing in wild delight, and next tears were streaming down their faces. For four long years they had been bond-slaves – now they were free. Relief long-expected had come at last. As one old man put it, 'They took our liberty; they took our food; they took our furniture, and now la bonne deliverance!'[19]

The 4th Battalion, New Zealand Rifle Brigade, sustained two officers and nine men killed, four missing and forty-two men wounded.[20] The 2nd Battalion, New Zealand Rifle Brigade, lost three officers and eighteen men killed, together with five officers and ninety-three men wounded.[21] Among those killed from the 2nd Battalion was Second Lieutenant George Bates DCM, from Wellington, who was twenty-one years old when he was killed at Le Quesnoy by an Allied shell that fell short, as previously mentioned.

Second Lieutenant Alan Wood was another officer from the 2nd Battalion who was killed at Le Quesnoy from the 2nd Battalion. Wood was born in Sydney, Australia, and his wife lived in Bexhill-on-Sea, Sussex, in England. Wood had seen action at Gallipoli and it is tragic that he should have died so close to the end of the war. Bates and Wood were buried at Le Quesnoy Communal Cemetery Extension together with forty-nine other New Zealand soldiers who were killed on 4 November 1918.

Chapter 10

Impact of Battle of Sambre
Upon German Forces

Although British forces had crossed the Sambre and Oise Canal and advanced through the German lines into the Forest of Mormal, the extent of their success was not realised, for on the evening on 4 November, orders were issued to the First, Third and Fourth Armies to continue their advance towards the Avesnes–Maubeuge–Mons road.

The defeat of German forces on the Sambre sector made it apparent to German commanders that the end was near. Orders were issued to withdraw towards a line that ran between Antwerp and the Meuse. Crown Prince Wilhelm recalled:

> From November 4 onwards, my four armies along their entire front, retreated towards the Antwerp-Meuse position, fighting hard as they retired and carrying out everything in perfect order and absolutely according to plan. At this time, General Groner, [sic Wilhelm Groener], the new First Quartermaster General, paid us a visit. The chiefs of my four armies reported upon the situation of their various fronts. All of them laid stress on the overstrained condition of their troops and the entire lack of fresh reserves. But they were quite confident that the retreat to the Antwerp-Meuse position would be accomplished successfully and that the position would be held.[1]

The British were pursuing routed German armies, however, despite their successes on the Sambre sector, with its damaged roads and sabotaged railway lines, Rawlinson was concerned that his advancing armies would outrun their own lines of supply. Without munitions, food and equipment and fresh reinforcements they would be unable to sustain those advances as well as bring forward artillery support. The infantry could cross country on foot, but lorries and guns were unable to keep up with the swift infantry advance because they could only use roads to move forward and many of those had been blocked by German engineers in an effort to slow the Allies and buy them more time to organise another line of defence. Some craters could be passed by lorries by going off road and going around them, however this would cause boggy, marshy conditions over soft ground, making the road impassable. Considering the limitations of what could be achieved, Rawlinson wrote:

> Such results are most satisfactory, and, if necessary, we could go on doing this all winter, when the weather permits. But we cannot do it continuously, weather or no, till the railways are repaired. My army is now thirty miles in front of our railheads, and the broken roads put a great strain upon the lorries. I can manage a farther advance of ten miles, but after that we must call a halt for a week or ten days.[2]

Lieutenant-Colonel Sutton, from the Quartermasters' Branch, 56th Division, wrote:

> The enemy has done his demolition work most effectively. Craters were blown at road junctions and render roads impassable, especially in villages, where the rim of the crater comes in many cases up to the walls of the houses. Culverts are blown on main roads, and a particularly effective blockage is caused in one place by blowing a bridge across a road and stream, so that all the material fell across the road and in the river.[3]

It was the responsibility of 1/5th Cheshires to fill the craters in with earth and strengthen the surfaces of roads on 56th Division's sector. The battalion war diary confirmed that on 5 November 'work continues to be repairing of roads, principally filling craters and removing obstructions. The enemy are in full retreat.'[4]

Despite the logistical limitations, Rawlinson was confident that the success of the Sambre offensive could bring an Armistice sooner. Reports from German prisoners captured during the operation brought him optimism that the German army would collapse. On 5 November, Rawlinson wrote:

> But before many days are past we shall have over a flag of truce asking for the terms of the armistice. Prisoners captured yesterday say the

Boche will accept any terms; and I think they are right, anyway, it would have been a great mistake to tone down the terms to encourage acceptance. Several German officers captured today were quite drunk when they were brought in. All prisoners were exceedingly glad to be captured, and in the cage there were great rejoicings as each successive batch came in, and friends met with handshakes and cheers.[5]

Retreating German forces were also attacked by French civilians who had been under occupation for four years and now had the opportunity to fight back. Captain Herbert Sulzbach recalled this danger in his diary as he approached Sains du Nord on 7 November:

Now the danger from civilian snipers or franco-tireurs is increasing again, because the French civilians of course know perfectly well what is going on, and would clearly like to pot one or two more of us. One Army order has been drafted with this in mind, enjoining us to keep the strictest march discipline and to let no troops stray or lag behind. Not, in future, may other ranks be sent out alone, or billeted alone, and no wounded man may be left even temporarily alone and unprotected. Corresponding regulations affecting civilians state that the latter have to keep indoors and that windows of houses must be kept shut.[6]

As the Armistice drew near, British soldiers were still being killed. Lance Corporal George Brooks, 2nd/4th York and Lancaster Regiment, was a former footballer who had played for Manchester City Football Club and at the outbreak of war was playing for Derby County. On 8 November 1918 he was killed in action and was buried at Maubeuge (Sous-le-Bois) Cemetery.[7]

Private Joe Phillips, from Hargrave, near Bury St. Edmunds, was killed by a stray bullet on 10 November. The *Bury Free Press* reported:

The deceased had not been in France long, and Sergeant Beaney writes that he had been killed by a stray shot, some little distance behind the lines less than 24 hours before the Armistice came into force. Death was instantaneous and the funeral was at Maubeuge.[8]

Field Marshal Sir Douglas Haig reported upon the Sambre offensive in his official despatch on 21 December 1918:

The military situation on the British front on the morning of the 11th November can be stated very shortly. In the fighting since

132

November 1st our troops had broken the enemy's resistance beyond possibility of recovery, and had forced on him a disorderly retreat along the whole of the front of the British Armies. Thereafter, the enemy was capable neither of accepting nor refusing battle. The utter confusion of his troops, the state of his railways, congested with abandoned trains, the capture of huge quantities of rolling stock and material, all showed that our attack had been decisive. It had been followed on the north by the evacuation of the Tournai salient, and to the south, where the French forces had pushed forward in conjunction with us, by a rapid and costly withdrawal to the line of the Meuse.

The strategic plan of the Allies had been realised with a completeness rarely seen in war. When the armistice was signed by the enemy his defensive powers had already been definitely destroyed. A continuance of hostilities could only have meant disaster to the German Armies and the armed invasion of Germany.[9]

Part III

ARMISTICE

Chapter 11

Negotiations for Armistice

On 4 November politicians from the Allied nations attended a conference in Paris to prepare for the end of the war and to finalise the content of their conditions in the event that Germany offered an Armistice. Among the delegates were British Prime Minister David Lloyd George, French Prime Minister Georges Clemenceau, Italian Premier Vittorio Emanuele Orlando, General Sir Henry Wilson and Marshal Ferdinand Foch and they met in a house on the Rue de l'Université that was the residence of Colonel Edward House, President Wilson's personal representative in Paris.

The terms for Armistice agreed by the Allied leaders were aimed to restore the frontiers violated by Germany and remove its ability to wage future war. It would be based upon the US President's fourteen-point proposal issued during January 1918 with the exception of two points. Germany must pay for the damage it had inflicted upon the Allies and Britain still contested the issue of Freedom of the Seas, which formed one of President Wilson's fourteen points. Britain wanted to preserve her naval supremacy across the globe and did not want Germany to be granted free navigational access in peace and war. It was agreed that this issue would be discussed during the eventual Peace Conference.

The Allies had to reach a consensus where the terms were not too lenient that the Germans would resume the war, or too severe that they would not be willing to accept. Lloyd George was fearful that the proposed terms were punitive to the extent that Germany would not sign. Foch was not perturbed and confident that he could beat the Germans on the battlefield and that the war would then come to a conclusion irrespective of harsh terms. The mood was optimistic since Turkey and Austria–Hungary had signed Armistices with the Allied

137

Entente nations, and it was expected that Germany would soon follow with an approach for peace.

Once the final draft of the Armistice terms was agreed by the leaders of the Allied nations, it was immediately cabled to President Woodrow Wilson in Washington DC. The Allies agreed that Wilson would approach the German Government advising it that if it wanted to know the terms of an armistice, it was to contact Foch, who was appointed representative of the Allied armies, while Admiral Sir Rosslyn Wemyss, First Sea Lord, was designated representative for the Allied Navies to meet the German delegates and hand to them the conditions for an Armistice. Foch was a private man, who spoke few words and shunned publicity. Wemyss held the rank of rear admiral during April 1915, when he was in command of a squadron that supported the Gallipoli landings. He also took part in the evacuation from Gallipoli later that year. Wemyss attained the rank of First Sea Lord during 1918.

These terms were communicated to the German Government on 5 November. Germany had no choice but to accept the terms of the Armistice; its allies, Turkey and Austria–Hungary, had signed one, the German Army was in retreat and the German people were revolting at home.

Foch alerted commanders in the field that German envoys might approach Allied lines to discuss Armistice terms. A specially designated train was shunted to the frontline on the French sector commanded by General Marie-Eugene Debeney between Givet and La Capelle-Guise. Within thirty-six hours Foch received a message that indicated that Germany wanted to send envoys to initiate an Armistice. Foch wrote:

> It was the night of November 6th-7th, at half past twelve, that I received the first wireless message from the German Supreme Command. It gave the names of the plenipotentiaries designated by the Berlin Government and asked me to fix a place of meeting. It added: 'The German Government would be glad if, in the interest of humanity, the arrival of the delegation before the Allied front might cause a provisional suspension of hostilities.'[1]

Foch refused the German request for a temporary ceasefire while discussions for an Armistice were taking place. He was in a commanding position and dictated the proceedings. Foch noted:

> I replied at once in these simple words: 'If the German plenipotentiaries wish to meet Marshal Foch to ask him for an armistice, they should present themselves at the French outposts on

the road Chimay-Fourmies-La Capelle-Guise. Orders have been given to receive and conduct them to the place selected for the meeting.[2]

This message was broadcast from the Eiffel Tower in Paris. Foch only granted a temporary truce along the Fourmies–La Capelle Road.

The politician Matthias Erzberger was surprised to learn that he had been appointed the leader of the German Armistice Commission. The commission did not contain any representative from German High Command because there was a fear that a military negotiator would be obstructive in negotiations with the Allies and risk the extension of the war. Approximately twenty-five officers were requested to accompany Erzberger, but he selected two; Major-General Detlof von Winterfeldt, who had been a former military attaché prior to the war, and Captain Ernst Vanselow, from the German Navy. The commission also included Count Alfred von Oberndorff, German envoy to Bulgaria, who was also a friend of Erzberger. They were accompanied by Staff Captain Geyer and Cavalry Captain de Cavalerie von Helldorf, who acted as interpreter.

The German delegates left Berlin for the German Headquarters at Spa in Belgium on 6 November. Shortly after they departed, Prince Max issued the following communication announcing their departure and purpose:

> PEACE AND ARMISTICE NEGOTIATIONS
> In order to put a stop to the bloodshed the German Delegation for the Conclusion of an Armistice and for the opening of Peace Negotiations has today been appointed and has started its journey westwards.[3]

Meanwhile, in London during the evening of 6 November, Wemyss had a final meeting with Prime Minister David Lloyd George before beginning the journey to Paris. Travelling overnight, he reached the French capital during the early hours of the morning on 7 November.

While Wemyss was travelling to Paris, Marshal Foch was at his headquarters at Senlis, 30 miles north of Paris. It was here during that morning that Foch received confirmation by wireless from Field Marshal Hindenburg that the German delegation would be crossing into the French lines to discuss the Armistice. Hindenburg requested the location where they were to cross the line. Foch recalled:

> On the morning of the 7th, I was informed that the German plenipotentiaries would leave Spa at noon and arrive before the

French lines between 4 and 5 o'clock in the afternoon. Measures were taken, both by French and German commanders, to stop the firing on each side during the passage of the enemy delegation.[4]

Roy Howard, an American journalist and President of the United Press Association, was travelling overnight from Paris to Brest on the Atlantic Coast by train. Before he boarded the train he was aware of Prince Max's communication announcing the German peace initiative and had wrongly assumed that a truce would take place within hours after the message was issued. On arriving at Brest at 09.00 hours on 7 November, he heard the inaccurate rumours amongst intelligence personnel that an Armistice had been discussed overnight and was implemented. Howard made various attempts to verify that an Armistice had been agreed, but the news was only a rumour. Howard went to lunch with General George Harrison, who was unable to confirm the news, but was certain that it was true. Later that afternoon, Howard visited Admiral Henry Wilson, commander of US Naval forces based in France. Wilson had received an incorrect report from Paris, sourced from the French Deuxième Bureau (Intelligence), confirming that the war had ended, which resulted in Howard believing that he had a scoop and cabled the news to New York at 16.20 hours:

UNIPRESS NEW YORK PARIS URGENT – ARMISTICE ALLIES SIGNED ELEVEN SMORNING [sic this morning] – HOSTILITIES CEASED TWO SAFTERNOON [sic this afternoon] – SEDAN TAKEN SMORNING [sic this morning] BY AMERICANS.

Within two hours of issuing the communiqué Howard realised that the message was premature and that an Armistice had not been signed, and neither had Sedan been captured by American troops. It was too late, because the news reached the New York office of United Press at 11.56 hours, Eastern Standard Time and within an hour it was broadcast in newspapers. The news rapidly spread across the continents of North America and within twenty-four hours, across the world. People in New York and Washington left their work and celebrated the news. Howard sent a second cable confirming that the first message was incorrect, but he could not stop it.

The news spread across the globe including Australia, which woke up to be told that the war was over. *The Sydney Morning Herald* reported:

Not for hours did it seem to dawn upon the crowd that there was somehow a jarring note. The Sydney populace was 'celebrating' with all heart and soul – but where were the official proceedings, the speeches, the march of sailors and soldiers, the bands? The crowds wedged themselves in Martin Place and Moore Street in a dense mass, swaying expectantly before the model destroyer and the recruiting stand, but neither civic nor official leaders appeared.

A most awkward and embarrassing position had developed. The signing of the Armistice had not been officially confirmed, and the authorities could not act on the unofficial Press message received from Paris, via America. As the day wore on it became apparent from the Press dispatches that the first message, reporting the cessation of hostilities and sending at least America and Australia into a delirium of joy, was completely inaccurate. The Germans had not yet agreed to the terms of the Armistice.

But who was to tell the joy-maddened crowds, surging over the city, convinced that the war was won and over? The people simply would not believe that the basis of their gladness was the error of a journalist in Europe. The news was told to a little group in Martin Place. 'Oh, well, if it isn't true it soon will be. Germany can't last. We're not going to stop now,' said the joyful ones.[5]

In New York, soldiers from the 71st New York Infantry, who heard the inaccurate news that an Armistice had been signed, tried to find their band in order to celebrate.

There was never a chance that the regiment would not celebrate Armistice Day in a fitting manner. When the false news of the Armistice was given out by the afternoon papers on 7 November, efforts were at once made to get in touch with the bandmaster, but it was found impossible to locate him until an hour when the falsity of the report had been demonstrated.[6]

The authorities found it difficult to control the civil population once the false Armistice had been declared. Problems were encountered by New York policeman to control the civil gatherings in the city.

The wild celebration of the people in the city on receipt of this false report, lasting from early afternoon until midnight, had shown that an element of danger existed in such unrestrained gathering of people and that when the Armistice should be truthfully announced gatherings of a most riotous nature might occur that would be beyond the control of the police.

One of the New York papers on 8 November stated:

> The city was in the hands of a mob in a way which had never been seen before – more completely than in the days of the draft riots.[7]

141

Meanwhile in Europe, on arriving in Paris, Wemyss continued his journey to Marshal Foch's headquarters at Senlis. Foch's HQ would have been the ideal location to meet the German delegation, but there were good reasons not to do so. Firstly, Senlis was close to Paris and could easily be reached by journalists and sightseers. Secondly, it would have been insensitive to discuss the Armistice at Senlis, because in 1914 the German Army executed the local mayor and several villagers who were held as hostages. It was therefore decided to meet the German delegation in a railway siding that was 56 miles north-east of Paris. Marshal Foch, Admiral Wemyss and the Allied delegation boarded a train at Senlis on 7 November that would take them to Compiègne. Wemyss wrote on that day:

> Arrived in Paris 7 a.m. and was met at Station by Brig-General Grant of General Du Cane's Staff. He is to accompany me to French G.H.Q. when the time arrives – probably today … In the afternoon we motored out to Senlis with Grant and called on Marshal Foch and then tea with Du Cane and I joined the Marshal's train at 5 p.m …We immediately steamed away and the train was taken into a siding in the Forest of Compiègne. The train containing the German delegates is expected during the night and will stand in a siding close to ours.
>
> The Frenchmen are all naturally very elated but dignified and calm, the Marshal quiet and confident. He told me he proposed to do as little talking as possible, to let the Germans do it all and then hand them the terms of the Armistice. If they accept the principles he may discuss details.[8]

Foch recalled the journey to Compiègne in his memoirs:

> Accompanied by General Weygand, three officers of my staff [Major Riedlinger, Captain de Mierry, Interpreter Laperche] and the British naval delegation headed by Admiral Wemyss, First Sea Lord of the Admiralty, I left Senlis at 5 o'clock in the afternoon and went by special train to the place chosen for meeting the German plenipotentiaries – a spot in the Compiègne Forest, north and near the station of Rethondes. My train was there run on to a siding built for the railroad artillery.[9]

The location designated for the rendezvous was secluded and in a clearing made specifically for heavy artillery. The area was secured and surrounded by sentries. It was isolated except for a telephone line that enabled Foch to communicate with his HQ in the field and the French Government in Paris. Foch's carriage bearing the number 2419D was converted into an office. Here they would be able to present the Armistice terms in a discreet, isolated location where there would be a calmness, ensuring that the defeated German delegation would be received with dignity and respect.

The German delegates were taken 90 miles from Spa to the German frontline at La Capelle in Belgium. They travelled in a convoy of five cars that were decorated with the Imperial Eagle. Their journey was hindered by the poor state of the roads behind the German frontline. Soon after they left the German Headquarters, the car carrying Erzberger careered off the road on a bend into a house on the suburbs of Spa. The car behind crashed into them. These two cars were badly damaged to the extent that it was necessary for the German Armistice Commission to continue their journey in the three remaining cars in the convoy. When they reached Haudroy they were invited to leave these cars and transfer into French cars that would take them across the frontline. Bugler Georges Labroche, 1st Coy, 19th Battalion Chasseur à Pieds, saw the procession of cars appear from out of the darkness:

> It rained more than we wanted when suddenly I hear of the sound of the bugle ringing the ceasefire … I saw the Krauts automobiles, all headlights, a large white flag in front.[10]

The French 171st Régiment d'Infantrie's war diary recorded the following on 7th November 1918:

> At 8.10 pm the mission of the German negotiators is seen on the road coming from Haudroy; this part of the road is held by the 3rd Company, 1st Platoon is spread on both sides by the sunken lane which passes by the Hill 232. Five cars move forward at top speed, lights are lit, a white flag is on the first car, one German trumpet plays appeals. Captain L'Huillier Co. of 1st Battalion advances and makes a sign in the convoy to stop. Lieut. De Jacobi gets out of the car and appearing says: Here is the Mission of negotiators; I am going to warn the General. General Von Winterfeld, head of mission of negotiators comes down from the second car. Having appeared, he says: 'My Commander, I apologize for being late the bad roads are the cause. May I make the introductions?' 'No my General,' answers Captain L'Huillier. 'I have no authority to receive you officially please go back to your car follow me I am going to lead you to the commanding officer of the outpost.'

Captain L'Huiller takes place in the 1st car, the Corporal Bugler Sellier of the 1st Battalion rises on the stepladder of the 1st car and the procession restarts towards La Capelle. On the road the bugler sounds the tune of the Regiment and the 'Stand To'. At the crossroad of La Capelle (crossing of the main road N°2 and the road coming from Buironfosse) the mission stops a second time, it is welcomed by the commanding officer of the outposts (Commandant Ducorny) and Lieut. Colonel Marquet of the 171st RI who, riding in a car of the army, accompanies the negotiators to the Pâques House, where they are received by Major Bourbon Busset from Headquarters of 1st Army. Shortly after two of the cars get across with Lieut. Von Jacobi. To allow the movement of the negotiators the order of cease fire had been given at first till midnight then until November 8th – 6 o'clock.[11]

They resumed their journey from La Capelle at 22.00 hours. The journey was further complicated by muddy roads that were ridden with potholes. As they drove through derelict villages, the headlights revealed the devastation that the war had caused. A member of the German Armistice Commission provided details of the journey by car and of the reception that they received from French officers:

> The motor drive with the French officers lasted ten hours, and it appeared to me that the drive was intentionally prolonged in order to carry us across devastated provinces and to prepare us for the hardest conditions which the feelings of hatred and revenge might demand. One of the Frenchman silently pointed out to us a heap of ruins, saying, 'Voila St Quentin'.[12]

They were taken to a ruined church at Homblièrees, close to St Quentin, where they were met by General Debeney, Commander of the First French Army. They ate a meal there, before continuing their journey to Tergnier.

Arriving at Tergnier at 03.00 hours on 8 November, the German delegation saw a glimpse of the devastation that had befallen the town, which was lit up by torches close to the station. Here they boarded a train that would take them to the Forest of Compiègne. The German delegation travelled in a saloon car that was once used by Napoleon III, but they were not told of their destination. The carriage windows had been screened. Foch recalled:

> The German delegation, having been constantly halted by the blocked roads behind the German front, reached the French lines only at 9 p.m., and arrived at their destination twelve hours late. It

was not until seven in the morning of November 8th that the train bringing them drew up near mine.[13]

The Allied and German trains were lying on sidings that were specially constructed for heavy railway artillery at Rethondes, which was 4 miles from Compiègne. Once the German delegation arrived the screens were removed from the carriage windows and they were informed that they were at the Forest of Compiègne. The ground was muddy and a duckboard connected the two carriages. A member of the German Armistice Commission recalled:

> In the evening a train was ready for us with blinds down, and when we arose next morning the train had stopped in the middle of a forest. We now know it was the Forest of Compiègne. It was perhaps a measure of precaution that we were not taken to some town. We were in a forest where there were no houses or tents, and we were obviously completely surrounded by troops. On the lines were two trains – one occupied by Marshal Foch and his staff, the other by us. In these two trains we lived, worked and negotiated for three days. Our train had a sleeping saloon and a dining car and was comfortably furnished. We had everything in abundance. The officer in charge of our train ordered everything we asked for, and there was nothing to find fault with. The great enmity and hatred that apparently prevailed against us was, however, shown in the negotiations and by the terms imposed upon us.[14]

Wemyss wrote of Foch's anxious state as they waited for the German delegation to arrive:

> The train containing the Germans arrived at 7 a.m. I saw the Marshal early and found him rather nervous, but dignified. A message was sent over to them to say that we would receive them at 9 a.m. The plenipotentiaries are Erzberger, Count von Oberndorff, General von Winterfield and Captain Vanselow. The mission walked over at 9 a.m. and were shown into the saloon by General Weygand. The Marshal and I were next door and came in when they were all present. Erzberger presented his people and the Marshal ours.[15]

The German delegation were ushered into the Allied railway carriage. The Allied representatives standing on the other side of the negotiating table were led by Marshal Foch and included Admiral Wemyss, General Maxime Weygand, Rear-Admiral George Hope and Captain Jack

145

Mariott R.N. Two interpreters were in attendance, Commander Bagot and Interpreter-Officer Captain Laperche. A member of the German delegation reported:

> Those of us who were soldiers wore the military uniform and the Iron Cross. Our presentation to the dozen French officers with whom we had to negotiate was made in a cool manner.[16]

Foch recalled:

> When I saw them at the other side of the table, I said to myself: 'There is the German Empire.' I thought: 'we shall be polite, but we must show them who we are.'[17]

Wemyss wrote:

> The Marshal then formally asked them what they had come for and had they their credentials. These they handed to the Marshal and he and I left the saloon to examine them. They were quite in order, were signed by Prince Max of Baden but gave no power to sign any Armistice.[18]

The contents of the letter signed by Prince Max of Baden, signed on 6 November, read:

> FULL POWER
> The undersigned Chancellor of the German Empire, Max Prince of Baden, hereby gives full power:
> To the Imperial Secretary of State, Matthias Erzberger, (as President of the Delegation),
> To Imperial Envoy Extraordinary and Minister Plenipotentiary, Count Alfred Oberndorff, and
> To Major-General Detlev von Winterfeldt, Royal Prussian Army, to conduct in the name of the German Government with the plenipotentiaries of the Powers allied against Germany, negotiations for an armistice and to conclude an agreement to that effect, provided the same be approved by the German government.[19]

Foch recalled his conversation with Erzberger:

> Then I asked them:
> 'What do you want?'

'We wish to know your proposals?'

'I have no proposals to make.'

'We should like to know on what conditions an armistice would be granted?'

'I have no conditions to give you.'

Erzberger wished to read me a paper – President Wilson's note – but I stopped him.

'Do you wish to ask for an armistice? If so, say so.'

'We ask for an armistice.'

'Good. We will read you the conditions drawn up by the Allied Governments.'[20]

Wemyss continued his account of their initial meeting with the German envoys by noting that 'General Weygand read out the terms of the Armistice and they were translated by interpreters – British and French'.[21] A member of the German delegation, meanwhile, recalled:

Marshal Foch, whom we only saw twice – at the beginning and at the end of the conference – is a stern plain man. He did not speak a single word to us in that polite tone which in former times distinguished the most chivalrous nation. He received us with the words, 'what do you desire Monsieurs?' and asked us to take a seat in the big car filled with map-covered tables. As it had been decided that everyone was to speak in his own language, and everything had to be interpreted, the reading of the terms lasted two hours. It is incorrect to say that Marshal Foch told us there could be no question of negotiations but only the imposition of conditions. Whatever coldness Marshal Foch may have shown, he was never ill-mannered or rough.[22]

Wemyss recalled that Winterfeldt, reading from a prepared statement, appealed for an immediate cessation to hostilities to prevent further loss of life:

General Winterfeldt, reading from a scrap of paper, then asked on behalf of the German High Command that hostilities might cease immediately. He said that such an action might save many lives.[23]

The content of the statement read by General von Winterfeldt was as follows:

The armistice terms which have just been brought to our knowledge require careful examination by us. As it is our intention to come to

147

a decision, this examination will be made as promptly as possible. Nevertheless, it will require a certain amount of time, especially as it will be necessary to consult our Government and the military Supreme Command.

During this time the struggle between our Armies will continue and it will result, both among soldiers and civilians, in numerous victims who will die in vain at the last minute, and who might be preserved to their families.

Therefore, the German Government and the German Supreme Command have the honour to revert the proposal made by them in their wireless message of the day before yesterday, viz: that Marshal Foch be kind enough to consent to an immediate suspension of hostilities on the entire front, to begin today at a certain fixed hour, the very simple details of which could be decided upon without loss of time.[24]

Foch was insistent that no ceasefire would not take place until the German delegation, with sanction from the German Government, had signed the Armistice. Besides, he was instructed by the governments who determined the terms of the Armistice that only a ceasefire would take place once the conditions were accepted by Germany. Foch responded as follows:

I am the Commander-in-Chief of the Allied Armies and representative of the Allied Governments. These Governments have decided upon their terms. Hostilities cannot cease before the signing of the Armistice. I am likewise desirous of reaching a conclusion and therefore I shall help you as far as possible toward this end. But hostilities cannot cease before the signing of the Armistice.[25]

The German delegation realised the consequences of the Armistice upon Germany and Erzberger tried to negotiate concessions. Foch wrote:

They were weary, tired out, like hunted animals ... Erzberger made me a long speech in order to secure concessions, explaining that revolution had broken out at home, that their soldiers would no longer obey orders, that the country was in a state of famine, that all authority had disappeared. I stopped him.

'You are suffering from a loser's malady, not a conqueror's. I am not afraid of it. I refuse everything.'[26]

Wemyss recollected:

> Foch replied that cessation of hostilities would only take place after the Armistice had been signed. Germans then formally asked for a copy of the terms, which were given them, and a short discussion took place as to the manner of transmitting them to Berlin. They have come without cyphers.[27]

A member of the German delegation recalled:

> We then withdrew to our train. As we had been sent out by the old Government, and had no instructions whatever to sign everything unconditionally, we divided under the direction of Herr Erzberger the various matters under the headings of military, diplomatic and naval affairs, and then negotiated separately with the members of the enemy commissions, which were composed solely of officers. All these officers showed the same cool correctness as Marshal Foch which was not once tempered by a friendly word, with the exception perhaps, of the Chief of Marshal Foch's Staff, who showed a little more politeness. The English admiral throughout adopted the same manner as the French. In reality there was nothing to negotiate. We only pointed out the impossibility of some of the conditions.[28]

The German delegates requested permission to send a message to the German Government by wireless and they were allowed to send coded messages, which were sent from the Eiffel Tower in Paris. The following message was sent to the German Chancellor in Berlin:

> *German Armistice Plenipotentiaries to the Imperial Chancellor and to the German Military and Naval High Commands:*
> The Plenipotentiaries received the armistice conditions on Friday morning at Allied General Headquarters; also the ultimatum that they be accepted or refused within seventy-two hours, expiring on Monday morning at 11 o'clock (French time).
> The German proposal for an immediate agreement to suspend hostilities provisionally was rejected by Marshal Foch.
> A German courier bearing the text of the armistice conditions has been sent to Spa, there being no other practical mode of communication. Please acknowledge receipt and send back the courier as soon as possible with your final instructions.
> It is not necessary for the time being to send new delegates.[29]

This message was wired to Berlin at 11.30 hours during that morning and Captain von Helldorf would act as courier to deliver the content of the Armistice terms to German General Headquarters at Spa.

Wemyss confirmed the conclusion of the meeting and the demeanour of the German delegates:

> An extra 24 hours was asked for, but this was refused. The time has been calculated and is sufficient … The meeting then was closed and the answer has to be given by 11 a.m. on Monday.
>
> All the Germans are very much distressed – naturally so. Erzberger showing most nervousness – but Winterfield and Vaneslow looked the most distressed. The General in his little speech asking for cessation of hostilities used the word 'déroute' in connection with the German Armies. The naval and military terms did not seem to affect them so much as the civil and financial ones. My impression is that they must and will sign. Bourbon-Busset [Colonel Comte de Bourbon-Busset, was a friend of Wemyss], who was in charge of them, said he thought they were all very down.[30]

Further discussions continued during the afternoon between the German and British naval officers and between Weygand and Winterfeld. The Germans were concerned of the threat from Bolshevism and persisted to demand the requirement to retain machine-guns in order to counter this threat.

As discussions continued between Allied and German delegates at Compiègne, Captain von Helldorf was traveling in a convoy of two cars towards the frontline and then on to Spa. One car was German and another was French, which would bring back the French party after it had escorted the German party across the frontline. Bugler Georges Labroche, 1st Company 19th Battalion Chasseur à Pieds, accompanied Captain von Helldorf on his journey. He later recalled:

> At about 1 p.m. in Fourmies Quartermaster Sergeant scolded me because he looked for me for exactly a quarter of an hour. My captain ordered me to leave my kitbag and my rifle and to take a place in the first car that was driven by a German. The driver was on my right; behind me, Captain von Helldorf and on his right, the captain of the General Staff. I seize the white flag of the negotiators and my bugle. For the first time in my life, I am riding in a luxury car.[31]

Captain von Helldorf's journey to the German lines was difficult and at one point the car transporting him came under hostile fire. The

French had to transmit the following wire to German General Headquarters:

> The German Captain von Helldorf, whose passage has been announced by General von Winterfeld, is waiting for the German fire to stop in order to return to the German lines by La Capelle-Fourmies road. The French fire has ceased on this road since 6 p.m..[32]

Bugler Georges Labroche recalled the moment when they eventually crossed the frontline:

> At the exit of Fourmies, while I played calls and while we moved forward slowly, a German soldier ran to meet us. He was one named Treuillaud of Château-Salins, native consequently of the annexed Lorraine, which came to warn us that bridges were going to explode. We kept him eight days with the company, dressed in 'Chasseur' and returned him directly to his home, well before us, the lucky man!
>
> We exceeded our first lines, but we do not know how we are to those of the Germans. The country is conducive to ambushes, hedges are numerous. As before with the German driver, I'm in the front row in case things get rough. My 'licks' redouble … In short, we are moving more and more on the road Trélon–Macon (Belgium). We pass a junction to 1500 meters south of Wallers-Trélon, having on our right a signpost to the Belgian border. Within 500 meters hundred meters later, we stop. The road is cut by a trench. We inspect the scene – time to find our way – when a German cyclist appears at the top of a ridge and descends towards us.
>
> Following the information given by this man, Captain von Helldorf decides to turn back. They pass in front of a ridge and take the road which leads to Wallers-Trélon, always followed by the second car. Halfway into this village, a very young German officer stops the negotiators, under the threat of a revolver, whereas his men open fire with a machine gun at French planes which fly over the place. Captain Von Helldorf orders cease-fire and both cars continue along the road until Wallers-Trélon where there is a whole German battalion.
>
> It is 2.20 pm. An Uhlan advances and greets. Both captains (French and German) join a group from seven to eight Germans.
>
> Two hundred boches come out of a barn, surround the car and quite merry speak to me. I hear 'Krieg fertig, Krieg fertig'. I do not know what that means. I answer to them by the unique word of German that I know: 'Ja, ja'. We learnt later that this was translated

to 'Finished war'. If that had been something else, it had been the same tobacco. What pleased me more was that where we were stopped, a woman came to offer me a cup of very hot coffee and a bunch of dahlias with three-colours and that, in front of every Fritz. And they gave me cigars, I had plenty of it in my cartridge belts.[33]

Captain von Helldorf continued his journey with details of the Armistice from Wallers-Trélon to Spa. The French party now had to return to the French lines without being shot by their own soldiers. Bugler Georges Labroche recalled:

Maybe one hour or two later, we took back the road to return with a car of the 166th Infantry Division. That fitted better, but needed to call all the same. That would have been too stupid to get bullets from our home. We returned into our lines and it is there that staff officer [Captain Marcel Le Lay] told me 'My little Chasseur, are you satisfied? You can boast to be the only one of the French Army to have this honor!' We were stopped by a patrol of the 2nd Chasseurs d'Afrique and the officers talked between them and from there, we return on to Trélon and to Ohain.[34]

Reports appeared in newspapers across Europe that the German delegation had crossed the frontline at La Capelle to receive Armistice conditions. Captain Herbert Sulzbach was pleased that the war would end, but he was hoping for a dignified peace, for he wrote in his diary on 8 November:

It's a splendid thought that it's all going to end some time, but we do hope for one thing: peace without humiliation![35]

The world waited for the German response that weekend. During the evening of 9 November, David Lloyd George addressed the Lord Mayor's banquet at the Guildhall, in the City of London, where he spoke of the implications if Germany did not accept the terms of the Armistice:

The issue for which the Allies have been fighting is settled. The greatest judgement in the history of the world has been given. I have just spent a week at Versailles, whilst emperors, kings and crowns were falling like withered leaves before the gale.
    What will Germany now do? Will she accept our terms or will she fight on? She has her choice today. She has no choice tomorrow.

Ruin is tearing at her vitals. She can avert it only by immediate surrender.

If she fights on her cities and towns will be devastated. That is her choice. She has no other. I was one of the believers of the 'knock-out blow'. The recklessness that placed the world in such awful agony must expect a stern reckoning.[36]

The railway siding in the Forest of Compiègne would be the home for the Allied and German delegates during that weekend. Wemyss described their accommodation:

The train is very comfortable. I have quite a good cabin, the size of two wagon-lits thrown into one. We have a whole wagon to ourselves. There is an office for the Staff, a dining-room and the Marshal's own bedroom and sitting-room. Baths are apparently not thought of!

It is a curious scene in the middle of the forest – raining and leaves falling, and yet there is nothing sad – at any rate for us. The two trains 200 yards off each other. Stray sentries in blue-grey can be seen amongst the trees. Nothing else in sight. We are in telephonic communications with Paris and the world.[37]

Foch left his carriage only one time during the morning of Sunday, 10 November, in order to attend mass at a nearby church. The Allied delegates only assembled together at dinner in the restaurant carriage of their train. At one dinner Foch generously shared a vintage bottle of Louis XVI 1778 brandy. During that weekend the Allied delegates speculated whether the Germans would sign the Armistice and upon the current state of the German Army and Navy. Wemyss wrote on 8 November:

Apparently the German Army is getting demoralised. Meanwhile, papers have arrived and the whole story of the Naval mutiny is out. How will it affect the Naval terms? It will be difficult for them to comply.

The Marshal told me, were the Armistice not signed, he would have the capitulation of the whole lot in three weeks. He also said that yesterday a whole regiment of Boches had laid down their arms and came in crying that now there was peace. Bourbon-Basset told me that the Germans were throwing away their arms and today a telegram came to say that they are actually leaving their field kitchens behind.[38]

153

Lieutenant-General Sir Henry Rawlinson wrote on 8 November:

> At 1 a.m. today the German delegates arrived at Debeney's headquarters. They were tired, hungry and humble. They were sent on at once by special train from Tergnier to Foch's headquarters at Senlis [Rawlinson was incorrect, because the meeting took place in a railway siding in the Forest of Compiègne], where at 11 a.m. he handed them the terms of the armistice. I hear from Du Cane this morning that they have found it necessary to refer the terms to the Government at Berlin. They have been given a time limit of seventy-two hours, which will expire at 11 a.m. on Monday. In view of the mutiny of the fleet at Kiel. I do not see how they can possibly do otherwise than accept the Armistice terms. We have again made good progress today on the whole army front against the hostile rear-guards, and have taken Avesnes. No serious opposition.[39]

On 9 November, as the German delegates awaited a response from Berlin, Foch wanted to demonstrate the Allies' determination to overwhelm all German resistance and issued the following message to encourage all Allied commanders to continue with their offensives:

> The enemy, disorganised by our repeated attacks, is giving way all along the front. It is urgent to hasten and intensify our efforts. I appeal to the energy and the initiative of Commanders-in-chief and of their Armies to make the result achieved decisive.[40]

While waiting for the German response to the Armistice, Wemyss visited Soissons on 9 November. As an admiral in the Royal Navy he would not have been exposed to the devastation and suffering that was caused on the Western Front.

> We motored to Soissons. Truly a dreadful sight – not one single house is habitable. The Cathedral is literally torn in two. Going through the streets gave one the impression of visiting Pompeii. We were shown some of the outlying houses which with great ingenuity and without any change in their external appearance had been made into regular fortresses.[41]

Also on 9 November, the German submarine *U-50*, commanded by Kapitänleutnant Heinrich Kukat, was returning to Kiel from Turkey via the Strait of Gibraltar when it encountered the British pre-Dreadnought battleship HMS *Britannia* off Cape Trafalgar. The latter was proceeding along the western approach to Gibraltar. Kukat fired three torpedoes; one missed, the other two successfully hit their target. *Britannia* returned fire at the submarine, which was on the surface, and forced it to submerge. As *Britannia* slowly sank, its destroyer escorts came alongside and evacuated thirty-nine officers and 673 men. It would take 3½ hours to sink. Two officers and forty-five ratings perished with her, many of whom were buried in Gibraltar Cemetery alongside sailors who died during the Battle of Trafalgar in 1805.

The last Royal Navy vessel to be torpedoed and sunk was the minesweeper HMS *Ascot*, together with her entire crew, close to Farne Island on 10 November. The Secretary of the Admiralty reported:

> His Majesties paddle minesweeper *Ascot* was torpedoed and sunk with all hands on the 10th inst. by a German submarine off the north-east coast of England. Five officers, including two mercantile Marine officers, and 47 men, including three mercantile marine ratings, lost their lives.[42]

Chapter 12

Kaiser Wilhelm Abdicates

Although the Allies were not seeking the abdication of Kaiser Wilhelm II as a condition for Armistice, the issue was discussed openly during October 1918 within Germany. The German Government was aware that there would be no peace so long as the Kaiser remained as ruler of Germany. It was its view that if Germany could convince the world that Germany had changed as a nation, then its enemies might treat it more leniently. The German Minister of the Interior, Wilhelm Drews, commented at a Cabinet meeting on 31 October:

> It cannot be denied that the movement for His Majesty's abdication is gaining daily strength among a large section of the people – not only among the workers, but also in the middle classes. The Kaiser and the Crown Prince are regarded as standing in the way of peace.[1]

On 7 November in Berlin a delegation of the Social Democratic Party comprising of Philipp Scheidemann, Secretary of State and Friedrich Ebert, presented an ultimatum to Prince Max. 'The Kaiser must abdicate at once or we shall have the revolution.'[2]

The pressure was mounting upon Prince Max, who felt his brief tenure as Chancellor beginning to collapse. He was unable to convince the Social Democrats to withdraw their ultimatum, and certainly was not prepared to advise the Kaiser to abdicate. He was therefore left impotent to perform the role of Chancellor and in a letter to the Kaiser he explained his predicament:

> In these circumstances it is impossible to preserve the unity of the present Government any longer ... I therefore beg Your Majesty in

the spirit of the deepest reverence most graciously to relieve me of my office as Imperial Chancellor.[3]

As Prince Max's letter of resignation was dispatched to the Kaiser, events were spiralling out of control as Germany continued to descend into a state of turmoil and rebellion. There was serious concern that Bolshevism would prevail in Germany unless the Kaiser abdicated and that the Bolsheviks could potentially become the dominant force in the revolution with the potential to usurp the Kaiser and undermine the Social Democratic Government. Prince Max received the following report on 8 November:

> The spread of the revolt through the length and breadth of the country is no longer to be avoided … It is owing to the success of the revolutionary movements at Hamburg and Kiel that the danger of infection is so overwhelming as it is. We must be prepared for civil war. The question of today is: Who is going to win it?
>
> There can be no doubt that Bolshevism will for the moment get the upper hand all over the country, unless indeed the popular Government is able to dispose of the necessary loyal troops. And that is unthinkable until the question of the Kaiser has been dealt with. The mass suggestion: 'The Kaiser is to blame!' provides a point of contact between the insurgents and the troops who are expected to put them down.
>
> We shall see wholesale desertions, even on part of troops who have proved their loyalty at the front.
>
> The Majority Socialists have acted rashly in issuing their ultimatum; but they really are not in a position to remain any longer in Government unless the question of the Kaiser is settled. Should the Kaiser remain, the Majority Socialists are today bound to join the revolutionary movement, if they are not to let the Independents and the Spartacus Group have it their own way with the masses. On the other hand, when the question of the Kaiser is once solved we can be quite sure that the Majority Socialist will put their whole organisation and propaganda resources at our service for the fight against Bolshevism.[4]

The Kaiser had not accepted Prince Max's request to resign as Chancellor. During the afternoon of 8 November, Prince Max spoke candidly to the Kaiser on the telephone to appeal for him to abdicate. He spoke not as Chancellor, but as a relative:

157

> Your abdication has become necessary to save Germany from civil war and to fulfil your mission as the Peacemaking Emperor to the end. The blood would be laid upon your head. The great majority of the people believes you to be responsible for the present situation. The belief is false, but it is held. If civil war and worse can be prevented through your abdication, your name will be blessed by future generations.[5]

The German Government had lost control completely. Prince Max continued his telephone conversation with the Kaiser, reporting the scale of the revolution as the Red Flag was now flying from the palace at Brunswick, the Workers' and Soldiers' Councils were in control of Cologne; and a republic had been proclaimed in Munich. They could no longer depend upon the German Army to regain control of the situation, because many of its soldiers had joined the revolution. He ended the conversation by reiterating that:

> Unless the abdication takes place today I can do no more; nor can the German Princes shield the Kaiser any more. Such is the terrible situation in which I am bound to speak out and not gloss over things … I speak to you today as your relative and as a German Prince. This voluntary sacrifice is necessary to save your good name before the bar of history.[6]

Deluded by the notion that as head of the German Army he could restore order and regain control of the country, the Kaiser remained resolute and was not going to abdicate. Feeling frustrated by his failure to persuade the Kaiser to see sense and do the right thing and abdicate, Prince Max repeated his request to be allowed to resign as Chancellor, but the Kaiser refused with the response 'You sent out the armistice offer, you will have to put your name to the conditions!'[7]

The situation worsened by the following day as Prince Max woke up to the news that Berlin was besieged and thousands of workers were massing on the streets. Only three Jäger battalions were defending the city and civil war could not be averted unless the Kaiser abdicated.

During the afternoon of 9 November German Socialists initiated a general strike and took control of Berlin. A German correspondent reported:

> The German Socialist Revolution may be said to be complete. In a few hours on Saturday the movement captured Berlin completely, and the events in the capital were of such an extraordinary nature

that the news of the abdication of the Kaiser was relegated to second place. In seven hours, to be exact, the capital of Germany capitulated to the Revolutionaries – certainly the most astounding feature of an extraordinary revolution.

This amazing event took place almost without bloodshed, the casualties being reported as four killed and two wounded. The taking possession of Berlin began at nine o'clock in the morning. At that hour a general strike started, and shortly afterwards thousands of soldiers carrying red flags, and accompanied by armed motor-cars, began to pour into the centre of the city from the outskirts. With them came workers from the outlying factories. A little later trains began to arrive, bring 3,000 sailors from Kiel. They were received in the streets with the utmost enthusiasm, and acting under the orders of the newly formed Council of Workers and Soldiers, they broke up into detachments and occupied many important parts of the city, such as bridges, public buildings, street corners, & co.

The streets in the meantime presented an extraordinary appearance. Almost as by magic, Red Flags appeared everywhere, and officers in the streets and barracks stripped off their cockades and epaulettes – in very few cases was compulsion necessary – and threw them away. Hundreds of Iron Crosses could be picked up in the streets. Socialist deputies went to the various barracks and addressed the soldiers, and in every case regiments signified their adhesion to the revolution. Enthusiastic scenes of fraternisation between soldiers, sailors, and workers followed, and the people everywhere gave vent to their joy by loud shouts of 'Long live the Republic!'

Towards midday a strong mixed force of soldiers and sailors marched along the Wilhelmstrasse and took possession, one after the other, of the Government buildings in the world-famous thoroughfare.

In front of the Reichstag a great demonstration was held. It was addressed by Herr Scheidemann, who had a tremendous reception. 'The Kaiser has abdicated,' he shouted 'the dynasty has fallen. It is a great and honourable victory for the German people.' ...

Events created enormous interest among the crowds. The first was the hoisting of the Red Flag over the Kaiser's Palace. Thunderous cheers came from the people as it was run up. Cheers were renewed when the happy idea was carried out displaying the Red Flag at the window of a balcony of the Palace through which the Kaiser came to address the crowd at the beginning of the war in August, 1914.[8]

At 14.00 hours on 9 November, Prince Max finally received confirmation that, after a thirty-year reign, Kaiser Wilhelm would abdicate as King of Germany. The following message, signed by the Kaiser, was communicated from German Headquarters in Spa:

1. His Majesty assents to the German Government's empowering the Armistice Commission now with the enemy, to conclude an Agreement immediately, even before the Armistice Conditions have become known here.
2. To avoid bloodshed His Majesty is ready to abdicate as German Kaiser, but not as King of Prussia. His Majesty also desires to remain King of Prussia in order to prevent the army becoming leaderless and breaking up, in consequence of the resignation of the majority of officers which would be simultaneous with such abdication.
3. His Majesty does not desire a civil war.
4. His Majesty, on abdication as German Kaiser, will command Field Marshal von Hindenburg to take over the Supreme Command of the German army, and will in August Person remain with the Prussian troops. Further decisions would be reserved for the Imperial Administrator.
5. The Army Commanders and the Supreme Command are of the opinion that the abdication of the German Kaiser and Supreme War Lord at this moment will provoke the gravest convulsions in the Army, and they can therefore no longer assume responsibility for the Army holding together.[9]

On that same day, Prince Max of Baden resigned as Chancellor and appointed Friedrich Ebert, leader of the Social Democrats, as his successor. Prince Max issued the following decree in Berlin:

The Kaiser and King has decided to renounce the throne. The Imperial Chancellor will remain in office until the questions connected with the abdication of the Kaiser, the renouncing by the Crown Prince of the throne of the German Empire and of Prussia, and the setting up of regency has been settled.

For the regency he intends to appoint Deputy Ebert as Imperial Chancellor and he proposes that a Bill shall be brought in for the establishment of a law providing for the immediate promulgation of general suffrage and for a Constituent German National Assembly, which will settle finally the future form of Government of the

German nation and of those peoples which may be desirous of coming within the Empire.[10]

In a final message Prince Max issued the following appeal to the German people:

Already in these difficult days the heart of many amongst you, my fellow countrymen, who outside the frontier of the German frontier are surrounded by manifestations of malicious joy and hatred, will be heavy. Do not despair of the German people. Our soldiers have fought to the last moment as heroically as any army has ever done. The homeland has shown unprecedented strength in suffering and endurance.

In the fifth year, abandoned by its Allies, the German people could no longer wage war against increasingly superior forces. The victory for which many had hoped has not been granted to us, but the German people has now a still greater victory, because it now has a victory over itself and its belief in the right of might. From this victory we shall draw new strength for the hard time which faces us, and which you can also build.

To those of you who have fought and suffered for the German Fatherland during these four hard years of war, the German Government will not be lacking in gratitude. As far as it lies in the power of the German Government and the German people to mitigate the sufferings of this war and its consequences, their care will be extended to the Germans abroad and at home.[11]

In a letter to his son Wilhelm, Crown Prince of Germany, Kaiser Wilhelm explained his reasons for abdicating the throne:

My Dear Boy,
As the Field-Marshal cannot guarantee my safety here and will not pledge himself for the reliability of the troops, I have decided, after a severe inward struggle, to leave the disorganised army. Berlin is totally lost; it is in the hands of the Socialists, and the two governments have been formed there – one with Ebert as Chancellor and one of the Independents. Till the troops start their march home, I recommend your continuing at your post and keeping the troops together! God willing, I trust we shall meet again. General von Marschall will give you further information.
Your sorely-stricken father,
Wilhelm.[12]

Hindenburg wrote:

> I was at the side of my All Highest War Lord during these fateful hours. He entrusted me with the task of bringing the Army back home. When I left my Emperor in the afternoon of November 9, I was never to see him again! He went to spare his Fatherland further sacrifices and enable it to secure more favourable terms of peace.[13]

The German People's Government was initiated in Berlin and most of the troops garrisoned in the capital aligned themselves with the new regime. Herr Ebert, deputy from the Social Democratic Party, assumed responsibilities of Imperial Chancellor and immediately issued this appeal to all authorities and officials:

> The new Government has taken over the conduct of affairs to save the German people from civil war and famine and to see that their right to self-determination is respected. It can only fulfil this task if all authorities and officials in town and country lend a helping hand.
>
> I know that for many it will be difficult to work with the new men who have taken over the Government of Empire, but I appeal to their love of our people. A break of organisation in this grave hour would hand Germany over to the extreme of anarchy and misery.
>
> Join me therefore in helping the Fatherland by working on fearlessly and tirelessly, each man at his post, until the time comes for him to be relieved.[14]

An article in the *Berlingske Tidende* stated that:

> Events have developed with such amazing rapidity in Berlin during the past twenty-four hours that it is impossible to describe them in chronological order. It is, however, clear that the Social Democrats are firmly fixed in the control of the affairs of government in Berlin, the security of the new regime being assured by the fact that they have the support of the whole of the workers and also of the soldiers stationed in Berlin. The Council of Workmen and Soldiers in Berlin has organised a kind of Red Guard for the maintenance of public order.
>
> A detachment of this guard yesterday took control of Wolff's Telegraph Agency in order to ensure the distribution of an impartial service of news. Other detachments of the Red Guard have taken possession of all the public buildings in Berlin.[15]

Another report noted the following:

> Travellers from Germany report that serious rioting has taken place in Berlin, and these statements are confirmed to some extent by similar reports received through the Amsterdam and Rotterdam banks. It is also declared that soldiers on furlough who had just returned to their garrison have now been sent home again, their passes being marked 'leave to the end of the war', and signed by the Soldiers' Council.[16]

A red banner was hoisted on the Royal Palace and a red flag was hoisted above the Brandenburg Gate in Berlin during the day. It was reported:

> On Saturday night there were frequent fights in the Unter den Linden between Royalist and Revolutionary troops, which continued also during Sunday. On Sunday morning the fighting began afresh at the Victoria Café and Café Bauer, both of which are still occupied by officers and cadets of the Jugendwehr. Royalist officers had also barricaded themselves in the Berlin Library, the arsenal, and the old museum. When towards 9.00 am shots were fired from these buildings the Soldiers' Council troops, who had taken up a position in the Opera House and the Neue Wache (guard house) in front of the Palace, opened a general fusillade, which lasted for forty minutes. Fighting also took place on the Square in front of the Royal Stables. The defenders availed themselves of the subterranean passages leading from the stables to the Palace. They occupied some rooms in the Palace, which is in the hands of the Council's troops, and fired from the street.[17]

Another newspaper reported:

> The streets near the Fredrichstrasse Station were also the scene of lively fighting, officers and cadets firing with machine guns from the roofs of houses in the Fredrichstrasse on patrols of labourers and soldiers, a considerable number being killed and wounded.[18]

The news of the Kaiser's abdication swiftly reached Brussels, where some disenchanted German soldiers took up arms against their officers and proclaimed their support for the new socialist government in Berlin. A correspondent in Brussels reported:

Events were moving with quite disconcerting rapidity, when on November 10 the news arrived in Brussels of the abdication of the German Emperor as a sequel to the revolutionary movement which was spreading in the Empire with incredible rapidity. The effect of this news was to create in the minds of all the feeling of supreme satisfaction demanded by universal conscience that the criminal had been punished.

Although the armistice terms had not yet been signed, it was evident that the Germans were already preparing for the evacuation of Belgium, for numerous transport convoys filled the roads crossing Brussels, and large numbers of soldiers were arriving in the town, alighting at the Gare du Nord, while many others blocked the approaches. Out of curiosity, people went to see them bivouacking, feeling that a settlement was approaching, and already counting on speedy deliverance.

About half-past two that afternoon an extraordinary spectacle met the eyes of the crowd, which was becoming denser and denser at this moment near the station in the centre of town. Starting from the Gare du Nord, a procession of soldiers, nearly all unarmed, was formed, and moved with the Red Flag at its head towards the great boulevards, singing revolutionary songs and raising cheers for Belgium and France, and announced their determination to fight no more. The procession was rapidly swelled by other soldiers who were met on the way. There were also numerous motor cars mounted by sailors and flying the Red Flag, while the cars were covered with the Belgian colours. The crowd, deliriously with enthusiasm and cheering frantically, saluted the colours which had been for so long forbidden, and as if by magic flags appeared everywhere.

An immense throng, delirious with joy, which was unfortunately premature, paraded the streets, and soon witnessed a stupefying spectacle.

The German soldiers decided to declare their adhesion to the German Republic. They resolved to get rid of their officers, and one saw them approach the latter, disarm them, and remove the insignia of their rank without the officers as a rule offering much resistance.

The movement, however, was not universal. Towards the end of the afternoon the soldiers constituted a Council, seized the Komandantur, secured the Governor-General and his staff, and made themselves masters of the situation.

Bands paraded the streets playing the 'Marseillaise.'[19]

The German infrastructure disintegrated rapidly and the descent into complete anarchy was unstoppable. General Ludendorff wrote:

> On 9 November, Germany, lacking any firm guidance, bereft of all will, robbed of her princes, collapsed like a house of cards. All that we had lived for, all that we had bled four long years to maintain, was gone. We no longer had a native land of which we might be proud of. Order in state and society vanished. All authority disappeared. Chaos, Bolshevism, terror, un-German in name and nature, make their entry into the German Fatherland. Soldiers' and Workmen's Councils, an institution prepared in long, systematic underground work, were now established. Men had worked at this who might by service at the Front have secured a successful issue of the war, but who had been dubbed 'indispensable', or had deserted.
>
> The L. of C. [depot] troops, including those stationed in the occupied territories, both in the East and West, who had no doubt also been prepared for the Revolution, lost all discipline and order, and streamed home in wild confusion plundering as they went. On the fighting front in the west, soldiers' Councils, with approval from high quarters, could not be formed fast enough.
>
> The new rulers and their bourgeois camp followers abandoned all resistance, and without a shred of authority signed our unconditional capitulation to a merciless enemy.[20]

During that day reports of the Kaiser's abdication were being received at Compiègne and Wemyss contemplated the impact of this news upon the Armistice:

> The news which reached us during Saturday was tremendous and varied. The abdication of the Emperor – at first was thought that Max of Baden remained as Chancellor. Then a manifesto to the German people and world, saying that a Socialist Democratic Government had been formed and that the functions of Chancellor had been taken over by Ebert. In the meantime a republic seems to have been proclaimed in Bavaria. All seems to be confusion. It would appear that the plenipotentiaries have no longer any powers and one would think that Erzberger at any rate has no longer any standing.[21]

Germany no longer held a strong military or political position to negotiate conditions for an Armistice. The German delegation learnt of the Kaiser's abdication while it was waiting for the government's response in the Forest of Compiègne. An anonymous member of the delegation reported:

> The enemy were thus able silently to present us with the Sunday morning newspapers announcing the abdication of the Kaiser. We observed no smile, no triumph, on their faces, but we saw their hatred. The revolution did not disturb our work. Our credentials signed by the German Government remained valid.[22]

Lieutenant Francis Jordan, 356th Infantry Regiment, US 89th Division, received an indication of German morale from a soldier who surrendered to him in the Meuse–Argonne sector:

> A German came down from where we had been the day before to give himself up. The first sergeant spoke to him in German and talked with him while our first aid man bandaged him. The German had the insides of both thighs chewed up from what appeared to be machine gun fire. Evidently he was among those sentenced to be executed because he had interfered with the determination of his comrades to continue fighting.
>
> After being wounded by machine gun fire directed toward him, he had played dead, and with these rather minor wounds he was able to wait until he could desert. He told us that the war was over, that the Kaiser had left Germany for Holland, and that Germany was giving up.[23]

Captain Herbert Sulzbach was at Beaumont on 9 November, where withdrawing German forces were attacked by Allied aeroplanes dropping bombs upon them. He recalled the depressing news that he had heard from home in his diary:

> News from home is quite clear: there is no way out on the home front either, we are moving towards an inevitable finish, and a very terrible one: part of the Navy is in a state of revolt; a proper mutiny broke out on one ship of the line, the *König*, and her colours were hauled down and replaced with the red flag; the Captain was shot defending the old colours, on which he had taken his oath of allegiance.
>
> Workers' Councils and Soldiers' Councils have been set up.
>
> The Kaiser and the Crown Prince are supposed to have abdicated.

We are sitting at the bottom of the abyss, and our splendid Germany has fallen to pieces! In the evening a mounted messenger arrives, bringing hard facts to confirm the rumour that a genuine revolution had broken out at home.

Mail is stopped from home, and letters home as well.

The Kaiser and the Crown Prince have now in fact abdicated. Germany is a Republic. The new Government has been formed, with Ebert as Chancellor.

You don't know whether you are dreaming or stumbling through reality. The events have tumbled past in such a rush that you can't grasp them all.[24]

On 10 November, the newly appointed Chancellor, Herr Friedrich Ebert, proclaimed the aim of the new Government and appealed for calm and stability:

Fellow citizens, I am planning to form a new Government which will be a People's Government. Its endeavour will necessary be to bring peace as speedily as possible to the German people, and to fortify the freedom they have won. Citizens I earnestly entreat you to maintain quiet and order.[25]

At 02.00 hours on 10 November, Kaiser Wilhelm began his journey to exile in Holland in a procession of motor cars that left Spa for the railway station close to the town. A journalist reported:

The Kaiser reached the Dutch frontier at Eysden from Spa at 7.30 a.m. on Sunday, with nine or ten motor cars with the imperial eagle in front. The first people to see him were Belgian night-staff engineers of a factory, the Maastrichtache Zinkwit, a large Belgian concern, the buildings of which are on either side of Eysden Station. The Kaiser was wearing uniform with a cap, not a helmet … On arrival the Kaiser, who did not look the least distressed, got out and walked up and down the platform smoking a cigarette and chatting with his staff. A few minutes later the imperial train ran into the station from Vise (south of Eysden). It consisted of about nine or ten carriages including restaurant, saloon and sleeping cars, but it contained only servants.[26]

The Queen of the Netherlands and the Dutch Government sanctioned granting Kaiser Wilhelm asylum in Holland and Count Bentinck allowed him to reside on his estate. The Crown Prince also followed his father to Holland on 12 November and there were rumours circulating in the press that he had been shot, which were verified to be inaccurate:

> The German ex-Crown Prince has not been shot as was reported. On Tuesday he crossed the frontier at Eysden, the party travelling in three motor cars. The ex-Prince was in uniform, and he wore large motor-goggles, evidently intended to prevent his being recognised. He was escorted to the residence of the Governor of the Province of Limburg at Maastricht.[27]

Chapter 13

The Canadians Advance
Upon Mons

While the world waited to see if the German delegation would obtain authority to agree to the Allied Armistice conditions, the fighting continued. The Canadian 20th Battalion (Central Ontario) was positioned at the village called Frameries, 3 miles south-west of Mons, on 10 November. Its war diary reported:

> The battalion moved from FRAMERIES at 06.15 hours on 10 November and arrived at the outpost line of resistance, held by the 18th Canadian Battalion, at about 09.15 hours … hostile M.G. fire was almost immediately encountered by our left company, and it was necessary for them to advance by short rushes. One platoon worked through carefully from house to house, along the road running through BELAIN and by using their L.G. [Lewis Gun] from the right flank, checked sniping to some extent.[1]

The 19th Battalion (Central Ontario) was also advancing upon Mons from the south-west. It had to leapfrog over the 18th Battalion (Western Ontario), which was holding a stretch of railway line 2,000 yards north-east of Frameries. The objectives of the 19th Battalion were to capture the village of Hyon and the high ground beyond, which was 600 yards south-west of Mons. The battalion war diary reported:

> The 19th Battalion passed through the 18th Battalion at 08.15 hours, without encountering serious opposition. At 10.27 hours a report was received that B Company were being held up by M.G. fire and had swung round to the left. At 10.45 hours the battalion had reached the outskirts of HYON, this was the location of a large

school for Machine Gunners and our advance met with heavy opposition as the Hun made use of every shelter for his guns.[2]

The post-operation report provided a detailed account of the strong resistance that 19th Battalion experienced in trying to secure Hyon:

> Little opposition was encountered until the Battalion reached MONT EREBUS, where it came under heavy enemy machine gun fire from both MONS and the high ground in rear of HYON. B and D Companies rushed the enemy posts around CHASSE ROYALE and established themselves along this road. Patrols were sent forward and on the left flank these made headway up to 300 yards east of the road. On the right, heavy machine gun fire from houses in HYON, coupled with hostile artillery fire, caused us heavy casualties. D Company made five attempts to work forward and eventually succeeded on the fifth attempt in capturing a strong machine gun post near the cemetery, which had been holding them up during the day.[3]

Georges Licope had lived in La Bascule, Mons, under occupation for four years.

He was a resident of the Belgian village where British soldiers fired their first shots in anger on European soil in the war. On Sunday, 10 November, the winds of war blew in Licope's direction once again, as he recalled:

> Since noon on November 9, 1918 we had been in the battle zone. We were surrounded by German guns, which fired ceaselessly towards the south west in the direction of Frameries, Pâturages and Noirchain. The noise was deafening. A battery of 7.7's, drawn up at the Carrefour de La Bascule (crossroads of Mons-Binche-Charleroi), 2 kilometres east of the town and hidden under acacias, was firing four shots every two minutes and each time the vibrations threatened to shatter all the windows of the house. As a precaution all the windows had been opened.[4]

Licope's testimony later shows that some German guns were being withdrawn, but its machine-gunners at Mons were resolute and determined to put up a strong defence on the penultimate day of the war. For the residents of Mons the sounds of war was prevalent; they were still living under German occupation and they questioned whether the war was coming to a close and if they would survive to see liberation. Licope recalled:

> A mile to the south a battery of 15's which had been firing the day before, was now silent. We learned from neighbours that one gun had been destroyed and that the others had been withdrawn. Behind our house on the summit of Mont Panisel, German machine-gunners were hastily digging emplacements for their guns. Without a doubt we were almost within rifle shot of the English troops. Was it possible that our liberation was so near?[5]

German forces were reluctant to give up ground, because it meant that the Allies would be getting closer to their own soil. German engineers were preparing mines and trees that could be felled easily to delay advancing Allied troops at Mons. Licope continued:

> At the crossroads at La Bascule, near some of the guns, German sappers had dug out great holes several metres deep, into which they had placed heavy steel cylinders bearing at each end a half sphere. There were mines destined to blow up the road. Other sappers had hewn large pieces out of the great elm trees bordering the three roads in such a manner that they could be felled at the first warning in order to hold up the progress of the British troops.[6]

Licope's home had been requisitioned by German officers, who used it as a temporary headquarters and as an artillery observation position. He and his family were now in a precarious position, for he recalled:

> In our house, several German officers were holding a council of war. An artillery captain had climbed into the attic with two soldiers and had installed a periscope in the skylight. He inspected the village of Hyon and its environs, which could be easily seen over the crest of Mont Panisel, about 2 kilometres away. The fire of the German artillery was unceasing. The empty shell cases piled up around the guns. Our friends did not reply.[7]

During that morning, Licope saw reconnaissance aeroplanes belonging to the RAF in the skies above Mons.

> Suddenly, about 10 o'clock, a zooming of engines caused us to look upwards. Aeroplanes bearing British colours were flying low above

our heads, so low, indeed, that the soldiers who were in the courtyard of our house grabbed their rifles and fired five or six shots in the direction of the pilots, who could be distinctly seen in their cockpits. An officer immediately ordered them to stop this fusillade, the only result of which was to give away their position.[8]

Meanwhile, the 19th and 20th Canadian battalions were preparing to advance into Hyon and the southern suburbs of Mons. Canadian artillery targeted German machine-gun positions at Hyon, but it proved ineffective and there was a risk of casualties being inflicted upon the civilian population of the town. There was an exposed stretch of land between the Chasse Royale Road and Hyon that was within the sights of the German machine guns defending this village. The 19th Canadian Battalion war diary reported:

> An artillery shoot was put on the town to silence his machine gunners. Major Hatch decided to move the battalion forward towards the village in small parties to avoid excessive casualties, it was soon found that it was impossible to get into the town under such heavy machine gun fire, so it was decided to wait for dusk.[9]

The sound of Canadian artillery was heard after midday and signalled to residents of Mons that the war was returning to their town once again: Licope recalled:

> At noon still nothing. Our friends had not yet opened fire. On the other hand, the German guns had not ceased fire. We sat down to table almost as calmly as in peace time. In the veranda some officers had spread out maps which they were consulting. Suddenly we heard an enormous explosion. Two panes of a window in the room in which we were sitting flew into splinters and fell just behind my father, whilst five other panes on the veranda were smashed to atoms by shell fragments. I had just time to notice a cloud of dust thrown up by a shell which had exploded on the edge of a field about 50 yards behind the house. We had a narrow shave.
>
> In less than a minute we took refuge in the cellar, but already a second shell had fallen near La Bascule and then a third. The walls trembled from top to bottom, and we thought that the house would be struck at any moment. It was exactly 12.30 p.m.
>
> Two German soldiers joined us in the cellar. One of them was crying: 'Zwei Kameraden kaput,' and explained that one of the

shells had just fallen at the La Bascule crossroads, killing two of his friends as well as two horses, and completely destroying a field kitchen. Ten yards nearer and it would have hit one of the guns. An officer called the two soldiers back. Very soon the tack-tack of the machine-guns posted on the summit of Mount Panisel told us that the battle line was drawing rapidly nearer.

The barrage set up across La Bascule by Allied artillery (we learned later that it was Canadian artillery) lasted only half an hour, but was of such violence that the German batteries fell back hastily towards the east, leaving in the immediate neighbourhood of the cross roads only a few particularly well protected guns.[10]

A further attempt to enter Hyon was made later that afternoon by the 19th Canadian Battalion. The battalion war diary reported:

An artillery shoot was arranged to take place between the hours of 16.00 and 16.30 on the BOIS LA HAUT to clean up the opposition from that quarter. Word was received that the 6th Brigade would pass through the 4th Brigade on the morning of the 11th.[11]

Patrols from the 20th Battalion were pushed forward towards the Bois La Haut, which sent back reports confirming that German forces were retreating. The diary added:

Late in the afternoon a barrage of heavy artillery was put down on BOIS LA HAUT, after which strong patrols were sent out, it was discovered that the enemy was retiring.[12]

As the afternoon progressed, the reality dawned upon the German occupiers that the war was drawing to a conclusion and that further resistance would be futile. Licope recalled:

The afternoon passed by in a fever of waiting. An officer said to us: 'Tomorrow your English friends will be here. We are beaten by a coalition of the whole world.'

At 5 pm we noticed the Germans putting on their equipment and marching off rapidly across the fields towards Saint-Symphorien. As night fell the noise of the gunfire diminished greatly in intensity, but never completely ceased.[13]

German machine-gunners continued to maintain fire into the Canadian lines as they withdrew from Hyon. The 19th Battalion was initially unaware that German forces were preparing to withdraw until it sent a patrol into the village. The battalion war diary reported:

> Heavy casualties from M.G. fire rendered a further advance impracticable so at 23.00 hours a patrol under the command of Lieut. Stuart entered the town of HYON and finding the Hun had evacuated, reported the town clear.[14]

The 19th Battalion's post-operation report provides further details of Lieutenant Stuart's reconnaissance into Hyon and described how the patrol came under machine-gun fire during the early hours of the last day of the First World War:

> At dusk, C Company (who were in support) were ordered to send forward patrols to work into HYON, Lieut. Stuart being in charge. Three patrols sent forward … were engaged with heavy machine gun fire but managed to work their way forward, reaching HYON at 1.45 hours, Nov 11th. Lieut. Stuart's patrol, finding that the enemy were withdrawing, sent back word to Report Centre, when A Company (who were in reserve) were sent forward with instructions to pass thought HYON and seize the high ground over the river, along the BOIS LA HAUT, the balance of C Company being ordered forward to occupy the village of HYON.
>
> This move was completed by 2.30 hours, A Company following closely behind the retreating enemy were able not only to secure the high ground in the BOIS LA HAUT, but placed their outposts along MONT PANISEL.[15]

The 20th Battalion also pushed forward its lines during that night:

> About midnight the reserve company sent out strong patrols, who succeeded in occupying SAINT SYMPHORIEN at about 02.00 hours on the 11th and at 03.00 hours a line of posts was established on the SAINT SYMPHORIEN– MONS ROAD.[16]

The 20th Battalion lost one officer, Lieutenant Russell Germain, and eleven men killed, along with thirty wounded. The war diary of 19th Battalion also reported the casualties sustained on the penultimate day of the war:

> 53 casualties occurred in the battalion of which were three officers killed, Capt. M.C. Roberts, MC, Lieut. W.C. McFaul and Lieut. C.E.G.

Robertson. 4 other ranks were killed, making a total of 7 killed and 46 wounded.[17]

Those killed from the battalion were initially buried close to where they fell in the presence of the local residents from Hyon two days after Armistice Day:

> On November 13th these brave men were buried in the cemetery at HYON where the Germans had temporarily held us up with machine guns. The civilian population of HYON turned out to a man to pay their last tribute of respect to those who had laid down their lives in freeing their country from the oppressors.[18]

After the war their remains were interred in Frameries Communal Cemetery.

Chapter 14

Signing of the Armistice
11 November 1918

Since the Kaiser had abdicated and a new government had been established under Chancellor Friedrich Ebert, Erzberger and the German Armistice Commission wondered whether Ebert and German High Command would accept the stern terms for Armistice issued by the Allies.

During the evening of 10 November Erzberger and the German delegation received wireless confirmation that Ebert had agreed to the Allied conditions for peace. The first message stated:

> The German Government to the plenipotentiaries at Headquarters of the Allied High Command:
> The German Government accepts the conditions of the Armistice communicated to it on November 8th.
> The Chancellor of the Empire – 3.084.[1]

The second message gave Erzberger authorisation to sign the Armistice, but requested that he highlight the plight of the German people who would suffer famine as a consequence and to negotiate provisions for food. The message stated:

> The German Government to the plenipotentiaries at Headquarters of the Allied High Command:
> The Government of the Empire transmits to the High Command the following for Under-Secretary of State Erzberger:
>
> Your Excellency is authorized to sign the Armistice. You will please, at the same time, have inserted in the record the following:

The German Government will do all in its power to fulfil the terms agreed upon. However, the undersigned deems in its duty to point out that the execution of some of the conditions will bring famine to the population of that part of the German Empire which is not to be occupied.

If all the provisions which had been accumulated for feeding the troops are left in the regions to be evacuated, and if the limitation (equivalent to complete suppression) of our means of transportation is maintained and the blockade continued, to feed the population and organize a food service will be impossible.

The undersigned requests, therefore, to be authorized to negotiate with a view to modifying certain points, in order that supplies may be assured.

The Chancellor of the Empire.[2]

General Weygand asked Erzberger if these messages were authentic and he confirmed that the number 3.084, which was added to the signature of the first message, was a previously agreed authenticity code. The delegation would not sign the Armistice until it received a further message from Hindenburg at Spa. This arrived at 21.00 hours and contained his reservations regarding some of the terms, however if there was no flexibility in negotiation of these points he instructed Erzberger to sign the Armistice. The German delegation was now ready to meet the Allied representatives and sign the Armistice. Wemyss recalled:

> On Sunday evening I had been talking to the Marshal for a long time after dinner and was just going to bed when an A.D.C. came and told me with the Marshal's compliments that he had thought the German Envoys had received instructions and would probably want to see us tonight and would I therefore be ready. Consequently I did not go to bed but lay down until midnight, when I was told that the Envoys had asked to be received immediately.[3]

The German delegates confirmed that they were ready to begin proceedings to sign the Armistice at 02.05 hours on 11 November. Ten minutes later, the meeting convened in Marshal Foch's carriage. Wemyss reported:

> They came into the train and we resumed our seats as we did on Friday morning. There was but slight inclination on the part of the

Germans to any protest. In one or two small matters, such as number of locomotives or aeroplanes to be delivered, they assured us that it was impossible to accede to the demands since we had over-estimated their strength and the Marshal showed reasonableness and to all intents and purposes the Military terms of the Armistice were signed. In the case of the German forces in East Africa the word capitulated which appeared in the original text of the Armistice was allowed to be altered.

When it came to discussing the Naval terms, Vaneslow showed a captiousness which was tiresome and quite unavailing. He made the remark, was it admissible that their fleet should be interned seeing that they had not been beaten? – the reply to this was obvious and it gave me a certain amount of pleasure to observe that they only had to come out!

On discussing the submarine situation, he told me, somewhat to my surprise, that there were not nearly a hundred and sixty to be had – this gave me the chance of getting what I had always wanted, viz, all the submarines. I may say here that the question of the Naval terms of the Armistice had caused a good deal of discussion. I had originally asked for the 'surrender' of eleven battleships, six battle cruisers, eight light cruisers, fifty destroyers and all the submarines. The politicians, however, were frightened and considered these terms as too heavy and desired to make them lighter, because they feared that there was a point beyond which the Germans would not go and they (very rightly) considered, so far as Great Britain was concerned, the present was the best psychological moment for obtaining a peace. I had many arguments with the Prime Minister on the subject and was quite aware that the French for the same reason wanted the general terms eased, and that this should be done at the expense of the British Navy rather than at the expense of the French Army. During some of the discussions on this subject Foch had said: 'Do you expect my men to go on fighting for the sake of ships that do not come out?' thereby displaying his entire ignorance of the general situation and of the part which the Navy had played in the war. Lloyd George had endeavoured to whittle down these terms and had suggested every sort and kind of compromise – a reduction of ships to be delivered, etc, and had eventually agreed to the internment of the surface vessels as a compromise. This I had accepted as the best to be got, and with an undertaking from him that these ships should never be returned to Germany but surrendered at the peace. It was the same with the question of the submarines; Lloyd George had objected to the word 'all'. By fixing a number which I felt sure would give us what they had got I had hoped to achieve my end – which I did. It was therefore a pleasure and a satisfaction to me to get the opportunity of inserting the word *all* in the terms.[4]

Due to the turbulent political events occurring in Germany, the Allied High Command wanted the following clause to be added to the Armistice terms:

In case the German vessels are not delivered within the periods agreed upon, The Governments of the Allies and the United States will have the right to occupy Heligoland in order to assume such delivery.[5]

The German delegates were opposed to this clause and could not sign it. This issue formed part of a separate document. Before the meeting was concluded, Erzberger sought permission to read the following declaration, for which Foch allowed:

The German Government will naturally make every effort within the power to see that the terms imposed are fulfilled.

The undersigned Plenipotentiaries acknowledge that on some points, upon their representation, a certain degree of benevolence has been shown. Therefore they feel that they can consider that the observations made by them on November 9th regarding the Armistice terms from Germany, and the answer made them on November 10th, constitute an integral part of the agreement as a whole.

But they cannot allow any doubt to exist as to the fact that the shortness of the time allowed for evacuation, and the surrender of indispensable transport equipment, threaten to create a situation such as may render it impossible for them to continue the fulfilment of the terms, through no fault of the German Government and people.

Referring to their repeated oral and written statements, the undersigned plenipotentiaries also deem it their duty to insist strongly on the fact that the carrying out of this agreement may plunge the German people into anarchy and famine.

In view of the discussions which brought about the Armistice, we might have expected terms which, while assuring our adversary complete and entire military security, would have terminated the sufferings of non-combatants of women and children.

The German nation, which for fifty months has defied the world of enemies, will preserve, in spite of every kind of violence, its liberty and unity.

A nation of seventy million suffers, but does not die.
Signed ERZBERGER, OBERNDORFF,
WINTERFELDT, VANSELOW.[6]

At 05.05 hours on 11 November 1918, the final text was agreed and five minutes later the Armistice was signed by the Allied and German plenipotentiaries. Wemyss, for his part, stated that the Armistice was signed nine minutes later:

> The Armistice was eventually signed at 5.19 a.m. and it was decided that the time should be taken as 5.00 a.m. and that hostilities would cease at 11 a.m. The Germans then went back to their train and we dispersed.[7]

Foch recalled the moment when Erzberger signed the Armistice:

> On November 11th they gave us what we asked for. The interview at Rethondes was not that a deed? It marked the disintegration of the German Empire, and I saw Erzberger brandish his pen and grind his teeth when he signed the document. I was then glad that I had exerted my will, and employed the means of exerting it, for the business was settled.[8]

The Armistice required Germany to evacuate from the territory that they occupied in France and Belgium, to withdraw their forces to the east bank of the River Rhine and to surrender arms and munitions. The complete terms of the signed Armistice are listed in Appendix 1. To ensure that Germany abided by the terms of the Armistice, the Allied armies would enter Germany to occupy territory west of the River Rhine, north of Cologne up to the Dutch border, and a blockade of Germany would be maintained until a peace treaty had been signed. The Armistice was valid for thirty-six days with the option to extend it, if further time was required to discuss peace terms.

As soon as the meeting was concluded and the German delegation returned to their train, Foch sent the following message, which was wired to commanders along the Western Front:

1. Hostilities will cease on the entire front on November 11th at 11 a.m. French time.
2. Allied troops are not to pass until further orders beyond the line reached on that day at that hour.
3. All communications with the enemy is forbidden until receipt of instructions by Army Commanders.[9]

Soon after the Armistice was agreed Wemyss immediately informed the Prime Minister, David Lloyd George, and King George V by telephone. Wemyss had very little sleep and once the Armistice had been signed he was scheduled to travel to Paris that morning. There was little point in going to bed. Instead he contemplated the fact that within hours the war would be over:

> Having to start for Paris at 7.30 a.m., I felt it was too late to go to bed, and so Hope [Admiral Sir George Hope] and I went for a walk in the forest, and it was a queer ꭇᴄᴌing that I had that the war was at last over and that bloodshed would cease at 11 o'clock.[10]

The following message was sent to the British Armies at 06.50 hours:

> Hostilities will cease at 11.00 hours today, November 11th. Troops will stand fast on the line reached at that hour, which will be reported by wire to Advanced G.H.Q. defensive precautions will be maintained. There will be no intercourse of any description with the enemy until the receipt of instructions from G.H.Q. Further instructions follow.[11]

It was a tremendous challenge to get this important message of ceasefire to the armies of both sides to the frontline, before the agreed ceasefire time. The headquarters of the five British armies received notification of the ceasefire between 07.00 hours and 07.35 hours, but it then had to be cascaded to brigade HQs and then filtered through to the battalions at the vanguard of the advance.

As news of the information was filtering through to the front lines the German envoys remained at Compiègne until their train left Rethondes station at 11.30 hours to return them to Tergnier. Once they arrived at Tergnier, they were driven to Germany in motor vehicles. Captain Geyer boarded an aeroplane at Tergnier airfield with maps and the text of the Armistice and was taken to German Headquarters. Some of the German delegates travelling to Spa received a negative response from their own officers and men.

Field Marshal Haig recalled in his diary on 11 November:

> The state of the German Army is said to be very bad, and the discipline seems to have become so low that the orders of the officers are not obeyed. Captain von Helldorf, who tried to get back to Spa from Compiègne with the terms of the Armistice by night, was fired at deliberately by the German troops marching on the road and he could not pass; while on another main road they broke up the bridges so that he could not proceed.[12]

Chapter 15

Morning of 11 November 1918
British Sector

As negotiations were taking place in the Forest of Compiègne during the night of 10/11 November, aeroplanes belonging to the Royal Air Force dropped 20 tons of bombs on railway stations and junctions. Raids were also conducted upon Liège and Enghien. Battles that had been fought during 10 November continued into the following day, the last day of the war.

The 156th Brigade advanced upon Herchies, 10 miles west of Mons, Belgium, during the afternoon of 10 November – but as it did so it came under sporadic hostile fire, which lasted into the early hours of 11 November. The *Dundee Evening Telegraph* later reported:

> While the Canadians were retaking Boringe and Mons, the 156th Infantry Brigade on 10 November, under orders of General Leggatt deployed from Condé, and, among other objectives moved on Herchies, the 7th Scottish Rifles, acting as advance guard, discovered the village strongly held with machine gun posts. In spite of the machine gun resistance the troops after a nine hours fight captured the village at one o'clock in the morning of what was to prove Armistice Day.[1]

The 156th Brigade's war diary reported:

> The enemy were reported to be holding HERCHIES and VACRESSE, and mg fire was heard from the western hedge of the Bois du BAVDOUR.
>
> At 14.00 the 7th Cameronians passed through the 4th Royal Scots, and advanced on HERCHIES. The right flank was protected by the 157th Brigade working through the Bois du BAVDOUR. Practically

no opposition was met in HERCHIES or VACRESSE which was reported clear by 18.00. The advance was pushed on, but was held up on the outskirts of ERBAUT by mg fire. At this time HERCHIES and the SIRAULT – HERCHIES road was subjected to harassing fire which continued intermittently until 01.00.

By 01.00 ERBAUT was cleared of the enemy in spite of some opposition, some dead and seventeen prisoners being left in our hands. Our casualties were twelve other ranks (four killed and eight wounded).[2]

Corporals A. Clark and R. Fisher, Privates H. Bertwistle and J. Quinn were the four casualties from the 7th Cameronians (Scottish Rifles) who were killed during the early hours of Armistice Day. They were buried at Herchies Communal Cemetery, where '11 November 1918' is inscribed on their headstones as their date of death.

On 11 November, 157th Brigade reached its objective of securing the Mons–Jurbise Road, encountering no opposition and without sustaining casualties:

At 08.00 the 5th H.L.I. [Highland Light Infantry] therefore advanced for the attack (the delay of one hour in commencing the attack having been caused through lateness in receipt of orders) and captured final objective i.e., the line of MONS – JURBISE road … without opposition, the enemy having withdrawn during the night. The 7th H.L.I. did not advance but were relieved by the 2nd Middlesex Regiment (23rd Inf. Bde. 8th Div.) who advanced through them … At 08.00 orders were received that an armistice would commence at 11.00 today, and that after capture of objectives, a defensive line would be taken up, the sentry groups being pushed out about 10.00 in front of the objective.[3]

Soldiers belonging to the 11th Manchester Regiment were consigned to the belief that they were marching into battle during that morning. On 11 November, Major S.C. Marriott wrote the following letter to his father describing how he learned of the Armistice:

We shall not forget the number 11, because by a curious coincidence hostilities closed officially on the 11th month at 11 o'clock in the morning of the 11th day and the 11th Battalion of the Manchesters, belonging to the 11th Division, were by that time back in their billets after going through a very hectic experience. We got orders late last night to push on at daybreak, and it was expected that we might be

Above: German delegates on their way, under the white flag, to the peace discussions that led to the Armistice on 11 November 1918. Their small convoy is depicted here passing through the French lines near Haudroy, 7 November 1918. (Everett Historical/Shutterstock)

Below: The Allied and German plenipotentiaries discussing the Armistice at Compiègne. Seated from left to right are: General Weygand, Marshal Ferdinand Foch, Admiral Sir Rosslyn Wemyss, Admiral George Hope, Captain Laperche (Interpreter), Captain de Cavalerie von Helldorf, Count Alfred von Oberndorff, Matthias Erzberger, Major-General Detlof von Winterfeldt and Captain Ernst Vanselow. (Author's Collection)

Above: Led by a band, almost certainly from the 42nd Battalion (Royal Highlanders of Canada) Canadian Expeditionary Force, Canadian troops march through the streets of Mons on 11 November 1918 having fought their way into the city in the last hours of the fighting on the Western Front. (Historic Military Press)

Below: This shell damage, from the last fighting on 10 or 11 November 1918, can still be seen on the exterior of the Institute of Hygiene and Bacteriology which is located on Boulevard Sainctecllette in the city of Mons. (Historic Military Press)

Above: Jubilant civilians and service personnel gather in front of Buckingham Palace on Armistice Day, 11 November 1918. (Historic Military Press)

Below: The Armistice of 11 November 1918, was welcomed in nations around the world – as illustrated by this picture of Canadians celebrating in Toronto.

Above: Crowds throng the streets of New York on 11 November 1918. (US Library of Congress)

Below: Allied personnel and civilians celebrate the news of the Armistice in Paris on 11 November 1918 - news that marked the end of the fighting of the First World War. (US Library of Congress)

Above: US troops in France celebrating the news of the Armistice on 11 November 1918. According to one source, these are men of the US 64th Regiment. (US Library of Congress)

Below: Defeated German soldiers pulling out from Luxembourg on 21 November 1918. They were replaced by US troops. (Courtesy of David Cade)

Above: German soldiers marching back towards the Rhine in November 1918, to comply with the terms of the Armistice. (Historic Military Press)

Below: Luxembourgers celebrating the liberation of their country and welcoming the arrival of Allied soldiers after the Armistice in November 1918. (US National Archives)

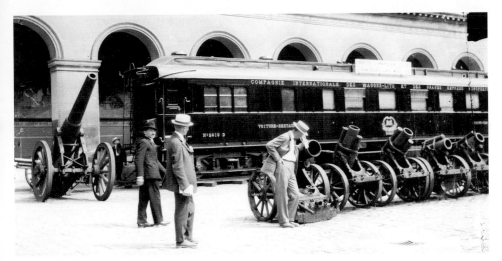

Above: The Armistice of 11 November 1918 was signed in a train carriage in the forest of Compiègne north of Paris. That same carriage, seen here on public display in the Cour des Invalides in Paris in the late 1920s, later became the setting of France's armistice in June 1940 – Hitler specifically chose the location as an irony for the defeated French. The rail car itself was ultimately destroyed in Berlin during the Allied bombing of the city. (US Library of Congress)

Above: Former British and Commonwealth prisoners of war in Germany at a service, following the Armistice, to honour their colleagues who died prior to being repatriated. (Historic Military Press)

Left: For some men there was still fighting to be done after the Armistice. In some cases this was because of the continuing internal struggle in Russia. In 1918, a large Allied force was sent to Vladivostok to help secure the port from the Bolsheviks. This photograph shows British troops that had just landed at Vladivostok marching through the grounds of the Czech Headquarters in the city. (Historic Military Press)

Below: The final confirmation of the end of the fighting with Germany in the First World War – the signing of the Treaty of Versailles in 1919. The Paris Peace Conference opened on 12 January 1919, and meetings were held at various locations in and around Paris until 20 January 1920. Leaders of thirty-two states, representing about 75% of the world's population, attended. Eventually five treaties emerged from the Paris Peace Conference, each one dealing with one of the defeated powers. Each of the five treaties was named after a Paris suburb. The one which dealt with Germany was the Treaty of Versailles, and was signed in the Hall of Mirrors in the Palace de Versailles. This picture shows the various delegations signing the Treaty of Versailles in the Hall of Mirrors. (US Library of Congress)

in action before long. So the battalion had fallen in and marched off. As 2nd in command I was busy at the end of the column getting the companies off at proper intervals, and marshalling the transport into place.

I was the last man to ride out of the village, next to Malplaquet, amidst cheers, handshakes and good wishes of the villagers, who had assembled to see us off. The column stretches about half a mile these days, because we march in file with long intervals between companies, to make it less deadly if bombed by aeroplanes and after marching about half a mile, I suddenly saw the C.O. and the Adjutant retreating back down the column, and then I heard terrific cheering, and saw hundreds of caps thrown into the air. I guessed at once what it was and my first thought was to tell those villagers, so I turned my horse round, and galloped like blazes down the road towards our last village. I shouted the news to a gang of R.E. repairing a blown up bridge, who threw their tools, picks, shovels, hats etc. into the air and cheered. The people in the village heard it, and as I came up I shouted 'C'est fini', somebody put a French flag into my hand, and on I went as far as my billet and Headquarters shouting the news to all around, and the people went absolutely mad. By this time the Battalion was forming up to march back, as hostilities had ceased, and with the C.O. who arrived about two minutes behind me, we went to rejoin it and bring it back. And back came the men amid indescribable scenes, they were cheering, firing off signal rockets, and one chap produced a Union Jack, and the band played a lively march.

We were accompanied by a whole squadron of planes, who swooped down, round and over us, sometimes only a couple of yards above us, looping the loop, firing signals and going completely mad, and in this fashion we marched through the village. Then came a march past and the Marseillaise, and the people wept and cheered alternately. We were decked with flowers and kissed. Everybody shook hands, and then a funny thing happened. The aeroplanes and the old men disappeared. The former to their aerodromes, the latter to dig up their hidden stores of wine, which had escaped the Germans systematic searchings' and for which the people had been frequently been beaten, fined and imprisoned. And now after four years it was being dug up in all directions, and of course it had to be drunk. Then came speeches, thanks, more flowers, more wine, and more coffee … In spite of all this it will take us a long time to realize that the war, which has been present to us for a long time, is now a thing of the past.[4]

185

In the British 66th Division sector, contact had been made with German forces close to Hestrud, where the attached South African Brigade was ordered to push forward its advance. The 1st South African Infantry Regiment war diary reported on 11 November:

> Orders were received to try and push on again at daybreak which was done, but no progress could be made. A patrol under 2/Lt Carwood pushed forward and did excellent work. Between 07.00 and 08.00 the village and locality were again shelled. At 10.15 when the B.G.C. was at Batt. H.Q., the G.S.O.2 arrived with orders that hostilities were to cease at 11.00 as an armistice had been signed. Orders were at once sent to the troops to cease fire at 11.00 and remain on the ground they were holding. At 10.30 orders were received to push on right up to 11.00. This was done but very little progress was made.[5]

The 1st South African Regiment's war diary also reported that German batteries intensified their artillery fire into its lines during the last hours of the war:

> Evidently he was determined not to have much surplus ammunition when the fateful hour arrived. The fighting continued right up to 11 when the enemy stood up in his trenches and then came towards our line and wanted to fraternise, but our troops ordered them back to their lines. Shortly after this two officers of the 443rd Regiment, Prussian Guard came to discuss the line we would hold. They were blindfolded and taken to the B.G.C. who discussed the matter with them. The battalion remained in the line during the night and a platoon was sent out towards SIVRY to link up with 199th Brigade. Our losses were 5 killed, 1 died of wounds, 26 wounded.[6]

The six soldiers who died from the 1st South African Regiment included Lance Corporal Crowley Thompson, Privates George de Kock, Ronald Haw, N. Johnson, Cecil Morris and T. Taylor. They all died on the day the Armistice was signed and were buried in Hestrud Churchyard.

In the 29th Division sector the fighting continued right up to the time of the Armistice. Brigadier-General Bernard Freyberg, commanding 88th Brigade, received orders to rush forward to seize the bridges over the River Dendre at Lessines, Belgium, because there was a risk they could be destroyed by German forces. Freyberg personally led the advanced guard, 'A' Squadron from 7th Dragoon Guards, to Lessines riding exhausted horses. Freyberg was the recipient of the Victoria Cross for his bravery during the Somme campaign in 1916. Continuing to demonstrate his dash and courage up to the last minutes of the war, Freyberg ignored German machine-gun outposts and succeeded in securing the bridges within minutes before the designated Armistice ceasefire time. The 29th Division war diary reported:

> Orders received that Armistice commenced at 11.00 and advance was to be pushed energetically up to that hour. G.S.O. III immediately started to inform G.O.C. 88th Infantry Brigade that he was to gain the line of the River Dendre if possible by that hour. He found G.O.C. 88th Infantry Brigade [Freyberg] and Major Chappell Commander A. Squadron, 7th D.Gs. [Dragoon Guards] at Flobecq at 09.30, they immediately galloped forward picking up the Squadron on their way at 10.45 reached a point about 300 yards from the outskirts of Lessines where they were fired upon by rifles and a M.G. The cavalry immediately charged and killed 4 Germans and capturing 2 officers and 98 men and reached the road bridges over the river Dendre at 10.57 establishing posts on the east of the river by 11.00. 2 Coys of the enemy who were captured in the east portion of the town after 11.00 were released and marched out.[7]

Major-General D.E. Cayley, commanding the 29th Division, reported:

REPORT ON THE SEIZING OF THE CROSSINGS OF THE DENDRE AT LESSINES ON 11TH NOVEMBER 1918

Orders as to the importance of getting on as far as possible by 11.00 hours and if possible, taking the crossing of the DENDRE at LESSINES by this hour, only reached Brig-General FREYBERG, O.C. Advanced Guard, about 9.30 hours. He immediately got 'A' Squadron, 7th Dragoon Guards, attached to him, under way. He accompanied them, and the Squadron moved as fast as possible (at a canter for most of the distance) towards Lessines. They arrived outside the town at about 10.45 hours and were met by machine gun fire. It was decided to rush the place, which was immediately done, a few of the enemy being killed and 2 officers and 98 other ranks being captured. The squadron pushed over the road bridges which were intact and established bridgeheads over the river, capturing two companies of the enemy on the East Bank, but as it was now 11.00 hours these were allowed to march out, after a request by the

Commander that they should receive protection against the inhabitants. This was refused unless they laid down their arms and surrendered. They decided to march out.

Considerable difficulty was experienced in LESSINES in protecting the prisoners captured in the town from the fury of the people.

That the important road crossings over the DENDRE were seized by 11.00 hours was entirely due to the energy of Brig-General FREYBERG, and to the dash and leadership of 'A' Squadron, 7th Dragoon Guards under the command of Major CHAPPELL.[8]

Both Freyberg and Major Wickam Chappell received a bar to their Distinguished Service Crosses for this action which took place during the final minutes of the war. The citation for Freyberg's award shows that he was Captain who should have been in charge of a company, but because of the shortage of high ranking officers he was elevated to the rank of Temporary Brigadier-General in command of a brigade. When he was appointed commander of a brigade, belonging to 58th Division, in April 1917 he was aged twenty-seven and considered to be the youngest Brigadier-General in the British Army. His citation recorded:

FREYBERG, BERNARD CYRIL, V.C., D.S.O., Capt. and Brevet Lieut-Colonel (Temporary Brigadier-General) Royal West Surrey Regt. (General Officer Commanding 88th Infantry Brigade). For marked gallantry and initiative on 11 Nov. 1918, at Lessines. He personally led the cavalry, and though at the time he had only nine men with him, he rushed the town, capturing 100 of the enemy and preventing the blowing up of the important road bridges over the Dendre.[9]

The advance of 55th Division came to a halt at the Blaton Canal and River Dendre during 10 November. The 55th Division's war diary reported:

At 11.30 a.m. Legard's force had cleared LIGNE and was moving on VILLERS ST. AMAND, and at 12.35 p.m. the advanced troops were checked by hostile guns covering the crossings of the canal at ATH and thence the river West and North of ATH.[10]

The 164th Brigade belonged to 55th Division and its war diary confirmed the efforts to cross the canal and river at Ath on 10 November:

The 3rd Cavalry Brigade went forward at 07.00, and our force got on the move at 07.30. The enemy was cleared of LEUZE and a couple of prisoners were taken. No more opposition was encountered till outside ATH. The cavalry came up against machine gun fire at 10.30 and attempted to force bridgeheads, but were unsuccessful, so at 14.30 the 2/5th Lan. Fus., went forward with two companies and tried to approach ATH through IRCHONWELZ. They could not make much progress, but prevented the enemy from blowing up the bridge, and having got into position kept up bursts of M.G. fire down the _____ at intervals during the night. Brigade H.Q. were at VILLERS ST.AMAND, Casualties: 2/5th Lan. Fus. 2/Lieuts. E.G.V. RIGHTON and R.S. LUSH wounded, 17 O.R. wounded, 2 O.R. wounded (at duty), 8 O.R. killed; 'C' Squadron King Edward's Horse, 3 O.R. wounded (gas); 'A' Coy., VII Corps Cyclist Bttn. 1 O.R. killed, 2 O.R. wounded.[11]

Eight soldiers from 2/5th Lancashire Fusiliers and one soldier from the Cyclist battalion who were mentioned in this report were all buried at Irchonwelz Communal Cemetery with 10 November 1918 inscribed on their headstones as date of death.

The 55th Division continued its efforts to establish a bridgehead across the Blaton Canal and River Dendre at Ath during the early hours of 11 November. The divisional war diary reported:

By nightfall on 10th November Legard's force had reached the line of the BLATON CANAL and DENDRE River, but further advance was checked by machine gun fire and the infantry attack had not made much progress. The enemy were holding the line of the railway from L'ARBRE to ATH, and thence the river west and north of ATH. The mounted troops of Legard's force were withdrawn for the night and the 2/5th Lancashire Fusiliers were left as outposts on the line reached, with orders to try and force a crossing during the night or in the early morning.

The Division had advanced over 13 miles since crossing the ESCAUT on the night of the 8th/9th November along the main TOURNAI – BRUSSELS Road, which the enemy had rendered impassable to all but pack transport by means of craters, inundations and mines. This road was effectually dealt with by the Field Companies and pioneers, who, in this stretch of road, filled 22 craters; over 500 mines being dealt with by them and the personnel attached from 170th Tunnelling Coy. As a result of this work no delay in getting up transport was experienced, even lorries being able to move along the road the day on which the ESCAUT was first crossed, a crib and rail bridge to take 17 tons being erected where the road crossed the River Dendre by the 422nd Field Coy.

On the night of the November 10th, orders were issued giving a general plan for the attack on ATH for November 11th should the crossings of the canal and river not have been forced during the night. The 165th and 166th Infantry Brigades were to attack immediately south and north of the town respectively. The 2/5th Lancashire Fusiliers were to hold the enemy frontally and the mounted troops were to make a turning movement as far north as circumstances permitted.

A conference for all commanders was ordered for 9 a.m. November 11th at Headquarters Legard's force at VILLERS ST. AMAND to settle details of the plan, by which time all troops taking part in the attack were ordered to be in preliminary assembly positions.

No crossings of the bridges into ATH was effected during the night 10th/11th November. Two bridges remained intact, namely that on the main LEUZE – ATH Road just south of ATH.

At 5.30 a.m. on November 11th the Lancashire Fusiliers reported that the iron bridge was barricaded and mined and still held by the enemy. By 7 a.m. however by means of daring action during which a Lewis Gun was mounted in a house close to the bridge, the enemy was driven from the bridge without being able to blow it up, and the barricade was destroyed. The Lancashire Fusiliers passed into the town and the mounted troops pushed on ahead reaching the line of PONCHAU – RENARD by 8 a.m. The Lancashire Fusiliers reached the line shortly afterwards and the mounted troops pushed on with little opposition eastward. At 9.05 a.m. a verbal message was received at Divisional Headquarters which was at BARRY and was telephoned from there to the Conference which was taking place at VILLERS ST. ARMAND, stating that hostilities would cease at 11 a.m. and troops would at that hour stand fast on the most easterly ground.

Orders were issued to this effect but did not reach the advanced mounted troops until 1.30 p.m. by which time they were on the line THORICOURT – BASSILLY, over 7 miles east of ATH.[12]

There were other British units that did not receive the news of the ceasefire and continued to advance after 11.00 hours. The 164th Brigade reported the action at Ath:

King Edward's Horse and Cyclists pushed forward, not knowing that Armistice commenced at 11.00, and a patrol of King Edward's Horse passed through SILLY, where an enemy gun was encountered. The Corporal was just going to attack and surround this when news of the Armistice came through, and much to his annoyance. The cavalry pushed forward to such lengths that a trooper was missing; he was wending his way to BRUSSELS, acting on the orders to go forward until opposition was encountered. A Corporal and six men of the Cyclist Bttn., on reaching SILLY Station found a German officer and 20 men. News of the cessation of hostilities came through, the Corporal called upon the Huns to retire, stating that his orders were to remain at the furthest point reached and that both he and the enemy could not remain in the same place! The officer did not fall in with the idea, so the Cyclists offered to fight the enemy for the Station; this argument proved sufficient and the Boche retired.[13]

The London Rifle Brigade was positioned at Erquennes, south-east of Mons. The troops found it difficult to focus upon their work as soldiers and were more concerned about surviving for the next hours until the ceasefire. An anonymous ranker recalled:

> What happened during the next few hours it is difficult to remember. Who could do an ounce of work or look at a harness when every man who passed down the road had some remark to make about 'keeping his head low for the next hour or so,' or 'being in Berlin within a week?' Everyone had got hold of the news: even Major Wallis said it was true. And at last we accepted it as an incontrovertible fact, like the statement that rations would be short for the next few weeks owing to the British feeding liberated Belgium.[14]

Cyril Dennys was a British officer serving with the 212nd Siege Battery, Royal Garrison Artillery, which was occupying gun positions overlooking the River Scheldt, when it received news of the Armistice.

> We got out through the salient and we were advancing towards the pack of towns, Quatre, Lille. I remember we had rather a close shave from a shell in a field of cabbages and I thought my God, I don't want to get killed now, the war is coming to an end.
>
> We were lumbering after the Germans, trying to catch them up. When we finally got them we were in a position, we and the other batteries, were overlooking across the Scheldt River. It was a terribly

exposed position and it seemed to us that if there was a battle, which was obviously blowing up, we were going to have a pretty rough time of it, but before it could come we had this news effected at 11 a.m. on the 11th of November 1918, hostilities were going to cease and there was to be no firing from then onwards. So we sat round and just bloody well couldn't believe it. It doesn't seem that this could be really happening and just before 11 a.m. it occurred to us and to a number of other batteries, that it would be very annoying to be left with loaded guns that we couldn't fire, because unloading is an awful nuisance with big guns, you have to be jolly careful what you do. So we and all the other batteries had the same idea because just before 11 o' clock there were a series of sounds of gunfire from up and down the line. What we did was to cock our guns up to an angle which we felt made it certain that no one was going to get killed, because at this time we did not want to slay someone in the last few minutes … everybody at the final moment did not want to do any more damage.

Until 11 o'clock arrived … we sat down and we had to talk about what we were going to do after the war. I said I was going to go back to Oxford and pick up my scholarship. Two colleagues of mine who were farmers were going back to their farms. The Major who was a regular said that he would look out for something else.[15]

Artillery batteries belonging to the 56th Division fired their guns for the last time before the war ended, as the unit history chronicled:

Just before 11 o'clock all batteries opened fire. Each gunner was determined to be the last man to fire a shot at the Germans. And then, in the midst of the rolling thunder of rapid fire, teams straining every nerve to throw the last shell into the breach of their guns before the 'cease fire' sounded, 11 o'clock struck, the first blast of the bugles pierced the air, and the last note silence reigned.[16]

The fatigued soldiers of the 56th Division were in a state of disbelief that the war was indeed over. Brigadier-General Elkington wrote:

There was no cheering or excitement amongst the men. They seemed too tired, and no one seemed able to realise that it was over.[17]

Private Edward Sullivan was among the last British soldiers of the war to be killed at Ath, just before the Armistice. Aged thirty-two, he was a dispatch carrier between headquarters and the front line. During 1915, while serving with the 2nd Essex Regiment, he had to hide in a shell hole for two days and nights in order to avoid the sights of a German sniper who knew his position. The *Essex County Chronicle* reported:

> The last British soldier killed in the war was Private Edward Sullivan, of A Co. 7th Corps Cyclist Battalion [should be Army Cyclist Corps, 7th Cyclist Battalion], son of Mr D. Sullivan of 10 Boleyn Road, East Ham. He met his death on Nov 11 at Ath, east of Tournai. He was killed by rifle fire just before the armistice was declared. He had served continuously since August 1914. Corporal F. Hawkins writes to the father. 'I think his grave is the most advanced in the British Army. We were shelled out of the position, but went forward again and found Ted. An old man living in the house close by had fetched him into the house. It was while pushing forward bravely with a Lewis gun that he fell.'[18]

Ted Sullivan had lost two brothers earlier during the war. Daniel was killed at Neuve Chapelle on 10 March 1915 and James was killed on 11 March 1918 at Amiens. Mr D. Thomas had four sons serving in the British Army during the war and the death of his third son, Ted, was another tragic blow that he had to deal with, a tragedy exacerbated by the fact that he was killed only hours away from the end of the war. The newspaper article claims that he was the last British soldier to be killed during the war and that he had died on 11 November, however his headstone at Irchonwelz Communal Cemetery states that he died on 10 November. Ted Sullivan's commanding officer, Major Grunant, confirmed that he was actually killed on the 11th. In a letter to Ted's father, he wrote:

> It is with deepest regret that I have to inform you of the death of your son, which took place on November 11 at a place called Ath, east of Tournai. He was killed by rifle fire just before the armistice was declared.[19]

Private George Edwin Ellison is officially regarded as the last British soldier to have been killed during the First World War. Ellison, who was born in York, was a former soldier working in the coal mines in 1914, but when war broke out he was recalled to duty and served with 5th (Royal Irish Lancers) throughout the war. The *National Roll of the Great War, Leeds Volume*, recorded that Ellison:

Already serving at the outbreak of war, he at once proceeded to France and fought in the Retreat from Mons. He also played a prominent part in engagements at Ypres, Armentières, La Bassée, Lens, Loos and Cambrai, but was unhappily killed only an hour and a half before the Armistice came into force. He was buried at St. Jean, and was entitled to the Mons Star, the General Service and Victory Medals. The path of duty is the way to glory.[20]

Ellison was aged forty when he died one hour before the Armistice while on a reconnaissance patrol of the suburbs of Mons. It is ironic that he was killed where the first British actions of the war in Europe took place in 1914. He was buried opposite Private John Parr at St Symphorien Military Cemetery, Parr being recognised as the first British soldier killed in the conflict in Europe.

Second Lieutenant Fred Perrett was seriously wounded on Armistice Day. Before the war, Perrett was a Welsh rugby international and also played for Hull. Serving with the 17th Battalion, Royal Welsh Fusiliers, he died from his wounds on 1 December 1918, leaving a wife and two young children in Hull. Perrett was buried at Terlincthun British Cemetery, Wimille, north of Boulogne.

With the loss of many soldiers during the last hours of the war questions were asked why they were killed so close to the end. Private Thomas Dewing, a signaller with 34th Division Signals Company Royal Engineers, was appalled that soldiers were sent into battle when their officers who issued those orders knew that the war would end that day:

> The thing I always remember, a ghastly thing, when they went to the signal office they got this message coming through, they knew that the war was going to stop at 11 o'clock the next morning and yet they sent men to attack and some of the men were killed on that day. I think that was a ghastly thing, they should have stopped it there and then. Think of someone at home, hearing that the war has ended and then get a message saying so and so has got killed the day it ended. I never forgive the people who sent people to attack something when they knew it was going to end.[21]

Chapter 16

Morning of 11 November 1918
Canadian Sector

Canadian forces advanced upon Mons during the evening of 10 November. Georges Licope, who lived in La Bascule, recalled the cheers of delighted Belgian citizens welcoming the Canadian troops as they entered the villages close to Mons:

> From midnight onwards everything was calm, as calm as in peace time. We were in No Man's Land. Everything was obscure. There was a frost during the night and it was cold and misty. Suddenly from the courtyard at about 5.00 a.m., we heard a far off and indistinct noise. It was rather like a humming which increased, grew louder and then stopped altogether, only to break out immediately afterwards.
>
> It was the cheer of the people at Hyon floating across the country. It sounded rather like the distant murmur of the sea. There was no longer any doubt. The English were arriving.
>
> Then with a peal of joy rang out the bells of the Belfry of Mons, our dear old bells which for centuries had sung or cried our joys and our sorrows. Our carillonneur, M. Fernand Redouté, had climbed the tower and at his keyboard played in succession the Brabançonne, the Marseillaise, God Save the King, and Le Doudon, the famous Mons anthem.[1]

Lieutenant Stuart's patrol from the Canadian 19th Battalion had confirmed that German forces had vacated Hyon, on the outskirts of Mons during the previous night. During the following morning the 19th Battalion entered Hyon. The battalion war diary reported:

> At 07.00 hours the battalion entered the town of HYON and established themselves in the eastern outskirts with battalion H.Q.

in the CHATEAU. At 08.00 hours a message was received that hostilities would cease at 11.00 hours and at 08.30 hours the 28th Battalion of the 6th C.I.B. [Canadian Infantry Brigade] passes through us, the 19th Battalion occupying the reserve position to the 6th Brigade. The remainder of the day was spent rejoicing. The civil population according the Battalion many impromptu celebrations. The 19th Battalion will ever be acclaimed as liberators of HYON on the dawn of armistice morning.[2]

Licope had lived under German occupation for four years and he decided to meet the liberators. Describing the moment and emotions felt during that morning, he recalled:

Daylight was breaking. A solitary horseman climbed cautiously the slope of La Bascule, coming from the direction of Mons. He was wearing the Khaki uniform and steel helmet of the British troops. Whilst we cheered him and our neighbours decorated the horse's harness with chrysanthemums, he asked: 'A quelle heure boches partis? Quelle direction? Plus de boches ici?' I tried to give him the necessary information in English, but I was too overcome. I fear my information was not very useful. This scout, I learned later, belonged to the 5th Royal Irish Lancers, attached to the Canadian Corps in November, 1918, as part of the Divisional Cavalry. This was the same regiment which in 1914 formed part of Allenby's famous Cavalry Division which covered itself with glory at the 1st Battle of Mons. A few minutes later we saw infantry troops crawling along and climbing through the ditch bordering the road. All were wearing steel helmets and box respirators at the alert. We greeted them with cries of 'Vivent les Anglais!' in just the same way as we had greeted 51 months before and in the same spot Allenby's cavalry: 'Pas Anglais, Canadiens nous sommes de l'Ontario central.' They showed us on their shoulders the word 'Canada'. Their collar badges bore the number C 19, for this advance party belonged to the 19th Infantry Battalion, 4th Brigade, 2nd Division of the Canadian Expeditionary Force. We could hardly believe our eyes. Whoever could have guessed that one day we should be set free by soldiers from over the seas, freed from more than four years of slavery?[3]

The 19th Battalion had arrived in La Bascule and formed up along the Chaussée de Beaumont opposite the home of Licope, who invited Lieutenant Stuart for breakfast. Stuart was the officer who led the reconnaissance patrol into Hyon.

The 42nd Battalion (Black Watch of Montreal) proceeded into the town centre at Mons during the night of 10/11 November and established outpost positions east of the town. Corporal Will Bird was among those soldiers from the battalion who cautiously ventured into Mons. During that night he narrowly escaped death when a shell exploded near to a brick building they were searching:

> Wheeee-crash! A slamming explosion. A shell had burst just beyond the building about fifteen feet in the air. Johnson was bowled over by the concussion. I was driven back with such force that both Old Bill and I went down heavily. We scrambled up, almost choked with fumes, 'That was too close for comfort' I said. No one answered me. I looked at Jones. He was seated where he had been, his chin in his hands, but blood was pouring from a great hole in his temple. He had been killed instantly.[4]

Bird was referring to Lance Corporal Bernard Jones, a native of Stoke-on-Trent in England, who died within hours of the Armistice being signed. This exploding shell also claimed another comrade. Corporal Bird later wrote:

> There was a despairing cry behind me. I swung around to see Tom Mills falling. His brother caught him, but had to let him down. 'I'm hit' Tom said, and held out his arm. His wrist was almost severed. But as he sank back on the floor I saw he had a fearful wound in the stomach. He died as we looked at him.[5]

Private Tom Mills died in the presence of his brother, Jim. Later that night, Bird attacked a German machine-gun position in Mons with a rifle grenade. Bird recalled:

> It was about fifty yards to where I could have a good view of the street and the last stretch took some time, as I kept as low as possible. At last I lay on my side and peered. Had I known exactly where the Germans were I could not have done better. Their gun was set up in the middle of the street. One German had his helmet off as if adjusting the strap. The other two watched him idly. Their backs were toward me and they were both big men. In a moment I had the rifle adjusted. It was not a long reach, but I did not know the time of the fuse and had to take a chance. The luck of the day stayed with me. Just as I shot, a large tin can or barrel crashed down nearby, in a backyard or possibly on a street. The next instant the grenade

197

exploded at shoulder height over the German gun. The gun crashed over, and I jumped up and ran back the way I had come.

There was no more sound. The three of us went forward, through a board gate and up to the street, our rifles ready. Two of the Germans lay as they had fallen. The third had crawled across the sidewalk and was lying there. The way was clear.[6]

Bird was awarded the Military Medal for this action. His citation stated:

This N.C.O. was in command of a section during the attack on Mons on the night of November 10/11th. When the advance was held up by two enemy machine-gun posts he worked his way forward, and by bringing heavy rifle grenade fire on the posts forced them to withdraw. He showed great gallantry and initiative throughout.[7]

Before dawn the population of Mons came out to welcome them after four years of German occupation. The celebrations of liberation began before official notification was received that the Armistice had been signed. The 42nd Battalion's war diary reported:

By daybreak on 11th the whole city of MONS had been mopped up and we had established outposts on the high ground on the eastern outskirts. Battalion Headquarters was established in the Hotel de Ville in the Grande Place. The pipe band played its way into the city about 07.00 hours and created tremendous enthusiasm. Thousands of civilians lined the streets and the Grand Place, and the Battalion was given such a welcome as it had never seen before. Men, women and children vied with one another in expressing their hospitality, hot coffee, cognac and wines were distributed with the utmost generosity. Soldiers everywhere were embraced and kissed. In a few moments the whole city was bedecked with flags flying from every window.

Lieut. L.H. Biggar and J.W. Cave were the first officers of the Battalion to actually enter the Hôtel de Ville, where they went forward to establish Headquarters and install telephone communication. As soon as they entered, the 'Gold Book' was taken from the vaults where it had lain for over four years and they had the honour of being the first British troops to sign it, the only other entry in this book up to that time was that of King Albert of Belgium who had signed it 1913, on his first visit to MONS after ascending the throne.[8]

At 07.30 hours, the 6th Canadian Infantry Brigade reported:

Wire from 2nd Canadian Division stating that an armistice had been signed by the enemy, and ordering hostilities to cease at 11.00 hours received. Troops to remain on line reached by them at that hour.[9]

Fifteen minutes later orders were issued to push forward the advance and gain as much ground before the ceasefire. At 07.45 hours, the 6th Canadian Infantry Brigade reported:

Instructions issued to all concerned. Attacking battalions ordered to push on with all possible speed in order to gain as much territory as possible before 11.00 hours.[10]

The 28th Battalion (Saskatchewan) was ordered to attack on the left, while the 31st Battalion assaulted the right flank in the 6th Infantry Brigade's sector. The advance of the 31st Battalion (Alberta) was obstructed by German machine gun positions, which continued to fire with vigour during the last hours of the war. The battalion war diary reported:

At 08.15 hours the attack commenced and for the first hour considerable progress was made by both front line companies, viz 'B' and 'D' Companies, in the face of considerable machine gun fire.
    At 09.00 hours a message was received from Brigade that hostilities would cease at 11.00 hours, and Battalion was advanced as far as possible before that time. This information was forwarded to the Companies, and instructed them to push ahead. At this time the Battalion had advanced ... having dislodged German enemy machine gun nests from the Chemical Works ... They then pushed forward over the slope in front of the village of BON VOULOIR and the BOIS DU RAPOIS where they met with concentrated fire from ten or twelve machine gun nests in the wood. In spite of this, the forward Companies worked steadily forward being well supported by fire from the 17th Battery stationed near the Chemical Works. These posts were gradually dislodged and they moved through the woods to the right. The left forward company worked around the left of the BOIS DU RAPOIS, the right forward company worked to the right of the woods along the road running ... in the direction of PETIT HAVRE and BOUSSOIT. One platoon of this Company being well in advance pushed into PETIT HAVRE and BOUSSOIT where they met with no enemy resistance.[11]

The Canadian 28th Battalion also pressed forward its advance. The battalion's war diary notes:

The particular task of the 28th Canadian Infantry Battalion was to pass through the advanced troops of the 19th Canadian Infantry Battalion on whatever line had been reached by then at 08.00 hours on November 11th 1918 and to advance between boundaries as are here under written and to make good the general line of the CANAL DU CENTRE to capture the village of HAVRE and to seize the bridge-heads over the CANAL DU CENTRE on the battalion front.[12]

As the 28th Battalion approached the suburbs of Mons the townsfolk came out of their homes to welcome them:

> As the troops moved through the outskirts of the city of MONS, large numbers of civilians flocked into the streets and received the men with scenes of remarkable enthusiasm. The bells of MONS could be heard ringing out in gladness for the deliverance of the city – a happy augury for the success of the operation to be undertaken.[13]

Before German forces evacuated Mons they made efforts to slow down the pursuing Canadians with mines and demolitions that obstructed roads. The citizens living in Mons assisted the Canadians in removing obstructions that lay in their path:

> Some considerable difficulty was experienced in bringing the Battalion forward to the deploying point owing to the enemy demolitions and the effect of his mines upon road junctions and crossings. The energetic efforts of Battalion Staff Officers and the organisation of willing civilian labour overcame the obstacle and long delay was avoided.[14]

Contrary to the 6th Infantry Brigade's report, the 28th Battalion had not received notification that a ceasefire would take place later that morning and it continued with its attack in accordance with its orders.

> At 08.00 hours the Battalion jumped off on what will probably prove to be the last attack of the Great War and made extremely rapid progress. Some opposition was encountered in the BOIS DE HAVRE which was quickly overcome. At 09.00 hours the Battalion was reported to be proceeding satisfactory through the BOIS DE HAVRE at this hour also an historic message was received at Battalion Headquarters to the effect that all hostilities would cease at 11.00 hours November 11th 1918. This information was communicated to the attacking troops. With splendid dash and overcoming somewhat

increased resistance the Battalion dashed forward and by 11.00 hours had reached its OBJECTIVE on the whole front and 'B' Company had crossed the canal. Large numbers of the enemy could be seen retreating over the high ground N.E. of the CANAL. The excitement of the civilian population of the village of HAVRE knew no bounds and scenes of indescribable enthusiasm ensued.[15]

However, while the people of Havre were celebrating as the 28th Battalion entered their village, the unit suffered its final casualty ten minutes before the ceasefire. His name was Private George Price, and he is regarded as the last Canadian and Commonwealth soldier casualty of the First World War. The 28th Battalion's war diary recorded:

The Battalion suffered on this operation one casualty only Pte. Price of 'A' Company being killed by an enemy machine gunner at 10.50 hours.[16]

Georges Licope recalled:

Private G.L. Price, of the 28th N. West Battalion, was the last to be killed. He was shot dead at 10.58 a.m. by a German bullet on the bridge of the Canal du Centre at Ville-sur-Haine (8km. E.N.E. of Mons) at the very moment at which, laden with flowers, he was thanking the inhabitants who were acclaiming him. The liberation of Mons cost the Canadian Corps 85 killed and 349 wounded.[17]

Price was originally buried at Havre Old Communal Cemetery, but his remains were later transferred for burial to St Symphorien Military Cemetery.

As soon as 42nd Battalion Headquarters received communications confirming the Armistice ceasefire, orders were immediately issued that no further offensive operations would take place:

At about 9 o'clock official word was received that the Armistice had been signed, and that hostilities would cease at 11.00 hours. Instructions were immediately sent out to Companies that no further offensive operations would take place, but that all precautions would be taken to defend the line then held, outposts would be established and the Companies distributed in depth.[18]

Private Jim Mills was grieving for his brother who was killed during the previous night. Distraught, he was looking for someone accountable

201

for his brother's death within hours of the war ending. Corporal Will Bird, who had to deal with this tragic situation, wrote:

> It had become full day when Old Bill came around the corner with Jim Mills. He beckoned me to him. Jim was wild eyed, white as if he had been ill. 'He says he is going to shoot whoever arranged to have his brother killed for nothing.' Whispered Bill. 'He really means it. He's hoping Currie [Lieutenant-General Sir Arthur Currie, Canadian Corps commander] comes here today. If he doesn't, he's going to shoot the next higher-up. He says his brother was murdered.'
>
> One of the 42nd officers was walking toward us and I went up to him. He was not the one I would have chosen, but something had to be done. I saluted him and told him about Jim. He was startled, for he had not known Jones and Tom Mills were dead. But he said there was no need to worry about Jim. Take him and get him drunk, so drunk he wouldn't know anything for twenty-four hours. When he came out of it he would be all right. He told me to say my piece to him. Bill agreed to get Jim plastered, and I gave him the money. Then the officer took me up the street to where the adjutant was standing. He said there was to be a parade shortly, but the two deaths must be reported. They asked me many questions, which ended in my having to show a party where to go for the bodies.[19]

Both Lance Corporal Bernhard Jones and Private Tom Mills were buried at Mons (Bergen) Communal Cemetery, where they lie in adjacent graves.

A Canadian soldier with the initials J.P.H., who originated from Coventry in Britain, wrote to his father describing the moment he entered Mons and the personal accounts he had obtained from the residents of the Belgian town of their ordeal under German occupation:

> We have been for three days on the outskirts of the town from which the great British retreat commenced at the beginning of the war. We entered it the day after the Germans left. The joy of the people at our arrival was pathetic. They decorated us with flowers and ribbons of the national colours – black, yellow and red: shaking hands and kissing us and each other.
>
> From the time we struck the inhabited places our progress has been a kind of triumphal procession. Everywhere flags were flying, which the owners has succeed in hiding from the Germans. To have flown those flags a few days earlier would have been to flirt with the undertaker.

At one town we were in, twenty-four civilians were lined up and shot at one time in 1914 pour encourager les autres. To realise what these people have suffered during the last four years or more, one must hear the tale from their own lips. Everything that could be of any use to them the Germans seized, even the bronze ornaments from their mantelpieces, the wool out of their mattresses, and the leather saddle and rubber tyres from their cycles. I have never seen people who bore such marks of starvation.

They have sunken cheeks, the prominent cheek bones, and the famished look that one associates with the last stages of consumption. Their meat allowance was half a pound for four persons per week. All civilians were required to step off the side walk and salute when a German officer passed. At eight o'clock in the evening a military patrol visited the houses of civilians to check that all had retired for the night. If not, they were fined the next day. In the same way they were liable to fines for singing the Marseillaise, the Brabançonne, or any of their national songs. It is no wonder that they are bitter against the Germans. But great as their sufferings have been, they all speak with pity of the sufferings of the British prisoners in German hands, whom they saw every day at work in the streets, or passing to and from their work elsewhere. These miserable men were so famished that the civilians would spare a crust from their own miserable allowance for them; but, if they were seen by the guard, the food would be taken from them.

Constantly the prisoners were abused by their guards with the butts of their rifles, in one case where a British prisoner had been given the butt-end of a cigarette it was knocked out of his mouth by the butt-end of a German rifle. The people have told me of many incidents of this kind, and though such hear-say evidence would not be accepted in a court of law, personally I believe it all.

The armistice was declared soon after we arrived here; but, though the people were glad to have peace, they willingly would have endured another year of war that the German people might suffer as they have suffered. That may not strike you as a very Christian attitude, but if ever a desire for vengeance were justified it is in this case.

I came to Belgium rather prejudiced against the Belgians, as the Canadians at Ypres have found them most disobliging. But the people there, it seems, are Flemish, speaking Flemish, while the people here are Walloon, speaking French. Nothing could exceed the kindness of the people here. They have taken up all into their own homes, giving us the best accommodation they have. In some cases, as we found out afterwards, they gave us their best bedrooms, making for themselves a 'shake-down' on the floor of another room. The women insist on doing our washing for us. They set their tables for us to eat our rations and brought out coffee that they have saved for years to celebrate the day of their liberation. There is not much that we can do for them to some extent. They have not, so far, received any help from France, or the unoccupied part of Belgium: but they expect that will be forthcoming very soon.

I suppose the armistice has been a great relief to all of you. I know very little about the terms of it, as I have not seen a newspaper for several weeks.[20]

Chapter 17

Morning of 11 November 1918
French Sector

The Régiment d'Infanterie Coloniale du Maroc was the most decorated French regiment and was positioned near Altkirch on the southern Alsace sector on 11 November 1918. Its war diary simply recorded:

> Signature of Armistice. The raid which had been scheduled à 8.30 am is cancelled. Ceasefire at 11 o'clock.[1]

The 25th Battalion, Chasseur à Pieds, had taken Malmaison fort on Chemin des Dames on 28 September 1918, and was the first unit to enter Laon on 13 October. On 11 November it was positioned at the village of Villacourt, near Charmes south of Metz. Its war diary reported:

> At 8 o'clock the battalion is officially informed that the Armistice has been signed at 5 am (!!!!!). This event is welcomed with great joy by all the men of the battalion. 8.30 am the band marched in the street of Villacourt and played la Marseillaise anthem of the Allies.[2]

The 219th Régiment d'Infanterie, at Mezières, recorded the moment when it heard that an Armistice had been signed:

> 11 November. Around 6 am a telephone message announces the signing of the Armistice. Hostilities must stop at 11 o'clock. Around 10 a.m. General Prax, commander in chief of the 11th Army Corps comes to tell his satisfaction to the regiment and especially to the 13th and 14th companies who yesterday succeeded to cross the canal and to repulse two enemy counter attacks on the railway line.[3]

Although the war was scheduled to end within three hours, French soldiers were still fighting and dying as the time approached 11.00 hours. Private Augustin Trébuchon is reputed to be the last French soldier to be killed during the First World War. Trébuchon was aged forty and worked as a shepherd before the war. Serving with the 415th Régiment d'Infanterie since he enlisted in August 1914, he had taken part in the second Battle of the Marne, Verdun, Artois and the Somme and was wounded on two occasions by shrapnel. Trébuchon crossed the River Meuse at Vrigne-sur-Meuse, through the fog during the morning of 11 November 1918. When the fog lifted around 10.30 hours, the 415th Régiment d'Infanterie became exposed to German fire from the surrounding ridges. Captain Charles de Berterèche de Menditte, from the 415th Régiment d'Infanterie, recalled in his diary that both French and German forces continued to fight during the last hours of the war:

> At about 6.30 am the sound of Armistice is going round. At 8.30 am, the notice is official. During that time on the front of the regiment we continue to fire and German shells fall on Dom-le–Mesnil. I announce the good news to the regiment then we wait!
> 10.45: The shells still fall on the village.
> 10.57: The machine guns still fire.[4]

At 10.45 hours Trébuchon was killed carrying a message 'Rassemblement à 11h 30 pour le ravitaillement', which in English translated into 'Assemble for food at 11:30 hours'. He knew that the war would be over within fifteen minutes when he died. Trébuchon was buried with his comrades who died on 11 November in the cemetery at Vrigne-sur-Meuse, however their headstones state 10 November 1918 as the date of their deaths. It is thought that the French Army was too embarrassed for the correct date to be cited because it had allowed men to die within minutes of the war ending. According to recent research conducted by French historian, René Richard, the last French soldier killed on Armistice Day was Auguste Renault, 411st Régiment d'Infanterie, at Robechies near Chimay Belgium, at 10.58 am.[5] Renault is buried in the French military plot of Dinant, Belgium.

Many French soldiers found it difficult to celebrate the Armistice because so many of their comrades had fallen during the war. Captain René Doucet, of the 106th Régiment d'Infanterie, wrote:

When bells sounded, on November 11th, my enjoyment was hardly moderated: I had lost too many friends in four years. The company, the men of which I had commanded, was decimated.[6]

At Vrigne-sur-Meuse the adjutant Chambaz for the 415th Régiment d'Infanterie declared that: 'It is the end of our youth.'[7]

207

Chapter 18

Morning of 11 November 1918
American Sector

Since there was uncertainty regarding whether Germany would agree to the terms of an Armistice, instructions for further attacks continued to be issued. The American First Army had received orders on the night of 10 November to maintain assaults upon German positions on the Meuse–Argonne sector. Major-General Hunter Liggett recalled:

> I received orders on November 10 for a general attack by the First Army the following morning. We went into battle knowing that the terms of an armistice were being discussed with higher authority; but with no assurance that the enemy would accept those terms in the few hours that remained before the offer would expire. Fighting was our concern and our only concern until we were ordered to stop.[1]

The 4th Marine Brigade, 2nd Division, began crossing the River Meuse at Bois de l'Hospice, between Pouilly and Mouzon on 10 November. The crossing was hindered by continuous machine-gun and artillery fire, causing further casualties during the final hours of the war. German batteries targeted the bridgehead established by 2nd Division and the adjacent 89th Division. Major-General John Lejeune, commanding 2nd Division, recalled:

> The plans were carried out as directed, except that the repeated attempts to throw across the two bridges near Mouzon were frustrated by intensive enemy artillery fire which swept the approaches to the river bank, and at daylight the troops withdrew to sheltered positions. At Letanne, our efforts were successful. The 2nd

208

Engineers, assisted by other troops, carried the rafts to the river from the place in which they had been hauled by wagon, and after lashing them end to end the bridges were floated across, the men in the up-stream end leaping ashore and fastening them securely to the farther bank. The inky darkness of the night was accentuated by an extremely dense fog, and in order that troops might find the bridges, it became necessary for the 2nd Engineers to form a chain of men to act as guides, from the Bois de l'Hospice, where the men had assembled, to the crossing point. The 1st and 2nd Battalions of the 5th Marines then crossed in the order named, in the face of a heavy artillery and machine gun fire, and were followed some hours later by the liaison battalion of the 89th Division and the 1st Battalion of the 9th Infantry.[2]

Commanders in the field had received Foch's orders to maintain pressure upon Germany's forces in order to force it to accept the terms of the Armistice. Major-General John Lejeune was hopeful that the Armistice would be agreed and signed before the scheduled time for the assault upon the eastern bank of the River Meuse in order to prevent anticipated and unnecessary losses among his men. Lejeune wrote:

> The night of this last battle of the war was the most trying night I have ever experienced. The knowledge that in all probability the Armistice was about to be signed caused the mental anguish, which I always felt because of the loss of life in battle, to be greatly accentuated, and I longed for the tidings of the cessation of hostilities to arrive before the engagement was initiated; but it was not to be, and many a brave man made the supreme sacrifice for his country in the last hours of the war.[3]

Lejeune, in a letter home written the following day, noted 'to me it was pitiful for men to go to their death on the evening of peace'.[4]

During the night of 10 / 11 November, the 89th Division received orders to cross the River Meuse at 18.00 hours. Rafts were launched by 314th Engineers into the stream known as Ruisseau la Wame, which leads into the River Meuse about a mile south from Pouilly. A raft was made using three pontoons and they were used to transport 356th Infantry Regiment across to the eastern bank. The first crossing was completed by 19.15 hours with a party of sixteen engineers and twenty-two infantrymen who rowed across. The empty rafts were pulled across the river by ropes. Further infantrymen were transported across the river from 20.00 hours. Twenty-five men were placed in each raft, therefore the pontoon comprised of three rafts and meant that seventy-five men could be transported on each crossing. Within ninety minutes 1st Battalion and part of 3rd Battalion, 356th Infantry Regiment, had reached the eastern bank and was establishing a bridgehead. The 3rd Battalion, 355th Infantry Battalion, later joined it.

At 21.30 hours, an artillery barrage started to bombard Pouilly as the 1st Battalion, 356th Infantry Regiment, advanced from the river bank following a creeping barrage. It had crossed the river, where it extended its bridgehead in a north-easterly direction in an effort to secure the ridge above Pouilly and Inor. The other two battalions followed. Using compasses to maintain direction, they reached the ridge north-east of Pouilly at midnight and extended their line from the river to 2nd Division boundary, a distance of approximately a mile. German forces occupying Pouilly were unaware that they were being encircled.

Sergeant Rudolph Forderhase, 356th Infantry Regiment, 89th Division, was among the soldiers that crossed the River Meuse during the night of 10/11 November:

> On the 10 of November all were checked for ammunition and rations. That night, after dark, we assembled and marched down the steep path to the road. We turned left and marched westward. Before we had covered half the distance to where the pontoon was located that was to ferry us across the river, our own machine guns laid a barrage on all known enemy positions across the river. Our engineers had finally located some positions and had concealed them in the small creek that emptied into the river where it made a bend, and had concealed them there the previous night. They had rigged a rope at either end, and paddled them into locations where each Battalion was to effect a crossing. Our crossing was without incident, but another Battalion that crossed, was observed by the enemy and suffered severe losses in men and officers by enemy artillery and machine gun fire. As soon as our Battalion got all men across they were formed in extended combat order and marched on a course that took us across the low ground along the river and pointed us toward the high ground to the north of the village of Pouilly.[5]

Lieutenant Francis Jordan, 356th Infantry Regiment, 89th Division, used bridges that were constructed by marines from 2nd Division:

> As dark was rapidly approaching, the marine battalion commander invited our officers to meet with him in a farmhouse on a slope

within a few yards of the Meuse River. He gave us the orders which he had received from higher headquarters – the Second Division would float bridges across the river over which we would cross the other side and prepare to advance at daylight.

These bridges had been developed by the Second Division engineering company and consisted of timbers the size of railway ties with three planks nailed across them so that they could be swung across the river by the force of the current and secured to the far bank (After the war I talked to the older son of the bookstore manager in Manhattan, Kansas. He had lost the sight of one eye and said that he was a member of that engineering company, all of whom had been killed or wounded in developing those bridges).

We crossed the river on one of these two bridges under very light enemy fire which did not seem directed at more than trying to frighten us. We waded in some water as we crossed, not surprising considering the weight of each man, his rifle, ammunition, and pack. By spacing the men on the bridge, it did not sink from their weight, and we had no losses crossing our bridge. The other bridge was cut by a German shell, and one or more men were lost, since there was no chance for a man to swim in the swift flow of the Meuse River when loaded with ammunition and weapons.

When we reached the far side of the river, we were located in a spongy, grassy area until near daybreak. I slept with my chin propped on my hands to keep it out of the water.[6]

Major Mark Hanna, commanding the 2nd Battalion, 356th Infantry Regiment, 89th Division, was ordered to maintain contact with the 2nd Division on its flank. During the early hours of 11 November, Major Hanna was overseeing the crossing of the Meuse when he was killed by shellfire. His posthumous citation for the Distinguished Service Cross recorded:

> While waiting to cross the River Meuse, Major Hanna's battalion was subject to terrific shell fire. During this period he walked up and down the line encouraging and steadying his men. Major Hanna was killed at the head of his command.[7]

Hanna, who was from Kansas City, was buried at the Meuse–Argonne American Cemetery.

At Pouilly some US engineers had constructed two footbridges across the remains of the old bridge that had been demolished by German engineers. Work on this bridging operation had to be temporarily suspended when German outpost positions close to the town discovered their presence and they came under a barrage of machine gun fire. Major-General William Wright, commanding the 89th Division, reported:

> The artillery repeated its program of brisk shelling of the river towns, and under the cover of this fire the Engineers proceeded with two footbridges, and the construction of a catamaran ferry. The enemy apparently took to the shelters believing the shelling to be but a repetition of that of the night before. The enemy outposts, however, located the footbridge work and called down on it machine gun and artillery fire of sufficient severity to stop the work temporarily.[8]

The 3rd Battalion, 356th Infantry Regiment, advanced from Pouilly towards the Bois du Hache, where it met strong resistance from German machine-gun nests during the early hours of 11 November. Lieutenant-Colonel English recorded:

> A machine gun nest from the right flank was causing losses and threatening complete annihilation of the battalion. A little group of five from Company 'I' was sent out to flank the nest. They were commanded by Lieutenant John H. Murphy and consisted of Corporal Augustine Martinez and Privates Benjamin T. Tubbs, Clarence E. Lauber, and Andrew W. Dilbeck. Moving to the flank of the nest under heavy fire, they worked to within thirty yards of the nest before opening fire. One of the enemy machine guns was turned upon them from this distance and the five, without an instant's hesitation, rushed directly upon it. When within a few feet the gun ceased firing and six Germans charged them with the bayonet. Corporal Martinez fired twice from a distance of only a few feet, killing the non-commissioned officer and one of the men. The others fled. Corporal Martinez pursued them until they were lost in the fog, and returned to the position to find Lieutenant Murphy wounded and the other three men dead within ten feet of the enemy's weapon. All the Germans had fled, leaving three hot machine guns. This gallant little attack undoubtedly saved the battalion extremely heavy losses.[9]

Lieutenant Murphy, who was from Detroit, and Corporal Martinez, a resident of Aztec, New Mexico, both received the Distinguished Service

Cross for their courage on that day. Lieutenant Murphy's citation recorded:

> Lieutenant Murphy and 4 soldiers flanked a machine-gun nest of three guns only to be fired on directly at 30 yards. Charging the guns they met hand-to-hand resistance, but repulsed the enemy, capturing the guns. Lieutenant Murphy was wounded twice, and 3 of his men were killed.[10]

It took three hours for news of the Armistice to reach the 1st Division's Headquarters, as Major Thomas Gowenlock, Intelligence Officer, recalled:

> On the morning of November 11 I sat in my dugout at Le Gros Faux, which was again our division headquarters, talking to our Chief of Staff, Colonel John Greely, and Lieutenant-Colonel Paul Peabody, our G-1. A signal corps officer entered and handed us the following message:
>
> Official Radio from Paris – 6:01 A.M., Nov. 11 1918.
> Marshal Foch to the Commander-in-Chief.
> Hostilities will be stopped on the entire front beginning at 11 o'clock, November 11th (French hour).
> The Allied troops will not go beyond the line reached at that hour on that date until further orders.
> [signed] MARSHAL FOCH
> 5.45 A.M.[11]

When an orderly from the 2nd Division's radio message station brought the same message to Major-General John Lejeune at 06.05 hours, he was reluctant to carry out the order because he doubted its authenticity. Lejeune recalled:

> I at once called up the Chief of Staff of the 5th Corps and, after repeating the message just quoted, I asked if it should be carried out. He replied that it might be a German hoax and would be disregarded, adding that no attention should be paid to any such message unless it came officially from Corps Headquarters.
>
> Upon leaving Division Headquarters, the orderly evidently told the men the contents of the message he had delivered, because I heard a great burst of cheering. The cheers were repeated by more

213

distant groups until they died out in the distance. At 8.45 a.m. Brigadier-General Burt, Chief of Staff, called me personally to the telephone and gave me the Armistice message officially, with the added instructions to hold all the ground gained up to 11 a.m., and not to permit any unofficial intercourse with the enemy.[12]

Once confirmation of the signing of the Armistice had been received it was a remarkable challenge to get out the message that a ceasefire would take place at 11.00 hours once the operations scheduled for 11 November had begun. Hunter Liggett wrote:

> At 6.25 o'clock that morning I received a message from G.H.Q. saying that an Armistice had been signed and would take effect at 11 a.m. In anticipation of such a possibility, we had taken what preparatory measures we could to get the news to the troops as promptly as possible, but the advance east of Beaumont had been so rapid that morning that, what with the obstacle of the river, the order did not reach isolated units until the last moment.[13]

Major Thomas Gowenlock was keen to see the end of the war in 1st Division's sector and he confirmed that, despite the declaration of the Armistice, American artillery continued to bombard German positions right until the end:

> My watch said nine o'clock. With only two hours to go, I drove to the bank of the Meuse River to see the finish. The shelling was heavy and, as I walked down the road, it grew steadily worse. It seemed to me that every battery in the world was trying to burn up its guns.[14]

D Battery, 129th Field Artillery, 35th Division, was positioned close to Verdun on 11 November. During that morning it fired 164 artillery shells into German positions. Its commanding officer was Captain Harry S. Truman, the future President of the United States. In a letter to his fiancé, Bess Wallace, Truman wrote:

> Their time for acceptance will be up in thirty minutes. There is a great big 155 Battery right behind me across the road that seems to want to get rid of all of its ammunition before the time is up. It has been banging away almost as fast as a 75 Battery for the last two hours. Every time one of the guns goes off it shakes my house like an earthquake.

I just got official notice that hostilities would cease at eleven o'clock. Everyone is about to have a fit. I fired 164 rounds at him before he quit this morning anyway. It seems that everyone was just about to blow up wondering if Heinie would come in. I knew that Germany could not stand the gaff. For all their preparedness and swashbuckling talk they cannot stand adversity. France was whipped for four years and never gave up and one good licking suffices for Germany. What pleases me most is the fact that I was lucky enough to take a Battery through the last drive. The Battery has shot something over ten thousand rounds at the Hun and I am sure they had a slight effect.[15]

The 4th Brigade, 2nd Division, received notification of the Armistice at 08.35 hours. Orders to establish a defensive line before then were emphasised because this was an Armistice, it was not permanent peace and there existed the possibility that the conflict would resume if peace terms were not successfully negotiated. Private Malcolm Aitken, with 'D' Company, 5th US Marine Regiment, 2nd Division, recalled:

Of course, strong rumour was around on the ninth and tenth as it had been ever since Champagne that the Armistice would be signed at 11 o'clock the 11th of November; but definite rumour setting the time did not show up until the evening of the tenth and just before we hopped off everyone was thanking his lucky stars that this was the last battle. It was for a large percentage. It always seemed a shame to me that GHQ had to send those boys through that scrap when by waiting an hour or so they would have gained the objective without loss. I suppose the very psychology, as well as the known fierceness of our attack, set the affair in motion. LeJune [Lejeune], our Commanding General, was quoted as remarking 'we'll cross the Meuse if I have to carry the last Marine over on my own back'. He almost had to do just that. It was a continuous rain all the two or three weeks we were in or near the Argonne. Needless to say we were wet most of the time. Visibility was terrible.[16]

Major-General John Lejeune questioned a Marine sergeant who had been wounded during the crossing of the River Meuse. Lejeune recalled:

He told me that he had been injured by a high explosive shell just after he had crossed the bridge over the Meuse during the last battle of the war. I asked him if he had heard before the battle that the

Armistice would probably be signed within a few hours. He replied that it was a matter of common knowledge among the men. I then said, 'What induced you to cross the bridge in the face of that terrible machine gun and artillery fire when you expected that the war would end in a few hours?' in answer, he said, 'Just before we began to cross the bridge our Battalion commander, Captain Dunbeck, assembled the companies around him in the ravine where we were waiting orders, and told us "Men, I am going across that river, and I expect you to go with me," The wounded man then remarked, 'What could we do but go across too? Surely we couldn't let him go by himself: we love him too much for that.'[17]

The US Marines crossed the River Meuse under hostile fire. Private Malcolm Aitken recalled:

The morning of the 11th at 4.30, I think, we endeavoured to cross the Meuse River. We finally crossed it, after considerable loss, for the enemy commanded the crossing and defended it quite nicely.

We swam across the Meuse, in the face of a galling and murderous fire, some five hours before the Armistice. We tried pontoons – shelled out. We tried a line of men – sniped. We finally made it ... seven per cent reported present on call. Pontoons were laid and most of the outfit crossed on them, but a few of the foolish ones swam.[18]

On the Marbache sector, reinforcements entered the Bois Frehaut to support Major Warner Ross and the African–American soldiers from the 2nd Battalion, 365th Infantry Regiment, 92nd Division, who were ordered to attack Champey, Bouières, le Côte and Bois Cheminot at 05.00 hours on 11 November. The Bois Frehaut was coming under a torrent of shells and gas from German artillery as they advanced. By 07.30 hours they had reached the perimeter of Bouières and the Bois Cheminot. As the clock ticked towards the hour of the Armistice, Ross recalled:

For twenty-eight long hours we advanced and held under a bombardment that in my opinion had not been surpassed if equalled on a similar area held by American troops during a similar length of time ... All day, all night and up to eleven o'clock next morning it lasted. By midnight the entire wood fairly reeked with gas. No one dared eat or drink because of it. Despite all our precautions and efforts, we were rapidly being wiped out. I have heard of officers and of men and of units – large ones and small ones, white and also colored, that became panic stricken and useless under fire that was feeble and light both in intensity and duration compared to this, but I am ready at any time to testify that twelve hundred and fifty officers and men (colored) did advance and that the command did hold without showing the faintest symptoms of panic or retreat.[19]

Major Ross was oblivious to the knowledge that the war would end that day. He recalled the moment when he discovered that the ordeal was coming to an end:

Not until ten thirty o'clock on the morning of November eleventh did I receive orders relative to an armistice. The third runner sent out got through to me with a Division order. I was in direct command of the principal advancing done in attempts on the tenth and eleventh toward Metz and this was the first definite word I had about the armistice. We had heard that such a thing was expected, but I supposed it would be several days, maybe weeks, before it went into effect. We knew that German officers had gone through the lines under a flag of truce to meet representatives of the High Allied Command, but we did not know what the result of those parleys had been. Some thought hostilities would not cease for months.

Therefore, imagine our joy in that unbearable shell hole, when we found the war had but thirty minutes to last. Of those with me at that time some shouted for happiness and some stared in amazement fearing it was too good to be true. I sent the word out to my leaders and sat looking at my watch. Artillery fire increased in intensity if any difference and enemy machine gunners elevated their pieces and were spraying the wood with bullets. It would have been hard luck to have been hit then. Promptly at eleven o'clock all fire began to lessen and in a few minutes ceased. The World War had stopped.

Not only our men but the Germans also seemed overjoyed. Soon after the buglers had sounded 'cease firing' the Huns rushed out of their positions and our men met them between lines. They actually shook hands and slapped backs. They traded trinkets and were holding a veritable reception until our officers succeeded in getting the men back into the lines. I wouldn't believe it if I hadn't seen it.[20]

Private Jim Irby, an African–American from Alabama serving with the 366th Infantry Regiment, 92nd Division, was killed by machine-gun fire while emerging from the Voivrotte Woods on 11 November. He was buried at St Mihiel American Cemetery.

The 104th Infantry Regiment, 26th Division, was just about to launch an attack when it received news of the Armistice. Corporal Harry Wright recalled in his diary:

> On the Monday Nov 11 1918 we had orders to push them over a hill that was in front of us. We were frozen, tired and hungry as the zero hour approached. But just before we started our last drive, which would have meant many more lives, an order came through to cease firing, an armistice had been signed for 11 o'clock. It is now 10.30, one half [hour] more of this hell on earth with us on the verge of going over the top again.[21]

Mist and fog appeared at dawn on 11 November and would provide some cover for the US engineers and infantry from 5th Division, who were about to prepare to launch an assault. The divisional history recorded the moment when news of the Armistice reached them:

> A heavy fog lay over the valley of the Loison and prevented the Tenth Brigade from beginning the attack against the strongly held hills ahead of them. When at 9 o'clock the fog dispersed, infantrymen and machine gunners of the Eleventh Infantry were crawling forward toward the Boche machine-gun nests previously located. Colonel Peck had carefully prepared his attack. A unit of the Chemical Warfare Service was in position ready to assist at the given signal. But the fog lifted and the Germans discovered all these preparations.
>
> Consternation reigned in the enemy's ranks. Immediately a white flag was waved and a man came forward from the opposing lines. He was an officer and he spoke good English. Upon being conducted to Colonel Peck he exclaimed. 'My God, Sir, what are you doing? Don't you know the Armistice goes into effect at 11 o'clock?'
>
> 'No; is that so,' replied Colonel Peck. 'Then that spoils all my schemes!' And just at that moment came the radio message from Colonel Malone, 'Armistice at 11 o'clock. All fighting called off.'[22]

The 79th Division continued to fight right until the deadline at 11.00 hours as it carried out orders to assault the Côte de Romagne and Côte de Mortimont. Captain Arthur Joel wrote:

In the fog, it was extremely difficult to keep the long waves advancing in the proper direction and to keep them together on the hill or in the woods and swamp.

Pop! Pop! Pop! Pop! Pop! Zing! Zing! Crack! Crack! Crack! The intense enemy machine gun barrage caught the advancing men just after clearing the woods and starting up the slope of Côte Romagne. The first bursts were over the troops' heads, for as the Germans told us after armistice, they knew of the truce and were testing the seriousness of our intentions.

But when a skirmish line had been formed behind a slight rise of ground and the men kept up a steady fire of rifles, automatics and rifle grenades, the Rhinelanders became angry, and began cutting up the dirt with more effective aim. There was still a dense fog so that the best any one could do was to fire into the haze in the direction of the general line he judged the enemy to hold.

For a short time the situation didn't look bad: but as the enemy range improved, the supply of ammunition rapidly decreased and no news whatever came from the major or 'E' company, due to the failure of a sergeant to carry out specific orders to hold contact at any cost. Exposed flanks were highly uncomfortable, even in a fog and would be extremely dangerous if the fog cleared and the enemy became aware of our unsupported position.

Where was the major and why hadn't he dispatched any runners with orders? Should we advance in the face of the deadly fire or hold? How long would ammunition last and when would the fog clear. What happened to 'E' Company on our left and to 'G' our support? If necessary, could we fall back to a safer position, without losing a number of men in the machine gun and artillery barrage that was falling behind? These were just a few of the things that had to be considered and decided as carefully and as quickly as possible.

Runners were dispatched to the major, the rate of fire cut down to intermittent volleys, and attempts made to locate the right flank of 'E' company.[23]

Private Americo Dipasquale, 315th Infantry Regiment, 79th Division, was assaulting the Côte de Romagne before the ceasefire and was killed by shellfire while trying to bring a message. He was posthumously awarded the Distinguished Service Cross:

> Private Dipasquale volunteered his services as a connecting file, and during the course of operations was obliged to cross and re-cross

fields swept by shell and machine-gun fire. His efforts were instrumental in keeping contact with the unit of his left. While he was thus engaged, Private Dipasquale was killed.[24]

The battle for Côte de Romagne continued after 11.00 hours and eventually a runner reached the forward waves to confirm that an Armistice had been signed and passed over orders to cease fire. Captain Arthur Joel wrote:

> Finally at 11.10 a.m. an exhausted runner, Latchet, crawled through the fog to the side of the company commander and gave his message: 'War's over – cease firing – Major's orders'. About the same moment Private Purcel was shot in the wrist. Very few seconds slipped by between the command 'Cease Firing' and the turning of the safety locks on the guns.
>
> At first there was a dead calm – no shells or bullets, but just the quiet of a peaceful countryside. But the calm quickly ended with the shouts and the voices of excited and happy men. The end of the fighting had come in one of the darkest hours of the company's history.
>
> The other companies of the battalion had received orders to fall back several hundred yards and to cease firing, but the runner dispatched to 'F; had never reached his destination. Men of the other companies had attempted to halt 'F' company fire, but the noise of battle drowned their voices. The outfit killed one German after eleven and blew up a keg of their liquor with a rifle grenade. They in turn shot Purcel in the wrist.
>
> With the aid of a Pennsylvannia Dutchman, acting as interpreter, arrangements were made with the Germans to ensure the end of the strife. There was an exchange of cigarettes and wine, some snappy saluting by the clean-cut, neatly-uniformed Germans who held this position, and a rather hopeless attempt at conversation. No one seemed sorry that the war had ended.
>
> Later, lines were established, with orders from headquarters to prevent intermingling or fraternizing with the enemy as it was only an armistice.[25]

On the 79th Division's right flank, despite notification of the Armistice being received, the 313th Infantry Regiment, 'Baltimore's Own', were still ordered to launch an attack during that morning and continue fighting until 11.00 hours. The Commanding Officer of the 2nd Battalion, 313th Infantry Regiment, received the following field message from Captain Thomas Bradlee, 313th US Infantry Adjutant, issued at 09.15 hours on 11 November 1918:

> You will proceed and attack VILLE-DEVANT-CHAUMONT; hostilities will cease on the whole front at 11 H today French time. Until that hour the operations ordered will be pressed vigorously. At 11 H lines will halt in place and no man will move one step backward or forward. He will stay exactly where he is. All men will cease firing and dig in. In case the enemy does not likewise suspend firing – firing will be resumed, but no further advance will be permitted. No fraternization will be allowed. Brigade and other commanders concerned are charged with the important duty of transmitting these orders to troops and securing their strict enforcement. Rockets or other signals may be used to notify frontline of the arrival of 11 H.[26]

Prior to receiving news of the Armistice, 313th Infantry Regiment on the Lorraine sector had orders to advance towards Metz. First Lieutenant Henry G. Thorn Jr., from 313th Infantry Regiment, reported that German resistance remained strong during that final morning of the war:

> In the morning of the November 11th at 6.00 a.m. the 1st Battalion moved out of the position in which they had been since the preceding morning with orders to make a demonstration or flank attack against the left flank of the enemy who were holding the Cote-de-Romagne, a high hill rising out of the swampy plains to the east. The Battalion moved out in the direction of Crepion, passed through the town and took up a position for the jump off. The left flank of the Battalion was at the village of Chaumont-devant-Damvillers and the right flank at Ville-devant-Chaumont. The Boche fire was very heavy and no sooner had the troops come into view than a barrage was put down. The Battalion kept pressing forward, the order being to 'mop up' any of the enemy who might remain in the villages or elsewhere. The soft, marshy ground was all that saved the Battalion from appalling casualties, as the shells sunk very deep upon impact, with the result that there was little dispersion of flying fragments. The bursts seemed to throw mud, water and iron into the air.[27]

German shells continued to rain down upon the 313th Infantry Regiment's positions, just as it received word that the Armistice had been signed. The 79th Division's history recorded:

221

Fortunately, the shells struck deep in the boggy ground, hurling great columns of water and mud when exploding, but did little damage. The Armistice message reached it at 10h44. At the same time the American artillery seemed to roar with more terrible concentration. Evidently the gunners were forcing their weapons to inflict as much damage to the Boche before the arrival of the Armistice hour.[28]

The individual recognised as the last American soldier to be killed during the war was, ironically, of German descent and served in the 79th Division.

Private Henry Gunther was born during June 1895 and raised in Baltimore, Maryland. When war broke out he suffered anti-German sentiment from the people in his neighbourhood, which made him reluctant to enlist. Gunther was also unwilling to fight his own countrymen from Germany. He was employed as a book keeper in the National Bank of Baltimore, but eventually he was conscripted into the US Army during September 1917. Assigned to 'A' Company, 313th Infantry Regiment, he climbed the ranks to sergeant, however he was not content with army life. He bore great resentment that he was serving his country while at the same time his countrymen had treated him with disdain because of his German origin. When he arrived in France during July 1918 he found it difficult to adapt to life in the frontline, for he wrote to a friend at home advising him not to enlist. This letter was intercepted by an army censor and, once it was passed to his commanding officer, Gunther was demoted to private. John Cain, journalist for the *Baltimore Sun*, had interviewed Gunther's comrades after the war. Cain reported:

> According to his comrades, Gunther brooded a great deal over his reduction in rank, and became obsessed with a determination to make good before his officers and fellow soldiers. Particularly he was worried because he thought himself suspected of being a German sympathizer. The regiment went into action a few days after he was reduced and from the start he displayed the most unusual willingness to expose himself to all sorts of risks.[29]

Within minutes of the ceasefire becoming effective, Gunther and his platoon, led by Sergeant Ernest Powell, were advancing towards the village of Ville-devant-Chaumont, north-east of Verdun. A German machine-gun post opened fire upon their line of advance. They may have been warning them to stay where they were until the time of the ceasefire as Gunther charged with bayonet fixed to his rifle. Sergeant Ernest Powell ordered his platoon to take cover, but Gunther continued to rush towards the machine-gun crew. First Lieutenant Henry G. Thorn Jr. reported:

> At sixteen minutes to eleven a runner from the Regimental Headquarters caught up with the Battalion Commander with orders to cease firing at 11 a.m. French time, hold the line at the spots and neither advance nor give way to the rear. The Armistice had been signed and the fighting was to stop. The Battalion still pressed the attack vigorously and kept gaining ground, the artillery of both sides were firing rapidly and the Boche were inflicting casualties with machine guns that were placed in depth along their front. At one minute to eleven, Private Gunther of A Company was killed while attempting to rush a Bosche machine gun. Promptly at eleven the firing ceased and all was quite along the front. Somewhat dazed by the suddenness, troops rested on their arms in wonder.[30]

John M. Cain, reporting for the *Baltimore Sun*, interviewed Gunther's comrades immediately after the war and it was thought that he may have charged the German position in order to prove himself in battle, to counter perception that he was a German sympathiser or maybe to redeem himself in order to get his demotion from sergeant to private overturned. Cain reported:

> Gunther still must have been fired by a desire to demonstrate, even at the last minute, that he was courageous and all-American. When the Germans saw him coming they waved at him and called out, in such broken English as they could, to go back, that the war was over. He paid no heed to them, however, and kept on firing a shot or two ... as he went. After several vain efforts to make him turn back, the Germans turned their machine gun on him.[31]

The German machine-gunners fired a warning shot and made futile efforts to wave him back, but he took no notice of their advice, nor did he listen to Powell's order to stop. These German machine-gunners may have received word that an Armistice was taking place, but as Gunther got closer, they had no option but to shoot him in self-defence.

At 10.59 hours, one minute before the agreed ceasefire, Gunther was killed, and was recorded to have been the last American soldier to have been killed and possibly the last soldier killed during the war. Private Will Schellberg witnessed Gunther's death:

So Gunther crawled out ahead of his platoon towards a German machine gun nest. By the time he started to crawl out, he had five minutes until 11. The rest of the men in the platoon shouted to him to come back. The Germans saw him; they shouted to him to keep away. But Gunther kept on and the war was not over yet by about two minutes, so they killed him.[32]

The 79th Division history chronicled:

Right ahead of the 313th were German machine gun nests being defended to the last. On the right of the line at 10h59, Private Henry Gunther, Company 'A', charging headlong upon the enemy weapon, was shot to death, and, almost as he fell, the firing died away and an appalling silence prevailed. The fighting was over. The roar of the guns had ceased as if by magic.[33]

Gunther was posthumously reinstated to the rank of sergeant. In 1923 his remains were returned to Baltimore, where he was buried at the Holy Redeemer Cemetery.

During the morning of 11 November, the 89th Division was fighting for control of Pouilly and Stenay. The 89th Division had received official confirmation at 08.30 hours of the ceasefire at 11.00 hours, but instead of preparing its soldiers to stand down, orders were issued for advanced parties to capture Stenay, on the eastern bank of the River Meuse. Major-General William Wright reported:

At 8.30 hours information was received at the Division P.C. from the Corps that an armistice would go into effect at 11.00 hours, and that fire should cease at that time. Word was immediately sent out by all available means of liaison, including officer couriers to the frontline battalions. Artillery was directed to cease firing at 10.45, in order to avoid mistakes and violations of the armistice.[34]

However, in the following paragraph of the same report Major-General Wright claimed that the division had received notification of the Armistice much later that morning, and justified continuing an attack upon Stenay as a means to secure adequate bathing facilities:

The terms of the armistice, or the letter of instructions giving the warning as to the approaching armistice, was not received at the Division P.C. until about 10.30 hours.
Since the Division had been in the line a considerable period

without proper bathing facilities, and since it was realised that if the enemy were permitted to remain in STENAY our troops would be deprived of the billets and of the probable bathing facilities there, instructions were sent to the Infantry Commander at LANEUVILLE, to push forward directly and take STENAY, not waiting for any assistance of support of the 90th Division.

There had been considerable discussion over the matter of taking this town. It is well established that troops of this Division entered this town from LANEUVILLE and occupied its northern portion about 10.00 o'clock. Those troops stated they met practically no resistance, and found no Americans in the town. The enemy, however, had patrols in the near vicinity, which was encountered near CERVISY.[35]

Soldiers from this division entered Stenay unopposed. The 90th Division claimed to have driven out German occupants holding this town before the arrival of the 89th Division. However, Major-General Wright reported that one of his battalion commanders 'was told that the town was strongly held by the Germans and that since operations were to cease later in the day, the 90th Division would not take the town'.[36]

With no one to oppose it, the 89th Division was therefore told to advance beyond Stenay until it made contact with German soldiers. It encountered German forces at Cervisy and Inor. Major-General Wright reported:

> Not being thoroughly familiar with the terms of the armistice, the Division commander directed that our troops push forward until the enemy was actually encountered: that the enemy would not be fired upon unless he attacked: that hostilities must cease, but that any terrain which might be of military value to us, and which had been abandoned by the enemy, would be taken and occupied. It was intended to complete the operation by occupying the heights east of the river between STENAY and MOULINS. The enemy however, was found to be in INOR and in CERVISY. Moreover, orders were later received not to advance beyond the line held at 11.00 hours, and those orders were enforced.
>
> The German High Command made an official complaint that the American troops on the STENAY – BEAUMONT front had not ceased attacking at 11.00 hours, but continued their advance.
>
> Orders once fully understood were, however, loyally obeyed, although there was no regret that the Division had up to the last

hour continued to carry its offensive instructions to the fullest possible extent.[37]

Captain R.C. Hilton, of the Machine Gun Company, 9th Infantry Regiment, 2nd Division, recalled the moment of ceasefire at Mouzon, when their former German adversaries attempted to fraternise:

> About 8.00 a.m., Nov. 11th, the glad tidings reached us that the Armistice had been signed and the firing wound cease at 11.00 o'clock that day. Words cannot express the happiness of those who had suffered so during the attack and who had missed death only by the Grace of God. Promptly at 11.00 o'clock the Germans at Mouzon began coming out of the buildings and celebrating on the street. They came to the river back and beckoned us to join them in their celebration; but we kept our distance and celebrated among ourselves.[38]

The 131st Infantry Regiment, 33rd Division, which comprised National Guard volunteers from Illinois, was ordered to attack Bulgnéville. Its commander, Colonel Joseph Sanborn, reported:

> While the troops were being assembled in the Bois de Warville, at 8.30 a.m., telephone notice was received that the armistice had been signed, that all firing on our part was to cease at once except to repel counter-attacks, the information being conveyed to troops in position and re-enforcing battalions successfully as they arrived. The enemy gradually ceased firing from the trenches and machine gun positions, but it was not until 11.00 o'clock sharp that a complete cessation was noticed. One machine gunner ran out into a position and shot at everybody in sight up to the last moment. Artillery fire with shrapnel also did not cease until a few minutes after eleven. Faithful to their trust, true to their traditions, noble in their sacrifice, the men of Illinois were suffering, wounded and dying, when the curtain came down at the end of the great world tragedy.[39]

First Lieutenant William Cary Sanger Jr, 131st Infantry Regiment, 33rd Division, reported:

> After ten a.m. the sound of the artillery fire increased and just before eleven a.m. the woods and the plain far and wide reverberated with intermittent rolling and concussion of the guns. And then, at eleven a.m., the tumult suddenly died away and all was still.[40]

Captain Morrill L. Cook, an infantry officer who originated from Pittsburgh, had been fighting throughout the previous day and night, so it was a welcome relief to know that the war would be coming to an end at 11.00 hours. In a letter to a friend in New York, Cook wrote of the emotions he felt when this news came through:

> The day before the Armistice we started an attack. All the afternoon we fought; all during the night we advanced through a deep fog, enemy machine-guns being our only guide, so blinded were we by the heavy mist. Daylight found us in the shell-eaten ruins of a little French village near the German border. It seemed that none could exist there, so filled by mustard gas was it, but nevertheless the Boches were still shelling it heavily. Four times the wall behind which we stood was struck with shells, and four times men standing near me paid the supreme price of battle on the morn of the Armistice.
>
> At eight o'clock the enemy artillery ceased firing. I could not understand it. The only evidence of battle was the drumming of the machine guns and occasional stretchers passing by. At nine-fifteen we received word that the Armistice had been signed. There was no excitement, no elation – we were too cold, too tired – our nerves had responded to too many sensations to respond even to this. But a strange, overwhelming sense of comfort, of thankfulness, of quiet joy, came over us. The war was over. We would have Peace! No longer would we walk the lines in apprehension. No longer would we hide the lights at night or live in caves, or go without food, or shiver because we could not build a fire, or wear wet clothes, or cling to our gas masks and helmets. There among the ruins we stood – thirty of us – tired, dirty, hungry – cheering our chaplain, who waived the emblem of our principles for which we had fought, while the sun struggled through the thinning mist to join our celebration.
>
> A grin – a hug, and we sat waiting for eleven o'clock to come. At ten o'clock there was absolute quiet for about one minute, and then all hell broke loose on both sides. For an hour it continued, as though everyone realised that it was the last opportunity to express the accumulated hatred of five years of desperate fighting. But at eleven it ceased as it had begun.[41]

The 115th Infantry Regiment had spent the past two weeks in Verdun on leave after fighting during the Meuse–Argonne offensive. During the morning of 11 November it was about to leave its billets and Chaplain F.C. Reynolds recalled:

Thus the old regiment, a veteran regiment now, tattered, depleted and exhausted as it came from the terrible ordeal of the Meuse–Argonne offensive, was fed up, rested up, patched up, equipped and in ten days' time was ready for another descent into hell.

From numerous rumours that reached us, it was evident that Germany was weakening and all but crushed. A report came saying that Germans had sent officers across the line to ask for an armistice. We were all delighted and hoped the end might really come before we were called into another killing drive. Word came that the old Kaiser had abdicated. It seemed too good to be true and yet all these reports sent our hopes high. On the night of November 10, however, all hopes were dashed to the ground; we received an order stating that the 29th Division had been transferred from the First to the Second American Army and should proceed by marching via certain villages to the left of Metz, the best of all Germany's fortified cities. It was an order sending us into another drive, probably worse than the Meuse–Argonne. To many of us it sounded like a death sentence: and it was, for had it been carried out, we would have lost another third of our regiment but in the army orders must be followed even though they mean death. So, on the morning of November 11, we rolled our packs, said goodbye to the few French friends we had made and with heavy hearts turned grim faces toward Metz, determined to battle on to decisive victory.

Just before we began our march into another big offensive, we received an official order from Divisional headquarters stating that the armistice had been signed, that all hostilities would cease at 11 o'clock that day, and that our regiment should remain comfortably in its billets rather than go into hell again. You can imagine – no, you can't imagine, it is impossible for anyone to imagine who did not experience it – the sense of relief and pure joy that came in our hearts. Although we had been expecting an armistice to be signed for some time, the full significance of it dawned upon us only gradually. At first we took it quietly. The feeling of gratitude was too deep for noisy expression. Instead of running out in the street, yelling and turning a hand spring, we felt like stealing away into some lonely spot and crying for sheer joy. We were happy, so happy, that the hellish enemy of justice and brotherhood had fallen into the dust of defeat and that it was no longer necessary to continue to kill and be killed, that we quietly looked at each other, whispered a 'Thank God' and wondered if it could really be true.[42]

Chapter 19

The Guns Fall Silent
11.00 Hours, 11 November 1918

The 1st Royal Scots Fusiliers was billeted close to Le Quesnoy and had received orders to move towards Maubeuge, where it was to support the Guards Division. Major Denys Reitz, commanding the battalion, wrote of the moment when he heard that an armistice had been agreed on 11 November:

> At daybreak on the morning of November 11th we marched out. In front and behind us were thousands of other troops going forward, and one could feel the suppressed excitement in the air, for every man realised that this was their final thrust. By 11 o'clock we were in the battle zone, British and German guns were firing, and there came the crackle of rifles and machine-guns ahead.
>
> Suddenly, far off, we heard the faint sound of cheering borne upon the wind. It gathered volume as it rolled towards us, and then we saw our Brigade-Major slowly making his way through the troops on the road. He carried good tidings, for around him the shouts grew deafening which I have carefully preserved. It contained momentous news:
>
> To 1st Royal Scots Fusiliers.
> M.2. 11 Nov
> Corps wire aaa. Hostilities will cease at 11.00 hours today 11th Nov. aaa Troops will stand fast on line reached at that hour which will be reported to Corps H.Q. aaa. There is to be no intercourse with the enemy and no Germans are to be allowed to enter our lines, any doing so will be taken prisoner.

From 8th Inf. Brig.

11.00 hours

G.H. Ewing, Capt.,and Actg. Brig-Major.[1]

Major Denys was excited by the implications of the Armistice, but his soldiers remained sombre. Denys recalled:

> Amid the demonstrations of the other troops, the Scots Fusiliers remained comparatively unmoved. A few cheers were raised, and there was solemn handshaking and slapping of backs, but otherwise they received the news with great calm. To me it was a supreme moment. I saw the beginnings of a new era for the world and for my country.[2]

An anonymous ranker from the London Rifle Brigade at Erquennes recalled the tense moments before the ceasefire as their eyes intently focused upon their watches as the clock ticked towards 11.00 hours and then their initial thoughts as they realised what the Armistice meant:

> Towards eleven o'clock we constantly looked at our watches to see how much longer the war had got to last and it was a difficult task for Watkins to walk up and down the lines urging men to erect harness racks in breathless moments like that. At about ten minutes to eleven a gun sounded in the far distance and we wondered whether any poor devil had 'gone west' as a result of that shot.
>
> Then the minutes ticked on and a clock struck eleven. Immediately the bells of the village church rang out and women came to their doorsteps literally weeping for joy: a feeble cheer went up from the section and men gathered in knots to discuss the turn of events. We were really too stunned for much gesticulation. To think there would be no more shells, no more bombs, no more gas, no more cold nights to be sent on picket through fear of lighting a fire. Of all the incredible announcements that had ever been made to us, this left us the most staggered. It must be only a dream! Surely we should hear the distant sound of guns in a minute or so, which would prove we had been deluded! We strained our ears for distant gunfire … Silence! Only the sound of church bells in other villages proclaiming the event.
>
> Armistice signed! If only we were in England now! Just picture the enthusiastic crowds in London, in the offices and restaurants and streets! Just picture the shouting and the singing and waving of

flags! What celebrations! What lovely girls would be blowing kisses to all and sundry! What crowds there would be round bars!

Erquennes! Fellows repeated the word contemptuously, as though there existed in the universe no more benighted spot in which to celebrate the occasion.[3]

Major Keith Officer, a staff officer serving with Australian Corps, recalled as he waited for 11 o'clock with an officer from the Scots Greys at Le Cateau:

At 11 o'clock on the 11 of November I was sitting in a room, in the Brewer's House at Le Cateau which had been Sir John French's headquarters at the time of the Battle of Mons. I was sitting at a table with a major in the Scots Greys who had a large map and an old fashioned hunting watch which he put on the table and watched the minutes going round. When 11 o'clock came, he shut his watch up and said, 'I wonder what we are all going to do next!' That was very much the feeling of everyone. What was one going to do next? To some of us it was the end of four years, to others three years, to some less. For many of us it was practically the only life we had known. We had started so young.[4]

Major Keith Officer also recalled that nearby a German machine-gun crew continued to fire upon the British lines at Le Cateau and the extraordinary moment when the clock stopped exactly at 11 o'clock:

Nearby there was a German machine-gun unit giving our troops a lot of trouble. They kept on firing until practically 11 o'clock. At precisely 11 o'clock an officer stepped out of their position, stood up, lifted his helmet and bowed to the British troops. He then fell in all his men in the front of the trench and marched them off. I always thought that this was a wonderful display of confidence in British chivalry, because the temptation to fire on them must have been very great.[5]

Naturally, German soldiers felt disappointment and dejection when they learned that the Armistice had been signed. Captain Herbert Sulzbach, of the German 9th Division, wrote:

The war is over ... How we looked forward to this moment, how we used to picture it at the most splendid event of our lives; and

231

here we are now, humbled, our souls torn and bleeding, and know that we've surrendered. Germany has surrendered to the Entente![6]

Meanwhile, in the French village of Escarmaine, Private Sydney Wratten, 23rd Royal Fusiliers, wrote about how he received the news in a letter to his sister:

I noticed no difference at all: everyone took his usual duties; here and there someone discussed it. At eleven o'clock someone quietly announced that the war was finished, and I went on washing my shirt. The solution, I should think, is that the men are dazed, too dazed to realize it. War to me, had become an everyday affair, and you must remember the boys had scrapped and walloped the Germans back 80 odd miles, and in about 60 miles one does about 600 miles marching. But here I am, intact, not even a trouser button missing, and since the armistice was concluded have sat in this busted French village scrubbing each strap and shining each buckle until it is finally filtering through my puny brain that I am indeed a peace time soldier. I've something like a fortnight's hefty marching to do, finishing up somewhere in the land of the Huns, and unless they send people on leave from there, I think I shall be an exile from the home of my father's for a few more weeks. When I sit thinking (sometimes I do these silly things) it soaks through that I have had a miraculous existence, especially the first 26 months: a whole skin through of bombing in the Somme, Ancre and Vimy battles, and a runner through the Arras and Cambrai battles and the 1918 retreat. I just sit down and test my tunic buttons to their utmost around my chest.[7]

War Correspondent Percival Philips was at Leuze and witnessed the events that took place in the town centre at 11.00 hours:

Just at eleven I came into the little town of Leuze, which had been one of the headquarters nearest the uncertain front. In the market place were British troopers on their horses drawn up in a hollow square, 3rd Dragoons, Royal Dragoons and 10th Hussars, of the 6th Cavalry Brigade, all in fighting kit. In the centre was the 1/4th Battalion of the King's Own, Barrow men, of the 51st Division, thrown across the square, their colonel at the head and the old Mayor of Leuze beside him. From the windows of all the houses round about and even from the roofs, the inhabitants looked down on the troops and heard uncomprehendingly the words of the colonel as he read from a sheet of paper the order that ended hostilities.

A trumpeter sounded 'Stand fast.' In the narrow high street at one end of the little square were other troops moving slowly forward, and as the notes of the bugle rose clear and crisp above the rumble of the gun carriages these men turned with smiles of wonder and delight and shouted to each other 'The war is over.'

The band of the Barrow men played 'God Save the King'. None heard it without a quiver of emotion. The mud stained troops paused in the crowded street. The hum of traffic was stilled. A rippling cheer was drowned in the first notes of the Belgian hymn; the 'Marseillaise' succeeded it, and the Army of each Ally was thus saluted in turn. I do not think that anyone heard the few choked words of the old Mayor when he tried to voice the thanks of Belgium for this day of happiness.

The Army 'carried' on briskly, as though a little ashamed of the emotion which had seized us all for an unforgettable moment. People shook hands in an embarrassed way and said to each other: 'Well, it's finished,' and the harassed traffic man at the corner resumed his weary task with even greater ferocity. Someone fired a Verey pistol into a field, and silver balls of light drifted over the heads of the troops – and that was the only outward sign of rejoicing.[8]

At Mons the Canadian 31st Battalion continued its advance upon German lines right up to the moment of the ceasefire. The war diary reported:

> The Battalion on our right was a considerable distance behind us, and the work of dislodging the enemy from the woods ... devolved upon us. At 11. hours 'B' Company had worked to within one hundred and fifty yards of the enemy posts at these points. The order cease fire was given, the enemy put up the white flag, shot up white flares, about sixty of them got out of their posts at the command of their officer, emptied the water out of their machine guns and marched away in formation.[9]

Meanwhile, the people of Mons and the Canadian liberators from 42nd Battalion continued their celebrations in the town centre:

> At 11 o'clock – the hour of 'Cease-fire' – in the Grand Place, the Mayor presented Brigadier-General J.A. Clark, DSO, G.O.Q., 7th

Canadian Inf. Brigade, with the keys of the city in honour of its capture by units of his Brigade. Such elements of the Brigade as could be withdrawn from the line were formed up en masse and after the celebrations were completed there was a formal march pass which was led by our Pipe Band. We were only able to have one Company and part of Headquarters on this parade as three of our Companies were still holding the Outpost Line and had not at that moment been relieved. The great square was filled with civilians and the troops got tremendous applause as they marched out.[10]

War correspondent H.W. Nevinson observed the scenes in Mons on Armistice Day:

It was fitting that the Armistice should be proclaimed at Mons, celebrated for the gallantry of our men at the very beginning of the war, the predecessors of those men whose steadiness and gallantry have won the war at last.

That was why I was determined to get to Mons at all costs today if possible, and, favoured by good fortune and first rate guide, I arrived there just in time.

It was just upon eleven when we entered Mons and behold the fine towers of its belfry and churches and Town Hall. High overhead a swarm of aeroplanes were dropping brilliant white stars, which fell slowly through the air. Perhaps they were Verey lights. Around us, on both sides of the road, the crowds stood thick, cheering and laughing and crying with joy.

On reaching the main square I found troops already drawn up in front of the beautiful old Town Hall. They were the 7th Brigade, 3rd Canadian Division, together with a squadron of the Hussars with their lances.

At 11.15, the General commanding the Canadian Brigade rode up. He called the parade to attention, they sloped arms, and led by the General, gave three cheers for King Albert. Then the National Anthems of Belgium and England were played, the population joining in the words of their own hymn. Except where the soldiers stood the whole square was crammed with people, and all the windows and roofs were crowded, too.

Flags hung from every point. The carillon in the belfry played the 'Marseillaise'. The people cheered as though they could never stop. The children clung to every British or Canadian band they could catch hold of. I was told that the General's duty was to hand over control of the town to the civil authorities. That was certainly a fitting end to the war, and all rejoiced that it was such an end.[11]

Private Reginald Johnson served with the 6th Battalion Tank Corps and was at Quivey heading for Mons when he learned that the talk of Armistice was now a reality:

> The rumour had been going for a day or two that the war was coming to an end and we was prepared for any news. We were advancing and we certainly got the Germans on the run. We could see that we had got the better of them, they were not making a stand at all …We were at a village called Quivey when we heard the news that the Armistice had been signed. Of course there was great rejoicing, I think there was some sort of heartburning as well, we had not got anything to do. We had a stock of Verey lights, these were the lights that were used for sending up signals at night, or even at daytime sometimes … at the Armistice we collected all these and had a proper firework display.[12]

On the French Sector, Captain Charles de Berterèche de Menditte, from the 415th Régiment d'Infanterie, recalled in his diary the moment when the guns fell silent at Vrigne-sur-Meuse:

> 11 o'clock: One of my bugles plays 'Cease Fire', 'Stand Up' then 'Face the flag'. The other bugles repeat. The Marseillaise is heard in the distance. Shouting of joy, and far away the shouts of the Boches who get out their holes and want to fraternize. What a joy and what emotion![13]

Private Ernest Brec, of the 77th Régiment d'Infanterie, recalled how they received the news of the Armistice on the French sector:

> Damn! A wave of joy swept over us. I don't know if I'd tears in my eyes. Like the others, I must have shouted 'Vive la France!' For a moment we were left breathless with happiness. Great sorrow is silent; so too is great joy. Then the shock passed, we recovered our power of speech and with it the reflex common to all Frenchmen, 'We'll have to drink a toast to that!' Yes, but with what? There was no red wine in this poor little place, just a bottle of lousy sparkling wine Bebert dug up in a shop where the bastard made us pay fifteen francs. We split it sixteen ways, hardly enough to wet your whistle! And that was how, on 11 November 1918, my battalion celebrated victory in a little town in the Meurthe-et-Moselle.[14]

As soon as the Armistice was announced, twenty unarmed German soldiers approached the French lines, held by the 163rd Régiment d'Infanterie at Metzeral near Belfort, and surrendered.

> At eleven o'clock, end of the hostilities, as a consequence of the Armistice entered into the Allied and German lines. The troops keep their fighting positions. Twenty or so Germans soon after the end of the hostilities put themselves forward without weapons in front of our lines, they are taken prisoners.[15]

Lieutenant Alden Brooks was an American citizen serving with the French 81st Regiment Heavy Artillery. Brooks participated in an experiment conducted by the French War Office to train Americans already in Europe and then return them to the American Army when US forces arrived in France. Brooks graduated, however his eyesight was so poor that he did not meet the standards needed to serve with the American artillery. The French Army accepted him and he was assigned to 81st Regiment Heavy Artillery. Brooks recalled:

> The Germans had agreed to sign the Armistice. It was the end, the war was over. It was a strange moment. Much as we had already discounted the event of late, it seemed to have come, now, all very suddenly. We were pleased of course, greatly pleased; yet we hardly knew what to say or what to do about it. The Colonel appeared even a trifle depressed. In these recent hours he had more and more stormed against this Armistice as the most idiotic of measures. What! Leave the Boche off now, just as we had him utterly licked and on the run? ...
> So at lunch we opened wine and quaffed each other's health and discussed future plans. We would surely go to Bocherie, we thought, and stay there while peace-terms were being discussed. Then many of us would be demobilized, allowed to return to civil life; and then ... then ... well, great heaven, only that moment come now as soon as it would.[16]

On the Meuse–Argonne sector, Major-General John Lejeune, 2nd Division, remembered:

> During the last two hours before the Armistice the enemy's artillery fire was intensified and our artillery sent as good as it received. A few minutes before eleven o'clock, there were tremendous bursts of fire from the two antagonists and then – suddenly – there was

complete silence. It was the most impressive celebration of the Armistice that could possibly have taken place. There was a solemn and an earnest joy in the hearts of every man at the front. We were satisfied with the terms of the Armistice. We were happy because fighting, death and destruction had ceased. I offered up a prayer of thanksgiving, to Almighty God.[17]

Lieutenant Francis Jordan, of the 356th Infantry Regiment, had been wounded after crossing the River Meuse during the morning on 11 November. He had made his way back across the river to Beaumont, where his wounds were being tended. It was here that he first heard about the Armistice. He recalled:

At 11 o'clock someone came in to announce that the war was over, but there was little cheering. Someone was able to play a hymn on the pipe organ, however, and somehow that helped us to realize that the war was over.[18]

A correspondent from *The Times* reported that close to Sedan in the American sector, German machine-gunners deliberately aimed high to avoid hitting American troops:

Punctually at eleven o'clock fighting on both sides stopped. The lasts shots fired on the German side were from machine-guns, which were aimed high in the air, the bullets falling two or three miles behind the lines.[19]

Captain Eddie Rickenbacker, commander of 94th Aero Squadron, was an American fighter ace and Medal of Honor recipient who had shot down twenty-one German aeroplanes and five observation balloons during the war. On 11 November he took to the skies to observe the moment when the war ended. He recalled:

I decided I wanted to see the real ending, and in spite of the fact that all combat units had been ordered to stay on the ground for twenty-four hours prior to 11.00 a.m. on November 11, I managed to wiggle my way up to the front alone, all unbeknownst to any other members of my squadron. I say 'wiggled' because there was a lot of fog between our aerodrome and no-man's land.

Reaching the village of Pont-à–Mousson on the Moselle river, I flew at about 100 feet along the front over no-man's land, passing to the left of Metz, and then over the village of Fontoy. I crossed the line about two minutes before the hour of eleven, and the troops on both sides – Germans and Americans – could be seen very clearly. Some shots were fired at me, but at the appointed hour all shooting ceased, and then slowly and cautiously, soldiers came out of the German and American trenches, throwing their rifles and helmets high into the air. They met in no-man's land and began fraternizing just as a group of school kids would after a football game – happy in the realization that they would not be killed in this terrible conflict. It was fantastic to them, and to me, to know that the war was over.[20]

There was apprehension about the prospect of an Armistice on the German side. Georg Bucher suffered from American artillery fire and bombing by US aeroplanes in the hours prior to the Armistice. One of his comrades, a youngster named Walter, had been wounded by a bomb. The German division on the adjacent sector was coming under further shelling. Bucher recounted:

All we could think of was how to survive the next three hours ... Walter was quite cheerful by the time 10.30 arrived. 'Only another half-hour,' he remarked.

Suddenly the bombardment came down on us. After a few hellish moments our own artillery joined in with the utmost ferocity, using up the reserves of ammunition upon the enemy's trenches and battery-position. The armistice would witness an orgy of burials.[21]

It was difficult for some German soldiers to believe that the Armistice was about to take place after the ferocious violence that had taken place that morning. As the minutes drew closer to 11.00 hours their only hope was that they would survive those final minutes of the war and live to see the peace. Bucher wrote:

The minutes seemed an eternity ... there was a great silence. We stood motionless gazing at the shell-fumes which drifted sluggishly across No-man's-land. Those minutes seemed eternal. I glanced at my watch – I felt that my staring eyes were glued to it. The hour had come. I turned round: 'Armistice!'

Then I went back to the youngster. I couldn't bear to go on staring at No-man's-land and at the faces of the men. We had lived through an experience which no one would ever understand who had not shared it.

'Armistice, Walter! It's all over!'[22]

238

In the American 71st Division's sector at Crepion, the divisional historian chronicled:

> Half out of a trench we found a young boy, perhaps not over sixteen years of age, killed on the morning of the Armistice. In his hand he clasped a letter written in German addressed from Umlaut and written by his mother. Translated it read, 'I have dreamed bad dreams of you. I am afraid that something has happened. Come home on a furlough if you can.' Her vision had come true.[23]

Some German soldiers were jubilant and attempted to fraternise with their former enemy. In particular, those who had lived in the United States prior to the war were keen to cross into the American lines and fraternise. Major-General Hunter Liggett recalled:

> The silence that fell at 11 o'clock was stunning to ears attuned to the infernal roar. Our men showed no particular elation; the full significance of the moment was not then apparent. But the German, who knew that he was well quit on any terms, was noisily jubilant. That night he burned up all his rockets and flares in a 'Fourth of July' celebration. We sent out rigid orders to the frontline troops against fraternisation, both for reasons of policy and because we were suspicious to the last, with good cause, of the enemy's good faith. Numbers of German soldiers, especially men who had lived in the United States or who had relatives here, attempted to visit our lines, but were warned back. They knew that we had many in our Army of German blood. One of the best fighting divisions was General Haan's Thirty-Second, a Wisconsin and Michigan National Guard unit, a majority of whom probably were of German extraction.[24]

German soldiers were also friendly on the sector of the line close to Ville-devant-Chaumont, where the last US soldier, Private Henry Gunther, was killed. First Lieutenant Henry Thorn Jr., of the 313th Infantry Regiment, wrote:

> The balance of November 11th seemed to impress different people in different ways. At first it seemed strange to be able to expose one's self without drawing fire. The Boche was inclined to be friendly, but the men all obeyed strictly the order against fraternizing and did not pay any attention to the enemy, except that there were no relaxing of vigilance. Boche would always bear watching and everyone realized it.[25]

A group of German soldiers approached French advanced posts on the 162nd Régiment d'Infanterie near Metz at 16.00 hours:

> During the day, at about 16 hours, a group of Germans among whom two appear to be officers advanced on the ford of the mill of Chambille and seemed to want to fraternize with our advanced elements. They were repelled.[26]

Although the clock struck 11.00 hours and the Armistice was enforced along most sectors across the Western Front, some units did not receive the notification that the ceasefire would take place at that designated time and as a consequence many soldiers died although hostilities had ceased. On the American 1st Division's front, Major Thomas Gowenlock, the division's intelligence officer, recalled:

> At last eleven o'clock came – but the firing continued. The men on both sides had decided to give each other all they had – their farewell to arms. It was a very natural impulse after their years of war, but unfortunately many fell after eleven o'clock that day.[27]

During the afternoon of 11 November, Major-General John Lejeune visited the 2nd Division Field Hospital, where he met soldiers who had been wounded a few seconds after the designated time for the ceasefire on 11 November:

> I asked a man who had been badly mangled by a shell to tell me how and when he had been wounded. He said he was in duty in the telephone exchange of one of the artillery regiments, and the message came over the wire, 'It is 11 o'clock and the war is _____.' At this point, he said, a shell landed and burst in the room killing his 'buddy' and seriously wounding him. So far as I have been able to learn, these were the last casualties of the war. The shell was doubtless fired a second or so before 11 o'clock, and reached its mark a few seconds after the clock had struck the hour which brought peace to more millions of people than had any other hour in the world's history.[28]

The 356th Infantry, 89th Division, did not receive notification that an Armistice would take place at 11.00 hours on that day until after the time of the ceasefire. It was difficult to communicate to these units because they were in the process of extending the bridgehead across the River Meuse. Sergeant Rudolph Forderhase was an American soldier of German descent, and could speak fluent German. Forderhase recalled the moment he approached a German machine-gun position, where he encountered two German soldiers with raised hands waiting to surrender:

> A dense fog had formed, during the night, and persisted until mid-morning, so Captain Ernsberger did not see the two young Germans, with their light machine gun, until he was close upon them. They were standing in the shallow pit they had dug with their hands held high in surrender. I could not see the incident, but the Captain called me to come. I was quite surprised to see them. The Captain knew I could speak a bit of German and told me to ask them why they had not fired on us. They informed me that all fighting was to end at eleven o'clock that morning and they saw no reason to sacrifice their lives, or ours, needlessly. Neither the Captain, not I, knew whether to believe them or not.[29]

There were some German soldiers who were determined to defend their positions until the end. As the 356th Infantry Regiment advanced forward through the fog it came under hostile fire. Lieutenant Francis Jordan recalled:

> We were then ordered forward and came under close machine gun fire not more than fifteen or twenty feet on our left. I received a minor flesh wound through the shoulder, which bullet continued on to hit my pack which was filled with cans of food. The impact tipped me over backwards, and, in falling, I threw up my hand and received a bullet at the base of my left thumb. The machine gun had been shifted quickly and killed the first sergeant immediately behind him. Our advance was stopped for the time being.
>
> Corporal Wicker crawled up beside me and put his rifle across my chest to fire in the direction of the German machine guns. The return fire was so accurate the wood on the corporal's rifle was splintered. Those of us who had been wounded remained there for some time, while those who were unwounded took up the advance to locate and kill the German machine gunner.[30]

Sergeant Rudolph Forderhase wrote:

> Our objective was the Autreville–Stenay Road, which was reached in less than a half-hour. On our way we were again under fire from the enemy on our left front and within fifty feet of the road. It was

from a machine gun and was too low so resulted in no casualties. We were not able to locate the gun which must have been at a considerable distance. We now proceeded along the road to a point above the hamlet of Inor, on the edge of the Bois de Sairy. The road ran parallel to the river but was generally at a level of about half way up the hill. A sniper located somewhere above us in the forest, was firing on our troops in the village below us. Apparently he could not see us and we could not see him. We were somewhat concerned about this when suddenly the sniper's firing ceased – everything became perfectly quiet, I then remembered what the two German prisoners had said earlier that morning. I took a look at the cheap wrist watch that I had been wearing. It stopped at eleven o'clock and I never did get it to run again. It was past 11.30 a.m. when we got orders to cease fire.[31]

It was in the 89th Division's sector that Lieutenant Thomä, of the German 19th Uhlans, was the last reported enemy casualty. He was killed after 11.00 hours on the Meuse–Argonne Sector, at Inor, 3½ miles north of Stenay. Thomä was shot as he approached a group of American soldiers, who were unaware of the Armistice, in order to inform them that the war was over and that he and his men would vacate their billets, so that the Americans could use them.

Lieutenant Colonel George English Jnr. chronicled this tragic episode in the American 89th Division's history:

> The delay in the receipt of orders in reference to the taking effect of the Armistice occasioned a regrettable incident. Inor was in the sector of the 356th Infantry and the mission of capturing it, after the crossing of the Meuse had been assigned by Colonel Allen to his 3rd Battalion, which was in support. Intense machine gun fire from the town had been directed on the flanks of the assault battalion as it passed. The operation for the capture of Inor was under way when the hour of the taking effect of the Armistice arrived, but Colonel Allen did not receive the orders until 11.40; and the commander of the 3rd Battalion did not receive them until 12.15. In this state of affairs the German commander of the troops in the vicinity, assuming that the town lay between the hostile positions, sent a detachment of an officer and two men into Inor for the purpose of finding out whether the town was required by us for the quartering of troops. The party consisted of Lieutenant Thomä, Sergeant Benz and Corporal Shweiker, all of the 19th Uhlan Regiment. When about to enter Inor from the north, at about noon, the party encountered a

detachment of Company 'L' 356th Infantry under the command of 1st Lieutenant Leon P. Shinn. The Americans, unaware of the armistice, opened fire upon them, wounding the officer. The wounded officer drew his pistol and ended his life by shooting himself through the head. The sergeant escaped, but the corporal was made prisoner and sent to the rear in accordance with the usual routine in the case of prisoners.[32]

One could ask the question, why would the wounded Lieutenant Thomä commit suicide when he knew that the war was over? Maybe officers belonging to the 89th Division wanted to cover up the fact that their soldiers had killed a German officer after the agreed ceasefire.

It is also thought that Unteroffizer Leonhard Eckel was the last German soldier to be killed during the war. Although he died in action at Maheulles, near Fresne-en-Woevre, on Armistice Day, he is buried in a mass grave at Maizeray German Cemetery, with the date of death listed as 10 November 1918. Eckel is commemorated in the village of his birth at Edesheim, where the square and an estate is named in his honour, as well as a plaque.

Fighting continued after 11.00 hours in the 2nd Division's sector. Major-General Lejeune recalled:

> About 1 p.m. on November 11th, a telephone call from Corps Headquarters caused quite a stir. The message originated with Marshal Foch, and was to the effect that the American troops on the east bank of the Meuse just south of Mouzon were still continuing their advance towards Moulins, and that they had not ceased firing at 11 a.m. The Marshal directed that all military operations cease immediately.[33]

Lejeune had no knowledge of reports of continued fighting, but he immediately dispatched officers to the frontline to investigate the situation, who reported that fighting had ceased. Months later, Lejeune spoke to Major George Hamilton DSC, who commanded the 1st Battalion, 5th Marine Regiment, on 11 November. Lejeune recalled:

> I questioned him about the report that that his men had not stopped advancing at 11 a.m. on November 11th, as ordered. He replied that he did not personally receive the message until about 11.30 a.m. and that it was fully noon before it reached all the advanced elements of the battalion, but as soon as the message was received he had ceased to advance, had drawn back his men to the positions which they had

reached at 11 a.m. and had thought no more about the matter, as there had been no casualties on either side after 11 o'clock.[34]

Private Malcolm Aitken, of the US 5th Marine Regiment, 2nd Division, recalled that his unit did not receive confirmation of the Armistice until 14.00 hours, which meant it had unknowingly continued the war three hours after the designated ceasefire time:

> We had about completed our first consolidation and most of us were taking pot-shots at anything we thought we saw up ahead, when the order 'Cease Firing but Stand-to' came hurling down the line, passed by word of mouth. Sometime later, I think it was about 2 pm, definite word was passed that an Armistice had been signed.
>
> We spent the afternoon fixing guard posts, general and special orders, established reliefs, and then proceeded to celebrate. We built a roaring fire, salvaged some wine and other rations that we had staked out; and saw the old year out and the new one in, in appropriate fashion. There was plenty of yelling and dancing around as we made bets as to who had fired the last shots. Several shots were fired during this time, until someone ordered us to be careful or we would start a war.[35]

An American, Lieutenant Alden Brooks, serving with the French artillery, recalled that late during the afternoon on 11 November American forces were still fighting several hours after the Armistice:

> Towards four o'clock our radio truck captured still another message: 'German Supreme Command to Allied Supreme Command. On the front Stenay-Beaumont, on the Meuse, the Americans are continuing attacks despite the armistice agreement. Please order suspension of hostilities. German Supreme Command.'
>
> The incident evoked smiles. Twenty minutes later there was the following answer: 'G.H.Q. of the Allies to German G.H.Q. Have received your radio of the 15.45. Orders have been given that American attacks signalled on the front Stenay-Beaumont cease immediately. G.H.Q. of the Allies.[36]

The German High Command made an official complaint that US soldiers did not adhere to the ceasefire at 11.00 hours and continued to advance into their lines between Beaumont and Stenay. The 89th Division's commander stated in his defence that there was not sufficient time to get word of the Armistice by 11.00 hours. The 89th Division suffered the following casualties during the last week of the war:

Final phase, Meuse–Argonne offensive, 1 to 6 November 1918:	1,646 casualties.
Holding the line along the River Meuse, 6 to 10 November 1918:	571 casualties.
Crossing the River Meuse, 10 to 11 November 1918:	362 casualties.
Total Casualties:	3,578.[37]

Major-General Robert Bullard, Commander of the US Second Army, wrote the following report regarding the fighting that took place after the ceasefire on 11 November 1918:

Today (November 11) the attack was renewed as ordered, but after 6 a.m. a telegram announced that an armistice would go into effect at 11 a.m. and all fighting and advance must then stop. I gave the corresponding orders. Some of our divisions of the line had already been pretty thoroughly committed to the attack, others not. The former continued, the latter desisted, though all were partially engaged. As on the 10th, the best work was done on the west by the 33rd Division, General George Bell. The others accomplished little. But the fighting continued until the last minute. I regard this day as the last fighting of the war. So I early went, with an aide, to near the front line, to see the last of it, to hear the crack of the last guns in the greatest war of all ages. It was an occasion of great history and great happening. Our men showed great zest in the striking of the last blows against the enemy. I stayed until 11 a.m., when all being over, I returned to my headquarters, thoughtful and feeling lost. It was over![38]

Bullard appeared disappointed that the war had come to an end. Lieutenant Alden Brooks was scathing of Bullard's conduct on the last day:

Although the General held in his hand at 6.30 a.m. the official announcement that the Armistice was signed and that the territory his men were attacking would be surrendered to them outright at eleven o'clock, he not only let many of them go to their death in that attack, but went out there himself near front lines to watch them. Notice that there is no question here of forcing the enemy to sign the

245

Armistice, of keeping hard after the enemy until he does sign. The Armistice has definitely been signed; the General knows it; it is all over. The hour of eleven has merely been set as a convenient one for a common cessation of hostilities.[39]

Booby traps laid by retreating German soldiers were also responsible for killing and maiming Allied troops after the Armistice. Private William Herzog, serving with the 4th Middlesex, recalled:

I remember the day of the Armistice. I went mad, so did we all, but some of our men got killed after the Armistice. Booby traps. I remember one young lad he said to me that day 'Thank God we will be home in a weeks' time,' next day he was dead, a lot of people died after the Armistice. It came as a great relief, although most of us got immune to the fighting.[40]

In most sectors the ceasefire successfully took effect, enabling soldiers and liberated citizens to celebrate the end of the war. During the afternoon in Mons, Lieutenant-General Sir Arthur Currie entered Mons accompanied by troops from the Canadian 42nd Battalion and the British 5th Lancers:

At 3.30 in the afternoon Lieut. General Sir Arthur Currie K.G.B., K.C.M.G., commanding the Canadian Corps rode into the city with his staff, escorted by a body of the 5th Lancers – men who had fought at Mons in 1914. Formed up in the Grand Place was a half-company of troops from every unit in the 3rd Division. General Currie's appearance provoked the wildest enthusiasm from the civilians who were packed solidly on four sides of the square and crowded on the balconies and windows. The band played the Belgian National Anthem which the crowd sang with great fervour.

The Corps Commander was met by the Mayor, the City Fathers and other prominent citizens. He was formally welcomed and presented with an address. Through an interpreter he conveyed the congratulations of the Corps to the Citizens and then presented the city with a Canadian Flag ... The day was the most memorable in the history of the 42nd Cdn. Battalion by virtue of the fact that it was our good fortune to have the honour to capture the most historic city in the annals of the war.[41]

The 164th Brigade participated in celebrations with the residents of the Belgian town of Ath. The brigade war diary reported:

Brigadier-General C.I. STOCKWELL was received by the Burgomeister during the afternoon and a dance was given at Brigade H.Q. in the evening. All the notabilities of ATH were present and the dance was a great success, the National Anthems at the close being heartily cheered and applauded. All members of 'Stockwell's force' were invited.[42]

While the world celebrated the Armistice, many of the soldiers holding their lines on the Western Front were reluctant to be jubilant. Some regarded this as a temporary truce and expected the resumption of hostilities. Major Thomas Gowenlock wrote:

All over the world on November 11, 1918, people were celebrating, dancing in the streets, drinking champagne, hailing the Armistice that meant the end of the war. But at the front there was no celebration. Many soldiers believed the Armistice only a temporary measure and that the war would so go on. As night came, the quietness, unearthly in its penetration, began to eat into their souls. The men sat around log fires, the first they had ever had at the front. They were trying to reassure themselves that there were no enemy batteries spying on them from the next hill and no German bombing planes approaching to blast them out of existence. They talked in low tones. They were nervous. After the long months of intense strain, of keying themselves up to the daily mortal danger, of thinking always in terms of war and the enemy, the abrupt release from it all was physical and psychological agony. Some suffered a total nervous collapse. Some, of a steadier temperament, began to hope they would someday return home to the embrace of their loved ones. Some could only think of the crude little crosses that marked the graves of their comrades. Some fell into an exhausted sleep. All were bewildered by the sudden meaninglessness of their existence as soldiers – and through their teeming memories paraded that swiftly moving cavalcade of Cantigny, St Mihiel, the Meuse-Argonne and Sedan. What was to come next? They did not know – and hardly cared. Their minds were numbed by the shock of peace. The past consumed their whole consciousness. The present did not exist – and the future was inconceivable.[43]

During the evening on 11 November, German units started to release Allied prisoners of war. The French 36th Régiment d'Infanterie, holding the line at Rocroi, received a convoy of motor vehicles carrying 130 British and French prisoners. The battalion war diary reported:

At 11 o'clock, the hostilities are suspended according to the clauses of the Armistice. The Colonel, the 2nd and 3rd Battalions settle in Rocroi. In the evening, the Germans sent a convoy of 130 French and British liberated prisoners.[44]

During the war, soldiers were not permitted to light fires close to the front because they would reveal their positions and attract German artillery fire. The Armistice allowed soldiers on the frontline to light fires in order to keep warm and to dry wet clothes during the night of 11 November. Major-General Lejeune recalled:

It was hard, at first, to realise fully that the war had actually ended, but on the evening of Armistice Day, I witnessed a striking demonstration of the men's appreciation of the restoration of peace. I had been to Beaumont on a visit of inspection and was returning after dark to Division's Headquarters. The highway on which I drove passed through an area where a division was in bivouac. Thousands of small fires were burning, and standing close to each fire were three or four men, warming their hands and drying their clothes. They had been drenched to the skin and chilled to the marrow over and over again, and now, for the first time in weeks, they were enjoying the comfort of a cheerful blaze.

To add to the brightness of the scene, the automobile's searchlights were turned on, and as we drove past bivouacs, thousands of men cheered from sheer joy, and many of them shouted remarks about the searchlights, 'It looks like Broadway,' 'The lights reminded me of home.' ...

Armistice evening was celebrated too in another way. The troops of all armies at the front acclaimed to return to peace by a display of fireworks which marked the lines from Belgium to Switzerland. As far as the eye could see, the sky was brilliantly illuminated with the flash of pyrotechnics. All the rockets must have gone up in smoke in that greatest of all the celebrations in history.[45]

Private Will Schellberg, of the American 313th Infantry Regiment, recalled:

For the first time, that night cigarettes glowed in the dark without a growl from the top and camp fires shed a cheerful warmth over shell hole and shelter half.[46]

German soldiers also participated in expressing their relief that the war was over. First Lieutenant Henry Thorn Jr, 313th Infantry Regiment, wrote:

When night fell, the bright camp fires burning on both sides produced a strange yet welcome sight. Later the Boche started sending up great quantities of rockets and flares by way of celebration. None who witnessed it will ever forget it.[47]

At the Côte de Romagne, Captain Arthur Joel, 79th Division, recalled:

On armistice night thousands of vari-coloured star shells, shot from German and American signal pistols, outlined the final battle positions as far as the eye could trace the line of fireworks; in no more effective way could one be impressed with the embarrassment of that final position than by this long curved line of exploding fireworks signals. One could easily see that the battalion was at the point of a dangerous salient, with the flank support a mile back on either side. Giving the German officers full credit for their statements. Côte Romagne had been defended with four machine gun companies and a strong force of infantry. The weakened battalion had apparently faced nothing short of capture or severe loss, if the fog had cleared and exposed conditions, and the fighting had lasted much longer.

From the German camp fires on the steep slope of Côte Romagne came the voices of an excellent quartet singing 'Silent Night, Holy Night' in the German tongue. The song sounded beautiful but out of keeping with the location and conditions. Sitting around the blazing camp fires – the first in the battle area for several years – there was a great deal of tobacco chewing, smoking and telling of jokes and stories. Those who sat silent, back in the shadows, or gazing into the coals of the fire, were probably dreaming of home, loved ones, and of the time when they could again live like real human beings, and get away from the nightmare of war.[48]

The French 202nd Régiment d'Infantry was holding positions in the Vosges Mountains on 11 November. Its war diary reported:

In the evening, the Germans are engaged in an enormous consumption of flares and rockets signals of all colours.[49]

Major S.C. Marriott, 11th Manchester Regiment, recalled:

Now tonight the whole countryside is ablaze with bonfires, and thousands of rockets and lights are going up in all directions, whilst away north of the town of … is burning with a great red glow in the sky.[50]

After four years of war, soldiers found it difficult to comprehend the fact that the war had ended. Those years had been focused upon defeating Germany and now that aim had been achieved they had lost a sense of purpose, leaving a void in their lives as they would have to contemplate their future in a world without war. Lieutenant-Colonel Bruce Puckle, commanding the 16th Battalion Machine Gun Corps, wrote on 12 November 1918:

> Things have been very quiet here and I've seen no signs of rejoicing or revelry by night whatever you would almost imagine. There had never been four years of war, people took it so quietly. I think perhaps it is because we have not collected our ideas as yet and have not quite realised what has happened to us. Everybody seemed to draw an extra deep breath and that was all there was to it. It is not till one sits down and really starts to think that one can appreciate the situation and all it means. It is a good business and a wonderful thing to have lived through … life and every routine all seems a little flat now that the 'motif' has been taken away and enthusiasm for parades and inspections is sadly lacking. The bottom seems to be knocked out of things in general.[51]

A Special War Correspondent from the Press Association attempted to explain the reason for the stoical, subdued mood of the British soldier from the British Army HQ in France:

> Now that full realisation of victory has had time to soak in, it is interesting to review how the great news has been received by the British Armies.
>
> I have found everywhere a soberness of spirit, which goes deeper than mere stoicism: indeed there is a sensual mood of depression in the demeanour of the very large proportion of our troops.
>
> Nor do I think explanation of this psychological condition is very far to seek. In the first place there is the natural reaction from the state of chronic subconscious tension in which the men have lived through this most terrible of all human wars.
>
> We have always been under the impalpable shadow of an imminent tragedy. The sudden lifting of this shadow has been followed by a sense of spiritual weariness.
>
> Further there is a haunting consciousness of the universal sorrow which has been caused. Scarcely a man out here but has lost a relative or a 'pal'. Jubilation is tinged with sadness.

Then again, the spectacle of the long-suffering inhabitants tramping back to their too often destroyed homes must needs have a depressing influence.

I think there is real grandeur in this subdued reception by the conquerors of the greatest victory in the history of the earth.[52]

There was also the relief felt for one's own personal salvation that they had endured those terrible times and saw the war through to its conclusion. Private Charlie Leeson was thankful that he had survived four years of war:

What stirring times are these! Stirring in a different manner from what they have been during the past four years. Thank God I have lived to see this time ... of an evening bonfires are lighted, and you know what thousands of rockets and lights of various kinds were used in the trenches and you can bet that now there is no use for them they are being used to enliven the festivities ... Rockets of every colour, parachute lights, Verey lights, etc. all are put to some use now. And the old moon – no longer an object of hatred to us all – shines down benignly, and we know there is no fear of 'Fritz' coming on bombing stunts. Batteries with guns pointing towards Germany stand devoid of purpose with the stacks of shells, which will never be used, behind them.[53]

On a strategic level, Lieutenant-General Sir Henry Rawlinson reflected upon the Allies' misfortunes during the series of offensives launched by German forces since March 1918 that brought them close to defeat. He was astonished that they had fought back and brought Germany to the brink of collapse, resulting in an Armistice eight months later. On 11 November he wrote:

The Armistice was signed this morning, and hostilities ceased at 11 a.m ... Looking back now on the events of March, it seems incredible that all this should have come to pass. We owe it to three things: to the spirit of the troops – their recovery after the events of the spring is a glorious testimony to British grit; to the way old Foch pulled the operations of the Allies together: and to D.H's [Douglas Haig] faith in victory this year – he believed in it long before I did, and when all the people at home were talking about plans for 1919. He not only believed in it, but went all out for it, and he must be a proud and thankful man today.[54]

Rawlinson also reflected upon the Fourth Army, and the units from various allied nations that he commanded. He thought about the role they had played in achieving that victory during 1918, and recognised their function in the future new world order:

> I have been looking at the figures of the Fourth Army since August 8. We have captured 79,000 prisoners and 1,100 guns, and our casualties have numbered 110,000. It had been very truly representative of the British speaking peoples. I have commanded British, Australians, Canadians, South Africans and Americans, and, if we make a proper peace, it is with these peoples the future of the world rest.[55]

Part IV

AFTERMATH

Chapter 20

Armistice Day
France and Belgium

Plans were swiftly implemented to celebrate the end of the First World War on 11 November. As soon as news of the Armistice had reached the French capital, the Mayor of Paris issued the following decree:

INHABITANTS OF PARIS!!
VICTORY! Triumphant victory! On all fronts the defeated enemy has laid down his arms. Blood will now cease to flow.
Let Paris throw off the noble reserve for which it has been admired by the whole world.
Let us give free course to our joy and enthusiasm, and hold back our tears.
To show our infinite gratitude to our magnificent soldiers and their incomparable leaders, let us decorate all our houses with the French colours and those of our dear Allies.
Our dead may rest in peace. The sublime sacrifice they have made of their lives to the future of the race and the salvation of France will not be in vain.
For them, as for us, 'the day of glory has arrived!'
Vive la République!
Vive la France immortelle![1]

Jules Pams, French Minister of the Interior, declared the following directive across France to mark the signing of the Armistice.

Put out flags immediately. Illuminate all public buildings this evening. Have all bells ring out in full peal and arrange with the military authorities to have guns fired, in order that the people may know of the signing of the Armistice.[2]

255

As civil dignitaries organised Armistice commemorations around France, Foch and the Allied delegation departed from the Forest of Compiègne by train at 07.00 hours and headed for Paris. General Maxime Weygand felt immense pride as their train approached their destination, for he recalled:

> This morning there when the train which brought us in Paris went on the bridge of the Oise, in a reduced speed, in a kind of highlight, our heart overflowed a pride without equal. In communion with the whole Army, we lived our Ideal of Soldier.[3]

On reaching the French capital, Foch immediately went to the Ministry of War at 10.45 hours to present President Raymond Poincaré and Prime Minister Georges Clemenceau with the signed Armistice. Foch later recalled:

> I had the Armistice in my pocket. It was a foggy morning, but the sun came out later! I called on M. Clemenceau and M. Poincaré.[4]

When he presented the signed Armistice to Clemenceau and Poincaré, Foch said: 'My work is finished. Your work begins.'[5] Wemyss accompanied Foch to the Ministry of War and recalled Clemenceau's elation:

> I drove back to Paris with the Marshal and went straight with him to the Ministry of War – where we were received by Clemenceau, whose joy and satisfaction he made no attempt to conceal, and taking my right hand in his left and the Marshal's left hand in his right, Foch and I joining hands equally, we all warmly congratulated one another.[6]

At 11.16 hours, the Armistice was officially announced in Paris and authorisation was given to release the news by telegraph. A Press Association journalist recalled the scenes when he heard the news that the war was officially over:

> All official buildings, Embassies and legations were at once beflagged and church bells pealed to the full. In every direction from all offices and workshops, processions surged up the main streets of the capital, preceded by flags, singing the Allied National Anthems with tremendous enthusiasm.[7]

A French submarine berthed opposite the Chamber of Deputies, along the banks of the River Seine, fired a gun salute to announce the Armistice. Vast crowds were descending upon the streets of Paris as official news of the Armistice was announced. In particular, crowds flocked to the Place de la Concorde and the Champs-Élysées. American soldier Private Prescott French recalled:

> Then in a twinkling, as if by magic, everybody seemed to know everybody else, regardless of nationality, color, civilian or military or for any other artificial barrier … Our group was caught up in the parade along the Avenue des Champs-Élysées and what a parade, row on row of civilians, male and female, soldiers of the different Allied Nations, often alternating with a soldier then a girl, then another soldier all the way across the broad Champs-Élysées, arms locked together, a singing, swinging, swaying, jolly jubilant mass of happy humanity.[8]

Once Foch left Clemenceau and Poincaré he immediately went to his home in the Avenue de Saxe, where he wanted to discuss the Armistice with his family over lunch. Monday was market day and the street outside his home was crowded. After identifying his car outside his home, the crowd interrupted his lunch and he was compelled to leave. As he drove down the Place de l'Opéra, he was welcomed by enthusiastic and joyous crowds who were celebrating the Armistice. Foch recalled that 'It seemed likely that they would drag me out of my car. But I wanted to get away.'[9]

Foch succeeded in evading the jubilant Parisians via the Rue Lafayette, where he took temporary refuge in the Army Headquarters. He later returned home, where he was again besieged by well-wishers. A journalist reported:

> All faces are beaming with laughter and joy. When Marshal Foch arrived at his house in the Avenue Saxe he was at once recognised by the crowd and received an ovation which for delirious enthusiasm could not be surpassed. The Marshal, who was in undress uniform, appeared at the window and briefly thanked the crowd, after which the plaudits doubled and redoubled.[10]

After leaving the French President and Premier at the Ministry of War, Wemyss went to the British Embassy in Paris to send a telegram to officially notify the British Government that an Armistice had been agreed. Before he began his journey to London he witnessed the joyous scenes in Paris:

> I went to the Embassy and sent a detailed telegram to the Government. On leaving the Embassy the news was beginning to get about and the streets were already full of people making merry. In the afternoon the crowds in the Place de la Concorde were enormous. I left Paris in the evening and arrived at Folkestone at 9.30 next morning.[11]

Major-General James Harbord arrived in Paris during 11 November. He provided a detailed account of the celebrations in the French capital:

> All Paris had given itself up to the delirious joy; all Paris except, perhaps, some thousands of women weeping at home for husbands, fathers and sons whose lives were given that Paris might on this day rejoice in freedom. A thousand church bells had pealed out at eleven o'clock in the morning, and twelve hundred guns had thundered news of victory ... Windows opened everywhere at the first peal of the bells and guns, and people listened to the music a few seconds in ecstasy before rushing down to mingle in the swelling throng in the streets. The streets became avenues of colour; flags waved from every apartment in the city, and Paris, sad for over four years, was transformed in an instant. Schools closed and pupils joined in joy. Munitions factories closed down and workers swarmed towards the centre of the capital. Shops shut up and offices ceased work. Florists' shops were taken by storm. Flowers were showered on every officer or soldier that passed; a form of tribute that was still paid as we drove into the city under lights that have not been so bright before for many months. It was a great manifestation of the Soul of Paris that words cannot reproduce. Taxicabs, trucks, vans and even field artillery pieces that have been on exhibition in the Place de la Concorde to help the Fourth Loan were seized and joined the processions, with scores of laughing, cheering Parisians clinging to them and singing 'La Marsellaise', the Lorraine March and other French airs.
>   Hundreds of thousands of excited people were on the streets. Groups of two or three hundred would form companies, French and American and British soldiers being arm in arm with each other or with French girls; soldiers of every colour and colony, marching together with French, British and American flags and an occasional Italian flag at their head. Yank and Aussie, Italian, Portuguese, Pulo,

Czecho-Slovak, British, Hindoo, Anamite, poliu, black, white, red, yellow and brown, arm in arm they paraded up and down the boulevards; tam o'shanters of the Chasseurs Alpins, Italian cocked hats, overseas caps, helmets, hats and bareheads, the four corners of the round earth; all glad that the war is ended. Nearly everybody in the city kissed by someone else. As one paper put it, to remain unkissed of any one, man, woman or child, the Allied soldier, whatever his badges or colour, had to descend to a cellar and hide. I myself am one of the few unkissed survivors.

Much of the mass centred around the craped statues of Strasbourg and Lille in the Place de la Concorde; so many years in mourning, and now redeemed and banked in flowers and ablaze with flags in honour of their deliverance. The crowd swept around the big obelisk in the centre of the Place. Italian airplanes flew overhead dropping flowers. People would pick them up, and then turn towards the sky and blow kisses at the aviators thousands or hundreds of feet above.

Improvised and uninvited orators climbed on the German guns on the Place de la Concorde and lectured the passing crowds on Peace and Armistice. The boulevards were almost impassable with the throngs. Flags waved, trumpets blew, bugles blared, and always one could hear the 'Marseillaise'. ...

... From many buildings luminous pictures were shown of Foch, Clemenceau, Wilson, Lloyd George, Pershing and other Allied leaders. Great singers appeared in the balconies. The Place de l'Opéra held thousands upon thousands of people while a great singer led in the 'Marseillaise' from an upper balcony of the great Opéra. Restaurants and cafés, for four years closed early, had permission to keep open until eleven. Tables were all full and late comers could get no places in well-known establishments. The city was given over to unrestrained rejoicing. Nor were our own countrymen missing from the demonstrations. American soldiers and French poilus dragged German guns from the Place de la Concorde and pulled them along the boulevards, sometimes with a French soldier astride the gun, to the great delight of the multitudes. Red Cross workers smothered the statue of Jeanne d'Arc with flowers, and here for the hundredth-thousandth time the 'Marseillaise' was sung. Three hundred Americans in the Café de la Paix, not all of them drunk, nearly stormed the place with the din of 'Hail, Hail, the Gang's all Here' following it with the well known inquiry as to 'What the Hell do we Care?'[12]

Euphoric crowds celebrated at Place de la Concord and some descended upon the Chamber of Deputies. One report confirmed:

> About 2.30 this afternoon a crowd invaded the precincts of the Chamber of Deputies dragging with them a cannon hung with flags. Cheers were given for M. Clemenceau, Marshal Foch, and for France and her Allies. M. Deschanel, President of the Chamber, appeared at a window, and called out to the crowd 'Citizens! Vive La France! Vive la République!'[13]

When the former French Premier, Aristide Briand, appeared at the same window he called for restraint. The report continued:

> M. Briand, an ex-premier, speaking to the crowd amid the greatest enthusiasm said that at this moment, when France had just achieved a most brilliant victory, they must beware of spoiling, by any undue exhibition of feeling, this sacred hour which should be lived through with becoming dignity. France, who in this hour has acted as of yore the part of a champion of justice and right, must not celebrate her triumph in a spirit of exultation and vain glory, but in a spirit of restraint and satisfaction at having done her duty, and in the conviction that she had laboured to secure reparation for the crimes committed and for liberty of the world.[14]

Inside the Chamber of Deputies, the galleries were crowded as the French Parliament took stock of the Armistice:

> The Chamber of Deputies today presented a scene of extraordinary animation. The Ministers were congratulated on all sides, and there was a general air of rejoicing. The public galleries were crowded to their utmost capacity.
>
> After reading the conditions of the Armistice, M. Clemenceau said: I will only add a word or two. In the name of the French people, in the name of the Republic, I send greetings from France unified and indivisible, to Alsace–Lorraine.
>
> After an outburst of wild enthusiasm the Premier added: Next let us render all honour to our great dead. France has been freed by the strength of their arms. All reverence to our heroes. Our soldiers will always be soldiers with an ideal.[15]

Sapper Granville Hampson, a wireless operator serving with the Royal Engineers Signal Section, was based at Wimereux, on the northern

French coast. Hampson reported how the news of the Armistice was announced and the celebrations that took place in the nearby coastal town of Boulogne:

My wireless operating duties still continued to claim most of my time. The whole outlook was rapidly becoming a case of good news daily. The British Army completely overpowering the German Army. It seemed now only a matter of time for the enemy to raise the white flag and call it a day... During the past few hours our wireless station has been kept unusually busy. Messages coming through all in code. Yes the writing was on the wall alright, capitulation was the topic being whispered all around. The troops all over France, each in their own depot or headquarters, garrison camp or wherever were instructed on the morning of the 11th November orders were issued to be on parade at 11 o'clock prompt for a special announcement. Guesswork was spot on. At precisely 11 o'clock the commanding officer addressed the troops saying that the Armistice had been signed, unconditional surrender.

That historic moment will never be forgotten in my lifetime. Minutes before that momentous announcement, anxious expectancy and unannounced silence conveyed what can best be described as a spontaneous reverence. Immediately after this victory announcement a gun boomed out by the Royal Garrison Artillery in the area. The Union Jack was hoisted, a trumpeter sounded the Last Post. Indeed a very moving moment, next came only one chorus, the National Anthem, God save the King and finally a resounding three cheers for victory, hats off and singing in the air with a hip hooray and so that went on three times almost a deafening cheer. The mental make-up now has to take it all in. Killing each other is at an end. The sense of victory yielded to the one expected outlet, celebration. The commanding officer handed over the parade to the Company Sergeant Major Ball, orders for the day were read out, essential duties would carry on as normal. Essential duties being the guard, the wireless section, orderlies, cooks and the duty officer. All others were free of duty until a 6 o'clock parade. A duty roster was quickly arranged for the wireless section so that each one could have a fair chance of joining in the celebrations. Quite a number of the boys went over to the Café Bon Air, drinking each others health and plenty of merry making, though it could be said that most of those based at Wimereux decided to go into Boulogne. Needless to say the jolly old tram car was soon overcrowded and doing roaring trade. The road from Wimereux into

Boulogne was just like, rather resembled, one huge route march, everyone flocking for Boulogne …

I got my old Triumph motor bike out and quickly journeyed into Boulogne …When I reached Boulogne, of course as a result of the good news the whole place had come alive. Flags and bunting had sprung up from everywhere, any of the hideouts where flags had been kept, and the whole place was one scene of excitement and jubilation. As you may imagine I soon had to drop into first gear and maintain only a very slow pace. The whole of dockland, which is virtually the main highway of Boulogne, was absolutely packed. Crowds there singing and dancing, it was with some difficulty really to get through the crowd … at the far end of Boulogne was a brewery with big double gates and quite a big yard, cobblestones incidentally, and it was there that I took a chance and parked my motor bike … Then in turn I joined in the crowds in all the enjoyment, the cafés were doing a roaring trade and all the pubs, as you might imagine revelry was quickly reaching fever pitch.

One would go into any of the estaminets there, or the pubs, one would never know who was paying for the drinks, but it was a case of hey fella well met, what are you going to drink, and so drinks galore were being handed round, no one knew who was paying for them, but it was really the carnival spirit, that this continued all through the day was no exaggeration at all. As the day went on, us wireless fellows ganged together as it were, joined in the singing and dancing, plenty of dancing in the road, oh and the dames, the dames galore, they came along and said 'you British Tommies come dance' and it was a case of girls galore and dancing. Talking about joviality and whoopee, it was one round of pleasure … the excitement was still carrying on as before and I suppose it had more or less reached the stage where the singsongs in the street, crowds arm in arm roaming along, couldn't care less whether it was today or tomorrow. That seemed to be the general spirit of things, although the revelry continued up to about 8 o'clock I had had enough. Celebrations are alright in their way, but of course one can overdo it. Hitherto I have never been drunk and I don't want to start now …[16]

While France celebrated, the mood in Brussels remained sombre on Armistice Day because the city was still occupied by German forces, where there were reports of conflict with Belgian citizens. The Antwerp correspondent from the *Handelshlad* reported:

Some collisions between the Germans and the inhabitants of Brussels took place on Nov 11, about 40 persons being killed. The German Soldiers' Council immediately took measures against the sale or purchase of arms. It is announced that all arms in hands of Belgian citizens must be surrendered, and that Belgians trying to purchase arms would be punished according to the laws of war. The Council also ordered all hotels and restaurants to close at 11 p.m.[17]

There was also dissent within the German Army that was garrisoned in Brussels. Many soldiers were supporting the revolution that was taking place in Germany. The *Nottingham Evening Post* reported the following:

German troops in Brussels have thrown 'iron discipline' to the dogs, and roughly handled the great Falkenhayn, one time idol of the Fatherland and chief of its army at the time of the disastrous Hun offensive against Verdun.

Members of the workmen and soldiers' council arrested him in the street and deprived him of his insignia and sword. They next made him agree that all military orders must be countersigned by the council. The German garrison is now under the red flag.[18]

There were also reports of German soldiers firing upon their own officers in the streets of Brussels:

Extraordinary scenes are said to be occurring in Brussels, where German snipers and machine gunners are ambushing their own officers from innumerable windows, making the streets rather unsafe to the populace.[19]

The situation in Brussels was extremely precarious as Belgian citizens tried to celebrate the end of the war, while their German occupiers continued to supress their joy. Another article from the Press Association reported:

Numerous flags were hoisted in many streets of the town and suburbs. In the afternoon, the animation was again extraordinary, but it was then that the situation, changing suddenly, became extremely grave. A reactionary movement having set in among the Germans, numerous conflicts took place between partisans of the new regime and those who did not adhere to it, and these conflicts rapidly degenerated into fights, in the course of which many shots were fired and machine guns were brought out into the streets.

The German soldiers ordered the removal of the flags which had been too hastily hoisted, and regular scenes of Bolshevism occurred among the German soldiers.

Pillaging, robbery under arms and acts of brigandage and savagery were committed, and this situation still continued on the following day. Among the civilian population, about fifteen prisoners were killed and 100 wounded.

The municipal authorities made a pressing appeal to the population to remain calm and several proclamations were placarded with this aim in view.

In the middle of these incidents came the news of the signing of the armistice and the evacuation by the German armies. A large array traversed the town of Brussels, tramping along the great boulevards. Motor lorries, gun carriages, cattle, disbanded soldiers, horsemen, and machine guns in incredible numbers went past without cessation day and night. Soldiers sold their helmets, equipment, arms, sugar, boots and cigars. The spectacle was an astonishing one. All these carried a red flag.[20]

German forces withdrew from Brussels around midday on Saturday, 16 November and the armies of the Entente entered the city the following day.

Chapter 21

Armistice Day
The United Kingdom

Commander Stephen King-Hall, who was a veteran of the Battle of Jutland, first learned of the Armistice aboard HMS *Maidstone*, a submarine depot ship berthed at Parkestone Quay, Harwich, in Essex. The swiftness of events leading to this day was difficult to comprehend, as King-Hall wrote in his diary on 11 November 1918:

> As I write these words it is over. I don't suppose I shall ever quite realize exactly what I do feel, and what the fact that it is all over really means. The past month has seen events rushing madly along the old-age path of history. It has been almost impossible to do more than follow the breathless excitement the successive stages of the collapses of Bulgaria, Turkey, and Austria–Hungary; finally at 5 a.m., this morning, just as I awoke with a strange feeling of unrest and remained wide-eyed till 7.30, it appears the Armistice was signed.[1]

Rumours of Armistice were being spoken in London during the morning of 11 November and crowds were assembling outside the Prime Minister's residence at 10 Downing Street. A journalist reported:

> The news that the Armistice had been signed spread throughout London with startling rapidity. At ten minutes past ten o'clock in the morning Downing Street was deserted. Half an hour later the crowd was so dense and of such dimensions that it touched the corner of Whitehall ... Mr Balfour left the Premier's residence at a quarter to eleven o'clock, and while a cheer was raised the crowd reserved its enthusiasm, and loud calls were now made for Mr Lloyd George.

The Premier responded, and as he appeared at the window the crowd let itself go. Mr. Lloyd George was greeted with burst after burst of cheering and singing of 'For he's a jolly good fellow'. When the cheering had died down somewhat, there were calls for a speech and the Premier, who was accompanied by Mr. Bonar Law, addressed a few words to the crowd. He said: 'At eleven o'clock this morning the war will be over, (loud and prolonged cheers). You are well entitled to rejoice. The people of this Empire, with their Allies have won a great victory. It is the sons and daughters of the people who have done it. It is a victory greater than has ever been known in history. We are entitled to a bit of shouting. Let us thank God!'

The Prime Minister then retired, and the crowd gave vent to another burst of loud cheering, followed by the singing of the National Anthem and 'Rule Britannia'.

It was in this way that London received the first official intimation of the signing of the Armistice.[2]

As the time for the Armistice approached, Winston Churchill, Minister of Munitions, was looking out of his office window in the requisitioned Hotel Metropole, close to Whitehall. He was pondering upon the challenges that the country faced in adjusting to peace. There was a plan in place to demobilise those soldiers who survived the war, but it had to be implemented. Contracts that were already in place for production of arms and munitions for war had to be cancelled. Military contracts earned companies in the arms industry vast sums of money. Would those companies flourish going forwards? There would be less demand for arms, so how would the British economy be sustained? Society had changed since 1914 and women played a prominent role in working in occupations, and were covering jobs that were once conducted by their menfolk before the war. Would those women be willing to give up their jobs so that their men returning from the war could work? Churchill recalled:

It was a few minutes before the eleventh hour of the eleventh day of the eleventh month. I stood at the window of my room looking up Northumberland Avenue towards Trafalgar Square, waiting for Big Ben to tell that the War was over … The minutes passed. I was conscious of reaction rather than elation. The material purposes on which one's work had been centred, every process of thought on which one had lived, crumbled into nothing. The whole vast business of supply, the growing outputs, the careful hoards, the secret future plans – but yesterday the whole duty of life – all at a stroke vanished like a nightmare dream, leaving a void behind. My mind mechanically persisted in exploring the problems of demobilization. What was to happen to our three million Munition workers? What would they make now? How would the roaring factories be converted? How in fact are swords beaten into ploughshares? How long would it take to bring the Armies home? What would they do when they got home? We had of course a demobilization plan for the Ministry of Munitions. It had been carefully worked out, but it had played no part in our thoughts. Now it must be put into operation.[3]

As the clock drew near to 11.00 hours the streets around Whitehall were silent and empty of people. The first stroke of chimes of Big Ben denoted the time of the Armistice. The war was now over and those working in offices in central London descended upon the streets to celebrate the end of the war. Churchill recalled:

Suddenly the first stroke of the chime. I looked again at the broad street beneath me. It was deserted. From the portals of one of the large hotels absorbed by Government Departments darted the slight figure of a girl clerk, distractedly gesticulating while another stroke resounded. Then from all sides men and women came scurrying into the street. Streams of people poured out of all the buildings. The bells of London began to clash. Northumberland Avenue was now crowded with hundreds, nay thousands, rushing hither and thither in a frantic manner, shouting and screaming with joy. I could see that Trafalgar Square was already swarming. Around me in our very headquarters, in the Hotel Metropole, disorder had broken out. Doors banged. Feet clattered down corridors. Everyone rose from the desk and cast aside pen and paper. All bounds were broken. The tumult grew. It grew like a gale, but from all sides simultaneously. The street was a seething mass of humanity. Flags appeared as if by magic. Streams of men and women flowed from the Embankment. They mingled with torrents coming from the Strand on their way to acclaim the King. Almost before the last stoke of the clock had died away, the strict, war straitened, regulated streets of London had become a triumphant pandemonium. At any rate it was clear that no more work would be done that day.[4]

When Churchill was driven to Downing Street to congratulate Lloyd George these jubilant crowds caused delays to his journey as his car was surrounded. In 1915 Churchill had left politics in disgrace after the failure of the ill-fated Gallipoli campaign, but three years later public opinion of him had changed. A journalist reported:

> Mr. Winston Churchill was greeted with vociferous cheering when he appeared in Whitehall. He stood up in his car waving his hat in acknowledgement of the cheers of the crowd.[5]

The sound of the maroons, an exploding firework, which were fired by police and fire brigade stations in London around 11.00 hours, was heard. It was at this point that Michael Macdonagh first became aware of the Armistice. Macdonagh was a member of *The Times'* parliamentary and reporting staff, and he recalled:

> I was stunned by the news, as if something highly improbable and difficult of belief had happened. It is not that what the papers have been saying about an Armistice had passed out of my mind, but that I had not expected the announcement of its success would have come so soon, and, above all, be proclaimed by the ill-omened maroons. Yet it was so. What is still more curious is that when I became fully seized of the tremendous nature of the event, though I was emotionally disturbed, I felt no joyous exultation. There was relief that the War was over, because it could not now end, as it might have done, in the crowning tragedy of the defeat of the Allies. I sorrowed for the millions of young men who had lost their lives; and perhaps more so for the living than for the dead – for the bereaved mothers and wives whose reawakened grief must in this hour of triumph be unbearably poignant.[6]

Macdonagh proceeded from south London to the Houses of Parliament, where he was able to listen to the bells of Big Ben strike at noon. The clock had already struck at 11.00 hours at the moment of Armistice, however the workings had to be adjusted in order to chime at every hour now that the war was over. Macdonagh wrote of the moment when Big Ben chimed at midday and the infectious effect it had upon the crowds in Westminster:

> In New Palace Yard I met my friend Wilson, Clerk of Works to the Houses of Parliament. 'You are just in time,' said he, 'to hear Big Ben after four years of silence.' I had heard Big Ben proclaiming War. I was now to hear him welcoming Peace. I looked up at the clock. It was less than five minutes to the midday hour. Men from Dent & Co., of Cockspur Street, the custodians of the clock, had just

completed the work of putting into action again the apparatus for striking the hours, though not the more complicated mechanism for the chiming of the quarters.

Then when the hands of the dials pointed to XII, Big Ben struck the hour, booming it in his deep and solemn tones, so old and so familiar. It was a most dramatic moment. The crowd that had assembled in Parliament Square stood silent and still the last stroke of the clock, when they burst into shouts of exultation.

Never did the welkin ring in London as it rang today. Parliament Street and Whitehall were packed with people. The day was grey and chilly with a threat of rain, but no one minded the weather. Besides, the streets were hot with excitement. There prevailed everywhere throughout London an irresistible impulse to let business go hang, to get into the streets and yell and sing and dance and weep – above all, to make oneself supremely ridiculous.[7]

The Prime Minister went to the House of Commons during that afternoon, where he announced to Parliament the terms of the Armistice, adding:

Thus at 11 o'clock this morning came to an end the cruellest and most terrible war that has ever scourged mankind. I hope we may say that thus, this fateful morning, came to an end of all wars. This is no time for words. Our hearts are too full of gratitude to which no tongue can give adequate expression. I will therefore, move: That this House do immediately adjourn until this time tomorrow, and that we proceed, as a House of Commons, to St. Margaret's to give humble and reverent thanks for the deliverance of the world from its great peril.[8]

Lloyd George wanted to keep the Armistice secret so that he could announce the end of the war during the afternoon of 11 November. He was unhappy that Admiral Sir Rosslyn Wemyss, by telephone from France, had informed King George V, who communicated this good news to the Royal Household, from which the news spread. Lloyd George felt he should have made the official announcement. When Wemyss arrived from France during the morning of 12 November he was immediately summoned to Buckingham Palace to report to King George V in person about the signing. Wemyss announced that he had arrived in London to Downing Street and expected a call from the Prime Minister to provide a similar report. However, the invite from Lloyd George never came forth as he was furious that he had informed the

King earlier during the morning on 11 November and the news of the Armistice was broadcast before he could announce it. Lady Wester Wemyss wrote of her husband's bewilderment as to why the Prime Minister did not want to meet to discuss the Armistice:

> When announcing his arrival to Buckingham Palace, Wemyss had done the same to the Prime Minister and spent all that afternoon and evening awaiting a summons, but – much to his astonishment – in vain. He deemed it beyond the bounds of reason that the Prime Minister should not desire to know what had passed on so momentous an occasion, and his astonishment turned into amazement when the following day, on attending the War Cabinet, instead of the congratulations he expected, he met with black looks and an icy reception.
>
> It was only on leaving the Cabinet that he was to discover the key to this enigma. The Prime Minister had apparently planned a spectacular announcement of the Armistice which he hoped to make at the Guildhall Banquet on November 9th; baulked of this by the Armistice not being signed, he projected doing so in the House of Commons on the afternoon of 11th – the news being meanwhile kept secret. This proved impossible after Wemyss' telephone to the King, who had announced the happy tidings to his entourage; the Armistice was accordingly made public at 11 a.m.; popular enthusiasm concentrated at Buckingham Palace – while his official statement in the House of Commons fell flat; hence his almost unconcealed fury.
>
> Wemyss shrugged his shoulders, the whole matter appeared to him so incredibly petty; indeed, he could hardly have believed it, had it not been vouched for by two unimpeachable authorities.[9]

Crowds descended upon Buckingham Palace in order to seek announcements regarding the Armistice. The crowds became euphoric once the Armistice was declared upon the noticeboard. A reporter recalled:

> Scenes of great enthusiasm were witnessed outside Buckingham Palace where a great assemblage of people of every rank had taken up their position in the hope of getting early information. The first indication of the good news was when the Master of the Household requested Inspector Smith, of the Palace Police, to announce the signing of the armistice and the ceasing of hostilities to the public

outside the Palace gates. Passing along the forecourt, the Inspector read the brief particulars from a board on which was pinned the Exchange's official message.

Shortly after this the guns commenced to fire, and then there was renewed cheering and flag-wagging, while a party of munition girls formed themselves into a ring and danced and sang in joyous holiday mood.[10]

A correspondent reported the scene outside Buckingham Palace:

Buckingham Palace was the centre of the greatest demonstration. People poured thither almost unconsciously as to the heart of the Empire, and by noon there was a throng which the police wisely made no effort to control. Everybody was happy and everybody was considerate, with the result that a crush of pedestrians and vehicles which might have been dangerous was harmless. All classes have been brought together by the war, and they mingled in the peace celebrations. Indeed in front of the Palace every type of war worker was to be seen from a Brigadier-General with the V.C. to the latest recruit for the W.R.A.F.[11]

Michael Macdonagh also described the jubilant scenes outside Buckingham Palace as the crowd chanted for the King in unison:

As on all occasions of national joyfulness the people had turned instinctively to the King and Queen to invite them to join with them in thanksgiving, and to tender them homage and devotion. The vast space in front of the Palace was occupied by a vaster crowd. Almost obliterated was the Victoria Memorial – rising in the centre – so thick were the swarming climbers to its very top. The crowd raised a staccato and mighty cry, often repeated, and emphasised by a pause between the words, 'We – want – King – George!'[12]

The crowd's request was soon answered when King George V eventually appeared on the balcony with his family. Another journalist reported:

The appearance of the King and Queen, with Princess Mary and the Duke of Connaught, on the centre balcony of the Palace, was the signal for a tremendous outburst of enthusiasm from the huge crowd of spectators. Addressing from the balcony of the Palace the

271

vast crowd, the King said 'With you I rejoice and thank God for the victories which the Allied Armies have won and brought hostilities to an end, and peace within sight.'

His Majesty's speech was received with tremendous cheering. At 12.30 the massed bands of the Guards assembled in the forecourt and played patriotic airs and other bright selections to the delight of the tremendous crowd assembled outside the Palace.[13]

Macdonagh described the Royal Family's response to the crowds and how the massed bands of the Guards led the crowd in singing patriotic songs:

> In response to the call of his lieges the King, accompanied by the Queen, appeared on the balcony of the Palace and was accorded a tumultuous greeting. It was plain to see that their Majesties were affected by the prevailing uncontrolled gaiety of spirits. The King was observed to be laughing heartily. The Queen waved a Union Jack over her head, and no doubt shouted 'Hurrah, hurrah!'
>
> Here the exultation of the Nation at the end of the War found its fitting expression. The immense concourse sang 'Land of Hope and Glory' to the accompaniment of the massed bands of the Guards in the forecourt of the Palace. The vainglorious exhortation, 'God, who made us mighty, make us mightier, yet,' was rendered in so tremendous a shout that it besieged the heavens. 'Tipperary' more modestly followed, with its sense of laughter and tears.
>
> What sad memories it now evokes! How many of the boys who sang it in the earlier years of the War will be coming home! Can any good that may come from the victory compensate for their loss! A gloomy reflection. Avaunt![14]

Arthur Mason reported in the *Sydney Morning Herald* of Australian soldiers on leave taking part in the celebrations in London:

> Down Westminster way Horseferry Road and the perilous thereof were a centre of definitely Australian demonstration, the AIF headquarters and the club loosing upon this great day, a timeless, tireless stream of exuberant activity. But as good as any Australian statement of us was one I caught sight of in the late afternoon as I struggled through Whitehall. The lofty equestrian statue of the late Duke of Cambridge will be remembered by many. It stands in the middle of Whitehall, just outside the Horse Guards. It is a big statue and the proportions of the horse upon his pedestal send it towering

high above the street. But on the horse's back sat two Australian soldiers, and a third had clamoured even higher until he sat astride the animal's head – and all three waved Australian flags to the roaring abyss below, when thousands of demonstrators surging along the highway shouted their joy at this adventure in progress far above their heads.[15]

The end of the war brought about immediate lifting of restrictions. Macdonagh noted that on Armistice Day:

At Westminster Bridge Underground Station, I saw an evening newspaper bill. It was the first I had seen for years, their use having been prohibited owing to the shortage of paper; and therefore it was a heartening sign of London's return to normal life. And what news it proclaimed: 'Fighting has ceased on all Fronts!' Hurrah![16]

As he moved through the crowds in London, Macdonagh noted:

As I moved about I heard not a single hard word of Germany, not a single expression of glee that she was lying crippled – perhaps for ever. Yet, as we all believed, she had caused the War. And what an atrocity the War was is implied in the universality of these rejoicings that it is at an end.[17]

By 11 November 1918 there were 888 conscientious objectors incarcerated in prisons around Britain. Some 464 of those prisoners had served two years and twenty had been declared insane. Walter Griffin was a conscientious objector detained in Canterbury Prison when the Armistice was signed. Isolated from the outside world, he was not told directly that the war was over until his release during April 1919. Griffin recalled:

We didn't know that the war was over for sure. We could hear rejoicing, we saw crackers, fireworks, which almost indicated that the war was over, but we had no real proof of it. We quite expected that we should hear about it in the church during one of the services, but we were not told at all.

The war must have been over for several months and of course we did not expect CO's [Conscientious objectors] to be doing the whole of their sentences, which in my case would have gone on for another two years, so we wondered what was going to happen and without any notice I was told that I would be going out tomorrow.[18]

Frank Merrick was another conscientious objector, who was imprisoned in Wandsworth Prison. On Armistice Day he recalled:

> We very naively hoped, supposed that we would be home by Christmas, but of course we weren't and I think the reason was that a lot of the soldiers who weren't demobbed would have been very angry if conscientious objectors were released if they were kept soldiering. I think that the Law Lords eventually persuaded the authorities to let us out, which was on April 22nd 1919, that I got home.[19]

Although many British servicemen had not been demobilised and were still serving, Churchill was keen to resolve the problem of conscientious objectors being released from prison. On 3 April 1919, he announced in the House of Commons:

> The Government have now decided that demobilisation is now sufficiently advanced to justify them in approving the proposal of the Army Council for dealing with soldiers of various classes who have committed offences under the Army Act, and in consequence have been sentenced to imprisonment. All such soldiers will be discharged from the Army for misconduct, and if and when they have served two years' imprisonment for misconduct in this country they will be released from prison.[20]

Production within armaments factories came to a sudden halt on 11 November. Munition workers stopped work as soon as the Armistice was confirmed. Amy May was a munitions worker at Woolwich Arsenal:

> It came through at eleven in the morning, we went to work the same of course, everyone was jolly ... a lot of jollification, tea parties in the street, flags all out, singing 'knees up mother brown'... all the old girls, streets looked quite nice with the flags out from the side of the road to that one's window.[21]

May carried on working until September 1919, and made jam tins instead of shells.

Private Harold Boughton was a Gallipoli veteran who landed at Suvla on 25 August 1915 with the 2nd/1st Battalion, City of London Regiment. When the Armistice was signed in 1918 he was serving with the Royal Defence Corps guarding a German prisoner of war camp at Leigh in Lancashire:

Everyone was talking about what we was going to do when we were discharged, what sort of life we was going to take up. We joined up as young men, we were 19 and here we were 22 and 23, to start life afresh. We were worried about what we were going to do.

We finally heard that on the 11th hour, of the 11th day, of the 11th month, the Armistice was going to be declared and we were all looking forward to that with great eagerness and of course when the time came on that 11th hour on the 11th day, pandemonium broke loose. Everybody went mad, work finished, all the factories poured out, sirens went, crowds rushed around the streets, even in the camp there was no discipline. Everybody just broke loose, they let the prisoners out into the compound and they all joined up and joined together and celebrated.

I got out and went into town. I was swamped with people and all the pubs and everything else was full up and in the evening I went to Bolton, to Bolton Hippodrome with my wife and there was a man there who played the organ, his name was Pattman and he used to travel around with one of those Wurlitzer organs. We had a wonderful time in that theatre singing all the patriotic songs.[22]

While London was rejoicing at the news of the Armistice, Lieutenant R.G. Dixon, of the 251st Siege Battery, 53rd Brigade, Royal Garrison Artillery, was aboard a leave ship. As he arrived at Folkestone harbour at midday on 11 November, he heard the sound of ships' sirens welcoming the Armistice – that is when he first became aware that the war had ended:

'Dickie,' said Captain Brown, 'The bloody war is over! It's over!'

And it was. We had left France with a war on and arrived in Blighty with a peace on! And all those ships letting off those sirens for us, as if we were a lot of conquering heroes coming home, that was the first intimation we had of it.

While we were going through the formalities of disembarking, a strange and unread thought was running through my mind. I had a future ahead of me, something I had not imagined for some years. I said as much to Captain Brown. He smiled at me, he was a man of about forty. 'Yes,' he agreed. 'You've got a future now, Dickie. And so have I. I wonder what we'll do with it, and what I will be like. Because, you know, things are not going to be the same as they were.'[23]

As Dixon contemplated his future, the realisation and the relief of what the end of the war meant, especially the end to the horrors experienced during that conflict, became suddenly apparent. Dixon recalled:

No more slaughter, no more maiming, no more mud and blood, and no more killing and disembowelling of horses and mules – which was what I found most difficult to bear. No more of those hopeless dawns with the rain chilling the spirits, no more crouching in inadequate dugouts scooped out of trench walls, no more dodging of snipers' bullets, no more of that terrible shell-fire. No more shovelling up bits of men's bodies and dumping them into sandbags; no more cries of 'Stretcher bearers!', and no more of those beastly gas-masks and the odious smell of pear-drops which was deadly to the lungs, and no more writing of those dreadfully difficult letters to the next-of-kin of the dead ... The whole vast business of the war was finished. It was over.[24]

Private Walter Spencer, 4th Grenadier Guards, had taken part in the attack upon Hill 70 during the Battle of Loos in 1915. Spencer was in Boulogne waiting to embark on a boat that would take him to England for some leave on 11 November 1918. He spoke of this leave:

I left the battalion and got down to Boulogne early 6 o'clock on November 11th, the day Armistice was declared. Our boat sailed at 11 a.m. and just before the boat sailed came a runner down to the officer in charge, there was always an officer in charge of a leave boat, and told him that an Armistice had been declared. He got up and told us all and there was a lot of cheering and everybody booed him and said it was a put up. Nobody would believe it although the sirens were all booming round at Boulogne. We finally got over to England, to Folkestone and it was confirmed there. I didn't believe it, nobody believed it, but when we got over to Folkestone there were flags out and people about everywhere and we came to believe it then that it was true. We got on the train for London, we got to Victoria Station, there were thousands in Victoria Station, we could hardly move when the leave train came in. Everybody's gone mad, dancing in the streets and all the pubs were open, there was birds and that kind of thing, I was pleased to get out of it. I did happen to get a bus and got straight across to Marylebone. Got a train at half past three and come up to Nottingham and got home at six o'clock that night. So I always remember November 11th.[25]

Many letters from the War Office were received by families on and around Armistice Day confirming the death of a loved one. Their bereavement was undoubtably exacerbated by the fact that their loved one had been killed so close to the end of the war. Private Edward

Griffin, 20th Manchester Regiment, had been killed on 23 October 1918 and was buried close to where he fell at Pommereuil British Cemetery. His parents, Lizzie and Wilson, of Hall Farm, Bawtry, Doncaster, received notification of his death on Armistice Day. It was reported in the *Hull Daily Mail*:

> During the rejoicings on Monday on the signing of the Armistice, news reached Mr. and Mrs. Wilson Griffin … from the War Office, by wire, that their youngest son, Pte Edward Griffin, Manchester Regiment, had been killed in action last month. Pte Griffin was only 19 years of age, and by his death 13 old scholars of Little Weighton School have fallen in action.
>
> Prior to joining up he was a wagonner, and it is only about a month ago he concluded his draft leave at home, and left in high spirits for France.[26]

Ada Long, from Walcot, Bath, learned that her twenty-two-year-old son, Sapper William Long, of the 19th Division Signal Company, Royal Engineers, was killed on 8 November close to Landrecies. The *Bath Chronicle* reported on 16 November 1918:

> Three days before the signing of the Armistice, a German shell entered a cellar in which a number of R.E. signallers were working, and all were killed, wounded or gassed. Among the killed was Sapper W.J. Long (22) … being keen on soldiering, deceased four years ago took a liberty with his age and was accepted for service. He was at the front for nearly 3½ years, and escaped all injury and illness until the fatal shell came along.
>
> Recently on home leave, he returned to France about ten days ago, telling his mother before he left that he would not for the worlds miss being out there with the boys when peace was proclaimed. The news of his death has been sent on by deceased's officer and by a chaplain, both of whom speak very highly of him. 'All our hearts are very heavy for his loss,' the officer wrote. 'He was a general favourite and loved by everyone.'[27]

Sapper Long was buried at Cross Roads Cemetery, Fontaine-au-Bois.

Spanish Flu, which would account for more deaths than the war itself, was spreading across Europe and many died throughout 1918. The *Burnley Express* reported the death of Sapper James Geldard on Armistice Day:

Sapper James Herbert Geldard, 210331, Royal Engineers, who died of pneumonia in Whalley Military Hospital on November 11. The deceased, whose wife lives at 228 Howard Street, joined up in 1916, going to France in December 1917, and whilst serving there had his leg broken. The deceased came home on leave for 14 days, and whilst here contracted influenza and was removed to Whalley Hospital where he died. Formerly he was a firebeater employed by Burnley Co-operative Centre.[28]

This article highlights inaccuracies in reporting, because his name is listed in the Commonwealth War Graves Commission's records as Herbert James Geldard. His service number was WR/206214 and the address of Lily, his wife, is confirmed as 228 Market Street, Whitworth. Geldard, who belonged to the Royal Engineers, Railway Operating Division, was buried in Burnley Cemetery.

During that evening people were celebrating the end of the war across the nation. There was an estimated 250,000 participating in these joyous scenes and in London the streets became impassable. Australian journalist Arthur Mason reported how the celebrations continued throughout the night in London:

> The day darkened early under a drizzling rain. No one cared neither for the darkness or the drizzle. No one cared for anything in the very midst of the swirling crowds, couples often joined hands and danced and many a time … Soldiers and sailors, youths out of khaki and girls of thousand-and-one war avocations made up the majority. Multitudes came up out of the East End and helped to fill the West End with the ceaseless clamour of the day and to mass the streets with the struggling jostling millions who congested them at night. Whitehall was a swaying sea of human beings. Trafalgar Square roared under its crowds.[29]

These celebrations continued throughout the following two evenings and descended into anarchy and civil disorder. The *Daily Mirror* reported:

> For the third night in succession huge cheering crowds perambulated the West End and indulged in all kinds of horse play. The West End of London last night presented a wonderful sight.
> Soon after seven o'clock huge crowds began to assemble in Whitehall, the Strand, Trafalgar Square, Piccadilly and other West End Streets. Scores of thousands of people formed a surging mass,

and they wondered aimlessly about, indulging in all sights of minor horse play.

The streets became impassable. Soldiers, munition girls and frenzied youths pushed their way through the crowd, making a deafening din, making weird noises on still weird instruments. Bells were rung, trumpets and bugles blown, and there was much banging of tins.

Jack tars climbed lamp-posts and hung flags therefrom, men and women perched on the water fountain at Piccadilly looked like the finale of a Japanese gymnastic troupe, while men and officers rushed here and there in battering-ram and chain formation.

Gun-fire – About 9.30 the wheels of a German gun, sprinkled with petrol commandeered earlier in the evening from taxi men, were set alight. As the fire developed wheels from other guns were added, and road-mender trestles, walking sticks, umbrellas, and, in one instance a kitchen broom.

Later the police formed a cordon about other guns and protected them from further damage. This fire was set in the middle of the road and clear of Nelson's Column.

A captured German gun was recaptured from the Mall and hauled into Piccadilly Circus. Just at the moment the wheels were to be stripped, a number of policemen arrived and took possession of it, and had it interned and another in a by-street.

It is estimated that 250,000 people were in Trafalgar Square and Piccadilly Circus.[30]

However, Nelson's Column did not escape from being damaged during the moments of lawlessness that occurred during the evening after Armistice Day, for the *Daily Mirror* reported:

The masonry of the Nelson Column in Trafalgar Square was damaged by two huge bonfires which were lighted at its base by a large crowd of 'peace' rejoicers on Tuesday night.

This act of vandalism, which is characterised by everyone as outrageous and inexcusable, even in the circumstances now prevailing is heartedly condemned as 'thoughtless folly'.

'The fire started,' said an eyewitness, 'with the advertisement canvas and the scaffolding of the big War Bond posters on the column. This blazed up pretty well, and the prime movers looked round for more fuel. They seized the heavy wood and iron seats in the square and piled them on to the flames. There was a contractors hut on wheels, wheelbarrows and a pitch tank standing near. The mob pushed the hut over and threw it onto the bonfire. Wheelbarrows, poles and trestles were all utilised. Then the soldiers filled barrels with wooden blocks and shot the lot on to the fire. The blazing pitch ran everywhere and the heat was terrific. In addition, blocks were torn up out of the road and made a lurid flame. Then someone thought of the German guns in the Mall, and the crowd ran there and returned, pushing a huge gun, which they wheeled on to one of the bonfires. The police were powerless, and when the fire brigade arrived soldiers prevented them getting to work. The firemen proceeded to keep the crowd back by turning the hose on them, but Australian soldiers wrested the pipe away and others slashed it with knives, causing the water to swerve high into the air.'[31]

Chapter 22

Armistice Day
Around the World

News that the Armistice had been signed was received before dawn on the eastern American coast on 11 November. President Woodrow Wilson was eating breakfast in the White House in Washington when he heard the news and immediately announced a public holiday, before spending the morning writing an address that he would deliver to Congress later that day. In New York a searchlight was switched on to light up Times Square and the Statue of Liberty was illuminated to celebrate the end of the war. A journalist reported:

> The news of the signing of the Armistice was ushered in an hour before dawn yesterday by the illumination of the Statue of Liberty, which has been in darkness since America's entry into the war and the din of sirens, bells and bombs, which roused the slumbering millions. The streets were soon thronged.
>
> Airmen from the neighbouring aerodromes soared above the Metropolis and dropped confetti on the people below. Many churches which had been thrown open, were thronged with men and women engaged in prayer and thanksgiving.[1]

The riotous celebrations in New York after the false Armistice on 7 November gave New York authorities an indication of the risk of potential civil disorder that might take place and they were able to implement contingencies for when the actual Armistice was signed:

> As a result of the experience obtained by the authorities, when the true armistice was announced in the morning papers on November 12th, the Sheriff hastened to the 71st Regiment Armory for consultation with Colonel Wells with a view to protecting the 5th

Avenue district if the revellers should get beyond the control of the police.

Arrangements had already been made with the band-leader to have a band at the armory on the evening of the true Armistice Day. The sheriff when he learned that it was the purpose of the 71st to parade in honor of the occasion was rather disposed to offer objection arguing that the regiment should be held at the armory to await any needed call. Colonel Wells, however, succeeded in convincing the Sheriff that a demonstration of a large body of armed men, such as the regiment would give in its parade, would be most effective in keeping the people within bounds, and the 71st, probably the only regiment in the city parading that day, covered the District. Fifth Avenue was occupied from house line to house line with joyous people, many of them with their spirits reinforced by refreshments that added to their joy, not their good judgement. It was necessary to march the regiment in the avenue in columns of squads in order to get through, but it was received with the greatest enthusiasm and also had the effect of informing the people that the regiment was mobilised ready for any rioting.[2]

At 13.00 hours on 11 November, President Wilson arrived at Capitol Hill, where he read out the terms of the Armistice to Congress. Before reading the terms the President delivered the following address:

Gentlemen of the Congress, in these anxious times of rapid and stupendous change it will in some degree lighten my senses of responsibility to perform in person the duty of communicating to you some of the larger circumstances of the situation with which it is necessary to deal.

The German authorities, who have at the invitation of the Supreme War Council been in communication with Marshal Foch, have accepted and signed the terms of the Armistice which he has authorised and instructed to communicate to them.

The war thus comes to an end for having accepted these terms of Armistice, it will be impossible for the German command to renew it.

It is not now possible to assess the consequences of this great consummation. We know only that this tragical war, whose consuming flames swept from one nation to another until all the world was on fire, is at an end, and it was the privilege of our own people to enter it at its most critical juncture, in such fashion and in such force as to contribute in a way of which we are all deeply proud to the great result.

We know, too, that the object of the war is attained – the object upon which all free men had set their hearts and attained with a sweeping completeness which even now we do not realise.

Imperialism such as the men conceived who were but yesterday the masters of Germany is at an end. His illicit ambitions engulfed in black disaster. Who will now seek to revive it? The arbitrary power of the military is discredited and destroyed.[3]

After reading the Armistice terms, the entire audience within Congress leapt to their feet and applauded President Wilson.

The scenes of joyous celebration that were seen in Europe and America were replicated in other parts of the world. A correspondent in Toronto, Canada, reported:

The news of the signing of the Armistice was received with demonstrations of joy, both here and all the other cities of the Dominion. Processions of women munition workers and others started before daybreak. The day was observed as a holiday by practically all the business firms. A favourite method of celebrating the event was the hanging and burning of the Kaiser's effigy in the streets.[4]

In South Africa the news that the Armistice had been signed was warmly received. It was reported:

The signing of the armistice has led to scenes of unprecedented enthusiasm throughout South Africa. In Cape Town the official news was intimated by gunfire. There was an immediate cessation of business and the streets were profusely decorated in record time, and were instantly filled with cheering crowds of all classes and races, who indulged in demonstrations of wild and unrestrained joy.

A large demonstration was held on the Grand Parade at which General Botha moved a resolution congratulating the King, the navy, the army and the Allies. There was tremendous enthusiasm throughout.[5]

Chapter 23

Armistice Day
Germany

As the Allied nations rejoiced on Armistice Day, Germany was in a state of turmoil and descending yet further into the abyss of revolution. A reporter from the *Handelsblad* newspaper reported:

> Since Saturday morning [9 November 1918], the aspect of Berlin, which is now under the authority of the Workers' and Soldiers' Council, has completely changed. Motor lorries filled with soldiers and civilians move slowly through the streets, which are crowded with sightseers, who, as yet, seem hardly able to comprehend the new spectacle. The soldiers carrying red flags in their hands, cheering and shouting 'Hurrah' and 'Long Live the Republic', and singing the 'Marseillaise'.
>
> In compact processions, soldiers proceed through streets, and thousands of workers join them, also singing. No police are to be seen, and the soldiers are trying to maintain order on Potsdamer Platz. The trams are still running. Some soldiers carry arms and ammunition, and I even saw a couple of soldiers with hand grenades, so far as I have learned, no serious incident has occurred.
>
> All the soldiers are compelled to remove the black, red and white cockades from their caps. A crowd of sightseers is concentrated in the Unter Den Linden and near the Schloss.
>
> The public was remarkably calm in the vicinity of the Schloss. From its main window is hanging a red cloth. From the Crown Prince's Palace and from various Ministerial buildings red flags are waving. The Workers' and Soldiers' Council have occupied the Imperial Bank, the main telegraph office. The Prefecture of Police, and the Town Hall.

The police have been disarmed. Civilians go about in the crowds armed with carbines, together with the soldiers. Thousands of processions are formed. At the head of one procession I saw Ledebour and Liebknecht in a carriage.

According to a report from Brunsbuettel, on the Kiel Canal, the sailors of the battleships *Posen*, *Ostfriesland*, *Nassau* and *Oldenburg*, which are lying off Brunsbuettel, have joined the revolution movement in Kiel.[1]

Seaman Richard Stumpf recalled the moment when he heard the news of the Armistice in the German port of Wilhelmshaven:

A delegate from the Sailors' Council with a crestfallen face ran up the gangplank and wordlessly handed me a broadsheet bearing the ominous title: Terms of a Cease-Fire. I read the fateful sheet with bated breath and growing amazement. What were the terms? Evacuation on the left bank of the Rhine as well as the right to an extent of forty kilometres ... 150,000 railroad cars ... the blockade to remain in effect ... the navy to be surrendered ... 10,000 ... 5,0000 ... 30,000. It can't be. This is ridiculous ... It means a fight to the end ... What a sudden change from the joy we had felt that morning! ... It was too much for me to bear and I hurried off to grieve in a lonely corner.[2]

Berlin newspapers were scathing about the signing of the Armistice. The *Berliner Tageblatt* wrote:

The terms of the Armistice are unprecedented in their inhumanity. We were ready to deliver up fortresses and surrender ships, but in addition a great part of our railway material which is absolutely necessary for our support is demanded. With these terms to support, a crisis is nearing.[3]

Pilots from the German Air Force found it difficult to come to terms with the Armistice. Jagdgeswader I, Manfred von Ricthofen's former squadron, known as the 'Flying Circus', was ordered to fly its aircraft and surrender to the French in Strasbourg. Instead, the pilots disobeyed this order and flew to Darmstadt in Germany, where they deliberately landed their aircraft badly in a determined effort to damage them so that they would be of no use to the Allies.[4] Pilots from the Jagdgeswader III were ordered to surrender their Fokker D.VIIs to British forces at Nivelles. The airmen were furious and wanted to burn their aeroplanes instead, but they were persuaded to comply and flew in formation towards Nivelles. Rittmeister Karl Bölle was the commander of Jasta 2 and an ace who had shot down thirty-six allied aeroplanes. He recalled:

> The handover followed. Each aircraft carried the glorious name of its pilot and the number of his victories. Thus they gave witness to the deeds which were accomplished with them.[5]

Gefreiter Adolf Hitler was still recovering from the effects of gas in a hospital at Pasewalk in Pomerania when he heard the news of the Armistice:

> The local pastor visited the hospital for the purpose of delivering a short address. And that was how we came to know the whole story. I was in a fever of excitement as I listened to the address. The reverend old gentleman seemed to be trembling when he informed us that the House of Hohenzollern should no longer wear the Imperial Crown, that the Fatherland had become a 'Republic', that we should pray to the Almighty not to withhold His blessing from the new order of things and not to abandon our people in the days to come. In delivering this message he could not do more than briefly express appreciation of the Royal House, its services to Pomerania, to Prussia, indeed, to the whole of the German Fatherland, and – here he began to weep. A feeling of profound dismay fell on the people in that assembly, and I do not think there was a single eye that withheld its tears. As for myself, I broke down completely when the old gentleman tried to resume his story by informing us that we must now end this long war, because the war was lost, he said, and we were at the mercy of the victor. The Fatherland would have to bear heavy burdens in the future. We were to accept the terms of the Armistice and trust to the magnanimity of our former enemies.
>
> It was impossible for me to stay and listen any longer. Darkness surrounded me as I staggered and stumbled back to my ward and buried my aching head between the blankets and pillow. I had not cried since the day that I stood beside my mother's grave. Whenever Fate dealt cruelly with me in my young days the spirit of determination within me grew stronger and stronger. During all those long years of war, when Death claimed many a true friend and comrade from our ranks, to me it would have appeared sinful to have uttered a word of complaint. Did they not die for Germany? And, finally, almost in the last few days of that titanic struggle, when

the waves of poison gas enveloped me and began to penetrate my eyes, the thought of becoming permanently blind unnerved me; but the voice of conscience cried out immediately: Poor miserable fellow, will you start howling when there are thousands of others whose lot is a hundred times worse than yours? And so I accepted my misfortune in silence, realizing that this was the only thing to be done and that personal suffering was nothing when compared with the misfortune of one's country.[6]

After dwelling upon the impact of the Armistice upon Germany, Hitler then went on to reflect upon those soldiers who had been consumed by the war and the sacrifices they had made during the past four years.

So all had been in vain. In vain all the sacrifices and privations, in vain the hunger and thirst for endless months, in vain those hours that we stuck to our posts though the fear of death gripped our souls, and in vain the deaths of two million who fell in discharging this duty. Think of those hundreds of thousands who set out with hearts full of faith in their Fatherland, and never returned; ought not their graves to open, so that the spirits of those heroes bespattered with mud and blood should come home and take vengeance on those who had so despicably betrayed the greatest sacrifice which a human being can make for his country? Was it for this that the soldiers died in August and September 1914, for this that the volunteer regiments followed the old comrades in the autumn of the same year? Was it for this that those boys of seventeen years of age were mingled with the earth of Flanders? Was this meant to be the fruits of the sacrifice which German mothers made for their Fatherland when, with heavy hearts, they said good-bye to their sons who never returned? Has all this been done in order to enable a gang of despicable criminals to lay hands on the Fatherland? Was this then what the German soldier struggled for through sweltering heat and blinding snowstorm, enduring hunger and thirst and cold, fatigued from sleepless nights and endless marches? Was it for this that he lived through an inferno of artillery bombardments, lay gasping and choking during gas attacks, neither flinching nor faltering, but remaining staunch to the thought of defending the Fatherland against the enemy?[7]

The dejection, disappointment and resentment felt by many German soldiers, including Hitler, would manifest itself into the creation of the right-wing Nazi organisation that would restore the honour of the

German nation and reverse the humiliating terms of the Treaty of Versailles within the following two decades after the First World War. The Armistice in 1918 and later the Peace Treaty in 1919 would sow the seeds for the Second World War. A special correspondent working for Association Press was the first American to enter Berlin since the signing of the Armistice. Within weeks of the signing he recognised the dangers of extremists, like Hitler, that would have disastrous consequences for Germany. He telegraphed the following report, which featured in newspapers across the world on 25 November.

> Berlin, crushed, broken and dispirited by privations, has accepted defeat with almost incredible apathy. It is demoralised, listless, hungry, and even abject. It is primarily this apathy, this feeling that nothing matters now, which is playing into the hands of a few energetic fanatics, and constitutes the gravest and greatest menace for the immediate future of the German people.[8]

Chapter 24

Prisoners of War

Approximately 180,000 British prisoners were incarcerated in German camps and they, unsurprisingly, welcomed the news that an Armistice had been agreed. Many had lived under poor conditions with little food, and some were malnourished, while they were imprisoned, so when the war ended, it meant that they would be returning home and their ordeal was over. Private Clarence Haydon recalled:

> When we heard about the signing of the Armistice, up went our caps and down went the wire. They respected the British Bulldog after that.[1]

Charles Laquiéze, of the French 55th Régiment d'Infanterie, was confined in a prisoner of war camp in Germany when he heard that the war was over.

> There was no shouting, no exuberance – we were all struck down by intense emotion. Our joy was too great to sing out loud … Can it be so? Can it be so?![2]

Although prisoners of war were now free, there were instances of violence carried out on Armistice Day. Private Frank Hodgson reported:

> Not a stroke of work was done after Armistice Day. We broke up our camp, containing 10,000 men. We had won our freedom. It was at this camp that three French soldiers were shot for insubordination. We threatened reprisals. The German sentry who had shot them was executed later by the German Government.[3]

Private John Strang, Royal Scots, had spent six months as a prisoner of war in a camp near Munster, Germany. When he returned home to Airdrie he recounted to a reporter the story of British PoWs being shot. The following article appeared in the *Sunday Post* during December 1918:

> There were about 500 Frenchmen, fifty-six British and a number of Portuguese and Italian prisoners in the camp, and all received brutal treatment in the camp from their guards.
>
> On the news of the armistice reaching the camp, four Englishmen in a steel work flung down their shovels and refused to work anymore. Their guards were so incensed that they took very summary measures to prevent others doing the same.
>
> The four Englishmen were immediately drawn up in the presence of the other prisoners and were shot down. The others including Private Strang, being informed that the same fate would befall any who refused to work.[4]

The soldiers who died at Munster were taken to Cologne Southern Cemetery for burial. There are thirteen soldiers listed as being killed on Armistice Day who are buried within this cemetery. Some of them may have died of influenza or malnutrition. Four of these men might have been those British soldiers shot on the 11 November.

On 19 November, Lieutenant-General Sir Henry Rawlinson intially gave a positive assessment of the condition of prisoners-of-war that had been released from German PoW camps:

> Our prisoners of war are coming back in large numbers, and they are in better condition than I expected to find them.[5]

However, three days later Rawlinson saw evidence that some Allied prisoners were suffering from malnutrition, for he wrote:

> Hearing that there were a number of our prisoners of war sick in Marche, I sent some of our doctors on there. They came in touch with the German rear-guard, and had to wait until it had cleared out. The treatment of our men in the German prisons seems to have been varied considerably. There are distinct cases of starvation among some of them.[6]

Major Deneys Reitz recalled the moment when the 1st Royal Scots Fusiliers encountered dishevelled Allied prisoners of war, showing symptoms of malnutrition:

From Frasnoy we marched to Maubeuge via Bavay. As soon as we got clear of the village we found the road thronged for miles with Allied prisoners of war, who had walked out of their camps, their German guards having disappeared. There were men from almost every nation. We saw British, French, Americans, Italians, Serbs, Roumanians [sic Romanians] and Belgians streaming by, mostly in rags, and half starved, but smiling cheerfully as they passed.[7]

The American 1st Division encountered Allied prisoners of war when they reached Etain, the first French village that they entered after crossing the Armistice line on 17 November. Major Thomas Gowenlock recalled:

The first settlement we came to was Etain. All around, the terrain was ripped up by shellfire, and most of the trees were splintery stubs and the farmhouses completely in ruins. As we neared the remains of the village, a large body of men appeared, marching toward us. When they came nearer we saw that they were Allied prisoners who had been released by the Germans according to terms of the Armistice. Most of them were Russians, Italians and French. They smiled and waved as they passed us, trying to show us appreciation of their liberty regained, and our men gave them a hearty welcome in return.[8]

As Allied troops marched through Belgium towards the German border they encountered prisoners of war who had been captured during 1914. Some of the French prisoners were still wearing the flamboyant uniforms they wore during the beginning of the war. Private John A. Hughes, C Battery, 15th Field Artillery, American 2nd Division, wrote:

We met hundreds of soldiers returning from Germany and some of them had been prisoners since 1914. Several had on their old uniforms of red pants and blue coats and they surely appeared funny looking to us. They had walked for days and we shared grub and smokes with them.[9]

Thomas Mitchell-Fox was a Royal Naval officer from the Hood Battalion, Royal Naval Division. He was a veteran from the Gallipoli campaign, who was later captured at Welsh Ridge during December 1917. Mitchell-Fox and fellow PoW's took advantage of the breakdown in the German infrastructure and discipline among their guards and walked out of the gates of their prisoner of war camp just before the

Armistice. Three weeks later they reached Cologne to find Allied soldiers occupying the German city and learned that the war had officially ended. Mitchell-Fox recalled:

> The German soldiers were obviously disgruntled about the way things were going, about the state of things at home, from letters from wives and families. Ultimately it broke out, we saw the German officers in civilian clothes for the first time. They went to their various and respective duties in the camp, coming in minus uniform; and the rumour got around; and a little bit of questioning here and there, we found that the German soldiers had taken over the army. They formed soldiers' councils and they ran everything from then on. They were so preoccupied with their own affairs they did not have the time to look after us as they might had done. That gave us the opportunity for skedaddling out of the main gate when it was wide open one night, about one hundred of us and we got away, just before the end of the war. We walked out, no one tried to stop us. We grabbed a Dutch barge on the Rhine, and we proceeded down the Rhine really slowly indeed, stopping at places from time to time, keeping under cover most of the way during the daylight and only appearing for a breath of air during the evening so that we would not be spotted. This was the routine from day to day until we ultimately found our way into Cologne. Having got to Cologne we spotted soldiers in British uniform. We thought 'hello, what the heck is this?' We found out that the war was over.[10]

The repatriation of thousands of prisoners of war from Germany to their respective nations was a major logistical task and would take time to administer and implement. Sergeant Harry Wright, who was captured on the Mole during the Zeebrugge raid on 23 April 1918, recalled:

> Owing to the breakdown of German transport, (Their rolling stock was then in very poor shape), the many thousands of Prisoner of War were sent home in alphabetical order, I landed in England early in the new year.[11]

Some PoWs were welcomed by royalty when they arrived in London. On 17 December, the Duke of Connaught, accompanied by Princess Beatrice, welcomed returning prisoners at Cannon Street Station. The *Daily Mirror* reported:

Mingling with the returned prisoners, the Duke was particularly interested in the experiences of men of the Rifle Brigade, of which he is Colonel-in-Chief. He chatted for some time and shook hands heartily with them as they left to take their seats in the trains. 'A Happy New Year, sir,' said a merry North-country youth. 'Thanks and the same to you lads,' responded the Duke with a wave of the hand. He and the Princess afterwards walked along the train, presenting the men with cigarettes and chocolates.[12]

Chapter 25

The Allied Armies
Enter Germany

The German Army was given six days to vacate from the territory it occupied in France and Belgium; and to withdraw to the eastern bank of the River Rhine. The Allies would march into Germany and occupy the industrial region of Germany while the politicians discussed peace. The presence of Allied armies would prevent Germany from changing its mind and resuming the war while these discussions were taking place. On 19 November, Field Marshal Sir Douglas Haig convened a meeting with his generals where they discussed plans for the Allied entry into Germany. Lieutenant-General Rawlinson, commanding the British Fourth Army, was in attendance and wrote:

> Archie met me with the news that the Fourth Army is not to go into Germany after all. Today we had a meeting of Army commanders at D.H.'s [Douglas Haig's] train, near Cambrai, and discussed the best way of carrying out Foch's orders. He has agreed with Hindenburg that only eleven British divisions are to cross the frontier, and there is to be only one British army in Germany; so Plumer is to go to Cologne, and I am to form a supporting army in Belgium behind the German frontier. Plumer is taking the Canadians with him and they are to be relieved later by the Australians, so that as many Dominion troops as possible may have been in Germany. There will be considerable heartburning over this, but there is no other solution. I shall have thirteen divisions in my army, and Plumer eleven in his. We are still having difficulties with supplies, as the roads to the Meuse are giving out, and the lorries are overworked, owing to the strain which the destruction of the railways puts on them. I have told Lawrence that I cannot take infantry across the Meuse till Charleroi is opened as a rail head. Cavalry can only be pushed on with great difficulty.[1]

Although the Armistice had been signed that ended the conflict, many soldiers who had considered their job done and were looking forward to returning home to their loved ones were now expected to march into Germany. Rawlinson had written the following order on 11 November, which alerted Fourth Army that in the weeks ahead it would enter Germany and advised it on how to behave to liberated French and German civilians under Allied occupation:

> The Fourth Army has been ordered to form part of the army of occupation on the Rhine in accordance with the terms of the Armistice. The march to the Rhine will shortly commence, and although carried out with the usual military precautions, will be generally undertaken as a peace march. The British Army through four years, and almost continuous and bitter fighting, has proved that it has lost none of that fighting spirit and dogged determination which have characterised the British Army in the past, and has won for it a place in history of which every soldier of the Empire has just reason to be proud. It has maintained the highest standard of discipline both in advances and in retreat. It has proved that British discipline, based on mutual confidence between officers and men, can stand the hard test of war far better than the Prussian discipline, based on fear of punishment. That is not all. The British has during the last four years on foreign soil, by its behaviour in billets, by its courtesy to women, by its ever ready help to old and weak, and by its kindness to children, earned a reputation in France that no army serving in a foreign land torn by the horrors of war has ever gained before.
>
> Till you reach the frontier of Germany, you will be marching through a country that has suffered grievously from all the depredations and exactions of a brutal enemy. Do all that is in your power to mitigate the hardships of these poor people, who will welcome you as deliverers and friends.
>
> I would further ask you as you cross the German frontier to show the world that the British soldiers, unlike those of Germany, do not wage war against women and children, or against the old and the weak. The Allied Governments have guaranteed that private property shall be respected by the army of occupation, and I rely on you to see that this engagement is carried out.
>
> In conclusion, I ask you one and all, men from all parts of the British Empire, to ensure that the fair name of the British Army, enhanced by your exertions in long years of trial and hardship, shall be fully maintained during the last exacting months that lie before you. I ask you to show the world that, as in war, so in peace, British

discipline is the highest form of discipline based on loyalty to our King, respect for authority, care for the well-being of sub-ordinates, courtesy and consideration for non-combatants, and true soldierly bearing in carrying out whatever duty we may be called upon to perform.[2]

General John Pershing issued a similar order to the American Expeditionary Force on 20 November 1918:

The mission entrusted to us by our country has not been ended by the armistice that is now in operation; and the same devotion to duty and sincere effort to attain efficiency which have marked your participation on the actual conflict are still demanded of you.

It is the desire of our Government to return us to our homes at the earliest possible moment, and every effort will be made to accomplish that purpose. It will be as difficult, however, to effect our return to America as it was to bring us to Europe: and any lack of enthusiasm in the tasks still to be accomplished will surely serve to postpone the hour of our departure for the United States.

I trust that each of you will continue to maintain the high standard of efficiency and conduct that has characterized your service in the past; and I expect every officer and soldier to undertake, with the same fine spirit they have always exhibited, the duties yet to be performed before the mission of these forces is successfully completed.[3]

Once the Allied Armies had crossed the Armistice line on 17th November, they received a warm welcome from French villages that had endured four years of German occupation. Major Deneys Reitz, 1st Royal Scots Fusiliers, wrote:

All along our course the prisoners and refugees cheered us, and often crowded round, nearly pulling me from my horse in their efforts to shake hands. The children clapped at the sound of the pipes, and their mothers held them up to see the soldiers go by, and in spite of their pinched faces, due to the trials which these poor people had endured, something of the courage of France still stood in their eyes.[4]

According to Major Thomas Gowenlock, an intelligence officer with the 1st Division, he was the first American officer to cross the Armistice line on 17 November:

It was a dramatic moment as we crossed the Armistice line and entered a no man's land more than four years old that had not seen Allied troops since 1914 ... I was the first American officer with combat troops to pass that historic mark and start the armed march into the land of the enemy.[5]

The American 5th Marine Regiment, 4th Marine Brigade, 2nd Division, received a rapturous welcome as it passed through French and Belgium towns and villages. Sergeant Karl McCune, 55th Company, 5th Marine Regiment, recalled the scene when they arrived at their first village:

Malandry, the first village of the repatriated area, was entered about 10.30. A sign of 'Welcome' stretched over the road. Civilians rushed out to greet the Marines with cries of 'Vive les Amércains' and 'Vive l'Amérique.' The column passed through Villy, a neighbouring village, receiving the same welcome, then turned off across swampy fields, over a footbridge across a small tributary of the Meuse. Here the battalion halted.

It was Sunday and the civilians, dressed up in their best clothes, crowded about, advancing greetings. A few assembled at the head of the 55th Company with accordions and played and sang the Marseillaise. Most of them were women. Meanwhile the company stacked arms and unslung equipment while the battalion billeting officer hunted billets. About this time the escort wagons and galleys, which had advanced by a different road, pulled up and the galleys began immediately to prepare chow.[6]

As they passed through Belgian towns, the American soldiers questioned the civilians about life under German occupation. Private John A. Hughes, C Battery, 15 Field Artillery, 2nd Division, recalled:

The Belgians could understand German as the Germans had occupied these parts for four years. We inquired about their treatment while under the German occupation and learned that during the first two years of the war the Germans took almost anything they wanted and set their own price on it, especially in regard to grain, hay and all kinds of forage; also that they were very domineering: but during the last two years the natives could bargain about the price of various foodstuffs. We also enquired about the way the women folks were treated regarding various abuses committed in other towns, but none around where they lived. Such was the answer through Belgium. I personally never came across one instance where such offenses had been committed. No doubt there had been some; couldn't expect anything different from an invading army, and I honestly believe that no army would be immune from such cases where four or five thousand men visit a city after possible months of fighting at the front, especially those that occupied the city as victors.[7]

On 18 November, the 5th Marine Regiment reached the French–Belgian Border. Sergeant Karl McCune wrote:

At 10.30, Villiers, a village perched on top of a high hill on the French border, was sighted. Great enthusiasm was shown by the civilians who ran far out beyond the town to meet the advancing column. A group of young boys and girls carrying flags, placed itself in advance of the leading unit and marched before the battalion into town. Cries of 'Vive les Américains' greeted the Marines on every hand. At ten o'clock the border was crossed and the battalion halted and ate its first meal on Belgian soil. We marched through hills into a rolling plain. We reached a demolished village, through which long lines of French wagons were passing, the streets lined with civilians who were very glad to see the Americans. At the outskirts of Tintigny many people thronged the road to escort the battalion into town. In the town itself, women, children, young girls and old folks were crowded about eight deep along the roadside who shouted the habitual cry 'Vive les Américains ', to be answered with 'Vive la Belgique' by the equally enthusiastic Marines.[8]

On 20 November at Bracquenies, the Canadian 20th Battalion had to quell civil strife between the local populace and German sympathisers:

In the evening there were some disturbances and small riots amongst the civilians who appeared to be agitating against German sympathisers. Accordingly the piquet was called out and all the other men were confined to their billets.[9]

During the following day some of the 20th Battalion remained in Braquenies to maintain order in the town:

On account of the disturbances amongst the civil population the Bourgmaster requested the battalion leave behind a piquet until the next troops arrived. Lieut. Edie and 50 troops were selected.[10]

The Canadian 19th Battalion received a warm welcome as it marched through Belgian towns and villages. For example, on 21 November, the battalion war diary reported:

> Battalion moved off at 10.30 hours and arrived in TRAZEGNIES at 16.15 hrs where everyone was again very comfortably billeted, all along the line of the march we were accorded a most generous welcome by civilian population of the various towns; the streets being very gaily decorated. Word was received from Bde that the Btn would remain here for 2 days. In the evening the town band paid an unexpected compliment when they serenaded the H.Q. officers mess. Major Hatch replied with a very appropriate impromptu speech.[11]

The 29th Division was one of two British divisions that advanced across the Armistice line through Belgium towards Germany. Their long march began on 18 November. After years of fighting, these soldiers expected that now the war was over, they would be sent home, but they were wrong. They had to endure further hardships after the Armistice. Chaplain Kenelm Swallow, who accompanied the divisional billeting officers as interpreter, recalled as they moved towards the German frontier:

> This march was probably the sternest test of sheer endurance, as apart from bravery, that the division ever encountered. Food and smokes were short all the way, the men were filthy and covered with lice, and utterly worn out. The marches were very severe – anything up to twenty miles a day, the roads bad, and the weather usually appalling. The food-supplies for some twenty thousand men depended upon one pontoon bridge across the Scheldt. I happened to be crossing the bridge on the occasion when it collapsed. It was crammed with heavy general service wagons drawn by mules. The whole structure groaned and cracked, and eventually sank into the river, the wagons, etc, just getting to the other bank in the nick of time.[12]

At each Belgian village they receive a rapturous welcome from the residents who had lived under German occupation for four years. Chaplain Kenelm Swallow wrote:

> A young second lieutenant and myself and the four N.C.O.s who made up the battalion's billeting party were the first Englishmen

the inhabitants of most of the previously occupied Belgian villages had seen in their lives. Many villages were quite unaware of our nationality or our purpose. As soon as this was realized, we received tremendous ovations. It was very difficult to get on with our job of arranging billets, owing to the numerous invitations to eat and drink in every house we entered … Most of the villages had bands – very bad ones. On the arrival of the battalion (the S.W.B.), it was met about half a mile outside the place by the local band, who escorted it in with great pomp. Then, as a rule, the entire civilian population assembled in the central spot of the place to witness the local burgomaster or maire greet the commanding officer as if he were royalty, while the band played the British National Anthem.[13]

The 1st Royal Scots Fusiliers crossed the River Meuse on 29 November at Yvoir and while billeted there for the night, Major Denys Reitz learned of an atrocity that took place in the village during 1914:

I was quartered in a neat little villa opposite the lock, whose owner told me that the Germans had executed a number of inhabitants of Yvoir in 1914, to keep the rest quiet, he said.[14]

When Reitz reached Spontin he discovered other atrocities that had taken place during the beginning of the war:

Spontin had been destroyed by the Germans in 1914. I had never believed all the German atrocities of which one read in the British newspapers during the war, but they had certainly acted with ruthless severity against this unfortunate little place. They had entered Spontin at daybreak on 23rd of August 1914. Alleging that the villagers had fired on them, they burned down every house. Then they arrested the Maire, the Curé, and forty-eight other men, and executed them against a bank at the railway station. The gravestone of each dead man in the little cemetery above the village reads 'victime de la terrible journée du 23 Août 1914', which was all that the survivors dared write on the tombs during the occupation of the enemy.[15]

Major Thomas Gowenlock spoke of the warm reception that the American 1st Division received from liberated French citizens as they marched through their villages towards Luxembourg:

For three days we saw only desolation and ruins. At each French village the people, who had not seen any uniform but the German gray in over four years, rushed out with tears of joy in their eyes. Again and again I found myself being hugged by the ragged and rhapsodical peasant women, who implored us to stop in their village. Many hearing of our coming, had hastily sewed together home-made American flags, which they now waved excitedly as they intermingled with the men in the ranks. Exultant strains of the Marseillaise greeted our ears in every village. In a few places we even marched under crudely constructed victory arches that had been erected in our honor.[16]

In some instances they were liberating French citizens who had lived under German occupation since the Franco–Prussian War fought during 1870. Major Gowenlock commented:

On November 20 we passed through a small strip of Lorraine where the people were wildly celebrating their freedom from forty-four years of bondage.[17]

Once they reached Luxembourg, the soldiers were offered better billets where they were able to sleep in proper beds, instead of sleeping in farm buildings. Gowenlock wrote:

When we entered Luxembourg the next day, the signs of desolation had completely disappeared. Here was a happy, prosperous and comfortable little nation, and in the villages where we now stopped nearly every soldier was given a bed to sleep in, instead of haylofts and barn floors which had been their usual lot in French villages. We took our time crossing Luxembourg, because the Armistice terms forbade our entering Germany proper until December 1.[18]

The American 5th Marine Regiment, 2nd Division, reached the German border on 1 December. Sergeant Karl McCune wrote:

At 7.00 a.m. we crossed into Germany by way of Wallendorf. It was Sunday and the people were going to church, and they looked curiously upon the column as it toiled up the road that led up the side of a hill towards the German interior. As we marched a number of Germans gazed at us without commenting on the passing column. Seimerich and Korperick were passed before 10.00 a.m. We

301

entered Neuerburg, a large sized town about 3.30 p.m. The men well nigh exhausted and famished. Our breakfast was negligible and the dinner very poor. The civilians stayed inside not daring to look upon the ferocious Americans.[19]

As the Allied armies entered Germany, their citizens were anxious and fearful that they would be mistreated. Major Thomas Gowenlock recalled their reaction as American soldiers from the 1st Division marched through their country.

On December 1 we at last entered our late enemy's homeland, heading northeast down the Moselle River toward Coblenz … The Germans at first were antagonistic toward us. Suspicious and sullen faces looked out from windows of houses we passed. When I had talked to some of the people, I found that most of this hostility was the result of propaganda directed against us. They had been told of atrocities practised by the American soldiers and of the cruel treatment they would suffer when we took over their country. They were afraid of us and hated the sight of the American flag. But when we billeted in one of their villages and they saw how well disciplined the soldiers were and how scrupulous they were in policing the vicinity, they soon became friendly. The good news preceded us as we marched forward. They were glad, they said, that we were Americans and not Frenchmen. Their traditional antipathy to the French would have prevented any such pleasant relations as we were to have with them.[20]

Chaplain Kenelm Swallow recalled the moment when the British 29th Division crossed the German border:

On December 4, 1918, I actually entered Germany with no more concern than one crosses a road at home. Near Malmédy we came to a place where posts were about six feet high, painted black and white, ran through the fields at intervals of about 200 yards. This was the frontier. Not a soul was to be seen. There were two houses, one on either side. The Belgian house flew colours. That on the German side had all the blinds drawn down, like a house of mourning and death.

When the battalion reached this point an hour or two later they marched over playing national and Welsh airs. Nobody came out to meet us at the first German village, Widerum. No one was to be seen save a few boys and girls. We came upon these somewhat unexpectedly round a corner, and they fled from us in terror. All the inhabitants evidently expected that unspeakable atrocities would be committed. We found them quiet, homely people, all of them hating the war, and most of them quite likeable. The battalion arrived soaked to the skin after a long march in a continuous downpour; hot drinks were waiting for them in every billet, and the men were provided with fresh clean straw in abundance. As we went further, and came to somewhat larger places, proclamations in German, bordered in deep black, were to be seen in all prominent walls. These gave the Germans the official intimation of their country's humiliation, coupled with instructions as to how to behave during occupation.[21]

The German inhabitants of Zweifel felt apprehension as the men of the 1/5th West Yorkshire Regiment arrived in their village. The streets were deserted and their window blinds were drawn. With the villagers reluctant to leave their homes, the battalion had to make efforts to reassure them that they would come to no harm. Private Ernest Law recalled:

The people there were scared to death because they heard we was going to kill them all, but the war was over. They would not come out. We had Sergeant Cox, he said when we go out take nothing with us, no guns, no rifles. In the end they got use to us, they took their blinds down.[22]

However, they were not permitted to talk to them, as Law recalled:

No fraternising for the first six months. You must not dare talk to a German and German soldiers must not come near you.[23]

Private Walter Spencer, 4th Grenadier Guards, learned about the Armistice on the leave boat to Folkestone on 11 November. Despite the war being over, he had to return to the battalion. He recalled the journey to Germany and gestures of goodwill from its civilians to British soldiers:

I re-joined our unit just in time for the march up to Germany and we marched from this place near Mons right up to Cologne, that was over 200 miles, in about 12 days, continuous marching ... we went over the border at Aachen ... One episode there I remember actually at Aachen, because we had a rest there for a night. We spent the night there in barns that were around to accommodate us while we were on the march … We all got down, our company, into a big barn, a farm barn. We used to carry candles in a tin to light us at night to see to get down. Of course there was all straw in the barn. Everyone had candles and settled down; and got to bed, the old farmer came in, looked at us and switched on the electric light. He lit up the whole barn … we gave him a good cheer. Anyhow, he and his wife, they were Germans of course, they made a great big two gallon thing full of soup, stew and brought to us hot and we had a good damned feed from them. That was from Germans, we had been killing them and they had been killing us two or three days before.[24]

The response was typical from the German people towards the British soldiers, according to Spencer:

The Germans were very subdued actually because when we got over the border at Aachen on the way to Cologne there were masses of people watching us going by and some were even cheering us, so they weren't anti of course, they were really for us.[25]

Lieutenant André Zeller, of the French 59th Régiment d'artillerie, recalled that the soldiers were given advice before they entered Germany:

The last billeting in Lorraine, in the north of Saint Avold, was the village of Coume. In the evening, I read to the officers and the men of the battery, the instructions to be applied in the country where we were going to occupy; including respect towards the inhabitants of both sexes, the strict guarding of the places containing weapons and ammunitions, night rounds, strict discipline. In the light lanterns, faces took a grave air. The entrance to Germany, more than the Armistice, better than the crossing of the Seille – marked the success.[26]

Zeller recalled that they received assistance from the residents of the first German village they entered:

First billets in Germany: the village of Kerling, near Saarlouis. Some elderly civilians, with grey hair, even came to help to stop and water horses.[27]

Lieutenant François Ingold recalled the reception received by the French Army as it entered the Rhineland on 7 December.

I had the honor to make the entrance into Kaiserslautern at the head of the 10th company of the 7th Colonial. The Rhenish population showed us no antipathy; so in spite of our first unfavorable reserve, let us give to her our cordiality. Accommodated one day with an old lady, in the charming small boudoir of a very beautiful house, I was amazed to see on the wall the miniature of an officer of Napoleonic time wearing the Legion of Honor. It was an ancestor of the old lady.[28]

Ingold would attain the rank of general twenty years later when he was in command of the 2nd Division d'Infanterie Coloniale of the French Free Forces during the Second World War.

Lieutenant Hanin Charles 3rd Régiment de Zouaves recalled:

In the overnight stay at Niederhausen; the Zouaves are busy. A German Bavarian light Infantryman recognizes my rank by my officer's sword, stands to attention marked with a beautiful and noble pride.[29]

By the time they reached the German Rhineland, the Allied armies had marched 200 miles. While in Germany many soldiers yearned to return home. Some were frustrated because they had not been demobilised, while there were jobs waiting for them in Britain. Private F. Irish expressed those frustrations from Germany to the editor of the *Western Times* on 29 March 1919.

I note that there is a great deal of complaint about the shortage of labour for agricultural work and this no doubt is greatly aggravated by the excessive wet weather. With matters as they are I cannot understand why so many men who have been applied for months – four months some of us – are not released to go back on the farms, to work that is awaiting us, and that is so sadly in arrears.

I wrote to you in January saying that we were anxious to get home for farm work and to plant our gardens, while young single men, mostly building hands were being released, first 1916 men at that. We are still here while the country at home is crying aloud for labour for the farms.

I was applied for by a leading agriculturist early in December. He has been expecting me home for at least three months, and I certainly thought I should have been home long before this. It makes me hot with anger when I read of farmers begging for men, and we are kept here doing about three hours of useless work when we could be at home doing so much good.

I have known cases here where men are doing about one or two hours' work a day, just to clean a pair of boots, polish a few buttons, etc. every day for an officer, while they are wanted and want to be at home for really useful and necessary work. So much for demobilisation.[30]

The American 2nd Division would remain in Germany until July 1919. Some British divisions returned to Britain during the summer of 1919. Despite orders not to fraternise with German civilians, there was evidence that this order had been disobeyed and intimate relationships between British soldiers and German women had developed. One article reported the following observations in Cologne:

A feature of the departure of the British troops from the Rhine is the number of German girls who come to the railway stations to see them off. Now and then the parting is very touching. Many girls are receiving letters from soldiers who have returned to England.[31]

One British officer explained the circumstances behind why many relationships developed between British soldiers and German women:

An officer, recently returned from Cologne, told us it was true that many of our soldiers had married or became engaged to German girls. His explanation was that 'Tommy' was billeted out among small households and had been captivated by the superior domestic efficiency of Gretchen ... there is another fact almost uniformly reported by officers from Rhineland, who have been through the war, that our men get on better with the Germans than the French and Belgians. This will be bad hearing for some of our journalists and politicians who are already declaring that these marriages are a plot by the German Government to poison Tommy, or to create an army of female spies.[32]

Chapter 26

Surrender of the German High Seas Fleet

When the Armistice had been signed there was a sense of dissatisfaction among officers within the Royal Navy because in their opinion a victory over Germany had been achieved without a large scale, epic naval battle similar to that fought by Nelson's navy at Trafalgar more than a century ago in 1805. The Battle of Jutland fought in 1916 saw the Royal Navy lose fourteen ships and 6,094 men, the German High Seas Fleet lost eleven ships and 2,551 men, with both sides claiming victory.

The argument over who was the victor at Jutland has been contested during the past century, but despite the Royal Navy sustaining the most losses in terms of ships and men, it could still operate and control the North Sea, while, despite it taking several months for the German High Seas Fleet to repair its vessels, throughout the remainder of the war it stayed berthed in port. In contrast, the Royal Navy was able to enforce a blockade of German ports, causing food shortages that contributed to the enemy's ultimate defeat. The British press was disappointed as it did not regard Jutland as a victory, and some officers were similarly underwhelmed by the result. However, in a letter to Admiral Sir David Beatty dated 14 November 1918, some two years after Jutland, Admiral Sir Rosslyn Wemyss wrote of his frustration at the perception of the battle, which was shared widely by fellow officers:

> There can be no naval officer who does not see the end of this war without the feeling of incompleteness, and that that incompleteness does not arise from any sense of failure. We feel it strongly at the Admiralty and realize how much more it must be the case with you and the Grand Fleet. The Navy has won a victory greater than Trafalgar, though less spectacular, and because of this lack of display

it feels that the unthinking do not perhaps realize what the nation – indeed the whole world – owes the British Navy.[1]

After the Armistice had been agreed, plans had to be formulated to implement the surrender of the German surface and submarine fleets. The governments of the neutral countries Norway and Spain were reluctant to accept responsibility for the internment of these German vessels within their shores. On 13 November, an emergency meeting of the Allied Naval Council was convened in London, where Wemyss suggested the German surface vessels be interned at Scapa Flow in the Orkneys and that the submarines be detailed to surrender at British ports to be specified.

On 15 November, Admiral Hugo Meurer was aboard the German light cruiser *Königsberg*, which was anchored close to May Island in the Firth of Forth. He had been sent by Admiral Franz von Hipper, commander of the German High Seas Fleet, to discuss the details of the internment process. Stoker Norbert McCrory had served in Gallipoli and with the Australian Artillery in France before transferring to the Royal Australian Navy towards the end of 1917, when he was drafted to HMAS *Australia*. In April 1918, he served as a stoker aboard the blockship HMS *Thetis* during the Zeebrugge Raid and several months later he witnessed *Königsberg* approach the Grand Fleet at May Island. McCrory wrote:

> On the 15-11-18 the German ship *Königsberg* arrived at the Firth of Forth about 10.30 am flying the white flag and carrying the German staff on board. She anchored on the starboard side of HMS *Queen Elizabeth*, flagship of the Grand Fleet. After paying the usual respect as a foreigner, the German Admiral and staff boarded the *Queen Elizabeth* to interview Admiral David Beatty who acted on behalf of the British Admiralty.[2]

Admiral Sir David Beatty met them aboard HMS *Queen Elizabeth* during that evening. At a further three meetings held on 16 November it was agreed that the German surface vessels would surrender to Beatty in the Firth of Forth, where they would then be taken to Scapa Flow for internment. The German submarine fleet would surrender to Admiral Tyrwhitt at Harwich. Once the plans for internment were agreed Admiral Meurer, and *Königsberg* returned to Germany.

The German High Seas Fleet departed from their ports on 19 November to surrender to the British Grand Fleet. Seaman Richard Stumpf witnessed their departure from Wilhelmshaven:

Today is a very sad day for me. At this moment *Frederich der Grosse* and *König Albert* are in the locks and the other ships are ready to follow. They are assembling at Schillig Roads for their final difficult voyage. The submarines will also go along. Now and then the wind carries a snatch of their sad songs over here. It is like a funeral. We shall not see them again. Impassively holding their seabags, the men who are being left behind stand at the pier. At the last minute they feared for their lives and threw down their weapons. I, too, feel too disgusted to remain here any longer. I wish I had not been born a German. This despicable act will remain a blot on Germany's good name forever.[3]

The first batch of German submarines appeared off the Essex coast to surrender on 20 November 1918. Commander Stephen King-Hall was waiting aboard the submarine depot ship HMS *Maidstone* at Harwich and recalled his thoughts that morning:

The surrender of these first ships of the German Navy had a double interest, firstly, in that, preceding as it did by twenty-four hours the surrender of the surface craft to the Grand Fleet, it was a test case as to the willingness of the German Navy to submit to this unprecedented humiliation; and secondly, there was something altogether incredible in the idea that submarines would arrive at a position on the sea and surrender. Most of us felt that a surface ship might possibly be expected to surrender; but we found it extraordinarily hard to imagine that very shy bird Fritz walking into the cage.[4]

Later that morning, King-Hall went aboard HMS *Firedrake*, where he witnessed the arrival of the German submarines at Harwich on 20 November. He recalled:

At 9.55 a hull appeared, which resolved itself into the *Danae*, one of the latest light cruisers. Close behind her, and looking sadly in need of a coat of paint, came a white transport. She was flanked on either side by destroyers. This seemed promising, but where were the Fritzes? A gap of half a mile, and then a smaller transport ambled out of the fog – more British destroyers – a 'Blimp' overhead, then a startled voice broke the silence with – 'By Jove: there's a ruddy Fritz.'

There was a rush to the port side of the *Firedrake* which heeled over like a paddle steamer full of tourists at a naval review. From the north, a long line of a hull with a dome-shaped conning tower in the centre slid across the water. No boat built in a British yard ever looked like that – the Huns had come. She was followed by five others in straggling order. One was a large vessel (*U-135*) elaborately camouflaged and mounting a 6-inch gun forward.

It is impossible to describe in words the feelings of the officers and men who witnessed this amazing sight. Try and imagine what you would feel like if you were told to go to Piccadilly at 10 a.m. and see twenty man-eating tigers walk up from Hyde Park Corner and lie down in front of the Ritz and let you cut their tails off and put their leads on – and it really was so. Add to these impressions the fact that many of those present had been hunting Fritz for over four years, in which period a man who could boast, 'I have seen six Fritzes and heard them four times on my hydrophones,' was favoured by the gods, and you may get an insight into what British crews felt.

More boats drifted out of the fog and anchored under the guns of the British destroyers. Motor-launches came alongside the *Firedrake* and *Melampus*, to take our crews over to the Huns. Each party consisted of two or three officers and about 15 men.[5]

King-Hall belonged to one of the boarding parties assigned to receive the surrender of the German submarines. He continued his detailed report:

I was with the party that boarded *U-90*, and as the proceedings in each case were similar, I shall describe what happened here.

The four officers composing of our party were armed, and it may safely be said that we were prepared for any eventuality except that which actually took place. The Hun submarine service is remarkable in many respects. It has a record of criminal brutality standing against it unequalled in the history of war.

It has been expanded from 20 to 30 boats to about 140 plus 180 to 200 lost, in the space of four years. During this period it has troubled the British Empire – no mean feat. At the end of this period it has submitted to humiliation unparalleled in history. A strange record.

I have said that the British parties were prepared for every eventuality save one. We were not prepared to find the Huns behaving for once as gentlemen. It is right to record that during those wonderful days their behaviour has been correct in every respect … In nearly every case the German officer has seemed genuinely anxious to assist in every way possible, and give as much information concerning the working of the boat as was feasible in the time at his disposal …

We left the *Firedrake* in a motor-launch and went alongside a fair sized Hun mounting two guns, one each side of the conning tower. K_____ (our senior officer) jumped on board, followed by the Engineer Commander, an Engineer Lieutenant-Commander, and myself. The two engineer officers had come out to try and pick up as much as they could about the Hun diesel engines during the trip in.

We were received by the German captain together with his torpedo officer and his engineer. They saluted us, which salutes were returned.

'Do you speak English?' said K_____.

'Yes, a little,' replied the Hun.

'Give me your papers.'

The German then produced a list of his crew and the signed terms of the surrender, which he translated into English. These terms were as follows:

1. The boat was to be in an efficient condition, with periscopes, main motors, diesel engines, and auxiliary engines in working order.
2. She was to be in surface trim, with all diving tanks blown.
3. Her torpedoes were to be on board, without their war heads and the torpedoes were to be cleared of the tubes.
4. Her wireless was to be complete.
5. There were to be no explosives on board.
6. There were to be no booby traps or infernal machines on board.

This last declaration stuck in his throat; he reported no 'hell engines' with great conviction. This captain was a well-fed-looking individual with quite a pleasant appearance, and he was wearing the Iron Cross of the first class. He had apparently sunk much tonnage in another boat, but had done only one trip in *U-90*. Curiously enough, his old boat was next ahead of us going up harbour.

K_____ then informed him that he would give him instructions where to go, but that otherwise the German crew would work the boat under the supervision of our people. This surprised the Hun, who showed us his orders, which stated that he was to hand the boat over to us and then leave at once for the transport. His subordinates urged him to protest, but he was too sensible and at once agreed to do whatever we ordered.

… Getting under way on the diesels, we proceeded towards Harwich, the White Ensign being run up as the anchor left the ground … We proceeded into Harwich and up to the head of the harbour, past Parkeston Quay, to what the reporters now say we call 'U-boat Avenue'. The ships in the harbour were crowded with spectators, but a complete silence was preserved which was more impressive than cheers. On arrival at our buoy the German manoeuvred his late command very skilfully on the oil engines … As soon as we had secured to the buoy, an operation which in every case the Germans had to do for themselves, the German was instructed to take us round the boat in a more detailed manner. This he did; and auxiliary machinery was started, periscopes raised and lowered, etc. etc.

At 4.00 p.m. a motor launch came alongside and the Germans were ordered to gather up their personal belongings and get into her. The captain, without a sign of that emotion which he must have felt, took a last look at his boat and saluted. We returned his salute, he bowed and then joined his crew in the motor-launch, which took them to the destroyer in which they made passage to the transport outside.[6]

A correspondent, also aboard HMS *Firedrake*, witnessed the surrender:

I have seen the surrender of the first of the German submarines to be delivered into our hands. Nameless, and of an inferior class, the slim grey ships were given up at sea at 10.30 this morning, and a little later the White Ensign, hoisted above the periscope, flickered in the breeze. So has ended Germany's dream of the capture of the oceans. So once more the sailors of our Fleet may travel the seas upon their lawful occasions in serenity and freedom.

At 5 o'clock this morning Admiral Tyrwhitt, 20 miles now, put another 50 miles to sea, so that his flotilla might be ready to escort the U-Boats to the appointed meeting place. Neither the Admiral nor his immediate officers took part in the reception of the submarines. A destroyer was detailed to guide them to the rendezvous. Those who were with the Admiral on his flagship, the *Curacao*, saw the twenty U-boats approaching through the haze, but their numbers had been painted out. No flags were carried, and the little grey fleet passed by the flagship without ceremony to the awaiting destroyer. Captain Addison, who was in charge of submarines at the Harwich base, directed the operations. Accompanied by Commander Kellett, he left the harbour in the destroyer *Firedrake* at 8 o'clock and as I had the happy privilege of joining the company on the ship I was able to watch the approach of the U boats, and to be present in the historic hour of their surrender. It was seemly that the valiant *Firedrake* should have been chosen for the day's work. She played her part in the Battle of Heligoland in the first month of the war, and she carried trophies from *UC-51*, one of her submarine victims. After breakfast on the *Maidstone*, the mothership of all the East Coast submarines, we were taken in motor launches to *Firedrake*. She made for sea very proudly, carrying the officers and men who were to man the German boats and bring them to port. Another destroyer, the *Melampus*, was also detailed for the mission, bearing ten crews. The *Firedrake* carried eight, and two were taken out on a small tug.

The rendezvous was between the South Cutler Buoy and the Cork Lightship, 5 miles off Felixstowe, and once Admiral Tyrwhitt's destroyer had conveyed the U-boats thither it was the duty of the *Firedrake* to receive them, occupy them with British officers and men, and take them to Harwich. It was a morning of a curious silver lights. The sea was quiet, and on starting out a filmy mist hung round us, which was not lifted for a couple of hours. 'There will be no cheers, no demonstration of any kind,' Commander Kellett remarked a little after we had left shore. 'We shall treat them with the stinking contempt they deserve; but that doesn't mean we shall get down to their level. There will be no outburst, and everything will be accomplished with strict regard for naval etiquette.' As the destroyer made its way delicately through the water the fog gradually vanished, and towards ten o'clock, the appointed hour, most of it had gone, and a wintery sun came out, and look down on us, smiling. For a while we could see nothing but a great airship and a seaplane that, dancing about, looked like a bird. The wireless had told us that the U boats were late, but on their way, and we leaned over the rope to starboard to watch for their coming.

Ten minutes passed, and then through glasses I saw a small ship approach. As it neared, its name, Sierra Ventana, became plain, and the green band and Red Cross showed that it had once been a hospital ship. I next sighted one of our own destroyers, and immediately behind came the first German submarine. Almost at once the rest of the German fleet followed, keeping a straight course, but the boats rather far from each other. There appeared, too, some of our own motor boats, by which officers from the destroyers were to journey to the submarines for the purpose of receiving the surrender.

The surrender was made in a strange silence. No sirens were sounded, and no words came from the British officers waiting for the launches, save those that were necessary for command. The bluejackets had been smoking and talking all the way out, but as the first motor boat came up to us they quickly put out their pipes and cigarettes, and with stolid, stoical faces waited for their orders. It was the hour of their just and great revenge. These men had seen their comrades go down to the floor of the sea in ships, and some of them had known the callousness of submarine commanders, who, laughing at the sight of drowning men, had refused to save them. But the sailors were perfect in their discipline, and not a sign came from them as they boarded the motor boats. In every act, even in the expression of their faces they acted like their officers – as gentlemen of the British Fleet. As soon as the crew embarked I jumped from the destroyer into the motor launch, and journeyed with them to a U boat which lay about 250 yards away. Its crew and officers were standing on the deck. No name was visible, and no flag was flown. The submarine was of a third class character and looked a tired, battered boat, which might have done murder on the high seas.

Lieutenant Borrowcroft, R.N., accompanied by Lieutenant Osborne, R.N.R., boarded the submarine and its commander came forward to meet him. The two officers saluted at once. There was a pause for a second. The German commander, a thin man with a gaunt face, looked up and waited. Behind him were his men who were gazing round with curious but not unhappy eyes. The commander was a lonely figure steeped in tragedy. It seemed he had difficulty in speaking. 'Your papers or forms if you please.' The clear distinct voice of the lieutenant broke the silence and the commander obeyed. Came there another pause while the two British officers inspected the papers. The lieutenant then asked questions about periscopes, wireless and infernal machines to which the commander replied in harsh but fairly fluent English. Orders were given that all men down below who were not wanted at engines must come on deck, and the position of the ship in relation to Harwich was explained. A crew from the motor boat then boarded the submarine while the commander stood aside to let them pass. The British officers carried revolvers in their pockets, but the crew were not armed, and so the brief act of surrender ended. The U boat made for Parkestone Quay, to be there interned.

According to the conditions of armistice, I returned to the *Firedrake* and from the bridge, where Captain Addison remained, I watched the surrender of ten more boats. Most of the submarines were 800 tons in displacement, 225ft. long, 22ft. beam, and 12ft. draft; but one submarine cruiser was 340ft. long and 2,800 tons displacement, and she carried a crew of 70. Among the boats was one of the latest models built only three months ago. The ceremony of surrender was the same in every instance. The officers and men detailed for the work carried it out quickly, and the little fleet of motor launches had soon accomplished its business. Standing there on the bridge, I could see the submarines making for land with their white ensigns moving with the wind. The immovable tragic figures of the commanders, standing on deck, with faces set in sullen sorrow, is a picture set for ever in the history of these days. As one of the U boats passed us, its commander gave an order to his men, and the crew, looking forwards to *Firedrake*, saluted.

At midday the *Firedrake* returned to Harwich, and a little way outside the harbour waited for the coming of the German crews, who were to join their transports. The submarines left them at Parkestone Quay, and the gay little motor boats set about their work again, and quickly collected the crews. I remained on the destroyer while the Germans were brought aboard. The men came on laughing and smoking, and, not waiting for orders or invitations, made themselves comfortable by sitting down on deck. They were dirty and unshaven, and, although they had not lost all sense of discipline, they appeared to have lost all sense of morale. Their officers followed, again remaining apart solitary, miserable figures. Fraternisation between the German crews and our men was forbidden, and the men of the U boats were left to themselves, stood over by half a dozen bluejackets armed with rifles. About 1 o'clock I returned to shore in a motor launch. The *Firedrake* put on her best speed. I watched her running through the sea, now of a clear wintry blue, till she was lost in the distance. She was to run alongside the German transports, where the men would be transferred without ceremony or delay, and then, her work over, she would return to land. There is no unwholesome sentiment in the Navy. Sailors do not measure their words when they talk to you of Germany's under-sea warfare. But it is the pride of the Navy that she has her flag unstained. In this day of victory she showed the enemy not the fierceness of her hatred, but simply the gentleness of her manners and I think the German commanders found her courtesy more unendurable than they would have found her hatred.[7]

As the German High Seas Fleet was steaming towards the Scottish coastline, the crews of the British Grand Fleet were preparing to meet them. On 20 November, King George V and the Prince of Wales visited the fleet before it set sail. During that evening the fleet received orders to proceed to sea to meet the High Seas Fleet at 2½ hours' notice and sailors aboard those ships were feeling anxious as they wondered whether the Germans would surrender, or would there be one last desperate act of hostility carried out. Stoker Norbert McCrory recalled:

> The night of the 20 November was one of anxious moments for all on board the ships of the Grand Fleet, because we expected any moment to receive our signal to attack the enemy, but time rolled kept a full head of steam and engines ready, but were not required until the middle watch of the morning of the 21.11.18. Each squadron, as previous details had been issued, they proceeded to sea.[8]

At dawn on 21 November the Grand Fleet sailed from Rosyth to rendezvous with the High Seas Fleet in the North Sea, 40 miles east of May Island, from where they would escort them to anchorages in the Firth of Forth. Admiral Sir David Beatty sailed in the flagship HMS *Queen Elizabeth*, flying the large battered and torn White Ensign that he flew when he commanded HMS *Lion* during the Battle of Jutland in 1916. The Grand Fleet was joined by warships from the American and Australian navies, the 6th Battle Squadron and two French destroyers. This amounted to 370 Allied vessels with 90,000 sailors aboard. This was the first time since Jutland that such an assembly of warships had taken place. Francis Perrot, London correspondent for the *Manchester Guardian*, was aboard HMS *Monarch* and reported:

> Two hundred and forty British ships of war were arrayed, and stole seawards in one immense line – one line as far as open water, and then in two lines six miles apart, so as to be ready to take the Germans into their midst and escort them decently and in order to their resting place.[9]

The Grand Fleet arrived at the agreed rendezvous at 08.30 hours and an hour later it established contact with the High Seas Fleet, which comprised nine battleships, five battle cruisers, seven light cruisers and forty-nine destroyers under the command of Admiral Ludwig von Reuter in the battleship SMS *Friedrich der Grosse*.

The light cruiser HMS *Cardiff* met the German warship SMS *Konigsberg* and arranged the surrender for the entire High Seas Fleet to the Grand Fleet. *Cardiff* was designated to lead the German fleet in between two columns of Allied warships. The German vessels were unarmed, however the crews of Allied vessels were standing by their guns at action stations, just as a precaution against any hostile acts carried out by the Germans. D.N. Burrows, from Derby, serving aboard *Cardiff* as observer, was the first sailor aboard to spot them. He recalled this unprecedented sight:

> We all lay at anchor at our advanced base in the Firth of Forth on Wednesday, Nov. 20, anxiously awaiting the signal to get under way, which was received at 2.30 a.m. on Thursday Nov. 21. We sighted the Huns about fifty miles east of May Island at 3 a.m. It was misty at the time, and as they slowly steamed out of the mist they presented a truly impressive scene. We could scarcely realise that the German Fleet was in sight, but under vastly different conditions from what we expected a few weeks ago. They were steaming single line ahead, followed by the remainder of the battle cruisers, battleships, light cruisers, and destroyers. About an hour elapsed between our first sight of them and the last destroyer passing us. As we assisted to escort them into harbour they gave one the impression of a flock of sheep being driven along, and the ships themselves appeared to have a shamed aspect about them. On Friday, the 20th, [should be 22nd], our search parties went aboard, and found that Admiral Beatty's instructions had been carried out to the letter. The general impression gained by them was that the German sailors were thankful the war was over.[10]

Stoker Norbert McCrory, aboard HMAS *Australia*, wrote:

> The morning was cold and a heavy mist of rain began to fall thickly forming a curtain around the downfall of the second greatest navy in the world. About six bells we surrounded the German fleet headed by the flagship 'Seyditz'. All guns of the German ships were trained fore and aft. Our guns trained on the beam ready for action. After a while the Germans trained their guns on the beam which made us think they were after business, but they had the laugh on us and came under instructions from the British Flag to an anchorage at the mouth of the Firth of Forth about three Bells (midday). After they had anchored and the British Fleet had surrounded them, then the British Fleet anchored and Admiral and senior officers boarded the different ships to give instructions of a hundred inspections. The German Fleet received orders from the *Queen Elizabeth* 'at sunset, you will lower your flag never to fly again

317

without my permission.' This is how the famous German Fleet came to an end before the British Fleet, that once they challenged for the supremacy of the seas, now the people may know what the largest is to the Empire.[11]

With the German fleet approaching the British coast, there was some anxiety that it might attack the British fleet instead of surrender. A naval correspondent reported:

> To those who may have wondered how we could allow the vast number of German ships to approach our shores so closely while our fighting ships remained at anchorage and the ceremonial of the King's visit take place, I may say that we never relaxed for a moment our network of patrols, and that if any nonsense was attempted the fleet, which for four years has kept steam up, has still the steam full up and ready for action should the signal be given at a moment.[12]

Francis Perrot, a correspondent aboard HMS *Monarch*, confirmed that the sailors aboard were primed and ready to go to action stations at a moment's notice if required.

> We were taking no risks today. Every ship in the Allied Fleet, went out to meet the Germans, ready for instant battle if need be, cleared for action. The order was that the guns were to be 'in securing position', the ordinary fore and aft arrangement; but the men on my ship, the battleship *Monarch*, told me that thirty seconds from then flashing of a signal was all that they needed to pour a broadside into anything that that wanted it.[13]

A German account of the surrender of the High Seas Fleet at Scapa Flow appeared in the 11 December edition of the *Hamburger Nachrichten*:

> On the morning of November 21 in nasty weather, the British forces which had been detailed for escort encountered the German Fleet. Great Britain had done its best to make an imposing demonstration in sending its most modern ships and most modern destroyers. Involuntarily the idea suggested itself – in over four years we have victoriously stood our ground with our weak forces against this most modern giant force. What would we not have done with this superabundance of small cruisers and destroyers?
>
> The British fleet received us with the greatest mistrust, cleared for action and torpedoes in tubes. A thick girdle of light and heavy

fighting forces was rapidly thrown around us, and we were caught. There were still some men who, with the officers, felt deeply this day of ignominy and humiliation, and who in impotent rage against the enemy and those responsible for this ignominy, did their duty to the Fatherland to the last.[14]

Perrot recalled the emotions of the sailors aboard HMS *Monarch* as they witnessed the High Seas Fleet pass them:

> Our sailors showed no emotion at all. There was not a cheer in all the British Fleet, although everywhere, on every turret and ledge, the men stood thickly, gazing silently or with some casual jest. One man who said to me: 'This is what we have been waiting for all these years' was an exception. The sailorman thought of peace to come and leave at last. There was chivalry in his heart for a beaten foe. I heard one say: 'It's a fine sight, but I wouldn't be on one of those ships for the world.'
>
> An officer said to me: 'We all feel this is an unparalleled humiliation to a great fleet. The High Seas Fleet has fought well, and we have nothing against it. The submarines are another story. We have won the greatest and the most bloodless victories in the history of the world. That's enough. No mafficking on the sea.'[15]

The ceremony began at 08.00 hours. The German warships were manned by navigating crews only and in compliance with the Armistice terms of surrender, they carried no munitions. Each German warship flew a White Ensign at its masthead, with their own flag beneath it.

As they proceeded along the Firth of Forth they were observed by civilians lined along the river bank. Once the Allied naval authorities inspected these vessels and confirmed that they complied with the surrender terms, they were then interned. One reporter commented 'thus ended the greatest and most humiliating naval surrender in history.'[16]

The German account of the surrender of the High Seas Fleet that appeared in the 11 December edition of the *Hamburger Nachrichten* continued:

> Anchor was cast in the Firth of Forth, and inspection commissions boarded the ships, led by superior officers. Polite, cold, scornful regards greeted us with no remnant of esteem for the past. Thus did the British officers and men bear themselves towards us.

Everything was carefully inspected. There was no attempt at private conversation, all questions being addressed to officers. The Soldiers' Councils were brusquely rejected. Around us lay the British Fleet at anchor. All intercourse between us was forbidden. We were not treated as though we were interned, but like prisoners.

In the evening we lowered the flags which hitherto no British guns had been able to lower, and were not permitted to replace them – a superfluous wounding of our feelings on the part of the British.[17]

It would take days for stringent inspections of all German vessels to take place before they were transferred to Scapa Flow for internment. Stoker Norbert McCrory was selected to form part of an inspection party from HMAS *Australia*. He recalled:

23.11.15. This day flagships and senior ships of the British Navy had picked parties detailed to search various ships of the German Fleet to make sure they had carried the terms of the armistice. I was serving on board HMAS *Australia*, flagship 2 Battle Cruiser Squadron. We were detailed to search the SMS *Hindenburg*. On arriving on board we were surprised to find a.b.s [able seamen] in charge of the ship. Of course, the German Navy had mutinied that is why the admirals had to take second place on board. We were treated with the greatest respect of courtesy. After making a thorough search we arrived on deck to return to our ship but not before we were surrounded by eager Germans asking for food and tobacco etc.[18]

On 21 November another batch of German submarines surrendered to Admiral Sir Reginald Tyrwhitt at Harwich. A correspondent aboard HMS *Firedrake* reported:

Nineteen more German submarines, including a large German submarine cruiser, have surrendered to Admiral Tyrwhitt, making with yesterday's batch, 39 of these underwater craft to pass into British hands. There would have been twenty today but one broke down on the other side. Twenty-one will surrender tomorrow, while the balance will come over next week.

It was 10.30 when we sighted the German battleship, *Helgoland*. She came over as a transport, and was unarmed. The Hun commander in one of the submarines today remarked to the British officer as he handed over his signed declaration: 'We shall be coming over again for them soon.'

A carrier pigeon was seen to be sent up from one of the U-boats today. When Commander Games, D.S.O., stepped aboard he saluted the Hun commander, a young man who spoke English. The latter promptly returned the salute. Commander Games asked what message was dispatched by the pigeon. The reply was: 'Dropped anchor; just being boarded.'

The second day's batch of submarines proceeded into harbour flying the British Ensign, with the German flag beneath.[19]

Twenty-eight German submarines surrendered at Harwich on 24 November. The following report from the Press Association featured in newspaper reports the following day:

28 U-BOATS ARRIVE – TOTAL NUMBER AT HARWICH NOW 87
Today saw the largest surrender of German submarines in one day. Twenty eight U-boats gave themselves up to the British Navy, the surrendered vessels, including several very large craft and four cruiser submarines, one of them nearly 350ft in length.

Sir Eric Geddes, the First Sea Lord of the Admiralty, was an interested spectator of the scene from the deck of a destroyer.

Among the boats arriving for internment was the noted cruiser submarine *Deutschland*, *U-153*, which brought to Harwich two American officers who were rescued from the United States transport *Triconderoga*, which was torpedoed on 30 September, when eight days out from America. The officers were taken to Kiel by *Deutschland* on her return from a three months' cruise in American waters.

Another large vessel was *U-139*, which carried a crew of 75, with 15 extra men for manning prizes, and mounted two 5.9-inch guns.

All vessels at the close of the day found a haven of rest in what has been locally designated the German Naval Cemetery, of Parkeston Quay. Today's surrenders brought the total up to 87 and it is expected that 14 others will arrive tomorrow.[20]

U-153 was later transported to London for public viewing at Tower Bridge. Another submarine, *U-64*, was displayed by the Houses of Parliament.[21]

Stoker Norbert McCrory aboard HMAS *Australia* recalled:

25.11.18. The German Fleet sails the seas once again, but under escort of the British Navy to Scapa Flow for internment. Their last sail in the North Sea.[22]

Only a small crew of German sailors remained aboard the interned German warships in order to maintain the vessels. One German sailor described Scapa Flow as 'no place could be more God-forsaken'.[23] The wireless equipment was removed and guns disabled aboard the interned vessels. Only a little fuel remained on board to ensure the crews did not make any efforts to escape.

A further twenty-seven German submarines surrendered on 27 November in the River Stour in Suffolk, bringing the total surrendering to 114. One young German officer aboard one of these U-boats was planning on returning to Britain as a businessman, for he declared:

> As soon as peace is signed you will find we shall all be over here. Thousands of German business men will return to England to resume their pre-war trade. Your people may say they do not want us, but it is your government who have the final word in that, and they will not be able to keep us out.[24]

A total of 176 German U Boats were surrendered and it was eventually decided during December 1919 that they would be distributed equally among the Allied nations and either be sunk or scrapped.

As the world deliberated the fate of the German surface fleets interned at Scapa Flow at the Paris Peace Conference and it looked likely that the vessels would either be sunk or retained for use by the Allied navies, Rear Admiral Ludwig von Reuter decided to take matters into his own hands and scuttle the ships under his command on 21 June 1919. He later wrote:'It was unthinkable to surrender defenceless ships to the enemy.'[25]

A skeleton crew comprising 1,800 German sailors remained aboard seventy-four warships belonging to the High Seas Fleet. Forbidden to go ashore, they were reliant upon food supplies shipped from Germany. When Admiral von Reuter gave the order to scuttle their vessels, the German flag was hoisted, before they opened torpedo tubes, water-tight doors, hatches and portholes, in one last act of defiance. Fifty-two of the seventy-four vessels anchored at Scapa Flow were successfully scuttled. The German casualties included ten killed and sixteen wounded. In an official statement, von Reuter explained his actions:

> I believed from what I saw in a German newspaper, that the Armistice had been terminated, and I personally gave the order for the ships to be sunk. This was done in the pursuance of orders given to the German Navy at an early stage of the war that no German man-of-war was to be surrendered.[26]

Chapter 27

Impact of the Armistice

The immediate impact of the Armistice meant that daily constraints that had been imposed upon the British populace could be lifted. Within an hour of the Armistice being declared on 11 November the government announced the end of wartime restrictions:

> Masking of public lights may be removed forthwith.
> Shading of house and shop lights withdrawn.
> Fireworks and bonfires permitted, subject to approval by military and police.
> Public clocks may strike and bells ring at night.
> The closing of restaurants at 9.30, and of theatres at 10.30 to be suspended.[1]

Soon after the Armistice, Lloyd George announced to Parliament that the government would be dissolved on 25 November and a General Election would take place on 14 December. There had not been an election since 1910 and with the prospect of negotiating a peace deal Lloyd George wanted to go to the future peace conference with the support of the British electorate behind him.

The Liberal Lloyd George and the Conservative Chancellor of the Exchequer, Andrew Bonar Law, wanted to maintain the coalition government during the transitional period from peace to war. Lloyd George reasoned:

> We must get the mandate immediately. Somebody will have to go to the Peace Conference with authority from the people of this country to speak in their name.[2]

The General Election saw the first admission of women to the electorate and provisions to enable absent soldiers and sailors to record their votes. When the results of the election were announced on 28 December, Lloyd George's coalition government had increased its majority in the House of Commons and had won the mandate of the British people to represent them at the future peace conference.

The signing of the Armistice meant that all conscription for the armed services in Britain was suspended immediately. The Secretary of the Local Government Board and the Ministry of National Service issued the following declaration:

> The Government has decided that all recruiting under the Military Services Acts is to be suspended. All outstanding calling-up notices, whether for medical or service are cancelled. All cases pending to tribunals are to be suspended.[3]

On 12 November, Dr Christopher Addison, Minister of Reconstruction, issued a detailed statement about the plans for demobilisations, now that the war had ended. The *Grantham Journal* reported:

> The following is a brief outline of the more important features of the general scheme for getting the soldiers back into civil employment without confusion and to the best advantage of the State:-
>
> Demobilisation will be governed by industrial requirements and broad social considerations.
>
> The first men to be recalled will be those who are actually needed to carry out the plan of demobilisation e.g. men employed in Labour Exchanges.
>
> Next to those will come the pivotal men, vis, men whose return is essential before a number of other men can be set to work.
>
> The various trades are being asked – workshop by workshop – to supply the names of these pivotal men, which will be sent to the Colonels of Regiments.
>
> The various trades are also being strictly graded according to their essential character, and the pivotal men of the most essential trades will come back first.
>
> In each group moreover, preference will be given to men with long periods of service to their credit, to married men, &c.
>
> A large proportion of soldiers – no less than 60 per cent – have the promise from their old employers that their places will be kept

open for them. These are known as 'slip' men, and the fact that so many will be provided for at once eases the problem enormously.

When drafts of men for mobilisation are made up they will go first to a concentration camp and then to a dispersal station at home, in the neighbourhood of their place. At the dispersal stations each will receive a protection certificate, a railway warrant, a cash payment, and an out-of-work donation policy.

Each soldier will have 28 days' furlough with full pay and ration allowance, and separation allowance for his family.

Soldiers at home will be treated exactly on the same lines as soldiers abroad. The amount of the gratuities will depend on length of service and other considerations.

Demobilised Officers

For a full year after demobilisation, nearly all permanent appointments in the Civil Service will be reserved for ex-officers and ex-soldiers. Assistance will be given to officers to enable them to complete their interrupted training for civil professions.

Help will be given towards to the repatriation of officers' families.

Help may be given to enable officers to meet their civil liabilities.

Provisions for Unemployment

A very important feature of the scheme is the provision of temporary unemployment pay for munition workers out of employment and ex-soldiers who do not succeed at once in finding situations.[4]

There were no objections to these proposals when they were announced, but it was difficult to implement them. During January 1919 soldiers began to show their dissatisfaction and impatience that they were not being demobilised sooner. They had fought the war, they had won the war; as far as they were concerned they had done their duty and wanted to return to civilian life. When service personnel on leave were ordered to return to the continent to form part of the Army of Occupation in Germany, they were understandably reluctant.

At Folkestone between 3 and 7 January 1919, 10,000 soldiers refused to embark on troopships bound for France and protested against the delays in demobilisation. This act of dissension within the British Army was reported in a local Folkestone newspaper under the headline SOLDIERS' DEMAND FOR DEMOBILISATION:

Remarkable scenes were witnessed at Folkestone yesterday, when several thousand soldiers joined in an impromptu protest against the delay of demobilisation. They were men who had been home on leave and were temporarily staying at the rest camps in the town whilst on the return journey. For some reason there had been a delay, and many of the troops had been in Folkestone since the earlier part of the week. Probably this delay accounted for the men becoming discontented, and determining to make a public protest. Any way it became evident early yesterday morning that something unusual was about to happen.

A drum was produced from somewhere, as likewise were some Union Jacks, and a procession was formed. The men marched through some of the principal streets, singing snatches of songs, and eventually a huge concourse assembled in front of the Town Hall. Vehicular traffic was completely stopped here for a while, and the public motors had to be diverted.

One or two soldiers 'gifted with the gab' climbed onto the columns supporting the Town Hall portico, and delivered speeches in ventilation of what they considered their grievances. A resolution asking for immediate demobilisation was proposed and declared carried. The speeches were not a violent or inflammatory nature and good order was maintained. It was intimated that there was no intimation to interfere with the civilian population.

The Mayor (Sir Stephen Penfold) put in an appearance and offered some advice to the soldiers in a friendly spirit, suggesting that they should go back to their rest camps. The Town Commandant (Lieut.-Colonel the Hon. E.J. Mills, D.S.O.) also arrived upon the scene and addressed the troops. He said he would do what he could to see that the men whose cases deserved special consideration received that consideration, and intimated that something could possibly be done in the cases of the men who had employment to go to.

Ultimately the soldiers formed up in procession and marched back to the rest camps ... One soldier put his complaint in the following words: 'We have been in the war from the start. Our grievance is that the men who have only been in the army three or four months have been discharged, whereas we are still kept in khaki.'[5]

There was no resolution to the soldiers' demands for demobilisation and there were further protests at Folkestone Harbour during the following day, when soldiers refused to board troopships to convey them to France and blocked the entrance to the port preventing other soldiers from entering the harbour arm. The local newspaper reported:

On Saturday morning there was a repetition at Folkestone of the demonstrations which had taken place on the previous day by discontented soldiers returning to France after being on home leave.

The boats engaged on the military cross-Channel service to Boulogne left as usual on Saturday morning but conveyed only a comparatively small number of soldiers – Colonials – who were permitted by the British soldiers to go on board. The Imperial men, as a whole, as on the preceding day, refused to embark, and picketed the approaches to the quay to prevent those willing to cross from returning. In the early parts of the day an armed guard was placed at the entrance to the Harbour, but this was withdrawn under the threat that if it remained there would be trouble, the soldiers who declined to embark intimating that they would procure arms from their quarters at rest camps. In the case of the street demonstrations the men were unarmed.

About ten o'clock on Saturday morning there was a great demonstration of soldiers in the centre of the town similar to that held on the previous day. On this occasion, however, a more business-like procedure was adopted. To the beating of a drum the men marched with flags flying to the Town Hall outside which a crowd some thousands strong gathered. The flags displayed were mostly Union Jacks. No red flags were to be seen. The leaders of the men mounted the balcony over the chief entrance of the Town Hall and delivered addresses to their comrades below. They said they only wanted justice. Many of them had enlisted as soon as the war broke out and now they were being kept in the Army, while other and younger men, who had only seen a few months' service were being demobilised first. A resolution to form was what was termed a Union was passed, and a committee of nine delegates was appointed to negotiate with the authorities. General Dallas and the Town Commandant (Lieut.-Colonel the Hon. E.J. Mills, D.S.O.) were present, and were engaged in conversation with some of the men. One of the men's leaders was a solicitor and another a Magistrate of the town where he resided. At the conclusion of the meeting the troops marched back to various rest camps. In the afternoon and evening there was a long conference between the authorities and the representatives of the men and matters were satisfactorily adjusted.

The men's delegates at the conference entered into a compact that there should be no more marching through streets or other demonstrations, and that they would not attempt to stop any soldiers who were willing to go back to France.[6]

Soldiers also protested in London and and across Britain demanding early demobilisation. A journalist reported:

> Following the weekend demonstrations by soldiers at Folkestone and Dover a number of men from the Army Service Corps on Monday broke camp at Osterley Park and driving to Whitehall in three service lorries demanded that demobilisation be speeded up.
>
> During the day there were several demonstrations by A.S.C. men at Bromley, Sydenham and Grove Park, and from Shoreham Camp 7,000 men marched into Brighton and explained their grievances to the Mayor.
>
> As at the weekend, the proceedings were conducted in good order and in each case after the protest had been made it was announced that the authorities would take no disciplinary action against the men.[7]

Soldiers from the Army Service Corps marched upon Whitehall on 8 January. Some commandeered motor vehicles and descended upon Whitehall bearing placards demanding 'We won the war, give us our tickets' or 'We want civvie suits'. They were fearful that they would be sent to Russia to fight the Bolsheviks and took their protest directly to the Prime Minister at 10 Downing Street, where they were received by General Sir William Robertson. The *Sheffield Independent* reported:

> Some 4,000 men of the ASC [Army Service Corps] at Park Royal yesterday morning sent a deputation to the General commanding demanding their immediate demobilisation and an assurance that they would not be sent to Russia.
>
> The General is stated to have told them that as regarded drafts to Russia, he could give no assurance. The men he said were soldiers, and would have to obey orders. This did not satisfy the men, who refused to 'carry on' and they marched in a body to Downing Street, where they demanded to see the Prime Minister.
>
> The scene in Downing Street was exciting. A number of staff officers mingled with the soldiers and urged them to return to their depot. The officials at No. 10 told the men who went to the door that if they would go to the Horse Guards Parade they would be addressed by General Fielding, commanding the London district. This they did forming a square on the parade.
>
> A large contingent of mounted police were brought up, and the big gates of the Horse Guards were closed. At a quarter past one General Sir William Robertson drove up and invited the men's committee

consisting of a corporal, a lance corporal, and ten drivers into his office to state their case.

After about a half an hour's interview the committee returned to the waiting men, accompanied by a major who wore the ribbon of the V.C., the D.S.O., the M.C. and other decorations.

The Major announced that the interview with the General had been in every way satisfactory, and that General Robertson had promised to send a General to the camp to investigate the complaints the men had regarding the conditions at Park Royal.

Amongst other things he had promised that no men over 41 should be put on draft overseas, but they should have their discharge as speedily as possible; that the A.S.C. should have a fair percentage of discharges on exactly the same basis as other units; and that the men who did not get their Christmas leave and were now on draft should have their leave before the draft departed.[8]

These demonstrations could have escalated and potentially undermine the victory that the Allies had won. If soldiers of the British Army revolted, then Germany might resume the war. Lloyd George and his government had to act quickly in order to quell any further dissension within the British armed services. The following statement was released by the government during the evening of 8 January:

The Prime Minister has been giving careful personal attention to the speed at which the process of demobilising the Army is being maintained.

He considers that his first duty is to make sure the fruits of the victory which has been won by the sacrifice of so many lives and by so many brave deeds are not jeopardised by any apparent weakness on the part of Britain during the critical months of the peace negotiations.

For this purpose it is imperative that we should maintain a strong Army on the Rhine, and, of course, the necessary services behind the front both in France and at home. Although the fighting has stopped the war is not over.

The German armies have not yet been demobilised, and are still very powerful.

No one can tell what the Germans will do or whether they will agree to the terms of the peace and reparation which we seek to impose upon them.

Impatience now might lose in a few weeks all that it is taken years of heroism and sacrifice to gain.

During these next few months we must be strong and united, in order that a firm settlement may be made with the enemy, and our country may exert its proper influence among the other nations at the peace conference.

Demobilisation cannot be carried out in any way that would undermine the military strength of Britain until final peace is secure.

No less, however, than 300,000 men have already been demobilised and steps have been taken to increase the speed as far as possible without injuring vital British interests in the world or impairing the safety of our troops in Germany.

No doubt there will be a great many hard cases and personal grievances. The troops may rest assured that everything possible will be done to listen to and remedy individual grievances of whatever nature, when presented through the authorised channels.

Instructions have been issued to ensure sympathetic hearing of all legitimate complaints. But inequalities and hardships are sure to remain, and the Prime Minister is confident that these will be endured in the same way as much harder trials have already been borne in order to make certain of a lasting and a just peace.

The men who have fought and shed their blood in this war would, rightly, hold the Government responsible if, after all the work they have done, it allowed the results to be frittered away, and the nation has a whole has unmistakably expressed its sentiments on that point.

Furthermore, fair and even treatment must be meted out as between men and bearing the hardships of the field and those whose duty is discharged at home.

One thing is certain: the work of demobilisation is not going to be quickened. On the contrary it is bound to be delayed by the men trying to take the law into their own hands.

It is not by these irregular assemblies or marches that anything can be put right.

The reason why public opinion has been tolerant of these demonstrations is because the country knows that all ranks would have cheerfully done their duty if actual fighting had been going on.

But a point has now been reached where real harm is being done to the national cause, and to the reputation of the British Army, and it is therefore essential that discipline should be maintained.[9]

There was a requirement for men to form the Army of Occupation while peace was being discussed by the leaders of the nations in Paris. The *Lancashire Evening Post* reported:

A million men will be needed for the new armies of occupation. It is not possible at present to raise this number by voluntary enlistment from the existing armies. Therefore, while demobilisation of the older men proceeds, younger men with shorter periods of service will be retained for the new armies.[10]

Plans for demobilisation of British service personal were swiftly reviewed by Winston Churchill, Minister of War, and his revised plans were duly announced on 29 January. The *Lancashire Evening Post* reported:

The Government has at length made known the intentions regarding the Armies of Occupation and these are clearly explained in the memorandum issued by Mr Winston Churchill. To put the matter briefly, we are to retain under arms 900,000 men of all ranks whose duty it will be to guard our interests during the transition period – at home, on the Rhine, in the Middle East and Egypt, in the far North and Siberia, and in the Crown Colonies and in India. The remainder of the three and a half million officers and men constituting our huge armies at the date of the signing of the Armistice are to be demobilised as speedily as possible. Length of service, age and wounds are to be the main considerations entitling to immediate or early release, and, therefore, the 900,000 men are to be chosen from those who did not enlist before January 1st, 1916, who are under 37 years of age, and who have not more than two wound stripes. Mr Churchill anticipates that these classes will supply a great many more men than the number specified, and in that case there will be further releases effected in accordance with the principle he lays down that those who are older, who have served the longest, or who have suffered most, have the first claim to consideration. Moreover, as time goes on, even the 900,000 will doubtless prove too large an army, and gradual reductions may be expected as circumstances justify them. As to the conditions of service, no soldier under 20 is to be asked to serve except at home or on the Rhine, and all ranks in the Armies of Occupation are to receive not merely generous leave but also increased pay in the shape of bonuses, the total cost of which in one year is estimated to be at not less than £29,000,000. Thus, roughly speaking, one in four of the men in our military forces as those stood on Armistice Day will be retained, and the great bulk of them will receive about double the existing rate of pay.[11]

Some soldiers were not demobilised until late 1919. Private Alexander Jamieson, 11th Royal Scots, was exasperated as he had a job waiting for him to occupy at home, but he was not released from the Army sooner:

> I got put into the wrong group for demobilisation. My friend who had joined up with me ... in every way we were the same and he was demobilised in March 1919 and in spite of my firm and my father at home applying to the War Office they would not take me. He was in group 2 and I was in group 49 and they would not change it. I wasn't demobilised until November 1919 – a year after the Armistice. There was a lot of dissatisfaction. During the summer of 1919 we had a military tattoo and Churchill was suddenly introduced, and was treated with loud booing because he had a great deal to do with drawing up the arrangements for demobilisation.[12]

When the Armistice was announced on 11 November, munition workers became demotivated to continue working. With the war ended there was no further purpose to produce weapons of war and factory owners in the munitions industry had to review how they could transform their operations from war production into a business that could flourish in peace time, producing items for the civilian market. *The Yorkshire Evening Post* reported the situation on 12 November, the day following Armistice Day:

> All, or nearly all, the munition works of Leeds and district were closed down from noon today, and some indeed suspended operations at a much earlier hour. At the Armley Shell Factory, the munition workers, both male and female, were very restless all the morning, and as many were going out and not returning it was deemed advisable at 11 o'clock to close the works for the day.
>
> At the neighbouring factory at Newley, work was never actually commenced, as so few of the workers turned up. There, however, as at other munition factories, there is expected to be a full resumption of work tomorrow ... but obviously the making of munitions will not be continued for long and the management of the various factories have announced that workers who desire to leave and go to other employment may do so.
>
> In the cloth factories of the West Riding the transition from military contracts to productions on civilian account is expected to be ordered any day, though no instructions have been sent out up to noon today. Sir Charles Sykes, the Director of Wool Textile Production, has gone to London to consult the higher authorities of

the War Office, and following upon his representations it is expected that there will be a considerable, if not complete stoppage, of khaki manufacture.

Meanwhile the weaving sheds everywhere today were as briskly engaged as ever upon the manufacture of khaki. Weavers, however, were expecting that after the next 'fell out' they would have to turn to other materials. It is officially announced that whereas during October the Department of Wool Textile Production were unable to supply the necessary quantity of tops for all the standard cloths intended for the special measure trade, the Department are making arrangements for all orders in respect to these to be fulfilled immediately.

This seems to suggest that the Department are already making provision against the needs of discharged soldiers by transferring to the production of standard goods the partially managed manufactured materials hitherto ear-marked for military purposes. Although it is realised that the civilian trade must 'come into its own' again soon, the needs of the next few weeks will be for cloth wherewith to make suits for the men discharged from the Army.

All the clothing factories of Leeds, where the girls were obviously unsettled by the excitement of yesterday, and very much inclined to take another half-day off, the work of making up khaki went on all the morning without interruption. Shortly before noon, however, orders suspending commencement on fresh work were received at several factories. Responsible men in the trade expect that at any hour they may be issued a general order stopping all khaki contracts beyond the completion of the work already in hand. From that moment the Leeds clothing firms for many months to come will be all activity, for before the ordinary civilian trade can be tackled, some millions of suits have to be made to be issued to the men as they are discharged from the Army.[13]

Factories that were making khaki uniforms had to swiftly transfer production to civilian clothes as there would be a huge demand with the advent of millions of demobilised soldiers returning to civilian life. It was reported:

Demobilisation will call for millions of new 'civvy' suits. Production of military clothing is to be curtailed without delay, and mills which have been turning out khaki by the millions for four years past will be able to devote more attention to the production of 'mufti'.

Whether there will be enough to go round really depends on the length of time demobilisation will take. A heavy rush back to civilian life would mean very short supplies, to say the least.

Already there has been a large increase in demand for civilian clothes. The head of a West End business house stated yesterday that for the last four years his trade has been 85 per cent military and 15 per cent civilian. Since the armistice the percentage is 90 civilian and 10 military.

He gave it as his opinion that it will take about 18 months for the clothing and tailoring trade to get back to its normal state. Establishments where fours year old suits can be made to 'look like new' for a few shillings were preparing for busy times.[14]

Many munition workers became unemployed as a consequence of the Armistice. Within days of it being signed, efforts to scale down munition work were taking place in Birmingham:

The demobilisation of women munition workers has begun in Birmingham, and it is expected that in a fortnight's time it will be in full swing ... The general plan for demobilisation is that married women whose husbands are employed in the works will be asked to leave first, then girls whose homes are at a distance and that widows will always be employed as long as possible.

Many Birmingham firms have established a forty hour week until their workers are demobilised, instead of, as formerly fifty or fifty five hours. By this method it is possible to continue to employ a large number of girls for a time and give them a living wage, at the same time allowing them an opportunity for rest and recreation.

On the completion of the night shift yesterday, from 60 to 80 men, it is said, were discharged without notice from the Midland and Birmingham Metal and Munitions Co. Ltd., Landor Street works. They were all employed in the rolling mill department and mostly unskilled.

In response to an inquiry at the head offices of the firm, it was stated that the men were given their legal notice. The cessation of the war and the completion of work in hand were the reasons for the discharge.[15]

In London on 19 November, women munition workers marched upon the Ministry of Munitions appealing for help for those discharged from their work and who were now unemployed. It was reported that:

A remarkable procession of 5,000 women munition workers from Woolwich Arsenal appeared suddenly in front of the Ministry of Munitions headquarters at the Hotel Metropole yesterday afternoon to impress upon the Government authorities the necessity of doing something promptly for the women who will be discharged from the Arsenal in consequence of the cessation of the demand for munitions of war.

As a result they learned that the Government's scheme for an unemployment donation of £1 a week for thirteen weeks is to come in operation next Monday.[16]

The end of the war brought unemployment across the British Isles. In Aberdeen the following article featured in a local newspaper:

The resources of the unemployment benefit department of the Aberdeen Exchange are being severely taxed today, especially the women's section, in the Music Hall Buildings. Munition workers from the large engineering establishments, members of Government clerical staffs, including the recruiting office staffs, have been thrown idle, their services being no longer required.

It is believed that over 500 workers joined the ranks of the unemployed in Aberdeen today, and the rush of applicants for the unemployed donation has been so great all day that they have had to be formed up in queues to await their turn for registration of claims.[17]

There would be periods of unemployment among men and women as munition factories made the transition from war to peace. Towards the end of November, however, there was optimism that most people would find employment as these factories now engaged in commercial non-military work. An article in the *Western Times* reported:

An interesting statement of the steps being taken by munition firms to revert to peace production was given, Thursday, by Mr. F.G. Kellaway, Parliamentary Secretary to the Ministry of Munitions. He hoped that by the time the process of transfer from war to peace work was completed, there would be sufficient employment for the whole of the men, and perhaps for the whole of the women. There was bound to be considerable unemployment, especially amongst the women, for a few weeks, because in the majority of cases, even where firms were going back to pre-war conditions, it would take some weeks to get their shops and machinery ready. A large establishment on the Tyne previously manufacturing aeroplanes were now making heavy toys and furniture, and employed 500 people. A firm at Newcastle-on-Tyne engaged in similar work had transferred its operations to the production of heavy furniture, finding work for 500 persons. In the same town a firm making guns was now building locomotives, and it was anticipated that 5,000 persons would be employed. A fuse-making house at Burnley was now manufacturing electric fittings, and at Leigh, (Lancashire) a similar concern had turned its activities into brick making. A Sheffield shell-making company was employing 1,000 people on the manufacture of files. Later, they would be making springs, a new industry to them. Recently making steel for mines and copper bands for shells, a Sheffield establishment was now producing dairy utensils. A Matlock munition shop was making cream separators, which had been imported from America and Sweden. Three firms at Leicester, Ilkeston and Nottingham respectively had taken up the manufacture of hosiery latch needles, which in pre-war days were practically imported from Germany. The output of these three places was 1,000,000 a week, which would be increased to 2,000,000. Three Loughborough factories were devoting themselves entirely to the manufacture of hosiery-bearded needles, a purely German industry. A Leicester firm which used to import typewriters was now making them, while another company in the same town had turned from the making of vulcanite pressings for magnetos to fountain pens. Hose-suspender fittings, another product of Germany, were to take the place of munition work in a factory in the same neighbourhood, while steel for war material used in an adjoining works was being replaced by corset steels. Another Leicester firm was taking up the manufacture of wood wool from old pit props, which was being done in a foundry formerly used for the casting of shells. Makers of aeroplane engines were turning out motor engines for cars and launches.[18]

During the 1914 campaign to recruit soldiers, men were promised that their jobs would be available to them once they returned home after the war. One demobilised soldier in Nottingham found it difficult to find employment, after his employer before the war was unable to keep its promise to re-employ him. In a letter to the editor of the *Nottingham Evening Post*, he wrote:

> Allow me also to express my disgust, after serving three years and eight months, and being promised my job on return, to find that the

firm has no work for me and that I am not wanted. Why make promises to men if they don't intend to carry them out. Walking about the streets I often hear the same story from other men. DISGUSTED.[19]

There were instances where soldiers were offered their previous jobs before they enlisted, but found that now the war was over, they were worse off financially. A Nottinghamshire miner who returned to the coalface was paid less than before the war. He wrote:

As a miner getting 8s. 6d. per day previous to the war, I enlisted in September 1914. Having now returned to the coal face I receive 7s. and 3d. war wage. It is the same with all demobilised soldiers who have started work again at our pit. Doubtless this will continue for some time unless something is done on our behalf.[20]

However, those service personnel who were seriously wounded, disfigured, mutilated and lost limbs during the war, were further disadvantaged. Some casualties would never recover and the wounds they had sustained would impact upon them for the rest of their lives. They would be affected physically and psychologically, making them unable to lead normal lives. They would have to deal with their life-changing injuries, try to assimilate back into civilian life and, if possible, find employment. Those who bore no physical scars had been affected psychologically by the war, suffering with symptoms that today are commonly diagnosed as post-traumatic stress disorder, and they now had to return to the normality of civilian life. Their families would have to adapt to their conditions, too.

Private Joseph Pickard, 1/5th Northumberland Fusiliers, had suffered severe leg, pelvic and facial wounds from shrapnel near Moreuil on 31 March 1918. He spent two years at Queen Mary's Hospital, Sidcup, which specialised in the treatment of facial injuries where doctors used cartilage from his rib to rebuild his mutilated nose. Feeling isolated as people stared at his disfigurement, he lost confidence. Pickard recalled:

Before I got the nose put on when I was down in Wales the first time I was out of the hospital, there was some kids playing about as I went past, a short time they galloped past me two or three streets; and when I got there, there was all the kids in the blinking neighboured had gathered; talking, looking, gawping at you ... I could have hit the whole bloody lot of them. I knew what they were looking at. So I turned around and walked back to the hospital. I lost confidence. I was sitting one day and thought this is no good, I could stop like this for the rest of my life, I thought you have got to face it sometime, so I went out again. After that I just walked out.[21]

When Pickard was discharged from the Army in 1921 he returned home to Alnwick. People continued to stare at his facial disfigurement:

They got used to it; I never used to mention it. I find gradually when you don't talk about what is wrong with you nobody bothers.[22]

Although his nose had been reconstructed, Pickard would permanently carry the scars of the war on his face for everyone to see, but he was determined to overcome his wound to his leg and his facial disfigurement. He regained his confidence, adapted to life as a civilian and spent the remainder of his life as a watchmaker.

Able Seaman Frederick Hide, who was part of the crew of HMS *Intrepid*, the blockship that was scuttled across the canal entrance at Zeebrugge with the purpose of bottling up the submarines of the Flanders Flotilla in Bruges, had to pawn his Distinguished Service Medal because he fell upon hard times. Hide was unable to use his right hand because of the wound he had sustained during the raid and it was this disability that deterred employers. By July 1926, Hide had no option but to pawn his medal, but as time went on, and with no hope of finding a job, he fell into rent arrears. His plight was reported in the *Portsmouth Evening News*:

Judge Sir Thomas Grainger at Greenwich County Court yesterday made an appeal on behalf of Frederick Henry Hide, of 69 Fordmill Road, Bellingham, S.E., who was sued by the London County Council for possession of his house on the ground of non-payment of rent.

'I have had inquiries made into this case,' said the Judge, 'and I have received a most excellent report. A woman has kindly given me some money to pay the arrears of rent and a week or two in advance, and it must be paid back.

'Hide is a skilled electrician and took part in the Zeebrugge operations – and only picked men were there. I ask publicly will anyone give this man a berth. It is a disgrace that a man who has done so well should be in this position.'

Mr. Hide said to a *Daily Mail* reporter last evening: 'I joined the Navy in 1906, and in 1918 volunteered to go on the Zeebrugge adventure. I was in HMS *Intrepid*, and was the man who sank her off the Mole by pressing the button which blew up the mines below-decks.

'I had to swim from the sinking ship, and when I boarded a small boat I discovered it was in the hands of Germans. One of them bayoneted and shot me in the right arm. I dived overboard again, and remembered nothing more until I was picked up by the submarine chaser commanded by Commander Dean, VC.

'I received the DSM for this exploit. His and my war medals are now at the pawnshop.

'People are not anxious to employ me, now because my right arm is not of much use, but I am able to do many things with it, and I have been doing odd jobs to eke out my pension of £1 1s. per week.

'I am an expert telephone operator and electrician's mate, but I would do any work that I was offered to keep my four young children.'[23]

Within a month of Judge Grainger's appeal, Hide was offered employment, as an article in the *Nottingham Evening Post* reported:

Mr. Frederick Henry Hide, who took a prominent part in the storming of the Zeebrugge, but because he could get no work had had to pawn the DCM he got for his service there, has now been given work by the London Electric Supply Corporation, Deptford.[24]

In America racial discrimination towards African–American citizens continued. Although this section of the community fought a war for the freedom and liberty of others in Europe, they were not treated equally because of the colour of their skin. Racial prejudice continued to flourish despite these soldiers displaying the same courage and making the same sacrifices as their white comrades. By the end of the war, Major Warner Ross, American 2nd Battalion, 365th Infantry Regiment, 183rd Brigade, 92nd Division, had many recommendations for honours for courage carried out by the soldiers under his command, but because they were African–Americans there were no medals awarded. Ross recalled:

I have a few citations and letters and one signed testimonial by white and colored who were witnesses, for coolness, bravery and the like. Thirty five or forty officers and men were cited for bravery in Division orders. Medals? No, I have received no medals or special decorations. Nor has any living member, officer or man, of my battalion. In fact, to my knowledge, not one living officer or man of the entire Three Hundred and Sixty-fifth Infantry has received any decoration or medal of any sort whatever – American, French, Belgian or any other kind. This, on the face of it, to anyone who knows the facts, would seem either a most glaring injustice or a mistake.[25]

This lack of recognition caused much resentment across the entire regiment, as Ross wrote:

> Many of the members of my Battalion and of the Regiment, especially those who were with us at the time of the armistice and during all or part of the awful days and weeks just preceding it, feel and resent this most keenly …
>
> The citations of which I am incomparably more proud of than the citations I did get or the medals I didn't get were not printed with ink nor stamped on metal. They were written with a point of fire into the brave, true hearts of my colored soldiers.
>
> And who knows (if I may indulge in a little sentiment)? Who can tell? Perhaps those who bravely endured the tortures of hell, because of the foolishness of the vain oppressors in this wicked world and who uncomplainingly and unselfishly gave all they had, all anyone could give – *gave their lives* – in defence of our great nation and in the cause of Democracy.
>
> Perhaps, I say, some of the spirits of that Battalion's dead have already whispered in the glorious Realm beyond where the great, all powerful God of justice, of love, of peace reigns supreme and with whom man's character is only thing that counts. Perhaps they have whispered, or will whisper, 'Our Commander not only braved the fury of the Hun, but he scorned the petty prejudices of a few white persons and treated us like officers and men.'[26]

On all sides, the end of the war was a sad time for many people – people who had either, as we have discussed, returned from the war severely wounded with life-changing injuries that would hinder their quality of life, or they had lost loved ones who were killed during the fighting. The German losses for the war were estimated to have been 1,580,000 killed, 4,000,000 wounded, 260,000 missing, with 490,000 taken prisoner, totalling 6,330,000 casualties overall.[27]

French losses were heavy and were announced towards the end of December 1918. These figures included their losses during the course of the war up to 1 November 1918, and were subject to addition because they did not include the casualties for the last ten days of the war. Their casualties amounted to 31,300 officers and 1,040,000 men killed, 3,000 officers and 311,000 men missing, and 8,300 officers and 438,000 men listed as prisoners. Exact figures for French wounded were unavailable, but it was estimated to have amounted to 1,831,600.[28] It was eventually estimated that France had suffered 3,595,000 casualties throughout the war.[29]

The war had a devastating impact upon the French nation and its citizens. In 1919 there were an estimated 600,000 war widows in France and 760,000 orphans.[30] The casualty number would increase even though the war had ended. It was difficult to estimate an accurate figure for casualty figures in 1918 because approximately 500,000 French veterans would die from their wounds during the period 1918 to 1933.[31]

We must not forget that France was the main battlefield and four years of war had a drastic effect upon the infrastructure. Many citizens in northern France had been displaced by the onset of war. Some 1,699 towns and villages had been destroyed during the conflict, including 319,269 houses and the partial destruction of another 313,675 homes. The war impacted upon French industry and communications, with the destruction of 9,332 factories, 58,967km of roads, 7,895km of railway lines and 4,875 bridges. Agriculture suffered, with 1,923,000 hectares of good soil devastated, reduced to a moonscape, and rendering it to such an extent that farmers were unable to farm on that land during 1919. The financial cost of that destruction was estimated to be worth 137 million French Francs. These statistics demonstrate why the French Government was seeking harsh peace terms and compensation from Germany.[32]

On 24 November General Peyton March announced the casualties of the American Expeditionary up to the signing of the Armistice. The total included 52,169 dead, 179,625 wounded, and 3,323 missing and prisoners.[33]

On 19 November the human cost of the war in relation to Britain and her Dominions within the Empire was announced to the House of Commons. The *Daily Mirror* reported:

> EMPIRES SACRIFICE: OUR 658,705 DEAD. The people of the Empire see figures today that will cause them to bow their heads in proud grief at the Noble Sacrifice of Our Great Dead; and our hearts go out to those Mothers and Fathers, Wives and Children whose splendid menfolk have by the selflessness opened the Portals of a New World ... In the House of Commons yesterday our total war casualties were announced as follows:
>
> | | Officers | Other Ranks |
> |---|---|---|
> | Killed | 37,876 | 620,829 |
> | Wounded | 92,644 | 1,939,478 |
> | Missing and Prisoners | 12,094 | 347,051 |
>
> Thus the grand total of casualties is 3,049,972.

Honour to the splendid living who have endured so much for Britain! Homage to those who have been maimed for Freedom's Cause! Honour to those who have lived with unconquerable spirit in the grim shadows of prison camp and slavery![34]

Private Charlie Leeson reflected upon those who made the supreme sacrifice and who now lay in foreign fields:

> Saddest of all, all over the country side are dotted graves where the dead have been buried after the battle just where they fell.[35]

While the world was celebrating the signing of the Armistice, Corporal Harry Wright, US 104th Regiment, 26th Division, was given the gruesome task of burying dead comrades:

> Got the toughest job of all, our service a job for other men than tired doughboys. There wasn't a man who could speak from hoarseness, but we had to move back over the ground we had just captured the last week and bury the dead, hundreds of them who got bumped off in that drive through the Argonne. Gee what a rotten job to bury bodies a week or two dead. We finished our burial detail in 2 days, burying the American in one group and the Germans in another.[36]

As the world celebrated the end of the war during Armistice Day, many families who had lost husbands, fathers, sons and fiancés had no cause to rejoice. The war may have come to a conclusion, but they would forever grieve for their loved ones and would have to live with the consequences of their loss. Phyllis Iliff had little to celebrate. She had lost her eighteen-year-old fiancé, Lieutenant Frederick Philip Pemble, 213 Squadron RAF, who had died in a tragic accident while flying a Sopwith Camel on 29 June 1918. He was buried at Andinkerk Military Cemetery, Belgium. His father, who lived in Birchington, Kent, renamed his home Andinkerk after the place where his son is buried. Iliff wrote on 11 November:

> So it has come – the day when this war which has wrecked my life and altered my whole character [has ended] and what does it mean to us, us, who have lost our all in this fight, a fight which is not won. It is wickedly unfair to our dead, you dear boy are the only one I think of, of course, but very soon will England have to answer for this base piece of treachery in which millions of brave lads like yourself went 'west' only to have been sold as the English

Government would sell anybody or anything. But England's day is over, the Throne shakes, Ireland openly hates England and will soon be out of their power, Scotland silently hates the English, and is working swiftly but steadily for the time when they will be free also. France, Italy and all other 'allied' countries turn away from England to – America, the country which will in a few years head the world. How America despises England which pretends to be so clever, while with her bad ruling, petty strikes and pig-headedness is losing trade and every other thing which makes a country famous.

And here – on the night when all are laughing and enjoying themselves, left alone I sit and think of what it would have been had you not been taken away and my heart were not slowly breaking. That night when 'everyone is happy' as people say. Dear Lord! Have mercy it is not in human nature to stand so much.[37]

The Armistice meant that the Allies could now consider how they would maintain the graves of their fallen soldiers. The *Bath Chronicle* reported:

The military situation will not for some time permit the restrictions imposed on visits to France and Belgium to be removed. This news may call some anxiety to many in whose thoughts a soldier's grave is continually present, and the following information is communicated by the War Office in the hope that it may do something to relieve the strain of suspense.

The north of France includes, so far as the British arms are concerned, a Western area which has been in Allied occupation, an Eastern area which was for four years in German occupation, and a middle area over which the campaign of 1916-1918 took place. In the Western area lie the graves of four years' fighting which have never been disturbed. In the Eastern area it is hoped that there may be found also some of the graves of the two corps which retreated from Mons to the Marne. In the middle area, which includes the Somme battlefield, the tide of war has dealt unequally with the graves of the British dead; some cemeteries are left in good order, while some are partly, and a few wholly, destroyed by shell-fire.

No wilful damage has been done by the enemy, so far as can be ascertained, to a single grave; but the inevitable effects of fierce fighting cannot be repaired as quickly as the ground has been recovered.

The armistice, however, has at least rendered it possible to make a thorough examination of the cemeteries in the middle area, and a thorough search for graves in and beyond the old front line of 1915. The Graves Registration Units, which for four years have marked and registered every grave that could be reached, have now been largely reinforced for the new work, and the trained officers who have carried out this duty under war conditions can now move more freely over the battlefields.

Arrangements have been made to inform the relatives of those who are buried in the middle area of the condition of any grave about which inquiry is made. There are complete records in the War Office, arranged by sections of maps, of every grave, whether marked and registered by the Graves Registration Units, or reported to them, but not yet found; and these records will be checked on the spot, section by section.

It is hoped that those relatives whose inquiries relate to areas not yet searched will not lose patience, but remember that the work on the ground which is of special interest to them can only be carried out in its turn.[38]

The end of the war meant that servicemen and women who had survived could return home to family and loved ones. Commander Stephen King-Hall had served throughout the conflict and had participated in the battles of Heligoland Bight and Jutland. He was contemplating life after the war and sharing it with his sweetheart, recalling:

> This ended my second life, which had lasted from 4th August, 1914 to 11th November, 1918. I hope my third life, for in the course of my second life, I found someone to share the third with me.[39]

Now that the war was over there was a rush for couples who had been separated by the conflict to reunite and resume relationships. As a result, there was a rush to get married before Christmas 1918. The *Daily Mirror* reported:

> There will be many pretty weddings at Christmas time. Many demobilised women hoped to become brides before the year is out. Munition girls, who have made their 'bit' hope to get their fiancés out of the Army before the New Year. Women engaged to prisoners of war are now putting their banns up. Many of the men have already returned, others are on their way home.
>
> A large number of girls working in factories are expecting their fiancés home every day.

'Many girls in khaki are arranging their weddings this month,' a welfare worker said to the *Daily Mirror* 'The khaki girl is almost irresistible in her uniform to some men. Waterloo Station is a happy hunting ground for Cupid. Brother and sisters who are in khaki meet and introduce their friends. Engagements follow. A large number of women who have seen service in France have been married already.'[40]

The Armistice signed on 11 November 1918 was only valid for thirty-six days, but because there was a delay in the Allies debating the final peace terms before presenting them to Germany, it had to be renewed several times. Once these extensions had expired the Allied nations reserved the right to terminate the Armistice at three days' notice, and maintained this agreement until the peace terms had been agreed. The Allies also added a further condition upon Germany in that its merchant fleet should be placed under the control of the Allies while the Armistice was taking place.

The Armistice was a mechanism to halt the war and prevent further bloodshed until peace terms were formally discussed and agreed. Those talks began on 18 January 1919 at the International Peace Conference in Paris. The leaders of thirty-two nations descended upon the French capital to attend this conference. President Wilson had to apply for a passport after the Armistice so that he could travel to Europe. It was reported in New York:

President Wilson has obtained his passport. It is the first passport ever issued to a President of the United States. It is valid for France, England and Italy. The President has also signed his own appointment as a peace delegate under his own commission, thus saving all doubts as to his exact status at the Versailles Conference.[41]

Prime Minister Georges Clemenceau presided over the conference, which ended with the signing of the Treaty of Versailles on 28 June 1919, five years to the day after Archduke Franz Ferdinand was assassinated in Sarajevo.

The treaty resulted in humiliating terms for Germany, which had to accept responsibility for beginning the war, relinquish control of territory and pay £6,000 million in reparations to the countries it invaded. It also resulted in the creation of the League of Nations, which was established to resolve international disputes though negotiation, with the purpose of removing the need to go to war. Although President Woodrow Wilson helped to establish the League, the United States declined to join. It had lost many casualties during the First World War and was reluctant to get embroiled in fresh problems aboard. The United States therefore adopted an isolationist foreign policy from then on.

The League of Nations was not a success. The Treaty of Versailles did allow the German Democratic Government and Germany as a nation to progress forward in a peaceful Europe. It caused resentment, creating the conditions in the next two decades for Hitler and Nazism to rise in Germany, which would result in the failure of other nations to prevent a burgeoning country from conducting a war of vengeance with a purpose of reversing the terms of that treaty and reclaiming the victory that it had lost in 1918; resulting in another world war fought twenty years later.

For those soldiers who had fought in the First World War, it was difficult to be jubilant on 11 November 1918, when they had seen so many comrades killed in terrible circumstances. Many of those soldiers who returned home were reluctant to talk about those experiences to their families. They would have to carry those horrific experiences with them throughout their lives and would find it difficult to discuss them with people who had not experienced that trauma. We will end this book with the contemplations of Sapper Granville Hampson. He did participate in the celebrations in Boulogne, but when he returned to his barracks in Wimereux he reflected upon those that fell during the war and considered whether their lives were worth sacrificing:

> Oh what a day, when I got back into the camp, back into the Nissen hut, just sort of sitting, browsing on the edge of my wire netting bed, meditating as it were, over what the day meant, what had happened, what it meant to think the end of the fighting. Jubilation for many, but one must not forget sadness for a good many more when one thought of the dead in the term of millions, not thousands, millions and that is what the position was. Millions who had been killed and literally slaughtered and you feel entitled to say for what? And the answer to that was a very thin one, was it worth it? Well of course the answer is, no it was not worth slaughtering all those human beings. No, I did not exactly sing 'Now the day is over, night is drawing nigh', nevertheless the day was over and the night was drawing nigh. November 11th came to an end.[42]

Appendix I

Terms of Armistice with Germany

Between MARSHAL FOCH, Commander-in-Chief of the Allied Armies, acting in the name of the Allied and Associated Powers with ADMIRAL WEMYSS, First Sea Lord, on the one hand, and

HERR ERZBERGER, SECRETARY OF STATE, President of the German Delegation,
COUNT VON OBERNDORFF, Envoy Extraordinary and Minister Plenipotentiary,
MAJOR-GENERAL VON WINTERFELDT,
CAPTAIN VANSELOW (German Navy),

duly empowered and acting with concurrence of the German Chancellor on the other hand.

An Armistice has been concluded on the following conditions:-

CONDITIONS OF THE ARMISTICE CONCLUDED WITH GERMANY
A.   Clauses Relating to the Western Front.

I.   Cessation of hostilities by land and in the air six hours after the signing of the Armistice.

II.   Immediate evacuation of the invaded countries – Belgium, France, Luxemburg, as well as Alsace-Lorraine – so ordered as to be completed within 15 days from the signature of the Armistice.
     German troops which have not left the above

mentioned territories within the period fixed shall be made prisoners of war.

Occupation by the Allied and United States Forces jointly shall keep pace with the evacuation in these areas.

All movements of evacuation and occupation shall be regulated in accordance with a Note (Annexe 1) determined at the time of the signing of the Armistice.

III. Repatriation, beginning at once, to be completed within 15 days, of all inhabitants of the countries above enumerated (including hostages, persons under trial, or condemned).

IV. Surrender in good condition by the German Armies of the following equipment: -

5,000 guns (2,500 heavy, 2,500 field).
25,000 machine-guns.
3,000 trench mortars.
1,700 aeroplanes (fighters, bombers – firstly all D.7s and night bombing machines).
The above to be delivered in *situ* to the Allied and United States troops in accordance with the detailed conditions laid down in the Note (Annexe 1) determined at the time of the signing of the Armistice.

V. Evacuation by the German Armies of the districts on the left bank of the Rhine. These districts on the left bank of the Rhine shall be administered by the local authorities under the control of the Allied and United States Armies of Occupation.

The occupation of these territories by Allied and United States troops shall be assured by garrisons holding the principle crossings of the Rhine (Mainz, Coblenz, Cologne), together with bridgeheads and at these points of a 30-kilometre (about 19 miles) radius on the right bank, and by garrisons similarly holding the strategic points of the area.

A neutral zone shall be reserved on the right bank of the Rhine, between the river and a line drawn parallel to the bridgeheads and to the river and 10 kilometers (6¼ miles) distant from them, between the Dutch frontier and Swiss frontier.

The evacuation by the enemy of the Rhine districts (right and left banks) shall be so ordered as to be completed within a further period of 16 days, in all 31 days, after the signing of the Armistice.

All movements of evacuation and occupation shall be regulated according to Note (Annexe 1) determined at the time of the signing of the Armistice.

VI. In all territories evacuated by the enemy, evacuation of the inhabitants shall be forbidden, no damage or harm shall be done to the persons or property of the inhabitants.

No person shall be prosecuted for having taken part in any military measures previous to the signing of the Armistice.

No destruction of any kind to be committed.

Military establishments of all kinds shall be delivered intact, as well as military stores, food, munitions and equipment, which shall not have been removed during the periods fixed for evacuation.

Stores of food of all kinds for the civil population, cattle &c., shall be left in *situ*.

No measure of a general character shall be taken, and no official order shall be given which would have as a consequence the depreciation of industrial establishments or a reduction of their personnel.

VII. Roads and means of communication of every kind, railroads, waterways, roads, bridges, telegraphs, telephones shall be in no manner impaired.

All civil and military personnel at present employed on them shall remain.

5,000 locomotives and 150,000 wagons, in good working order, with all necessary spare parts and fittings, shall be delivered to the Associated Powers within the period fixed in Annexe No.2 (not exceeding 31 days in all).

5,000 motor lorries are also to be delivered in good condition within 36 days.

The railways of Alsace-Lorraine shall be handed over within 31 days, together with all personnel and material belonging to the organisation of this system.

Further, the necessary working material in the territories on the left bank of the Rhine shall be left in *situ*.

All stores of coal and material for the upkeep of permanent way, signals and repair shops shall be left in *situ* and kept in an efficient state by Germany, so far as the working means of communication on the left bank of the Rhine is concerned.

All lighters taken from the Allies shall be restored to them.

The note attached as Annexe 2 defines the details of these measures.

VIII.   The German Command shall be responsible for revealing within 4 hours after the signing of the Armistice, all mines or delay-action fuses disposed on territories evacuated by the German troops, and shall assist in their discovery and destruction.

The German Command shall also reveal all destructive measures that may have been taken (such as poisoning or pollution of wells, springs, &c.)

Breaches of these clauses will involve reprisals.

IX.   The right of requisition shall be exercised by the Allied and United States Armies in all occupied territories, save for settlement of accounts with authorised persons.

The upkeep of the troops of occupation in the Rhine districts (excluding Alsace-Lorraine) shall be charged to the German Government.

X.   The immediate repatriation, without reciprocity, according to details conditions which shall be fixed, of all Allied and United States prisoners of war, including those under trial and condemned. The Allied Powers and the United States of America shall be able to dispose of these prisoners as they think fit. The condition annuls all other conventions regarding prisoners of war, including that of July, 1918, now being ratified. However, the return of German prisoners of war interned in Holland and Switzerland shall continue as heretofore. The return of German prisoners of war shall be settled at the conclusion of the Peace preliminaries.

XI.   Sick and wounded who cannot be removed from territory evacuated by the German forces shall be cared for by

German personnel, who shall be left on the spot with the material required.

B. Clauses relating to the Eastern Frontiers of Germany

XII. All German troops present in any territory which before the war formed part of the Austria-Hungary, Roumania [sic Romania], or turkey, shall withdraw within the frontiers of Germany as they existed on 1st August 1914, and all German troops at present in territories, which before the war formed part of Russia, must likewise return to within the frontiers of Germany, as above defined, as soon as the Allies shall think the moment suitable, having regard to the internal situation of these territories.

XIII. Evacuation of German troops, to begin at once, and all German instructors, prisoners and agents, civilian as well as military, now on the territory of Russia (frontiers as defined on 1st August 1914), to be recalled.

XIV. German troops to cease at once all requisitions and seizures and any other coercive measures with a view to obtaining supplies intended for Germany in Roumania [sic Romania], and Russia (frontiers as defined on 1 August 1914).

XV. Annulment of the treaties of Bucharest and Brest-Litovsk and of the supplementary treaties.

XVI. The Allies shall have free access to the territories evacuated by the Germans on their Eastern frontier, either through Danzig or by the Vistula, in order to convey supplies to the population of these territories or for the purpose of maintaining order.

C. Clause relating to East Africa

XVII. Evacuation of all German forces operating in east Africa within a period specified by the Allies.

D. General Clauses

XVIII.   Repatriation without reciprocity, within a maximum period of one month, in accordance with detailed conditions hereafter to be fixed, of all interned civilians, including hostages and persons under trial and condemned, who may be subjects of Allied or Associated States other than those mentioned in Clause III.

Financial Clauses

XIX.   With the reservation that any subsequent concessions and claims by the Allies and United States remain unaffected, the following financial conditions are imposed:-

Reparation for damage done.
      While the Armistice lasts, no public securities shall be removed by the enemy which can serve as a pledge to the Allies to cover reparation for war losses.
      Immediate restitution of the cash deposit in the National Bank of Belgium and, in general, immediate return of all documents., specie, stock, shares, paper money, together with plant for the issue thereof, affecting public or private interests in the invaded countries.
      Restitution of the Russian and Roumanian [sic Romanian], gold yielded to Germany or taken by that Power.
      This gold to be delivered in trust to the Allies until peace is concluded.

E.   Naval Conditions

XX.   Immediate cessation of all hostilities at sea, and definite information to be given as to the position and movements of all German ships.
      Notification to be given to neutrals that freedom of navigation in all territorial waters is given to the Navies and Mercantile Marines of the Allied and Associated powers, all question of neutrality being waived.

XXI.   All naval and Mercantile Marine prisoners of war of the Allied and Associated Powers in German hands to be returned, without reciprocity.

XXII. To surrender at the ports specified by the Allies and the United States all submarines at present in existence (including all submarine cruisers and minelayers) with armament and equipment complete. Those that cannot put to sea shall be deprived of armament and equipment, and shall remain under the supervision of the Allies and the United States. Submarines ready to put to sea shall be prepared to leave German ports immediately on receipt of a wireless order to sail to the port of surrender, the remainder to follow as early as possible. The conditions of this Article shall be completed within 14 days of the signing of the Armistice.

XXIII. The following German surface warships. Which shall be designated by the Allies and the United States of America, shall forthwith be disarmed and thereafter interned in neutral ports, or, failing them, Allied ports, to be designated by the Allies and the United States of America, and placed under the surveillance of the Allies and the United States of America, only care and maintenance parties being left on board, namely:-

6 battle cruisers.
10 battleships.
8 light cruisers (including two minelayers).
50 destroyers of the most modern types.

All other surface warships (including river craft) are to be concentrated in German Naval bases, to be designated by the Allies and the United States of America, completely disarmed and placed under the supervision of the Allies and the United States of America. All vessels of the Auxiliary Fleet are to be disarmed. All vessels specified for internment shall be ready to leave German ports seven days after the signing of the Armistice. Directions for the voyage shall be given to wireless.

XXIV. The Allies and the United States of America shall have the right to sweep up all minefields and destroy all obstructions laid by Germany outside German territorial waters, and the position of these are to be indicated.

353

XXV.   Freedom of access to and from the Baltic to be given to the Navies and Mercantile Marines of the Allied and Associated Powers. This to be secured by the occupation of all German forts from the Cattegat into the Baltic, and by the sweeping up and destruction of all mines and obstructions within and without German territorial waters without any questions of neutrality being raised by Germany, and the positions of all such mines and obstructions to be indicated, and the plans relating thereto are to be supplied.

XXVI.   The existing blockade conditions set up by the Allied and Associated Powers are to remain unchanged, and all German merchant ships found at sea are to remain liable to capture. The Allies and United States contemplate the provisioning of Germany during the Armistice as shall be found necessary.

XXVII.   All Aerial Forces are be concentrated and immobilized in German bases to be specified by the Allies and the United States of America.

XXVIII.   In evacuating the Belgian coasts and ports, Germany shall abandon, in situ and intact, the port material and material for inland waterways, also all merchant ships, tugs and lighters, all Naval aircraft and air materials and stores, all arms and armaments and all stores and apparatus of all kinds.

XXIX.   All Black Sea ports are to be evacuated by Germany: all Russian warships of all description seized by Germany in the Black Sea are to be handed over to the Allies and the United States of America: all neutral merchant ships seized in the Black Sea are to be released; all warlike and other materials of all kinds seized in those ports are to be returned, and German materials as specified in Clause XXVIII are to be abandoned.

XXX.   All merchant ships at present in German hands belonging to the Allied and Associated Powers are to be restored to ports specified by the Allies and the United States of America without reciprocity.

XXXI.   No destruction of ships or of materials to be permitted before evacuation, surrender or restoration.

XXXII. The German Government shall formally notify all the neutral Governments, and particularly the Governments of Norway, Sweden, Denmark and Holland, that all restrictions placed on the trading of their vessels with the Allied and Associated countries, whether by the German Government or by private German interests, and whether in return for specific concessions, such as the export of shipbuilding materials or not, are immediately cancelled.

XXXIII. No transfer of German merchant shipping, of any description, to any neutral flag are to take place after signature of the Armistice.

F.   Duration of Armistice

XXXIV. The duration of the Armistice is to be 36 days, with option to extend. During this period, on failure of execution of any of the above clauses, the Armistice may be repudiated by one of the contracting parties on 48 hours' previous notice. It is understood that failure to execute Articles III and XVIII completely in the periods specified is not to give reason for a repudiation of the Armistice, save where such failure is due to malice aforethought.

To ensure the execution of the present convention under the most favourable conditions, the principle of a permanent International Armistice Commission is recognised. This Commission shall act under the supreme authority of the High Command, military and naval, of the Allied Armies.

The present Armistice was signed on the 11th day of November, 1918, at 5 o'clock a.m. (French time).

F. FOCH.   ERZBERGER.
R.E. WEMYSS   OBERNDORFF.
                    WINTERFELDT.
                    VANSELOW.
                            11th November, 1918.

The representatives of the Allies declare that, in view of fresh events, it appears necessary to them that the following condition shall be added to the clauses of the Armistice:-

'In case the German ships are not handed over within the periods specified, the Governments of the Allies and of the United States shall have the right to occupy Heligoland to ensure their delivery.'

R.E. WEMYSS,   F. FOCH
Admiral.

'The German delegates declare that they will forward this declaration to the German Chancellor, with the recommendation that it will be accepted, accompanying it with the reasons by which the Allies have been actuated in making this demand.'

ERZBERGER.
OBERNDORFF.
WINTERFELDT.
VANSELOW.

Notes and References

Abbreviations:
AWM   Australian War Memorial
IWM   Imperial War Museum
TNA   The National Archives

Introduction
1. Hindenburg, Field Marshal Paul von, *Out of My Life* (Cassell & Co., London, 1920), p.340.
2. Foch, Marshal Ferdinand, *The Memoirs of Marshal Foch* (William Heinemann Ltd, London, 1931), p.300.
3. ibid, p.301.
4. Field Marshal Sir Douglas Haig, Special Order of the Day, 11 April 1918.
5. Ludendorff, General Erich, *My Memories 1914–18* (Hutchinson & Co., London, 1922), p.679.
6. TNA: CAB 28/5/2; Allied War Conferences and Councils minutes.
7. Foch, Marshal Ferdinand, *op. cit.*, p.490.
8. *Birmingham Gazette*, 11 November 1918.
9. Blake, Robert (Ed.), *The Private Papers of Douglas Haig 1914–1918* (Eyre & Spottiswoode, London 1952), p.329.

Chapter 1: German Approaches to Peace – 1916–17
1. Ludendorff, General Erich, *My Memories 1914–18* (Published Hutchinson & Co. London, 1922), p.244.
2. ibid, p.241-2.
3. Hindenburg, Field Marshal Paul von, *Out of My Life* (Cassell & Co. London, 1920), pp.241-2.
4. ibid, p.244.
5. Ludendorff, General Erich, *op. cit.*, p.308.
6. Hindenburg, Field Marshal Paul von, *op. cit.*, pp.241-2.
7. Max, Prince of Baden, *The Memoirs of Prince Max of Baden, Volume 1* (Constable & Co. Ltd, 1928), p.22.
8. Hindenburg, Field Marshal Paul von, *op. cit.*, p.426-7.
9. Lloyd George, David, *War Memoirs of David Lloyd George, Volume 1* (Odhams Press Limited, London, 1938), pp.653-4.

10. Anon, *Official Communications and Speeches Relating to Peace Proposals 1916–17* (Endowment, Washington 1917), p.5.
11. *Birmingham Gazette*, 14 December 1916.
12. Lloyd George, David, *op. cit.*, pp.653-4.
13. *Birmingham Gazette*, 14 December 1916.
14. Hindenburg, Field Marshal Paul von, *op. cit.*, p.132.
15. Anon, *Official Communications and Speeches Relating to Peace Proposals 1916–17*, p.19; *The Morning Post*, 20 December 1916.
16. Max, Prince of Baden, *op. cit.*, p.52.
17. *Sunday Mirror*, 31 December 1916.
18. ibid.
19. Max, Prince of Baden, *op. cit.*, p.52.

Chapter 2: Proposals for Peace – 1918
1. Wilson, H.H. *The Great War, Volume XII* (Amalgamated Press, London, 1919), p.548.
2. Max, Prince of Baden, *op. cit.*, p.52.
3. Ludendorff, General Erich, *op. cit.*, p.677.
4. Toland, John, *No Man's Land, The Story of 1918* (Eyre Methuen, London, 1980), p.369.
5. Charteris, Brigadier-General, *Field Marshal Earl Haig* (Cassell & Company Ltd, London, 1929), p.350.
6. Ludendorff, General Erich, *op. cit.*, p.679.
7. Hindenburg, Field Marshal Paul von, *op. cit.*, p.393.
8. Ludendorff, General Erich, *op. cit.*, p.684.
9. Pitt, Barrie, *1918: The Last Act* (The Reprint Society, London, 1962), p.241.
10. Ulrich Bernd and Ziemann, Benjamin *German Soldiers in the Great War: Letters and Eyewitness Accounts* (Pen & Sword, Barnsley, 2010), p.179.
11. Hindenburg, Field Marshal Paul von, *op. cit.*, pp.426-7.
12. Foch, Marshal Ferdinand, *op. cit.*, p.490.
13. Charteris, Brigadier-General, *op. cit.*, p.358.
14. Blake, Robert, *op. cit.*, p.329.
15. Wilhelm II, Kaiser, *The Kaiser's Memoirs Wilhelm II Emperor of Germany 1888–1918* (Cassell & Company Ltd., London, 1922), pp.273-4.
16. Max, Prince of Baden, *The Memoirs of Prince Max of Baden, Volume 2* (Constable & Co. Ltd, 1928), p.3.
17. ibid, p.6.
18. ibid, p.23.
19. Hindenburg, Field Marshal Paul von, *op. cit.*, pp.426-7.
20. ibid, p.431.
21. Wilhelm, Crown Prince, *Memoirs of the Crown Prince of Germany* (Thornton Butterworth Ltd., London, 1922), pp.216-7.
22. Anon, *The Year 1918 Illustrated* (Headley Bros. Publishers Ltd, London, 1918), pp.172-3.
23. TNA: CAB 28/5/2, Allied War Conferences and Councils minutes.
24. ibid.
25. ibid.
26. Blake, Robert, *op. cit.*, p.330.
27. *Anon, The Year 1918 Illustrated* (Headley Bros. Publishers Ltd, London, 1918), p.174.

28. Wilhelm, Crown Prince, *op. cit.*, p.218.
29. Sulzbach, Herbert, *With the German Guns: Four Years on the Western Front* (First published in Germany 1935, published by Pen & Sword, Barnsley, 2003), pp.231-2.
30. *Dover Express*, 18 October 1918.
31. Wilson, Woodrow, *The Messages and Papers of Woodrow Wilson, Volume One* (The Review of Reviews Corporation, 1924), p.539.
32. Wilhelm, Crown Prince, *op. cit.*, p.219.
33. Brooks, Alden, *As I Saw It* (Alfred A. Knopf, 1930), p.280.
34. ibid, pp.281-2.
35. Liddle Collection, University of Leeds: WW1/GS/1467A, Captain Oliver Sichel.

Chapter 3: Allied Response to the German Peace Initiative
1. Blake, Robert, *op. cit.*, p.331.
2. TNA: CAB 23/17/29, Minutes of War Cabinet 19 October 1918.
3. ibid.
4. ibid.
5. ibid.
6. ibid.
7. ibid.
8. ibid.
9. ibid.
10. ibid.
11. ibid.
12. Wilhelm, Crown Prince, *op. cit.*, p.222.
13. TNA: CAB 23/14/36: Minutes of War Cabinet 21 October 1918.
14. ibid.
15. ibid.
16. ibid.
17. ibid.
18. Hindenburg, Field Marshal Paul von, *op. cit.*, p.432.
19. Wilhelm, Crown Prince, *op. cit.*, pp.220-1.
20. TNA: CAB 23/14/40, Minutes of War Cabinet 26 October 1918.
21. ibid.
22. ibid.
23. ibid.
24. ibid.
25. ibid.
26. ibid.
27. ibid.
28. ibid.
29. ibid.
30. ibid.
31. TNA: CAB 28/5/2, Allied War Conferences and Councils minutes.
32. Blake, Robert, *op. cit.*, p.339.

Chapter 4: German Situation at Home and at the Front
1. Bayerisches Hauptstaatsarchiv *München*/Abt. IV. Kriegsarchiv: BHStA/IV Kriegbriefe 340, war letters of Hans Spieß; Ulrich Bernd and Ziemann, Benjamin *German Soldiers in the Great War: Letters and Eyewitness Accounts* (Pen & Sword,

Barnsley, 2010), p.165.

2. ibid.
3. Max, Prince of Baden, *op. cit.*, Volume 2, p.196.
4. ibid.
5. Ludendorff's other stepson, Heinz Pernot, was a lieutenant who survived the war and was a prominent figure during the Beer Hall Putsch in November 1923. He was among nine men tried and convicted in 1924. Heinz Pernot died in 1973.
6. Ludendorff, General Erich, *op. cit.*, p.602.
7. Max, Prince of Baden, *op. cit.*, Volume 2, p.55.
8. Ludendorff, General Erich, *op. cit.*, p.759.
9. ibid, p.762.
10. Hindenburg, Field Marshal Paul von, *op. cit.*, p.433.
11. Wilhelm, Crown Prince, *op. cit.*, p.224.
12. Stumpf, Richard, *The Private War of Seaman Stumpf* (Leslie Frewin, London, 1969), p.417.
13. Max, Prince of Baden, *op. cit.*, Volume 2, p.275.
14. ibid, p.286-7.
15. Young, Peter, *The History of the First World War, Volume 7, Number 16* (Purnell, London, 1971), p.3115.
16. *Aberdeen Evening Express*, 9 November 1918.
17. Hitler, Adolf, *Mein Kampf* (Germany, 1924, published in the United Kingdom by Hurst and Blackett/Hutchinson, translated by James Murphy 1939), pp.188-9.
18. *Aberdeen Daily Journal*, 9 November 1918.
19. *Daily Gazette for Middlesbrough*, 9 November 1918.
20. Max, Prince of Baden, *op. cit.*, Volume 2, pp.331-2.
21. Young, Peter, *op. cit.*, p.3116.
22. Wilhelm II, Kaiser, *op. cit.*, p.277.

Chapter 5: Battle of Valenciennes – 1 November 1918

1. Hammerton, Sir John, *The Great War: I Was There* (The Amalgamated Press, 1938), p.1862.
2. ibid, p.1863.
3. ibid, p.1863.
4. Library and Archives, Canada: 44th Battalion War Diary.
5. Library and Archives, Canada: 47th Battalion War Diary.
6. Library and Archives, Canada: 47th Battalion War Diary.
7. Library and Archives, Canada: 46th Battalion War Diary.
8. McWilliams, James L. and Steel, R. James, *The Suicide Battalion* (Hurtig Publishers, Edmonton, 1978), p.198.
9. Library and Archives, Canada: 46th Battalion War Diary.
10. *The London Gazette*, 28 January 1919.
11. Library and Archives, Canada: 72nd Battalion War Diary.
12. Library and Archives, Canada: 38th Battalion War Diary.
13. TNA: WO 95/2793, 146th Brigade War Diary.
14. TNA: WO 95/3057, 2/8th Worcestershire Regiment War Diary.
15. TNA: WO 95/3057, 2/8th Worcestershire Regiment War Diary.
16. Hammerton, Sir John, *op. cit.*, p.1864.
17. TNA: WO 95/2768, 146th Brigade War Diary.
18. Hammerton, Sir John, *op. cit.*, pp.1864-5.
19. McWilliams, James L. and Steel, R. James, *op. cit.*, p.202.

20. *Nottingham Evening Post*, 2 November 1918.
21. *Daily Record*, 4 November 1918.

Chapter 6: American Sector – Meuse–Argonne offensive
1. TNA: CAB 23/14/36, Minutes of War Cabinet, 21 October 1918.
2. ibid.
3. English, Lieutenant Colonel George H., *History of the 89th Division, U.S.A.* (War Society of 89th Division, 1920), p.150.
4. Foch, Marshal Ferdinand, *op. cit.*, p.490.
5. Liggett, Major-General Hunter, *AEF Ten Years Ago in France* (Dodd, Mead & Company, 1928), p.206.
6. ibid, p.202.
7. ibid, p.202.
8. ibid, pp.218-19.
9. President Harry S. Truman Library and Museum.
10. Spaulding, Colonel Oliver and Wright, Colonel John, *The Second Division, American Expeditionary Force in France 1917–1919* (The Hillman Press, New York, 1937), p.283.
11. Catlin, Brigadier General A.W., *With the Help of God and a Few Marines* (Doubleday, Page & Company, New York, 1919), p.132.
12. WW1 Veterans Survey Collection/ U.S. Army Heritage and Education Centre, Carlisle, PA: Sergeant Rudolph Forderhase.
13. English, Lieutenant Colonel George H., *op. cit.*, p.182.
14. *American Decorations* (United States Government Printing Office, Washington, 1927), p.34.
15. ibid, p.35.
16. ibid, p.213.
17. US Army War College Library: Private Malcolm Aitken, 5th Marine Regiment, 2nd Division.
18. English, Lieutenant Colonel George H., *op. cit.*, p.188.
19. Major General William Wright's report on Operations 19 October 1918 to 11 November 1918, inclusive; English, Lieutenant-Colonel George H., *op. cit.*, p.346.
20. WW1 Veterans Survey Collection/ U.S. Army Heritage and Education Centre, Carlisle, PA: Sergeant Rudolph Forderhase.
21. ibid
22. Liggett, Major General Hunter, *op. cit.*, p.208-9.
23. Spaulding, Colonel Oliver and Wright, Colonel John, *op. cit.*, pp.283-4.
24. English, Lieutenant Colonel George H., *op. cit.*, p.200.
25. Spaulding, Colonel Oliver and Wright, Colonel John, *op. cit.*, pp.283-4.
26. *American Decorations*, p.612.
27. ibid, p.2.
28. Liggett, Major-General Hunter, *op. cit.*, p.230.
29. MacArthur, General Douglas, *Reminiscences* (Mcgraw-Hill, New York, 1964), p.70.
30. ibid, p.69.
31. WW1 Veterans Survey Collection/U.S. Army Heritage and Education Centre, Carlisle, PA: Sergeant Rudolph Forderhase.
32. ibid.
33. ibid.
34. English, Lieutenant Colonel George H., *op. cit.*, p.205.

35. *American Decorations*, p.325.
36. English, Lieutenant Colonel George H., *op. cit.*, p.215.
37. *American Decorations*, p.45.
38. ibid, p.4.
39. ibid.
40. ibid, p.110.
41. Ross, Major Warner A., *My Colored Battalion: Dedicated to the American Colored Soldier* (Warner A. Ross, 1920), pp.53-2.
42. ibid, p.100-1.
43. ibid, p.61-2.
44. ibid, p.67-9.
45. Sanborn, Colonel Joseph B., *The 131st U.S. Infantry in the World War* (privately published, Chicago, 1919), p.149.
46. Catlin, Brigadier General A.W., *op. cit.*, p.133.
47. Liggett, Major-General Hunter, *op. cit.*, pp.223-4.
48. Hindenburg, Field Marshal Paul von, *op. cit.*, p.437.

Chapter 7: French Sector – Meuse–Argonne Offensive

1. Service Historique de l'Armée de Terre Archives: 26 N718010, 219e Régiment d'Infanterie War Diary.
2. ibid.
3. ibid.
4. ibid.
5. ibid.
6. Service Historique de l'Armée de Terre Archives: 26 N699 0110049, 93rd Régiment d'Infanterie War Diary.
7. ibid.
8. Service Historique de l'Armée de Terre Archives: 26 N718010, 219th Régiment d'Infanterie War Diary.
9. Service Historique de l'Armée de Terre Archives: 26 N 732 004 00039, 264th Régiment d'Infanterie War Diary.

Chapter 8: British Assault Upon the Sambre Canal

1. TNA: WO 95/1269, 2nd Royal Sussex Regiment War Diary.
2. TNA: WO 95/1234, 1st Division War Diary.
3. TNA: WO 95/1246, 1st Division Commander Royal Engineers.
4. TNA: WO 95/2232, 25th Division Commander Royal Engineer's War Diary.
5. ibid.
6. TNA: WO 95/1246, 1st Division Commander Royal Engineers.
7. TNA: WO 95/1269, 2nd Royal Sussex Regiment War Diary.
8. ibid.
9. IWM Department of Sound: 1044, Private Walter Grover.
10. TNA: WO 95/1269.
11. TNA: WO 95/1246.
12. TNA: WO 95/1269.
13. TNA: WO 95/1246.
14. *The London Gazette*, 15 May 1919.
15. ibid, 6 January 1919.
16. IWM Department of Sound: 10441, Private Walter Grover.
17. O.H. Woodward, 'With the Tunnellers', *Reveille*, 1 July 1935.

18. AWM: AWM4 16/2/23, 1st Australian Tunnelling Company R.E. War Diary.
19. TNA: WO 95/1269.
20. *The London Gazette*, 13 February 1919.
21. ibid, 6 January 1919.
22. TNA: WO 95/2397, 2nd Manchester Regiment War Diary.
23. *London Gazette*, 6 January 1919.
24. ibid, 13 February 1919.
25. TNA: WO 95/2397: 16th Lancashire Fusiliers War Diary.
26. IWM Department of Documents: Misc 3 Item 42 (VC Box 50 (M21).
27. IWM Department of Sound: 10922, Private Frank Holding.
28. IWM Department of Documents: Misc 3 Item 42 (VC Box 50 (M21).
29. ibid.
30. Anon, *The Tank Corps Honour & Awards 1916–1919* (Midland Medals Birmingham, 1982), p.330.
31. ibid, p.331.
32. *The London Gazette*, 4 October 1919.
33. TNA: WO 95/2045, 11th Royal Fusiliers War Diary.
34. TNA: WO 95/2042, 2nd Bedfordshire Regiment War Diary.
35. Anon, *The Tank Corps Honour & Awards 1916–1919*, p.160.
36. ibid, pp.331-2.
37. ibid, pp.160-1.
38. ibid, pp.329-30.
39. Depree, Major-General H.D., *A History of the 38th (Welsh) and 33rd Divisions in the Last Five Weeks of the Great War* (The Naval & Military Press, Uckfield), p.192.
40. ibid, p.193.
41. ibid, p.191.
42. TNA: WO 95/2533, 13th King's Royal Rifle Corps War Diary.
43. ibid.
44. Maurice, Major-General Sir Frederick, *The Life of General Lord Rawlinson of Trent* (Cassell & Company Ltd, London, 1928), pp.244-5.

Chapter 9: The New Zealanders Capture Le Quesnoy

1. Edmonds, Brigadier Sir James and Maxwell-Hyslop, Lieutenant Colonel R., *Military Operations France & Belgium 1918: Volume V* (HMSO, London, 1947), p.482.
2. Stewart, Colonel H., *The New Zealand Division 1916–1919* (Whitcombe & Tombs Ltd, Auckland, 1921), pp.584-5.
3. National Library of Australia: *Northern Advocate*, 27 November 1918.
4. TNA: WO 95/3708, 1st New Zealand Battalion Rifle Brigade War Diary.
5. TNA: WO 95/3707, 3rd New Zealand Rifle Brigade War Diary.
6. TNA: WO 95/3709, 2nd Battalion, New Zealand Rifle Brigade War Diary.
7. ibid.
8. TNA: WO 95/3711, 4th Battalion New Zealand Rifle Brigade War Diary.
9. ibid.
10. Stewart, Colonel H., *op. cit.*, p.584-5.
11. National Library of Australia: *Northern Advocate*, 27 November 1918.
12. Austin, Lieutenant-Colonel W.S., *The Official History of the New Zealand Rifle Brigade* (L.T. Watkins Ltd, Wellington, 1924), p.456.
13. National Library of Australia: *Northern Advocate*, 27 November 1918.
14. TNA: WO 95/3711.

15. National Library of New Zealand: *Auckland Star*, 8 April 1939.
16. TNA: WO 95/3709.
17. Edmonds, Brigadier-General Sir James and Maxwell-Hyslop, *op. cit.*, p.483.
18. TNA: WO 95/3711.
19. National Library of Australia: *Northern Advocate*, 27 November 1918.
20. TNA: WO 95/3711.
21. TNA: WO 95/3709.

Chapter 10: Impact of Battle of Sambre Upon German Forces
1. Wilhelm, Crown Prince, *op. cit.*, pp.224-5.
2. Maurice, Major General Sir Frederick, *op. cit.*, pp.247-8.
3. Dudley Ward, Major C.H., *The Fifty-Sixth Division 1914–1918* (Murray, London, 1921), p.305.
4. TNA: WO 95/2943, 1/5th Pioneers Battalion, Cheshire Regiment War Diary.
5. Maurice, Major-General Sir Frederick, *op. cit.*, p.248.
6. Sulzbach, Herbert, *op. cit.*, p.243.
7. *Manchester Evening News*, 26 November 1918.
8. *Bury Free Press*, 23 November 1918.
9. John Grehan and Martin Mace, *Despatches from the Front: Western Front 1917–1918* (Pen & Sword, Barnsley, 2014), pp.190-1.

Chapter 11: Negotiations for Armistice
1. Foch, Marshal Ferdinand, *op. cit.*, pp.544-5.
2. ibid, p.545.
3. Best, Nicholas, *The Greatest Day in History* (Weidenfeld & Nicolson, London, 2008), p.56.
4. Foch, Marshal Ferdinand, *op. cit.*, p.545.
5. National Library of Australia: *Sydney Morning Herald*, 9th November 1918.
6. Sutcliffe, Robert, *Seventy-First New York in the World War* (privately published 1922), p.497.
7. ibid.
8. Wemyss, Lady Wester, *The Life and Letters of Lord Wester Wemyss* (Eyre and Spottiswoode, London, 1935), pp.389-90.
9. Foch, Marshal Ferdinand, *op. cit.*, p.545.
10. *L'ancien combattant, journal de l'association des mutilés et victimes de guerre* (Nancy, 1938).
11. Service Historique de l'Armée de Terre Archives: 26 N708 11, 171st French Régiment d'Infanterie War Diary, 7 November 1918.
12. *Liverpool Daily Post and Mercury*, 28 November 1918.
13. Foch, Marshal Ferdinand, *op. cit.*, p.545.
14. *Liverpool Daily Post and Mercury*, 28 November 1918.
15. Wemyss, Lady Wester, *op. cit.*, p.390.
16. *Liverpool Daily Post and Mercury*, 28 November 1918.
17. Aston, Major-General Sir George, *The Biography of the Late Marshal Foch* (The Macmillan Company, New York, 1929), p.402-3.
18. Wemyss, Lady Wester, *op. cit.*, p.390.
19. Foch, Marshal Ferdinand, *op. cit.*, p.547.
20. Aston, Major-General Sir George, *op. cit.*, pp.402-3.
21. Wemyss, Lady Wester, *op. cit.*, p.390.
22. *Liverpool Daily Post and Mercury*, 28 November 1918.

23. Wemyss, Lady Wester, *op. cit.*, p.390.
24. Foch, Marshal Ferdinand, *op. cit.*, pp.550-1.
25. ibid, p.551.
26. Aston, Major-General Sir George, *op. cit.*, pp.402-3.
27. Wemyss, Lady Wester, *op. cit.*, p.390.
28. *Liverpool Daily Post and Mercury*, 28 November 1918.
29. Foch, Marshal Ferdinand, *op. cit.*, p.551.
30. Wemyss, Lady Wester, *op. cit.*, p.390-1.
31. *L'ancien combattant, journal de l'association des mutilés et victimes de guerre* (Nancy, 1938).
32. *Aberdeen Journal*, 9 November 1918.
33. *L'ancien combattant, journal de l'association des mutilés et victimes de guerre* (Nancy, 1938).
34. ibid.
35. Sulzbach, Herbert, *op. cit.*, p.243.
36. *Daily Mirror*, 10 November 1918.
37. Wemyss, Lady Wester, *op. cit.*, p.391.
38. ibid.
39. Maurice, Major General Sir Frederick, *op. cit.*, p.248.
40. Foch, Marshal Ferdinand, *op. cit.*, p.546.
41. Wemyss, Lady Wester, *op. cit.*, p.392.
42. *Dundee Courier*, 20 November 1918.

Chapter 12: Kaiser Wilhelm Abdicates
1. Edmonds, Brigadier-General Sir James and Maxwell-Hyslop, Lieutenant Colonel R., *op. cit.*, p.516.
2. Max, Prince of Baden, *op. cit.*, Volume 2, p.318.
3. ibid, pp.320-1.
4. ibid.
5. ibid, p.341.
6. ibid, p.342.
7. ibid.
8. *Liverpool Daily Post and Mercury*, 12 November 1918.
9. Max, Prince of Baden, *op. cit.*, Volume 2, p.360.
10. *Western Daily Press*, 11 November 1918.
11. *Aberdeen Daily Journal*, 9 November 1918.
12. Wilhelm, Crown Prince, *op. cit.*, p.258.
13. Hindenburg, Field Marshal Paul, *op. cit.*, p.439.
14. Max, Prince of Baden, *op. cit.*, Volume 2, p.362.
15. *The Birmingham Post*, 11 November 1918.
16. ibid.
17. *Coventry Evening Telegraph*, 12 November 1918.
18. *Daily Record*, 13 November 1918.
19. *Dundee Courier*, 19 November 1918.
20. Ludendorff, General Erich, *op. cit.*, p.766.
21. Wemyss, Lady Wester, *op. cit.*, p.393.
22. *Liverpool Daily Post and Mercury*, 28 November 1918.
23. WW1 Veterans Survey Collection/U.S. Army Heritage and Education Centre, Carlisle, PA: Lieutenant Francis Jordan.
24. Sulzbach, Herbert, *op. cit.*, p.245.

25. *Western Daily Press*, 11 November 1918.
26. *Taunton Courier*, 13 November 1918.
27. *Nottingham Evening Post*, 14 November 1918.

Chapter 13: Canadians Advance Upon Mons
1. Library and Archives, Canada: 20th Battalion War Diary.
2. Library and Archives, Canada: 19th Battalion War Diary.
3. ibid.
4. Hammerton, Sir John, *op. cit.*, p.1867.
5. ibid.
6. ibid.
7. ibid.
8. ibid.
9. Library and Archives, Canada: 19th Battalion War Diary.
10. Hammerton, Sir John, *op. cit.*, p.1868.
11. Library and Archives, Canada: 19th Battalion War Diary.
12. Library and Archives, Canada: 20th Battalion War Diary.
13. Hammerton, Sir John, *op. cit.*, p.1868.
14. Library and Archives, Canada: 19th Battalion War Diary.
15. ibid.
16. Library and Archives, Canada: 20th Battalion War Diary.
17. Library and Archives, Canada: 19th Battalion War Diary.
18. ibid.

Chapter 14: Signing of the Armistice – 11 November 1918
1. Foch, Marshal Ferdinand, *op. cit.*, p.547.
2. ibid.
3. Wemyss, Lady Wester, *op. cit.*, p.393.
4. ibid, pp.393-4.
5. Foch, Marshal Ferdinand, *op. cit.*, p.569.
6. ibid, pp.569-70.
7. Wemyss, Lady Wester, *op. cit.*, p.394-5.
8. Aston, Major General Sir George, *op. cit.*, p.409.
9. Foch, Marshal Ferdinand, *op. cit.*, p.571.
10. Wemyss, Lady Wester, *op. cit.*, p.395.
11. Edmonds, Brigadier General Sir James and Maxwell-Hyslop, Lieutenant Colonel R., *op. cit.*, p.552.
12. Blake, Robert, *op. cit.*, p.340.

Chapter 15: Morning of 11 November 1918 – British Sector
1. *Dundee Evening Telegraph*, 19 October 1919.
2. TNA: WO 95/2897, 156th Infantry Brigade War Diary.
3. TNA: WO 95/2898, 157th Infantry Brigade War Diary.
4. Liddle Collection, University of Leeds: WW1/GS/1052, S.C. Marriott.
5. TNA: WO 95/3147, 1st South African Infantry Regiment War Diary.
6. ibid.
7. TNA: WO 95/2285, 29th Division War Diary.
8. TNA: WO 95/1155, 7th Dragoon Guards (Princess Royal) War Diary.
9. The *London Gazette*, 4 October 1919.
10. TNA: WO 95/2907, 55th Division War Diary.

11. TNA: WO 95/2921, 164th Infantry Brigade War Diary.
12. TNA: WO 95/2907, 55th Division War Diary.
13. TNA: WO 95/2921, 164th Infantry Brigade War Diary.
14. Anon, *Four Years on the Front* (Odhams Press Ltd, London, 1922), p.399.
15. IWM Department of Sound: 9876, Cyril Dennys.
16. Dudley Ward, Major C.H., *op. cit.*, p.313.
17. ibid.
18. *Essex County Chronicle*, 20 December 1918.
19. *Aberdeen Evening Express*, 21 December 1918.
20. National Roll of the Great War, Leeds Volume.
21. IWM Department of Sound: 19073, Private Thomas Dewing.

Chapter 16: Morning of 11 November 1918 – Canadian Sector
1. Hammerton, Sir John, *op. cit.*, p.1868.
2. Library and Archives, Canada: 19th Battalion War Diary.
3. Hammerton, Sir John, *op. cit.*, pp.1868-9.
4. Bird, Will, *Ghosts Have Warm Hands* (CEF Books, 1997), pp.156-7.
5. ibid, p.157.
6. ibid, p.158.
7. ibid, p.177.
8. Library and Archives, Canada: 42nd Battalion War Diary.
9. Library and Archives, Canada: 6th Brigade War Diary.
10. ibid.
11. Library and Archives, Canada: 31st Battalion War Diary.
12. Library and Archives, Canada: 28th Battalion War Diary.
13. ibid.
14. ibid.
15. ibid.
16. ibid.
17. Hammerton, Sir John, *op. cit.*, pp.1870-1.
18. Library and Archives, Canada: 42nd Battalion War Diary.
19. Bird, Will, *op. cit.*, p.158.
20. *Coventry Evening Telegraph*, 23 November 1918.

Chapter 17: Morning of 11 November 1918 – French Sector
1. Service Historique de l'Armée de Terre Archives: 26 N 868/2, Régiment d'Infanterie Coloniale du Maroc War Diary.
2. Service Historique de l'Armée de Terre Archives: 26 N 825/9, 25th Battalion de Chasseur à Pieds War Diary.
3. Service Historique de l'Armée de Terre Archives: 26 N718010, 219th Régiment d'Infanterie War Diary.
4. Chauveau, Alain, *Le Vagabond de la Grande Guerre, Souvenirs de Guerre 1914–1918 de Charles de Berterèche de Menditte, officier d'Infanterie* (Geste editions, La Crèche, 2008).
5. *Ouest France*, 17 June 2016.
6. 'L'année de l'Armistice 1918–1998', Brochure DMIH (Délégation à la Mémoire, Paris, 1998), p.98.
7. ibid.

Chapter 18: Morning of 11 November 1918 – American Sector
1. Liggett, Major General Hunter, *op. cit.*, p.234.

2. Lejeune, Major General John A., *The Reminiscences of a Marine* (Dorrance & Company, 1930), pp.399-400.
3. ibid, p.400.
4. ibid, p.410.
5. WW1 Veterans Survey Collection/U.S. Army Heritage and Education Centre, Carlisle, PA: Sergeant Rudolph Forderhase.
6. WW1 Veterans Survey Collection/U.S. Army Heritage and Education Centre, Carlisle, PA: Lieutenant Francis Jordan.
7. *American Decorations, op. cit.*, p.325.
8. Major General Wright's report; English, Lieutenant Colonel George H., *op. cit.*, p.350.
9. English, Lieutenant Colonel George H., *op. cit.*, p.223.
10. *American Decorations, op. cit.*, p.466.
11. Gowenlock, Thomas R., *Soldiers of Darkness* (Doubleday Doran & Co., New York, 1937), p.264.
12. Lejeune, Major General John A., *op. cit.*, p.402.
13. Liggett, Major General Hunter, *op. cit.*, p.236.
14. Gowenlock, Thomas R., *op. cit.*, pp.264-5.
15. President Harry S. Truman Library and Museum.
16. WW1 Veterans Survey Collection/U.S. Army Heritage and Education Centre, Carlisle, PA: Private Malcolm Aitken.
17. Lejeune, Major General John A., *op. cit.*, pp.405-6.
18. WW1 Veterans Survey Collection/U.S. Army Heritage and Education Centre, Carlisle, PA: Private Malcolm Aitken.
19. Ross, Major Warner A., *op. cit.*, p.64.
20. ibid, pp.76-8.
21. WW1 Veterans Survey Collection/U.S. Army Heritage and Education Centre, Carlisle, PA: Corporal Harry Wright.
22. Stevenson, 2nd Lieutenant Kenyon, *Official History of the Fifth Division U.S.A.* (The Society of the Fifth of the Fifth Division, 1920), p.255.
23. Joel, Arthur H., *Under the Lorraine Cross* (privately published, Lancing, Michigan, 1920), p.46.
24. *American Decorations*, p.252.
25. Joel, Arthur H., *op. cit.*, pp.46-7.
26. Thorn, Henry G. Jr., *History of 313th U.S. Infantry* (Wynkoop Hallenbeck Crawford Company, 1920) p.67.
27. ibid, p.50.
28. Anon, *History of the 79th Division AEF During the War 1917–19* (Steinman & Steinman, Lancaster, 1922), p.316.
29. *Baltimore Sun*, 11 November 2008.
30. Thorn, Henry G. Jr., *op. cit.*, p.50.
31. *Baltimore Sun*, 11 November 2008.
32. Private Will Schellberg's diary, quoted in the *Baltimore Sun*, 6 May 1993.
33. Anon, *History of the 79th Division AEF During the War 1917–19*, p.316.
34. Major-General Wright's report/English, Lieutenant-Colonel George H., *op. cit.*, p.351.
35. ibid
36. ibid
37. ibid
38. Spaulding, Colonel Oliver and Wright, Colonel John, *op. cit.*, p.284.

39. Sanborn, Colonel Joseph B., *op. cit.*, p.149.
40. ibid, p.237.
41. *Ballymena Observer*, 23 April 1919.
42. Reynolds, Chaplain F.C., *115th Infantry U.S.A. in the World War* (privately published, 1920), pp.163-4.

Chapter 19: The Guns Fall Silent: 11.00 Hours, 11 November 1918
1. Reitz, Deneys, *Trekking On* (Faber & Faber, London, 1933), pp.320-1.
2. ibid.
3. Anon, *Four Years on the Front*, p.399.
4. IWM Department of Sound: 4191, Major Keith Officer.
5. ibid.
6. Sulzbach, Herbert, *op. cit.*, p.248.
7. *Hastings & St Leonards Observer*, 21 December 1918.
8. *Western Gazette*, 15 November 1918.
9. Library and Archives, Canada: 31st Battalion War Diary.
10. Library and Archives, Canada: 42nd Battalion war diary.
11. *Taunton Courier*, 20 November 1918.
12. IWM Department of Sound: 9172, Private Reginald Johnson.
13. Chauveau, Alain, *op. cit.*
14. Sumner, Ian, *They Shall Not Pass: The French Army on the Western Front 1914–15* (Pen & Sword, Barnsley, 2012), pp.210-1.
15. Service Historique de l'Armée de Terre Archives : 26 N 702/13, 163rd Régiment d'Infanterie War Diary.
16. Brooks, Alden, *As I Saw It* (Alfred A. Knopf, New York, 1930), pp.292-3.
17. Lejeune, Major-General John A., *op. cit.*, p.402.
18. WW1 Veterans Survey Collection/U.S. Army Heritage and Education Centre, Carlisle, PA: Lieutenant Francis Jordan.
19. *Taunton Courier*, 20 November 1918.
20. Rickenbacker, Captain Eddie V., *Fighting the Flying Circus* (Stokes, New York, 1919).
21. Georg Bucher, *In the Line* (Naval and Military Press, Uckfield, 2005), p.315.
22. ibid, pp.317-8.
23. Sutcliffe, Robert, *op. cit.*, p.288.
24. Liggett, Major General Hunter Liggett, *op. cit.*, p.237.
25. Thorn, Henry G. Jr., *op. cit.*
26. Service Historique de l'Armée de Terre Archives : 26 N 702/8, 162nd Régiment d'Infanterie War Diary.
27. Gowenlock, Thomas R., *op. cit.*, p.265.
28. Lejeune, Major General John A., *op. cit.*, p.405.
29. WW1 Veterans Survey Collection/U.S. Army Heritage and Education Centre, Carlisle, PA: Sergeant Rudolph Forderhase.
30. WW1 Veterans Survey Collection/U.S. Army Heritage and Education Centre, Carlisle, PA: Lieutenant Francis Jordan.
31. WW1 Veterans Survey Collection/U.S. Army Heritage and Education Centre, Carlisle, PA: Sergeant Rudolph Forderhase.
32. English, Lieutenant Colonel George H. *op. cit.*, p.244.
33. Lejeune, Major-General John A., *op. cit.*, p.404.
34. ibid, p.404-5.
35. WW1 Veterans Survey Collection/U.S. Army Heritage and Education Centre,

Carlisle, PA: Private Malcolm Aitken.
36. Brooks, Alden, *op. cit.*, p.293.
37. English, Lieutenant Colonel George H., *op. cit.*, p.325.
38. Brooks, Alden, *op. cit.*, p.294.
39. ibid, pp.294-5.
40. IWM Department of Sound: 14879, Private William Herzog.
41. Library and Archives, Canada: 42nd Battalion War Diary.
42. TNA: WO 95/2921, 164th Infantry Brigade War Diary.
43. Gowenlock, Thomas R., *op. cit.*, pp.264-5.
44. Service Historique de l'Armée de Terre Archives : 26 N 612/6, 36th Régiment d'Infanterie War Diary.
45. Lejeune, Major-General John A., *op. cit.*, pp.405-6.
46. Private Will Schellberg's diary, quoted in the *Baltimore Sun*, 6 May 1993.
47. Thorn, Henry G. Jr., *op. cit.*
48. Joel, Arthur H., *op. cit.*, p.47.
49. Service Historique de l'Armée de Terre Archives : 26 N 702/8, 202nd Régiment d'Infanterie War Diary.
50. Liddle Collection, University of Leeds: WW1/GS/1052, S.C. Marriott.
51. Liddle Collection, University of Leeds: WW1/GS/1310, Lieutenant Colonel Bruce Hale Puckle.
52. *Taunton Courier*, 20 November 1918.
53. Liddle Collection, University of Leeds: WW1/GS/0944, C.L. Leeson.
54. Maurice, Major General Sir Frederick, *op. cit.*, pp.249-50.
55. ibid, p.250.

Chapter 20: Armistice Day – France and Belgium

1. Harbord, Major General James, *Leaves from a War Diary* (Dodd, Mead & Company, 1925), pp.392-3.
2. ibid, p.393.
3. Weygand, Captain Maxime, *Ideal Vécu* (Flammarion, Paris. 1953).
4. Aston, Major-General Sir George, *op. cit.*, pp.402-3.
5. ibid.
6. Wemyss, Lady Wester, *op. cit.*, p.395.
7. *Daily Record*, 12 November 1918.
8. Quoted in Toland, John, *No Man's Land* (Eyre Methuen, London, 1980).
9. Aston, Major-General Sir George, *op. cit.*, pp.410-11.
10. *Daily Record*, 13 November 1918.
11. Wemyss, Lady Wester, *op. cit.*, p.395.
12. Harbord, Major General James, *op. cit.*, pp.394-6.
13. *Coventry Evening Telegraph*, 12 November 1918.
14. ibid.
15. *Daily Record*, 13 November 1918.
16. IWM Department of Sound: 10067, Sapper Granville Hampson.
17. *Western Times*, 30 November 1918.
18. *Nottingham Evening Post*, 14 November 1918.
19. *Aberdeen Journal*, 16 November 1918.
20. *Dundee Courier*, 19 November 1918.

Chapter 21: Armistice Day – The United Kingdom

1. King-Hall, Commander Stephen, *A North Sea Diary 1914–1918* (Newnes,

London), p.226.
2. *Daily Record*, 12 November 1918.
3. Churchill, Winston, *The World Crisis 1911–1918* (Odhams Press, 1938), pp.1399-400.
4. ibid.
5. *Derby Daily Telegraph*, 11 November 1918.
6. Hammerton, Sir John, *op. cit.*, p.1889.
7. ibid.
8. George, David Lloyd, *op. cit.*, Volume II, p.1986.
9. Wemyss, Lady Wester, *op. cit.*, pp.396-7.
10. *Daily Record*, 12 November 1918.
11. *Liverpool Daily Post*, 12 November 1918.
12. Hammerton, Sir John, *op. cit.*, p.1891.
13. *Daily Record*, 12 November 1918.
14. Hammerton, Sir John, *op. cit.*, p.1891.
15. National Library of Australia: *Sydney Morning Herald*, 27 December 1918.
16. Hammerton, Sir John, *op. cit.*, p.1891.
17. ibid.
18. IWM Department of Sound: 9790, Walter Griffin.
19. IWM Department of Sound: 381, Frank Merrick.
20. *Gloucestershire Echo*, 4 April 1919.
21. IWM Department of Sound: 684, Amy May.
22. IWM Department of Sound: 8667, Private Harold Boughton.
23. IWM Department of Documents: 2001, Papers of Lieutenant R.G. Dixon.
24. ibid.
25. IWM Department of Sound: 10170, Private Walter Spencer.
26. *Hull Daily Mail*, 16 November 1918.
27. *Bath Chronicle*, 16 November 1918.
28. *Burnley Express*, 23 November 1918.
29. National Library of Australia: *Sydney Morning Herald*, 27 December 1918.
30. *Daily Mirror*, 14 November 1918.
31. ibid.

Chapter 22: Armistice Day – Around the World
1. *Daily Record*, 13 November 1918.
2. Sutcliffe, Robert, *op. cit.*, p.497.
3. *Coventry Evening Telegraph*, 12 November 1918.
4. *Daily Record*, 13 November 1918.
5. *Dundee Evening Telegraph*, 20 November 1918.

Chapter 23: Armistice Day – Germany
1. *Daily Record*, 12 November 1918.
2. Stumpf, Richard, *op. cit.*, p.428.
3. *Evening Dispatch*, 13 November 1918.
4. Wyngarden, Greg van, *Richtofen Circus Jagdgeswader Nr 1* (Osprey, London, 2004), p.117.
5. ibid, p.119.
6. Hitler, Adolf, *op. cit.*, p.190.
7. ibid.
8. *Birmingham Gazette*, 25 November 1918.

Chapter 24: Prisoners of War
1. *Daily Mirror*, 18 December 1918.
2. Sumner, Ian, *op. cit.*, p.210.
3. *Daily Mirror*, 18 December 1918.
4. *The Sunday Post*, 22 December 1918.
5. Maurice, Major General Sir Frederick, *op. cit.*, p.251.
6. ibid.
7. Reitz, Deneys, *op. cit.*, pp.324-5.
8. Gowenlock, Thomas R., *op. cit.*, pp.269-70.
9. Spaulding, Colonel Oliver and Wright, Colonel John, *op. cit.*, p.288.
10. IWM Department of Sound: 315, Thomas Mitchell-Fox.
11. Royal Marines Museum: Arc 11/12/5(5), Sergeant Harry Wright.
12. *Daily Mirror, 18 December 1918.*

Chapter 25: The Allied Armies Enter Germany
1. Maurice, Major-General Sir Frederick, *op. cit.*, p.251.
2. *Western Times*, 21 November 1918.
3. Papers of Sergeant Albert Cade, 131st Infantry Regiment, US 33rd Division.
4. Reitz, Deneys, *op. cit.*, p.325.
5. Gowenlock, Thomas R., *op. cit.*, pp.269-70.
6. Spaulding, Colonel Oliver and Wright, Colonel John, *op. cit.*, p.284.
7. ibid, p.288.
8. ibid, p.285.
9. Library and Archives, Canada: 20th Battalion War Diary.
10. ibid.
11. Library and Archives, Canada: 19th Battalion War Diary.
12. Gillon, Captain Stair, *The Story of the 29th Division, A Record of Gallant Deeds* (Thomas Nelson & Sons, 1925), pp.220-1.
13. ibid, p.221.
14. Reitz, Deneys, *op. cit.*, p.321.
15. ibid, pp.321-2.
16. Gowenlock, Thomas R., *op. cit.*, pp.269-70.
17. ibid, p.270.
18. ibid.
19. Spaulding, Colonel Oliver and Wright, Colonel John, *op. cit.*, p.286.
20. Gowenlock, Thomas R., *op. cit.*, p.270.
21. Gillon, Captain Stair, *op. cit.*, pp.223-4.
22. IWM Department of Sound: 10616, Private Ernest Law.
23. ibid
24. IWM Department of Sound: 10170, Private Walter Spencer.
25. ibid.
26. André Zeller, *Dialogues avec un Lieutenant* (Plon Editions, 1971).
27. ibid.
28. Ingold, Général François, *Le Chemin* (Editions Escale, 1958).
29. Giovanangeli, Bernard (Ed.), *Souvenirs d'un officier de Zouaves 1915-1918* (2014).
30. *Western Times*, 11 April 1919.
31. *Dundee Evening Telegraph*, 27 August 1919.
32. *Yorkshire Telegraph & Star*, 27 September 1919.

Chapter 26: Surrender of the German High Seas Fleet
1. Wemyss, Lady Wester, *op. cit.*, pp.389-90.
2. AWM: 1 DRL 429, File No: 12/11/4812, Stoker N. McCrory, Royal Australian Navy.
3. Stumpf, Richard, *op. cit.*, p.430.
4. King-Hall, Commander Stephen, *op. cit.*, p.229.
5. ibid, pp.231-2.
6. ibid, pp.232-5.
7. *Liverpool Daily Post & Mercury*, 21 November 1918.
8. AWM: 1 DRL 429, File No: 12/11/4812.
9. Hammerton, Sir John, *op. cit.*, p.1893.
10. *Derby Daily Telegraph*, 26 November 1918.
11. AWM: 1 DRL 429, File No: 12/11/4812.
12. *Dundee Evening Telegraph*, 21 November 1918.
13. Hammerton, Sir John, *op. cit.*, p.1893.
14. *Dundee Courier*, 14 December 1918.
15. Hammerton, Sir John, *op. cit.*, p.1900.
16. *Dundee Evening Telegraph*, 21 November 1918.
17. *Dundee Courier*, 14 December 1918.
18. AWM: 1 DRL 429, File No: 12/11/4812.
19. *Dundee Evening Telegraph*, 21 November 1918.
20. *Birmingham Gazette*, 25 November 1918.
21. *The Great War*, Volume 12, p.573.
22. AWM: 1 DRL 429, File No: 12/11/4812.
23. *Dundee Courier*, 14 December 1918.
24. *Yorkshire Evening Post*, 27 November 1918.
25. Young, Peter, *The History of the First World War*, Volume 8, Number 12 (Purnell, London, 1971), p.3453.
26. *Hull Daily Mail*, 24 June 1919.

Chapter 27 – Impact of the Armistice
1. *Grantham Journal*, 16 November 1918.
2. Young, Peter, *op. cit.*, p.3148.
3. *Derby Daily Telegraph*, 11 November 1918.
4. *Grantham Journal*, 16 November 1918.
5. *Folkestone, Hythe, Sandgate and Cheriton Herald*, 4 January 1919.
6. ibid, 11 January 1919.
7. *Driffield Times*, 11 January 1919.
8. *Sheffield Independent*, 9 January 1919.
9. ibid.
10. *Lancashire Evening Post*, 29 January 1919.
11. ibid, 30 January 1919.
12. IWM Department of Sound: 10434, Private Alexander Jamieson.
13. *Yorkshire Evening Post*, 12 November 1918.
14. *Lancashire Daily Post*, 16 November 1918.
15. *Birmingham Gazette*, 20 November 1918.
16. ibid.
17. *Aberdeen Evening Express*, 29 November 1918.
18. *Western Times*, 30 November 1918.

19. *Nottingham Evening Post*, 22 January 1919.
20. ibid.
21. IWM Department of Sound: 8946, Private Joseph Pickard.
22. ibid.
23. *Portsmouth Evening News*, 31 July 1918.
24. *Nottingham Evening Post*, 7 August 1926.
25. Ross, Major Warner A., *op. cit.*, pp.8–9.
26. ibid, p.9.
27. *Aberdeen Journal*, 22 November 1918.
28. *Chelmsford Chronicle*, 3 January 1919.
29. Becker, Jean Jacques, *Les destructions de la guerre de 1914–1918; coût ampleur, conséquences démographiques, Reconstruction et modernisation, Direction des Archives de France* (Edition Archives Nationales, Paris, 1991).
30. ibid.
31. George Pineau and André Galland, *Journal des Mutilés et Combattants* (Paris, 1934).
32. Jacques Becker, Jean, *op. cit.*
33. *Sunday Mirror*, 24 November 1918.
34. *Daily Mirror*, 20 November 1918.
35. Liddle Collection, University of Leeds: WW1/GS/0944, C.L. Leeson.
36. WW1 Veterans Survey Collection/U.S. Army Heritage and Education Centre, Carlisle, PA: Corporal Harry Wright.
37. Liddle, Peter, *At the Eleventh Hour* (Leo Cooper, Barnsley, 1998) pp.69-70; Liddle Collection, University of Leeds: WW1/DF/069, Phyllis Iliff.
38. *Bath Chronicle*, 23 November 1918.
39. King-Hall, Commander Stephen, *op. cit.*, p.228.
40. *Daily Mirror*, 18 December 1918.
41. *Aberdeen Evening Express*, 29 November 1918.
42. IWM Department of Sound: 10067, Sapper Granville Hampson.

Bibliography

PRINTED SOURCES

Anon, *American Armies and Battlefields in Europe, A History, Guide and Reference Book* (American Battle Monuments Commission, 1933).

Anon, *History of the 79th Division AEF during the war 1917–19* (Steinman and Steinman, Lancaster PA, 1922), p.316.

American Decorations: A List of Awards of the Congressional Medal of Honor, the Distinguished Service Cross and the Distinguished Service Medal Awarded under the Authority of the Congress of the United States 1862–1926 (United States Government Printing Office, Washington, 1927).

Anon, *Four Years on the Front* (Odhams Press Ltd, London, 1922).

Anon, *Official Communications and Speeches Relating to Peace Proposals 1916–17* (Endowment, Washington, 1917).

Anon, *The Tank Corps Honour and Awards 1916–1919* (Midland Medals, Birmingham, 1982).

Anon, *The Year 1918 Illustrated* (Headley Bros. Publishers Ltd, London, 1918).

Aston, Major-General Sir George, *The Biography of the Late Marshal Foch* (The Macmillan Company, New York, 1929).

Austin, Lieutenant Colonel W.S., *The Official History of the New Zealand Rifle Brigade* (L.T. Watkins Ltd, Wellington, 1924).

Becker, Jean Jacques, *Les destructions de la guerre de 1914–1918; coût ampleur, conséquences démographiques, Reconstruction et modernisation, Direction des Archives de France* (Edition Archives Nationales, Paris, 1991).

Bird, William Richard, *Ghosts Have Warm Hands* (CEF Books, 1997).

Blake, Robert, *The Private Papers of Douglas Haig 1914–1918* (Eyre and Spottiswoode, London 1952).

Brooks, Alden, *As I Saw It* (Alfred A. Knopf, 1930).

Bucher, Georg, *In the Line* (Naval and Military Press, Uckfield, 2005).

Catlin, Brigadier General A.W., *With the Help of God and a Few Marines* (Doubleday, Page and Company, New York, 1919).

Cecil, Hugh and Liddle, Peter, *At the Eleventh Hour* (Leo Cooper, Barnsley, 1998).

Charteris, Brigadier-General, *Field Marshal Earl Haig* (Cassell and Company Ltd, London, 1929).

Chauveau, Alain, *Le Vagabond de la Grande Guerre, Souvenirs de Guerre 1914–1918 de Charles de Berterèche de Menditte, officier d'Infanterie* (Geste Editions, La Crèche, 2008).

Churchill, Winston, *The World Crisis 1911–1918* (Odhams Press, London, 1938).

Depree, Major-General H.D., *A History of the 38th (Welsh) and 33rd Divisions in the Last Five Weeks of the Great War* (Naval and Military Press, Uckfield).

Dudley Ward, Major C.H., DSO MC, *The Fifty-Sixth Division 1914–1918* (Murray, London, 1921).

Edmonds, Brigadier-General Sir James and Maxwell-Hyslop, Lieutenant-Colonel R., *Military Operations France and Belgium 1918, Volume V* (Naval and Military Press, Uckfield).

English, Lieutenant Colonel George H., *History of the 89th Division, U.S.A.* (War Society of 89th Division, 1920).

Foch, Marshal Ferdinand, *The Memoirs of Marshal Foch* (William Heinemann Ltd, London, 1931).

Galland, André and Pineau, George, *Journal des Mutilés et Combattants* (Paris, 1934).

George, David Lloyd, *War Memoirs of David Lloyd George, Volume I and II* (Odhams Press Ltd, London, 1938).

Gibson, R.H. and Prendergast, R.H., *The German Submarine War 1914–18* (Naval and Military Press, Uckfield, 2015).

Gillon, Captain Stair, *The Story of the 29th Division, A Record of Gallant Deeds* (Thomas Nelson and Sons, London, 1925).

Gowenlock, Thomas R., *Soldiers of Darkness* (Doubleday Doran and Co., 1937)

Grehan, John and Mace, Martin, *Despatches from the Front: Western Front 1917–1918* (Pen and Sword, Barnsley, 2014).

Haig, Douglas, *The Private Papers of Douglas Haig 1914–19* (Eyre and Spottiswoode, London, 1952).

Hammerton, Sir John Hammerton, *The Great War: I Was There* (The Amalgamated Press, London, 1938).

Harbord, Major-General James, *Leaves from a War Diary* (Dodd, Mead and Company, 1925).

Hindenburg, Field Marshal Paul von, *Out of My Life* (Cassell and Co., London, 1920).

Hitler, Adolf, *Mein Kampf* (Germany, 1924; published in Britain by Hurst and Blackett/Hutchinson, translated by James Murphy 1939).

Houseman, Laurence, *War Letters of Fallen Englishmen* (Victor Gollance, 1930).

Ingold, Général François, *Le Chemin* (Editions Escale, 1958).

Joel, Arthur H., *Under the Lorraine Cross* (Lancing, Michigan, private published 1920).

King-Hall, Commander Stephen, *A North Sea Diary 1914–1918* (Newnes, London).

Lejeune, Major-General John A., *The Reminiscences of a Marine* (Dorrance and Company, 1930).

Liggett, Major General Hunter, *AEF Ten Years Ago in France* (Dodd, Mead and Company, 1928).

Ludendorff, General Erich, *My Memories 1914–18* (Published Hutchinson and Co., London, 1922).

MacArthur, General Douglas, *Reminiscences* (Mcgraw-Hill, New York, 1964).

Maurice, Major-General Sir Frederick, *The Life of General Lord Rawlinson of Trent* (Cassell and Company Ltd, 1928).

Max, Prince of Baden, *The Memoirs of Prince Max of Baden, Volumes 1 and 2* (Constable and Co. Ltd, London, 1928).

Mead, Gary, *The Doughboys: America and the First World War* (Allen Lane, London, 2000).

Pitt, Barrie, *1918: The Last Act* (The Reprint Society, London, 1962).

Reitz, Deneys, *Trekking On* (Faber and Faber, London, 1933).

Reynolds, Chaplain F.C., *115th Infantry U.S.A. in the World War* (privately published 1920).

Rickenbacker, Captain Eddie V., *Fighting the Flying Circus* (Stokes, New York, 1919).

Ross, Major Warner A., *My Colored Battalion: Dedicated to the American Colored Soldier* (Warner A. Ross, 1920).

Sanborn, Colonel Joseph B., *The 131st U.S. Infantry in the World War* (privately published, Chicago, 1919).

Spaulding, Colonel Oliver and Wright, Colonel John, *The Second Division, American Expeditionary Force in France 1917–1919* (The Hillman Press, New York, 1937).

Stevenson, 2nd Lieutenant Kenyon, *Official History of the Fifth Division U.S.A.* (The Society of the Fifth of the Fifth Division, 1920).

Stewart, Colonel H., *The New Zealand Division 1916–1919* (Whitcombe and Tombs Ltd, Auckland, 1921).

Stumpf, Richard, *The Private War of Seaman Stumpf* (Leslie Frewin, London, 1969).

Sulzbach, Herbert, *With the German Guns: Four Years on the Western Front* (First published in Germany 1935, published by Pen and Sword, Barnsley, 2003).

Sumner, Ian, *They Shall Not Pass: The French Army on the Western Front 1914–15* (Pen and Sword, Barnsley 2012).

Sutcliffe, Robert, *Seventy-First New York in the World War* (privately published 1922).

Taylor, A.J.P., *The First World War: An Illustrated History* (Penguin, London, 1966).

Thorn, Henry G. Jr., *History of 313th U.S. Infantry* (Wynkoop Hallenbeck Crawford Company, 1920).

Toland, John, *No Man's Land, The Story of 1918* (Eyre Methuen, London, 1980).

Ulrich Bernd and Ziemann, Benjamin, *German Soldiers in the Great War: Letters and Eyewitness Accounts* (Pen and Sword, Barnsley, 2010).

Venson, Anne Capriano, *The United States in the First World War: An Encyclopedia* (Garland Publishing, Inc. New York, 1995).

Wemyss, Lady Wester, *The Life and Letters of Lord Wester Wemyss* (Eyre and Spottiswoode, London, 1935).

Weygand, Captain Maxime, *Idéal Vécu* (Flammarion, Paris, 1953).

Wilhelm II, Kaiser, *The Kaiser's Memoirs Wilhelm II Emperor of Germany 1888–1918* (Cassell and Company Ltd., London, 1922).

Wilhelm, Crown Prince, *Memoirs of the Crown Prince of Germany* (Thornton Butterworth Ltd., London, 1922).

Wilson, H.H. *The Great War, Volume XII* (Amalgamated Press, London, 1919).

Wilson, Woodrow, *The Messages and Papers of Woodrow Wilson, Volume One* (The Review of Reviews Corporation, 1924).

Woods, William Seaver, *Colossal Blunders of the War* (The Macmillan Company, New York, 1930).

Wylly, Colonel H.C., *The 1st and 2nd Battalions The Sherwood Foresters in the Great War* (Naval and Military Press, Uckfield).

Wyngarden, Greg Van, *Richtofen Circus Jagdgeswader Nr 1* (Osprey, London, 2004).

Young, Peter, *The History of the First World War, Volume 7, Number 16* (Purnell, London, 1971).

_____, *The History of the First World War, Volume 8, Number 1* (Purnell, London, 1971).

_____, *The History of the First World War, Volume 8, Number 12* (Purnell, London, 1971).

Zeller, André, *Dialogues avec un Lieutenant* (Plon Editions, 1971).

NEWSPAPERS

Aberdeen Daily Journal, 9 and 22 November 1918.

BIBLIOGRAPHY

Aberdeen Evening Express, 9 and 29 November, 21 December 1918.
Ballymena Observer, 23 April 1919.
Baltimore Sun, 6 May 1993, 11 November 2008.
Bath Chronicle, 23 November 1918.
Birmingham Gazette, 16 December 1916, 11, 20 and 25 November 1918.
Birmingham Post, 11 November 1918.
Burnley Express, 23 November 1918.
Bury Free Press, 23 November 1918.
Cambridge Daily News, 22 November 1918.
Coventry Evening Telegraph, 12 and 23 November 1918.
Daily Gazette for Middlesbrough, 9 November 1918.
Daily Mirror, 10, 12 and 20 November and 18 December 1918.
Daily Record, 4, 12, 13 November 1918.
Derby Daily Telegraph, 11 November 1918.
Dover Express, 18 October 1918.
Driffield Times, 11 January 1919.
Dundee Courier, 20 November and 14 December 1918.
Dundee Evening Telegraph, 20, 21 November 1918, 27 August and 19 October 1919.
Essex County Chronicle, 20 December 1918.
Evening Dispatch, 13 November 1918.
Folkestone, Hythe, Sandgate and Cheriton Herald, 4 and 11 January 1919.
Gloucestershire Echo, 4 April 1919.
Grantham Journal, 16 November 1918.
Hastings and St Leonards Observer, 21 December 1918.
Hull Daily Mail, 16 November 1918; 4 April and 24 June 1919.
Lancashire Daily Post, 16 November 1918.
Lancashire Evening Post, 29 and 30 January 1919.
Liverpool Daily Post and Mercury, 12, 21 and 28 November 1918.
Morning Post, 20 December 1916.
Nottingham Evening Post, 2 and 14 November 1918 and 22 January 1919.
Sheffield Independent, 9 January 1919.
Sunday Mirror, 24 November, 31 December 1918.
Sunday Post, 22 December 1918.
Taunton Courier, 13 and 20 November 1918.
Western Daily Press, 11 November 1918.
Western Gazette, 15 November 1918.
Western Times, 18, 21 and 30 November 1918 and 11 April 1919.
Yorkshire Evening Post, 12 and 27 November 1918.
Yorkshire Telegraph and Star, 27 September 1919.

MAGAZINES
L'ancien combattant, journal de l'association des mutilés et victimes de guerre, Nancy, 1938
    – Georges Labroche account.
Reveille, 'With the Tunnellers' by O.H. Woodward, published 1 July 1935.

AUSTRALIAN WAR MEMORIAL
1st Australian Tunnelling Company R.E., War Diary., Ref: AWM4 16/2/23.
Papers of Stoker N. McCrory, Royal Australian Navy, Ref: 1 DRL 429 File No:
    12/11/4812

HOUSE OF COMMONS ARCHIVE
Hansard: HC Deb 31 May 1916 vol 82 cc2706-72706.

IMPERIAL WAR MUSUEM DEPARTMENT OF DOCUMENTS
Documents 2001: Papers of Lieutenant R.G. Dixon.
Misc 3 Item 42 (VC Box 50 (M21).

IMPERIAL WAR MUSEUM DEPARTMENT OF SOUND
315: Thomas Mitchell-Fox.
381: Frank Merrick.
4191: Major Keith Officer.
684: Amy May.
8667: Private Harold Boughton.
9172: Private Reginald Johnson.
9876: Cyril Dennys
10067: Sapper Granville Hampson.
10170: Private Walter Spencer.
10434: Private Alexander Jamieson.
10441: Private Walter Grover.
10616: Private Ernest Law.
14879: Private William Herzog.
19073: Private Thomas Dewing.

LIBRARY AND ARCHIVES CANADA
19th Battalion War Diary.
20th Battalion War Diary.
28th Battalion War Diary.
31st Battalion War Diary.
38th Battalion War Diary.
42nd Battalion War Diary.
44th Battalion War Diary.
46th Battalion War Diary.
47th Battalion War Diary.
72nd Battalion War Diary.

LIDDLE COLLECTION, UNIVERSITY OF LEEDS
WW1/DF/069: Phyllis Iliff.
WW1/GS/0944: C.L. Leeson.
WW1/GS/1052: S C Marriott.
WW1/GS/1310: B.H. Puckle.
WW1/GS/1467A: Captain Oliver Sichel.

NATIONAL LIBRARY OF AUSTRALIA
Northern Advocate, 27 November 1918.
Sydney Morning Herald, 9 November and 27 December 1918.

NATIONAL LIBRARY OF NEW ZEALAND
Auckland Star, 8 April 1939.

PRESIDENT HARRY S. TRUMAN LIBRARY AND MUSEUM
Letters to Bess Truman, 1 and 11 November 1918.

PRIVATE PAPERS
Papers of Sergeant Albert Cade, 131st Infantry Regiment, US 33rd Division, courtesy of David Cade.

ROYAL MARINES MUSEUM
ARCH 11/12/5(5): Papers of Sergeant Harry Wright.

SERVICE HISTORIQUE DE L'ARMÉE DE TERRE ARCHIVES
26 N 612/6: 36e Régiment d'Infanterie War Diary.
26 N 697/6: 152e Régiment d'Infanterie War Diary.
26 N 702/8: 162e Régiment d'Infanterie War Diary.
26 N 702/13: 163e Régiment d'Infanterie War Diary.
26 N 708 11: 11e Régiment d'Infanterie War Diary.
26 N 825/9: 25 Bataillon de Chasseur à Pieds War Diary.
26 N 699 0110049: 93e Régiment d'Infanterie War Diary.
26 N 718010: 219e Régiment d'Infanterie War Diary.
26 N 732 004 00039: 264e Régiment d'Infanterie War Diary.

THE LONDON GAZETTE
6 and 28 January 1919.
13 February 1919.
15 May 1919.
4 October 1919.

THE NATIONAL ARCHIVES
CAB 13/14/36: Minutes of War Cabinet meeting, 21 October 1918.
CAB 23/14/40: Minutes of War Cabinet meeting, 26 October 1918.
CAB 23/17/29: Minutes of War Cabinet meeting, 19 October 1918.
CAB 28/5/2: Allied War Conferences and Councils minutes.
WO 95/1234: 1st Division War Diary.
WO 95/1246: 1st Division Commander Royal Engineer's War Diary.
WO 95/1269: 2nd Royal Sussex Regiment War Diary.
WO 95/1155: 7th Dragoon Guards (Princess Royal) War Diary.
WO 95/2042: 2nd Bedfordshire Regiment War Diary.
WO 95/2045: 11th Royal Fusiliers War Diary.
WO 95/2232: 25th Division Commander Royal Engineer's War Diary.
WO 95/2285: 29th Division War Diary.
WO 95/2397: 2nd Manchester Regiment War Diary.
WO 95/2397: 16th Lancashire Fusiliers War Diary.
WO 95/2533: 13th King's Royal Rifle Corps War Diary.
WO 95/2793: 146th Brigade War Diary.
WO 95/2897: 156th Infantry Brigade War Diary.
WO 95/2898: 157th Infantry Brigade War Diary.
WO 95/2907: 55th Division War Diary.
WO 95/2921: 164th Infantry Brigade War Diary.
WO 95/2943: 1/5 Pioneers Battalion, Cheshire Regiment War Diary.
WO 95/3057: 2/8th Worcestershire Regiment War Diary.

WO 95/3146: South African Brigade War Diary.
WO 95/3147: 1st South African Infantry Regiment War Diary.
WO 95/3707: 3rd New Zealand Rifle Brigade War Diary.
WO 95/3709: 2nd Battalion, New Zealand Rifle Brigade War Diary.
WO 95/3711: 4th Battalion New Zealand Rifle Brigade War Diary.

WW1 VETERANS SURVEY COLLECTION, US ARMY HERITAGE AND EDUCATION CENTRE, CARLISLE BARRACKS, PENNSYLVANNIA
Papers of Private Malcolm Aitken.
Papers of Sergeant Rudolph Forderhase.
Papers of Lieutenant Francis Jordan.
Papers of Corporal Harry Wright.

Index

382